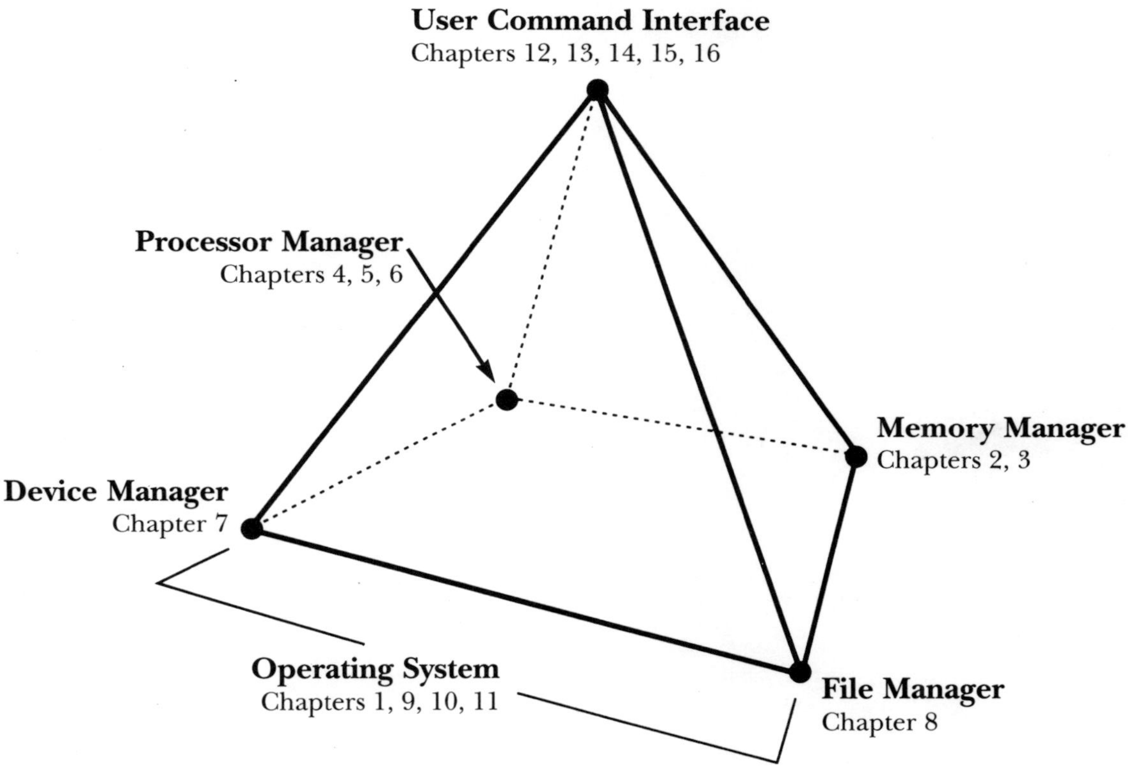

This pyramid graphically illustrates how the four components of every operating system—the Memory Manager, Processor Manager, Device Manager, and File Manager—support the User Command Interface. For more details, see pages 3–7.

UNDERSTANDING OPERATING SYSTEMS

SECOND EDITION

Ida M. Flynn, Ph.D.
University of Pittsburgh

Ann McIver McHoes
Carlow College

PWS PUBLISHING COMPANY

I(T)P *An International Thomson Publishing Company*

Boston • Albany • Bonn • Cincinnati • Detroit • London
Madrid • Melbourne • Mexico City • New York • Pacific Grove
Paris • San Francisco • Singapore • Tokoyo • Washington

THIS IS DEDICATED TO THE ONES I LOVE...(ESPECIALLY NEAL, GEN, AND KATHERINE). AMM

TO ROGER, ANTHONY, AND CHRISTOPHER: FOR KEEPING ME IN A STABLE STATE. IMF

PWS PUBLISHING COMPANY
20 Park Plaza, Boston, MA 02116-4324

Library of Congress Cataloging-in-Publication Data

Flynn, Ida M.
Understanding operating systems / Ida M. Flynn, Ann McIver McHoes.
p. cm.
Includes bibliographical references and index.
ISBN 0-534-95093-0 (alk. paper)
1. Operating systems (Computers). I. McHoes, Ann McIver. II. Title
QA76.76.063F598 1996 96-27705
005.4′3 — dc20 CIP

This book is printed on recycled, acid-free paper.

Printed and bound in the United States of America.
11 – 01

Sponsoring Editor: *David Dietz*
Marketing Manager: *Nathan Wilbur*
Production Editor/Interior Designer: *Andrea Goldman*
Manufacturing Buyer: *Andrew Christensen*
Compositor/Illustrator: *Shepard Poorman Comm. Corp.*
Cover Designer: *Jay Shippole*
Text Printer: *Phoenix Color Corp-BTP*
Cover Printer: *Phoenix Color Corp-BTP*

For more information, contact:
PWS Publishing Company
20 Park Plaza
Boston, MA 02116

International Thomson Publishing Europe
Berkshire House I68-I73
High Holborn
London WC1V 7AA
England

Thomas Nelson Australia
102 Dodds Street
South Melbourne, 3205
Victoria, Australia

Nelson Canada
1120 Birchmont Road
Scarborough, Ontario
Canada M1K 5G4

International Thomson Editores
Campos Eliseos 385, Piso 7
Col. Polanco
11560 Mexico D.F., Mexico

International Thomson Publishing GmbH
Königswinterer Strasse 418
53227 Bonn, Germany

International Thomson Publishing Asia
221 Henderson Road
#05-10 Henderson Building
Singapore 0315

International Thomson Publishing Japan
Hirakawacho Kyowa Building, 31
2-2-1 Hirakawacho
Chiyoda-ku, Tokyo 102
Japan

Contents

Preface

We believe that operating systems can be understood and appreciated by anyone who uses a computer. So we wrote a book that explains this very technical subject in a not-so-technical manner, putting the concepts and theories of operating systems into a concrete format that the reader can quickly grasp.

For readers new to the subject, this text demonstrates what operating systems are, what they do, how they do it, how their performance can be evaluated, and how they compare with each other. In the following pages we show the overall view and tell the readers where to find more detailed information, if they so desire.

For those with more background, this text introduces the subject concisely, describing the complexities of the operating systems without going into intricate detail. One might say this book leaves off where other operating systems textbooks begin.

Of course, we've made some assumptions about our audiences. First, we assume our readers have some familiarity with computing systems. Second, we assume they have a working knowledge of an operating system and how it interacts with its users. We recommend (although we don't require) that readers be familiar with at least one operating system and one computer language. In a few places we found it necessary to include examples using assembler language to illustrate the inner workings of the operating systems. For our readers who are unfamiliar with assembler we've added a prose description to each example that explains the events in more familiar terms.

ORGANIZATION AND FEATURES

This book is structured to explain the functions of an operating system regardless of the hardware that will house it. The organization addresses a recurring problem with textbooks about technologies that continue to evolve — that is, constant advances in the subject matter make the textbook outdated. To address this problem we've divided the material into two sections: first, the theory of the subject — which does not change much — and second, the specifics of operating systems — which change and evolve with the technology. Our goal is to give readers the ability to apply the topics intelligently, realizing that although the command, or series of commands, used by one operating system may be slightly different from that of another, their goals are the same and the functions of the operating systems are also the same.

Although it is more difficult to understand how operating systems work than to memorize the details of a single operating system, understanding it is a longer-lasting achievement. It also pays off in the long run, because it allows one to adapt as technology changes — as, inevitably, it does. Therefore, the purpose of this book is to give users of computer systems a solid background in the components of the operating system, their functions and goals, and how they interact and interrelate.

Part I, the first eleven chapters, describes the theory of operating systems. It concentrates on the four "managers" in turn and shows how they work together. It introduces network organization concepts and management of network functions. Part II examines actual operating systems, how they apply the theories presented in Part I, and how they compare with each other.

The meat of the text begins in Chapters 2 and 3 with main memory management because it is the simplest component of the operating system to explain and has historically been tied to the advances from one operating system to the next. We explain the role of the processor manager in Chapters 4, 5, and 6, first discussing simple systems and then expanding the discussion to include multiuser systems. By the time we reach device management in Chapter 7 and file management in Chapter 8 readers will have been introduced to the complexities of large computing systems. Chapters 9 and 10 introduce terms and concepts related to networking of computer systems and the functions assumed by those operating systems. Chapter 11 shows the interaction among the four managers and some of the tradeoffs operating system designers have to make to satisfy the needs of users.

Each chapter includes key terms (definitions are available in the glossary), and chapter conclusions, several of which include tables to compare facets of the operating system that have already been discussed. For example, Table 3.8 compares memory allocation schemes that were discussed in Chapters 2 and 3.

Throughout the book we've added "real-life" examples to illustrate the theory. This is an attempt on our part to bring the concepts closer to home. Let no one confuse our conversational style with our considerable respect for the subject matter. Operating systems is a complex subject that cannot be covered completely in these few pages. This textbook does not attempt to give an in-depth treatise of operating systems theory and applications. This is the overall view.

For our more technically oriented readers, the exercises at the end of each chapter include problems for advanced students. Please note that some of them assume knowledge of matters not presented in the book — but they're good for those who enjoy a challenge. We expect our more general audience will cheerfully pass them by.

Part II looks at several specific operating systems and how they apply the theories discussed in Part I. The structure of each chapter is similar so that each operating system can be roughly compared with the others. We have tried to include the advantages and disadvantages of each. Again, we must stress that this is a general discussion — an in-depth examination of an operating system would require details based on its current standard version, which can't be done here. We strongly suggest that readers use our discussion as a guide, a base to work from, when researching the pros and cons of a specific operating system.

The text concludes with several reference aids. The extensive glossary includes brief definitions for hundreds of terms used in these pages. Each of these terms is boldfaced in the text the first time it is used. Those terms that are important within a chapter are listed at its conclusion as Key Terms. The bibliography can guide the reader to basic research on the subject. Finally, the appendices feature a guide to acronyms used by IBM and Microsoft operating systems and a "translation table" showing a few comparable commands from the operating systems described in Part II. Caveat: the commands in Section this table are not precisely comparable, but they can be used as a guide from system to system. Of course, the command structure and syntax for many systems vary from version to version, and the appendix can't be considered a definitive guide. But for someone who is knowledgeable in one system and anxious to try another, our translation table should be of some assistance.

Not included in this text is a discussion of databases and data structures, except as examples of process synchronization problems, because they do not relate directly to operating systems. We suggest that readers begin by learning the basics as presented in the following pages before pursuing these complex subjects in depth.

CHANGES TO THE SECOND EDITION

The most notable change is the addition of Chapters 9 and 10, on networking theory. While we realize that no one can adequately describe such a complex subject in so small a space, we felt that the exclusion of network operating systems from the first edition didn't give students the needed exposure to these systems, which are commonly used in many schools and organizations. We have designed these chapters to provide a general basis in network theory, hoping interested students will explore the subject in much greater detail in more advanced texts.

The new chapter on Windows NT was added for two reasons. First, as an example of a current network operating system, it demonstrates the theory explained in Part I of the book. Second, its graphical user interface is similar to those used by several other popular systems including OS/2, Macintosh System 7, Windows 3.1, Windows 95, and Windows for Workgroups. Therefore, by reviewing this chapter readers can become acquainted with both networking and GUIs.

A new Appendix D compares common graphical user interfaces.

The chapter on device management has been updated to reflect the technology most current at the time of this writing. With the industry's legendary speed in hardware improvements, it isn't surprising that this chapter is the most dynamic in Part I and will be the first to go out of date. We suggest readers supplement our text with the most current industry literature for up-to-date device management theory.

Other changes throughout the text are minor editorial clarifications, expanded captions, improved illustrations, and the most current historical information for chapters in Part II. We appreciate the comments of those readers and reviewers who helped us refine this book.

A NOTE FOR INSTRUCTORS

An instructor's manual that includes many helpful teaching aids including exercises, answers, and an expanded reference section is available. If you're teaching from this text, be sure to order the accompanying manual.

This text has a modular construction. Chapters 2 through 11 are the core of the book; Chapter 1 may be assigned as preliminary reading or may be covered in the introductory lecture. The order of presentation in a classroom does not need to follow the table of contents in sequence. Other than Chapters 2 and 3, and Chapters 4 and 5, which are best understood when they are presented in that order, an instructor can present the chapters in any order. Chapter 6 may be omitted for less technical audiences. If you don't want to explore networks, skip Chapters 9 and 10. In addition, instructors have the option of integrating one or all of the operating systems described in Part II depending on the individual's preferences, the course direction, and time availability.

ACKNOWLEDGMENTS

Special thanks go to Alan Kent and Roger Flynn of the University of Pittsburgh for their comments and encouragement; Richard Feingold for his assistance with the section on security issues discussed in Chapter 11; and our support staff of Donald A. McIver, Neal McHoes, Karen Esch, Jennifer Ramaley, Annette Anderson, and Mary McIver Puthawala.

Our gratitude to all of our friends and colleagues, particularly those at the University of Pittsburgh, who were so generous with their encouragement, advice, and support. Special thanks also to those at PWS Publishing who made significant contributions to this effort: Mike Sugarman, David Dietz, Mary Thomas Stone, Sarah Zobel, and Andrea Goldman.

For their comments and suggestions we are deeply indebted to the following reviewers: Linda Boettner, Slippery Rock University, Slippery Rock, Pennsylvania; Albert B. Cawns, Webster University, St. Louis, Missouri; Pauline K. Cushman, University of Louisville; Tony Fabbri, University of Louisville; Charles H. Garrison, Saginaw Valley State University, University Center, Michigan; Fran Gustavson, Pace University; David J. Jones, Trident Technical College, Charleston, South Carolina; Janet L. Kourik, Webster University, St. Louis, Missouri; Gene Kwatny, Temple University; Gary Locklair, Concordia University, Mequon, Wisconsin; Michael Lyle, Sonoma State University; James Silver, Indiana-Purdue University; Andrea J. Wachter, Point Park College, Pittsburgh, Pennsylvania; Greg Wagner, Chatham College; Les Waguespack, Bentley College, Waltham, Massachusetts; Ronald Wyllys, University of Texas, Austin; Ronald J. Zucker, University of North Florida, Jacksonville; and Bruce W. Derr, Syracuse University.

Ida M. Flynn
ida@lis.pitt.edu
Ann McIver McHoes
mchoes@acm.org

Part One

OPERATING SYSTEMS THEORY

Part I, the first eleven chapters of the book, is an overview of operating systems: what they are, how they work, their goals, and how they achieve those goals. Each chapter covers a primary part of the operating system, beginning with the management of main memory and moving on to processors, devices, files and networks. Finally, Chapter 11 explores system management and the interaction of the operating system's components.

Although this is a technical subject, we tried to include in our discussions the definitions of the terms that might be unfamiliar to you. However, it isn't always possible to describe a function *and* define the technical terms while keeping the explanation clear. Therefore, we've included an extensive glossary at the end of this book for your reference. Items listed in the glossary are indicated in the text by boldface type.

For the purposes of this book we kept our descriptions and examples as simple as possible so we could introduce you to the system's complexities without getting bogged down in the technical detail. Therefore, be aware that for almost every topic we'll explain in the following pages there is much more information we could have passed along, but didn't. Our goal is to introduce you to the subject, and we encourage you to pursue your interest using other texts if you need more detail.

In Part II we'll look at specific operating systems and how they apply the theory described in Part I.

Chapter One

OVERVIEW

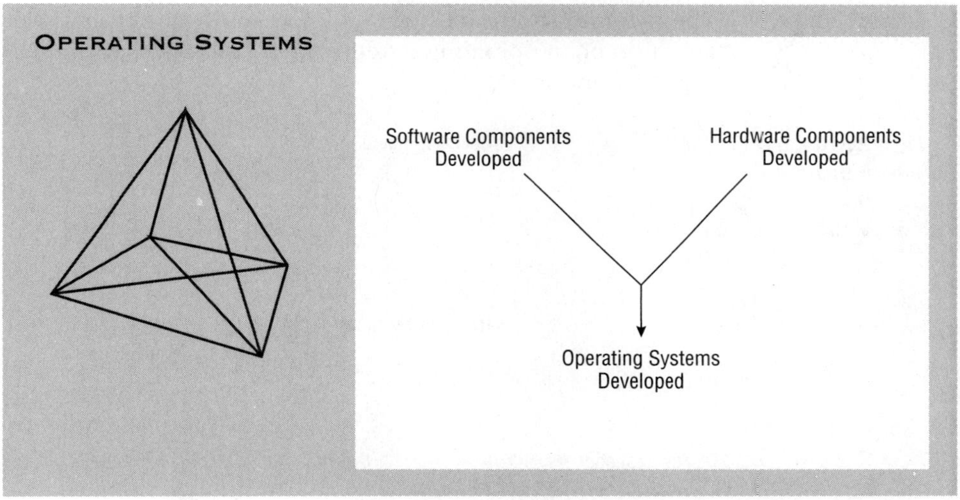

To understand the operating system is to understand the workings of the entire computer system, because it is the operating system that manages each and every piece of hardware and software. In this text we'll explore what operating systems are, how they work, what they do, and why.

In this chapter we'll show briefly how operating systems work and how, in general, they have evolved. The following chapters will explore each component in more depth and show how its function relates to the other parts of the operating system. In other words, we'll see how the pieces work harmoniously to keep the computer system humming smoothly. Note: throughout this text, boldface type indicates terms that are defined in the glossary.

INTRODUCTION

Let's begin with a definition: What is an **operating system**? To put it in the simplest terms, it is the "executive manager," the part of the computing system that manages all of the hardware and all of the software. To be specific, it controls every file, every device, every section of main memory, and every nanosecond of processing time. It controls who can use the system and how. In short, it's the boss.

Therefore, when the user sends a command, the operating system must make sure that the command is executed or, if it's not executed, must arrange for the user to get a message explaining the error. This does not necessarily mean that the operating system executes the command or sends the error message — but it does control the parts of the system that do.

OPERATING SYSTEM COMPONENTS

The pyramid shown in Figure 1.1 and inside the front cover is an abstract representation of an operating system and demonstrates the interrelationships of its five major components.

FIGURE 1.1
The operating system and its four subsystem managers.

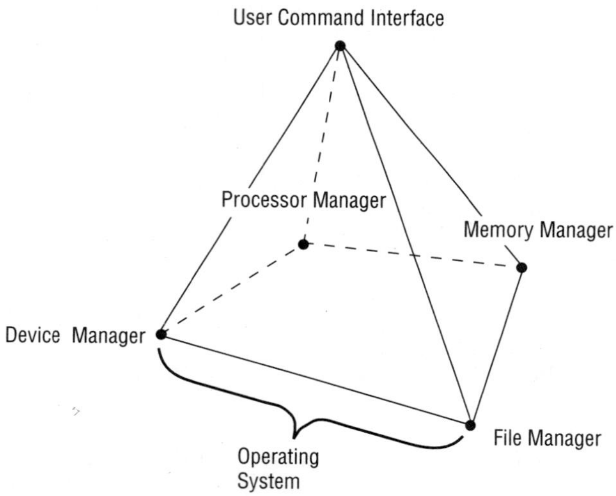

The base of the pyramid shows the four primary "managers": the **Memory Manager**, the **Processor Manager**, the **Device Manager**, and the **File Manager**. In fact, these managers are the basis of all operating systems and each is discussed in detail throughout the first part of this book. Each of these managers works closely with all of the others and performs its unique role regardless of which specific operating system is being discussed. Network functions were not always an integral part of operating systems; they were normally mounted over existing operating systems. Hence, we have not identified a separate corner in the pyramid but have incorporated the chapters related to these functions under the heading of "operating systems." On the other hand, the **User Command Interface**, from which users issue commands to the operating system, is the component that is unique to each operating system and is very different from one operating system to the next — sometimes even between different versions of the same operating system. (For your convenience, Figure 1.1 is repeated inside the front cover showing the chapters in which each component is discussed.)

Regardless of the size or configuration of the system, each of the subsystem managers, shown in Figure 1.2, must perform these tasks:

1. Monitor its resources continuously
2. Enforce the policies that determine who gets what, when, and how much
3. Allocate the resource when it's appropriate
4. Deallocate the resource — reclaim it — when appropriate

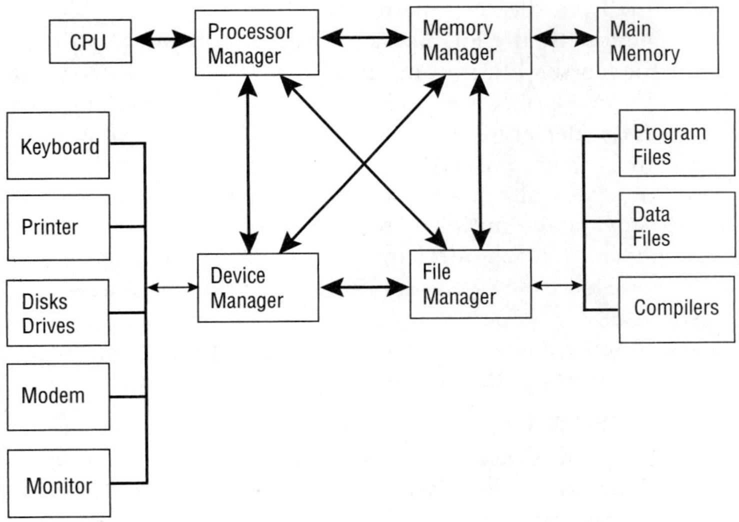

FIGURE 1.2 *Each subsystem manager at the base of the pyramid must take responsibility for its own tasks while working harmoniously with every other manager.*

For instance, the Memory Manager is in charge of **main memory**. It checks the validity of each request for memory space and, if it is a legal request, the Memory Manager allocates a portion that isn't already in use. In a multiuser environment, the Memory Manager sets up a table to keep track of who is using which section of memory. Finally, when the time comes to reclaim the memory the Memory Manager "deallocates" memory.

Of course, one of the Memory Manager's primary responsibilities is to preserve the space in main memory that's occupied by the operating system itself — it can't allow any part of it to be accidentally or intentionally altered.

The Processor Manager decides how to allocate the **Central Processing Unit (CPU)**. An important function of the Processor Manager is to keep track of the status of each process (a process is defined here as an "instance of execution" of a program). It monitors whether the CPU is executing a process or waiting for a READ or WRITE command to finish execution. Because it handles the processes' transitions from one state of execution to another, it can be compared to a traffic controller. Once the Processor Manager allocates the processor, it sets up the necessary registers and tables and, when the job is finished or the maximum amount of time has expired, it reclaims the processor.

Conceptually, the Processor Manager has two levels of responsibility: one is to handle jobs as they enter the system and the other is to manage each of the processes within those jobs. The first part is handled by the **Job Scheduler**, the high-level portion of the Processor Manager, which accepts or rejects the incoming jobs. The second part is handled by the **Process Scheduler**, the low-level portion of the Processor Manager, which is responsible for deciding which process gets the CPU and for how long.

The Device Manager monitors every device, channel, and control unit. Its job is to choose the most efficient way to allocate all of the system's devices, printers, terminals, disk drives, and so forth, based on a scheduling policy chosen by the system's designers. The Device Manager makes the allocation, starts its operation, and, finally, deallocates the device.

The fourth, the File Manager, keeps track of every file in the system including data files, assemblers, compilers, and application programs. By using predetermined access policies, it enforces access restrictions on each file. (When created, every file is declared: system only, user only, group only, or general access, and the operating system enforces these restrictions.) The File Manager also controls the amount of flexibility each user is allowed with that file (such as read only, read and write only, or the authority to create and/or delete records). Also, the File Manager allocates the resource by opening the file and deallocates it by closing the file.

However, it is not enough for each of these managers to perform its individual tasks. It must also be able to work harmoniously with every other manager. Here's a simplified example. Let's say someone types a command to execute a program. The following are the major steps that must occur:

1. The Device Manager must receive the electrical impulses from the keyboard, decode the keystrokes to form the command, and send the command to the User Command Interface, where the Processor Manager validates the command.
2. The Processor Manager then sends an acknowledgment message to be displayed on the video monitor so the typist will realize the command has been sent.
3. When the Processor Manager receives the command, it determines whether the program must be retrieved from storage or is already in memory, and then notifies the appropriate manager.
4. If the program is in storage, the File Manager must calculate its exact location on the disk, pass this information to the Device Manager which will retrieve, and send the program on to the Memory Manager, which must find space for it and record its exact location in memory.
5. Once the program is in memory, the Memory Manager must track its location and progress as it is executed by the Processor Manager.
6. When the program has finished executing, it must send a "finished" message back to the Processor Manager.
7. Finally, the Processor Manager must forward the "finished" message back to the Device Manager, which displays it on the video monitor for the user to see.

Although this is an oversimplified demonstration of a complex operation, it illustrates the incredible precision required by the operating system. Remember, no single manager could perform its tasks without the active cooperation of every other part.

MACHINE HARDWARE

To appreciate the role of the operating system we need to define the essential aspects of the computer system's **hardware**, the physical machine and its electronic components including memory chips, input/output devices, storage devices, and the central processing unit. Hardware contrasts with **software**, which refers to programs written for computer systems.

Main memory is where the data and instructions must reside to be processed.

I/O devices, short for "input/output devices," include every peripheral unit in the system such as terminals, printers, card readers, disk drives, drums, and magnetic tape devices.

The CPU, the central processing unit, is the "brains," with the circuitry (sometimes called the "chips") to control the interpretation and execution of instructions. In essence, it controls the operation of the entire computer system, as illustrated in Figure 1.3. All storage references, data manipulations, and I/O operations are initiated or performed by the CPU.

FIGURE 1.3
A typical computer system hardware configuration.

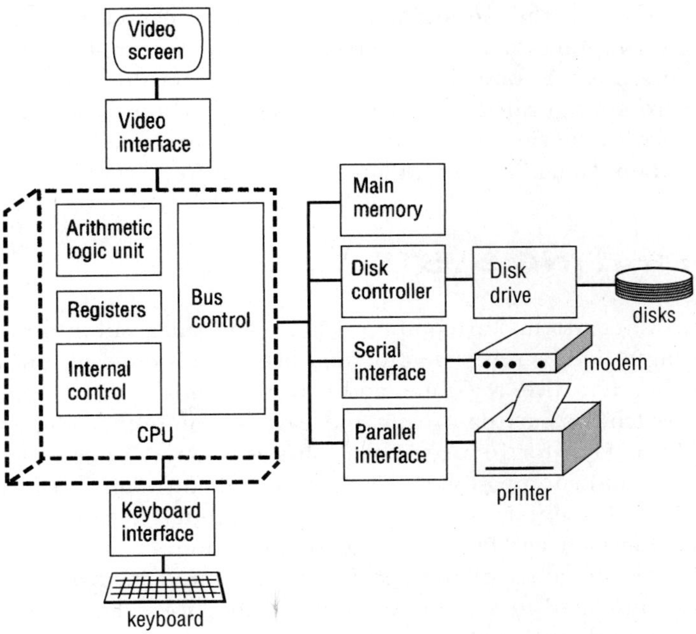

Until 1975, computers were classified by capacity and price. A **mainframe** was a large machine — both physically and in terms of internal memory capacity. The IBM 360, introduced in 1964, is a classic example of an early mainframe. The IBM 360 model 30, the smallest in the 360 family (Prasad, 1989), required an air-conditioned room about 18 feet square to house the CPU, the operator's console, a printer, a card reader, and a keypunch machine. The CPU was five feet high and six feet wide, had an internal memory of 64K (considered large at that time), and a price tag of $200,000 in 1964 dollars. Because of its size and price, its applications were generally limited to large computer centers belonging to the federal government, universities, and very large businesses.

The **minicomputer** was developed to meet the needs of smaller institutions, those with only a few dozen users. One of the early minicomputers was marketed by Digital Equipment Corporation to satisfy the needs of large schools and small colleges that began offering computer science courses in the early 1970s (its PDP-8, Peripheral Device Processor-8, was priced at under $18,000). Minicomputers were smaller in size and memory capacity and cheaper than a mainframe.

The **microcomputer** was developed for single users in the late 1970s. Tandy Corporation and Apple Computer, Inc. were the first to offer microcomputers for sale to the general public. The former targeted the small business market and the latter aimed for the elementary education market. These early models had very little memory by today's standards: 64K was the maximum capacity. Their physical size was smaller than the minicomputers of that time, though larger than the microcomputers of today.

Since the mid-1970s rapid advances in computer technology have blurred the distinguishing characteristics of early machines: physical size, cost, and memory capacity. The most powerful mainframes today have multiple processors coordinated by the Processor Manager. Simple mainframes still have a large main memory, but now they're available in desk-sized cabinets. Minicomputers look like microcomputers, and the smallest can now accomplish tasks once reserved for mainframes. At one time computers were classified by memory capacity; now they're distinguished by processor capacity. Of course, we emphasize that these are relative categories and what is "large" today will eventually become "medium" and then "small" sometime in the near future.

TYPES OF OPERATING SYSTEMS

Operating systems for computers large and small fall into four distinct categories distinguished by response time and how data is entered into the system. They are batch, interactive, real-time, and hybrid systems.

Batch systems date from the earliest computers, which relied on punched cards or tape for input when a job was entered by assembling the cards into a "deck" and running the entire deck of cards through a card reader as a group — a "batch." Present-day batch systems aren't limited to cards or tapes, but the jobs are still processed serially, without user interaction.

The efficiency of the system was measured in **throughput** — the number of jobs completed in a given amount of time (for example, 30 jobs per hour) and turnaround was measured in hours or even days. Today it's uncommon to find a system that is limited to batch programs.

Interactive systems (also called "time-sharing" systems) give a faster turnaround than batch systems but are slower than the real-time systems we'll talk about next. They were introduced to satisfy the demands of users who needed fast turnaround when debugging their programs. The operating system required the development of time-sharing software, which would allow each user to interact directly with the computer system via commands entered from a typewriter-like terminal (Shelly & Cashman, 1984).

The operating system provides immediate feedback to the user and response time can be measured in minutes or seconds, depending on the number of active users. A personal computer can be defined as a single-user interactive system.

Real-time systems are the fastest of the four and are used in "time-critical" environments where data must be processed extremely quickly because the output will influence immediate decisions. Real-time systems are used for space flights, airport traffic control, high-speed aircraft, industrial processes, sophisticated medical equipment, distribution of electricity, and telephone switching. A real-time system must be 100 percent responsive 100 percent of the time. Response time is measured in fractions of a second, although this is an ideal not often achieved in practice.

Hybrid systems are a combination of batch and interactive. They appear to be interactive because individual users can access the system via terminals and get fast response, but such a system actually accepts and runs batch programs in the background when the interactive load is light. A hybrid system takes advantage of the free time between demands for processing to execute programs that need no significant operator assistance. Many large computer systems are hybrids.

BRIEF HISTORY OF OPERATING SYSTEMS DEVELOPMENT

The evolution of operating systems parallels the evolution of the computers they were designed to control.

The **first generation** of computers (1940–1955) was a time of vacuum tube technology and computers the size of classrooms. Each computer was unique in structure and purpose. There was little need for standard operating system software because each computer's use was restricted to a few professionals working on mathematical, scientific, or military applications, all of whom were familiar with the idiosyncrasies of their hardware.

A typical program would include all the instructions the computer needed to perform the tasks requested. It would give explicit directions to the card reader (when to begin, how to interpret the data on the cards, when to end), the CPU (how and where to store the instructions in memory, what to calculate, where to find the data, where to send the output), and the output device (when to begin, how to print out the finished product, how to format the page, and when to end).

The machines were operated by the programmers from the main console — it was a "hands-on" process. In fact, to debug a program, the programmer would stop the processor, read the contents of each register, make the corrections in memory locations, and then resume operation.

To run programs, the programmers would have to reserve the machine for the length of time they estimated it would take the computer to execute the program. As a result, the machine was poorly utilized. The CPU was processing for only a fraction of the available time and, in fact, the entire system sat idle between reservations.

In time computer hardware and software became more standard and the execution of a program required fewer steps and less knowledge of the internal workings of the computer.

- Assemblers and compilers were developed to translate into binary code the English-like commands of the evolving high-level languages.
- Rudimentary operating systems started to take shape with the creation of macros, library programs, standard subroutines, and utility programs.
- Device driver subroutines were written to standardize the use of input and output devices.

The disadvantage of the early programs was that they were designed to use the available resources conservatively, but at the expense of understandability, and the finished product was impossible to debug or adapt later on.

Second generation computers (1955–1965) were developed to meet the needs of a new market — businesses. The business environment placed much more importance on the cost effectiveness of the system. Computers were still very expensive, especially when compared to other office equipment (the IBM 7094 was priced at $200,000). Therefore, throughput had to be maximized to make such an investment worthwhile for business use, which meant dramatically increasing the usage of the system.

Two improvements were widely adopted: (1) computer operators were hired to facilitate each machine's operation, and (2) job scheduling was instituted. *Job scheduling* is a productivity improvement scheme that groups together programs with similar requirements. For example, the FORTRAN programs would be run together while the FORTRAN compiler was still resident in memory. Or all of the jobs using the card reader for input might be run together, and those using the tape drive would be run later. Some operators found that a mix of I/O device requirements was the most efficient; by mixing tape input programs with card input programs, the tapes could be mounted or rewound while the card reader was busy.

Job scheduling introduced the need for "control cards," which defined the exact nature of each program and its requirements. This was one of the first uses of **job control language (JCL)**, which helped the operating system coordinate and manage the system's resources by identifying the users and their jobs and specifying the resources required to execute each job.

The following is an example of a simple program set-up for the DEC-10:

```
$JOB (insert user number)               <— identify job and user
$PASSWORD (insert user password)        <— positively identify user
$LANGUAGE (indicate compiler needed     <— specify resource
  [source deck]
$DATA                                   <— identify resource
  [data deck]
$EOJ                                    <— identify end of job and
                                           release resources
```

But even with batching techniques the faster second-generation computers allowed expensive time lags between the CPU and the I/O devices. For example, a job with 1600 cards could take 79 seconds to be completely read by the card reader and only 5 seconds of CPU time to assemble (compile). That meant the CPU was idle 94 percent of the time and actually processing only 6 percent of the time it was dedicated to that job.

Eventually several factors helped improve the performance of the CPU. First, the speed of I/O devices like tape drives, disks, and drums gradually became faster. Second, to use more of the available storage area in these devices, records were "blocked" before they were retrieved or stored. (**Blocking** means that several logical records are grouped within one physical record.) Of course, when the records were retrieved, they had to be "deblocked" before the program could use them. To aid programmers in these blocking and deblocking functions, access methods were developed and added to object code by the linkage editor.

Third, to reduce the discrepancy in speed between the I/O and the CPU an interface called the "control unit" was placed between them to perform the function of buffering. A "buffer" is an interim storage area that works like this: as the slow input device reads a record, the control unit places each character of the record into the buffer. When the buffer is full, the entire record is quickly transmitted to the CPU. The process is just the opposite for output devices: the CPU places into the buffer the entire record, which is then passed on by the control unit at the slower rate required by the output device.

If a control unit has more than one buffer, the I/O process can be speeded up even more. For example, if the control unit has two buffers, while the first buffer is transmitting its contents to the CPU the second can be loaded. Ideally, by the time the first has been transmitted the second is ready to go, and so on. In this example, input time is cut in half.

Fourth, in addition to buffering, an early form of "spooling" was developed by moving off-line the operations of card reading, printing, and card punching. For example, incoming jobs would be transferred from card decks to tape off-line. Then they would be read into the CPU from the tape at a speed much faster than that of the card reader.

Also during the second generation, techniques were developed to manage program libraries, create and maintain data files and indexes, randomize direct access addresses, and create and check file labels. Sequential, indexed sequential, and direct access files were supported and facilitated by standardized macros that relieved programmers of the need to write customized open and close routines for each program.

Timer interrupts were developed to protect the CPU from infinite loops on programs that were mistakenly instructed to execute a single series of commands forever, and to allow sharing of jobs. A fixed amount of execution time was allocated to each program upon entry into the system and was monitored by the operating system. If any programs were still running when the time expired, they were terminated and the user was notified by an error message.

During the second generation, programs were still run in serial batch mode — one at a time. The next step toward better use of the system's resources was the move to shared processing.

Third-generation computers date from the mid-1960s. They were designed with faster CPUs, but their speed caused problems with the relatively slow I/O devices. The solution was multiprogramming, which introduced the concept of many programs sharing the attention of a single CPU.

The first multiprogramming systems allowed each program to be serviced in turn, one after another. The most common mechanism for implementing multiprogramming was the introduction of the "interrupt" concept, which is when the CPU is notified of events needing operating systems services. For example, when a program issues an I/O command, it generates an interrupt requesting the services of the I/O processor and the CPU is released to begin execution of the next job. This was named **passive multiprogramming** because the operating system didn't control the interrupts but waited for each job to end an execution sequence. It was less than ideal because if a job was "CPU-bound" (meaning that it performed a great deal of nonstop processing before issuing an interrupt) it would tie up the CPU for long periods of time while all other jobs had to wait.

To counteract this effect, the operating system was soon given a more active role with the advent of **active multiprogramming**. The system allowed each program to use only a preset slice of CPU time. When time expired, the job was interrupted and another job was allowed to begin execution. The interrupted job had to wait its turn until it was allowed to resume execution later. The idea of time slicing became common in many time-sharing systems.

Program scheduling, which was begun with second-generation systems, was complicated by the fact that main memory was occupied by many jobs. The solution was to sort the jobs into groups and then load the programs according to a preset rotation. The groups were usually determined by priority or memory requirements — whichever was found to be the most efficient use of resources.

In addition to scheduling jobs, handling interrupts, and allocating memory, the operating systems had to resolve conflicts when two jobs requested the same device at the same time.

Few major advances were made in data management during this period. Library functions and access methods were still the same as in the last years of the second generation. The operating system for third-generation machines consisted of many modules from which a user could select; thus the total operating system was customized to suit its user's needs. The most-used modules were made core resident, and those less frequently used resided in secondary storage and were called in only as needed.

Post–third-generation computers developed during the late 1970s and had faster CPUs, thus creating an even greater disparity between processing speed and I/O access time. Multiprogramming schemes to increase CPU use were limited by the physical capacity of the main memory, which was both a limited resource and very expensive.

A solution to this physical limitation was **virtual memory**, which took advantage of the fact that the CPU could process only one instruction at a time. With virtual memory, the entire program didn't have to reside in memory before execution could begin. A system with virtual memory would divide the programs into segments and keep them in secondary storage, bringing each segment into memory only as it was needed. (Programmers of second-generation computers had used this concept with the "roll in/roll out" programming method to execute programs that exceeded the physical memory of those computers.)

At this time there was also growing attention to the need for data resource conservation. Database management software became a popular tool because it organized data in an integrated manner, minimized redundancy, and simplified updating and access of data. A number of query systems were introduced that allowed even the novice user to retrieve specific pieces of the database. These queries were usually made via a terminal, which in turn, mandated a growth in terminal support and data communication software.

Programmers soon became more removed from the intricacies of the computer, and application programs started using English-like words, modular structures, and standard operations. This trend toward the use of standards improved program management because program maintenance became faster and easier.

Development in the 1980s dramatically improved the cost/performance ratio of computer components. Hardware was more flexible, with logical functions built on easily replaceable cards. It was also less costly, so more operating system functions were made part of the hardware itself, giving rise to a new concept — **firmware**, a word used to indicate that a program is permanently held in ROM (read only memory), as opposed to being held in secondary storage. The job of the programmer, as it had been defined in previous years, changed dramatically because many programming functions were being carried out by the system's software, hence making the programmer's task simpler.

Eventually the industry moved to **multiprocessing** (more than one processor), and more complex languages were designed to coordinate the activities of the multiple processors servicing a single job. As a result, it became possible to execute programs in parallel, and eventually operating systems for computers of every size were routinely expected to accommodate multiprocessing.

The evolution of personal computers and high-speed communications sparked the move to distributed processing and networked systems enabling users in remote locations to share hardware and software resources. These systems required a new kind of operating system — one capable of managing multiple sets of subsystem managers, as well as hardware that might reside half a world away.

With network operating systems' users generally are aware of the existence of multiple resources, can log in to remote locations, and can copy files from one networked computer to another. Network operating systems are similar to single-processor operating systems in that each machine runs its own local operating system and has its own users. The difference is in the addition of a network interface controller with low-level software to drive the local operating system, as well as programs to allow remote log in and remote file access. Still, even with these additions the basic structure of the network operating system is quite close to that of a stand-alone system.

On the other hand, with distributed operating systems users might think that they are working with a typical uniprocessor system when in fact they are connected to a web consisting of many processors working closely together. With these systems, users need not be aware of which processor is running their applications or which device is storing their files. These details are all handled transparently by the operating system — something that requires more than just adding a few lines of code to a uniprocessor operating system. The disadvantage of such a complex operating system is the requirement for more complex processor-scheduling algorithms. In addition, communications delays within the network sometimes mean that scheduling algorithms must operate with incomplete or outdated information.

CHAPTER ONE CONCLUSION

In this chapter we've looked at the overall function of operating systems and how they have evolved to run increasingly complex computers and computer systems. Of course we've only seen the general picture — an overview of the hardware and the role of the operating system software. In the following chapters we'll explore in detail how each segment of the operating system works, its features, functions, benefits, and costs.

We'll begin with the part of the operating system that is the heart of every computer, the module that manages main memory.

KEY TERMS

operating system
Memory Manager
Processor Manager
Device Manager
File Manager
main memory
central processing unit (CPU)
hardware
software
mainframe
minicomputer
microcomputer
batch system
interactive system
real-time system
hybrid system
multiprocessing

EXERCISES

1. Name five current operating systems and the computers or configurations each operates.
2. Name the five key concepts about an operating system that you think a user needs to know and understand.
3. Explain the impact of the evolution of computer hardware with respect to the evolution of operating systems software.
4. Explain the fundamental differences between interactive, batch, and real-time systems.
5. List three situations that might demand a real-time operating system and explain why.
6. Give an example of an organization that might find batch-mode processing useful and explain why.

ADVANCED EXERCISES

7. Briefly compare active and passive multiprogramming.
8. Compare the development of two operating systems described in Part II of this text including design goals and evolution.
9. Draw a system flowchart illustrating the steps performed by an operating system as it executes the instruction to back up a disk on a single-user computer system. Begin with the user typing the command on the keyboard and conclude with the display of the result on the monitor.

Chapter Two

MEMORY MANAGEMENT, EARLY SYSTEMS

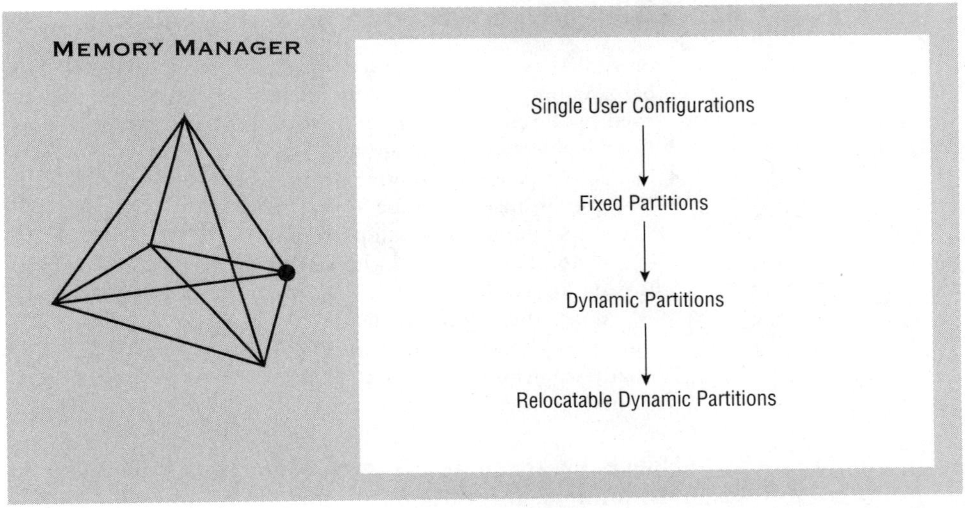

The management of main memory is critical. In fact, the performance of the *entire* system has historically been directly dependent on two things: how much memory is available and how it is optimized while jobs are being processed.

This chapter introduces the Memory Manager and four types of memory allocation schemes: single-user systems, fixed partitions, dynamic partitions, and relocatable dynamic partitions. We start with the most simple — it's the one used in the earliest generations of computer systems.

SINGLE-USER CONTIGUOUS SCHEME

The first **memory allocation scheme** worked like this: each program to be processed was loaded in its entirety into memory and allocated as much contiguous space in memory as it needed. The key words here are *entirety* and *contiguous.* If the program was too large and didn't fit the available memory space, it couldn't be executed. And, although early computers were physically large, they had very little memory.

This demonstrates a significant limiting factor of all computers — they have only a finite amount of memory and if a program doesn't fit, then either the size of the main memory must be increased or the program must be modified — this latter by making it smaller or by using methods that allow program segments (partitions made to the program) to be overlayed (the transfer of segments of a program from secondary storage into main memory for execution, so that two or more segments occupy the same storage locations at different times).

Even today's **single-user systems** work the same way. Each user is given access to all available main memory for each job, and jobs are processed sequentially, one after the other. To allocate memory the operating system uses a simple **algorithm**:

ALGORITHM TO LOAD A JOB IN A SINGLE-USER SYSTEM

1 Store first memory location of program into base register (for memory protection)
2 Set program counter (it keeps a running sum of the amount of memory locations used by the program) equal to address of first memory location
3 Load instructions of program
4 Increment program counter by number of bytes in instructions
5 Has the last instruction been reached?
    if yes, then stop loading program
    if no, then continue with step 6
6 Is program counter greater than memory size?
    if yes, then stop loading
    if no, then continue with step 7
7 Load instruction in memory
8 Go to step 3

Notice that the amount of work done by the operating system's Memory Manager is minimal, the code to perform the functions is straightforward, and the logic is quite simple. Only two hardware items are needed: a register to store the "base **address**" and an "accumulator" to keep track of the size of the program as it's being read into memory. Once the program is entirely loaded into memory, it remains there until execution is complete, either through normal termination or by intervention of the operating system.

One of the major problems with this type of memory allocation scheme is that it doesn't support **multiprogramming** (discussed in detail in Chapter 4); it can handle only one job at a time.

When they were first made available commercially in the late 1940s and early 1950s, these single-user configurations were used in research institutions but proved unacceptable for the business community — it wasn't cost effective to spend almost $200,000 for a piece of equipment that could be used by only one person at a time. Therefore, in the late 1950s and early 1960s a new scheme was needed to manage memory.

The next design used partitions to take advantage of the computer system's resources by overlapping independent operations.

FIXED PARTITIONS

The first attempt to allow for multiprogramming was to create **fixed partitions** (also called **static partitions**) within the main memory — one partition for each job. Because the size of each partition was designated when the system was powered on, each partition could only be reconfigured when the computer system was shut down, reconfigured, and restarted. Thus, once the system was in operation the partition sizes remained static.

A critical factor was introduced with this scheme: protection of the job's memory space. Once a partition was assigned to a job, no other job could be allowed to enter its boundaries, either accidentally or intentionally. This problem of "partition intrusion" didn't exist in single-user contiguous allocation schemes because only one job was present in main memory at any given time so only the portion of the operating system residing in main memory had to be protected. However, for the fixed partition allocation schemes, protection was mandatory for each partition present in main memory. Typically this was the joint responsibility of the hardware of the computer and the operating system (Madnick & Donovan, 1974).

The algorithm used to store jobs into memory requires a few more steps than the one used for a single-user system because the size of the job must be matched with the size of the partition to make sure it fits completely. Then, when a block of sufficient size is located, the status of the partition must be checked to see if it's available.

ALGORITHM TO LOAD A JOB IN A FIXED PARTITION

```
1 Determine job's requested memory size
2 If job_size > size of largest partition
    then reject the job
      print appropriate message to operator
      go to step 1 to handle next job in line
    else continue with step 3
3 Set counter to 1
4 Do while counter <= number of partitions in memory
      If job_size > memory_partition_size(counter)
        then counter = counter + 1
      else
        If memory_partition_status(counter) = "free"
          then load job into memory_partition(counter)
            change memory_partition_status(counter) to "busy"
            go to step 1
        else counter = counter + 1
    end do
5 No partition available at this time, put job in waiting queue
6 Go to step 1
```

This partition scheme is more flexible than the single-user scheme because it allows several programs to be in memory at the same time. However, it still requires that the *entire* program be stored *contiguously* and *in memory* from the beginning to the end of its execution. In order to allocate memory spaces to jobs, the operating system's Memory Manager must keep a table such as Table 2.1 showing each memory partition size, its address, its access restrictions, and its current status (free or busy) for the system illustrated in Figure 2.1.

TABLE 2.1 *A simplified fixed partition memory table. (A more in-depth discussion of this topic is presented in Chapter 8.)*

Partition size	Memory address	Access	Partition status
100K	200K	Job 1	Busy
25K	300K	Job 4	Busy
25K	325K		Free
50K	350K	Job 2	Busy

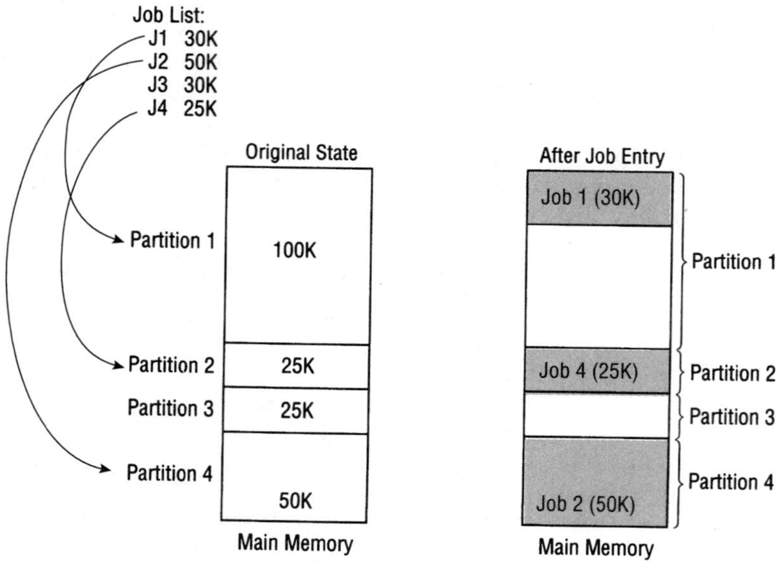

FIGURE 2.1 *Main memory use during fixed partition allocation of Table 2.1. Job 3 must wait even though there's 70K of free space available in Partition 1 where Job 1 is only occupying 30K of the 100K available. The jobs are allocated space on the basis of "first available partition of required size."*

As each job terminates, the status of its memory partition is changed from busy to free so an incoming job can be assigned to that partition.

The fixed partition scheme works well if all of the jobs run on the system are of the same size or if the sizes are known ahead of time and don't vary between reconfigurations. Ideally, that would require accurate advance knowledge of all the jobs to be run on the system in the coming hours, days, or weeks. However, unless the operator can accurately predict the future, the size of the partitions are determined in an arbitrary fashion and they might be too small or too large for the jobs coming in.

There are significant consequences if the partitions sizes are too small; larger jobs will be rejected if they're too big to fit into the largest partitions or will wait if the large partitions are busy. As a result, large jobs may have a longer turnaround time as they wait for free partitions of sufficient size.

On the other hand, if the partitions sizes are too big, memory is wasted. If a job does not occupy the entire partition, the unused memory in the partition will remain idle; it can't be given to another job because each partition is allocated to only one job at a time. It's an indivisible unit. Figure 2.1 demonstrates one such circumstance.

This phenomenon of partial usage of fixed partitions and the coinciding creation of unused spaces within the partition is called **internal fragmentation**, and it's one of the major drawbacks to the fixed partition memory allocation scheme.

DYNAMIC PARTITIONS

With **dynamic partitions**, available memory is still kept in contiguous blocks but jobs are given only as much memory as they request when they are loaded for processing. Although this is a significant improvement over fixed partitions because memory isn't wasted within the partition, it doesn't entirely eliminate the problem, as illustrated in Figure 2.2 (page 22).

As shown in Figure 2.2, a dynamic partition scheme fully utilizes memory when the first jobs are loaded. But as new jobs enter the system that are not of the same size as those that just vacated memory, they are fit into the available spaces on a priority basis. Figure 2.2 demonstrates "**first-come first-served**" priority. Therefore, the subsequent allocation of memory creates fragments of free memory between blocks of allocated memory (Madnick & Donovan, 1974). This problem is called **external fragmentation** and, like internal fragmentation, it lets memory go to waste.

In the last snapshot, (e) in Figure 2.2, there are three free partitions of 5K, 10K, and 20K — 35K in all — enough to accommodate Job 8, which only requires 30K. However they are not contiguous and, because the jobs are loaded in a contiguous manner, this scheme forces Job 8 to wait.

Before we go to the next allocation scheme, let's examine how the operating system keeps track of the free sections of memory.

BEST-FIT VERSUS FIRST-FIT ALLOCATION

For both fixed and dynamic memory allocation schemes, the operating system must keep lists of each memory location noting which are free and which are busy. Then as new jobs come into the system the free partitions must be allocated.

These partitions may be allocated on the basis of **first-fit** (first partition fitting the requirements) or **best-fit** (closest fit, the smallest partition fitting the requirements). For both schemes the Memory Manager organizes the memory lists of the free and used partitions (free/busy) either by size or by location. The best-fit allocation method keeps the free/busy lists in order by size, smallest to largest. The first-fit method keeps the free/busy lists organized by memory locations, low-order memory to high-order memory. Each has advantages depending on the needs of the particular allocation scheme — best-fit usually makes the best use of memory space; first-fit is faster in making the allocation.

FIGURE 2.2 *Main memory use and fragmentation during dynamic partition allocation. Five snapshots of main memory as eight jobs are submitted for processing and allocated space on the basis of "first-come first-served." Job 8 has to wait (see part (e)) even though there's enough free memory between partitions to accommodate it.*

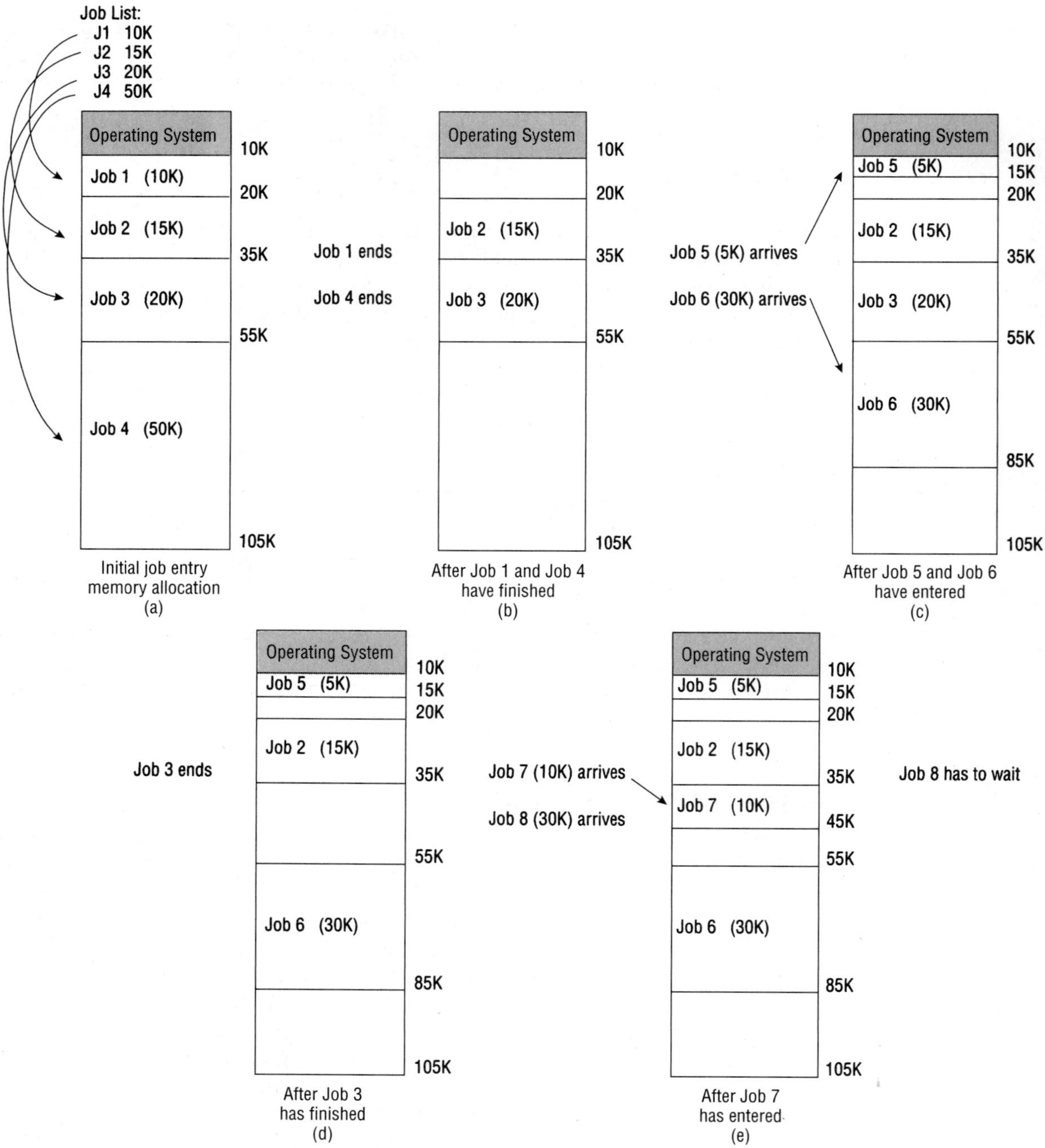

To understand the trade-offs, imagine that you've turned your collection of books into a lending library. Let's say you have books of all shapes and sizes, and let's also say there's a continuous stream of people taking books out and bringing them back — someone's always waiting. It's clear that you'll always be busy, and that's good, but you never have time to rearrange the bookshelves.

You need a system. Your shelves have fixed partitions with a few tall spaces for oversized books, several shelves for paperbacks, and lots of room for textbooks. You'll need to keep track of which spaces on the shelves are full and where you have spaces for more. For the purposes of our example, we'll keep two lists: a free list showing all the available spaces, and a busy list showing all the occupied spaces. Each list will include the size and location of each space.

So as each book is removed from its shelf you'll update both lists by removing the space from the busy list and adding it to the free list. Then as your books are returned and placed back on a shelf, the two lists will be updated again.

There are two ways to organize your lists — by size or by location. If they're organized by size, the spaces for the smallest books are at the top of the list and those for the largest are at the bottom. When they're organized by location, the spaces closest to your lending desk are at the top of the list and the areas farthest away are at the bottom. Which option is best? It depends on what you want to optimize: space or speed of allocation.

If the lists are organized by size, you're optimizing your shelf space: as books arrive, you'll be able to put them in the spaces that fit them best. This is a best-fit scheme. If a paperback is returned, you'll place it on a shelf with the other paperbacks or at least with other small books. Similarly, oversized books will be shelved with other large books. Your lists make it easy to find the smallest available empty space where the book can fit. The disadvantage of this system is that you're wasting time looking for the best space. Your other customers have to wait for you to put each book away, so you won't be able to process as many customers as you could with the other kind of list.

In the second case, a list organized by shelf location, you're optimizing the time it takes you to put books back on the shelves. This is a first-fit scheme. This system ignores the size of the book that you're trying to put away. If the same paperback book arrives, you can quickly find it an empty space. In fact, any nearby empty space will suffice if it's large enough — even an encyclopedia rack can be used if it's close to your desk because you are optimizing the time it takes you to reshelve the books.

Of course, this is a fast method of shelving books, and if speed is important it's the best of the two alternatives. It is not a good choice if your shelf space is limited or if many large books are returned, because large books must wait for the large spaces. If all of your large spaces are filled with small books, the customers returning large books must wait until a suitable space becomes available. (Eventually you'll need time to rearrange the books and compact your collection.)

Table 2.2 shows how a large job can have problems with a first-fit memory allocation list.

Jobs 1, 2, and 4 are able to enter the system and begin execution; Job 3 has to wait even though, if all of the fragments of memory were added together, there would be more than enough room to accommodate it. First-fit is fast in allocation, but it is not always efficient.

TABLE 2.2 *First-fit free list. Job 2 claimed the first partition large enough to accommodate it, but by doing so it took the last block large enough to accommodate Job 3, so Job 3 (indicated by the asterisk) must wait even though there's 75K of unused memory space. Notice that the list is ordered according to memory location.*

Job List:
J1 10K
J2 20K
J3 30K*
J4 10K

Memory location	Memory block size	Job number	Job size	Status	Internal fragmentation
10K	30K	J1	10K	Busy	20K
40K	15K	J4	10K	Busy	5K
55K	50K	J2	20K	Busy	30K
105K	20K			Free	
Total Available:	115K	Total Used:	40K		

On the other hand, the same job list using a best-fit scheme would use memory more efficiently, as shown in Table 2.3. In this particular case a best-fit scheme would yield better memory utilization.

TABLE 2.3 *Best-fit free list. Job 1 is allocated to the closest-fitting free partition, as are Job 2 and Job 3. Job 4 is allocated to the only available partition although it is not the best-fitting one. In this scheme all jobs are served without waiting. Notice that the list is ordered according to memory size. It uses memory more efficiently but it is slower to implement.*

Job List:
J1 10K
J2 20K
J3 30K
J4 10K

Memory location	Memory block size	Job number	Job size	Status	Internal fragmentation
40K	15K	J1	10K	Busy	5K
105K	20K	J2	20K	Busy	None
10K	30K	J3	30K	Busy	None
55K	50K	J4	10K	Busy	40K
Total Available:	115K	Total Used:	70K		

Memory use has been increased but the memory allocation process takes more time. What's more, while internal fragmentation has been diminished, it hasn't been completely eliminated.

The first-fit algorithm assumes that the Memory Manager keeps two lists, one for free memory blocks and one for busy memory blocks. The operation consists of a simple loop that compares the size of each job to the size of each memory block until a block is found that's large enough to fit the job. Then the job is stored into that block of memory, and the Memory Manager moves out of the loop to fetch the next job from the entry queue. If the entire list is searched in vain, then the job is placed into a waiting queue. The Memory Manager then fetches the next job and repeats the process (Madnick & Donovan, 1974).

The algorithms for best-fit and first-fit are very different. Here's how first-fit is implemented.

FIRST-FIT ALGORITHM

```
1 Set counter to 1
2 Do while counter <= number of blocks in memory
    If job_size > memory_size(counter)
        then counter = counter + 1
    else
        load job into memory_size(counter)
          adjust free/busy memory lists
          go to step 4
  End do
3 Put job in waiting queue
4 Go fetch next job
```

In Table 2.4 a request for a block of 200 spaces has just been given to the Memory Manager. (The spaces may be words, bytes, or any other unit the system handles.) Using the first-fit algorithm and starting from the top of the list, the Memory Manager locates the first block of memory large enough to accommodate the job, which is at location 6785. The job is then loaded, starting at location 6785 and occupying the next 200 spaces. The next step is to adjust the free list to indicate that the block of free memory now starts at location 6985 (not 6785 as before) and that it contains only 400 spaces (not 600 as before).

TABLE 2.4 *Memory request satisfied using first-fit algorithm. The original free list before and after the request has been satisfied. (Note: All values are in decimal notation unless specifically noted otherwise.)*

Before request		**After request**	
Beginning address	**Memory block size**	**Beginning address**	**Memory block size**
4075	105	4075	105
5225	5	5225	5
6785	600	*6985	400
7560	20	7560	20
7600	205	7600	205
10250	4050	10250	4050
15125	230	15125	230
24500	1000	24500	1000

The algorithm for best-fit is slightly more complex because the goal is to find the smallest memory block into which the job will fit (Madnick & Donovan, 1974).

BEST-FIT ALGORITHM

```
1 Initialize memory_block(0) = 99999
2 Compute initial_memory_waste = memory_block(0) – job_size
3 Initialize subscript = 0
4 Set counter to 1
5 Do while counter <= number of blocks in memory
  If job_size > memory_size(counter)
    Then counter = counter + 1
  Else
    memory_waste = memory_size(counter) – job_size
    If initial_memory_waste > memory_waste
      Then subscript = counter
        initial_memory_waste = memory_waste
      counter = counter + 1
  End do
6 If subscript = 0
    Then put job in waiting queue
  Else
    load job into memory_size(subscript)
    adjust free/busy memory lists
7 Go fetch next job
```

One of the problems with the best-fit algorithm is that the entire table must be searched before the allocation can be made because the memory blocks are physically stored in sequence according to their location in memory (and not by memory block sizes as shown in Table 2.3). The system could execute an algorithm to continuously rearrange the list in ascending order by memory block size, but that would add more overhead and might not be an efficient use of processing time in the long run.

As above, the best-fit algorithm is illustrated showing only the list of free memory blocks. Table 2.5 shows the free list before and after the best-fit block has been allocated to the same request presented in Table 2.4.

TABLE 2.5

Memory request satisfied using best-fit algorithm. The original free list before and after the request has been satisfied.

Before request		After request	
Beginning address	**Memory block size**	**Beginning address**	**Memory block size**
4075	105	4075	105
5225	5	5225	5
6785	600	6785	600
7560	20	7560	20
7600	205	*7800	5
10250	4050	10250	4050
15125	230	15125	230
24500	1000	24500	1000

In Table 2.5, a request for a block of 200 spaces has just been given to the Memory Manager. Using the best-fit algorithm and starting from the top of the list, the Memory Manager searches the entire list and locates a block of memory starting at location 7600, which is the smallest block that's large enough to accommodate the job. The choice of this block minimizes the wasted space (only 5 spaces are wasted, which is less than in the four alternative blocks). The job is then stored, starting at location 7600 and occupying the next 200 spaces. Now the free list must be adjusted to show that the block of free memory starts at location 7800 (not 7600 as before) and that it contains only 5 spaces (not 205 as before).

Which is best — first-fit or best-fit? For many years there was no way to answer such a general question because performance depends on the job mix. Note that while the best-fit resulted in a better "fit," it also resulted (and does so in the general case) in a smaller "free" space (5 spaces), which is known as a "sliver."

In the exercises at the end of this chapter, two other hypothetical allocation schemes are explored: next-fit, which starts searching from the last allocated block for the next available block when a new job arrives; and worst-fit, which allocates the largest free available block to the new job. Worst-fit is the opposite of best-fit but, although it's a good way to explore the theory of memory allocation, it might not be the best choice for an actual system.

In recent years access times have become so fast that the scheme that saves the more valuable resource, memory space, may be the best in some cases. Research continues to focus on finding the optimum allocation scheme. This includes optimum page size — a fixed allocation scheme that we will cover in the next chapter and which is the key to improving the performance of the best-fit allocation scheme.

DEALLOCATION

Until now we've considered only the problem of how memory blocks are allocated, but eventually there comes a time when memory space must be released, or **deallocated**.

For a fixed partition system, the process is quite straightforward. When the job is completed the Memory Manager resets the status of the memory block where the job was stored to "free." Any code — for example, binary values with 0 indicating free and 1 indicating busy — may be used so the mechanical task of deallocating a block of memory is relatively simple.

A dynamic partition system uses a more complex algorithm because the algorithm tries to combine free areas of memory whenever possible. Therefore, the system must be prepared for three alternative situations (Madnick & Donovan, 1974):

1. When the block to be deallocated is adjacent to another free block
2. When the block to be deallocated is between two free blocks
3. When the block to be deallocated is isolated from other free blocks

The deallocation algorithm must be prepared for all three eventualities with a set of nested conditionals. The following algorithm is based on the fact that memory locations are listed using a lowest-to-highest address scheme. The algorithm would have to be modified to accommodate a different organization of memory locations.

ALGORITHM TO DEALLOCATE MEMORY BLOCKS

```
If job_location is adjacent to one or more free blocks
  Then
  If job_location is between two free blocks
    Then merge all three blocks into one
      memory_size(counter–1) = memory_size(counter–1) +
          job_size + memory_size(counter+1)
        Set status of memory_size(counter+1) to null entry
  Else merge both blocks into one
    memory_size(counter–1)=memory_size(counter–1)+job_size
Else search for null entry in free memory list
  Enter job_size and beginning_address in the entry slot
  Set its status to "free"
```

Here "job_size" is the amount of memory being released by the terminating job and "beginning_address" is where the first instruction of the job was located.

Situation 1 Table 2.6 shows how deallocation occurs in a dynamic memory allocation system when the job to be deallocated is next to one free memory block.

TABLE 2.6 *Original free list before deallocation for Situation 1. Asterisk indicates the free memory block adjacent to the "soon-to-be-free" memory block.*

Beginning address	Memory block size	Status
4075	105	F
5225	5	F
6785	600	F
7560	20	F
(7600)	(200)	(Busy)[1]
* 7800	5	F
10250	4050	F
15125	230	F
24500	1000	F

Note: 1. Although this entry isn't in the free list, it has been inserted here for clarity. The job size is 200 and its beginning location is 7600.

Using the deallocation algorithm presented above, the system sees that the memory to be released is next to a free memory block, which starts at location 7800. Therefore the list must be changed to reflect the starting address of the new free block, 7600, which was the address of the first instruction of the job that just released this block. In addition, the memory block size for this new free space must be changed to show its new size, that is, the combined total of the two free partitions (200 + 5).

After deallocation the free list looks like the one shown in Table 2.7.

Situation 2 When the deallocated memory space is between two memory blocks, the process is similar, as shown in Table 2.8.

Using the deallocation algorithm, the system learns that the memory to be deallocated is between two free blocks of memory. Therefore, the sizes of the three free partitions (20 + 20 + 205) must be combined and the total stored with the smallest beginning address, 7560.

TABLE 2.7 *Free list after deallocation for Situation 1. Asterisk indicates the free memory block after changes have occurred.*

Beginning address	Memory block size	Status
4075	105	F
5225	5	F
6785	600	F
7560	20	F
* 7600	205	F
10250	4050	F
15125	230	F
24500	1000	F

TABLE 2.8 *Original free list before deallocation for Situation 2. Asterisks indicate the two free memory blocks adjacent to the "soon-to-be-free" memory block.*

Beginning address	Memory block size	Status
4075	105	F
5225	5	F
6785	600	F
* 7560	20	F
(7580)	(20)	(Busy)[1]
* 7600	205	F
10250	4050	F
15125	230	F
24500	1000	F

Note: 1. Although this entry isn't shown in the free list, it has been inserted here for clarity. The job size is 20 and its beginning location is 7580.

Because the entry at location 7600 has been combined with the previous entry we must "empty out" this entry, and we do that by changing the status to N, for **null entry**, with no beginning address and no memory block size as indicated by an asterisk in Table 2.9. This avoids rearranging the list at the expense of memory.

TABLE 2.9 *Free list after a job has released memory for Situation 2.*

Beginning address	Memory block size	Status
4075	105	F
5225	5	F
6785	600	F
7560	245	F
*		N
10250	4050	F
15125	230	F
24500	1000	F

Situation 3 The third alternative is when the space to be deallocated is isolated from all other free areas.

For this example we need to know more about how the "busy" memory list is configured. To simplify matters let's look at the busy list for the memory area between locations 7560 and 10250. Remember that starting at 7560 there's a free memory block of 245, so the busy memory area includes everything from location 7805 (7560 + 245) to 10250, which is the address of the next free block. The free list and busy list are shown in Table 2.10 and Table 2.11.

TABLE 2.10 *Original free list before deallocation for Situation 3. The soon-to-be-free memory block is not adjacent to any blocks already free.*

Beginning address	Memory block size	Status
4075	105	F
5225	5	F
6785	600	F
7560	245	F
		N
10250	4050	F
15125	230	F
24500	1000	F

TABLE 2.11 *Busy memory list for Situation 3. The job to be deallocated is of size 445 and begins at location 8805. Asterisk indicates "soon-to-be-free" memory block.*

Beginning address	Memory block size	Status
7805	1000	B
*8805	445	B
9250	1000	B

Using the deallocation algorithm, the system learns that the memory block to be released is not adjacent to any free blocks of memory; it is between two other busy areas. Therefore it must search the table for a null entry: N.

The scheme presented in this example creates null entries in both the busy and the free lists during the process of allocation or deallocation of memory. An example of a null entry occurring as a result of deallocation was presented in Situation 2. A null entry in the busy list occurs when a memory block between two other busy memory blocks is returned to the free list (as shown in Table 2.13). This mechanism ensures that all blocks are entered in the lists according to the beginning address of their memory location from smallest to largest.

When the null entry is found, the beginning memory location of the terminating job is entered in the beginning address column, the job size is entered under the memory block size column, and the status is changed from N to F to indicate that a new block of memory is free and available, as shown in Table 2.12.

TABLE 2.12 *Free list after the job has released its memory. Asterisk indicates "new free block" entry replacing null entry.*

Beginning address	Memory block size	Status
4075	105	F
5225	5	F
6785	600	F
7560	245	F
* 8805	445	F
10250	4050	F
15125	230	F
24500	1000	F

TABLE 2.13 *Busy list after the job has released its memory. Asterisk indicates new null entry in busy list.*

Beginning address	Memory block size	Status
7805	1000	B
*		N
9250	1000	B

RELOCATABLE DYNAMIC PARTITIONS

Both of the fixed and dynamic memory allocation schemes described thus far shared some unacceptable fragmentation characteristics that had to be resolved before the number of jobs waiting to be accepted became unwieldy. In addition, there was a growing need to use all the "slivers" of memory often left over.

The solution to both problems was the development of **relocatable dynamic partitions**. With this memory allocation scheme, the Memory Manager relocates programs to gather together all of the empty blocks and compact them to make one block of memory that's large enough to accommodate some or all of the jobs waiting to get in.

The compaction of memory, sometimes referred to as "garbage collection" or "defragmentation," is performed by the operating system to reclaim fragmented sections of the memory space. Remember our earlier example of the makeshift lending library? If you stopped lending books for a few moments and rearranged the books in the most effective order, you would be compacting your collection. But this demonstrates its disadvantage — it's an overhead process, so that while compaction is being done everything else must wait.

Compaction isn't an easy task. First, every program in memory must be relocated so they're contiguous, and then every address, and every reference to an address, within each program must be adjusted to account for the program's new location in memory. However, all other values within the program (such as data values) must be left alone. In other words, the operating system must distinguish between addresses and data values, and the distinctions are not obvious once the program has been loaded into memory.

To appreciate the complexity of **relocation**, let's look at a typical program. Remember, all numbers are stored in memory as binary values, and in any given program instruction it's not uncommon to find addresses as well as data values. For example, an assembly language program might include the instruction to add the integer 1 to I. The source code instruction looks like this:

```
ADDI  I, 1
```

However, after it has been translated into actual code it could look like this (for readability purposes the values are represented here in octal code, not binary):

```
000007    271 01 0 00 000001
```

It's not immediately obvious which are addresses and which are instruction codes or data values. In fact, the address is the number on the left (000007). The instruction code is next (271), and the data value is on the right (000001).

The operating system can tell the function of each group of digits by its location in the line and the operation code. However, if the program is to be moved to another place in memory each address must be identified, or flagged. So later the amount of memory locations by which the program has been displaced must be added to (or subtracted from) all of the original addresses in the program.

This becomes particularly important when the program includes loop sequences, decision sequences, and branching sequences, as well as data references. If, by chance, not all the addresses were adjusted by the same value, the program would branch to the wrong section of the program or to a section of another program, or it would reference the wrong data.

The program in Figure 2.3 shows how the operating system flags the addresses so they can be adjusted if and when a program is relocated.

Internally, the addresses are marked with a special symbol (indicated in Figure 2.3 by apostrophes) so the Memory Manager will know to adjust them by the value stored in the relocation register. All of the other values (data values) are not marked and won't be changed after relocation. Other numbers in the program, those indicating instructions, registers, or constants used in the instruction, are also left alone.

The original assembly language program looks like this:

```
A:      EXP 132, 144,125, 110    ;the data values
BEGIN:  MOVEI           1,0      ;initialize register 1
        MOVEI           2,0      ;initialize register 2
LOOP:   ADD             2,A(1)   ;add (A + reg 1) to reg 2
        ADDI            1,1      ;add 1 to reg 1
        CAIG            1,4-1    ;is reg 1 > 4-1?
        JUMPA           LOOP     ;if not, go to Loop
        MOVE            3,2      ;if so, move reg 2 to reg 3
        IDIVI           3,4      ;divide reg 3 by 4,
                                 ;remainder to register 4
        EXIT                     ;end
        END
```

Once it's loaded into memory it looks like this:

FIGURE 2.3 *The original assembly language program (shown on page 32) performs a simple incremental operation. To run the program, the compiler software must translate it into machine-readable code (shown at bottom left) with addresses marked by a special symbol (shown here as an apostrophe) to distinguish addresses from data values. This program was run on a DEC system 1099 tri-processor with TOPS-10 monitor version 7.01A operating system.*

```
000000' 000000 000132               A:        EXP 132,144,125,110
000001' 000000 000144
000002' 000000 000125
000003' 000000 000110

000004' 201 01 0 00 000000          BEGIN:    MOVEI     1,0
000005' 201 02 0 00 000000                    MOVEI     2,0
000006' 270 02 0 01 000000'         LOOP:     ADD       2,A(1)
000007' 271 01 0 00 000001                    ADDI      1,1
000008' 307 01 0 00 000003                    CAIG      1,4-1
000009' 324 00 0 00 000006'                   JUMPA     LOOP
000010' 200 03 0 00 000002                    MOVE      3,2
000011' 231 03 0 00 000004                    IDIVI     3,4
000012' 047 00 0 00 000012                    EXIT

              000000                          END
```

Figure 2.4 illustrates what happens to a program in memory during compaction and relocation.

Our discussion raises three questions:

1. What goes on behind the scenes when relocation and compaction take place?
2. What keeps track of how far each job has moved from its original storage area?
3. What lists have to be updated?

The last question is easiest to answer. After relocation and compaction, both the free list and the busy list are updated. The free list is changed to show the partition for the new block of free memory: the one formed as a result of compaction that will be located in memory starting after the last location used by the last job. The busy list is changed to show the new locations for all of the jobs already in process that were relocated. Each job will have a new address except for those that were already residing at the lowest memory locations.

To answer the other two questions we must learn more about the hardware components of a computer, specifically the registers. Special-purpose registers are used to help with the relocation. In some computers two special registers are set aside for this purpose: the bounds register and the relocation register.

FIGURE 2.4 *Three snapshots of memory before and after compaction. When Job 6 arrives requiring 84K, the initial memory layout in (a) shows external fragmentation totaling 96K of space. Immediately after compaction (b), external fragmentation has been eliminated, making room for Job 6 (c).*

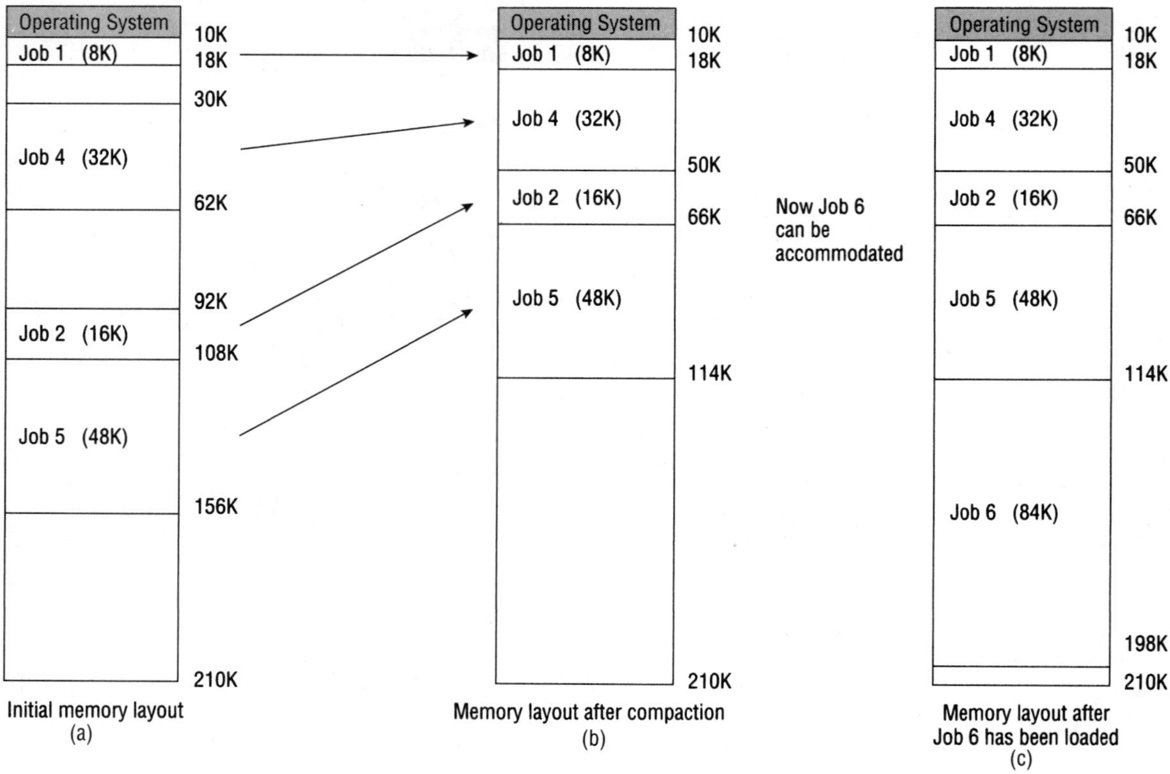

The **bounds register** is used to store the highest (or lowest, depending on the specific system) location in memory accessible by each program. This ensures that during execution, a program won't try to access memory locations that don't belong to it — that is, those that are "out of bounds." The **relocation register** contains the value that must be added to each address referenced in the program so it will be able to access the correct memory addresses after relocation. If the program isn't relocated, the value stored in the program's relocation register is zero.

Figure 2.5 illustrates what happens during relocation by using the relocation register (all values are shown in decimal form).

Originally, Job 4 was loaded into memory starting at memory location 30K. (**K** = 1024 bytes so the exact starting address is: 30 * 1024 = 30,720.) It required a block of memory of 32K (or 32 * 1024 = 32,768) addressable locations. Therefore, when it was originally loaded, the job occupied the space from memory location 30720 to memory location 63488-1. Now, suppose that within the program, at memory location 31744, there's an instruction that looks like this:

```
LOAD 4, ANSWER
```

FIGURE 2.5 *Contents of relocation register and close-up of Job 4 memory area (a) before relocation and (b) after relocation and compaction.*

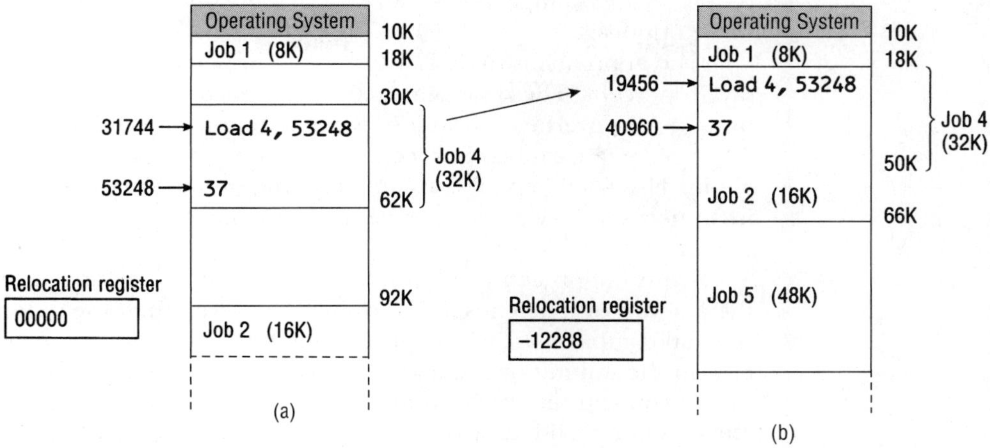

This assembly language command asks that the data value known as `ANSWER` be loaded into Register 4 for later computation. `ANSWER`, the value 37, is stored at memory location 53248. (In this example Register 4 is a working/computation register, which is distinct from either the relocation or the bounds register.)

After relocation, Job 4 has been moved to a new starting memory address of 18K (actually 18 * 1024 = 18,432). Of course, the job still has its 32K addressable locations, so it now occupies memory from location 18432 to location 51200-1 and, thanks to the relocation register, all of the addresses will be adjusted accordingly.

What does the relocation register contain? In this example it contains the value −12288. As calculated previously, 12288 is the size of the free block that has been "moved forward" toward the high addressable end of memory. The sign is negative because Job 4 has been "moved back," closer to the low addressable end of memory, as shown at the top of Figure 2.5(b).

However, the program instruction (`LOAD 4,ANSWER`) has not been changed. The original address 53248 where `ANSWER` had been stored remains the same in the program no matter how many times it is relocated. Before the instruction is executed, however, the "true" address must be computed by adding the value stored in the relocation register to the address found at that instruction. If the addresses are not adjusted by the value stored in the relocation register, then even though memory location 31744 is still part of the job's accessible set of memory locations, it would not contain the `LOAD` command. Not only that, but location 53248 is now "out of bounds." The instruction that was originally at 31744 has been moved to location 19456. That's because all of the instructions in this program have been "moved back" by 12K (12 * 1024 = 12,288), which is the size of the free block. Therefore, location 53248 has been displaced by −12288 and `ANSWER`, the data value 37, is now located at address 40960.

In effect, by compacting and relocating, the Memory Manager optimizes the use of memory and thus improves throughput — one of the measures of system performance. An unfortunate side effect is that more overhead is incurred than with the two previous memory allocation schemes. The crucial factor here is the timing of the compaction — when and how often it should be done. There are three options.

One approach is to do it when a certain percentage of memory becomes busy, say 75 percent. The disadvantage of this approach is that the system would incur unnecessary overhead if no jobs were waiting to use the remaining 25 percent.

A second approach is to compact memory only when there are jobs waiting to get in. This would entail constant checking of the entry queue, which might result in unnecessary overhead and slow down the processing of jobs already in the system.

A third approach is to do it after a prescribed amount of time has elapsed. If the amount of time chosen is too small, however, then the system will spend more time on compaction than on processing. If it's too large, too many jobs will congregate in the waiting queue and the advantages of compaction are lost.

As you can see, each option has its good and bad points. The best choice for any system is decided by the operating system designer who, based on the job mix and other factors, tries to optimize both processing time and memory use while keeping overhead as low as possible.

CHAPTER TWO CONCLUSION

Four memory management techniques were presented in this chapter: single-user systems, fixed partitions, dynamic partitions, and relocatable dynamic partitions. They have three things in common: they all require that the entire program (1) be loaded into memory, (2) be stored contiguously, and (3) remain in memory until the job is completed.

Consequently, each puts severe restrictions on the size of the jobs because they can only be as large as the biggest partitions in memory.

These schemes were sufficient for the first three generations of computers, which processed jobs in batch mode. Turnaround time was measured in hours, or sometimes days, but that was a period when users expected such delays between the submission of their jobs and pick up of output. As we'll see in the next chapter, a new trend emerged during the third-generation computers of the late 1960s and early 1970s: users were able to connect directly with the central processing unit via remote job entry stations, loading their jobs from on-line terminals that could interact more directly with the system. New methods of memory management were needed to accommodate them.

We'll see that the memory allocation schemes that followed had two new things in common. First, programs didn't have to be stored in contiguous memory locations: they could be divided into "segments" of variable sizes or "pages" of equal size. Each page, or segment, could be stored wherever there was an empty block big enough to hold it. Second, not all the pages, or segments, had to reside in memory during the execution of the job. These were significant advances for system designers, operators, and users alike.

KEY TERMS

memory allocation scheme
single-user system
address
multiprogramming
fixed partitions
internal fragmentation
dynamic partitions
first come first served
external fragmentation
first-fit memory allocation
best-fit memory allocation
deallocation
relocatable dynamic partitions
compaction
relocation
bounds register
relocation register
K

EXERCISES

1. Explain the following:
   - **a.** Multiprogramming. Why is it used?
   - **b.** Internal fragmentation. How does it occur?
   - **c.** External fragmentation. How does it occur?
   - **d.** Compaction. Why is it needed?
   - **e.** Relocation. How often should it be performed?
2. Describe the major disadvantages for each of the four memory allocation schemes presented in the chapter.
3. Describe the major advantages for each of the memory allocation schemes presented in the chapter.
4. Given the following information:

Job list		Memory list	
Job stream	**Memory requested**	**Memory blocks**	**Size**
Job 1	740K	Block 1	610K (low-order memory)
Job 2	500K	Block 2	850K
Job 3	700K	Block 3	700K (high-order memory)

   - **a.** Use the best-fit algorithm to allocate the memory blocks to the three arriving jobs.
   - **b.** Use the first-fit algorithm to allocate the memory blocks to the three arriving jobs.

5. Given the following information:

Job list		Memory list	
Job stream	**Memory requested**	**Memory blocks**	**Size**
Job 1	700K	Block 1	610K (low-order memory)
Job 2	500K	Block 2	850K
Job 3	740K	Block 3	700K (high-order memory)

a. Use the best-fit algorithm to allocate the memory blocks to the three arriving jobs.
b. Use the first-fit algorithm to allocate the memory blocks to the three arriving jobs.

6. "Next-fit" is an allocation algorithm that keeps track of the last allocated partition and starts searching from that point on when a new job arrives.
a. What might be an advantage of this algorithm?
b. How would it compare to best-fit and first-fit for the conditions given in exercise 4?
c. How would it compare to best-fit and first-fit for the conditions given in exercise 5?

7. "Worst-fit" is an allocation algorithm that is the opposite of best-fit. It allocates the largest free block to a new job.
a. What might be an advantage of this algorithm?
b. How would it compare to best-fit and first-fit for the conditions given in exercise 4?
c. How would it compare to best-fit and first-fit for the conditions given in exercise 5?

8. The relocation example presented in the chapter implies that compaction is done entirely in memory, without secondary storage. Can all free sections of memory be merged into one contiguous block using this approach? Why or why not?

9. One way to compact memory would be to copy all existing jobs to a secondary storage device and then reload them contiguously into main memory, thus creating one free block after all jobs have been recopied (and relocated) into memory. Is this viable? Could you devise a better way to compact memory? Write your algorithm and explain why it is better.

ADVANCED EXERCISES

10. Given the following memory configuration:

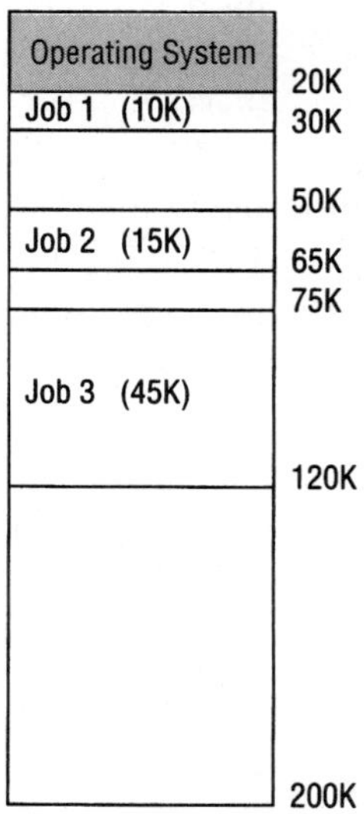

At this point, Job 4 arrives requesting a block of 100K. Answer the following:

a. Can Job 4 be accommodated? Why or why not?

b. If relocation is used, what are the contents of the relocation registers for Job 1, Job 2, and Job 3 after recompaction?

c. What are the contents of the relocation register for Job 4 after it has been loaded into memory?

d. The instruction `ADDI 4,10` is part of Job 1 and was originally loaded into memory location 22K. What is its new location after compaction?

e. The instruction `MUL 4,NUMBER` is part of Job 2 and was originally loaded into memory location 55K. What is its new location after compaction?

f. The instruction `MOVE 3,SUM` is part of Job 3 and was originally loaded into memory location 80K. What is its new location after compaction?

g. If `SUM` was originally loaded into memory location 110K, what is its new location after compaction?

h. If the instruction `MOVE 3,SUM` is stored as follows (this is in octal instead of binary for compactness):

```
200      03  00    334000
```

where the rightmost value indicates the memory location where `SUM` is stored, what would that value be after compaction?

11. You have been given the job of determining whether the current fixed partition memory configuration in your computer system should be changed.

a. What information do you need to help you make that decision?

b. How would you go about collecting this information?

c. Once you had the information, how would you determine the best configuration for your system?

PROGRAMMING EXERCISES

12. Here is a long-term programming project. Use the information that follows to complete this exercise.

Job list

Job stream number	Time	Job size
1	5	5760
2	4	4190
3	8	3290
4	2	2030
5	2	2550
6	6	6990
7	8	8940
8	10	740
9	7	3930
10	6	6890
11	5	6580

Memory list

Memory block	Size
1	9500
2	7000
3	4500
4	8500
5	3000
6	9000
7	1000
8	5500
9	1500
10	500

Job list *(continued)*

Job stream number	Time	Job size
12	8	3820
13	9	9140
14	10	420
15	10	220
16	7	7540
17	3	3210
18	1	1380
19	9	9850
20	3	3610
21	7	7540
22	2	2710
23	8	8390
24	5	5950
25	10	760

At one large batch-processing computer installation the management wants to decide what storage placement strategy will yield the best possible performance. The installation runs a large real storage (as opposed to "virtual" storage, which will be covered in the following chapter) computer under fixed partition multiprogramming. Each user program runs in a single group of contiguous storage locations. Users state their storage requirements and time units for CPU usage on their Job Control Card (it used to, and still does, work this way, although cards may not be used). The operating system allocates to each user the appropriate partition and starts up the user's job. The job remains in memory until completion. A total of 50,000 memory locations are available, divided into blocks as indicated in the table above.

a. Write (or calculate) an event-driven simulation to help you decide which storage placement strategy should be used at this installation. Your program would use the job stream and memory partitioning as indicated previously. Run the program until all jobs have been executed with the memory as is (in order by address). This will give you the first-fit type performance results.

b. Sort the memory partitions by size and run the program a second time; this will give you the best-fit performance results. For both parts **a.** and **b.** you are investigating the performance of the system using a typical job stream by measuring:

1. Throughput (how many jobs are processed per given time unit)
2. Storage utilization (percentage of partitions never used, percentage of partitions heavily used, etc.)
3. Waiting queue length
4. Waiting time in queue
5. Internal fragmentation

Given that jobs are served on a first-come first-served basis:

c. Explain how the system handles conflicts when jobs are put into a waiting queue and there are still jobs entering the system — who goes first?

d. Explain how the system handles the "job clocks," which keep track of the amount of time each job has run, and the "wait clocks," which keep track of how long each job in the waiting queue has to wait.

e. Since this is an event-driven system, explain how you define "event" and what happens in your system when the event occurs.

f. Look at the results from the best-fit run and compare them with the results from the first-fit run. Explain what the results indicate about the performance of the system for this job mix and memory organization. Is one method of partitioning better than the other? Why or why not? Could you recommend one method over the other given your sample run? Would this hold in all cases? Write some conclusions and recommendations.

13. Suppose your system (as explained in exercise 12) now has a "spooler" (storage area in which to temporarily hold jobs) and the job scheduler can choose which will be served from among 25 resident jobs. Suppose also that the first-come first-served policy is replaced with a "faster-job first-served" policy. This would require that a sort by time be performed on the job list before running the program. Does this make a different in the results? Does it make a difference in your analysis? Does it make a difference in your conclusions and recommendations? The program should be run twice to test this new policy with both best-fit and first-fit.

14. Suppose your spooler (as described in exercise 13) replaces the previous policy with one of "smallest-job first-served." This would require that a sort by job size be performed on the job list before running the program. How do the results compare to the previous two sets of results? Will your analysis change? Will your conclusions change? The program should be run twice to test this new policy with both best-fit and first-fit.

Chapter Three

MEMORY MANAGEMENT, RECENT SYSTEMS

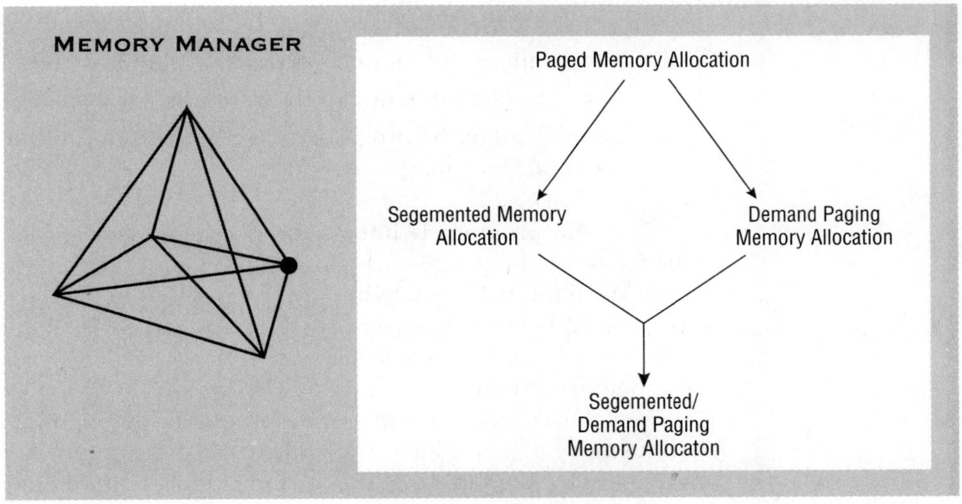

In the previous chapter we looked at the first memory allocation schemes. Each one required that the Memory Manager store the entire program in main memory in contiguous locations, and as we pointed out each scheme solved some problems but created others, such as fragmentation or the overhead of relocation.

In this chapter we'll examine more sophisticated memory allocation schemes that first remove the restriction of storing the programs contiguously and then eliminate the requirement that the entire program reside in memory during its execution. These four schemes are paged, demand paging, segmented, and segmented/demand paged allocation. Finally, we'll discuss virtual memory and how it affects main memory allocation.

PAGED MEMORY ALLOCATION

Paged memory allocation is based on the concept of dividing each incoming job into **pages** of equal size. Some operating systems choose a page size that's the same as the memory block size and that is also the same size as the sections of the disk on which the job is stored.

The sections of a disk are called "sectors" (or sometimes "blocks"), and the sections of main memory are called **page frames**. The scheme works quite efficiently when the pages, sectors, and page frames are all the same size. The exact size (the number of bytes that can be stored in each of them) is usually determined by the disk's sector size. Therefore, one sector will hold one page of job instructions and fit into one page frame of memory.

Before executing a program, the Memory Manager prepares it by:

1. Determining the number of pages in the program;
2. Locating enough empty page frames in main memory;
3. Loading all of the program's pages into them (in "static" paging the pages need not be contiguous).

When the program is initially prepared for loading its pages are in logical sequence — the first pages contain the first lines of the program and the last page has the last lines. But the loading process is different from the schemes we studied in Chapter 2 because the pages do not have to be loaded in adjacent memory blocks. In fact, each page can be stored in any available page frame anywhere in main memory (Madnick & Donovan, 1974).

The primary advantage of storing programs in noncontiguous locations is that main memory is used more efficiently because an empty page frame can be used by any page of any job. In addition, the compaction scheme used for relocatable partitions is eliminated because there's not external fragmentation between page frames (and no internal fragmentation in most pages).

However, with every new solution comes a new problem: because a job's pages can be located anywhere in main memory, the Memory Manager now needs a mechanism to keep track of them — and that means enlarging the size and complexity of the operating system software, which increases overhead.

The example in Figure 3.1 shows how the Memory Manager keeps track of a program that's four pages long. To simplify the arithmetic, we've arbitrarily set the page size at 100 lines (or bytes). Job 1 is 350 lines (or bytes) long and is being readied for execution.

Notice in Figure 3.1 that the last page (Page 3) is not fully utilized because the job is less than 400 lines — the last page uses only 50 of the 100 lines available. In fact, very few jobs would perfectly fill all of the pages, so internal fragmentation is still a problem (but only in the last page of a job).

In Figure 3.1 (with seven free page frames), the operating system can accommodate jobs that vary in size from 1 to 700 lines because they can be stored in the seven empty page frames. But a job that's larger than 700 lines can't be accommodated until Job 1 ends its execution and releases the four page frames it occupies.

FIGURE 3.1 *Programs too long to fit on a single page are split into equal-sized pages that can be stored in free page frames. In this example each page frame can hold 100 lines. This job is 350 lines long and is divided among four page frames, leaving internal fragmentation in the last page frame. The Page Map Table for this job is shown later in Table 3.2.*

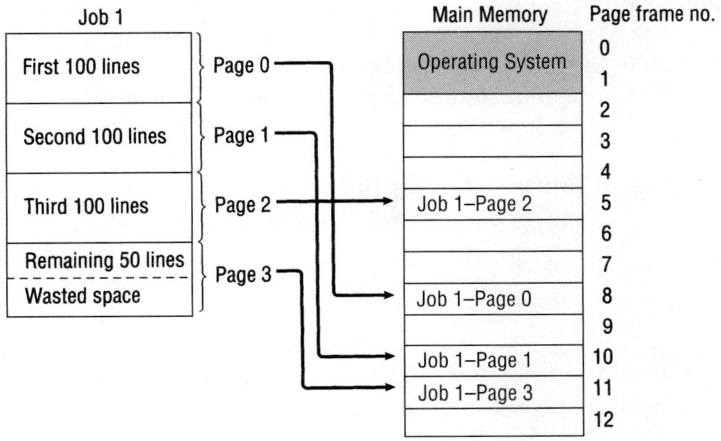

And a job that's larger than 1100 lines will never fit into memory. Therefore, although paged memory allocation offers the advantage of noncontiguous storage, it still requires that the entire job be stored in memory during its execution, in this scheme.

Figure 3.1 uses arrows and lines to show how a job's pages fit into page frames in memory, but the Memory Manager uses tables to keep track of them. There are essentially three tables that perform this function: Job Table (JT), Page Map Table (PMT), and Memory Map Table (MMT). All three tables reside in the part of main memory that's reserved for the operating system.

As shown in Table 3.1, the **Job Table** contains two entries for each active job: the size of the job and the memory location where its Page Map Table is stored. This is a dynamic list that grows as jobs are loaded into the system and shrinks as they're later completed.

TABLE 3.1 *This section of the Job Table (a) initially has three entries, one for each job in process. When the second job ends, (b) its entry in the table is released and it is replaced (c) by information about the next job that is processed.*

Job Table

Job size	PMT location
400	3096
200	3100
500	3150

(a)

Job Table

Job size	PMT location
400	3096
500	3150

(b)

Job Table

Job size	PMT location
400	3096
700	3100
500	3150

(c)

Each active job has its own **Page Map Table** that contains the vital information for each page: the page number and its corresponding page frame memory address. Actually, the PMT includes only one entry per page. The page numbers are sequential (Page 0, Page 1, Page 2, through the last page) so it isn't necessary to list each page number in the PMT. The first entry in the PMT lists the page frame memory address for Page 0, the second entry is the address for Page 1, and so on.

The **Memory Map Table** has one entry for each page frame listing the location and free/busy status for each one.

At compilation time every job is divided into pages. Using Job 1 from Figure 3.1 we can see how this works:

Page 0 contains the first hundred lines

Page 1 contains the second hundred lines

Page 2 contains the third hundred lines

Page 3 contains the last fifty lines

As you can see, the program has 350 lines, but when they're stored the system numbers them starting from 0 through 349, so they're referred to by the system as line 0 through line 349.

The **displacement**, or **offset**, of a line (that is, how far away a line is from the beginning of its page) is the factor used to locate that line within its page frame. It's a relative factor.

For example, lines 0, 100, 200, and 300 are the first lines for pages 0, 1, 2, and 3 respectively so each has a displacement of zero. This is shown in Figure 3.2. Likewise, if the operating system needed to access line 214 it would first go to page 2 and then go to line 14 (the fifteenth line).

The first line of each page has a displacement of zero, the second line has a displacement of one, and so on to the last line (or byte), which has a displacement of 99. So once the operating system finds the right page, it can access a line using the job's relative position within its page.

In this example, it's easy for us to see, intuitively, that all of the line numbers less than 100 will be on Page 0, all line numbers greater than or equal to 100 but less than 200 will be on Page 1, and so on. (That's the advantage of choosing a fixed page size, e.g., 100 lines.) The operating system uses an algorithm to calculate the page and displacement; it's a simple arithmetic calculation.

To find the address of a given program line, the line number is divided by the page size, keeping the remainder as an integer. The resulting quotient is the page number and the remainder is the displacement within that page. When it's set up as a long division problem, it looks like this:

```
                 page number
page size ) line number to be located
            xxx
              xxx
              xxx
                displacement
```

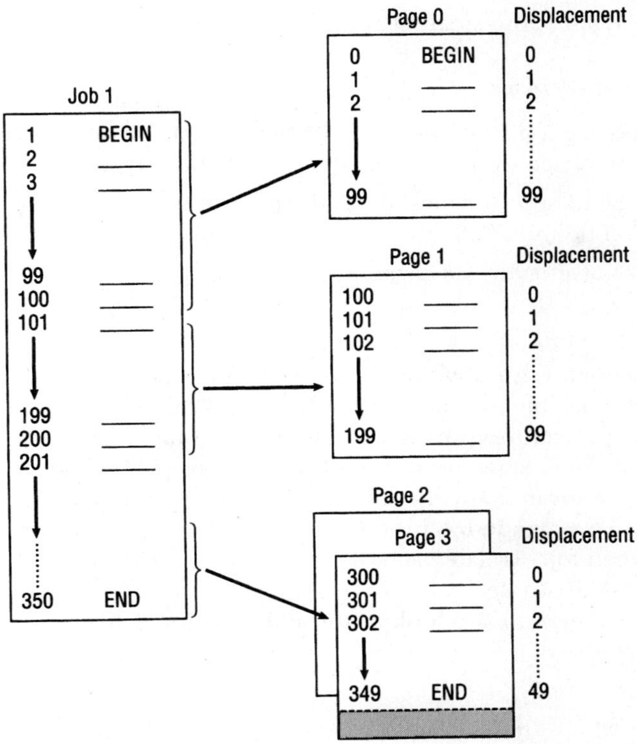

FIGURE 3.2 *Job 1 is 350 lines long and divided into four pages of 100 lines each.*

EXAMPLE 1 For example, if we use 100 lines as the page size, the page number and the displacement (the location within that page) of Line 214 would be calculated like this:

$$\begin{array}{r} 2 \\ 100\,\overline{)214} \\ \underline{200} \\ 14 \end{array}$$

The quotient (2) is the page number and the remainder (14) is the displacement. So the line is located on Page 2, 15 lines (Line 14) from the top of the page.

EXAMPLE 2 Likewise, we could calculate the page number and displacement of Line 36 by dividing 36 by 100. We find that the page number is 0 and the displacement is 36. So the line will be found on Page 0, Line 36, the 37th line from the top of the page.

Using the concepts just presented, and using the same parameters from Example 1, answer these questions:

1. Could the operating system (or the hardware) get a page number that's greater than 3, if the program intended Line 214?
2. If it did, what should the operating system do?
3. Could the operating system get a remainder of more than 99?

4. What is the smallest remainder possible?

The answers are:

1. No, not if the application program was written correctly. (For the exception, see exercise 14 at the end of this chapter.)
2. Send an error message and stop processing the program (the page is "out-of-bounds").
3. Not if it divides correctly.
4. Zero.

In actuality, the division is carried out in the hardware but the operating system is responsible for maintaining the tables (allocating and deallocating storage).

This procedure gives the location of the line with respect to the job's pages. However, these pages are only relative; each page is actually stored in a page frame that can be located anywhere in available main memory. Therefore, the algorithm needs to be expanded to find the exact location of the line in main memory. To do so, we need to correlate each of the job's pages with their page frame numbers via the Page Map Table.

For example, if we look at the PMT for Job 1 from Figure 3.1, we see that it looks like the data in Table 3.2.

TABLE 3.2
Page Map Table for Job 1 in Figure 3.1.

Job page no.	Page frame no.
0	8
1	10
2	5
3	11

In example 1 we were looking for an instruction with a displacement of 14 on Page 2. To find its exact location in memory, the operating system (or the hardware) has to do the following.

Step 1 Do the arithmetic computation from the algorithm described previously to determine the page number and displacement of the line. (In actuality, the operating system identifies the lines, or data values and instructions, as addresses [bytes or words]. We refer to them here as "lines" to make them easier to explain.)

Page number = the integer quotient from the division of the job space address by the page size

Displacement = the remainder from the page number division above

The computation shows that the page number is 2 and the displacement is 14.

Step 2 Refer to this job's PMT and find out which page frame contains Page 2. According to Table 3.2, Page 2 is located in Page Frame 5.

Step 3 Get the address of the beginning of the page frame by multiplying the page frame number by the page frame size.

```
ADDR_PAGE_FRAME = PAGE_FRAME_NUM * PAGE_SIZE
```

Step 4 Now add the displacement (calculated in step 1) to the starting address of the page frame to compute the precise location in memory of the line:

```
INSTR_ADDR_IN_MEM = ADDR_PAGE_FRAME + DISPL
```

The result of this maneuver tells us exactly where Line 14 is located in main memory.

Figure 3.3 follows the hardware (and the operating system) as it runs an assembly language program that instructs the system to load into Register 1 the value found at Line 518.

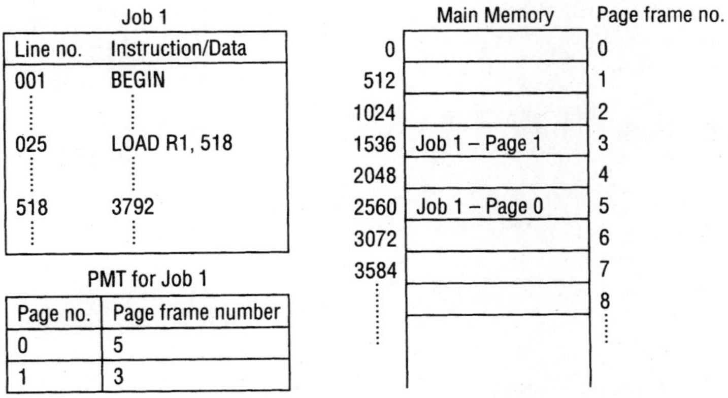

FIGURE 3.3
Job 1 with its Page Map Table. Main memory showing allocation of page frames to Job 1.

In Figure 3.3 the page frame sizes in main memory are set at 512 bytes each and the page size is 512 bytes for this system. From the PMT we can see that this job has been divided into two pages. To find the exact location of Line 518 (where the system will find the value to load into Register 1), the system will do the following:

1. Compute the page number and displacement: the page number is 1, the displacement is 6.
2. Go to the Page Map Table and retrieve the appropriate page frame number for Page 1. It's Page Frame 3.
3. Compute the starting address of the page frame by multiplying the page frame number times the page frame size: (3 * 512 = 1536).
4. Calculate the exact address of the instruction in main memory by adding the displacement to the starting address: (1536 + 6 = 1542). Therefore, memory address 1542 holds the value that should be loaded into Register 1.

As you can see, this is a lengthy operation. Every time an instruction is executed, or a data value is used, the operating system (or the hardware) must translate the job space address, which is relative, into its physical address, which is absolute. This is called "resolving the address" or **address resolution**. Of course, all of this processing is overhead, which takes processing capability away from the jobs waiting to be completed. However, in most systems the hardware does the paging, although the operating system is involved in dynamic paging, which will be covered later.

The advantage of a paging scheme is that it allows jobs to be allocated in noncontiguous memory locations so that memory is used more efficiently and more jobs can fit in the main memory (which is synonymous). However, there are disadvantages: overhead is increased and internal fragmentation is still a problem, although only in the last page of each job. The key to the success of this scheme is the size of the page: a page size too small will generate very long PMTs while a page size too large will result in excessive internal fragmentation. Determining the best page size isn't easy — there are no hard and fast rules that will guarantee optimal use of resources — and it's a problem we'll see again as we examine other paging alternatives. The best size depends on the actual job environment, the nature of the jobs being processed, and the constraints placed on the system.

DEMAND PAGING

Demand paging takes advantage of the fact that programs are written sequentially so that while one section, or module, is being processed all of the other modules are idle (Madnick & Donovan, 1974). Not all the pages are necessary at once, for example:

1. User-written error handling modules are processed only when a specific error is detected during execution. (For instance, they are often used to indicate to the operator that input data was incorrect or that a computation resulted in an invalid answer). If no error occurs, and we hope this is generally the case, these instructions are never processed.
2. Many modules are mutually exclusive. For example, if the input module is active then the processing module isn't being used. Similarly, if the processing module is active then the output module is idle.
3. Certain program options are either mutually exclusive or not always accessible. This is easiest to visualize in menu-driven programs. For example, a program used to maintain a data file may give the user four menu choices as shown in Figure 3.4 on page 51. The system allows the operator to make only one selection at a time. If the user selects number 1 then only the module with the program instructions to add new records to the file will be used, so only that module needs to be in memory. All of the other

modules can remain in secondary storage until they are called from the menu.

4. Many tables are assigned a large fixed amount of address space even though only a fraction of the table is actually used. For example, a symbol table for an assembler might be prepared to handle 100 symbols. If only 10 symbols are used then 90 percent of the table remains unused.

FIGURE 3.4 *Menu-driven programs allow users to work with only one program module at a time. Modules that are not currently available can be moved out of memory and reloaded later, when they're needed.*

```
        DATA FILE MAINTENANCE MENU

SELECT ONE:
  1)  To add a new record
  2)  To delete existing records
  3)  To update existing records
  4)  To return to previous menu

PLEASE ENTER YOUR CHOICE:
```

One of the most important innovations of demand paging was that it made virtual memory widely available. (Virtual memory is explained in detail at the conclusion of this chapter.) The demand paging scheme allows the user to run jobs with less main memory than would be required if the operating system was using the paged memory allocation scheme described earlier. In fact, a demand paging scheme can give the appearance of an almost-infinite or nonfinite amount of physical memory when, in reality, physical memory is significantly less than infinite.

The key to the successful implementation of this scheme is the use of a high-speed direct access storage device that can work directly with the CPU. That's vital because pages must be passed quickly from secondary storage to main memory and back again.

How and when the pages are passed (or "swapped") depends on predefined policies that determine when to make room for needed pages and how to do so. The operating system relies on tables (the Job Table, the Page Map Table, and the Memory Map Table) to implement the algorithm. These tables are basically the same as for paged memory allocation but with the addition of three new fields for each page in the PMT: one to determine if the page being requested is already in memory or not; a second to determine if the page contents have been modified or not; and a third to determine if the page has been referenced recently.

The first field tells the system where to find each page. If it's already in memory, the system will be spared the time required to bring it from secondary storage. It's faster for the operating system to scan a table located in main memory than it is to retrieve a page from a disk.

The second field, noting if the page has been modified, is used to save time when pages are removed from main memory and returned to secondary storage. If the contents of the page haven't been modified then the page doesn't need to be rewritten to secondary storage. The original, already there, is correct.

The third field, which indicates any recent activity, is used to determine which pages show the most processing activity, and which are relatively inactive. This information is used by several page-swapping policy schemes to determine which pages should remain in main memory and which should be swapped out when the system needs to make room for other pages being requested.

For example, in Figure 3.5, the number of total job pages is 15, and the number of total available page frames is 12. (The operating system occupies the first four of the 16 page frames in main memory.)

FIGURE 3.5 *Demand paging requires that the Page Map Table for each job keep track of each page as it is loaded or removed from main memory. Each PMT tracks the status of the page, whether or not it has been modified, whether or not it has been recently referenced, and the page frame number for each page currently in main memory. (Note: For this illustration the Page Map Tables have been simplified. See Table 3.5 for more detail.)*

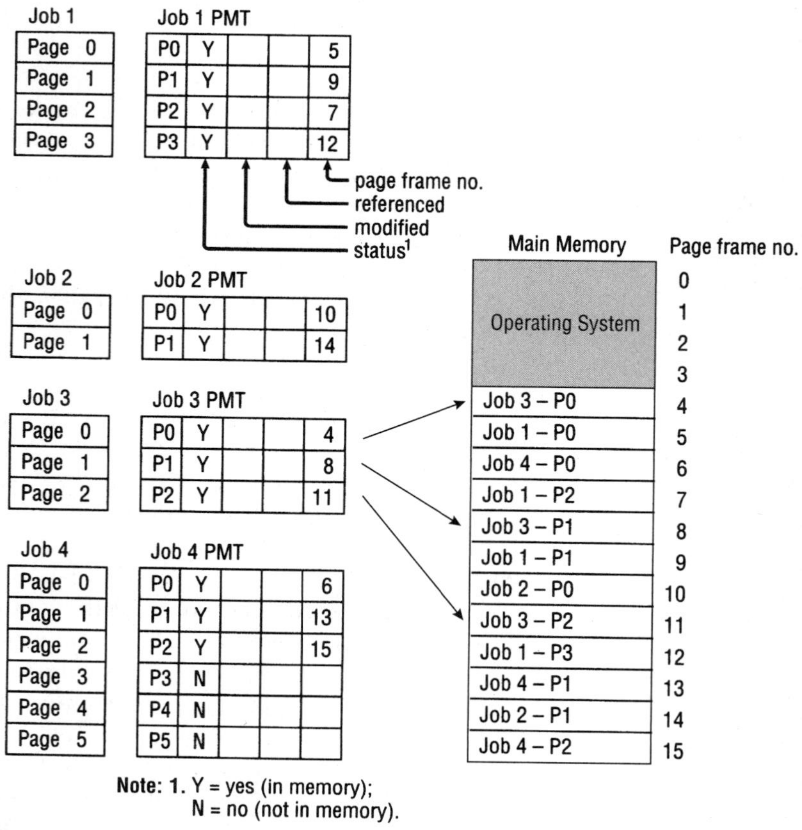

Assuming the processing status illustrated in Figure 3.5, what happens when Job 4 requests that Page 3 be brought into memory if there are no empty page frames available?

To move in a new page, a resident page must be swapped back into secondary storage. Specifically, that includes copying the resident page to the disk (if it was modified), and writing the new page into the empty page frame. Such a swap requires close interaction between hardware components, software algorithms, and policy schemes.

The hardware components generate the address of the required page, find the page number, and determine whether or not it's already in memory. The following steps make up the hardware instruction processing cycle.

```
1 Start processing instruction
2 Generate data address
3 Compute page number
4 If page is in memory
     then
        get data and finish instruction
        advance to next instruction
        return to step 1
  else
     generate page interrupt
     call page interrupt handler
```

The same process is followed when "fetching" an instruction.

When the test fails (meaning that the page is in secondary storage, but not in memory), the operating system software takes over. The section of the operating system that resolves these problems is called the **page interrupt handler**. It determines if there are empty page frames in memory so the requested page can be immediately copied from secondary storage. If all page frames are busy, the page interrupt handler must decide which page will be swapped out. (This decision is directly dependent on the predefined policy for page removal.) Then the swap is made.

PAGE INTERRUPT HANDLER ALGORITHM

```
1 If there is no free page frame
     then
        select page to be swapped out using page removal algorithm
        update job's Page Map Table
        if content of page had been changed then
             write page to disk
        end if
  end if
2 Use page number from step 3 on page 53 to get disk address where requested
  page is stored (the File Manager, to be discussed later, uses the page number to
  get the disk address)
3 Read page into memory
```

4 Update job's Page Map Table
5 Update Memory Map Table
6 Restart interrupted instruction

Before continuing, three tables must be updated: the Page Map Tables for both jobs (the PMT with the page that was swapped out and the PMT with the page that was swapped in) and the Memory Map Table. Finally, the instruction that was interrupted is resumed and processing continues. The algorithm for the page interrupt handler is shown on the next page.

Although demand paging is a solution to inefficient memory utilization, it's not free of problems. When there is an excessive amount of page swapping back and forth between main memory and secondary storage, the operation becomes inefficient. This is a phenomenon called **thrashing**. It uses a great deal of the computer's energy but accomplishes very little and it's caused when a page is removed from memory but is called back shortly thereafter. Thrashing can occur across jobs, when a large number of jobs are vying for a relatively few number of free pages (the ratio of job pages to free memory page frames is high), or it can happen within a job, for example, in loops that cross page boundaries. We can demonstrate this with a simple example shown in Figure 3.6: suppose the beginning of a loop falls at the bottom of a page, and is completed at the top of the next page, as in the FORTRAN program:

FIGURE 3.6 *An example of demand paging that results in a page swap each time the loop is executed and results in thrashing. If only a single page frame is available, this program will have one page fault each time the loop is executed.*

```
. . .
DO I = 1,100                     Page 0
  K = I * I
```

```
  M = A * I                      Page 1
  WRITE (6,*) I,K,M
END DO
```

The situation in Figure 3.6 assumes there's only one empty page frame available. The first page is loaded into memory and execution begins, but after executing the last command on Page 0, the page is swapped out to make room for Page 1. Now execution can continue with the first command on Page 1, but at the END DO statement, Page 1 must be swapped out so Page 0 can be brought back in to continue the loop. Before this program is completed, swapping will have occurred 100 times (unless another page frame becomes free so both pages can reside in memory at the same time). A failure to find a page in memory is often called a **page fault** and this example would generate 100 page faults (and "swaps").

In extreme cases, the rate of useful computation could be degraded by a factor of 100. Ideally, a demand paging scheme is most efficient when users are aware of the page size used by their operating system and are careful to design their programs to keep page faults to a minimum, but in reality this is not often feasible.

PAGE REPLACEMENT POLICIES AND CONCEPTS

As we just learned, the policy that selects the page to be removed, the **page replacement policy**, is crucial to the efficiency of the system, and the algorithm to do that must be carefully selected.

Several such algorithms exist and it's a subject that enjoys a great deal of theoretical attention and research. Two of the most well-known are first-in first-out (FIFO) and least-recently-used (LRU). The **first-in first-out policy** is based on the theory that the best page to remove is the one that has been in memory the longest. The **least-recently-used policy** chooses the pages least recently accessed to be swapped out.

To illustrate the difference between FIFO and LRU, let's imagine a dresser drawer filled with your favorite sweaters. The drawer is full, but that didn't stop you from buying a new sweater. Now you have to put it away. Obviously it won't fit in your sweater drawer unless you take something out, but which sweater should you remove to the storage closet? Your decision will be based on a "sweater removal policy."

You could take out your oldest sweater (the one that was "first in"), figuring that you probably won't use it again — hoping you won't discover in the following days that it's your most used, most treasured possession. Or, you could remove the sweater that you haven't worn recently and has been idle for the longest amount of time (the one that was "least recently used"). It's readily identifiable because it's at the bottom of the drawer. But just because it hasn't been used recently doesn't mean that a once-a-year occasion won't demand its appearance soon.

What guarantee do you have that once you've made your choice you won't be trekking to the storage closet to retrieve the sweater you stored yesterday? You could become a victim of thrashing.

Which is the best policy? It depends on the weather, the wearer, and the wardrobe. Of course, one option is to get another drawer. For an operating system (or a computer), this is the equivalent of having more accessible memory, and we'll explore that option after we discover how to more effectively use the memory we already have.

The examples presented in the following sections related to FIFO and LRU have been adapted from Madnick & Donovan (1974).

FIRST-IN FIRST-OUT

The first-in first-out (FIFO) page replacement policy will remove the pages that have been in memory the longest.

To show how the FIFO algorithm works, let's follow a job of four pages as it's processed by a system with only two available page frames. Let's watch how each of the program's pages are swapped into and out of memory and count the number of page interrupts. Then we'll compute the failure rate and the success rate.

Note: Tables 3.3 and 3.4 are simplified illustrations of how page removal works. In reality, each of the four pages retains its place in secondary storage. And while pages are in memory they're never swapped between page frames — they're moved from Page Frame 1 to Page Frame 2 in this example for illustration purposes only. In reality they constitute the page frame request queue.

In Table 3.3 the job will request that its pages be processed in the following order:

```
A, B, A, C, A, B, D, B, A, C, D
```

When both page frames are occupied, each new page brought into memory will cause an existing one to be swapped out to secondary storage. A page interrupt, which we'll identify with an asterisk (*), is generated when a new page is brought into memory (whether a page is swapped out or not).

TABLE 3.3 *Memory management using a FIFO page removal policy for a four-page program and main memory with two available page frames. When the program is ready to be processed (when Time = 1) all four pages are on the disk. Throughout the program, 11 page requests are issued. When the program calls a page that is not already in memory, a page interrupt is issued, as shown by the asterisks. This program resulted in nine page interrupts.*

	Page Requests		A	B	A	C	A	B	D	B	A	C	D
	Page Interrupts		*	*		*	*	*	*		*	*	*
Main Memory	Contents of Page Frame 1		A	B	B	C	A	B	D	D	A	C	D
	Contents of Page Frame 2			A	A	B	C	A	B	B	D	A	C
	Contents of Secondary Storage:	A B C D	B C D	C D	C D	A D	B D	C D	A C	A C	B C	B D	A B
	Time	1	2	3	4	5	6	7	8	9	10	11	12

The efficiency of this configuration is dismal: there are nine page interrupts out of 11 page requests due to the few page frames available and the need for many new pages. To calculate the failure rate we divide the number of page requests into the number of interrupts. The failure rate of this system is 9/11, which is 82 percent. Stated another way, the success rate is 2/11, or 18 percent. A failure rate this high is usually unacceptable.

We're not saying FIFO is bad. We chose this example to show how FIFO works, not to diminish its appeal as a swapping policy. The high failure rate here is caused by both the limited amount of memory available and the order in which pages are requested by the program. The page order can't be changed by the system, although the size of main memory can be changed. But buying more memory may not always be the best solution — especially when you have many users and each one wants an unlimited amount of memory. There is no guarantee that buying more memory will always result in better performance; this is known as the **FIFO anomaly** or **Belady's anomaly**.

LEAST RECENTLY USED

The least recently used (LRU) page replacement policy swaps out the pages that show the least amount of recent activity, figuring that these pages are the least likely to be used again in the immediate future. Conversely, if a page is used, it's likely to be used again soon; this is the basis for the "theory of **locality**," which will be explained later in this chapter.

To see how it works, let's follow the same job in Table 3.3 but using the LRU policy. The results are shown in Table 3.4. For illustration purposes, we'll move each page to Page Frame 1 as it's requested. When each page is retained, it "goes" to the head of the queue (Page Frame 1). Remember that in a working system pages are not swapped between page frames. In reality, a queue of the requests is kept in FIFO order, or a "time stamp" of when the job entered the system is saved, or a "mark" in the job's PMT is made periodically to implement this policy.

TABLE 3.4 *Memory management using an LRU page removal policy for the program shown in Table 3.3. Throughout the program 11 page requests are issued, but they cause only eight page interrupts.*

	Page Requests		A	B	A	C	A	B	D	B	A	C	D
	Page Interrupts		*	*		*		*	*		*	*	*
Main Memory	Contents of Page Frame 1		A	B	A	C	A	B	D	B	A	C	D
	Contents of Page Frame 2			A	B	A	C	A	B	D	B	A	C
	Contents of Secondary Storage:	A B C D	B C D	C D	C D	B D	B D	C D	A C	A C	C D	B D	A B
	Time	1	2	3	4	5	6	7	8	9	10	11	12

The efficiency of this configuration is only slightly better than with FIFO. Here, there are eight page interrupts out of 11 page requests, so the failure rate is 8/11, or 73 percent. In this example, an increase in main memory by one page frame would increase the success rate of both FIFO and LRU (you'll have the opportunity to calculate the exact increase in exercises 6 and 7 at the end of this chapter). However, we can't conclude on the basis of only one example that one policy is better than the others. In fact, LRU is a **stack algorithm** removal policy, which functions in such a way that increasing main memory will cause either a decrease in or the same number of page interrupts. In other words, an increase in memory will never cause an increase in the number of page interrupts.

On the other hand, it has been shown (Belady, Nelson, & Shelder, 1969) that under certain circumstances adding more memory can, in rare cases, actually cause an increase in page interrupts when using a FIFO policy. As noted before, it's called the FIFO anomaly. But although it's an unusual occurrence, the fact that it exists, coupled with the fact that pages are removed regardless of their activity (as was the case in Table 3.3), has removed FIFO from the most favored policy position it held in some cases.

Other page removal algorithms, MRU (most recently used) and LFU (least frequently used), are given as exercises at the end of this chapter.

THE MECHANICS OF PAGING

Before the Memory Manager can determine which pages will be swapped out, it needs specific information about each page in memory — information included in the Page Map Tables.

For example, in Figure 3.5, the Page Map Table for Job 1 included three bits: the status bit, the referenced bit, and the modified bit (these were the three middle columns: the two empty columns and the Y/N [in memory or not]column), but the representation of the table was simplified for illustration purposes; it would look something like the one in Table 3.5.

TABLE 3.5 *Page Map Table for Job 1 shown in Figure 3.5.*

Page	Status bit	Referenced bit	Modified bit	Page frame
0	1	1	1	5
1	1	0	0	9
2	1	0	0	7
3	1	1	0	12

As we said before, the status bit indicates whether the page is currently in memory or not. The referenced bit indicates whether the page has been "called" (referenced) recently. This bit is important because it's used by the LRU algorithm to determine which pages should be swapped out.

The modified bit indicates whether the contents of the page have been altered and is used to determine if the page must be rewritten to secondary storage when it's swapped out before its page frame is released (a page frame whose contents have not been modified can be overwritten directly). That's because when a page is swapped into memory, it isn't removed from secondary storage. The page is merely copied — the original remains intact in secondary storage. Therefore, if the page isn't altered while it's in main memory (in which case the modified bit remains unchanged, zero), the page needn't be copied back to secondary storage when it's swapped out of memory — the page that's already there is correct. However, if modifications were made to the page, the new version of the page must be written over the older version — and that takes time.

Each of the bits can be either 0 or 1 as shown in Table 3.6.

TABLE 3.6 *Meaning of the bits in the Page Map Table. As shown in Figure 3.5, each PMT must track the status of, and modifications and references to its pages. It does so with three bits, each of which can be either 0 or 1.*

Status bit		Modified bit		Referenced bit	
Value	Meaning	Value	Meaning	Value	Meaning
0	not in memory	0	not modified	0	not called
1	resides in memory	1	was modified	1	was called

The status bit for all pages in memory is 1. A page must be in memory before it can be swapped out so all of the candidates for swapping have a 1 in this column. The other two bits can be either 0 or 1, so there are four possible combinations of the referenced and modified bits (Table 3.7).

TABLE 3.7 *Four possible combinations of modified and referenced bits and the meaning of each.*

	Modified	Referenced	Meaning
Case 1	0	0	Not modified AND not referenced
Case 2	0	1	Not modified BUT was referenced
Case 3	1	0	Was modified BUT not referenced [impossible?]
Case 4	1	1	Was modified AND was referenced

The FIFO algorithm uses only the modified bit and status bits when swapping pages, but the LRU looks at all three before deciding which pages to swap out.

Which page would the LRU policy choose first to swap? Of the four cases described in Table 3.7, it would choose pages in Case 1 as the ideal candidates for removal because they've been neither modified nor referenced. That means that they wouldn't need to be rewritten to secondary storage, and they haven't been referenced recently. So the pages with zeros for these two bits would be the first to be swapped out.

What's the next most likely candidate? The LRU policy would choose Case 3 next because the other two, Case 2 and Case 4, were recently referenced. The bad news is that Case 3 pages have been modified so it'll take more time to swap them out. By process of elimination, then, we can say that Case 2 is the third choice and Case 4 would be the pages least likely to be removed.

You may have noticed that Case 3 presents an interesting situation: apparently these pages have been modified without being referenced. How is that possible? The key lies in how the referenced bit is manipulated by the operating system. When the pages are brought into memory, they're all usually referenced at least once and that means that all of the pages soon have a referenced bit of 1. Of course the LRU algorithm would be defeated if every page indicated that it had been referenced. Therefore, to make sure the referenced bit actually indicates *recently* referenced, the operating system periodically resets it to 0. Then, as the pages are referenced during processing the bit is changed from 0 to 1 and the LRU policy is able to identify which pages actually are frequently referenced. As you can imagine, there's one brief instant, just after the bits are reset, in which all of the pages (even the active pages) have reference bits of 0 and are vulnerable. But as processing continues, the most-referenced pages soon have their bits reset to 1 so the risk is minimized.

THE WORKING SET

One innovation that improved the performance of demand paging schemes was the concept of the **working set**. A job's working set is the set of pages residing in memory that can be accessed directly without incurring a page fault.

When a user requests execution of a program, the first page is loaded into memory and execution continues as more pages are loaded: those containing variable declarations, others containing instructions, others containing data, and so on. After a while, most programs reach a fairly stable state and processing continues smoothly with very few additional page faults. At this point the job's working set is in memory, and the program won't generate many page faults until it gets to another phase requiring a different set of pages to do the work — a different working set.

Of course, it's possible that a poorly structured program could require that every one of its pages be in memory before processing can begin.

Fortunately most programmers structure their work, and this leads to a "locality of reference" during the program's execution, meaning that during any phase of its execution the program references only a small fraction of its pages. For example, if a job is executing a loop then the instructions within the loop are referenced extensively while those outside the loop aren't used at all until the loop is completed — that's locality of reference. The same applies to sequential instructions, subroutine calls (within the subroutine), stack implementations, or access to variables acting as counters or sums, or multidimensional variables such as arrays and tables (only a few of the pages are needed to handle the references).

It would be convenient if all of the pages in a job's working set were loaded into memory at one time to minimize the number of page faults and to speed up processing. But that's easier said than done. To do so the system needs definitive answers to some difficult questions: How many pages comprise the working set? What's the maximum number of pages the operating system will allow for a working set?

The second question is particularly important in time-sharing systems, which regularly swap jobs (or pages of jobs) into memory and back to secondary storage to accommodate the needs of many users. The problem is this: every time a job is reloaded back into memory (or has pages swapped) it has to generate several page faults until its working set is back in memory and processing can continue. It's a time-consuming task for the CPU, which can't be processing jobs during the time it takes to process each page fault, as shown in Figure 3.7.

FIGURE 3.7 *Time line showing the amount of time required to process page faults. The program in this example takes 120 ms to execute but 900 ms to load the necessary pages into memory. Therefore, job turnaround is 1,020 ms.*

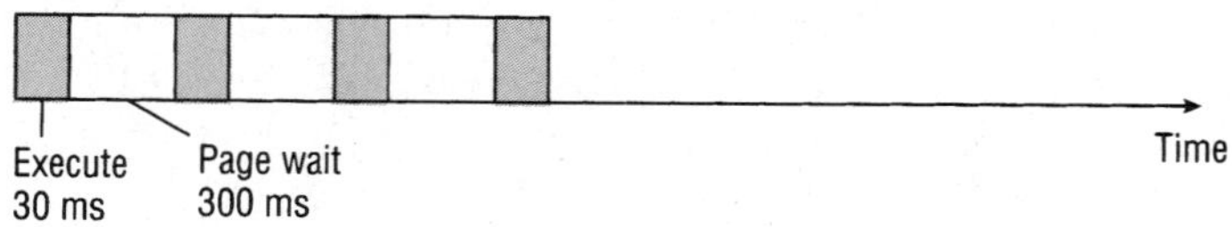

One solution adopted by many paging systems is to begin by identifying each job's working set and then loading it into memory in its entirety before allowing execution to begin. This is difficult to do before a job is executed but can be identified as its execution proceeds.

In a time-sharing system this means the operating system must keep track of the size and identity of every working set, making sure that the jobs destined for processing at any one time won't exceed the available memory. Some operating systems use a variable working set size and either increase it when necessary (the job requires more processing) or decrease it when necessary. This may mean that the number of jobs in memory will need to be reduced if, by doing so, the system can ensure the completion of each job and the subsequent release of its memory space.

We've looked at several examples of demand paging memory allocation schemes. Demand paging had two advantages. It was the first scheme in which a job was no longer constrained by the size of physical memory; it introduced the concept of virtual memory. The second advantage was that it utilized memory more efficiently than the previous schemes because the sections of a job that were used seldom or not at all (such as error routines) weren't loaded into memory unless they were specifically requested. Its disadvantage was the increased overhead caused by the tables and the page interrupts. The next allocation scheme built on the advantages of both paging and dynamic partitions.

SEGMENTED MEMORY ALLOCATION

The concept of segmentation is based on the common practice by programmers of structuring their programs in **modules** — logical groupings of code. With **segmented memory allocation**, each job is divided into several **segments** of different sizes, one for each module that contains pieces that perform related functions. A **subroutine** is an example of one such logical group. This is fundamentally different from a paging scheme, which divides the job into several pages all of the same size, each of which often contains pieces from more than one program module.

A second important difference is that main memory is no longer divided into page frames because the size of each segment is different — some are large and some are small. Therefore, as with the dynamic partitions discussed in Chapter 2, memory is allocated in a dynamic manner.

When a program is compiled or assembled, the segments are set up according to the program's structural modules. Each segment is numbered and a **Segment Map Table (SMT)** is generated for each job; it contains the segment numbers, their lengths, access rights, status, and (when each is loaded into memory) its location in memory. Figures 3.8 and 3.9 show a job, Job 1, composed of a main program and two subroutines, together with its Segment Map Table and actual main memory allocation.

As in demand paging, the referenced, modified, and status bits are used in segmentation and appear in the SMT but they aren't shown in Figures 3.9 and 3.11.

The Memory Manager needs to keep track of the segments in memory and this is done with three tables combining aspects of both dynamic partitions and demand paging memory management:

1. The Job Table lists every job in process (one for the whole system).
2. The Segment Map Table lists details about each segment (one for each job).

FIGURE 3.8 *Segmented memory allocation. Job 1 includes a main program, Subroutine A and Subroutine B, so it's divided into three segments.*

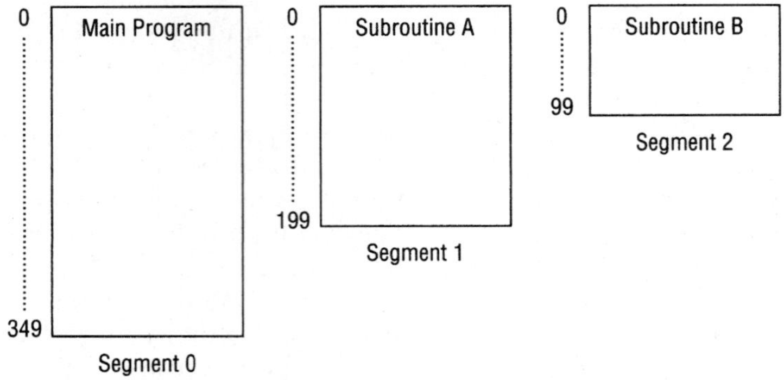

FIGURE 3.9 *The Segment Map Table tracks each of the segments for Job 1.*

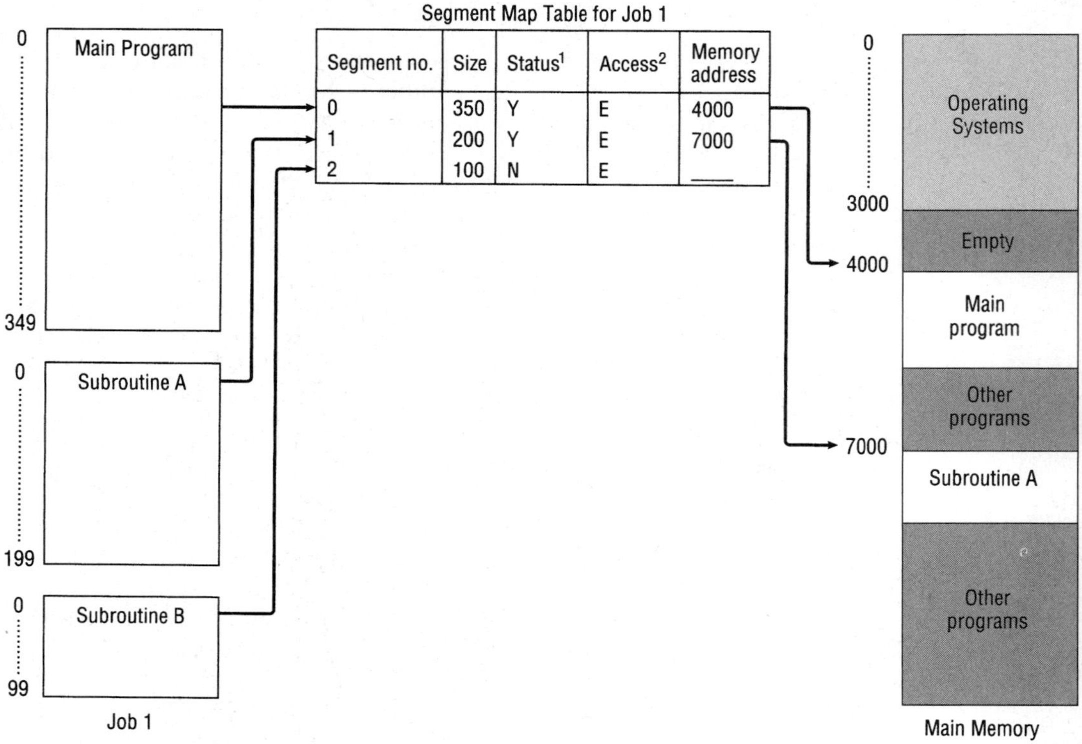

Segment Map Table for Job 1

Segment no.	Size	Status[1]	Access[2]	Memory address
0	350	Y	E	4000
1	200	Y	E	7000
2	100	N	E	____

Notes: 1. Y = in memory;
N = not in memory.

2. E = Execute only.

3. The Memory Map Table monitors the allocation of main memory (one for the whole system).

Like demand paging, the instructions within each segment are ordered sequentially, but the segments don't need to be stored contiguously in memory. We only need to know where each segment is stored. The contents of the segments themselves are contiguous (in this scheme).

To access a specific location within a segment we can perform an operation similar to the one used for paged memory management. The only difference is that we work with segments instead of pages. The addressing scheme requires the segment number and the displacement within that segment, and, because the segments are of different sizes, the displacement must be verified to make sure it isn't outside of the segment's range.

In Figure 3.10, Segment 1 is (includes all of) Subroutine A so the system finds the beginning address of Segment 1, address 7000, and it begins there. If the instruction requested that processing begin at Line 100 of Subroutine A (which is

FIGURE 3.10 *During execution, the main program calls Subroutine A, which triggers the SMT to look up its location in memory.*

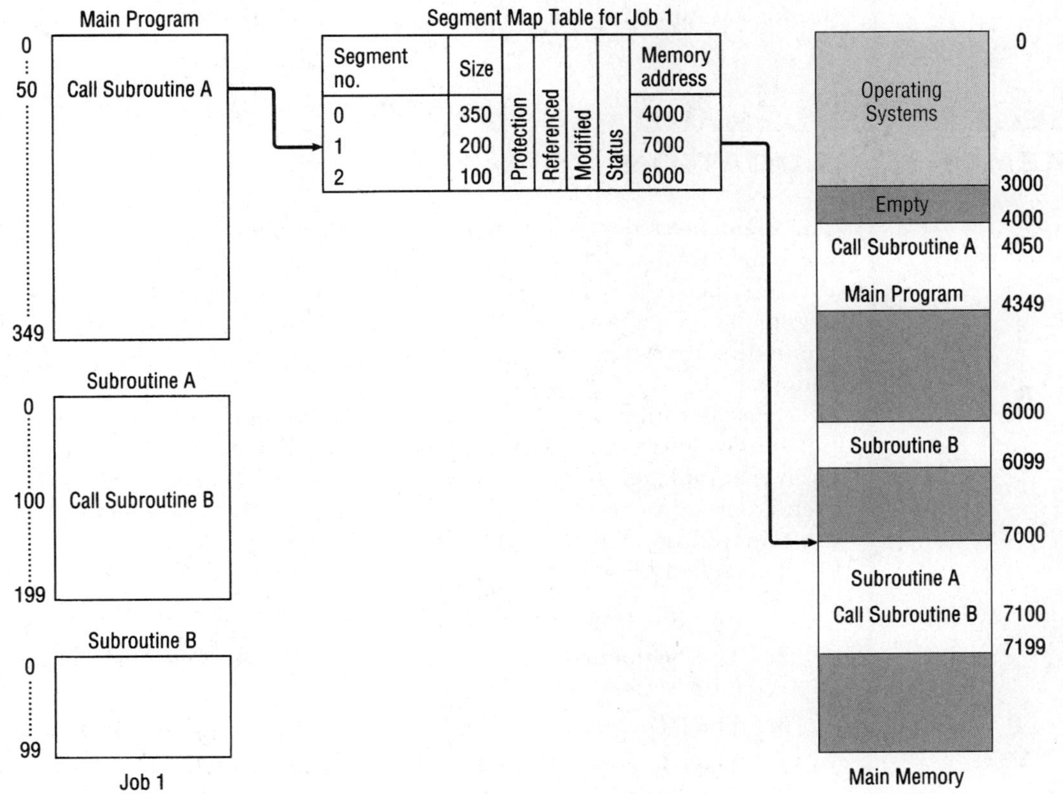

possible in languages that support multiple entries into subroutines) then, to locate that line in memory, the Memory Manager would need to add 100 (the displacement) to 7000 (the beginning address of Segment 1). In code it would look like this:

```
ACTUAL_MEM_LOC = BEGIN_MEM_LOC_OF_SEG + DISPLACEMENT
```

Can the displacement be larger than the size of the segment? No, not if the program is coded correctly; however, accidents do happen and the Memory Manager must always guard against this possibility by checking the displacement against the size of the segment, verifying that it's not out of bounds.

To access a location in memory when using either paged or segmented memory management, the address is composed of two entries: the page or segment number and the displacement. Therefore, it's a two-dimensional addressing scheme: SEGMENT NUMBER — DISPLACEMENT.

The disadvantage of any allocation scheme in which memory is partitioned dynamically is the return of external fragmentation. Therefore, recompaction of available memory is necessary from time to time (if that schema is used).

As you can see, there are many similarities between paging and segmentation, so they're often confused. The major difference is a conceptual one: pages are physical units that are invisible to the user's program and of fixed sizes; segments are logical units that are visible to the user's program and of variable sizes.

SEGMENTED/DEMAND PAGED MEMORY ALLOCATION

The **segmented/demand paged memory allocation** scheme evolved from the two we've just discussed. It's a combination of segmentation and demand paging, and it offers the logical benefits of segmentation, as well as the physical benefits of paging. The logic isn't new. The algorithms used by the demand paging and segmented memory management schemes are applied here with only minor modifications.

This allocation scheme doesn't keep each segment as a single contiguous unit but subdivides it into pages of equal size, smaller than most segments, and more easily manipulated than whole segments. Therefore, many of the problems of segmentation (compaction, external fragmentation, and secondary storage handling) are removed because the pages are of fixed length.

This scheme, illustrated in Figure 3.11, requires four tables:

1. The Job Table lists every job in process (one for the whole system).
2. The Segment Map Table lists details about each segment (one for each job).
3. The Page Map Table lists details about every page (one for each segment).
4. The Memory Map Table monitors the allocation of the page frames in main memory (one for the whole system).

FIGURE 3.11 *How the Job Table, Segment Map Table, Page Map Table, and main memory interact in a segment/paging scheme.*

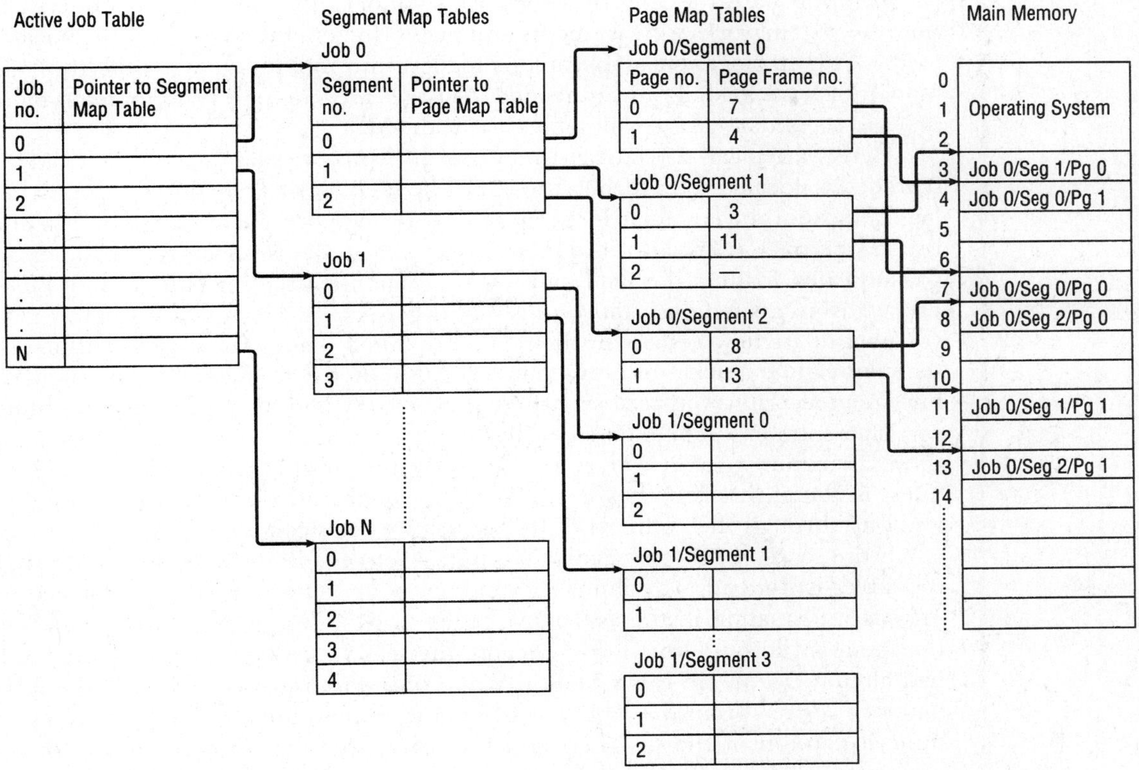

Note that the tables in Figure 3.11 have been simplified. The SMT actually includes additional information regarding protection (such as the authority to read, write, execute, and delete parts of the file), as well as which users have access to that segment (user only, group only, or everyone — some systems call these access categories "owner," "group," and "world," respectively). In addition, the PMT includes the status, modified, and referenced bits.

To access a location in memory, the system must locate the address, which is composed of three entries: segment number, page number within that segment, and displacement within that page. It's a three-dimensional addressing scheme: SEGMENT NUMBER — PAGE NUMBER — DISPLACEMENT.

The major disadvantages of this memory allocation scheme are the overhead required for the extra tables and the time required to reference the segment table and the page table. To minimize the number of references, many systems use associative memory to speed up the process.

Associative memory is a name given to several registers that are allocated to each job that's active. Their task is to associate several segment and page numbers belonging to the job being processed with their main memory addresses. These associative registers reside in main memory, and the exact number of registers varies from system to system.

To appreciate the role of associative memory, it's important to understand how the system works with segments and pages. In general, when a job is allocated to the CPU its Segment Map Table is loaded into main memory while the Page Map Tables are loaded only as needed. As pages are swapped between main memory and secondary storage all tables are updated.

Here's a typical procedure: when a page is first requested, the job's SMT is searched to locate its PMT; then the PMT is loaded and searched to determine the page's location in memory. If the page isn't in memory, then a page interrupt is issued, the page is brought into memory, and the table is updated. (As the example indicates, loading the PMT can cause a page interrupt, or fault, as well.) This process is just as tedious as it sounds, but it gets easier. Since this segment's PMT (or part of it) now resides in memory, any other requests for pages within this segment can be quickly accommodated because there's no need to bring the PMT into memory. However, accessing these tables (SMT and PMT) is time-consuming.

That's the problem addressed by associative memory, which stores in memory the information related to the most-recently-used pages. Then, when a page request is issued, two searches begin — one through the segment and page tables and one through the contents of the associative registers.

If the search of the associative registers is successful, then the search through the tables is stopped (or eliminated) and the address translation is performed using the information in the associative registers. However, if the search of associative memory fails, no time is lost because the search through the SMTs and PMTs had already begun (in this schema). When this search is successful and the main memory address from the PMT has been determined, the address is used to continue execution of the program and the reference is also stored in one of the associative registers. If all of the associative registers are full, then an LRU (or other) algorithm is used and the least-recently-referenced associative register is used to hold the information on this requested page.

For example, a system with eight associative registers per job will use them to store the SMT and PMT for the last eight pages referenced by that job. When an address needs to be translated from segment and page numbers to a memory location, the system will look first in the eight associative registers. If a match is found the memory location is taken from the associative register; if there is no match then the SMTs and PMTs will continue to be searched and the new information will be stored in one of the eight registers as a result.

If a job is swapped out to secondary storage during its execution, then all of the information stored in its associative registers is saved, as well as the current PMT and SMT, so the displaced job can be resumed quickly when the CPU is reallocated to it. The primary advantage of a large associative memory is increased speed. The disadvantage is the high cost of the complex hardware required to perform the parallel searches. In some systems the searches do not run in parallel, but the search of the SMT and PMT follows the search of the associative registers.

VIRTUAL MEMORY

Demand paging made it possible for a program to execute even though only a part of it was loaded into main memory. In effect it removed the restriction imposed on maximum program size. The capability of moving pages at will between two storage areas (main memory and secondary storage) gave way to a new concept appropriately named **virtual memory**. It gives the users the appearance that their programs are being completely loaded in main memory during their entire processing time — a feat that would require an incredible amount of main memory — while, in reality, only a portion of each is stored there.

Until the implementation of virtual memory, the problem of making programs fit into available memory was left to the users. In the early days, programmers had to limit the size of their programs to make them fit into main memory, but sometimes that wasn't possible because the amount of memory allocated to them was too small to get the job done. Clever programmers solved the problem by writing "tight" programs wherever possible. It was the size of the program that counted most — and the instructions for these tight programs were nearly impossible for anyone but their authors to understand or maintain. The useful life of the program was limited to the employment of its programmer.

During the second generation, programmers started dividing their programs into sections that resembled working sets, really segments, called "**overlays**." The program could begin with only the first overlay loaded into memory. As the first section neared completion it would instruct the system to lay the second section of code over the first section already in memory. Then the second section would be processed. As that section would finish, it would call in the third section to be overlayed, and so on until the program was finished. Some programs had multiple overlays in main memory at once.

Although the swapping of overlays between main memory and secondary storage was done by the system, the tedious task of dividing the program into sections was done by the programmer. It was the concept of overlays that suggested paging and segmentation and led to virtual memory, which was then implemented through demand paging and segmentation schemes.

Segmentation allowed for "sharing" of files among users (see exercise 12 for an example). This means that the shared segment contains: (1) an area where unchangeable (called "reentrant") code is stored, and (2) several data areas, one for each user. In this schema, users share the code, which cannot be modified, and can modify the information stored in their own data areas as needed without affecting the data stored in other users' data areas.

Before virtual memory, sharing meant that copies of files were stored in each user's account. This allowed them to load their own copy and work on it at any time. This scheme created a great deal of unnecessary system cost — the I/O overhead in loading the copies and the extra secondary storage needed. With virtual memory, those costs are substantially reduced because shared programs and subroutines are loaded "on demand," satisfactorily reducing the storage requirements of main memory (although this is accomplished at the expense of the Memory Map Table).

Virtual memory works well in a multiprogramming environment because most programs spend a lot of time waiting — they wait for I/O to be performed; they wait for pages to be swapped in or out; and, in a time-sharing environment, they wait when their "time slice is up" (their turn to use the processor is expired). In a multiprogramming environment, the waiting time isn't lost, and the CPU simply moves to another job; this was the advantage of partitions.

Virtual memory has increased the use of several programming techniques. For instance, it aids the development of large software systems because individual pieces can be developed independently and linked together later on.

Virtual memory management has several advantages:

1. A job's size is no longer restricted to the size of main memory (or the free space within main memory).
2. Memory is used more efficiently because the only sections of a job stored in memory are those needed immediately, while those not needed remain in secondary storage.
3. It allows an unlimited amount of multiprogramming (which can apply to many jobs, as in dynamic and static partitioning, or many users in a time-sharing environment).
4. It eliminates external fragmentation and minimizes internal fragmentation by combining segmentation and paging (internal fragmentation occurs in the program).
5. It allows the sharing of code and data.
6. It facilitates dynamic linking of program segments.

The advantages far outweigh these disadvantages:

1. Increased hardware costs.
2. Increased overhead for handling paging interrupts.
3. Increased software complexity to prevent thrashing.

CHAPTER THREE CONCLUSION

The Memory Manager has the task of allocating memory to each job to be executed, and reclaiming it when execution is completed.

Each of the schemes we've discussed in Chapters 2 and 3 was designed to address a different set of pressing problems but, as we've seen, when some problems were solved, others were created. Table 3.8 shows how they compare.

The Memory Manager is only one of four "managers" that make up the operating system. Once the jobs are loaded into memory using a memory allocation scheme, the Processor Manager must allocate the processor to process each job in the most efficient manner possible. We'll see how that's done in the next chapter.

TABLE 3.8 *Comparison of memory allocation schemes discussed in Chapters 2 and 3.*

Scheme	Problem solved	Problem created	Changes in software
Single-user Contiguous		Job size limited to physical memory size CPU often idle	None
Fixed Partitions	Idle CPU time	Internal fragmentation Job size limited to partition size	Add Processor Scheduler Add protection handler
Dynamic Partitions	Internal fragmentation	External fragmentation	None
Relocatable Dynamic Partitions	Internal fragmentation	Compaction overhead Job size limited to physical memory size	Compaction algorithm
Paged	Need for compaction	Memory needed for tables Job size limited to physical memory size Internal fragmentation returns	Algorithms to handle Page Map Tables
Demand Paging	Job size no longer limited to memory size More efficient memory use Allows large-scale multiprogramming and time-sharing	Larger number of tables Possibility of thrashing Overhead required by page interrupts Necessary paging hardware	Page replacement algorithm Search algorithm for pages in secondary storage
Segmented	Internal fragmentation Dynamic linking Sharing of segments	Difficulty managing variable-length segments in secondary storage External fragmentation	Dynamic linking package Two-dimensional addressing scheme
Segmented/Demand Paged	Large virtual memory Segment loaded on demand	Table handling overhead Memory needed for page and segment tables	Three-dimensional addressing scheme

KEY TERMS

paged memory allocation
page
page frame
Job Table (JT)
Page Map Table (PMT)
Memory Map Table (MMT)
displacement
address resolution
demand paging
page interrupt handler
thrashing
page swap
page fault
page replacement policy
first-in first-out (FIFO) policy
least-recently-used (LRU) policy
FIFO anomaly
working set

segmented memory allocation
segment
Segment Map Table (SMT)
segmented/demand paged memory allocation
associative memory
virtual memory

EXERCISES

1. Explain the differences between a page and a segment.
2. List the advantages and disadvantages for each of the memory management schemes presented in this chapter. (Although this was done in the summary, expand on it.)
3. What purpose does the modified bit serve in a demand paging system?
4. Answer these questions:
   - **a.** What is the cause of thrashing?
   - **b.** How does the operating system detect thrashing?
   - **c.** Once thrashing is detected, what can the operating system do to eliminate it?
5. What purpose does the referenced bit serve in a demand paging system?
6. Given that main memory is composed of three page frames for public use and that a program requests pages in the following order:

   `d c b a d c e d c b a e`

   - **a.** Using the FIFO page removal algorithm, do a page trace analysis indicating page faults with asterisks (*). Then compute the failure and success ratios.
   - **b.** Increase the size of memory so it contains four page frames for public use. Using the same page requests as above and FIFO, do another page trace analysis and compute the failure and success ratios.
   - **c.** Did the result correspond with your intuition? Explain.
7. Given that main memory is composed of three page frames for public use and that a program requests pages in the following order:

   `a b a c a b d b a c d`

   - **a.** Using the FIFO page removal algorithm, do a page trace analysis indicating page faults with asterisks (*). Then compute the failure and success ratios.
   - **b.** Using the LRU page removal algorithm do a page trace analysis and compute the failure and success ratios.
   - **c.** Which is better? Why do you think it's better? Can you make general statements from this example? Why or why not?
   - **d.** Let's define "most-recently-used" (MRU) as a page removal algorithm that removes from memory the most recently used page. Do a page trace analysis using the same page requests as before and compute the failure and success ratios.

e. Which of the three page removal algorithms is best, and why do you think so?

8. To implement LRU each page needs a referenced bit. If we wanted to implement a "least-frequently-used" (LFU) page removal algorithm, in which the page that was used the least would be removed from memory, what would we need to add to the tables? What software modifications would have to be made to support this new algorithm?

ADVANCED EXERCISES

9. Given that main memory is composed of four page frames for public use, use the following table to answer all parts of this problem:

Page frame	Time when loaded	Time when last referenced	Referenced bit	Modified bit
0	126	279	0	0
1	230	280	1	0
2	120	282	1	1
3	160	290	1	1

a. The contents of which page frame would be swapped out by FIFO?

b. The contents of which page frame would be swapped out by LRU?

c. The contents of which page frame would be swapped out by MRU?

d. The contents of which page frame would be swapped out by LFU?

10. Given that main memory is composed of four page frames and that a program has been divided into eight pages (numbered 0 through 7):

a. How many page faults will occur using FIFO with a request list of: `0, 1, 7, 2, 3, 2, 7, 1, 0, 3` if the four page frames are initially empty?

b. How many page faults will occur with the same conditions but using LRU?

11. Given three subroutines of 700, 200, and 500 words each, if segmentation is used then the total memory needed is the sum of the three sizes (if all three routines are loaded). However, if paging is used then some storage space is lost because subroutines rarely fill the last page completely, and that results in internal fragmentation.

Determine the total amount of wasted memory due to internal fragmentation when the three subroutines are loaded into memory using each of the following page sizes:

a. 200 words

b. 500 words

c. 600 words

d. 700 words

12. Given the following Segment Map Tables for two jobs:

SMT for Job 1

Segment no.	Memory location
0	4096
1	6144
2	9216
3	2048
4	7168

SMT for Job 2

Segment no.	Memory location
0	2048
1	6144
2	9216

a. Which segments, if any, are shared between the two jobs?

b. If the segment now located at 7168 is swapped out and later reloaded at 8192, and the segment now at 2048 is swapped out and reloaded at 1024, what would the new segment tables look like?

PROGRAMMING EXERCISES

13. This problem will study the effect of changing page sizes in a demand paging system.

The following sequence of requests for program words is taken from a 460-word program: `10, 11, 104, 170, 73, 309, 185, 245, 246, 434, 458, 364`. Main memory can hold a total of 200 words for this program and the page frame size will match the size of the pages into which the program has been divided.

Calculate the page numbers according to the page size; divide by the page size, and the quotient gives the page number. The number of page frames in memory is the total number, 200, divided by the page size. For example, in problem **a.** the page size is 100, which means that requests `10` and `11` are on Page 0, and requests `104` and `170` are on Page 1. The number of page frames is two.

a. Find the success frequency for the request list using a FIFO replacement algorithm and a page size of 100 words (there are two page frames).

b. Find the success frequency for the request list using a FIFO replacement algorithm and a page size of 50 words (10 pages, 0 through 9).

c. Find the success frequency for the request list using a FIFO replacement algorithm and a page size of 200 words.

d. What do your results indicate? Can you make any general statements about what happens when page sizes are halved or doubled?

e. Are there any overriding advantages in using smaller pages? What are the offsetting factors? Remember that transferring 200 words of information takes less than twice as long as transferring 100 words because of the way secondary storage devices operate (the "transfer" rate is higher than the "access" [search/find] rate).

f. Repeat (a) through (c) above, using a main memory of 400 words. The size of each page frame will again correspond to the size of the page.

g. What happened when more memory was given to the program? Can you make some general statements about this occurrence? What changes might you expect to see if the request list was much longer, as it would be in real life?

h. Could this request list happen during the execution of a real program? Explain.

i. Would you expect the success rate of an actual program under similar conditions to be higher or lower than the one in this problem?

14. Given the following information for an assembly language program:

Job size = 3126 bytes
Page size = 1042 bytes
instruction at memory location 532: `Load 1,2098`
instruction at memory location 1156: `Add 1, 4087`
instruction at memory location 2086: `Sub 1, 1052`

data at memory location 1052: 015672
data at memory location 2098: 114321
data at memory location 4087: 077435

a. How many pages are needed to store the entire job?

b. Compute the page number and displacement for each of the byte addresses where the data is stored (remember that page numbering starts at zero).

c. Determine if the page number and displacements are legal for this job.

d. Explain why the page number and displacements may not be legal for this job.

e. Indicate what action the operating system might take when a page number is not legal.

Chapter Four

PROCESSOR MANAGEMENT

PROCESSOR MANAGER

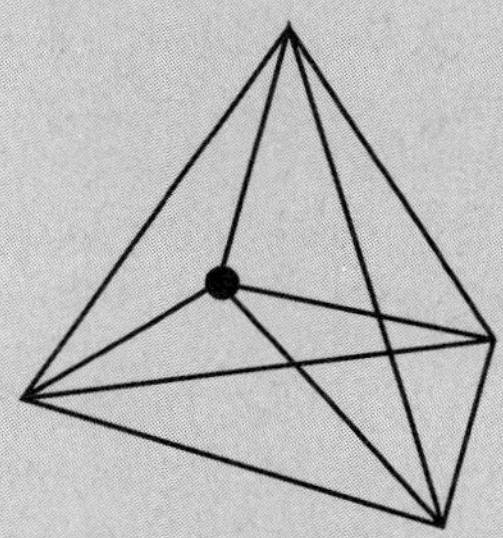

Job Scheduling

↓

Process Scheduling

↓

Interrupt Management

In the last two chapters we explained how main memory is allocated to the system's users. In this chapter we'll see how the Processor Manager allocates a single CPU to execute the jobs of those users.

In single-user systems, the processor is busy only when the user is executing a job — at all other times it is idle. Processor management in this environment is simple. However, when there are many users with many jobs on the system (this is known as a **multiprogramming** environment) the processor must be allocated to each job in a fair and efficient manner, which can be a complex task, as we'll see in this chapter.

Before we begin, let's clearly define some of the terms we'll be using in the following pages. The **processor**, also known as the CPU (for central processing unit), is the part of the machine that does the calculations and executes the programs. A **process** is a single instance of an executable program — for example, a single mathematical calculation is a process. (IBM prefers to use the term "task" instead of process, and UNIVAC calls it an "activity.") A **job**, or **program** in an operating systems environment, is a unit of work that's submitted by the **user**.

Multiprogramming requires that the processor be "allocated" to each job or to each process for a period of time and "deallocated" at an appropriate moment. If the processor is deallocated during a program's execution, it must be done in such a way that it can be restarted later as easily as possible. It's a delicate procedure. To demonstrate, let's look at an everyday example.

Here you are, confident you can put together a toy despite the warning that "some assembly is required." Armed with the instructions and lots of patience, you embark on your task — to read the directions, collect the necessary tools, follow each step in turn, and turn out the finished product.

The first step is to "join Part A to Part B with a 2-inch screw," and as you complete it you check off Step 1 as "done." Inspired by your success, you move on to Step 2 and then Step 3. You've only just completed the third step when a neighbor is injured while working with a power tool and cries for help.

Quickly you check off Step 3 in the directions so you know where you left off, then you drop your tools and race to your neighbor's side. After all, someone's immediate need is more important than your eventual success with the toy. Now you find yourself engaged in a very different task: following the instructions in a first-aid book using bandages and antiseptic.

Once the injury has been successfully treated you return to your previous job. As you pick up your tools you refer to the instructions and see that you should begin with Step 4. You then continue with this project until it is finally completed.

In operating system terminology, you played the part of the *CPU* or *processor*. There were two *programs,* or *jobs* — one was the mission to assemble the toy and the second was to bandage the injury. When you were assembling the toy (Job A), each of the steps you performed was a *process.* The call for help was an *interrupt* and when you left the toy to treat your wounded friend, you left for a *higher priority program.* When you were interrupted, you performed a *context switch* when you marked Step 3 as the last completed instruction and put down your tools. Attending to the neighbor's injury became Job B. While you were executing the first-aid instructions each of the steps you executed was again a *process.* And, of course, when each of the two jobs was completed it was *finished* or terminated.

The Processor Manager would identify the series of events as follows:

get the input for Job A	(find the instructions in the box)
identify resources	(collect the necessary tools)
execute the process	(follow each step in turn)
interrupt	(neighbor calls)
context switch to Job B	(mark your place in the instructions)
get the input for Job B	(find your first-aid book)
identify resources	(collect the medical supplies)
execute the process	(follow each first-aid step)
terminate Job B	(return home)
context switch to Job A	(prepare to resume assembly)

resume executing interrupted process	(follow remaining steps in turn)
terminate Job A	(turn out the finished toy)

As we've shown, a single processor can be shared by several jobs, or several processes, but if, and only if, the operating system has a scheduling policy, as well as a scheduling algorithm, to determine when to stop working on one job and proceed to another.

In this example, the scheduling algorithm was based on priority: you worked on the processes belonging to Job A until a higher priority job came along. Although this was a good algorithm in this case, a priority-based scheduling algorithm isn't always best, as we'll see later in this chapter.

JOB SCHEDULING VERSUS PROCESS SCHEDULING

The Processor Manager is a composite of two submanagers: one in charge of job scheduling and the other in charge of process scheduling. They're known as the **Job Scheduler** and the **Process Scheduler**.

Typically a user views a job either as a series of global job steps — compilation, loading, and execution — or as one all-encompassing step: execution. However, the scheduling of jobs is actually handled on two levels by most operating systems. If we return to the example presented earlier, we can see that a hierarchy exists between the Job Scheduler and the Process Scheduler.

The scheduling of the two "jobs," assemble the toy and bandage the injury, was on a first-come first-served and priority basis. Each job is initiated by the Job Scheduler based on certain criteria. Once a job is selected for execution, the Process Scheduler determines when each step, or set of steps, is executed — a decision that's also based on certain criteria. When you started assembling the toy, each step in the assembly instructions would have been selected for execution by the Process Scheduler.

This is an important function. For example, if the Job Scheduler selected several jobs to run consecutively and each had a lot of **I/O**, then the I/O devices would be kept very busy and the CPU might be busy handling the I/O, if an I/O controller were not used, so that little computation might get done. On the other hand, if the Job Scheduler selected several consecutive jobs with a great deal of computation, then the CPU would be very busy but the I/O devices would be idle waiting for I/O requests. Therefore, the Job Scheduler strives for a balanced mix of jobs that require large amounts of I/O interaction and jobs that require large amounts of computation. Its goal is to keep most of the components of the computer system busy most of the time.

PROCESS SCHEDULER

Most of this chapter is dedicated to the Process Scheduler because after a job has been placed on the READY queue by the Job Scheduler, it's the Process Scheduler that takes over. It determines which jobs will get the CPU, when, and for how long. It also decides when processing should be interrupted, determines which queues the job should be moved to during its execution, and recognizes when a job has concluded and should be terminated.

The Process Scheduler is the **low-level scheduler** that assigns the CPU to execute the processes of those jobs placed on the ready queue by the Job Scheduler. This becomes a crucial function when the processing of several jobs has to be orchestrated—just as when you had to set aside your assembly and rush to help your neighbor.

To schedule the CPU, the Process Scheduler takes advantage of a common trait among most computer programs: they alternate between CPU cycles and I/O cycles. Notice that the following job has one relatively long CPU cycle and two very brief I/O cycles:

```
READ A,B              <——— I/O cycle
C = A+B               }
D = (A*B)-C           }    CPU cycle
E = A-B               }
F = D/E               }
WRITE A,B,C,D,E,F     <——— I/O cycle
STOP                  <——— terminate execution
END
```

Although the duration and frequency of CPU cycles vary from program to program, there are some general tendencies that can be exploited when selecting a scheduling algorithm. For example, **I/O-bound** jobs (such as printing a series of documents) have many brief CPU cycles and long I/O cycles, whereas **CPU-bound** jobs (such as finding the first 300 prime numbers) have long CPU cycles and shorter I/O cycles. The total effect of all CPU cycles, from both I/O-bound and CPU-bound jobs, approximates a Poisson distribution curve as shown in Figure 4.1.

In a highly interactive environment there's also a third layer of the Processor Manager called the **middle-level scheduler**. In some cases, especially when the system is overloaded, the middle-level scheduler finds it is advantageous to remove active jobs from memory to reduce the degree of multiprogramming and thus allow jobs to be completed faster. The jobs that are swapped out and eventually swapped back in are managed by the middle-level scheduler.

In a single-user environment, there's no distinction made between job and process scheduling because only one job is active in the system at any given time. So the CPU and all other resources are dedicated to that job until it is completed.

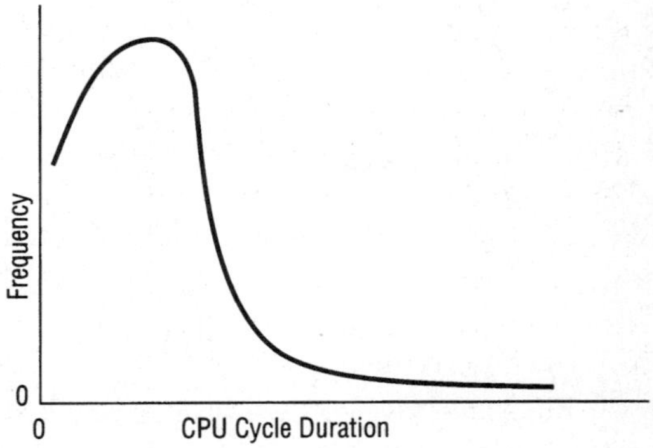

FIGURE 4.1
Distribution of CPU cycle times. This distribution shows that there is a greater number of jobs requesting short CPU cycles (the frequency peaks close to the low end of the CPU cycle axis), and a lesser number of jobs requesting long CPU cycles.

JOB AND PROCESS STATUS

As a job moves through the system it's always in one of five states (or at least three) as it changes from HOLD to READY to RUNNING to WAITING and eventually to FINISHED as shown in Figure 4.2. These are called the **job status** or the **process status**.

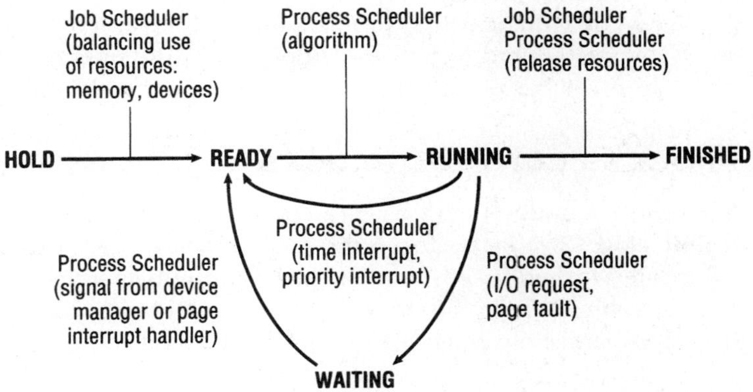

FIGURE 4.2
A typical job (or process) changes status as it moves through the system from HOLD *to* FINISHED.

Here's how the job status changes when a user submits a job to the system via batch or interactive mode. When the job is accepted by the system it's put on HOLD and placed in a queue. In some systems the job spooler (or disk controller) creates a table with the characteristics of each job in the queue and notes the important features of the job, such as an estimate of CPU time, priority, special I/O devices required, and maximum memory required. This table is used by the Job Scheduler to decide which job is to be run next.

From HOLD, the job moves to READY when it's ready to run but is waiting for the CPU. In some systems, the job (or process) might be placed on the READY list directly. RUNNING, of course, means that the job is being processed. In a single processor system this is one "job" or process. WAITING means that the job can't continue until a specific resource is allocated or an I/O operation has finished. Upon completion, the job is FINISHED and returned to the user.

The transition from one job or process status to another is initiated by either the Job Scheduler or the Process Scheduler:

- The transition from HOLD to READY is initiated by the Job Scheduler according to some predefined policy. At this point the availability of enough main memory and any requested devices are checked.
- The transition from READY to RUNNING is handled by the Process Scheduler according to some predefined algorithm (i.e., FCFS, SJN, priority scheduling, SRT, or round robin — all of which will be discussed shortly).
- The transition from RUNNING back to READY is handled by the Process Scheduler according to some predefined time limit or other criterion, for example a "priority" interrupt.
- The transition from RUNNING to WAITING is handled by the Process Scheduler and is initiated by an instruction in the job such as a command to READ, WRITE, or other I/O request, or one that requires a page fetch.
- The transition from WAITING to READY is handled by the Process Scheduler and is initiated by a signal from the I/O device manager that the I/O request has been satisfied and the job can continue. In the case of a page fetch, the page interrupt handler will signal that the page is now in memory and the process can be placed on the READY queue.
- Eventually, the transition from RUNNING to FINISHED is initiated by the Process Scheduler or the Job Scheduler either when (1) the job is successfully completed and it ends execution or (2) the operating system indicates that an error has occurred and the job is being terminated prematurely.

PROCESS CONTROL BLOCKS

Each process in the system is represented by a data structure called a **Process Control Block (PCB)** that performs the same function as a traveler's passport. The PCB (illustrated in Figure 4.3) contains the basic information about the job including what it is, where it's going, how much of its processing has been completed, where it's stored, and how much it has "spent" in using resources.

FIGURE 4.3
Contents of each job's Process Control Block.

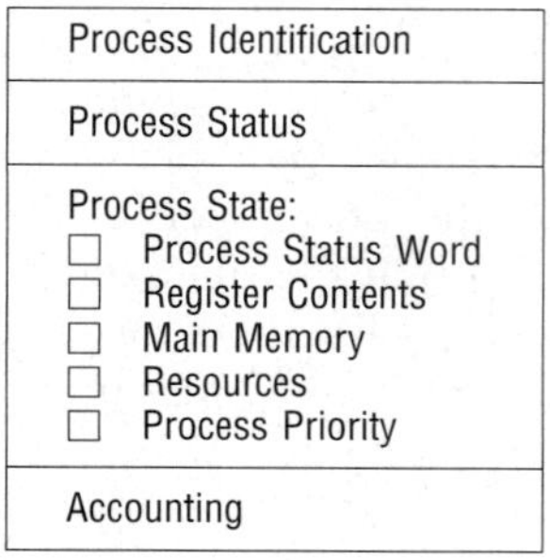

Process Identification Each job is uniquely identified by the user's identification and a pointer connecting it to its descriptor (supplied by the Job Scheduler when the job first enters the system and is placed on HOLD).

Process Status This indicates the current status of the job — HOLD, READY, RUNNING, or WAITING — and the resources responsible for that status.

Process State This contains all of the information needed to indicate the current state of the job such as:

- *Process Status Word,* which is the current instruction counter and register contents when the job isn't running but is either on HOLD or is READY or WAITING. If the job is RUNNING this information is left undefined.
- *Register contents* if the job has been interrupted and is waiting to resume processing.
- *Main memory,* pertinent information, including the address where the job is stored and, in the case of virtual memory, the mapping between virtual and physical memory locations.
- *Resources,* information about all allocated to this job. Each resource has an identification field listing its type and a field describing details of its allocation such as the sector address on a disk. These resources can be hardware units (disk drives, or printers, for example) or files.
- *Process priority* used by systems using a priority scheduling algorithm to select which job will be run next.

Accounting Contains information used mainly for billing purposes and performance measurement. It indicates what kind of resources the job used and for how long. Typical charges include:

1. Amount of CPU time used from beginning to end of its execution.
2. Total time the job was in the system until it exited.
3. Main storage occupancy, how long the job stayed in memory until it finished execution. This is usually a combination of time and space used; for example, in a paging system it may be recorded in units of page-seconds.
4. Secondary storage used during execution. This, too, is recorded as a combination of time and space used.
5. System programs used such as compilers, editors, or utilities.
6. Number and type of I/O operations, including I/O transmission time, that includes utilization of channels, control units, and devices.
7. Time spent waiting for I/O completion.
8. Number of input records read (specifically, those entered on-line or coming from optical scanners, card readers, or other input devices), and number of output records written (specifically, those sent to the line printer). This last one distinguishes between secondary storage devices and typical I/O devices.

PCBs AND QUEUEING

A job's PCB is created when the Job Scheduler accepts the job and is updated as the job progresses from the beginning to the end of its execution.

Queues use PCBs to track jobs the same way customs officials use passports to track international visitors. The PCB contains all of the data about the job needed by the operating system to manage the processing of the job. As the job moves through the system its progress is noted in the PCB.

The PCBs, not the jobs, are linked to form the queues as shown in Figure 4.4. Although each PCB is not drawn in detail the reader should imagine each queue as a linked list of PCBs. The PCBs for every ready job are linked on the READY queue, and all of the PCBs for the jobs just entering the system are linked on the HOLD queue. The jobs that are WAITING, however, are linked together by "reason for waiting," so the PCBs for the jobs in this category are linked into several queues. For example, the PCBs for jobs that are waiting for I/O on a specific disk drive are linked together, while those waiting for the line printer are linked in a different queue. These queues need to be managed in an orderly fashion and that's determined by the process scheduling policies and algorithms.

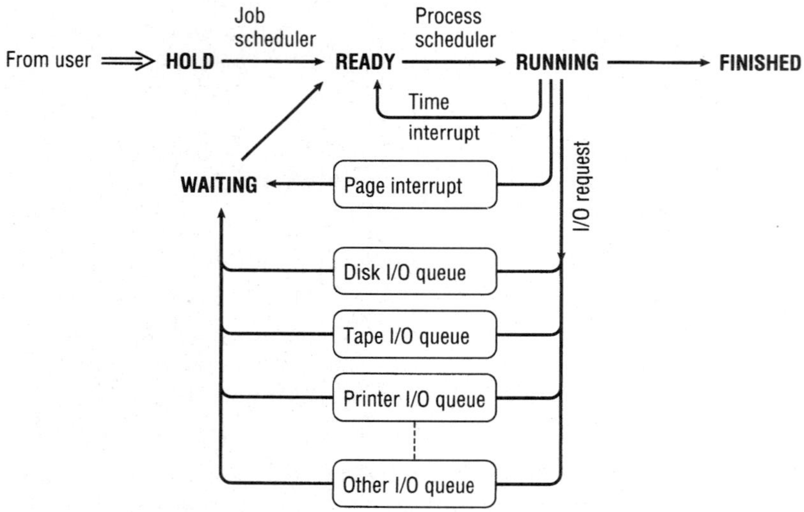

FIGURE 4.4
Queuing paths from HOLD *to* FINISHED.

PROCESS SCHEDULING POLICIES

In a multiprogramming environment there are usually more jobs to be executed than could possibly be run at one time. Before the operating system can schedule them, it needs to resolve three limitations of the system: (1) there are a finite number of resources (such as disk drives, printers, and tape drives); (2) some resources, once they're allocated, can't be shared with another job (such as printers); and (3) some resources require operator intervention — that is, they can't be reassigned automatically from job to job (such as tape drives).

What's a "good" **process scheduling policy**? There are several criteria that come to mind, but notice in the list below that some of them contradict each other:

- *Maximize throughput* by running as many jobs as possible in a given amount of time. This could be accomplished easily by running only short jobs or by running jobs without interruptions.
- *Minimize response time* by quickly turning around interactive requests. This could be done by running only interactive jobs and letting the batch jobs wait until the interactive load ceases.
- *Minimize turnaround time* by moving entire jobs in and out of the system quickly. This could be done by running all batch jobs first (because batch jobs can be grouped to run more efficiently than interactive jobs).
- *Minimize waiting time* by moving jobs out of the READY queue as quickly as possible. This could only be done by reducing the number of users allowed on the system so the CPU would be available immediately whenever a job entered the READY queue.
- *Maximize CPU efficiency* by keeping the CPU busy 100 percent of the time. This could be done by running only CPU-bound jobs (and not I/O-bound jobs).
- *Ensure fairness for all jobs* by giving everyone an equal amount of CPU and I/O time. This could be done by not giving special treatment to any job, regardless of its processing characteristics or priority.

As we can see from this list, if the system favors one type of user then it hurts another or doesn't efficiently use its resources. The final decision rests with the system designer, who must determine which criteria are most important for that specific system. For example, you might decide to "maximize CPU utilization while minimizing response time and balancing the use of all system components through a mix of I/O-bound and CPU-bound jobs." So you would select the scheduling policy that most closely satisfies your criteria.

Although the Job Scheduler selects jobs to ensure that the READY and I/O queues remain balanced, there are instances when a job claims the CPU for a very long time before issuing an I/O request. If I/O requests are being satisfied (this is done by an I/O controller and will be discussed later), this extensive use of the CPU will build up the READY queue while emptying out the I/O queues, which creates an unacceptable imbalance in the system.

To solve this problem the Process Scheduler often uses a timing mechanism and periodically interrupts running processes when a predetermined slice of time has expired. When that happens, the scheduler suspends all activity on the currently running job and reschedules it into the READY queue; it will be continued later. The CPU is now allocated to another job that runs until one of three things happens: the timer goes off, the job issues an I/O command, or the job is finished. Then the job moves to the READY queue, the WAIT queue, or the FINISHED queue, respectively. An I/O request is called a "**natural wait**" in multiprogramming environments (it allows the processor to be allocated to another job).

A scheduling strategy that interrupts the processing of a job and transfers the CPU to another job is called a **preemptive scheduling policy**; it is widely used in time-sharing environments. The alternative, of course, is a **nonpreemptive schedul-**

ing policy, which functions without external interrupts (interrupts external to the job). Therefore, once a job captures the processor and begins execution, it remains in the RUNNING state uninterrupted until it issues an I/O request (natural wait) or until it is finished (with exceptions made for infinite loops, which are interrupted by both preemptive and nonpreemptive policies).

PROCESS SCHEDULING ALGORITHMS

The Process Scheduler relies on a **process scheduling algorithm**, based on a specific policy, to allocate the CPU and move jobs through the system.

Early operating systems used nonpreemptive policies designed to move batch jobs through the system as efficiently as possible. Most current systems, with their emphasis on interactive use and **response time**, use an algorithm that takes care of the immediate requests of interactive users.

Here are six process scheduling algorithms that have been used extensively.

FIRST COME FIRST SERVED

First come first served (FCFS) is a nonpreemptive scheduling algorithm that handles jobs according to their arrival time: the earlier they arrive, the sooner they're served. It's a very simple algorithm to implement because it uses a FIFO type of queue. This algorithm is fine for most batch systems, but it is unacceptable for interactive systems because interactive users expect quick response times.

With FCFS, as a new job enters the system its PCB is linked to the end of the READY queue and it is removed from the front of the queue when the processor becomes available — that is, after it has processed all of the jobs before it in the queue.

In a strictly FCFS system there are no WAIT queues (each job is run to completion), although there may be systems in which control ("context") is switched on a natural wait (I/O request) and then the job resumes on I/O completion.

The following examples presume a strictly FCFS environment (no multiprogramming). **Turnaround time** is unpredictable with the FCFS policy; consider the following three jobs:

Job A has a CPU cycle of 15 milliseconds.

Job B has a CPU cycle of 2 milliseconds.

Job C has a CPU cycle of 1 millisecond.

For each job, the CPU cycle contains both the actual CPU usage and the I/O requests. That is, it is the total run time. Using a FCFS algorithm with an arrival sequence of A, B, C the time line (Gantt Chart) is shown in Figure 4.5.

If all three jobs arrive almost simultaneously, we can calculate that the turnaround time for Job A is 15, for Job B is 17, and for Job C is 18. So the average turnaround time is:

$$\frac{15 + 17 + 18}{3} = 16.67$$

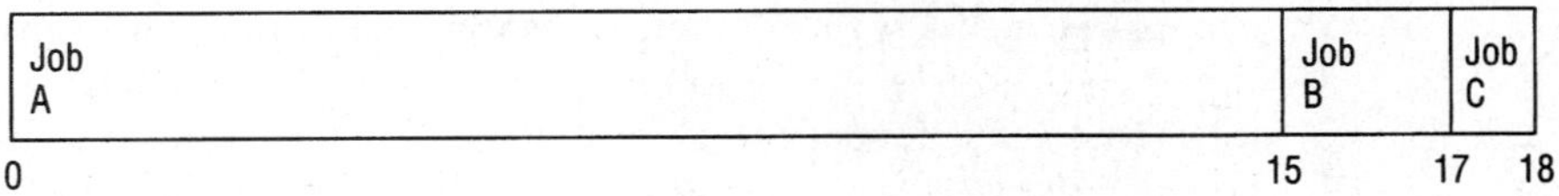

FIGURE 4.5
Time line for job sequence A, B, C using the FCFS algorithm.

However, if the jobs arrived in a different order, say C, B, A, then the results using the same FCFS algorithm would be as shown in Figure 4.6.

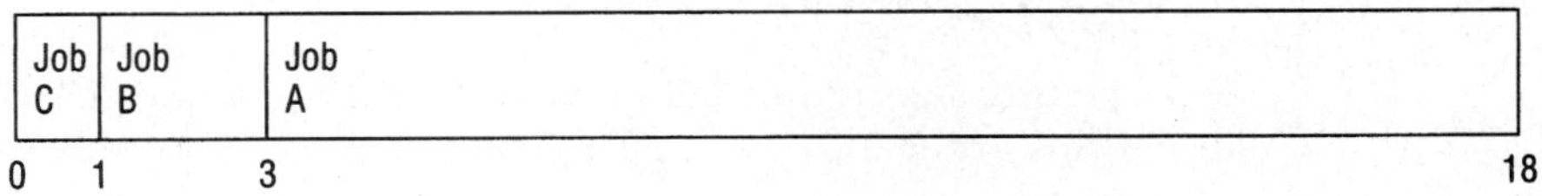

FIGURE 4.6
Time line for job sequence C, B, A using the FCFS algorithm.

In this example the turnaround time for Job A is 18, for Job B is 3, and for Job C is 1 and the average turnaround time is:

$$\frac{18 + 3 + 1}{3} = 7.3$$

That's quite an improvement over the first sequence. Unfortunately, these two examples illustrate the primary disadvantage of using the FCFS concept — the average turnaround times vary widely and are seldom minimized. In fact, when there are three jobs in the `READY` queue, the system has only a 1 in 6 chance of running the jobs in the most advantageous sequence (C, B, A). With four jobs the odds fall to 1 in 24, and so on.

If one job monopolizes the system, the extent of its overall effect on system performance depends on the scheduling policy and whether the job is CPU-bound or I/O-bound. While a job with a long CPU cycle (in this example, Job A) is using the CPU, the other jobs in the system are waiting for processing or finishing their I/O requests (if an I/O controller is used) and joining the `READY` queue to wait for their turn to use the processor. If the I/O requests are not being serviced, the I/O queues would remain stable while the `READY` list "grew" (with new arrivals). In extreme cases, the `READY` queue could fill to capacity while the I/O queues would be empty, or stable, and the I/O devices would sit idle.

On the other hand, if the job is processing a lengthy I/O cycle, the I/O queues quickly build to overflowing and the CPU could be sitting idle (if an I/O controller is used). This situation is eventually resolved when the I/O-bound job finishes its I/O cycle, the queues start moving again, and the system can recover from the bottleneck.

In a strictly FCFS algorithm, neither situation occurs. However, the turnaround time is variable (unpredictable). For this reason, FCFS is a less attractive algorithm than one that would serve the shortest job first, as the next scheduling algorithm does, even in a nonmultiprogramming environment.

SHORTEST JOB NEXT

Shortest job next (SJN) is a nonpreemptive scheduling algorithm (also known as **shortest job first**, or **SJF**) that handles jobs based on the length of their CPU cycle time. It's easiest to implement in batch environments where the estimated CPU time required to run the job is given in advance by each user at the start of each job. However, it doesn't work in interactive systems because users don't estimate in advance the CPU time required to run their jobs. For example, here are four batch jobs, all in the READY queue, for which the CPU cycle, or run time, is estimated as follows:

Job:	A	B	C	D
CPU cycle:	5	2	6	4

The SJN algorithm would review the four jobs and schedule them for processing in this order: B, D, A, C. Their time line is shown in Figure 4.7.

FIGURE 4.7 *Time line for job sequence B, D, A, C using the SJN algorithm.*

The average turnaround time is:

$$\frac{2 + 6 + 11 + 17}{4} = 9.0$$

Let's take a minute to see why this algorithm can be proved to be optimal and will consistently give the minimum average turnaround time. We'll use the example above to derive a general formula.

If we look at Figure 4.7 we can see that Job B finishes in its given time (2), Job D finishes in its given time plus the time it waited for B to run (4 + 2), Job A finishes in its given time plus D's time plus B's time (5 + 4 + 2), and Job C finishes in its given time plus that of the previous three (6 + 5 + 4 + 2). So when calculating the average we have:

$$\frac{[(2) + (4 + 2) + (5 + 4 + 2) + (6 + 5 + 4 + 2)]}{4} = 9.0$$

As you can see, the time for the first job appears in the equation four times—once for each job. Similarly, the time for the second job appears three times (the number of jobs minus one). The time for the third job appears twice (number of jobs minus 2) and the time for the fourth job appears only once (number of jobs minus 3).

So the above equation can be rewritten as:

$$\frac{[4 * 2 + 3 * 4 + 2 * 5 + 1 * 6]}{4} = 9.0$$

Because the time for the first job appears in the equation four times, it has four times the effect on the average time than does the length of the fourth job, which appears only once. Therefore, if the first job requires the shortest computation time, followed in turn by the other jobs, ordered from shortest to longest, then the result will be the smallest possible average. The formula for the average is as follows:

$$\frac{[t_1(n) + t_2(n-1) + t_3(n-2) + \ldots + t_n(1)]}{n}$$

where n is the number of jobs in the queue and $t_j(j = 1, 2, 3, \ldots, n)$ is the length of the CPU cycle for each of the jobs.

However, the SJN algorithm is optimal only when all of the jobs are available at the same time and the CPU estimates are available and accurate.

PRIORITY SCHEDULING

Priority Scheduling is a nonpreemptive algorithm and one of the most common scheduling algorithms in batch systems, even though it may give slower turnaround to some users. This algorithm gives preferential treatment to important jobs. It allows the programs with the highest priority to be processed first, and they aren't interrupted until their CPU cycles (run times) are completed or a natural wait occurs. If two or more jobs with equal priority are present in the READY queue, the processor is allocated to the one that arrived first (first come first served within priority).

Priorities can be assigned by a system administrator using characteristics extrinsic to the jobs; for example, they can be assigned based on the position of the user (researchers first, students last) or, in commercial environments, they can be purchased by the users who pay more for higher priority to guarantee the fastest possible processing of their jobs. With a priority algorithm, jobs are usually linked to one of several READY queues by the Job Scheduler based on their priority so the Process Scheduler manages multiple READY queues instead of just one. Details about multiple queues are presented later in this chapter.

Priorities can also be determined by the Processor Manager based on characteristics intrinsic to the jobs such as:

- *Memory requirements.* Jobs requiring large amounts of memory could be allocated lower priorities than those requesting small amounts of memory, or vice versa.
- *Number and type of peripheral devices.* Jobs requiring many peripheral devices would be allocated lower priorities than those requesting fewer devices.
- *Total CPU time.* Jobs having a long CPU cycle, or estimated run time, would be given lower priorities than those having a brief estimated run time.
- *Amount of time already spent in the system.* This is the total amount of elapsed time since the job was accepted for processing. Some systems increase the priority of jobs that have been in the system for an unusually long time to expedite their exit. This is known as "aging."

These criteria are used to determine default priorities in many systems. The default priorities can be overruled by specific priorities named by users.

There are also preemptive priority schemes. These will be discussed later in this chapter in the section on multiple queues.

SHORTEST REMAINING TIME

Shortest remaining time (SRT) is the preemptive version of the SJN algorithm. The processor is allocated to the job closest to completion — but even this job can be preempted if a newer job in the READY queue has a "time to completion" that's shorter.

This algorithm can't be implemented in an interactive system because it requires advance knowledge of the CPU time required to finish each job. It is often used in batch environments, when it is desirable to give preference to short jobs, even though SRT involves more overhead than SJN because the operating system has to frequently monitor the CPU time for all the jobs in the READY queue and must perform "context switching" for the jobs being swapped ("switched") at preemption time (not necessarily swapped out to the disk, although this might occur as well).

The example in Figure 4.8 shows how the SRT algorithm works with four jobs that arrived in quick succession (1 CPU cycle apart).

Arrival time:	0	1	2	3
Job:	A	B	C	D
CPU cycle:	6	3	1	4

FIGURE 4.8
Time line for job sequence A, B, C, D using the preemptive SRT algorithm.

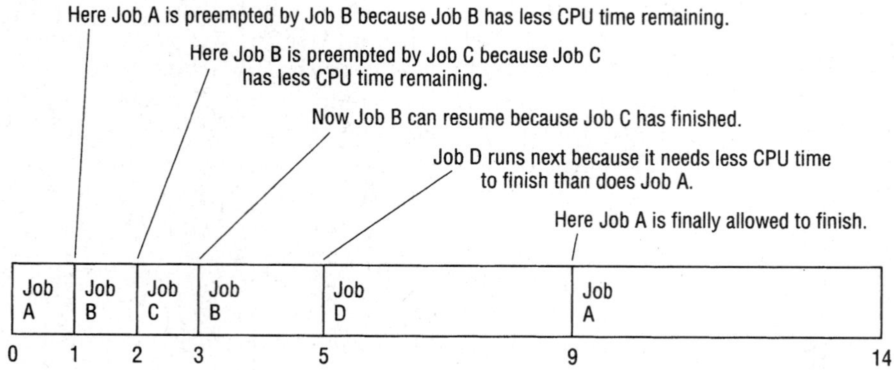

In this case the turnaround time is the completion time of each job minus its arrival time:

Job:	A	B	C	D
Turnaround:	14	4	1	6

So the average turnaround time is:

$$\frac{14 + 4 + 1 + 6}{4} = 6.25$$

How does that compare to the same problem using the nonpreemptive SJN policy? Figure 4.9 shows the same situation using SJN.

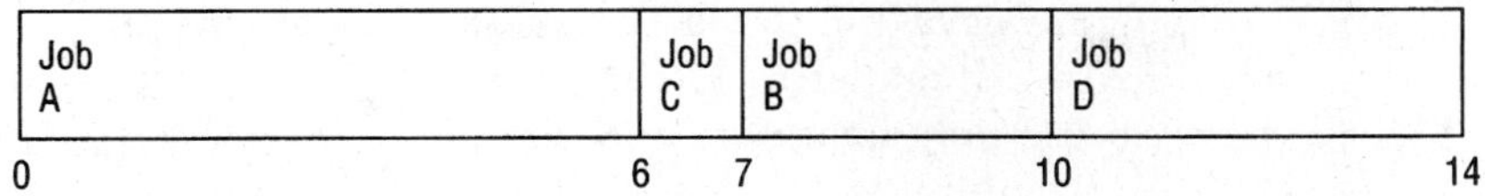

FIGURE 4.9
Time line for the same job sequence A, B, C, D using the nonpreemptive SJN algorithm.

In this case the turnaround time is:

Job:	A	B	C	D
Turnaround:	6	9	5	11

So the average turnaround time is:

$$\frac{6 + 9 + 5 + 11}{4} = 7.75$$

Note in Figure 4.9 that initially A is the only job in the READY queue so it runs first and continues until it's finished because SJN is a nonpreemptive algorithm. The next job to be run is C because when Job A is finished (at time 6), all of the other jobs (B, C, and D) have arrived. Of those three, C has the shortest CPU cycle, so it is the next one run, then B, and finally D.

Therefore, with this example, SRT at 6.25 is faster than SJN at 7.75. However, we neglected to include the time required by the SRT algorithm to do the context switching. **Context switching** is required by all preemptive algorithms. When Job A is preempted, all of its processing information must be saved in its PCB for later, when Job A's execution is to be continued, and the contents of Job B's PCB are loaded into the appropriate registers so it can start running again; this is a context switch. Later when Job A is once again assigned to the processor another context switch is performed; this time the information from the preempted job is stored in its PCB, and the contents of Job A's PCB are loaded into the appropriate registers.

How the context switching is actually done depends on the architecture of the CPU; in many systems there are special instructions that provide quick saving and restoring of information. The switching is designed to be performed efficiently but, no matter how fast it is, it still takes valuable CPU time. So although SRT appears to be faster, in a real operating environment its advantages are diminished by the time spent in context switching. A precise comparison of SRT and SJN would have to include the time required to do the context switching.

ROUND ROBIN

Round robin is a preemptive process scheduling algorithm that is used extensively in interactive systems because it's easy to implement and it isn't based on job characteristics but on a predetermined slice of time that's given to each job to ensure that the CPU is equally shared among all active processes and isn't monopolized by any one job.

This **time slice** is called a **time quantum** and its size is crucial to the performance of the system. It usually varies from 100 milliseconds to 1 or 2 seconds (Pinkert & Wear, 1989).

Jobs are placed in the READY queue using a first-come first-served scheme and the Process Scheduler selects the first job from the front of the queue, sets the timer to the time quantum, and allocates the CPU to this job. If processing isn't finished when time expires, the job is preempted and put at the end of the READY queue and its information is saved in its PCB.

In the event that the job's CPU cycle is shorter than the time quantum, one of two actions will take place: (1) if this is the job's last CPU cycle and the job is finished, then all resources allocated to it are released and the completed job is returned to the user; (2) if the CPU cycle has been interrupted by an I/O request, then information about the job is saved in its PCB and it is linked at the end of the appropriate I/O queue. Later, when the I/O request has been satisfied, it is returned to the end of the READY queue to await allocation of the CPU.

The example in Figure 4.10 illustrates a round robin algorithm with a time slice of 4 milliseconds (I/O requests are ignored):

Arrival time:	0	1	2	3
Job:	A	B	C	D
CPU cycle:	8	4	9	5

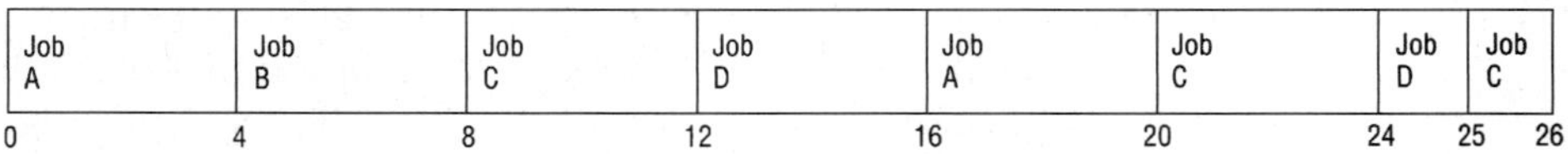

FIGURE 4.10
Time line for job sequence A, B, C, D using the preemptive round robin algorithm using time slices of 4 ms.

The turnaround time is the completion time minus the arrival time:

Job:	A	B	C	D
Turnaround:	20	7	24	22

So the average turnaround time is:

$$\frac{20 + 7 + 24 + 22}{4} = 18.25$$

Note that in Figure 4.10 Job A was preempted once because it needed 8 milliseconds to complete its CPU cycle, while Job B terminated in one time quantum. Job C was preempted twice because it needed 9 milliseconds to complete its CPU cycle, and Job D was preempted once because it needed 5 milliseconds. In their last execution or swap into memory, both Jobs D and C used the CPU for only 1 millisecond and terminated before their last time quantum expired, releasing the CPU sooner.

The efficiency of round robin depends on the size of the time quantum in relation to the average CPU cycle. If the quantum is too large — that is, if it's larger than most CPU cycles — then the algorithm reduces to the FCFS scheme. If the quantum is too small, then the amount of context switching slows down the execution of the jobs and the amount of overhead is dramatically increased, as the three examples in Figure 4.11 demonstrate. Job A has a CPU cycle of 8 milliseconds. The amount of context switching increases as the time quantum decreases in size.

In Figure 4.11 the first case (a) has a time quantum of 10 milliseconds and there is no context switching (and no overhead). The CPU cycle ends shortly before the time quantum expires and the job runs to completion. For this job with this time quantum, there is no difference between the round robin algorithm and the FCFS algorithm.

FIGURE 4.11
Context switches for Job A with three different time quantums.

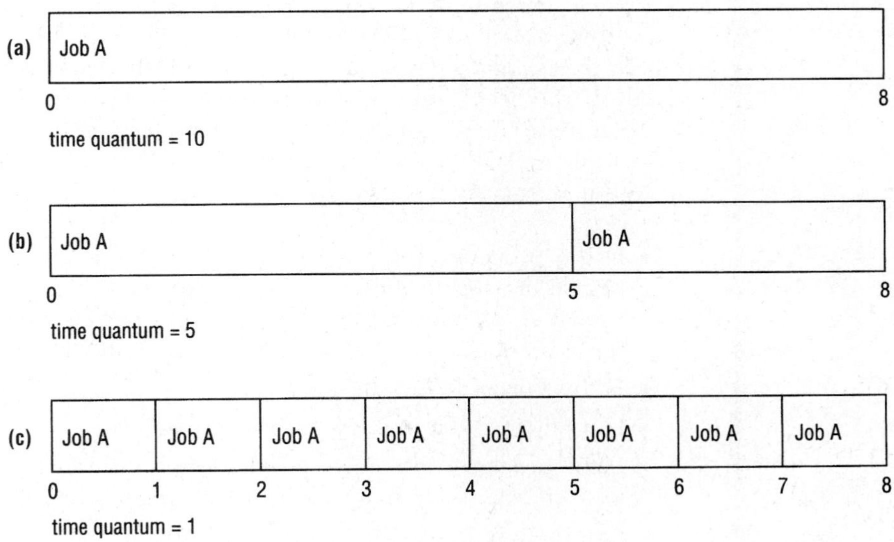

In the second case (b), with a time quantum of 5 milliseconds, there is one context switch. The job is preempted once when the time quantum expires, so there is some overhead for context switching and there would be a delayed turnaround based on the number of other jobs in the system.

In the third case (c), with a time quantum of 1 millisecond, there are seven context switches because the job is preempted every time the time quantum expires; overhead becomes costly and turnaround time suffers accordingly.

What's the best time quantum size? The answer should be predictable by now: it depends on the system. If it's an interactive environment the system is expected to respond quickly to its users, especially when they make simple requests. If it's a batch system, response time is not a factor (turnaround is) and overhead becomes very important.

Here are two general rules of thumb for selecting the "proper" time quantum: (1) it should be long enough to allow 80 percent of the CPU cycles to run to completion, and (2) it should be at least 100 times longer than the time required to perform one context switch. These rules are used in some systems, but they are not inflexible (Finkel, 1986).

MULTIPLE LEVEL QUEUES

Multiple level queues isn't really a separate scheduling algorithm but works in conjunction with several of the other schemes already discussed and is found in systems with jobs that can be grouped according to a common characteristic. We've already introduced at least one kind of multiple level queue — that of a priority-based system with different queues for each priority level.

Another kind of system might gather all of the CPU-bound jobs in one queue and all I/O-bound jobs in another. The Process Scheduler then alternately selects jobs from each queue to keep the system balanced.

A third common example is one used in a hybrid environment that supports both batch and interactive jobs. The batch jobs are put in one queue called the "background queue" while the interactive jobs are put in a "foreground queue" and are treated more favorably than those on the background queue.

All of these examples have one thing in common: the scheduling policy is based on some predetermined scheme that allocates special treatment to the jobs in each queue. Within each queue, the jobs are served in FCFS fashion.

Multiple level queues raise some interesting questions.

- Is the processor allocated to the jobs in the first queue until it is empty before moving to the next queue or does it "travel" from queue to queue until the last job on the last queue has been served and then go back to serve the first job on the first queue, or something in between?
- Is this fair to those who have earned, or paid for, a higher priority?
- Is it fair to those in a low priority queue?
- If the processor is allocated to the jobs on the first queue and it never empties out, when will the jobs in the last queues be served?
- Can the jobs in the last queues get "time off for good behavior" and eventually move to better queues?

The answers depend on the policy used by the system to service the queues. There are four primary methods to the movement: not allowing movement between queues; moving jobs from queue to queue; moving jobs from queue to queue and increasing the time quantums for "lower" queues; and giving special treatment to jobs that have been in the system for a long time. The latter is known as **aging**. The following examples are derived from Yourdon (1972).

No movement between queues is a very simple policy that rewards those who have high-priority jobs. The processor is allocated to the jobs in the high-priority queue in FCFS fashion and it is allocated to jobs in lower priority queues only when the high-priority queues are empty. This policy can be justified if there are relatively few users with high-priority jobs so the top queues quickly empty out, allowing the processor to spend a fair amount of time running the low-priority jobs.

Movement between queues is a policy that adjusts the priorities assigned to each job: high-priority jobs are treated like all the others once they are in the system (their initial priority may be favorable). When a time quantum interrupt occurs, the job is preempted and it is moved to the end of the next lower queue. A job may also have its priority increased; for example, when it issues an I/O request before its time quantum has expired.

This policy is fairest in a system in which the jobs are handled according to their computing cycle characteristics: CPU-bound or I/O-bound. This assumes that a job that exceeds its time quantum is CPU-bound and will require more CPU allocation than one that requests I/O before the time quantum expires. Therefore, the CPU-bound jobs are placed at the end of the next lower queue when they're preempted because of the expiration of the time quantum, while I/O-bound jobs are returned to the end of the next higher level queue once their I/O request has finished. This facilitates I/O-bound jobs (and is good in interactive systems).

Variable time quantum per queue is a variation of the Movement Between Queues and it allows for faster turnaround of CPU-bound jobs.

In this scheme, each of the queues is given a time quantum twice as long as the previous queue. The highest queue might have a time quantum of 100 milliseconds. So the second-highest queue would have a time quantum of 200 milliseconds, the third would have 400 milliseconds, and so on. If there are enough queues, the lowest one might have a relatively long time quantum of 3 seconds or more.

If a job doesn't finish its CPU cycle in the first time quantum, it is moved to the end of the next lower level queue and when the processor is next allocated to it, the job executes for twice as long as before. With this scheme a CPU-bound job can execute for longer and longer periods of time, thus improving its chances of finishing faster.

Aging is used to ensure that jobs in the lower level queues will eventually complete their execution. The operating system keeps track of each job's waiting time and when a job gets too old — that is, when it reaches a certain time limit — it moves the job to the next highest queue, and so on until it reaches the top queue. A more drastic aging policy is one that moves the "old" job directly from the lowest queue to the end of the topmost queue. Regardless of its actual implementation, an aging policy guards against the indefinite postponement of unwieldy jobs. As you might expect, **indefinite postponement** means that a job's execution is delayed indefinitely because it is repeatedly preempted so other jobs can be processed. (We all know examples of an unpleasant task that's been indefinitely postponed to make time for a more appealing pastime). Eventually the situation could lead to the old job's "starvation." Indefinite postponement is a major problem when allocating resources and one that will be discussed in detail in Chapter 5.

A WORD ABOUT INTERRUPTS

We first encountered **interrupts** in Chapter 3 when the Memory Manager issued page interrupts to accommodate job requests. In this chapter we examined another type of interrupt that occurs when the time quantum expires and the processor is deallocated from the running job and allocated to another one.

There are other interrupts that are caused by events internal to the process. I/O interrupts are issued when a `READ` or `WRITE` command is issued. (We'll explain them in detail in Chapter 7.) **Internal interrupts**, or **synchronous interrupts**, also occur as a direct result of the arithmetic operation or job instruction currently being processed.

Illegal arithmetic operations such as the following can generate interrupts:

- Attempts to divide by zero;
- Floating point operations generating an overflow or underflow;
- Fixed-point addition or subtraction that causes an arithmetic overflow.

Illegal job instructions such as the following can also generate interrupts:

- Attempts to access protected or nonexistent storage locations;
- Attempts to use an undefined operation code;
- Operating on invalid data;
- Attempts to make system changes, such as trying to change the size of the time quantum.

The control program that handles the interruption sequence of events is called the **interrupt handler**. When the operating system detects a nonrecoverable error, the interrupt handler typically follows this sequence:

1. The type of interrupt is described and stored — to be passed on to the user as an error message.
2. The state of the interrupted process is saved, including the value of the program counter, the mode specification, and the contents of all registers.
3. The interrupt is processed: the error message and state of the interrupted process are sent to the user; program execution is halted; any resources allocated to the job are released; and the job exits the system.
4. The processor resumes normal operation.

If we're dealing only with internal interrupts, which are nonrecoverable, the job is terminated in Step 3. However, when the interrupt handler is working with an I/O interrupt, time quantum, or other recoverable interrupt, Step 3 simply halts the job and moves it to the appropriate I/O device queue, or `READY` queue (on "time out"). Later, when the I/O request is finished, the job is returned to the `READY` queue. If it was a time out (quantum interrupt), the job (or process) is already on the `READY` queue.

CHAPTER FOUR CONCLUSION

The Processor Manager must allocate the CPU among all the system's users. In this chapter we've made the distinction between job scheduling, the selection of incoming jobs based on their characteristics, and process scheduling, the instant-by-instant allocation of the CPU. We've also described how interrupts are generated and resolved by the interrupt handler.

Each of the scheduling algorithms presented in this chapter has unique characteristics, objectives, and applications. A system designer can choose the best policy and algorithm only after carefully evaluating their strengths and weaknesses. Table 4.1 shows how the algorithms presented in this chapter compare.

TABLE 4.1 *Comparison of scheduling algorithms.*

Algorithm	Policy type	Best for	Disadvantages	Advantages
FCFS	Nonpreemptive	Batch	Unpredictable turnaround times	Easy to implement
SJN	Nonpreemptive	Batch	Indefinite postponement of some jobs	Minimizes average waiting time
Priority scheduling	Nonpreemptive	Batch	Indefinite postponement of some jobs	Ensures fast completion of important jobs
SRT	Preemptive	Batch	Overhead incurred by context switching	Ensures fast completion of short jobs
Round robin	Preemptive	Interactive	Requires selection of "good" time quantum	Provides reasonable response time to interactive users; provides "fair" CPU allocation
Multiple level queues	Preemptive/ Nonpreemptive	Batch/ interactive	Overhead incurred by monitoring of queues	Flexible scheme; counteracts indefinite postponement with aging or other queue movement; gives "fair" treatment to CPU-bound jobs by incrementing time quantums on lower priority queues or other queue movement

In the next chapter we'll explore the demands placed on the Processor Manager as it attempts to synchronize execution of all the jobs in the system.

KEY TERMS

multiprogramming
processor
process
Job Scheduler
Process Scheduler
high-level scheduler
low-level scheduler
I/O-bound
CPU-bound
middle-level scheduler
job status
process status
Process Control Block (PCB)
queue
process scheduling policy
preemptive scheduling policy
nonpreemptive scheduling policy
process scheduling algorithm
response time
first come first served (FCFS)
turnaround time
shortest job next (SJN)

priority scheduling
shortest remaining time (SRT)
context switching
round robin
time slice
time quantum
multiple level queues
aging
indefinite postponement
interrupt
internal interrupts
synchronous interrupts
interrupt handler

EXERCISES

1. What information about a job needs to be kept in the PCB?
2. What information about a process needs to be saved, changed, or updated when context switching takes place?
3. Five jobs are in the READY queue waiting to be processed. Their estimated CPU cycles are as follows: 10, 3, 5, 6, and 2. Using SJN, in what order should they be processed to minimize average waiting time?
4. A job running in a system, with variable time quantums per queue, needs 30 milliseconds to run to completion. If the first queue has a time quantum of 5 milliseconds and each queue thereafter has a time quantum that is twice as large as the previous one, how many times will the job be interrupted and on which queue will it finish its execution?
5. The following diagram (adapted from Madnick & Donovan, 1974) is a simplified process model of you, in which there are only two states: sleeping and waking.

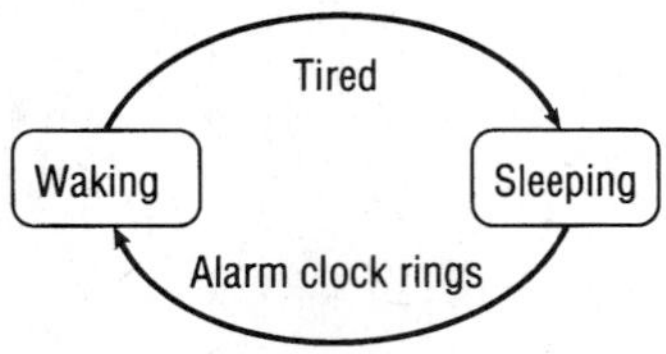

   You make the transition from waking to sleeping when you are tired, and from sleeping to waking when the alarm clock goes off.

   a. Add three more states to the diagram (for example, one might be eating).

   b. State all of the possible transitions among the five states.
6. What is the relationship between turnaround time, CPU cycle time, and waiting time? Write an equation to express this relationship, if possible.
7. Given the following information:

Job #	Arrival time	CPU cycle
1	0	10
2	1	2
3	2	3
4	3	1
5	4	5

Draw a time line for each of the following scheduling algorithms. (It may be helpful to first compute a start and finish time for each job.)

a. FCFS

b. SJN

c. SRT

d. Round robin (using a time quantum of 2, ignore context switching and natural wait)

8. Using the same information given for exercise 7, complete the chart by computing waiting time and turnaround time for every job for each of the following scheduling algorithms (ignoring context switching overhead).

a. FCFS

b. SJN

c. SRT

d. Round robin (using a time quantum of 2)

9. Using the same information given for exercise 7, compute the average waiting time and average turnaround time for each of the following scheduling algorithms and determine which one gives the best results.

a. FCFS

b. SJN

c. SRT

d. Round robin (using a time quantum of 2)

ADVANCED EXERCISES

10. Consider a variation of round robin in which a process that has used its full time quantum is returned to the end of the READY queue, while one that has used half of its time quantum is returned to the middle of the queue and one that has used one-fourth of its time quantum goes to a place one-fourth of the distance away from the beginning of the queue.

a. What is the objective of this scheduling policy?

b. Discuss the advantage and disadvantage of its implementation.

11. In a single-user dedicated system, such as a personal computer, it's easy for the user to determine when a job is caught in an infinite loop. The typical solution to this problem is for the user to manually intervene and terminate the job. What mechanism would you implement in the Process Scheduler to automate the termination of a job that's in an infinite loop? Take into account jobs that legitimately use large amounts of CPU time; for example, one "finding the first 10,000 prime numbers."

12. Some guidelines for selecting the "right" time quantum were given in this chapter. As a system designer, how would you know when you have chosen the "best" time quantum? What factors would make this time quantum best from the user's point of view? What factors would make this time quantum best from the system's point of view?

13. Using the process state diagrams of Figure 4.2, explain why there's no transition:

    a. From the READY state to the WAITING state.

    b. From the WAITING state to the RUNNING state.

PROGRAMMING EXERCISES

14. Write a program that will simulate FCFS, SJN, SRT, and round robin scheduling algorithms. For each algorithm, the program should compute waiting time and turnaround time of every job as well as the average waiting time and average turnaround time. The average values should be consolidated in a table for easy comparison. You may use the following data to test your program:

Arrival time	CPU cycle (in milliseconds)
0	6
3	2
5	1
9	7
10	5
12	3
14	4
16	5
17	7
19	2

time quantum for round robin = 4 ms
context switching time = 0

15. Using your program from exercise 14, change the context switching time to 0.4 milliseconds. Compare outputs from both runs and discuss which would be the best policy. Describe any drastic changes encountered or a lack of changes and why.

Chapter Five

PROCESS MANAGEMENT

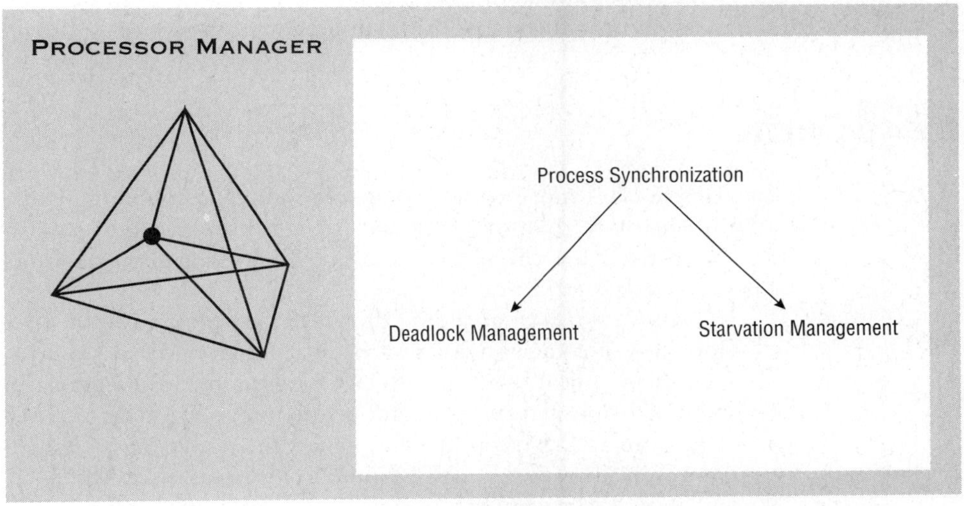

We've already looked at two aspects of resource sharing — memory management and processor sharing. In this chapter, we'll address the problems caused when many processes compete for relatively few resources and the system is unable to service all of the processes in the system.

A lack of **process synchronization** can result in two extreme conditions: deadlock or starvation.

In early operating systems, deadlock was known by the more descriptive phrase **deadly embrace**. It's a systemwide tangle of resource requests that begins when two or more jobs are put on hold, each waiting for a vital resource to become available. The problem builds when the resources needed by those jobs are the resources held by other jobs that are also waiting to run but cannot because they're waiting for other unavailable resources. The jobs come to a standstill. The deadlock is complete if the remainder of the system comes to a standstill as well. Usually the situation can't be resolved by the operating system and requires outside intervention by either operators or users who must take drastic actions, such as manually preempting or terminating a job.

A **deadlock** is most easily described with an example — a narrow staircase in a building (we'll return to this example throughout this chapter). The staircase was built as a fire escape route, but people working in the building often take the stairs instead of waiting for the slow elevators. Traffic on the staircase moves well unless two people, traveling in opposite directions, need to pass on the stairs; there's room for only one person on each step. There's a landing between each floor and it's wide enough for passing, but the stairs are not. Problems occur when someone going up the stairs meets someone coming down, and each refuses to retreat to a wider place. This creates a deadlock, which is the subject of much of our discussion on process synchronization.

On the other hand, if a few patient people wait on the landing for a break in the opposing traffic, and that break never comes, they could wait there forever. That's **starvation**, an extreme case of indefinite postponement, and it is discussed near the conclusion of this chapter.

DEADLOCK

Deadlock is more serious than indefinite postponement or starvation because it affects more than one job. Because resources are being tied up, the entire system (not just a few programs) is affected. The example most often used to illustrate deadlock is a traffic jam.

As shown in Figure 5.1, there's no simple and immediate solution to a deadlock; no one can move forward until someone moves out of the way, but no one can move out of the way until either someone advances or the rear of a line moves back. Obviously it requires an outside intervention to remove one of the four vehicles from an intersection or to make a line move back. Only then can the deadlock be resolved.

Deadlocks were infrequent in the early batch systems because users would include in the job control cards that preceded the job a complete list of the specific system resources (tape drives, disks, printers, etc.) required to run the job. The operating system would then make sure that all requested resources were available and allocated to that job before moving the job to the `READY` queue; and then the system did not release these resources until the job was completed. If the resources weren't available, the job wasn't moved to the `READY` queue until they were.

Deadlocks became more prevalent with the growing use of interactive systems because they are more flexible than batch environments. Interactive systems generally improve the use of resources through dynamic resource sharing, but it's this resource-sharing capability that also increases the possibility of deadlocks.

SEVEN CASES OF DEADLOCK

A deadlock usually occurs when nonsharable, nonpreemptable resources, such as files, printers, or tape drives are allocated to jobs that eventually require other nonsharable, nonpreemptive resources — resources that have been locked by other jobs. However, deadlocks aren't restricted to files, printers, and tape drives. They can also occur on sharable resources such as disks and databases, as we'll see in the following examples (Bic & Shaw, 1988).

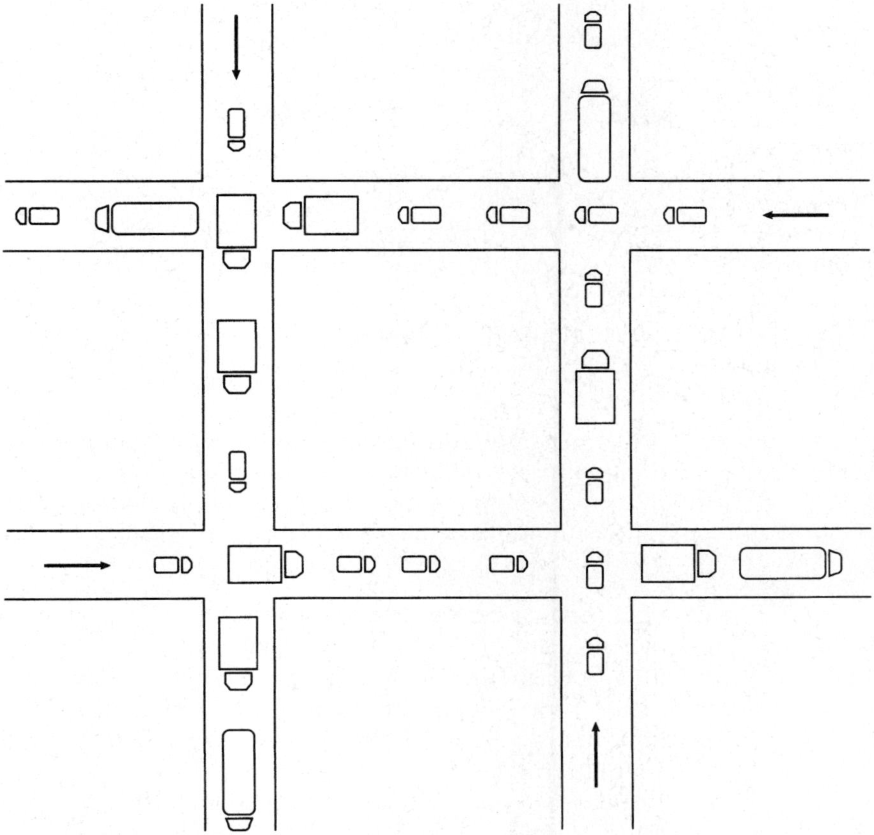

FIGURE 5.1
A classic case of deadlock. This is "gridlock," where all the cars are entangled.

CASE 1: DEADLOCKS ON FILE REQUESTS If jobs are allowed to request and hold files for the duration of their execution, a deadlock can occur. For example, consider the case of a home construction company with two application programs, purchasing (P1) and sales (P2), which are active at the same time. They each need to access two files, inventory (F1) and suppliers (F2), to update daily transactions. One day the system deadlocks when the following sequence of events takes place.

1. Purchasing (P1) accesses the supplier file (F2) to place an order for more lumber.
2. Sales (P2) accesses the inventory file (F1) to reserve the parts that will be required to build the home ordered that day.
3. Purchasing (P1) doesn't release the supplier file (F2) but requests the inventory file (F1) to verify the quantity of lumber on hand before placing its order for more, but P1 is blocked because F1 is being held by P2.
4. Meanwhile, sales (P2) doesn't release the inventory file (F1) but requests the supplier file (F2) to check the schedule of a subcontractor. At this

point P2 is also blocked because F2 is being held by P1. Figure 5.2 shows the deadlock.

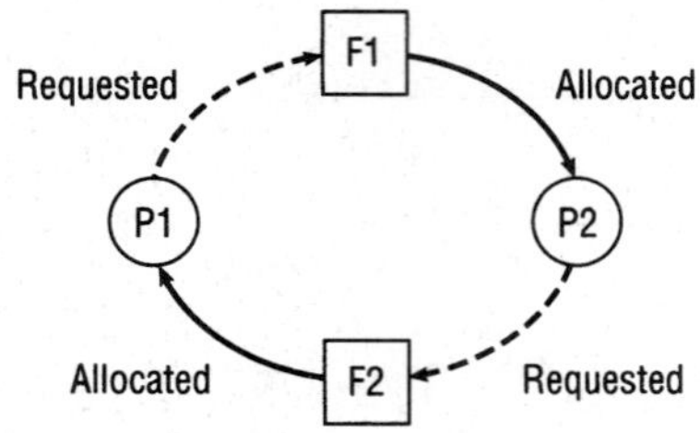

FIGURE 5.2
A deadlock in action, using a modified representation of directed graphs that will be discussed in more detail in the "Modeling Deadlocks" section.

Any other programs that require F1 or F2 will be put on hold as long as this situation continues. This deadlock will remain until one of the two programs is withdrawn or forcibly removed and its file is released. Only then can the other program continue and the system return to normal.

CASE 2: DEADLOCKS IN DATABASES A deadlock can also occur if two processes access and lock records in a database.

To appreciate the following scenario it is necessary to remember that database queries and transactions are often relatively brief processes that either search or modify parts of a database. Requests usually arrive at random and may be interleaved arbitrarily.

Locking is a technique used to guarantee the integrity of the data through which the user locks out all other users while working with the database. Locking can be done at three different levels: the entire database can be locked for the duration of the request; a subsection of the database can be locked; or only the individual record can be locked until the process is completed. If the entire database is locked (the most extreme and most successful solution) it prevents a deadlock from occurring but access to the database is restricted to one user at a time and, in a multiuser environment, response times are significantly slowed; this then is normally an unacceptable solution. When the locking is performed on only part of the database, access time is improved but the possibility of a deadlock is increased because different processes sometimes need to work with several parts of the database at the same time.

Here's a system that locks each record when it is accessed until the process is completed. There are two processes (P1 and P2), each of which needs to update two records (R1 and R2) and the following sequence leads to a deadlock:

1. P1 accesses R1 and locks it.
2. P2 accesses R2 and locks it.
3. P1 requests R2, which is locked by P2.
4. P2 requests R1, which is locked by P1.

An alternative, of course, is to not use locks — but that leads to other difficulties. If locks are not used to preserve their integrity, the updated records in the database might include only some of the data — and their contents would depend on the order in which each process finishes its execution. This is known as a **"race"** between processes and is illustrated in the following example.

Let's say you are a veteran student who knows the university maintains most of its files on a database that can be accessed by several different programs, including one for grades and another listing home addresses. Let's say you're a student on the move so you send the university a change of address form at the end of the fall term, shortly after grades are submitted. And one fateful day both programs race to access your record in the database:

1. The grades process (P1) is the first to access your record (R1) and it copies the record to its work area.
2. The address process (P2) accesses your record (R1) and copies it to its work area.
3. P1 changes R1 by entering your grades for the fall term and calculating your new grade average.
4. P2 changes R1 by updating the address field.
5. P1 finishes its work first and rewrites its version of your record back to the database. Your grades have been changed, but your address hasn't.
6. P2 finishes and rewrites its updated record back to the database. Your address has been changed, but your grades haven't. According to the database you didn't attend school this term.

Figure 5.3 illustrates this process and the outcome of the race.

If we reverse the order and say that P2 won the race, your grades will be updated but not your address. Depending on your success in the classroom you might prefer one mishap over the other, but from the operating system's point of view either alternative is unacceptable because incorrect data is allowed to pollute the database. The system can't allow the integrity of the database to depend on a random sequence of events.

CASE 3: DEADLOCKS IN DEDICATED DEVICE ALLOCATION The use of a group of dedicated devices can deadlock the system.

Let's say two users from the local board of education are each running a program (P1 and P2), and both programs will eventually need two tape drives to copy files from one tape to another. The system is small, however, and when the two programs are begun, only two tape drives are available and they're allocated on an "as requested" basis. Soon the following sequence transpires:

1. P1 requests tape drive 1 and gets it.
2. P2 requests tape drive 2 and gets it.
3. P1 requests tape drive 2 but is blocked.
4. P2 requests tape drive 1 but is blocked.

Neither job can continue because each is waiting for the other to finish and release its tape drive — an event that will never occur. A similar series of events could deadlock any group of dedicated devices.

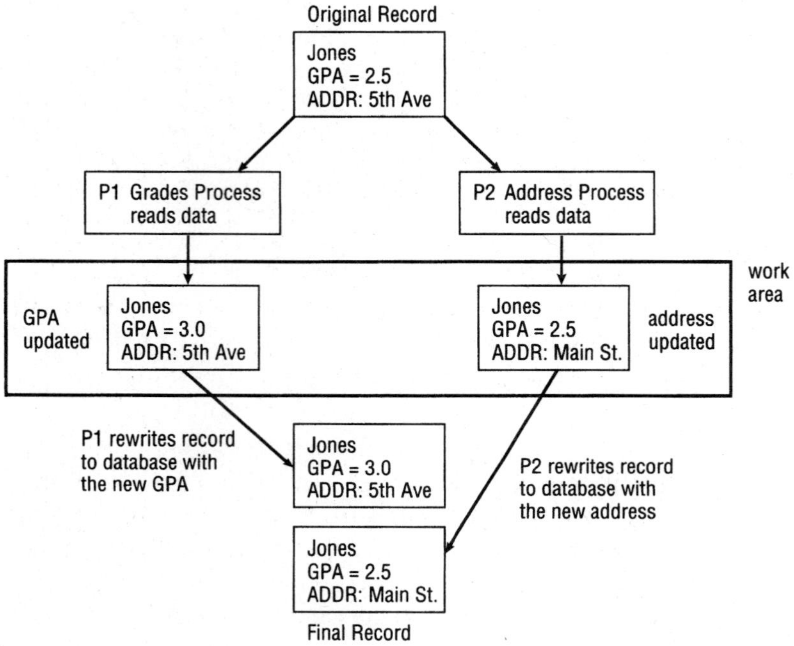

FIGURE 5.3
If P1 finishes first it will win the race but its version of the record will soon be overwritten by P2.

CASE 4: DEADLOCKS IN MULTIPLE DEVICE ALLOCATION Deadlocks aren't restricted to processes contending for the same type of device; they can happen when several processes request, and hold on to, dedicated devices while other processes act in a similar manner.

Consider the case of an engineering design firm with three programs (P1, P2, and P3) and three dedicated devices: tape drive, printer, and plotter. The following sequence of events will result in deadlock:

1. P1 requests and gets the tape drive.
2. P2 requests and gets the printer.
3. P3 requests and gets the plotter.
4. P1 requests the printer but is blocked.
5. P2 requests the plotter but is blocked.
6. P3 requests the tape drive but is blocked.

Figure 5.4 depicts this problem graphically.

As in the earlier examples, none of the jobs can continue because each is waiting for a resource being held by another.

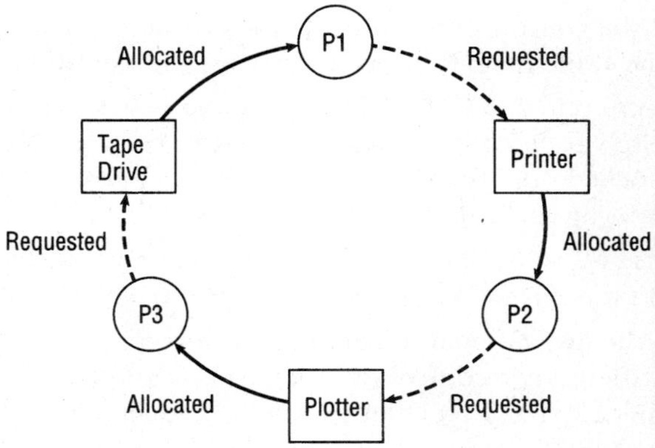

FIGURE 5.4 *Three devices deadlocked by three processes. The dashed and solid lines, as well as the arrows, have the same meaning as those used in Figure 5.2.*

CASE 5: DEADLOCKS IN SPOOLING Although in the previous example the printer was a dedicated device, most systems have transformed the printer into a sharable device (also known as a "virtual device") by installing a high-speed device, a disk, between it and the CPU. The disk accepts output from several users and acts as a temporary storage area for all output until the printer is ready to accept it. This process is called **spooling**. If the printer needs all of a job's output before it will begin printing, but the spooling system fills the available disk space with only partially completed output, then a deadlock can occur. It happens like this.

Let's say it's one hour before the big project is due for a computer class. Twenty-six frantic programmers key in their final changes and, with only minutes to spare, issue print commands. The spooler receives the pages one at a time from each of the students but the pages are received separately, several page one's, page two's, etc. The printer is ready to print the first completed program it gets, but as the spooler canvasses its files it has the first page for many programs but the last page for none of them. Alas, the spooler is full of partially completed output so no other pages can be accepted, but none of the jobs can be printed out (which would release their disk space) because the printer only accepts completed output files. An unfortunate state of affairs.

This scenario isn't limited to printers. Any part of the system that relies on spooling, such as one that handles incoming jobs or transfers files over a network, is vulnerable to such a deadlock.

CASE 6: DEADLOCKS IN DISK SHARING Disks are designed to be shared, so it's not uncommon for two processes to be accessing different areas of the same disk. Without controls to regulate the use of the disk drive, competing processes could send conflicting commands and deadlock the system.

For example, at an insurance company the system performs many daily transactions. One day the following series of events ties up the system:

1. Process P1 wishes to show a payment so it issues a command to read the balance, which is stored in cylinder 20 of a disk pack.

2. While the control unit is moving the arm to cylinder 20, P1 is put on hold and the I/O channel is free to process the next I/O request.
3. P2 gains control of the I/O channel and issues a command to write someone else's payment to a record stored in cylinder 310. If the command is not "locked out," P2 will be put on hold while the control unit moves the arm to cylinder 310.
4. Because P2 is "on hold," the channel is free to be captured again by P1, which reconfirms its command to "read from cylinder 20."
5. Since the last command from P2 had forced the arm mechanism to cylinder 310, the disk control unit begins to reposition the arm to cylinder 20 to satisfy P1. The I/O channel would be released because P1 is once again put on hold, so it could be captured by P2, which issues a `WRITE` command only to discover that the arm mechanism needs to be repositioned.

As a result, the arm is in a constant state of motion, moving back and forth between cylinder 20 and cylinder 310 as it responds to the two competing commands, but satisfies neither, as shown in Figure 5.5.

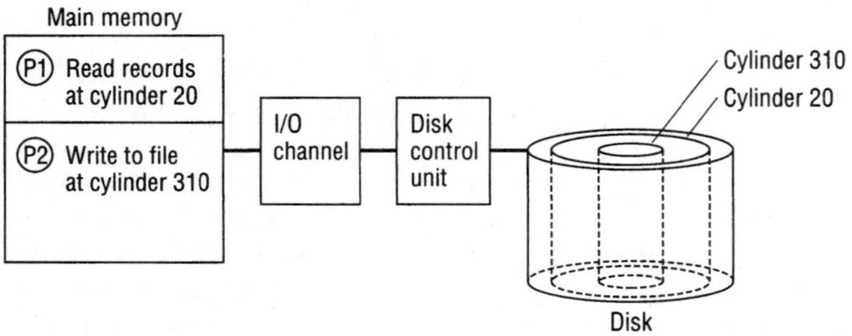

FIGURE 5.5 *The I/O channel and disk control unit can work independently from the CPU, so a new command can be waiting before the first one is completed and create a deadlock.*

CASE 7: DEADLOCKS IN A NETWORK A network that's congested or has a large percentage of its I/O buffer space full can be deadlocked if it doesn't have protocols to control the flow of messages through the network.

For example, a medium-sized word processing center has seven computers on a network, each on different nodes. C1 receives messages from nodes C2, C6, and C7 and sends messages to only one: C2. C2 receives messages from nodes C1, C3, and C4 and sends messages to C1 and C3. The direction of the arrows in Figure 5.6 indicates the flow of messages.

Messages received by C1 from C6 and C7 and destined for C2 are buffered in an output queue. Messages received by C2 from C3 and C4 and destined for C1 are buffered on an output queue. As the traffic increases, the length of each output queue increases until all of the available buffer space is filled. At this point C1 can't accept any more messages (from C2 or any other computer) because there's no more buffer space available to store them. For the same reason, C2 can't accept any messages from C1 or any other computer, not even a request to send. The communication path between C1 and C2 becomes deadlocked and since C1 can receive messages only from C6 and C7 those routes also become deadlocked. C1

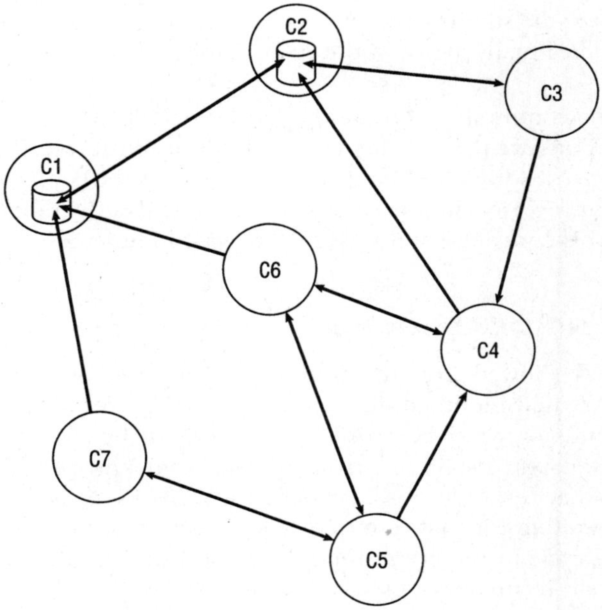

FIGURE 5.6
Typical network flow. Each circle represents a node; each line represents a communication line; arrows indicate the direction of the flow of traffic.

can't send word to C2 about the problem and so the deadlock can't be resolved without outside intervention.

CONDITIONS FOR DEADLOCK

In each of these seven cases, the deadlock involved the interaction of several processes and resources, but each deadlock was preceded by the simultaneous occurrence of four conditions that the operating system (or other systems) could have recognized: mutual exclusion, resource holding, no preemption, and circular wait.

To illustrate them, let's review the staircase example from the beginning of the chapter and identify the four conditions required for a deadlock.

- When two people met between landings they couldn't pass because the steps can hold only one person at a time. **Mutual exclusion**, the act of allowing only one person (or process) to have access to a step (or resource), is the first condition for deadlock.
- When two people met on the stairs and each one held ground and waited for the other to retreat that was an example of **resource holding** (as opposed to resource sharing), the second condition for deadlock.
- In this example, each step was dedicated to the climber (or the descender); it was allocated to the holder for as long as needed. This is called **no preemption**, the lack of temporary reallocation of resources, and is the third condition for deadlock.
- These three lead to the fourth condition of **circular wait** in which each person (or process) involved in the impasse is waiting for another to voluntarily

release the step (or resource) so that at least one will be able to continue on and eventually arrive at the destination.

All four conditions are required for the deadlock to occur and as long as all four conditions are present the deadlock will continue; but if one condition can be removed the deadlock will be resolved. In fact, if the four conditions can be prevented from ever occurring at the same time, deadlocks can be prevented, but although this concept is obvious it isn't easy to implement.

MODELING DEADLOCKS

Holt (1972) showed how the four conditions can be modeled using **directed graphs**. (We used modified directed graphs in Figures 5.2 and 5.4.) These graphs use two kinds of symbols: processes represented by circles and resources represented by squares. A solid line from a resource to a process means that the process is holding that resource. A solid line from a process to a resource means that the process is waiting for that resource. The direction of the arrow indicates the flow. If there's a cycle in the graph then there's a deadlock involving the processes and the resources in the cycle, as shown in Figure 5.7(c).

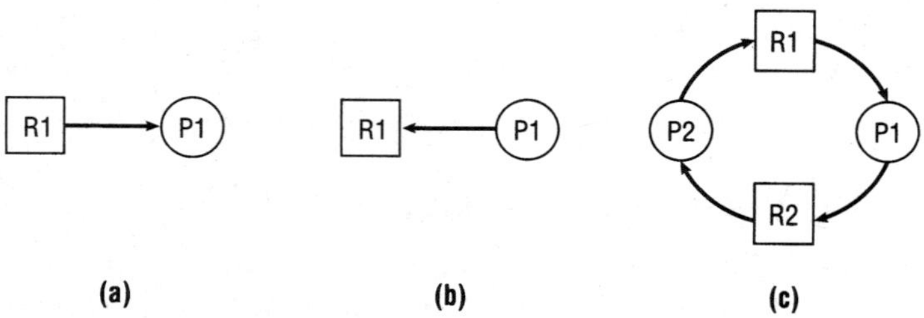

FIGURE 5.7 *In (**a**) process P1 is holding resource R1. In (**b**) process P1 is waiting for resource R1. In (**c**) P1 holds R1 and is waiting for R2, while P2 holds R2 and is waiting for R1 — creating a deadlock.*

The following system has three processes — P1, P2, P3 — and three resources — R1, R2, R3 — each of a different type: printer, tape drive, and plotter. Because there is no specified order in which the requests are handled we'll look at three different possible scenarios using graphs to help us detect any deadlocks.

The first scenario is:

1. P1 requests and is allocated the printer R1.
2. P1 releases the printer R1.
3. P2 requests and is allocated the tape drive R2.
4. P2 releases the tape drive R2.
5. P3 requests and is allocated the plotter R3.
6. P3 releases the plotter R3.

This is shown in Figure 5.8. Therefore, we can safely conclude that a deadlock can't occur even if each process requests every resource *if* the resources are released before the next process requests them.

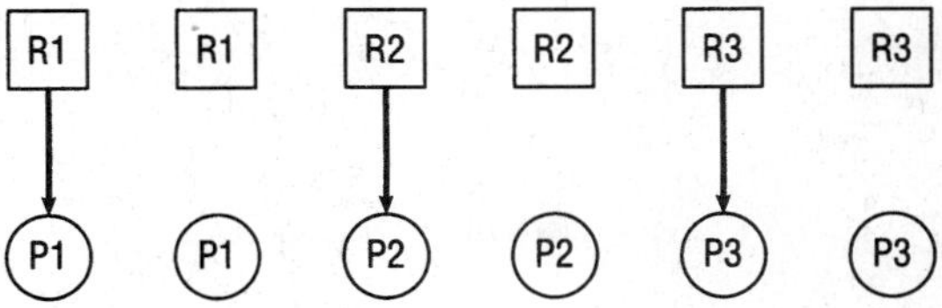

FIGURE 5.8 *The system will stay free of deadlocks if all resources are released before they're requested by the next process.*

Now, consider a second scenario:

1. P1 requests and is allocated R1.
2. P2 requests and is allocated R2.
3. P3 requests and is allocated R3.
4. P1 requests R2.
5. P2 requests R3.
6. P3 requests R1.

This is shown in Figure 5.9. In this case there *is* a deadlock because every process is waiting for a resource being held by one of the other processes, but none will be released without operator intervention.

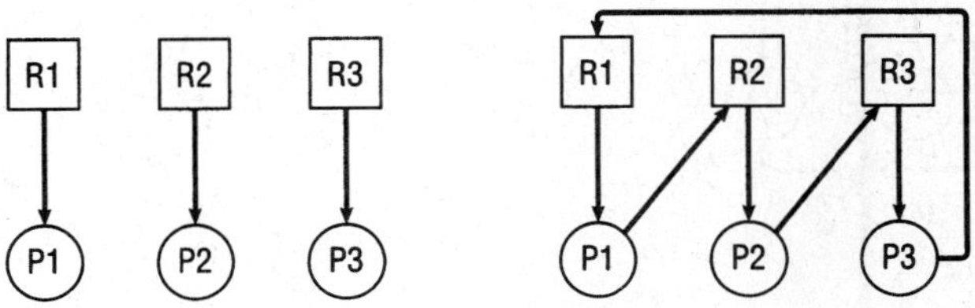

FIGURE 5.9 *A deadlocked system; note the circular wait.*

Here's a third scenario:

1. P1 requests and is allocated R1.
2. P1 requests and is allocated R2.
3. P2 requests R1.
4. P3 requests and is allocated R3.
5. P1 releases R1, which is allocated to P2.
6. P3 requests R2.
7. P1 releases R2, which is allocated to P3.

In the scenario shown in Figure 5.10 the resources are released before deadlock can occur.

The examples presented so far have examined cases in which one or more resources of different types were allocated to a process. However, the graphs can be expanded to include several resources of the same type, such as tape drives, which can be allocated individually or in groups to the same process. These graphs cluster the devices of the same type into one node, and the arrows show the links between the single resource and the processes using it.

FIGURE 5.10
After step 4 the diagram looks like (**a**) *and P2 is blocked because P1 is holding onto R1. However, step 5 breaks the impasse and the diagram soon looks like* (**b**). *Again there is a blocked process, P3, which must wait for the release of R2 in step 7 when the diagram looks like* (**c**).

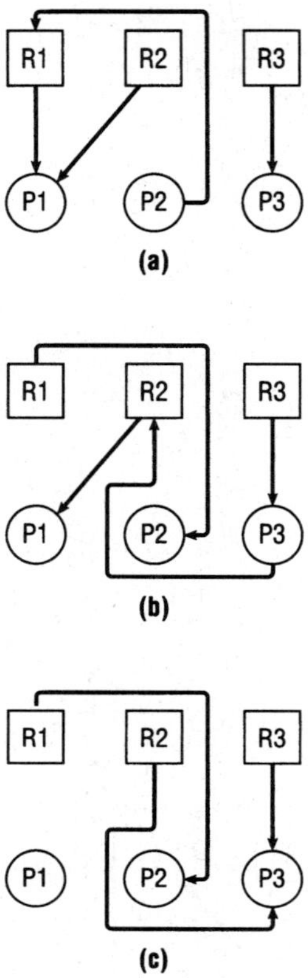

Figure 5.11 gives an example of a node with three resources of the same type, each allocated to a different process. Although Figure 5.11(**a**) seems to be stable (no deadlock can occur), this is not the case because if all three processes request one more resource, without releasing the one they are using, then deadlock will occur as shown in Figure 5.11(**b**).

STRATEGIES FOR HANDLING DEADLOCKS

As these examples show, the requests and releases are received in an unpredictable order, which makes it very difficult to design a foolproof preventive policy. In general, operating systems use one of three strategies to deal with deadlocks:

1. Prevent one of the four conditions from occurring.
2. Avoid the deadlock if it becomes probable.
3. Detect the deadlock when it occurs and recover from it gracefully.

PREVENTION To prevent a deadlock the operating system must eliminate one of the four necessary conditions, a task complicated by the fact that the same condition can't be eliminated from every resource.

Mutual exclusion is necessary in any computer system because some resources

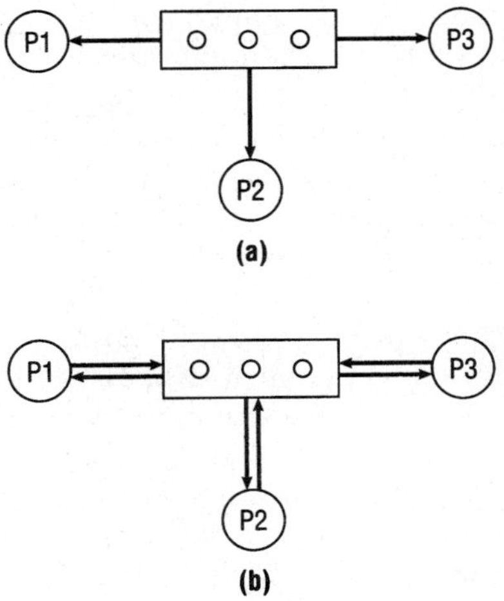

FIGURE 5.11
*(**a**) A fully allocated resource node; there are as many lines coming out of it as there are units in it. The state of (**a**) is uncertain because a request for another resource by all three processes would create a deadlock, as shown in (**b**).*

such as memory, CPU, and dedicated devices must be exclusively allocated to one user at a time. In the case of I/O devices such as printers the mutual exclusion may be bypassed by spooling so the output from many jobs may be stored into separate temporary spool files at the same time, and each complete output file is then selected for printing when the device is ready. However, we may be trading one type of deadlock (Case 3: Deadlocks in Dedicated Device Allocation) for another (Case 5: Deadlocks in Spooling).

Resource holding, where a job holds on to one resource while waiting for another one that's not yet available, could be sidestepped by forcing each job to request, at creation time, every resource it will need to run to completion. For example, if every job in a batch system is given as much memory as it needs, then the number of active jobs will be dictated by how many can fit in memory — a policy that would significantly decrease the degree of multiprogramming. In addition, peripheral devices would be idle because they would be allocated to a job even though they wouldn't be used all the time. As we've said before, this was used successfully in batch environments although it reduced the effective use of resources and restricted the amount of multiprogramming. But it doesn't work as well in interactive systems.

No preemption could be bypassed by allowing the operating system to deallocate resources from jobs. This can be done if the state of the job can be easily saved and restored, as when a job is preempted in a round robin environment or a page is swapped to secondary storage in a virtual memory system. On the other hand, preemption of a dedicated I/O device (printer, plotter, tape drive, and so on), or of files during the modification process, can require some extremely unpleasant recovery tasks.

Circular wait can be bypassed if the operating system prevents the formation of a circle. One such solution was proposed by Havender (1968) and is based on a numbering system for the resources such as: printer = 1, disk = 2, tape = 3, plotter = 4, and so on. The system forces each job to request its resources in ascending order: any "number one" devices required by the job would be requested first; any "number two" devices would be requested next; and so on. So if a job needed a printer and then a plotter, it would request them in this order: printer (#1) first and then the plotter (#4). If the job required the plotter first and then the printer, it would still request the printer first (which is a #1) even though it wouldn't be used right away. A job could request a printer (#1) and then a disk (#2) and then a tape (#3), but if it needed another printer (#1) late in its processing, it would still have to anticipate that need when it requested the first one, and before it requested the disk.

This scheme of "hierarchical ordering" removes the possibility of a circular wait and therefore guarantees the removal of deadlocks. It doesn't require that jobs state their maximum needs in advance, but it does require that the jobs anticipate the order in which they will request resources. From the perspective of a system designer, one of the difficulties of this scheme is discovering the best order for the resources so the needs of the majority of the users are satisfied. Another difficulty is that of assigning a ranking to nonphysical resources such as files or locked database records where there is no basis for assigning a higher number to one over another (Lane & Mooney, 1988).

AVOIDANCE Even if the operating system can't remove one of the conditions for deadlock, it can avoid one if the system knows ahead of time the sequence of requests associated with each of the active processes. As was illustrated in the graphs presented in Figures 5.7 through 5.11 there exists at least one allocation of resources sequence that will allow jobs to continue without becoming deadlocked.

One such algorithm was proposed by Dijkstra (1965) to regulate resource allocation to avoid deadlocks. The Banker's Algorithm is based on a bank with a fixed amount of capital that operates on the following principles:

1. No customer will be granted a loan exceeding the bank's total capital.
2. All customers will be given a maximum credit limit when opening an account.
3. No customer will be allowed to borrow over the limit.
4. The sum of all loans won't exceed the bank's total capital.

Under these conditions the bank isn't required to have on hand the total of all maximum lending quotas before it can open up for business (we'll assume the bank will always have the same fixed total and we'll disregard interest charged on loans). For our example the bank has a total capital fund of $10,000 and has three customers, C1, C2, and C3, who have maximum credit limits of $4,000, $5,000, and $8,000, respectively. Table 5.1 illustrates the state of affairs of the bank after some loans have been granted to C2 and C3. This is called a **safe state** because the bank still has enough money left to satisfy the maximum requests of C1, C2, and C3.

A few weeks later after more loans have been made, and some have been repaid, the bank is in the **unsafe state** represented in Table 5.2.

This is an unsafe state because with only $1,000 left, the bank can't satisfy anyone's maximum request and if the bank lent the $1,000 to anyone then it would be deadlocked (it can't make a loan). An unsafe state doesn't necessarily

TABLE 5.1 *The bank started with $10,000 and has remaining capital of $4,000 after these loans. Therefore it's in a "safe state."*

Customer	Loan amount	Maximum credit	Remaining credit
C1	0	4,000	4,000
C2	2,000	5,000	3,000
C3	4,000	8,000	4,000

Total Loaned: $6,000
Total Capital Fund: $10,000

TABLE 5.2 *The bank only has remaining capital of $1,000 after these loans and therefore is in an "unsafe state."*

Customer	Loan amount	Maximum credit	Remaining credit
C1	2,000	4,000	2,000
C2	3,000	5,000	2,000
C3	4,000	8,000	4,000

Total Loaned: $9,000
Total Capital Fund: $10,000

lead to deadlock, but it does indicate that the system is an excellent candidate for one. After all, none of the customers is required to request the maximum, but the bank doesn't know the exact amount that will eventually be requested, and as long as the bank's capital is less than the maximum amount available for individual loans it can't guarantee that it will be able to fill every loan request.

If we substitute jobs for customers and dedicated devices for dollars we can apply the same banking principles to an operating system. In this example the system has ten devices.

Table 5.3 shows our system in a safe state and Table 5.4 depicts the same system in an unsafe state. As before, a safe state is one in which at least one job can finish because there are enough available resources to satisfy its maximum needs. Then, using the resources released by the finished job, the maximum needs of another job can be filled and that job can be finished, and so on until all jobs are done.

TABLE 5.3 *Resource assignments after initial allocations. A safe state: six devices are allocated and four units are still available.*

Job no.	Devices allocated	Maximum required	Remaining needs
1	0	4	4
2	2	5	3
3	4	8	4

Total no. devices allocated: 6
Total devices in system: 10

The operating system must be sure never to satisfy a request that moves it from a safe state to an unsafe one. Therefore, as users' requests are satisfied, the operating system must identify the job with the smallest number of remaining resources and make sure that the number of available resources is always equal to, or greater than, the number needed for this job to run to completion. Requests that would

TABLE 5.4 *Resource assignments after later allocations. An unsafe state: only one unit is available but every job requires at least two to complete its execution.*

Job no.	Devices allocated	Maximum required	Remaining needs
1	2	4	2
2	3	5	2
3	4	8	4
Total no. devices allocated: 9			
Total devices in system: 10			

place the safe state in jeopardy must be blocked by the operating system until they can be safely accommodated. If the system is always kept in a safe state, all requests will eventually be satisfied and a deadlock is avoided.

If this elegant solution is expanded to work with several classes of resources the system sets up a "resource assignment table" for each type of resource and tracks each table to keep the system in a safe state.

Although the Banker's Algorithm has been used to avoid deadlocks in systems with a few resources, it isn't always practical for most systems for several reasons (Tanenbaum, 1987)

1. As they enter the system jobs must state in advance the maximum number of resources needed. As we've said before, this isn't practical in interactive systems.
2. The number of total resources for each class must remain constant. If a device breaks and becomes suddenly unavailable the algorithm won't work (the system may already be in an unsafe state).
3. The number of jobs must remain fixed, something that isn't possible in interactive systems where the number of active jobs is constantly changing.
4. The overhead cost incurred by running the avoidance algorithm can be quite high when there are many active jobs and many devices because it has to be invoked for every request.
5. Resources aren't well utilized because the algorithm assumes the worst case and, as a result, keeps vital resources unavailable to guard against unsafe states.
6. Scheduling suffers as a result of the poor utilization and jobs are kept waiting for resource allocation. A steady stream of jobs asking for a few resources can cause the indefinite postponement of a more complex job requiring many resources.

DETECTION The directed graphs presented earlier in this chapter showed how the existence of a circular wait indicated a deadlock, so it's reasonable to conclude that deadlocks can be detected by building directed resource graphs and looking for cycles. Unlike the avoidance algorithm, which must be performed every time there is a request, the algorithm used to detect circularity can be executed whenever it is appropriate: every hour, once a day, only when the operator notices that throughput has deteriorated, or when an angry user complains.

The detection algorithm can be explained by using directed resource graphs and "reducing" them. The steps to reduce a graph are these (Lane & Mooney, 1988):

1. Find a process that is currently using a resource and *not waiting* for one. This process can be removed from the graph (by disconnecting the link tying the resource to the process), and the resource can be returned to the "available list." This is possible because the process would eventually finish and return the resource.
2. Find a process that's waiting only for resource classes that aren't fully allocated. This process isn't contributing to deadlock since it would eventually get the resource it's waiting for, finish its work, and return the resource to the "available list."
3. Go back to Step 1 and continue the loop until all lines connecting resources to processes have been removed.

If there are any lines left, this indicates that the request of the process in question can't be satisfied and that a deadlock exists. Figure 5.12 illustrates a system in which three processes — P1, P2, and P3 — and three resources — R1, R2, and R3 — aren't deadlocked.

Figure 5.12 shows the stages of a graph reduction from (**a**), the original state. In (**b**) the link between P3 and R3 can be removed because P3 isn't waiting for any other resources to finish, so R3 is released and allocated to P2 (Step 1). In (**c**) the links between P2 and R3 and between P2 and R2 can be removed because P2 has all of its requested resources and can run to completion — and then R2 can be allocated to P1. Finally in (**d**) the links between P1 and R2 and between P1 and R1 can be removed because P1 has all of its requested resources and can finish successfully. Therefore, the graph is completely resolved. In Figure 5.13, the same system is deadlocked.

The deadlocked system in Figure 5.13 can't be reduced. In (**a**) the link between P3 and R3 can be removed because P3 isn't waiting for any other resource, so R3 is released and allocated to P2. But in (**b**) P2 has only two of the three resources it needs to finish and it is waiting for R1. But R1 can't be released by P1 because P1 is waiting for R2, which is held by P2; moreover, P1 can't finish because it is waiting for P2 to finish (and release R2), and P2 can't finish because it's waiting for R1. This is a circular wait.

RECOVERY Once a deadlock has been detected it must be untangled and the system returned to normal as quickly as possible. There are several recovery algorithms, but they all have one feature in common: they all require at least one **victim**, an expendable job, which, when removed from the deadlock, will free the system. Unfortunately for the victim removal generally requires that the job be restarted from the beginning or from a convenient midpoint (Calingaert, 1982).

The first and simplest recovery method, and the most drastic, is to terminate all of the jobs active in the system and restart them from the beginning.

The second method is to terminate only the jobs involved in the deadlock and ask their users to resubmit them.

The third method is to identify which jobs are involved in the deadlock and

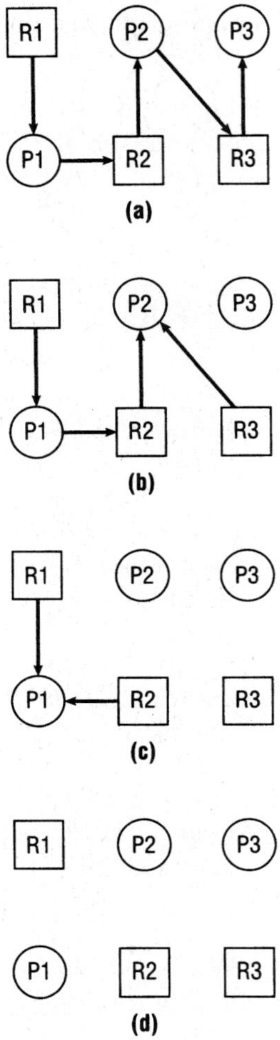

FIGURE 5.12 *The system is deadlock-free because the graph can be completely reduced.*

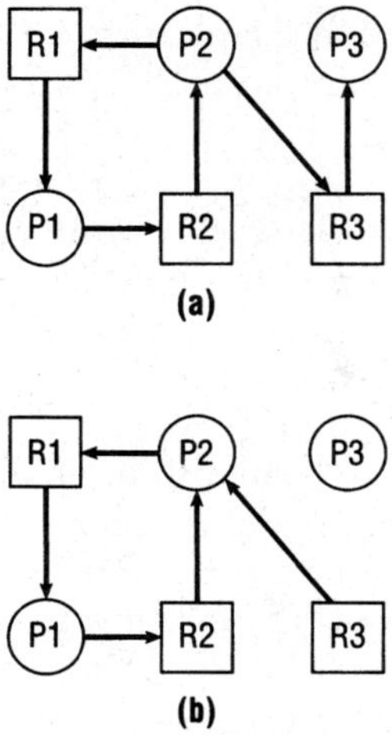

FIGURE 5.13 *The graph can't be reduced any further, indicating a deadlock.*

terminate them one at a time, checking to see if the deadlock is eliminated after each removal, until the deadlock has been resolved. Once the system is freed, the remaining jobs are allowed to complete their processing and later the halted jobs are started again from the beginning.

The fourth method can be put into effect only if the job keeps a record, a snapshot, of its progress so it can be interrupted and then continued without starting again from the beginning of its execution. The snapshot is like the landing in our staircase example: instead of forcing the deadlocked stairclimbers to return to the bottom of the stairs, they need to retreat only to the nearest landing and wait until the others have passed. Then the climb can be resumed. In general, this method is favored for long-running jobs to help them make a speedy recovery.

Until now we've offered solutions involving the jobs caught in the deadlock. The next two methods concentrate on the nondeadlocked jobs and the resources they hold. One of them, the fifth method in our list, selects a nondeadlocked job, preempts the resources it's holding, and allocates them to a deadlocked process so it can resume execution, thus breaking the deadlock. The sixth method stops new jobs from entering the system, which allows the nondeadlocked jobs to run to completion so they'll release their resources. Eventually, with fewer jobs in the system, competition for resources is curtailed so the deadlocked processes get the resources they need to run to completion. This method is the only one listed here that doesn't rely on a victim, and it's not guaranteed to work unless the number of available resources surpasses that needed by at least one of the deadlocked jobs to run (this is possible with multiple resources).

Several factors must be considered to select the victim that will have the least-negative effect on the system. The most common are:

1. The priority of the job under consideration — high-priority jobs are usually untouched.
2. CPU time used by job — jobs close to completion are usually left alone.
3. The number of other jobs that would be affected if this job were selected as the victim.

In addition, programs working with databases also deserve special treatment. Jobs that are modifying data shouldn't be selected for termination because the consistency and validity of the database would be jeopardized. Fortunately, designers of many database systems have included sophisticated recovery mechanisms so damage to the database is minimized if a transaction is interrupted or terminated before completion (Finkel, 1986).

STARVATION

So far we have concentrated on deadlocks, the result of liberal allocation of resources. At the opposite end is starvation, the result of conservative allocation of resources where a single job is prevented from execution because it's kept waiting for resources that never become available. To illustrate this, the case of "the dining philosophers" was introduced by Dijkstra (1968).

Five philosophers are sitting at a round table, each deep in thought, and in the center lies a bowl of spaghetti that is accessible to everyone. There are forks on the table — one between each philosopher, as illustrated in Figure 5.14. Local custom dictates that each philosopher must use two forks, the forks on either side of the plate, to eat the spaghetti, but there are only five forks — not the ten it would require for all five thinkers to eat at once — and that's unfortunate for Philosopher 2.

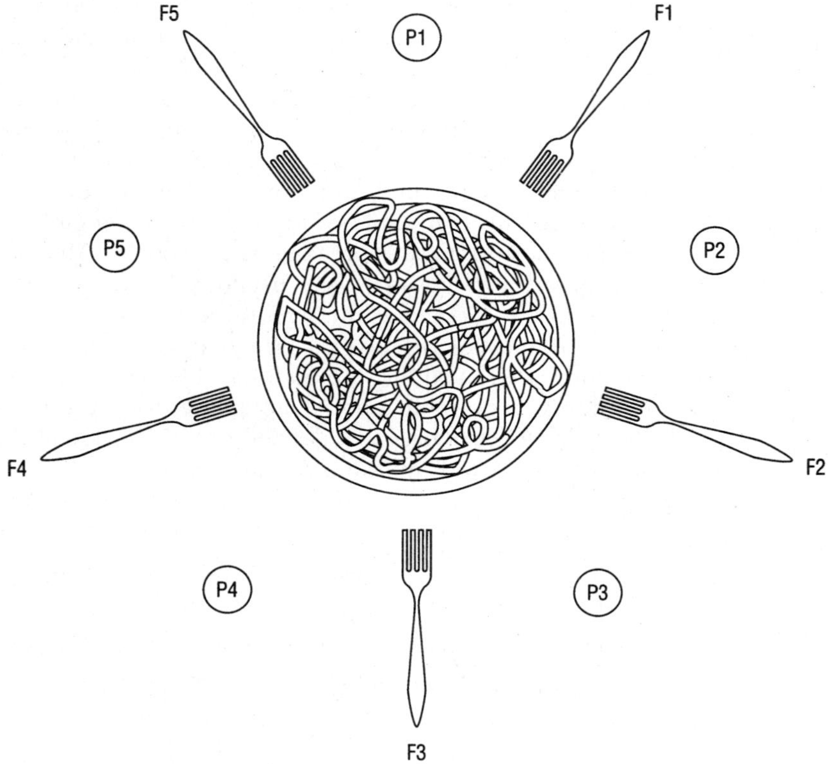

FIGURE 5.14 *The dining philosophers' table, before the meal begins.*

When they sit down to dinner, Philosopher 1 (P1) is the first to take the two forks (F1 and F5) on either side of the plate and begins to eat. Inspired by his colleague, Philosopher 3 (P3) does likewise, using F2 and F3. Now Philosopher 2 (P2) decides to begin the meal but is unable to start because no forks are available: F1 has been allocated to P1 and F2 has been allocated to P3, and the only remaining fork can be used only by P4 or P5. So Philosopher 2 must wait.

Soon, P3 finishes eating, puts down his two forks and resumes his pondering. Should the fork beside him (F2), that's now free, be allocated to the hungry philosopher (P2)? Although it's tempting, such a move would be a bad precedent because if the philosophers are allowed to tie up resources with only the hope that the other required resource will become available, the dinner could easily slip into an unsafe state; it would be only a matter of time before each philosopher held a single fork — and nobody could eat. So the resources are allocated to the philosophers only when both forks are available at the same time. The status of the "system" is illustrated in Figure 5.15.

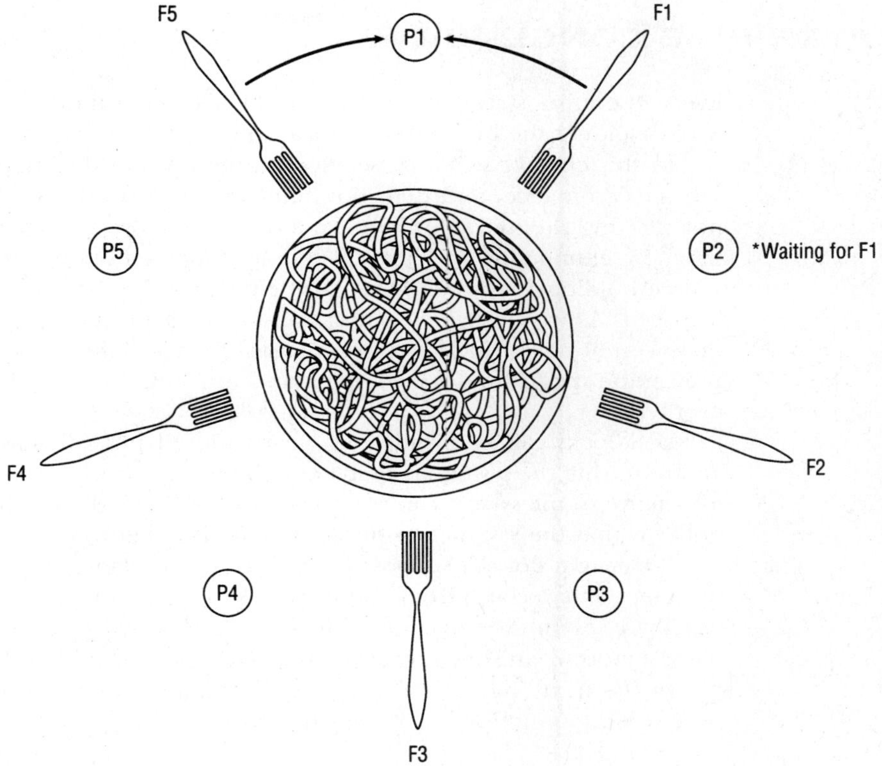

FIGURE 5.15
Each philosopher must have both forks to begin eating, the one on the right and the one on the left. Unless the resources, the forks, are allocated fairly, some philosophers may starve.

P4 and P5 are quietly thinking and P1 is still eating when P3 (who should be full) decides to eat some more and because the resources are free he is able to take F2 and F3 once again. Soon thereafter, P1 finishes and releases F1 and F5, but P2 is still not able to eat because F2 is now allocated. This scenario could continue forever, and as long as P1 and P3 alternate their use of the available resources P2 must wait. P1 and P3 can eat any time they wish while P2 starves — only inches from nourishment.

In a computer environment, the resources are like forks and the competing processes are like dining philosophers. If the resource manager doesn't watch for starving processes and jobs, and plan for their eventual completion, they could remain in the system forever waiting for the right combination of resources.

To address this problem, an algorithm designed to detect starving jobs can be implemented, which tracks how long each job has been waiting for resources (this is the same as **aging** described in Chapter 4). Once starvation has been detected, the system can block new jobs until the starving jobs have been satisfied. This algorithm must be monitored closely: if it's done too often then new jobs will be blocked too frequently and throughput will be diminished. If it's not done often enough starving jobs will remain in the system for an unacceptably long period of time.

CHAPTER FIVE CONCLUSION

Every operating system must dynamically allocate a limited number of resources while avoiding the two extremes of deadlock and starvation.

In this chapter we discussed several methods of dealing with deadlocks: prevention, avoidance, and detection and recovery. Deadlocks can be prevented by not allowing the four conditions of a deadlock to occur in the system at the same time. By eliminating at least one of the four conditions (mutual exclusion, resource holding, no preemption, and circular wait) the system can be kept deadlock-free. As we've seen, the disadvantage of a preventive policy is that each of these conditions is vital to different parts of the system at least some of the time, so prevention algorithms are complex and to routinely execute them involves high overhead.

Deadlocks can be avoided by clearly identifying safe states and unsafe states and requiring the system to keep enough resources in reserve to guarantee that all jobs active in the system can run to completion. The disadvantage of an avoidance policy is that the system's resources aren't allocated to their fullest potential.

If a system doesn't support prevention or avoidance then it must be prepared to detect and recover from the deadlocks that occur. Unfortunately, this option usually relies on the selection of at least one "victim" — a job that must be terminated before it finishes execution and restarted from the beginning.

In the next chapter we'll look at problems related to the synchronization of processes in a multiprocessing environment.

KEY TERMS

process synchronization
deadly embrace
deadlock
starvation
locking
race
spooling
mutual exclusion
resource holding
no preemption
circular wait
directed graphs
prevention
avoidance
safe state
unsafe state
victim
detection
recovery

EXERCISES

1. What are the major differences between deadlock, starvation, and race?
2. Give some "real life" examples (not related to a computer system environment) of deadlock, starvation, and race.

3. Select one example of deadlock from Exercise 2 and list the four necessary conditions needed for the deadlock.
4. Suppose the narrow staircase (used as an example in the beginning of this chapter) has become a major source of aggravation. Design an algorithm for using it so that both deadlock and starvation are not possible.
5. The following figure shows a tunnel going through a mountain and two streets parallel to each other at each entrance/exit of the tunnel. Traffic lights are located at each end of the tunnel to control the crossflow of traffic through each intersection.

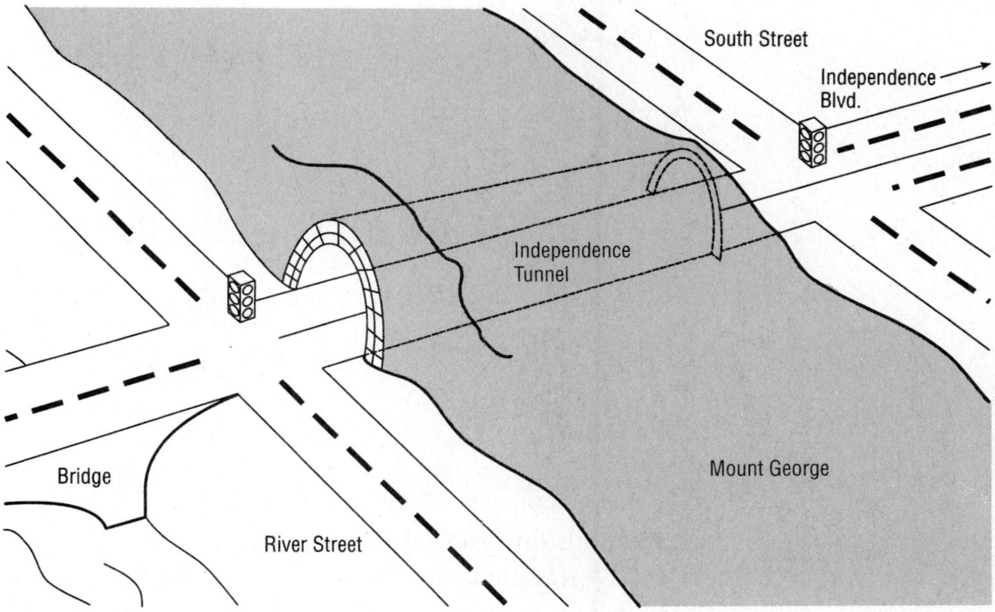

   a. Can deadlock occur? How and under what circumstances?
   b. How can deadlock be detected?
   c. Give a solution to prevent deadlock but watch out for starvation.
6. Consider the following directed resource graph:

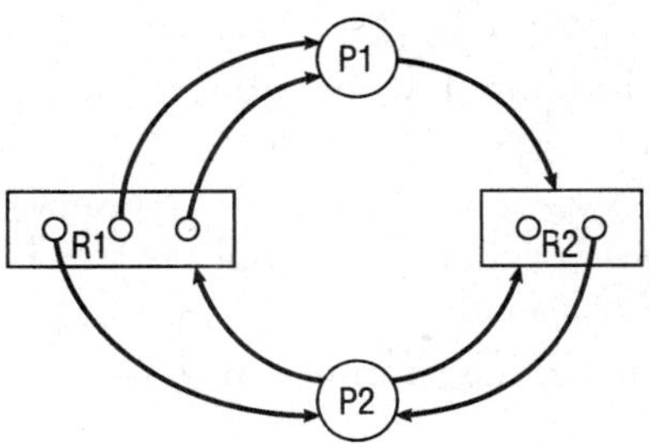

a. Is this system deadlocked?

b. Are there any blocked processes?

c. What is the resulting graph after reduction by P1?

d. What is the resulting graph after reduction by P2?

e. Both P1 and P2 have requested R2:

  1. What is the status of the system if P2's request is granted before P1's?
  2. What is the status of the system if P1's request is granted before P2's?

7. Consider the following directed resource graph:

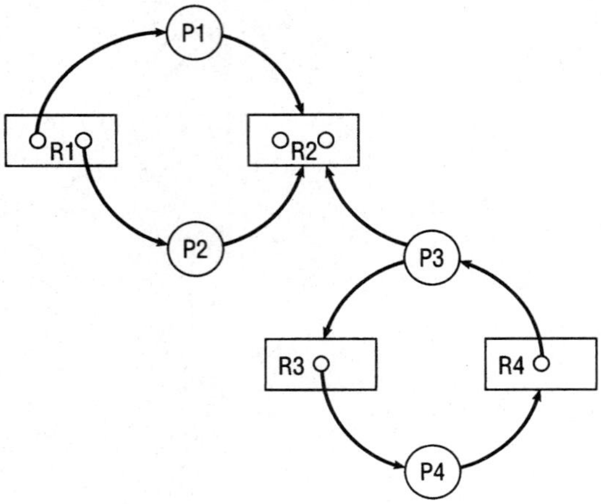

a. Is this system, as a whole, deadlocked?

b. Are there any deadlocked processes?

c. Three processes — P1, P2, and P3 — are requesting resources from R2.

  1. Which requests would you satisfy to minimize the number of processes involved in the deadlock?
  2. Which requests would you satisfy to maximize the number of processes involved in deadlock?

d. Can the graph be reduced, partially or totally?

e. Can the deadlock be resolved without selecting a victim?

8. Consider a computing system with 13 tape drives. All jobs running on this system require a maximum of 5 tape drives to complete but they each run for long periods of time with just 4 drives and request the fifth one only at the very end of the run. The job stream is endless.

a. If your operating system supports a very conservative device allocation policy no job will be started unless all tapes required have been allocated to it for the duration of its run:

  1. What is the maximum number of jobs that can be active at once?

   2. What are the minimum and maximum number of tape drives that may be idle as a result of this policy?
   3. Explain your answer.

b. If your operating system supports the Banker's Algorithm:
   1. What is the maximum number of jobs that can be in progress at once?
   2. What are the minimum and maximum number of tape drives that may be idle as a result of this policy?
   3. Explain your answer.

For the systems described in exercises 9 through 11, given that all of the devices are of the same type, and using the definitions presented in the discussion of the Banker's Algorithm, answer these questions.

a. Determine the "remaining needs" for each job in each system.
b. Determine whether each of the systems is safe or unsafe.
c. If the system is in a safe state, list the sequence of requests and releases that will make it possible for all processes to run to completion.
d. If the system is in an unsafe state, show how it's possible for deadlock to occur.

9. System number 1 has 12 devices; only 1 is available.

Job no.	Devices allocated	Maximum required	Remaining needs
1	5	6	
2	4	7	
3	2	6	
4	0	2	

10. System number 2 has 14 devices; only 2 are available.

Job no.	Devices allocated	Maximum required	Remaining needs
1	5	8	
2	3	9	
3	4	8	

11. System number 3 has 12 devices; only 2 are available.

Job no.	Devices allocated	Maximum required	Remaining needs
1	5	8	
2	4	6	
3	1	4	

ADVANCED EXERCISES

12. Suppose you are an operating system designer and have been approached by the operator to help solve the recurring deadlock problem in your installation's spooling system. What features might you incorporate into the operating system so that deadlocks in the spooling system can be resolved without loss of work done by the processes involved?
13. A system in an unsafe state is not necessarily deadlocked. Explain why this is true. Give an example of a system in an unsafe state and show how all the processes could be completed without having deadlock occurring.
14. State how you would design and implement a mechanism to allow the operating system to detect which of the processes are starving.
15. Given the four primary types of resources — CPU, memory, storage devices, and files — select for each one the most suitable technique for fighting deadlock and briefly explain why it is your choice.
16. State the limitations imposed on programs (and on systems) that have to follow a hierarchical ordering of resources; for example, disks, printers, terminals, and files.

Chapter Six

CONCURRENT PROCESSES

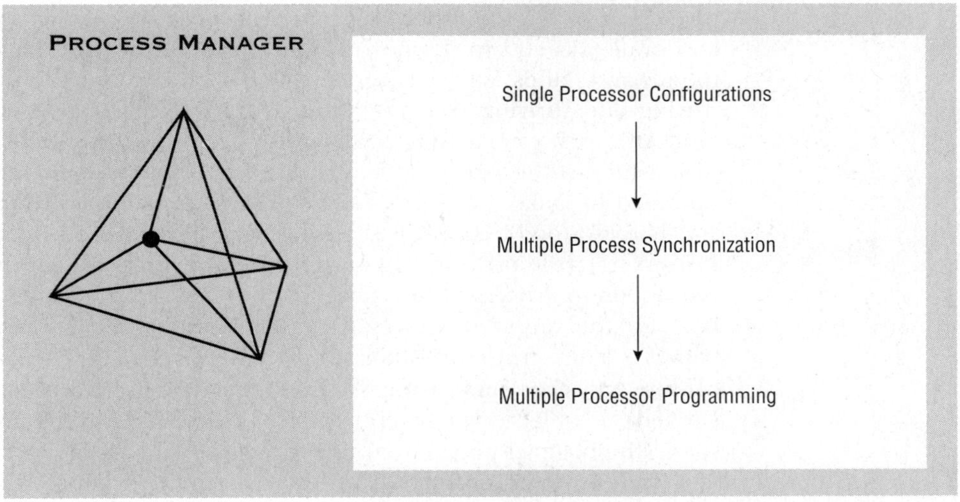

In Chapters 4 and 5 we described systems that used only one CPU. In this chapter we will look at multiprocessing systems, those with more than one CPU. We'll discuss the reasons for their development, their advantages, and their problems.

As we will see in this chapter, the key to multiprocessing has been the object of extensive research. We'll examine several configurations of processors and review the classic problems of concurrent processes, such as: "producers and consumers," the "readers and writers" and the "missed waiting customer." While the problems occur in single processor systems, they are presented here because they apply to multiprocesses in general, whether they involve a single processor (with two or more processes) or more than one processor (hence multiprocesses). The chapter concludes with a brief look at the Ada programming language and concurrent processing programming.

WHAT IS PARALLEL PROCESSING?

Parallel processing, also called **multiprocessing**, is a situation in which two or more processors operate in unison. That means two or more CPUs are executing instructions simultaneously. Therefore, with more than one process executing at the same time, each CPU can have a process in the RUNNING state at the same time. For multiprocessing systems, the Processor Manager has to coordinate the activity of each processor, as well as synchronize the interaction among the CPUs.

The complexities of the Processor Manager's task when dealing with multiple processors or multiple processes are easily illustrated with an example: You're late for an early afternoon appointment and you're in danger of missing lunch, so you get in line for the drive-through window of the local fast-food shop. When you place your order, the order clerk confirms your request, tells you how much it will cost, and asks you to drive to the pick-up window where a cashier collects your money and hands over your order. All's well and once again you're on your way — driving and thriving. You just witnessed a well-synchronized multiprocessing system. Although you came in contact with just two processors — the order clerk and the cashier — there were at least two other processors behind the scenes who cooperated to make the system work — the cook and the bagger.

The fast-food restaurant is similar to an information retrieval system in which Processor 1 (the order clerk) accepts the query, checks for errors, and passes the request on to Processor 2 (the bagger). Processor 2 (the bagger) searches the database for the required information (the hamburger). Processor 3 (the cook) retrieves the data from the database (the meat to cook for the hamburger) if it's kept off-line in secondary storage. Once the data is gathered (the hamburger is cooked), it's placed where Processor 2 can get it (in the hamburger bin). Processor 2 (the bagger) passes it on to Processor 4 (the cashier). Processor 4 (the cashier) routes the response (your order) back to the originator of the request — you.

Synchronization is the key to the system's success because many things can go wrong in a multiprocessing system: What if the communications system broke down and you couldn't speak with the order clerk? What if the cook produced hamburgers at full speed all day, even during slow periods? What would happen to the extra hamburgers? What if the cook got badly burned and couldn't cook anymore? What would the bagger do if there were no hamburgers? What if the cashier decided to take your money but didn't give you any food? Obviously, the system won't work unless every processor communicates and cooperates with every other processor.

Multiprocessors were developed for high-end models of IBM mainframes and VAX computers where the operating system treated additional CPUs as another resource that could be scheduled for work. These systems, some with as few as two CPUs, have been in use for many years (Lane & Mooney, 1988).

Since the mid-1980s, when the costs of CPU hardware declined, multiprocessor systems with dozens of CPUs have found their way into business environments. What's more, systems containing tens of thousands of CPUs (systems that had once been available only for research) can now be found in production environments. Today multiprocessor systems are available on systems of every size (Lane & Mooney, 1988).

There are two major forces behind the development of multiprocessing: to enhance throughput and to increase computing power. And there are two primary benefits: increased reliability and faster processing.

The reliability stems from the availability of more than one CPU: if one processor fails the others can continue to operate and absorb the load. This isn't simple to do; the system must be carefully designed so that, first, the failing processor can inform the other processors to take over and, second, the operating system can restructure its resource allocation strategies so the remaining system doesn't become overloaded.

The increased processing speed is achieved because instructions can be processed in parallel, two or more at a time, and it's done in one of several ways. Some systems allocate a CPU to each program or job. Others allocate a CPU to each working set or parts of it. Still others subdivide individual instructions so each subdivision can be processed simultaneously (this is called "concurrent programming" and will be discussed in detail at the conclusion of this chapter).

Increased flexibility brings increased complexity, however, and two major challenges are how to connect the processors (configurations) and how to orchestrate their interaction. This latter issue, the orchestration of the interaction, applies to multiple interacting processes as well. (It might help if you think of each process as being run on a separate processor although, in reality, there is only one doing all the work.)

TYPICAL MULTIPROCESSING CONFIGURATIONS

Much depends on how the multiple processors are configured within the system. Three typical configurations are: master/slave, loosely coupled, and symmetric.

MASTER/SLAVE CONFIGURATION

The **master/slave multiprocessing system** is an asymmetric configuration. Conceptually it's a single-processor system with additional "slave" processors, each of which is managed by the primary "master" processor. The master processor is responsible for managing the entire system: all files, all devices, memory, and all processors. Therefore it maintains the status of all processes in the system, performs storage management activities, schedules the work for the other processors, and executes all control programs. This configuration is well suited for computing environments in which processing time is divided between front-end and back-end processors; in these cases the front-end processor takes care of the interactive users and quick jobs, and the back-end processor takes care of those with long jobs using the batch mode.

Figure 6.1 (page 128) shows a typical master/slave configuration. The primary advantage of this configuration is its simplicity. However, it has three serious disadvantages:

1. Its reliability is no higher than for a single processor system because if the master processor fails, the entire system fails.

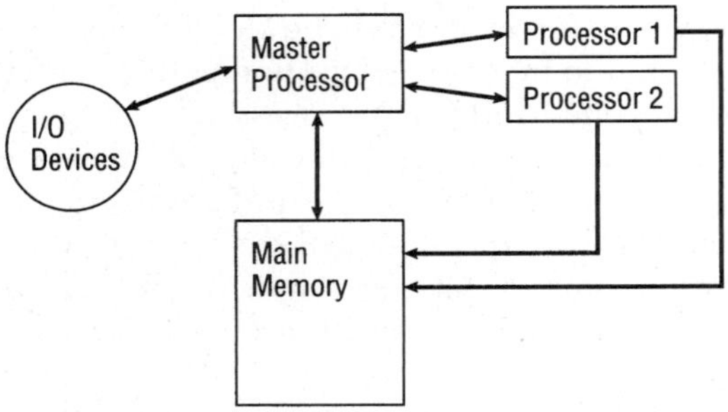

FIGURE 6.1
"Master/slave" multiprocessing configuration.

2. It can lead to poor use of resources because if a slave processor should become free while the master processor is busy, the slave must wait until the master becomes free and can assign more work to it.
3. It increases the number of interrupts because all slave processors must interrupt the master processor every time they need operating system intervention, such as for I/O requests. This creates long queues at the master processor level when there are many processors and many interrupts.

LOOSELY COUPLED CONFIGURATION

The **loosely coupled configuration** features several complete computer systems, each with its own memory, I/O devices, CPU, and operating system, as shown in Figure 6.2.

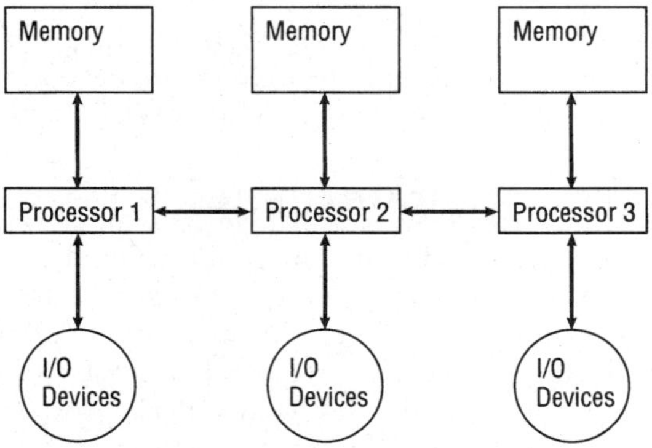

FIGURE 6.2
Loosely coupled multiprocessing configuration.

It is called loosely coupled because each processor controls its own resources — its own files and its own I/O devices — and that means that each processor maintains its own commands and I/O management tables. The only difference between a loosely coupled multiprocessing system and a collection of independent single processing systems is that each processor can communicate and cooperate with the others.

When a job arrives for the first time, it's assigned to one processor. Once allocated, the job will remain with the same processor until it's finished. Therefore each processor must have "global" tables that indicate to which processor each job has been allocated.

To keep the system well-balanced and to ensure the best use of resources, job scheduling is based on several requirements and policies. For example, new jobs might be assigned to the processor with the lightest load or the best combination of output devices available.

This system isn't prone to catastrophic system failures because even when a single processor fails the others can continue to work independently from it. However, it can be difficult to detect when a processor has failed.

SYMMETRIC CONFIGURATION

The **symmetric configuration** is best implemented if the processors are all of the same type. It has four advantages over loosely coupled: (1) it's more reliable; (2) it uses resources effectively; (3) it can balance loads well; and (4) it can degrade gracefully in the event of a failure (Forinash, 1987). However, it is the most difficult to implement because the processes must be well synchronized to avoid the problems of races and deadlocks that we discussed in Chapter 5.

In a symmetric configuration processor scheduling is decentralized (as depicted in Figure 6.3). A single copy of the operating system and a global table listing each process and its status is stored in a common area of memory so every processor has access to it. Each processor uses the same scheduling algorithm to select which process it will run next.

FIGURE 6.3 *Symmetric multiprocessing with homogeneous processors.*

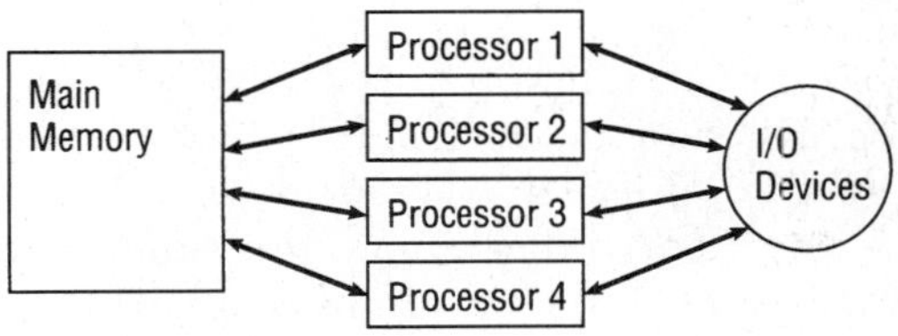

Whenever a process is interrupted, whether it's because of an I/O request or another type of interrupt, its processor updates the corresponding entry in the process list and finds another process to run. This means that the processors are kept quite busy. But it also means that any given job or task may be executed by several different processors during its run time. And because each processor has access to all I/O devices and can reference any storage unit, there are more conflicts as several processors try to access the same resource at the same time.

This presents the obvious need for algorithms to resolve conflicts between processors — that's "process synchronization."

PROCESS SYNCHRONIZATION SOFTWARE

The success of **process synchronization** hinges on the capability of the operating system to make a resource unavailable to other processes while it's being used by one of them. These "resources" can include I/O devices, a location in storage, or a data file. In essence, the used resource must be locked away from other processes until it is released. Only when it is released is a waiting process allowed to use the resource. This is where synchronization is critical. A mistake could leave a job waiting indefinitely.

It is the same thing that happens in a crowded ice cream parlor. Customers take a number to be served. The numbers on the wall are changed by the clerks who pull a chain to increment them as they attend to each customer. But what happens when there is no synchronization between serving the customers and changing the number? Chaos. This is the case of the "missed waiting customer" (Madnick & Donovan, 1974).

Let's say your number is 75. Clerk 1 is waiting on customer 73 and Clerk 2 is waiting on customer 74. On the wall the sign says "Now Serving #74" and you're ready with your order. Clerk 2 finishes with customer 74 and pulls the chain to "Now Serving #75" — but just then the clerk is called to the telephone (an interrupt). Meanwhile Clerk 1 pulls the chain and proceeds to wait on #76 — and you're history. If you're quick you can correct the mistake gracefully, but when it happens in a computer system the outcome isn't as easily remedied.

Consider the scenario in which Processor 1 and Processor 2 finish with their current jobs at the same time. To run the next job each processor must:

1. Consult the list of jobs to see which one should be run next;
2. Retrieve the job for execution;
3. Increment the READY list to the next job;
4. Execute it.

Both go to the READY list to select a job. Processor 1 sees that Job 74 is the next job to be run, and goes to retrieve it. A moment later, Processor 2 also selects Job 74 and goes to retrieve it. Shortly thereafter, Processor 1, having retrieved Job 74, returns to the READY list and increments it, moving Job 75 to the top. A moment later Processor 2 returns; it has also retrieved Job 74 and is ready to process it, so it increments the READY list and now Job 76 is moved to the top and becomes the next job in line to be processed. Job 75 has become the "missed waiting customer" and will never be processed — an unacceptable state of affairs.

There are several other places where this problem can occur: memory and page allocation tables, I/O tables, application databases, and any shared resource.

Obviously, this situation calls for synchronization. Several synchronization mechanisms are available to provide cooperation and communication among processes. The common element in all synchronization schemes is to allow a process to finish work on a **critical region** of the program before other processes have access to it. This is applicable both to multiprocessors and to two or more processes in a single-processor (time-shared) processing system. It is called a critical region because its execution must be handled as a unit. As we've seen, the processes within a critical region can't be interleaved without threatening the integrity of the operation.

Synchronization is sometimes implemented as a "lock-and-key" arrangement: before a process can work on a critical region, it's required to get the "key." And once it has the key, all other processes are "locked out" until it finishes, when it unlocks the entry to the critical region and returns the key so another process can get the key and begin work. This sequence consists of two actions: (1) the process must first see if the key is available and (2) if it is available, it must pick it up and put it in the lock to make it unavailable to all other processes. For this scheme to work both actions must be performed in a single machine cycle; otherwise it is conceivable that while the first process is ready to pick up the key, another one would find the key available and prepare to pick up the key — and each could block the other from proceeding any further.

Several locking mechanisms have been developed including test-and-set, WAIT and SIGNAL, and semaphores.

TEST-AND-SET

Test-and-set is a single indivisible machine instruction known simply as "TS" and was introduced by IBM for its multiprocessing System 360/370 computers. In a single machine cycle it tests to see if the key is available and, if it is, sets it to "unavailable."

The actual key is a single bit in a storage location that can contain a zero (if it's free) or a one (if busy). We can consider TS to be a function subprogram that has one parameter (the storage location) and returns one value (the condition code: busy/free), with the exception that it takes only one machine cycle.

Therefore, a process (P1) would test the condition code using the TS instruction before entering a critical region. If no other process was in this critical region, then P1 would be allowed to proceed and the condition code would be changed from zero to one. Later, when P1 exits the critical region, the condition code is reset to zero so another process can enter. On the other hand, if P1 finds a busy condition code, then it's placed in a "waiting loop" where it continues to test the condition code and waits until it's free (Calingaert, 1982).

Although it's a simple procedure to implement, and works well for a small number of processes, test-and-set has two major drawbacks. First, when many processes are waiting to enter a critical region, starvation could occur because the processes gain access in an arbitrary fashion. Unless a first-come first-served policy were set up, some processes could be favored over others. A second drawback is that waiting processes remain in unproductive, resource-consuming wait loops. This is known as **busy waiting** — which not only consumes valuable processor time but also relies on the competing processes to test the key, something that is best handled by the operating system or the hardware.

WAIT AND SIGNAL

WAIT and SIGNAL is a modification of test-and-set that's designed to remove busy waiting. Two new operations, which are mutually exclusive and become part of the process scheduler's set of operations, are WAIT and SIGNAL.

WAIT is activated when the process encounters a busy condition code. WAIT sets the process's process control block (PCB) to the blocked state and links it to the queue of processes waiting to enter this particular critical region. The Process Scheduler then selects another process for execution. SIGNAL is activated when a process exits the critical region and the condition code is set to "free." It checks the queue of processes waiting to enter this critical region and selects one, setting it to the READY state. Eventually the Process Scheduler will choose this process for running. The addition of the operations WAIT and SIGNAL frees the processes from the "busy waiting" dilemma and returns control to the operating system, which can then run other jobs while the waiting processes are idle (WAIT).

SEMAPHORES

A **semaphore** is a nonnegative integer variable that's used as a flag (Calingaert, 1982).

The most well-known semaphores are the flag-like signaling devices used by railroads to indicate whether or not a section of track is clear. When the arm of the semaphore is raised, the track is clear and the train can proceed. When the arm is lowered, the track is busy and the train must wait until the arm is raised, as shown in Figure 6.4.

FIGURE 6.4
The semaphore used by railroads indicates whether the train can proceed. If it is raised the train can continue, but when it's lowered an oncoming train is expected.

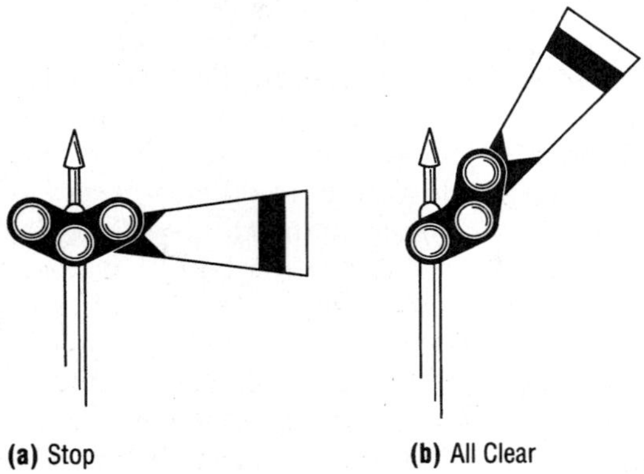

In an operating system a semaphore performs a similar function: it signals if and when a resource is free and can be used by a process. Dijkstra (1965) introduced two operations to operate the semaphore to overcome the process synchronization problem we've discussed. Dijkstra called them **P** and **V** and that's how they're known today. The P stands for the Dutch word *proberen* (to test) and the V stands for *verhogen* (to increment). The P and V operations do just that: they test and increment.

Here's how they work. If we let s be a semaphore variable, then the V operation on s is simply to increment s by 1. The action can be stated as:

$$V(s): s: = s + 1$$

This in turn necessitates a fetch, increment, and store sequence. Like the test-and-set operation, the V operation must be performed as a single indivisible action to avoid deadlocks. And that means that s cannot be accessed by any other process during the operation.

The operation P on s is to test the value of s and, if it's not zero, to decrement it by one. The action can be stated as:

$$P(s): \text{If } s > 0 \text{ then } s := s - 1$$

which involves a test, fetch, decrement, and store sequence. Again this sequence must be performed as an indivisible action in a single machine cycle or have it arranged that the process cannot take action until the operation (P or V) is finished.

The operations P and V are executed by the operating system in response to calls issued by any one process naming a semaphore as parameter (this alleviates the process from having control). If $s = 0$, the process calling on the P operation must wait until the operation can be executed and that's not until $s > 0$.

As shown in Table 6.1, P3 is placed in the WAIT state (for the semaphore) on State 4. As also shown in Table 6.1, for States 6 and 8, when a process exits the critical region, the value of *s* is reset to 1. This, in turn, triggers the awakening of one of the blocked processes, its entry into the critical region, and the resetting of *s* to zero. In State 7, P1 and P2 are not trying to do processing in that critical region and P4 is still blocked (Madnick & Donovan, 1974).

TABLE 6.1

The sequence of states for four processes calling P and V operations on the binary semaphore s. *(Note: the value of the semaphore before the operation is on the line preceding the operation. The current value is on the same line.)*

	Actions		Results		
State number	**Calling process**	**Operation**	**Running in critical region**	**Blocked on *s***	**Value of *s***
0					1
1	P1	P (*s*)	P1		0
2	P1	V (*s*)			1
3	P2	P (*s*)	P2		0
4	P3	P (*s*)	P2	P3	0
5	P4	P (*s*)	P2	P3, P4	0
6	P2	V (*s*)	P3	P4	0
7			P3	P4	0
8	P3	V (*s*)	P4		0
9	P4	V (*s*)			1

After State 5 of Table 6.1 the longest waiting process, P3, was the one selected to enter the critical region, but that isn't necessarily the case unless the system is using a first-in first-out selection policy. In fact, the choice of which job will be processed next depends on the algorithm used by this portion of the Process Scheduler.

As you can see from Table 6.1, P and V operations on semaphore *s* enforce the concept of mutual exclusion, which is necessary to avoid having two operations attempt to execute at the same time. The name traditionally given to this semaphore in the literature is **mutex** and it stands for MUTual EXclusion. So the operations become:

P(mutex): if mutex > 0 then mutex: = mutex – 1

V(mutex): mutex: = mutex + 1

In Chapter 5 we talked about the requirement for mutual exclusion when several jobs were trying to access the same shared physical resources. The concept is the same here, but we have several processes trying to access the same shared critical region. The procedure can generalize to semaphores having values greater than zero and one.

Thus far we've looked at the problem of mutual exclusion presented by interacting parallel processes using the same shared data at different rates of execution. This can apply to several processes on more than one processor, or interacting (codependent) processes on a single processor. In this case the concept of a "critical region" becomes necessary because it ensures that parallel processes will modify shared data only while in the critical region.

In sequential computations mutual exclusion is achieved automatically because each operation is handled in order, one at a time. However, in parallel computations the order of execution can change, so mutual exclusion must be explicitly stated and maintained. In fact, the entire premise of parallel processes hinges on the requirement that all operations on common variables consistently exclude one another over time (Brinch Hansen, 1973).

PROCESS COOPERATION

There are occasions when several processes work directly together to complete a common task. Two famous examples are the problems of "producers and consumers" and "readers and writers." Each case requires both mutual exclusion and synchronization, and they are implemented by using semaphores.

PRODUCERS AND CONSUMERS

The classic problem of **producers and consumers** is one in which one process produces some data that another process consumes later. Although we'll describe the case with one producer and one consumer, it can be expanded to several pairs of producers and consumers.

Let's return for a moment to the fast-food fiasco at the beginning of this chapter because the synchronization between two of the processors (the cook and the bagger) represents a significant problem in operating systems. The cook *produces* hamburgers to be *consumed* by the bagger. Both processors have access to one common area, the hamburger bin, which can hold only a finite number of hamburgers (this is called a buffer area). The bin is a necessary storage area because the speed at which hamburgers are produced is independent from the speed at which they are consumed.

Problems arise at two extremes: when the producer attempts to add to an already full bin (as when the cook tries to put one more hamburger into a full bin) and when the consumer attempts to draw from an empty bin (as when the bagger tries to take a hamburger that hasn't been made yet). In real life, the people watch the bin and if it's empty or too full the problem is recognized and quickly resolved. However, in a computer system such resolution is not so easy.

Consider the case of the prolific CPU: the CPU can generate output data much faster than a line printer can print it. Therefore, since this involves a producer and a consumer of two different speeds, we need a buffer where the producer can temporarily store data that can be retrieved by the consumer at a more appropriate speed. Figure 6.5 shows three typical buffer states.

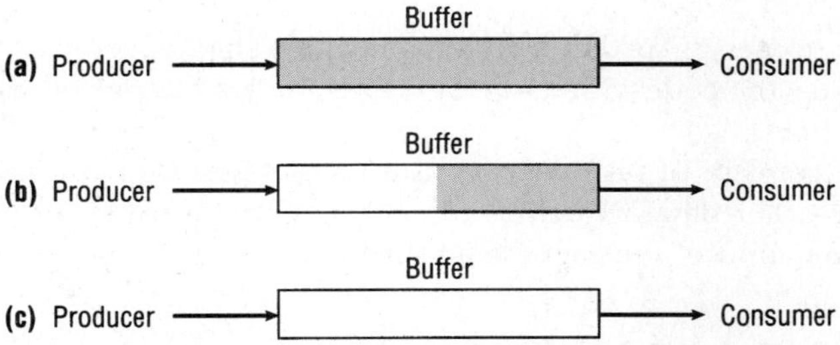

FIGURE 6.5
The buffer can be in any one of these three states: (**a**) *full buffer,* (**b**) *partially empty buffer, or* (**c**) *empty buffer.*

Because the buffer can hold only a finite amount of data, the synchronization process must delay the producer from generating more data when the buffer is full. And it must also be prepared to delay the consumer from retrieving data when the buffer is empty. This task can be implemented by two counting semaphores—one to indicate the number of full positions in the buffer and the other to indicate the number of empty positions in the buffer.

A third semaphore, mutex, will ensure mutual exclusion between processes. Here are the definitions of the producer and consumer processes:

PRODUCER	CONSUMER
produce data	P (full)
P (empty)	P (mutex)
P (mutex)	read data from buffer
write data into buffer	V (mutex)
V (mutex)	V (empty)
V (full)	consume data

Here are the definitions of the variables and functions used in the following algorithm:

Given:	Full, Empty, Mutex defined as semaphores
n:	maximum number of positions in the buffer
V (x):	$x := x + 1$ (x is any variable defined as a semaphore)
P (x):	if $x > 0$ then $x := x - 1$

COBEGIN and COEND are delimiters used to indicate sections of code to be done concurrently

mutex = 1 means the process is allowed to enter critical region

And here is the algorithm that implements the interaction between producer and consumer:

```
empty:= n
full:= 0
mutex:= 1
COBEGIN
  repeat until no more data PRODUCER
  repeat until buffer is empty CONSUMER
COEND
```

The processes (producer and consumer) then execute as described previously. You can try the code with $n = 3$, or try an alternate order of execution to see how it actually works.

The concept of producer/consumer can be extended to buffers that hold records or other data, as well as other situations in which direct process-to-process communication of messages is required.

READERS AND WRITERS

The problem of **readers and writers** was first formulated by Courtois, Heymans, and Parnas (1971) and arises when two types of processes need to access a shared resource such as a file or database. They called these processes "readers" and "writers."

An airline reservation system is a good example. The readers are those who want flight information. They're called readers because they only read the existing data; they don't modify it. And because no one is changing the database, the system can allow many readers to be active at the same time — there's no need to enforce mutual exclusion among them.

The writers are those who are making reservations on a particular flight. Writers must be carefully accommodated because they are modifying existing data in the database. The system can't allow someone to be writing while someone else is reading (or writing). Therefore, it must enforce mutual exclusion if there are groups of readers and a writer, and also if there are several writers, in the system. Of course the system must be fair when it enforces its policy to avoid indefinite postponement of readers or writers.

In the original paper, Courtois, Heymans, and Parnas offered two solutions using P and V operations. The first gives priority to readers over writers so readers are kept waiting only if a writer is actually modifying the data. However, this policy results in writer starvation if there is a continuous stream of readers. The second policy gives priority to the writers. In this case, as soon as a writer arrives, any readers that are already active are allowed to finish processing, but all additional readers are put on hold until the writer is done. Obviously this policy results in reader starvation if a continuous stream of writers is present. Either scenario is unacceptable.

To prevent either type of starvation from occurring Hoare (1974) proposed the following combination priority policy. When a writer is finished, any and all readers who are waiting, or "on hold," are allowed to read. Then, when that group of readers is finished, the writer who is "on hold" can begin, and any *new* readers who arrive in the meantime aren't allowed to start until the writer is finished.

The state of the system can be summarized by four counters initialized to zero:

1. Number of readers who have *requested* a resource and haven't yet released it (R1=0);
2. Number of readers who are *using* a resource and haven't yet released it (R2=0);
3. Number of writers who have *requested* a resource and haven't yet released it (W1=0);
4. Number of writers who are *using* a resource and haven't yet released it (W2=0).

This can be implemented using two semaphores to ensure mutual exclusion between readers and writers. A resource can be given to all readers (R1=R2), provided that no writers are processing (W2=0). A resource can be given to a writer, provided that no readers are reading (R2=0) and no writers are writing (W2=0).

Readers must always call two procedures: the first checks whether the resources can be immediately granted for reading; and then, when the resource is released, the second checks to see if there are any writers waiting. The same holds true for writers. The first procedure must determine if the resource can be immediately granted for writing, and then, upon releasing the resource, the second procedure will find out if any readers are waiting.

CONCURRENT PROGRAMMING

Until now we've looked at multiprocessing as several jobs executing at the same time on a single processor (which interacts with I/O processors, for example) or on multiprocessors. Multiprocessing can also refer to one job using several processors to execute sets of instructions in parallel. The concept isn't new, but it requires a programming language and a computer system that can support this type of construct. This type of system is referred to as a **concurrent processing system**.

APPLICATIONS OF CONCURRENT PROGRAMMING

Most monoprogramming languages are serial in nature — instructions are executed one at a time. Therefore, to resolve an arithmetic expression, every operation is done in sequence following the order prescribed by the programmer and compiler as shown in Table 6.2.

For many computational purposes, serial processing is sufficient; it's easy to implement and fast enough for most users.

However, arithmetic expressions can be processed differently if we use a language that allows for concurrent processing. Let's define two terms — `COBEGIN` and `COEND` — that will indicate to the compiler which instructions can be processed concurrently; then we'll rewrite our expression to take advantage of a concurrent processing compiler.

TABLE 6.2 *The sequential computation of the expression requires several steps. (In this case there are seven steps, but each step may involve more than one machine operation.)*

Compute: A = 3 * B * C + 4 / (D+E)**(F–G)

Step no.	Operation	Result
1	(F–G)	Store difference in T1
2	(D+E)	Store sum in T2
3	(T2)**(T1)	Store power in T1
4	4/(T1)	Store quotient in T2
5	3*B	Store product in T1
6	(T1)*C	Store product in T1
7	(T1)+(T2)	Store sum in A

```
COBEGIN
  T1 = 3*B
  T2 = D+E
  T3 = F-G
COEND
COBEGIN
  T4 = T1*C
  T5 = T2**T3
COEND
  A = T4+4/T5
```

As shown in Table 6.3, the first three operations can be done at the same time (if our computer system has three processors). The next two operations are done at the same time, and the last expression is performed serially with the results of the first two steps.

TABLE 6.3 *With concurrent processing the seven-step instruction can be processed in only four steps, which reduces execution time.*

Compute: A = 3 * B * C + 4 / (D+E)**(F–G)

Step no.	Processor	Operation	Result
1	1	3*B	Store product in T1
	2	(D+E)	Store sum in T2
	3	(F–G)	Store difference in T3
2	1	(T1)*C	Store product in T4
	2	(T2)**(T3)	Store power in T5
3	1	4/ (T5)	Store quotient in T1
4	1	(T4)+(T1)	Store sum in A

With this system we've increased the computation speed, but we've also increased the complexity of the programming language and the hardware (both machinery and communication among machines). In fact, we've also placed a large burden on the programmer — that of explicitly stating which instructions can be executed in parallel. This is **explicit parallelism**.

Early concurrent processing programs relied on the programmer to write the parallel instructions, but there were problems: coding was a time-consuming task and led to missed opportunities for parallel processing. It also led to errors where parallel processing was mistakenly indicated. And from a maintenance standpoint the programs were difficult to modify. The solution: automatic detection by the *compiler* of instructions that can be performed in parallel. This is called **implicit parallelism**.

With a true concurrent processing system, the example presented in Table 6.2 and Table 6.3 is coded as a single expression. It is the compiler that translates the algebraic expression into separate instructions and decides which can be performed in parallel and which serially.

For example, the equation $Y = A + B * C + D$ could be rearranged by the compiler as $A + D + B * C$ so that two operations $A + D$ and $B * C$ would be done in parallel, leaving the final addition to be calculated last.

Concurrent processing can also dramatically reduce the complexity of working with array operations within loops, of performing matrix multiplication, of conducting parallel searches in databases, and of sorting or merging files. Some of these systems use parallel processors that execute the same type of tasks (Ben-Ari, 1982).

EXAMPLE 1 *Array operations*

To perform an array operation within a loop, the instruction might say:

```
DO I=1,3
  A(I) = B(I)+C(I)
ENDDO
```

If we use three processors, the instruction can be performed in a single step like this:

Processor #1 performs: $A(1) = B(1)+C(1)$

Processor #2 performs: $A(2) = B(2)+C(2)$

Processor #3 performs: $A(3) = B(3)+C(3)$

EXAMPLE 2 *Matrix multiplication*

To perform $C = A * B$ where A and B represent two matrices:

Matrix A			Matrix B		
1	2	3	1	2	3
4	5	6	4	5	6
7	8	9	7	8	9

Several elements of the first row of matrix A could be multiplied by corresponding elements of the first column of matrix B. This process could be repeated until all of the products for the first element of matrix C would be computed and the result obtained by summing the products. The actual number of products that could be computed at the same time would depend on the number of processors available. Serially the answer can be computed in 45 steps. With three processors it takes only 27 steps by doing the multiplications in parallel.

EXAMPLE 3 *Searching databases*

Searching is a common nonmathematical application of concurrent processing. Each processor searches a different section of the database or file. It's a very fast way to find terms in a thesaurus, authors in a bibliographic database, or terms in inverted files. (Inverted files are generated from full document databases. Each record in an inverted file contains a subject term and the document numbers where that subject is found.)

EXAMPLE 4 *Sorting/ merging files*

By dividing a large file into sections, each with its own processor, every section can be sorted at the same time. Then pairs of sections can be merged together until the entire file is whole again — and sorted (Ben-Ari, 1982).

ADA

In the early 1970s the U.S. Department of Defense (DoD) needed a programming language that could perform concurrent processing. They decided to fight the rising cost of software by commissioning the design of an original language suited for **embedded computer systems**. These are systems that reside in jet aircraft or ships, so they must be small and fast and usually must work with real-time constraints, fail-safe execution, and nonstandard input and output devices; they must be able to manage concurrent activities, which requires parallel processing. The software took 10 years to complete. **Ada**, the final form of the high-level programming language, was made available to the public in 1980 (MacLennan, 1987).

The language was named after Augusta Ada Byron, the Countess of Lovelace and daughter of the renowned poet Lord Byron. She was a skilled mathematician and is regarded as the world's first programmer for her work on Charles Babbage's Analytical Engine in the 1830s. The Analytical Engine was an early prototype of a computer (Barnes, 1980).

During the first 4-year span the specifications for the new language underwent five sets of modifications, each more specific than the last. Some of the general requirements placed on the design of the language were readability and simplicity. Three more specific requirements were:

1. Its modules would support "information hiding" so the user would know how to use a module (through the "information" interface or argument list) without knowing how the module achieved its result (the procedure). Therefore, the user would have all the information needed to use a module correctly, but *no more*, and the processor would have all the information needed to process a module, but *no more*.
2. It would contain mechanisms to implement **concurrent programming**.
3. Its design would make it easy to verify the correctness of a program (MacLennan, 1987).

Ada was designed to be modular so several programmers could work on sections of a large project independently of one another. Therefore, an Ada program may contain one or more program units that can be compiled separately and are typically composed of (1) a specification part, which has all the information that must be visible to other units (the argument list) and (2) a body part made up of implementation details that don't need to be visible to other units.

Program units can fall into any one of three types: "subprograms," which are executable algorithms, "packages," which are collections of entities (i.e., procedures or functions), and "tasks," which are concurrent computations (MIL-STD-1815, 1982).

It is the *task* that is the heart of the language's parallel processing ability — this is the basic unit that defines a sequence of instructions that may be executed in parallel with other similar units.

The key is the synchronization of the tasks. To synchronize the concurrently executing processes several statements were designed. A "delay" statement is used to delay the execution of a task for a specified amount of time. A "select" statement can be used to allow conditional or timed "entry calls." "Entry calls" are used by tasks to communicate between one another. For example, a task will issue a call when it needs to "rendezvous" with another task that has the entry declaration. While the rendezvous is in effect the tasks are synchronized. The called task will accept the entry call when it reaches a corresponding accept statement that specifies the actions to be performed. After the rendezvous is completed both tasks (the one calling and the one having the entry) may continue their execution, either in parallel or independently (MIL-STD-1815, 1982).

An attractive feature of Ada is its ability to handle exceptional situations during execution of a program unit that would prevent its normal execution from continuing. These situations include arithmetic computations that yield values that exceed the maximum or those that attempt to access array elements using index values that exceed the size of the array. To handle these problems, statements can be followed by "exception handlers," which indicate what to do when an exception occurs (MIL-STD-1815, 1982).

During the early stages of the project the Department of Defense realized that its new language would prosper only if it could stifle the growth of mutually incompatible subsets and supersets of the language — enhanced versions of the standard compiler with extra "bells and whistles" that make them incompatible with each other.

Therefore, the DoD officially registered the name "Ada" as a trademark so it can control the use of the name. It has rigidly controlled which compilers can use the name, thus guaranteeing that anything called "Ada" will be part of the standard language. To make sure that a compiler implements Ada exactly as it's designed, the DoD uses a validation procedure that includes 2,500 tests. Several dozen compilers have passed these tests and therefore are validated (MacLennan, 1987).

Is Ada the wave of the future? As of this writing, it is too early to tell what impact Ada will have on those who don't deal directly with the DoD. It certainly has all the elements of a landmark language. Researchers find it helpful because of its parallel processing power. Its modular design is appealing to application programmers and systems analysts alike. Its tasking capabilities appeal to designers of database systems and others with applications that require parallel processing. Some universities have introduced Ada courses to their students majoring in business computer information systems.

CHAPTER SIX CONCLUSION

Multiprocessing systems have two or more CPUs that must be synchronized by the Processor Manager. Each processor must communicate and cooperate with the others. These systems can be configured in a variety of ways. From the simplest to the most complex they are master/slave, loosely coupled, and symmetric. By definition these are multiprocessing systems.

Multiprocessing also occurs in single processor systems between interacting processes that obtain control of the CPU at different times.

The success of any multiprocessing system depends on the success of the system to synchronize the processors or processes and the system's other resources. The concept of mutual exclusion helps keep the processes having the allocated resources from becoming deadlocked. Mutual exclusion is maintained with a series of techniques including test-and-set, `WAIT` and `SIGNAL`, and semaphores (P, V, and mutex).

Hardware and software mechanisms are used to synchronize the many processes but they must be careful to avoid the typical problems of synchronization: missed waiting customers, the synchronization of producers and consumers, and the mutual exclusion of readers and writers.

In the next chapter we'll look at the module of the operating system that manages the printers, disk drives, tape drives, and terminals: the Device Manager.

KEY TERMS

parallel processing
multiprocessing
master/slave configuration
loosely coupled configuration
symmetric configuration
process synchronization
critical region
test-and-set
busy waiting
`WAIT` and `SIGNAL`
semaphore
P
V
mutex
producers and consumers
readers and writers
concurrent processing
`COBEGIN`
`COEND`
explicit parallelism
implicit parallelism
embedded computer systems
Ada
concurrent programming

EXERCISES

1. What is the central goal of most multiprocessing systems?
2. What is the meaning of the term "busy waiting"?
3. Explain the need for mutual exclusion.
4. Describe "explicit parallelism."
5. Describe "implicit parallelism."
6. Rewrite each of the following arithmetic expressions to take advantage of con-

current processing and then code each. Use the terms `COBEGIN` and `COEND` to delimit the sections of concurrent code.

a. (X(Y*Z*W*R)+M+N+P)

b. ((J+K*L*M*N)*I)

7. Use the P and V semaphore operations to simulate the traffic flow at the intersection of two one-way streets. The following rules should be satisfied:

- Only one car can be crossing at any given time.
- A car should be allowed to cross the intersection only if there are no cars coming from the other street.
- When cars are coming from both streets, they should take turns to prevent indefinite postponements in either street.

ADVANCED EXERCISES

8. Consider the following program segments for two different processes executing concurrently:

```
    P1                  P2
DO  A=1,3           DO  B=1,3
   x=x+1               x=x+1
ENDDO               ENDDO
```

where B and A are not shared variables, but *x* starts at zero and is a shared variable.

If the processes P1 and P2 execute only once at any speed, what are the possible resulting values of *x*? Explain your answers.

9. Examine one of the programs you have written recently and indicate which operations could be executed concurrently. How long did it take you to do this? When might it be a good idea to write your programs in such a way that they can be run concurrently?

10. Consider the following segment taken from a FORTRAN program:

```
DO I=1,12
READ *,x
  IF (x .EQ. 0) Y(I) = 0
  IF (x .NE. 0) Y(I) = 10
ENDDO
```

a. Recode it so it will run more efficiently in a single-processor system.

b. Given that a multiprocessing environment with four symmetrical processors is available, recode the segment as an efficient concurrent program that performs the same function as the original FORTRAN program.

c. Given that all processors have identical capabilities, compare the execution speeds of the original FORTRAN segment with the execution speeds of your segments for parts (a) and (b).

PROGRAMMING EXERCISES

11. Dijkstra introduced the Sleeping Barber Problem (Dijkstra, 1965): A barbershop is divided into two rooms. The waiting room has *n* chairs and the work room only has the barber chair. When the waiting room is empty, the barber goes to sleep in the barber chair. If a customer comes in and the barber is asleep, he knows it's his turn to get his hair cut. So he wakes up the barber and takes his turn in the barber chair. But if the waiting room is not empty then the customer must take a seat in the waiting room and wait his turn.

Write a program that will coordinate the barber and his customers.

12. Patil introduced the Cigarette Smokers Problem (Patil, 1971): Three smokers and a supplier make up this system. Each smoker wants to roll a cigarette and smoke it immediately. However, to smoke a cigarette the smoker needs three ingredients — paper, tobacco, and a match — and to the great discomfort of everyone involved, each smoker has only one of the ingredients: Smoker 1 has lots of paper; Smoker 2 has lots of tobacco; and Smoker 3 has the matches. And, of course, the rules of the group don't allow hoarding, swapping, or sharing.

All three ingredients are provided by the supplier, who doesn't smoke, and he has an infinite amount of all three items. But he only provides two of them at a time — and only when no one is smoking. Here's how it works. The supplier randomly selects and places two different items on the table (which is accessible to all three smokers), and the smoker with the remaining ingredient immediately takes them, rolls, and smokes a cigarette. When he's finished smoking he signals the supplier, who then places another two randomly selected items on the table, and so on.

Write a program that will synchronize the supplier with the smokers. Keep track of how many cigarettes each smoker consumes. Is this a fair supplier? Why or why not?

Chapter Seven

DEVICE MANAGEMENT

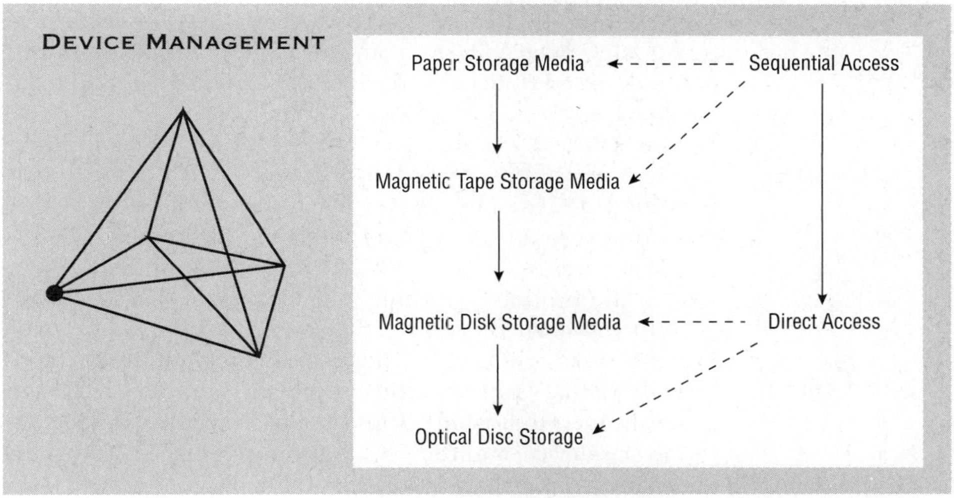

To put it simply: the Device Manager manages every peripheral device of the system. To do this, the Device Manager must maintain a delicate balance of supply and demand — balancing the system's finite supply of devices with the users' infinite demand for them.

Device management involves four basic functions: (1) tracking the status of each device (such as tape drives, disk drives, printers, plotters, and terminals); (2) using preset policies to determine which process will get a device and for how long; (3) allocating the devices; and (4) deallocating them at two levels — at the process level when an I/O command has been executed and the device is temporarily released and at the job level when the job is finished and the device is permanently released.

SYSTEM DEVICES

The system's peripheral devices generally fall into one of three categories: dedicated, shared, and virtual. The differences are a function of the characteristics of the devices, as well as how they're managed by the Device Manager.

Dedicated devices are assigned to only one job at a time; they serve that job for the entire time it's active. Some devices, such as tape drives, printers, and plotters, demand this kind of allocation scheme, because it would be awkward to let several users share them. A shared plotter might produce half of one user's graph and half of another. The disadvantage of dedicated devices is that they must be allocated to a single user for the duration of a job's execution, and that can be quite inefficient, especially when the device isn't used 100 percent of the time. Devices from the next two device categories are generally preferred.

Shared devices can be assigned to several processes. For instance, a disk pack, or any other direct access storage device, can be shared by several processes at the same time by interleaving their requests, but this interleaving must be carefully controlled by the Device Manager. All conflicts — such as when Process A and Process B each need to read from the same disk pack — must be resolved based on predetermined policies to decide which request will be handled first. We'll examine some of these policies later in this chapter.

Virtual devices are a combination of the first two: they're dedicated devices that have been transformed into shared devices. For example, printers (which are dedicated devices) are converted into sharable devices through a spooling program that reroutes all print requests to a disk. Only when all of a job's output is complete, and the printer is ready to print out the entire document, is the output sent to the printer for printing. (This procedure has to be managed carefully to prevent the occurrence of a deadlocked system, as we explained in Chapter 5.) Because disks are sharable devices, this technique can convert one printer into several "virtual" printers, thus improving both its performance and use. Spooling is a technique that is often used to speed up slow dedicated I/O devices.

Every device is different. The most important differences among them are their speeds and degrees of sharability. By minimizing the variances among the devices, a system's overall efficiency can be dramatically improved.

Storage media are divided into two groups: **sequential access media**, which store records sequentially, one after the other; and **direct access storage devices** (DASD), which can store either sequential or direct access files. There are vast differences in their speed and sharability.

SEQUENTIAL ACCESS STORAGE MEDIA

The first storage medium was paper in the form of printouts, punch cards, and paper tape. However, the bulk and price of paper soon made this primitive medium unacceptable for large systems.

Magnetic tape was then developed for early computer systems for routine secondary storage; it is now used for routine archiving and for storing back-up data.

Records on magnetic tapes are stored serially, one after the other, and each record can be of any length. The length is usually determined by the application program. Each record can be identified by its position on the tape. Therefore, to access a single record the tape must be mounted and "fast-forwarded" from its beginning until the desired position is located. This is a time-consuming process because it can take several minutes to read the entire tape.

To see just how long it takes, let's look at a typical large computer system that uses a reel of tape 1/2 inch wide and 2400 feet long (see Figure 7.1). Data is recorded on eight of the nine parallel tracks that run the length of the tape. (The ninth track holds a parity bit; a **parity bit** is used for routine error checking.)

FIGURE 7.1 *Nine-track magnetic tape with three characters recorded using odd parity. A 1/2-inch wide reel of tape, typically used to back up a mainframe computer, can store thousands of characters, or bytes, per inch.*

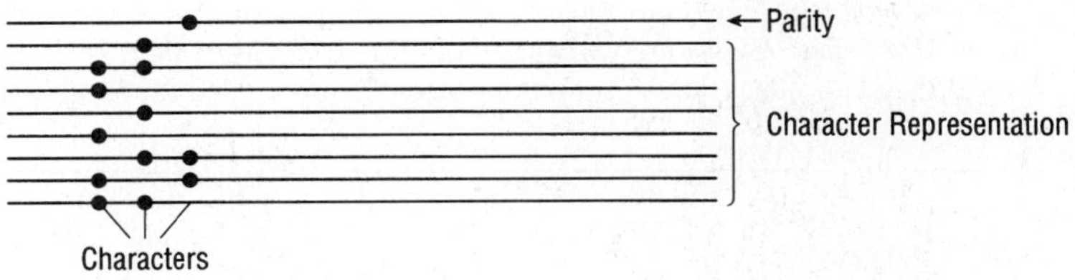

The number of characters that can be recorded per inch is determined by the density of the tape, such as 1600 or 6250 bytes per inch (bpi). For example, if you had records of 160 characters each and were storing them on a tape with a density of 1600 bpi, then theoretically you could store ten records on one inch of tape. However, in actual practice it would depend on how you decided to store the records: individually or grouped into blocks. If the records are stored individually, each record would need to be separated by a space to indicate its starting and ending places. If the records are stored in blocks, then the entire block is preceded by a space and followed by a space, but the individual records are stored sequentially within the block.

To appreciate the difference between the two alternatives, let's take a minute to look at the mechanics of reading and writing on magnetic tape. Magnetic tape moves under the read/write head only when there's a need to access a record; at all other times it's standing still. So the tape moves in jerks: read a record and stop, read another record and stop again, and so on. Records would be written in the same way.

The tape needs time and space to stop, so a gap is inserted between each record. This **interrecord gap (IRG)** is about 1/2 inch long regardless of the sizes of the records it separates. Therefore, if ten records are stored individually, there will be nine 1/2-inch IRGs between each record. (In this example we assume the records are only 1/10 inch each.)

In Figure 7.2, 5 1/2 inches of tape were required to store one inch of data — not a very efficient way to use the storage medium.

An alternative is to group the records into blocks before recording them on tape. This is called **blocking** and it's performed when the file is created. (Of course, you must take care to "deblock" them later.)

The number of records in a block is usually determined by the application program, and it's often set to take advantage of the **transfer rate**, which is the density of the tape, multiplied by the tape **transport speed**, which is the speed of the tape:

transfer rate = density * transport speed

A typical transport speed is 200 inches per second. Therefore, at 1600 bpi, a total of 320,000 bytes can be transferred in one second, so theoretically the optimal size of a block is 320,000 bytes. But there's a catch: this technique requires that the *entire* block be read into a buffer in main memory, so the buffer must be at least as large as the block. In actual operating environments the buffers range from 1000 to 2000 bytes, so most blocks are 1K to 2K.

FIGURE 7.2 *IRGs in magnetic tape. Each record requires only 1/10 inch of tape, for a total of one inch. When these records are stored individually on magnetic tape, each is separated by an IRG, which add up to 4 1/2 inches of tape. This totals 5 1/2 inches of tape.*

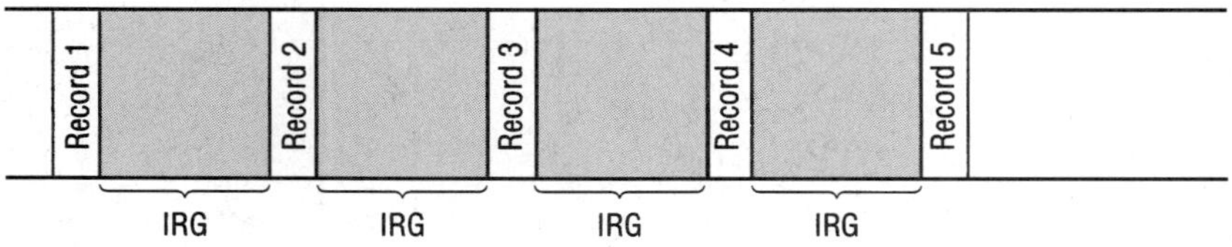

Notice in Figure 7.3 that the gap (now called an **interblock gap** or **IBG**) is still 1/2 inch long, but the data from each ten records is now stored on only one inch of tape — so we've used only 1 1/2 inches of tape (instead of the 5 1/2 inches used in Figure 7.2), and we've wasted only 1/2 inch of tape (instead of 4 1/2 inches).

FIGURE 7.3 *Two blocks of records stored on magnetic tape, each preceded by an interblock gap (IBG) of 1/2 inch. Each block holds ten records, each of which is still 1/10 inch. The block, however, is one inch, for a total of 2 1/2 inches.*

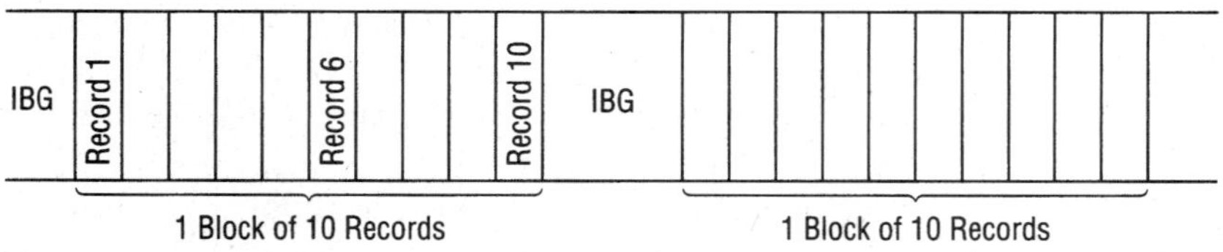

Blocking has two distinct advantages:

1. Fewer I/O operations are needed because a single READ command can move an entire block, the physical record that includes several logical records, into main memory.
2. Less tape is wasted because the size of the physical record exceeds the size of the gap.

The two disadvantages of blocking seem mild by comparison:

1. Overhead and software routines are needed for blocking, deblocking, and record keeping.

2. Buffer space may be wasted if you need only one logical record but must read an entire block to get it.

How long does it take to access a block or record on magnetic tape? Of course it depends on where it's located, but we can make some general calculations. A 2400-foot reel of tape with a tape transport speed of 200 inches per second can be read without stopping in approximately $2^1/_2$ minutes. Therefore, it would take $2^1/_2$ minutes to access the last record on the tape. On the average, then, it would take $1^1/_4$ minutes to access a record. And to access one record after another sequentially would take as long as it takes to start and stop a tape — which is 0.003 seconds, or 3 milliseconds (ms).

As we can see from Table 7.1, **access times** can vary widely. That makes magnetic tape a poor medium for routine secondary storage except for files with very high sequential activity — that is, those requiring that 90 to 100 percent of the records be accessed sequentially during an application.

TABLE 7.1 *Access times for 2400-foot magnetic tape with a tape transport speed of 200 inches/second.*

Maximum access	= 2.5 minutes
Average access	= 1.25 minutes
Sequential access	= 3 milliseconds

The advantage of magnetic tape is its compact storage capabilities, so it is the preferred medium for many "backup" duties and long-term archival file storage. For most other applications, a direct access medium is preferable.

DIRECT ACCESS STORAGE DEVICES

Direct access storage devices (DASDs) are any devices that can directly read or write to a specific place on a disk. (They're also called **random access storage devices**.) They're generally grouped into two major categories: those with fixed read/write heads and those with movable read/write heads. Although the variance in DASD access times isn't as wide as with magnetic tape, the location of the specific record still has a direct effect on the amount of time required to access it.

FIXED-HEAD DRUMS AND DISKS

Although drums are no longer routinely used as DASDs, they were the first of these devices. They are presented here to give a historical perspective on the development of DASDs and to help illustrate the abstract concept of "cylinders" used in our discussions about disk packs later in this chapter.

Fixed-head drums were developed in the early 1950s and their access times of 5 to 25 ms were considered very fast. Early versions of the IBM 650, for example, used a drum with a storage capacity of 2000 bytes, which was increased to 4000 bytes for later models. The speed of this device was on the order of 200 rpm, which was considered high when compared to only 50–60 rpm for other drums of that time. By the late 1970s the storage capacity of drums had increased to 1 megabyte and their speed was almost 3000 rpm (Habermann, 1976).

A drum resembles a giant coffee can covered with magnetic film and formatted so the tracks run around it (as shown in Figure 7.4). Data is recorded serially on each track by the read/write head positioned over it.

FIGURE 7.4
A fixed-head drum with seven read/write heads, one per track.

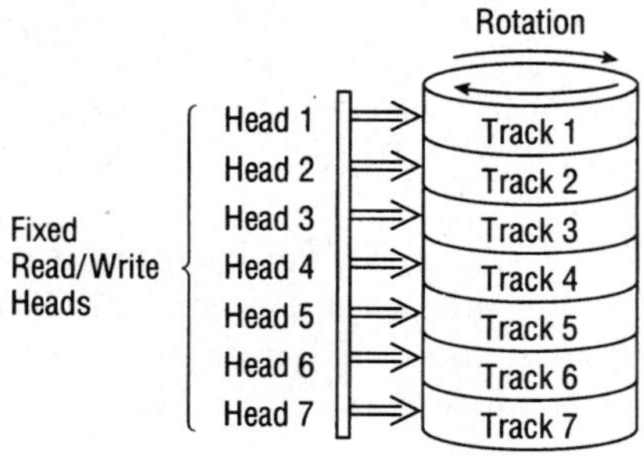

Fixed-head drums were very fast but also very expensive, and they did not hold as much data as other DASDs so their popularity waned.

Fixed-head disks use a similar concept but on a different plane. Each disk looks like a phonograph album covered with magnetic film that has been formatted, usually on both sides, into concentric circles. Each circle is a **track**. Data is recorded serially on each track by the fixed read/write head positioned over it. Again, there's one head for each track.

A fixed-head disk, shown in Figure 7.5, is also very fast — faster than the movable-head disks we'll talk about in a minute. Its major disadvantages are its high cost and its reduced storage space compared to a moveable-head disk (because the tracks must be positioned farther apart to accommodate the width of the read/write heads).

FIGURE 7.5
A fixed-head disk with four read/write heads, one per track.

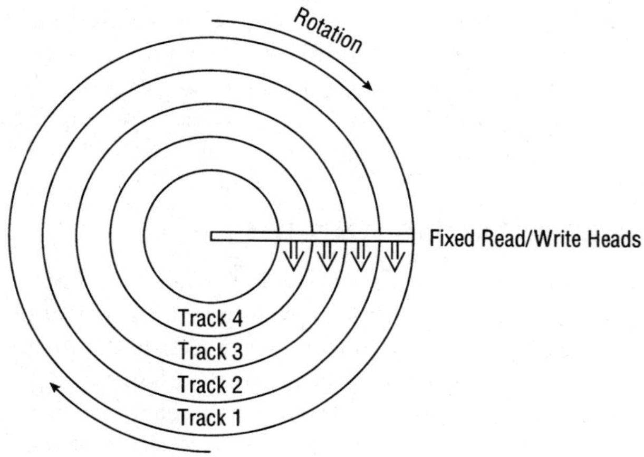

Fixed-head disks are used today only when extremely high performance is required, such as when implementing virtual memory (Lane & Mooney, 1988).

MOVABLE-HEAD DRUMS AND DISKS

Movable-head drums have only a few read/write heads that move from track to track to cover the entire surface of the drum. Figure 7.6 shows two drums with movable read/write heads. Figure 7.6(**a**) shows the least expensive device, with only one read/write head for the entire drum; Figure 7.6(**b**) shows the more conventional design with several read/write heads that move together.

FIGURE 7.6 *Two designs of movable-head drums:* (**a**) *with one head and* (**b**) *with several heads on a single arm, which moves them in unison. A drum with several read/write heads can access a record faster, but it's also a more expensive unit.*

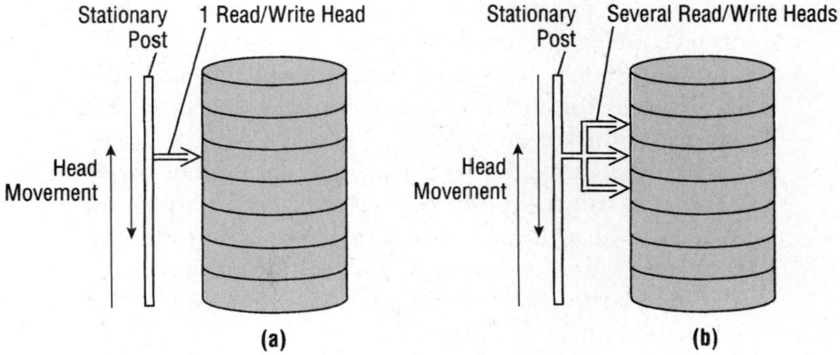

Movable-head disks have one read/write head that floats over the surface of the disk. Disks can be individual units, such as those used with many personal computers, or part of a **disk pack**, which is a stack of disks. Figure 7.7 shows a typical disk pack — several platters stacked on a common central spindle, 1/2 inch apart, so the read/write heads can move between each pair of disks.

FIGURE 7.7 *A disk pack is a stack of magnetic platters. The read/write heads move between each pair of surfaces, and all of the heads are moved in unison by the arm.*

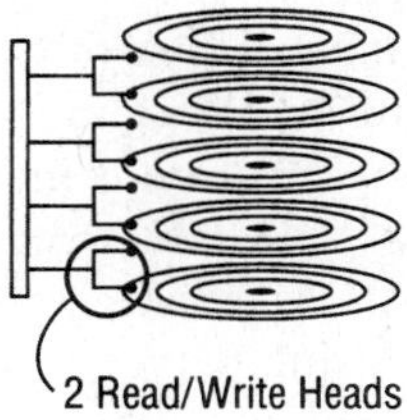

As shown in Figure 7.7, each platter (except those at the top and bottom of the stack) has two surfaces for recording, and each surface is formatted with a specific number of concentric tracks where the data is recorded. The number of tracks varies from manufacturer to manufacturer but typically they range from 200 to 800 tracks. Each track on each surface is numbered: Track 0 identifies the outermost concentric circle on each surface; the highest-numbered track is in the center.

The arm moves two read/write heads between each pair of surfaces: one for the surface above it and one for the surface below. The arm moves all of the heads in unison, so if one head is on Track 36, then all of the heads are on Track 36 — in other words, they're all positioned on the same track but on their respective surfaces.

This raises some interesting questions: Is it more efficient to write a series of records on surface one and, when that surface is full, to continue writing on surface two, and then on surface three, and so on? Or is it better to fill up every outside track of every surface before moving the heads inward to the next track position to continue writing?

It's slower to fill a disk pack surface-by-surface than it is to fill it up track-by-track — and this leads us to a valuable concept. If we fill Track 0 of all of the surfaces, we've got a virtual **cylinder** of data — this is the cylinder concept illustrated in Figure 5.5. There are as many cylinders as there are tracks, and the cylinders are as tall as the disk pack. You could visualize the cylinders as a series of drums, one inside the other.

To access any given record, the system needs three things: its cylinder number, so the arm can move the read/write heads to it; a surface number, so the proper read/write head is activated; and a record number, so the read/write head knows the instant when it should begin reading or writing.

One clarification: we've used the term "surface" in this discussion because it makes the concepts easier to understand. However, conventional literature generally uses the term "track" to identify both the surface and the concentric track. Therefore, our use of "surface/track" coincides with the term "track" or "head" used in many other texts.

OPTICAL DISC STORAGE

Optical storage DASDs, including **CD-ROM**, provide high-density storage and are reliable media in which to store very large databases, reference works such as encyclopedias, complex games, large software packages, system documentation, and user training material. (Optical storage devices are referred to as "discs," to differentiate them from magnetic storage "disks.")

According to market reports, the first major users of CD-ROMs were libraries and corporations that needed text-based information and reference works. However, as more CD-ROM publishers began incorporating multimedia in their discs and marketing "edutainment"-type products, CD-ROMs became widespread in the microcomputer market. By mid-1995 CD-ROM drives were ubiquitous and the technology had evolved to support CD-ROM jukeboxes (also called autochangers or libraries) capable of handling multiple discs and networked to distribute multimedia and reference works to distant users.

As of 1995 optical disc drives were widely used as *read only* drives. Recordable drives, known as CD-Rs, were not popular because of their high cost, so this discussion will center on read only drives.

The **optical disc drive** functions in a manner similar to the magnetic disk drive: it has a head — in this case it's a read head instead of a read/write head —

on an arm that moves forward and backward from track to track. Two of the most important measures of performance of CD-ROM drives are sustained data-transfer rate and average access time. Data-transfer rate is measured in kilobytes per second (Kbps) and refers to the speed at which massive amounts of data can be read off the disc. For applications requiring sequential access, such as for audio and video playback, this factor is crucial. For example, a CD-ROM with a fast transfer rate will drop fewer frames when playing back a recorded video segment than will a unit with a slower transfer rate, creating an image that's much smoother.

However, if you want to retrieve data that is *not* stored sequentially, the drive's access time may be more important. Access time, which indicates the average time required to move the read head to a specific place on the disc, is expressed in milliseconds (ms). The fastest units have the lowest numbers.

Access time is most important when searching for information in random fashion, such as in an encyclopedia. Both access time and data-transfer rate have improved over the years as optical disc technology has evolved from single-speed to hex-speed drives, as shown in Table 7.2.

TABLE 7.2 *Typical data-transfer rates and average access times for CD-ROM drives. A fast data-transfer rate is most important for sequential disk access, such as for video playback, whereas fast access time is crucial when retrieving data that's widely dispersed on the optical disc.*

Speed designation	Data transfer rate	Average access time
Single	150 Kbps	450 ms
Double	300 Kbps	280 ms
Quadruple	600 Kbps	150 ms
Hex	900 Kbps	<150 ms

A third important feature of optical disc drives is **cache size**. Although it's not a speed measurement, cache size has a substantial impact on perceived performance. A hardware cache acts as a buffer by transferring blocks of data from the disc, anticipating that the user may want to reread some recently retrieved information. Hardware caches vary in size from 64 KB in single-speed drives to 1 MB in quad-speed drives. In some cases the cache can also act as a read-ahead buffer, looking for the next block of information on the disc. Read-ahead caches might appear to be most useful for multimedia playback, where a continuous stream of data is flowing. However, because they fill up quickly, read-ahead caches actually become more useful when paging through a database or electronic book. In these cases, the cache has time to recover while the user is reading the current piece of information.

ACCESS TIME REQUIRED

Depending on whether the device has fixed or movable heads, there can be as many as three factors that contribute to the time required to access a file: seek time, search time, and transfer time.

Seek time is the slowest of the three factors. It's the time required to position the read/write head on the proper track. Obviously, seek time doesn't apply to devices with fixed read/write heads.

Search time, also known as **rotational delay**, is the time it takes to rotate the drum or disk until the requested record is moved under the read/write head.

Transfer time is the fastest of the three; that's when the data is actually transferred from secondary storage to main memory.

FOR FIXED-HEAD DEVICES Fixed-head devices can access a record by knowing its track number and record number. The total amount of time required to access data depends on two factors: (1) the rotational speed, which, although it varies from device to device, is constant within each device, and (2) the position of the record relative to the position of the read/write head. Therefore, total access time is the sum of search time plus transfer time.

$$\begin{array}{rl} & \text{search time (rotational delay)} \\ + & \underline{\text{transfer time (data transfer)}} \\ & \text{access time} \end{array}$$

Because drums and disks rotate continuously, there are three basic positions for the requested record relative to the read/write head position. Figure 7.8(**a**) shows the best possible situation because the record is next to the read/write head when the I/O command is executed; this gives a rotational delay of zero. Figure 7.8(**b**) shows the average situation because the record is directly opposite the read/write head when the I/O command is executed; this gives a rotational delay of $t/2$ where t (time) is one full rotation. Figure 7.8(**c**) shows the worst situation because the record has just rotated past the read/write head when the I/O command is executed; this gives a rotational delay of t because it will take one full rotation for the record to reposition itself under the read/write head.

FIGURE 7.8 *As a disk rotates, Record 1 may be near the read/write head and ready to be scanned, as seen in* (**a**)*; in the farthest position just past the head, as in* (**c**)*; or somewhere in between, as seen in the average case, shown in* (**b**).

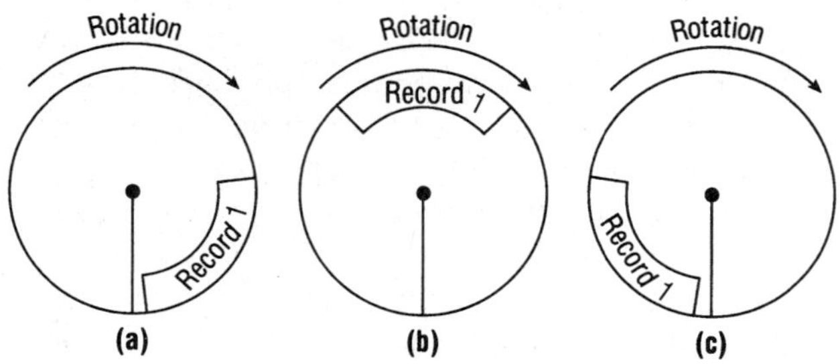

How long will it take to access a record? Typically, one complete revolution takes 16.8 ms, so the average rotational delay, as shown in Figure 7.8(**b**), is 8.4 ms. The data transfer time varies from device to device, but a typical value is 0.00094

ms per byte — the size of the record dictates this value. For example, it takes 0.094 ms (almost 0.1 ms) to transfer a record with 100 bytes. Therefore, using these numbers, the access times would be as shown in Table 7.3.

TABLE 7.3
Access times for a fixed-head DASD at 16.8 ms/revolution.

Maximum access	= 16.8 ms + 0.00094 ms/byte
Average access	= 8.4 ms + 0.00094 ms/byte
Sequential access	= depends on the length of the record, generally less than 1 ms (known as the transfer rate)

Because there's little variance in access, DASDs are good for files with low activity or for users who access records in a random fashion.

Data recorded on DASDs may or may not be blocked at the discretion of the application programmer. With DASDs blocking isn't used to save space because there are no IRGs between records; instead, blocking is used to save time.

To illustrate the advantages to blocking the records, let's use the same values shown in Table 7.3 for a record containing 100 bytes and blocks containing ten records. If we were to read ten records individually, we would multiply the access time for a single record by ten:

$$\begin{aligned} \text{access time} &= 8.4 + 0.094 &&= 8.494 \text{ ms for one record} \\ \text{total access time} &= 10(8.4 + 0.094) &&= 84.940 \text{ ms for ten records} \end{aligned}$$

On the other hand, to read one block of ten records we would make a single access, so we'd compute the access time only once, multiplying the transfer rate by ten:

$$\begin{aligned} \text{access time} &= 8.4 + (0.094 * 10) \\ &= 8.4 + 0.94 \\ &= 9.34 \text{ ms for ten records in one block} \end{aligned}$$

Once the block is in memory the software that handles blocking and deblocking takes over. Of course, the amount of time used in deblocking must be less than what you saved in access time (75.6 ms) for this to be a productive move.

FOR MOVABLE-HEAD DEVICES Movable-head disks and drums add the third time element to the computation of access time: the time required to move the arm into position over the proper track — that's called seek time. So now the formula for access time is:

$$\begin{array}{r l} & \text{seek time (arm movement)} \\ & \text{search time (rotational delay)} \\ + & \text{transfer time (data transfer)} \\ \hline & \text{access time} \end{array}$$

Of the three components of access time in this equation, seek time is the longest. It's been the subject of many studies to find the seek strategy that will move the arm in the most efficient manner possible. We'll examine several seek strategies in a moment.

The calculations to figure search time (rotational delay) and transfer time are the same as those presented for fixed-head DASDs. The maximum seek time, the maximum time required to move the arm, is typically 50 ms. Table 7.4 compares typical access times for movable-head DASDs.

TABLE 7.4
Typical access times for a movable-head DASD.

Maximum access	= 50 ms + 16.8 ms + 0.00094 ms/byte
Average access	= 25 ms + 8.4 ms + 0.00094 ms/byte
Sequential access	= depends on the length of the record, generally less than 1 ms

The variance in access time has increased in comparison to that of the fixed-head DASD, but it's relatively small — especially when compared to tape access, which varies from milliseconds to minutes.

Again, blocking is a good way to minimize access time. If we use the same example as for fixed-head disks and consider the worst possible case with ten seeks followed by ten searches, we would get:

$$\begin{aligned} \text{access time} &= 25 + 8.4 + 0.094 = 33.494 \text{ ms for one record} \\ \text{total access time} &= 10 * 33.494 \\ &= 334.94 \text{ ms for ten records (that's about } 1/3 \text{ of a second)} \end{aligned}$$

But when we put the ten records into one block, the access time is significantly decreased:

$$\begin{aligned} \text{total access time} &= 25 + 8.4 + (0.094 * 10) \\ &= 33.4 + 0.94 \\ &= 34.34 \text{ ms for ten records} \end{aligned}$$

We stress that these figures wouldn't apply in an actual operating environment. For instance, we haven't taken into consideration what else is happening in the system while I/O is taking place. Therefore, although we can show the comparable performance of these components of the system, we're not seeing the whole picture. Exercises 8 and 9 at the end of this chapter show the interaction between I/O commands and processing of the data retrieved with those commands. In fact, Exercise 9 gives you the opportunity to design a more efficient order of data storage that will take advantage of this interaction.

Overall, moveable-head devices are much more common than fixed-head DASDs because they're less costly and have larger capacities, even though retrieval time is longer. The system designer must make a choice: a less expensive movable-head unit with more storage and slower retrieval, or a more expensive fixed-head unit with less storage and faster retrieval.

COMPONENTS OF THE I/O SUBSYSTEM

The pieces of the I/O subsystem all have to work harmoniously together, and it works in a manner similar to the mythical "McHoes and Flynn Taxicab Company" shown in Figure 7.9.

Many requests come in from all over the city to the taxi company dispatcher.

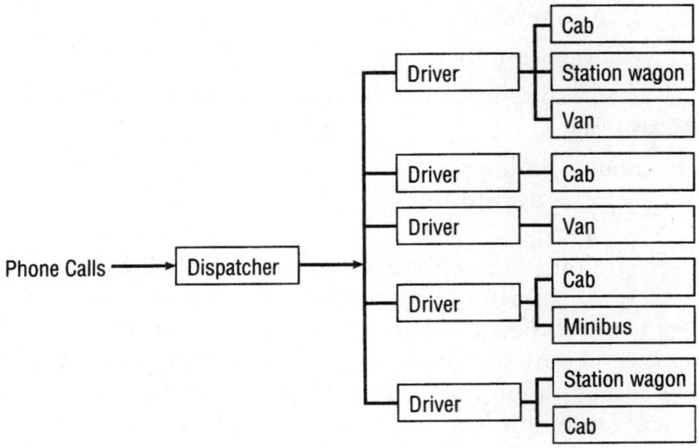

FIGURE 7.9
The McHoes and Flynn Taxicab Company works in a manner similar to an I/O subsystem. One driver can operate several vehicles just as an I/O control unit can operate several devices, as shown in Figure 7.10.

It's the dispatcher's job to handle the incoming calls as fast as they arrive and to find out who needs transportation, where they are, where they're going, and when. Then the dispatcher organizes the calls into an order that will use the company's resources as efficiently as possible. That's not easy, because the cab company has several drivers and a variety of vehicles at its disposal: ordinary taxicabs, station wagons, vans, and a minibus. Once the order is set, the dispatcher calls the drivers who, ideally, jump into the appropriate vehicles, pick up the waiting passengers, and deliver them quickly to their respective destinations.

That's the ideal — but problems sometimes occur; rainy days mean too many phone calls, cabs can break down, and sometimes there are several calls for the minibus.

The **I/O subsystem**'s components perform similar functions. The channel plays the part of the dispatcher in this example. Its job is to keep up with the I/O requests from the CPU and pass them down the line to the appropriate control unit. The control units play the part of the drivers. The I/O devices play the part of the vehicles.

I/O channels are programmable units placed between the CPU and the control units — their job is to synchronize the fast speed of the CPU with the slow speed of the I/O device, and they make it possible to overlap I/O operations with processor operations so the CPU and I/O can process concurrently. Channels use **channel programs**, which can range in size from one to many instructions. Each channel program specifies the action to be performed by the devices and controls the transmission of data between main memory and the control units (Calingaert, 1982).

The channel sends one signal for each function, and the **I/O control unit** interprets the signal, which might say "go to the top of the page" if the device is a printer or "rewind" if the device is a tape drive. Although a control unit is sometimes part of the device, in most systems a single control unit is attached to several similar devices, so we distinguish between the control unit and the device.

At the start of an I/O command, the information passed from the CPU to the channel is this:

1. I/O command (READ, WRITE, REWIND, etc.)
2. Channel number
3. Address of the physical record to be transferred (from or to secondary storage)
4. Starting address of a memory buffer from which or into which the record is to be transferred

Because the channels are as fast as the CPU they work with, each channel can direct several control units by interleaving commands (just as we had several cab drivers being directed by a single dispatcher). In addition, each control unit can direct several devices (just as a single taxi driver could operate several vehicles). A typical configuration might have one channel and up to eight control units, each of which communicates with up to eight I/O devices. Channels are often shared because they're the most expensive items in the entire I/O subsystem.

The system shown in Figure 7.10 requires that the entire path be available when an I/O command is initiated. However, there's some flexibility built into the system because each unit can end independently of the others, as will be explained in the next section. This figure also shows the hierarchical nature of the interconnection and the one-to-one correspondence between each device and its transmission path.

FIGURE 7.10
Typical I/O subsystem configuration.

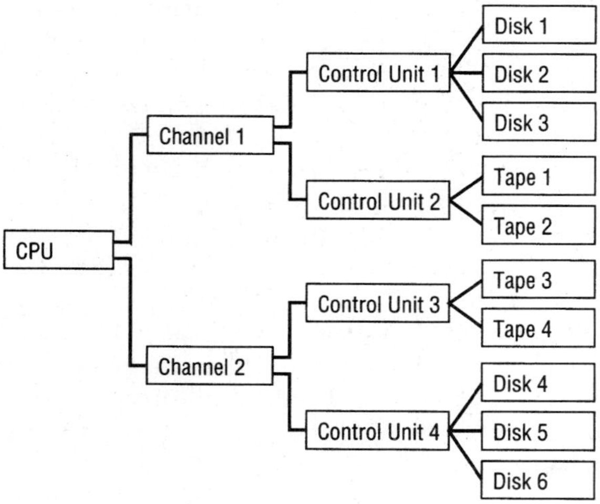

Additional flexibility can be built into the system by connecting more than one channel to a control unit or by connecting more than one control unit to a single device. That's the same as if the taxi drivers of the McHoes and Flynn Taxicab Company could also take calls from the ABC Taxicab Company, or if its cabs could be used by ABC drivers (or if the drivers in our company could share vehicles).

These multiple paths increase the reliability of the I/O subsystem by keeping communication lines open even if a component should malfunction. Figure 7.11

FIGURE 7.11
I/O subsystem configuration with multiple paths, which increase both flexibility and reliability. With these two additional paths, if Control Unit 2 malfunctions then Tape 2 can still be accessed via Control Unit 3.

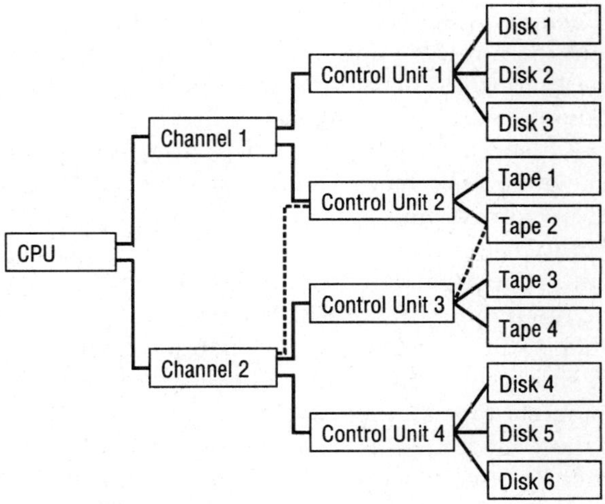

shows the same system presented in Figure 7.10, but with one control unit connected to two channels and one device connected to two control units.

COMMUNICATION AMONG DEVICES

The Device Manager relies on several auxiliary features to keep running efficiently under the demanding conditions of a busy computer system, and there are three problems that must be resolved: (1) it needs to know which components are busy and which are free; (2) it must be able to accommodate the requests that come in during heavy I/O traffic; and (3) it must accommodate the disparity of speeds between the CPU and the I/O devices. The last two problems are handled by "buffering" records and queueing requests. The first is solved by structuring the interaction between units.

As we mentioned previously, each unit in the I/O subsystem can finish its operation independently from the others. For example, after a device has begun writing a record, and before it has completed the task, the connection between the device and its controller can be cut off so the controller can initiate another I/O task with another device. Meanwhile, at the other end of the subsystem, the CPU is free to process data while I/O is being performed, which allows for concurrent processing and I/O.

The success of the operation depends on the system's ability to know when a device has completed an operation. It's done with a hardware flag that must be tested by the CPU.

This flag is made up of three bits and resides in the **Channel Status Word (CSW)**, which is in a predefined location in main memory and contains information indicating the status of the channel. Each bit represents one of the components of the I/O subsystem, one each for the channel, control unit, and device. Each bit is changed from zero to one to indicate that the unit has changed from free to busy. Each component has access to the flag, which can be tested before proceeding with the next I/O operation to ensure that the entire path is free and vice versa. There are two common ways to perform this test: polling and using interrupts (Prasad, 1989).

Polling uses a special machine instruction to test the flag. For example, the CPU periodically tests the channel status bit (in the CSW). If the channel is still busy, the CPU performs some other processing task until the test shows that the channel is free; then the channel performs the I/O operation. The major disadvantage with this scheme is determining how often the flag should be polled. If polling is done too frequently, the CPU wastes time testing the flag just to find out that the channel is still busy. On the other hand, if polling is done too seldom, the channel could sit idle for long periods of time.

The use of **interrupts** is a more efficient way to test the flag. Instead of having the CPU test the flag, a hardware mechanism does the test as part of every machine instruction executed by the CPU. If the channel is busy the flag is set so that execution of the current sequence of instructions is automatically interrupted and control is transferred to the interrupt handler, which resides in a predefined location in memory (Bic & Shaw, 1988).

The interrupt handler's job is to determine the best course of action based on the current situation because it's not unusual for more than one unit to have caused the I/O interrupt. So the interrupt handler must find out which unit sent the signal, analyze its status, restart it when appropriate with the next operation, and finally return control to the interrupted process.

Some sophisticated systems are equipped with hardware that can distinguish between several types of interrupts. These interrupts are ordered by priority, and each one can transfer control to a corresponding location in memory. The memory locations are ranked in order according to the same priorities. So if the CPU is executing the interrupt-handler routine associated with a given priority, the hardware will automatically intercept all interrupts at the same or at lower priorities. This "multiple-priority" interrupt system helps improve resource utilization because each interrupt is handled according to its relative importance (Calingaert, 1982).

Direct memory access (DMA) is an I/O technique that allows a control unit to access main memory directly. This means that once reading or writing has begun, the remainder of the data can be transferred to and from memory without CPU intervention. To activate this process the CPU sends enough information to the control unit to initiate the transfer of data; the CPU then can go on to another task while the control unit completes the transfer independently. This mode of data transfer is used for high-speed devices such as disks.

Without DMA, the CPU is responsible for the physical movement of data between main memory and the device — a time-consuming task that results in significant overhead and decreased CPU utilization.

Buffers are used extensively to better synchronize the movement of data between the relatively slow I/O devices and the very fast CPU. Buffers are temporary storage areas residing in convenient locations throughout the system: main memory, channels, and control units. They're used to store data read from an input device before it's needed by the processor and to store data that will be written to an output device. A typical use of buffers (mentioned earlier in this chapter) occurs when blocked records are either read from, or written to, an I/O device. In this case one logical record contains several physical records and must reside in memory while the processing of each individual record takes place. For example, if a block contains five records then a "physical READ" occurs with every six READ commands; all other READ requests are directed to retrieve information from the buffer (this buffer may be set by the application program).

To minimize the idle time for devices and, even more importantly, to maximize their throughput the technique of **double buffering** is used as shown in Figure 7.12. In this system two buffers are present in main memory, channels, and control units. The objective is to have a record ready to be transferred to or from memory at any time to avoid any possible delay that might be caused by waiting for a buffer to fill up with data. Thus, while one record is being processed by the CPU another can be read or written by the channel.

FIGURE 7.12
*Example of double buffering: (**a**) the CPU is reading from Buffer 1 as Buffer 2 is being filled; (**b**) once Buffer 2 is filled it can be read quickly by the CPU while Buffer 1 is being filled again.*

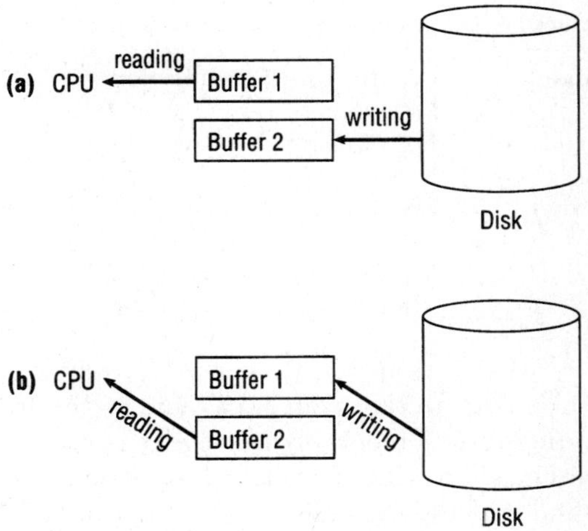

When using blocked records, upon receipt of the command to "READ last logical record," the channel can start reading the next physical record, which results in overlapped I/O and processing. When the first READ command is received, two records are transferred from the device to fill both buffers right away. Then, as the data from one buffer has been processed, the second buffer is ready. As the second is being read, the first buffer is being filled with data from a third record, and so on.

MANAGEMENT OF I/O REQUESTS

Although most users think of an I/O request in terms of elementary machine actions, the Device Manager actually divides the task into three parts, with each one handled by a specific software component of the I/O subsystem. The I/O traffic controller watches the status of all devices, control units, and channels. The I/O scheduler implements the policies that determine the allocation of, and access to, the devices, control units, and channels. The I/O device handler performs the actual transfer of data and processes the device interrupts (Madnick & Donovan, 1974). Let's look at these in more detail.

The **I/O traffic controller** monitors the status of every device, control unit, and channel. It's a job that becomes more complex as the number of units in the I/O subsystem increases and as the number of paths between these units increases. The traffic controller has three main tasks: (1) it must determine if there's at least one path available; (2) if there's more than one path available, it must determine which to select; and (3) if the paths are all busy, it must determine when one will become available.

To do all this, the traffic controller maintains a database containing the status and connections for each unit in the I/O subsystem, grouped into Channel Control Blocks, Control Unit Control Blocks, and Device Control Blocks, as shown in Table 7.5.

TABLE 7.5 *Each of the three control blocks contains the information it needs to manage its part of the I/O subsystem.*

Channel Control Block	Control Unit Control Block	Device Control Block
Channel identification status List of control units connected to it List of processes waiting for it	Control Unit Identification status List of channels connected to it List of devices connected to it List of processes waiting for it	Device identification status List of control units connected to it List of processes waiting for it

To choose a free path to satisfy an I/O request, the traffic controller "traces backward" from the control block of the requested device through the control units to the channels. If no path is available, a common occurrence under heavy load conditions, the process (actually its Process Control Block, or PCB, as described in Chapter 4) is linked to the queues kept in the control blocks of the requested device, control unit, and channel. This creates multiple wait queues with one queue per path. Later, when a path becomes available, the traffic controller quickly selects the first PCB from the queue for that path.

The **I/O scheduler** performs the same job as the Process Scheduler described in Chapter 4 on processor management — that is, it allocates the devices, control units, and channels.

Under heavy loads, when the number of requests is greater than the number of available paths, the I/O scheduler must decide which request will be satisfied first. Many of the criteria and objectives discussed in Chapter 4 also apply here. In many systems the major difference between I/O scheduling and process scheduling is that I/O requests are not preempted: once the channel program has started, it's allowed to continue to completion even though I/O requests with higher priorities may have entered the queue. This is feasible because channel programs are relatively short, 50 to 100 ms. Other systems subdivide an I/O request into several stages and allow preemption of the I/O request at any one of these stages.

Some systems allow the I/O scheduler to give preferential treatment to I/O requests from "high-priority" programs. In that case, if a process has high priority then its I/O requests would also have high priority and would be satisfied before other I/O requests with lower priorities.

The I/O scheduler must synchronize its work with the traffic controller to make sure that a path is available to satisfy the selected I/O requests.

The **I/O device handler** processes the I/O interrupts, handles error conditions, and provides detailed scheduling algorithms, which are extremely device dependent. Each type of I/O device has its own device handler algorithm.

DEVICE HANDLER SEEK STRATEGIES

A **seek strategy** for the I/O device handler is the predetermined policy that the device handler uses to allocate access to the device among the many processes that may be waiting for it; it determines the order in which the processes get the device, and the goal is to keep seek time to a minimum. We'll look at some of the most commonly used seek strategies: first come first served (FCFS); shortest seek time first (SSTF); and SCAN and its variations: LOOK, N-Step SCAN, C-SCAN, and C-LOOK (Peterson & Silberschatz, 1987).

Every scheduling algorithm should do the following:

1. Minimize arm movement
2. Minimize mean response time
3. Minimize the variance in response time

These goals are only a guide. In actual systems, the designer must choose the strategy that makes the system as fair as possible to the general user population while using the system's resources as efficiently as possible.

First come first served (FCFS) is the simplest device-scheduling algorithm: easy to program and essentially fair to users. However, on average, it doesn't meet any of the three goals of a seek strategy. To illustrate, consider a single-sided disk with one recordable surface where the tracks are numbered from zero to 49. It takes 1 ms to travel from one track to the next adjacent one. For this example, let's say that while retrieving data from Track 15, the following list of requests has arrived: Track 4, 40, 11, 35, 7, and 14. Let's also assume that once a requested track has been reached, the entire track is read into main memory. The path of the read/write head looks like the graph shown in Figure 7.13.

In Figure 7.13, it takes a long time, 135 ms, to satisfy the entire series of requests — and that's before considering the work to be done when the arm is finally in place: search time and data transfer.

FCFS has an obvious disadvantage — extreme arm movement: from 15 to 4, up to 40, back to 11, up to 35, back to 7, and, finally, up to 14. Remember, seek time is the most time-consuming of the three functions performed here, so any algorithm that can minimize it is preferable to FCFS.

Shortest seek time first (SSTF) uses the same underlying philosophy as shortest job next (described in Chapter 4), where the shortest jobs are processed first and longer jobs are made to wait.

With SSTF the request with the track closest to the one being served (that is,

FIGURE 7.13
The arm makes many time-consuming moves as it travels from track to track to satisfy all requests in FCFS order.

Head path	Tracks Traveled
15 to 4	11
4 to 40	36
40 to 11	29
11 to 35	24
35 to 7	28
7 to 14	7
	135

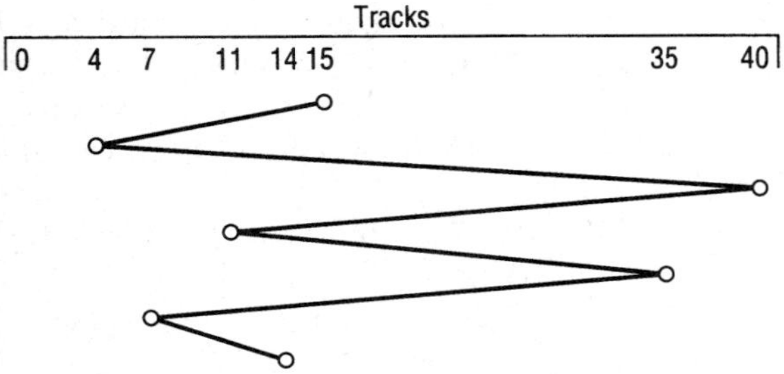

Total Number of Tracks = 135 ms
Average Number of Tracks Traveled = 22.50 ms

the one with the shortest distance to travel) is the next to be satisfied, thus minimizing overall seek time. Figure 7.14 shows what happens to the same track requests that took 135 ms to service using FCFS.

Again, without considering search time and data transfer time, it took 47 ms to satisfy all seven requests — which is about one third of the time required by FCFS. That's a substantial improvement.

But SSTF has its disadvantages. Remember that the SJN process scheduling algorithm had a tendency to favor the short jobs and postpone the long unwieldy jobs. The same holds true for SSTF: it favors easy-to-reach requests and postpones traveling to those that are out of the way.

For example, let's say that in the previous example the arm is at Track 11 and is preparing to go to Track 7 when the system suddenly gets a deluge of requests, including requests for Tracks 22, 13, 16, 29, 1, and 21. With SSTF, the system notes that Track 13 is closer to the arm's present position (only two tracks away) than the older request for Track 7 (five tracks away), so Track 13 is handled first. Of the requests now waiting, the next closest is Track 16, so off it goes — moving farther and farther away from Tracks 7 and 1. In fact, during periods of heavy loads the arm stays in the center of the disk, where it can satisfy the majority of requests easily and it ignores (or indefinitely postpones) those on the outer edges of the disk. Therefore, this algorithm meets the first goal of seek strategies but fails the other two.

FIGURE 7.14
Using the SSTF algorithm, arm movement is reduced by almost one third while satisfying the same requests shown in Figure 7.13 (using the FCFS algorithm).

Head path	Tracks Traveled
15 to 14	1
14 to 11	3
11 to 7	4
7 to 4	3
4 to 35	31
35 to 40	5
	47

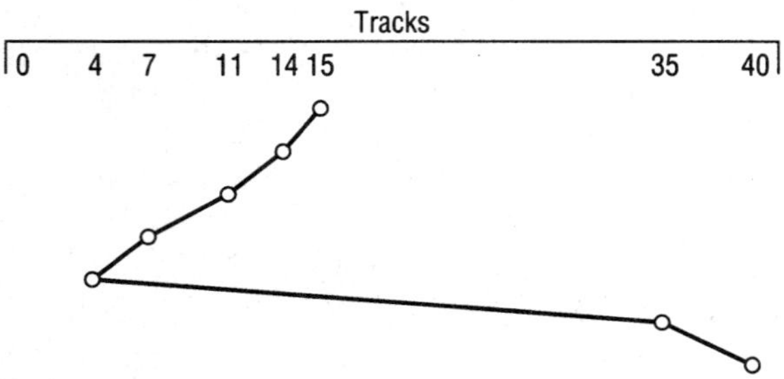

Total Number of Tracks = 47 ms
Average Number of Tracks Traveled = 7.83 ms

SCAN uses a directional bit to indicate whether the arm is moving toward the center of the disk or away from it. The algorithm moves the arm methodically from the outer to the inner track servicing every request in its path. When it reaches the innermost track it reverses direction and moves toward the outer tracks, again servicing every request in its path. The most common variation of SCAN is **LOOK**, sometimes known as the **elevator algorithm**, in which the arm doesn't necessarily go all the way to either edge unless there are requests there. In effect, it "looks" ahead for a request before going to service it. In Figure 7.15 we assume that the arm is moving first toward the inner (higher-numbered) tracks before reversing direction.

FIGURE 7.15
The LOOK algorithm makes the arm move systematically from the first requested track at one edge of the disk to the last requested track at the other edge.

Head path	Tracks Traveled
15 to 35	20
35 to 40	5
40 to 14	26
14 to 11	3
11 to 7	4
7 to 4	3
	61

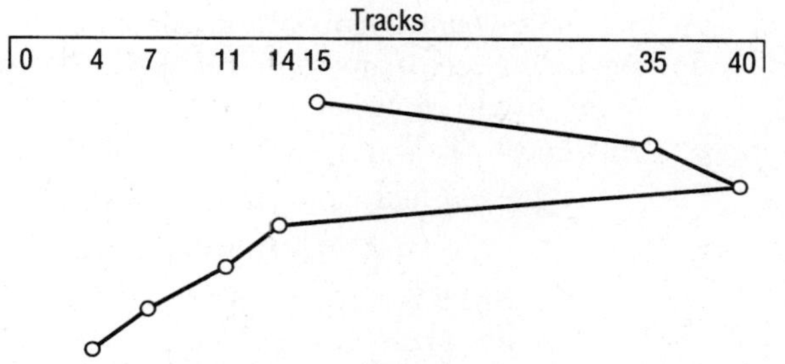

Total Number of Tracks = 61 ms
Average Number of Tracks Traveled = 10.16 ms

Again, without adding search time and data transfer time, it took 61 ms to satisfy all requests, 14 ms more than with SSTF. Does this make SCAN a less attractive algorithm than SSTF? For this particular example, the answer is "yes." But for the overall system, the answer is "no" because it eliminates the possibility of indefinite postponement of requests in out-of-the-way places — at either edge of the disk.

Also, as requests arrive each is incorporated in its proper place in the queue and serviced when the arm reaches that track. Therefore, if Track 11 is being served when the request for Track 13 arrives, the arm continues on its way to Track 7 and then to Track 1. Track 13 must wait until the arm starts on its way back, as does the request for Track 16. This eliminates a great deal of arm movement and saves time in the end. In fact, SCAN meets all three goals for seek strategies.

Variations of SCAN, in addition to LOOK, are N-Step SCAN, C-SCAN, and C-LOOK.

N-Step SCAN doesn't incorporate requests into the arm's path as it travels, but holds all the requests until the arm starts on its way back. Any requests that arrive while the arm is in motion are grouped together for the arm's next sweep.

With **C-SCAN** (an abbreviation for Circular SCAN), the arm picks up requests on its path during the inward sweep. When the innermost track has been reached it immediately returns to the outermost track and starts servicing requests that had arrived during its last inward sweep. With this modification, the system can provide quicker service to those requests that had accumulated for the low-numbered tracks while the arm was moving inward. The theory here is that by the time the arm reaches the highest-numbered tracks there are few requests immediately behind it. However, there are many requests at the far end of the disk and these have been waiting the longest. Therefore, C-SCAN is designed to provide a more uniform wait time.

C-LOOK is an optimization of C-SCAN, just as LOOK is an optimization of SCAN. In this algorithm the sweep inward stops at the last high-numbered track request, so the arm doesn't move all the way to the last track unless it's required to do so. In addition, the arm doesn't necessarily return to the lowest-numbered track; it returns only to the lowest-numbered track that's requested.

Which strategy is best? It's up to the system designer to select the "best" algorithm for each environment. It's a job that's complicated because the day-to-day performance of any scheduling algorithm depends on the load it must handle, but some broad generalizations can be made based on simulation studies (Teorey & Pinkerton, 1972):

1. FCFS works well with light loads, but as soon as the load grows, service time becomes unacceptably long.
2. SSTF is quite popular and intuitively appealing. It works well with moderate loads but has the problem of localization under heavy loads.
3. SCAN works well with light to moderate loads and eliminates the problem of indefinite postponement. SCAN is similar to SSTF in throughput and mean service times.
4. C-SCAN works well with moderate to heavy loads and has a very small variance in service times.

The best scheduling algorithm for a specific computing system may be a combination of more than one scheme. For instance, it might be a combination of two schemes: SCAN or LOOK during light to moderate loads, and C-SCAN or C-LOOK during heavy load times.

SEARCH STRATEGIES: ROTATIONAL ORDERING

So far we've only tried to optimize seek times. To complete the picture we'll now look at a way to optimize search times by ordering the requests once the read/write heads have been positioned. This **search strategy** is called "**rotational ordering**."

To help illustrate the abstract concept of rotational ordering, let's return to the discussion of a movable head drum introduced earlier in the chapter. By understanding how reordering requests work on a drum, we'll understand how it works with "virtual drums" — disk pack cylinders.

Figure 7.16 illustrates the list of requests arriving at a movable-head drum for different sectors on different tracks. For this example we'll assume that the drum has only five tracks, numbered 0 through 4, and that each track contains five **sectors**, numbered 0 through 4. We'll take the requests in the order in which they arrive (Madnick & Donovan, 1974).

FIGURE 7.16 *This movable-head drum takes 5 ms to move the read/write head from one track to the next. The read/write head is initially positioned at Track 0, Sector 0. It takes 5 ms to rotate the drum from Sector 0 to Sector 4 and 1 ms to transfer one sector from the drum to main memory.*

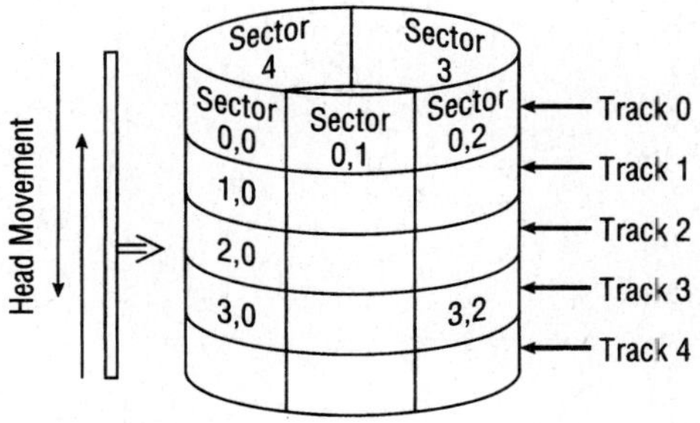

Request list

Track	Sector
0	1
1	4
1	3
2	0
2	3
2	4
3	2
3	0

Each request is satisfied as it comes in with the results shown in Table 7.6.

TABLE 7.6 *It takes 36 ms to fill the eight requests on the movable-head drum shown in Figure 7.16.*

	Request (track, sector)	Seek time		Search time		Data transfer		Total time
1.	0,1	0		1		1		2
2.	1,4	5		2		1		8
3.	1,3	0		3		1		4
4.	2,0	5		1		1		7
5.	2,3	0		2		1		3
6.	2,4	0		0		1		1
7.	3,2	5		2		1		8
8.	3,0	0		2		1		3
	TOTALS	15ms	+	13ms	+	8ms	=	36ms

Although nothing can be done to improve the time spent moving the read/write head because it's dependent on the hardware, the amount of time wasted due to rotational delay can be reduced. If the requests are ordered within each track so that the first sector requested on the second track is the next number higher than the one just served, rotational delay will be minimized as shown in Table 7.7.

To properly implement this algorithm, the device controller must provide "rotational sensing" so the device driver can "see" which sector is currently under the read/write head. Under heavy I/O loads this kind of ordering can significantly increase throughput, especially if the device has fixed read/write heads rather than movable heads.

Disk pack cylinders are similar conceptually to fixed-head drums: once the heads are positioned on a cylinder each surface has its own read/write head. So

TABLE 7.7
It takes 28 ms to fill the same eight requests shown in Table 7.6 after the requests are ordered to minimize search time, reducing it to 5 ms.

	Request (track, sector)	Seek time		Search time		Data transfer		Total time
1.	0,1	0		1		1		2
2.	1,3	5		1		1		7
3.	1,4	0		0		1		1
4.	2,0	5		0		1		6
5.	2,3	0		2		1		3
6.	2,4	0		0		1		1
7.	3,0	5		0		1		6
8.	3,2	0		1		1		2
	TOTALS	15ms	+	5ms	+	8ms	=	28ms

rotational ordering can be accomplished on a surface-by-surface basis and the read/write heads can be activated in turn with no additional movement required.

Only one read/write head can be active at any one time, so the controller must be ready to handle mutually exclusive requests such as Request 2 and Request 5 in Table 7.7. They're mutually exclusive because both are requesting Sector 3, one at Track 1 and the other at Track 2, but only one of the two read/write heads can be transmitting at any given time. So the policy could state that the tracks will be processed from low-numbered to high-numbered and then from high-numbered to low-numbered in a sweeping motion such as that used in SCAN. Therefore, to handle requests on a disk pack there would be two orderings of requests: one to handle the position of the read/write heads making up the cylinder and the other to handle the processing of each cylinder.

CHAPTER SEVEN CONCLUSION

The Device Manager's job is to manage all of the system's devices as effectively as possible despite their unique characteristics: they have varying speed and degrees of sharability; some can handle direct access and some only sequential access; they can have one or many read/write heads; and they can be in a fixed position or the heads can have the ability to move across the surface.

Balancing the demand for these devices is a complex task that's divided among several hardware components: channels, control units, and the devices themselves. The success of the I/O subsystem depends on the communications that link these parts.

In this chapter we reviewed several seek strategies, each with distinct advantages and disadvantages, as shown in Table 7.8.

Thus far in this text we've reviewed three of the operating system's managers: the Memory Manager, the Processor Manager, and the Device Manager. In the next chapter we'll meet the fourth, the File Manager, which is responsible for the health and well-being of every file used by the system: the system's files, those submitted by users, and those generated as output.

TABLE 7.8 *Comparison of seek strategies.*

Strategy	Advantages	Disadvantages
FCFS	Easy to implement Sufficient for light loads	Doesn't provide best average service Doesn't maximize throughput
SSTF	Throughput better than FCFS Tends to minimize arm movement Tends to minimize response time	May cause starvation of some requests Localizes under heavy loads
SCAN/LOOK	Eliminates starvation Throughput similar to SSTF Works well with light to moderate loads	Needs directional bit More complex algorithm to implement, more overhead
N-Step SCAN	Easier to implement than SCAN	The newest requests wait longer than with SCAN
C-SCAN/C-LOOK	Works well with moderate to heavy loads No directional bit Small variance in service time C-LOOK doesn't travel to unused tracks	May not be fair to recent requests for high-numbered tracks More complex algorithm than N-Step SCAN, so there's more overhead

KEY TERMS

dedicated device
shared device
virtual device
sequential access media
direct access storage devices (DASDs)
magnetic tape
interrecord gap (IRG)
blocking
transfer rate
transport speed
interblock gap (IBG)
access time
track
sector
cylinder
optical disc drive
CD-ROM
seek time
search time
transfer time
I/O subsystem
I/O channel
channel program
I/O control unit
Channel Status Word (CSW)
polling
interrupts
direct memory access (DMA)
buffers
I/O traffic controller
I/O scheduler
I/O device handler
seek strategy
first come first served (FCFS)
shortest seek time first (SSTF)
SCAN
LOOK
search strategy
rotational ordering

EXERCISES

1. What is the difference between buffering and blocking?
2. Given the following characteristics for a magnetic tape:

density = 1600 bpi
speed = 200 inches/second
size = 2,400 feet
start/stop time = 3 ms
number of records to be stored = 200,000 records
size of each record = 160 bytes
block size = 10 logical records
IBG = 0.5 inch

Find the following:

a. Number of blocks needed.

b. Size of the block in bytes.

c. Time required to read one block.

d. Time required to write all of the blocks.

e. Amount of tape used for data only, in inches.

f. Total amount of tape used (data + IBGs), in inches.

3. Given the following characteristics for a disk pack with 10 platters yielding 18 recordable surfaces:

rotational speed = 10 ms
transfer rate = 0.1 ms/track
density per track = 19,000 bytes
number of records to be stored = 200,000 records
size of each record = 160 bytes
block size = 10 logical records
number of tracks per surface = 500

Find the following:

a. Number of blocks per track.

b. Waste per track.

c. Number of tracks required to store the entire file.

d. Total waste to store the entire file.

e. Time to write all of the blocks. (Use rotational speed; ignore the time it takes to move to the next track.)

f. Time to write all of the records if they're not blocked. (Use rotational speed; ignore the time it takes to move to the next track.)

g. Optimal blocking factor to minimize waste.

h. What would be the answer to (e) if the time it takes to move to the next track were 5 ms?

i. What would be the answer to (f) if the time it takes to move to the next track were 5 ms?

4. Given that it takes 1 ms to travel from one track to the next, and that the arm is originally positioned at track 15 moving toward the low-numbered tracks, compute how long it will take to satisfy the following requests — 4, 40, 11, 35, 7, 14 —

using the SCAN scheduling policy. (Ignore rotational time and transfer time; just consider seek time.) How does your result compare to the one in Figure 7.15?

5. Interactive systems must respond quickly to users. Minimizing the variance of response time is an important goal, but it doesn't always prevent an occasional user from suffering indefinite postponement. What mechanism would you incorporate into a disk scheduling policy to counteract this problem and still provide reasonable response time to the user population as a whole?

ADVANCED EXERCISES

6. Would a drum be a better device than a disk when paging is used? Why or why not?
7. Under very light loading conditions, every disk scheduling policy discussed in this chapter tends to approximate one of the policies discussed in this chapter. Which one is it and why?
8. Given a file of ten records (identified as A, B, C, . . . J) to be stored on a drum that holds ten records per track. Once the file is stored, the records will be accessed sequentially: A, B, C, . . . J. It takes 2 ms to process each record once it has been transferred into memory. It takes 10 ms for the drum to complete one rotation. It takes 1 ms to transfer the record from the drum to main memory. Suppose you store the records in the order given: A, B, C, . . . J.

   Compute how long it will take to process all ten records. Break up your computation into (1) time to transfer a record, (2) time to process a record, and (3) time to access the next record.
9. Given the same situation described in Exercise 8:
   a. Organize the records so that they're stored in nonsequential order (not A, B, C, . . . J) to reduce the time it takes to process them sequentially.
   b. Compute how long it will take to process all ten records using this new order. Break up your computation into (1) time to transfer a record, (2) time to process a record, and (3) time to access the next record.
10. Track requests are not usually equally or evenly distributed. For example, the tracks where the disk directory resides are accessed more often than those where the user's files reside. Suppose that you know that 50 percent of the requests are for a small fixed number of cylinders.
    a. Which one of the scheduling policies presented in this chapter would be "the best" under these conditions?
    b. Can you design one that would be better?

PROGRAMMING EXERCISE

11. Write a program that will simulate the FCFS, SSTF, LOOK, and C-LOOK seek optimization strategies. Assume that:
    a. The disk's outer track is the 0 track and the disk contains 200 tracks per surface. Each track holds eight sectors numbered 0 through 7.

b. A seek takes 10 + 0.1 * T ms, where T is the number of tracks of motion from one request to the next, and 10 is a movement time constant.

c. One full rotation takes 8 ms.

d. Transfer time is 1 ms.

Use the following data to test your program:

Arrival time	Track requested	Sector requested
0	45	0
23	132	6
25	20	2
29	23	1
35	198	7
45	170	5
57	180	3
83	78	4
88	73	5
95	150	7

For comparison purposes compute the average, variance, and standard deviation of the time required to service all requests under each of the strategies. Consolidate your results into a table.

Optional: Run your program again with different data and compare your results. Recommend the best policy and explain why.

Chapter Eight

FILE MANAGEMENT

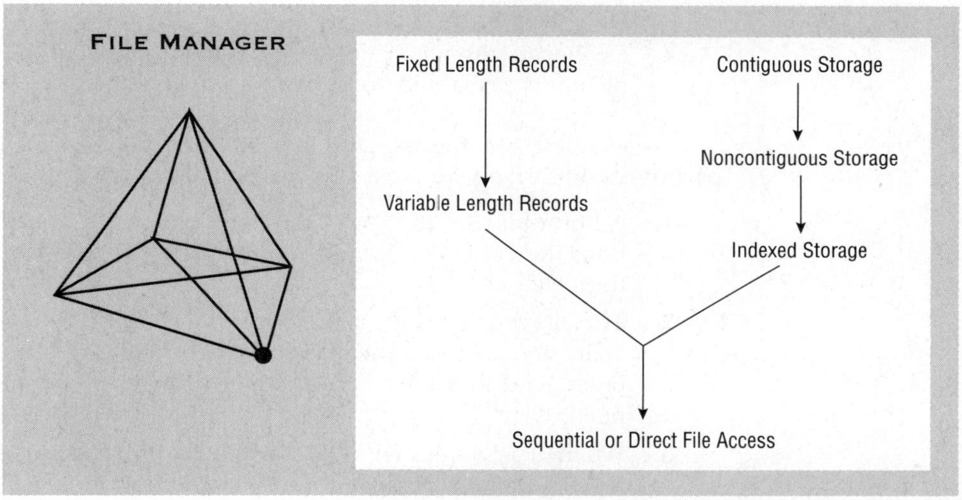

The File Manager controls every file in the system. In this chapter we'll learn how files are organized logically, how they're stored physically, how they're accessed, and who is allowed to access them. We'll also study the interaction between the File Manager and the Device Manager.

The efficiency of the File Manager depends on how the system's files are organized (sequential, direct, or indexed sequential); how they're stored (contiguously, noncontiguously, or indexed); how each file's records are structured (fixed-length or variable-length); and how access to these files is controlled. We'll look at each of these variables in this chapter.

THE FILE MANAGER

The file management system is the software responsible for creating, deleting, modifying, and controlling access to files — as well as for managing the resources used by files. It is the File Manager that provides support for libraries of programs and data to on-line users, for spooling operations, and for interactive computing. These functions are performed in collaboration with the Device Manager.

RESPONSIBILITIES OF THE FILE MANAGER

The File manager has a complex job. It is in charge of the system's physical components, its information resources, and the policies used to store and distribute the files. To carry out its responsibilities it must perform these four tasks:

1. Keep track of where each file is stored.
2. Use a policy that will determine where and how the files will be stored, making sure to efficiently use the available storage space and provide efficient access to the files.
3. Allocate each file when a user has been cleared for access to it, then record its use.
4. Deallocate the file when the file is to be returned to storage, and communicate its availability to others who may be waiting for it.

For example, the file system is like a library, with the File Manager playing the part of the librarian who performs the same four tasks:

1. A librarian uses the card catalog to keep track of each item in the collection; the cards list the call number and the details that help the patrons find each book.
2. The library relies on a predetermined policy to store everything in the collection including oversized books, magazines, recordings, maps, and tapes. And they must be physically arranged so people can find what they need.
3. When it is requested, the book is retrieved from its shelf and the borrower's name is recorded in the circulation file.
4. When the book is returned, the librarian deletes the entry from the circulation file and reshelves the item.

In a computer system, the File Manager keeps track of its files with directories that contain the file name, its physical location in secondary storage, and important information about each file.

The File Manager's predetermined policy determines where each file is stored and how the system, and users, will be able to access them simply — via commands that are independent from device details. In addition, the policy must determine who will have access to what material, and this involves two factors: flexibility of access to the information and its subsequent protection. The File Manager does this by allowing access to shared files, providing distributed access, and allowing users to browse through "public" directories. Meanwhile, the operating system must protect its files against system malfunctions and provide security checks via account numbers, passwords, and lockwords to preserve the integrity of the data and safeguard against tampering. Lockwords are explained at the conclusion of this chapter.

The computer system allocates a file by activating the appropriate secondary storage device and loading the file into memory while updating its records of who is using what file.

Finally, the File Manager deallocates a file by updating the file tables and rewriting the file (if revised) to the secondary storage device. Any processes waiting to access the file are then notified of its availability.

DEFINITIONS

Before we continue, let's take a minute to review some basic definitions that relate to our discussion of the File Manager.

A **field** is a group of related bytes that can be identified by the user with a name, type, and size. A **record** is a group of related fields.

A **file** is a group of related records that contains information to be used by specific application programs to generate reports. This type of file contains data and is sometimes called a "flat" file because it has no connections to other files; unlike databases, it has no dimensionality.

A **database** appears to the File Manager to be a type of file, but databases are more complex because they are actually groups of related files that are interconnected at various levels to give users flexibility of access to the data stored. If the user's database requires a specific structure, the File Manager must be able to support it.

Program files contain instructions and **data files** contain data, but as far as storage is concerned, the File Manager treats them exactly the same way. **Directories** are listings of file names and their attributes and are treated in a manner similar to files by the File Manager. Data collected to monitor system performance and provide for system accounting is collected into files. In fact, every program and data file accessed by the computer system, as well as every piece of computer software, is treated as a file.

INTERACTING WITH THE FILE MANAGER

The user communicates with the File Manager via specific commands that may be either embedded in the user's program or submitted interactively by the user.

Examples of embedded commands are `OPEN`, `CLOSE`, `READ`, `WRITE`, and `MODIFY`. `OPEN` and `CLOSE` pertain to the availability of a file for the program invoking it. `READ` and `WRITE` are the I/O commands. `MODIFY` is a specialized `WRITE` command for existing data files that allows for appending records or for rewriting selected records in their original place in the file.

Examples of interactive commands are `CREATE`, `DELETE`, `RENAME`, and `COPY`. `CREATE` and `DELETE` deal with the system's knowledge of the file. Actually, files can be created with other system-specific terms: for example, the first time a user gives the command to `SAVE` a file, it's actually created. In other systems the `OPEN NEW` command within a program indicates to the File Manager that a file must be created. Likewise, an `OPEN . . . FOR OUTPUT` command instructs the File Manager to create a file by making an entry for it in the directory and to find space for it in secondary storage. `RENAME` allows users to change the name of an existing file, and `COPY` lets them make duplicate copies of existing files.

These commands and many more, which are the interface between the user and the hardware, were designed to be as simple as possible to use so they're devoid of the detailed instructions required to run the device where the file may be stored. That is, they are **device independent**. Therefore, to access a file, the user doesn't need to know its exact physical location on the disk pack (the cylinder, surface, and sector) or even the medium in which it's stored (tape or disk). And that's fortunate because file access is a complex process. Each logical command is broken down into a sequence of low-level signals that trigger the step-by-step actions performed by the device and supervise the progress of the operation by testing the device's status. For example, when a user's program issues a command to read a record from a movable-head disk, the `READ` instruction has to be decomposed into:

1. Move the read/write heads to the cylinder where the record is to be found.
2. Wait for the rotational delay until the sector containing the desired record passes under the read/write head.
3. Activate the appropriate read/write head and read the record.
4. Transfer the record to main memory.
5. Send a flag to indicate that the device is free to satisfy another request.

While all this is going on the system must check for possible error conditions.

The File Manager frees the user from including in each program the low-level instructions for every device to be used: the terminal, keyboard, printer, disk drive, etc. Without the File Manager every program would need to include instructions to operate all of the different types of devices, and all of the different models within each type. Considering the rapid development and increased sophistication of I/O devices it would be impractical, and certainly not very "user friendly," to require each program to include these minute operational details.

Fortunately, with device independence, users can manipulate their files by using a simple set of commands such as `OPEN`, `CLOSE`, `READ`, `WRITE`, and `MODIFY`.

TYPICAL VOLUME CONFIGURATION

Normally the active files for a computer system reside on secondary storage units. Some devices accommodate removable storage units — such as tapes, floppy disks, and removable disk packs — so files that are not frequently used can be stored offline and mounted only when the user specifically requests them. Other devices feature an integrated storage unit, such as drums, hard disks, and nonremovable disk packs.

Each storage unit, whether it's removable or not, is considered a **volume** and each volume can contain several files so, of course, they're called "multifile volumes." However, some files are extremely large and are contained in several volumes; not surprisingly these are called "multivolume files."

Generally, each volume in the system is given a name, just as files are named. The File Manager writes this name and other descriptive information on an easy-to-access place on each unit, as shown in Figure 8.1: the beginning of the magnetic

FIGURE 8.1 *The volume descriptor, stored at the beginning of each volume, includes the volume name and other vital information about the storage unit.*

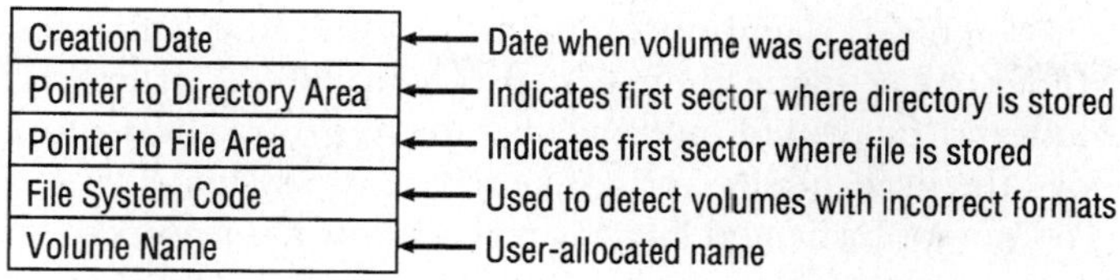

tape or the first sector of the outermost track of the disk pack. Once identified, the operating system can interact with the storage unit.

The **master file directory (MFD)** is stored immediately after the volume descriptor and it lists the names and characteristics of every file contained in that volume. The file names in the MFD can refer to program files, data files, and/or system files. And if the File Manager supports subdirectories, they're listed in the MFD as well. The remainder of the volume is used for file storage.

Early operating systems supported only a single directory per volume. This directory was created by the File Manager and contained the names of files, usually organized in alphabetical, spatial, or chronological order. Although it was simple to implement and maintain, this scheme had some major disadvantages.

1. It would take a long time to search for an individual file, especially if the MFD was organized in an arbitrary order.
2. If the user had many small files stored in the volume, the directory space would fill up before the disk storage space filled up. The user would then be told "disk full" when only the directory was full.
3. Users couldn't create subdirectories to group the files that were related.
4. Multiple users couldn't safeguard their files from "browsers" because the entire directory was listed on request.
5. Each program in the entire directory needed a unique name, even those directories serving many users, so only one person using that directory could have a program named `PROG1`.

For example, imagine the havoc in an introductory computer science class. The first person on the system would, as usual, name the first assignment `PROG1`, and the rest of the class would have an interesting choice: find unique names for their programs; write a new program and name it `PROG1` (which would erase the original version); or simply modify `PROG1` as it was most recently saved. Eventually, the entire class could end up with a single, though perhaps terrific, program.

ABOUT SUBDIRECTORIES

Semi-sophisticated File Managers create an MFD for each volume that can contain entries for both files and for subdirectories. A **subdirectory** is created when a user opens an account to access the computer system. Although this "user directory" is treated as a file, its entry in the MFD is flagged to indicate to the File Manager that this "file" is really a subdirectory and has unique properties — in fact, its records are file names pointing to files.

Although this is an improvement from the single directory scheme (now all of the students can name their first program PROG1), it doesn't solve the problems encountered by prolific users who want to group their files in a logical order to improve the accessibility and efficiency of the system.

Today's sophisticated File Managers allow their users to create their own subdirectories so related files can be grouped together. This is an extension of the previous "two-level" directory structure and it's implemented as an upside-down tree, as shown in Figure 8.2.

FIGURE 8.2 *File directory tree structure. The "root" is the MFD shown at the top, each "node" is a directory file, and each "branch" is a directory entry pointing to either another directory or to a "real" file. All program and data files subsequently added to the tree are the "leaves," represented by circles.*

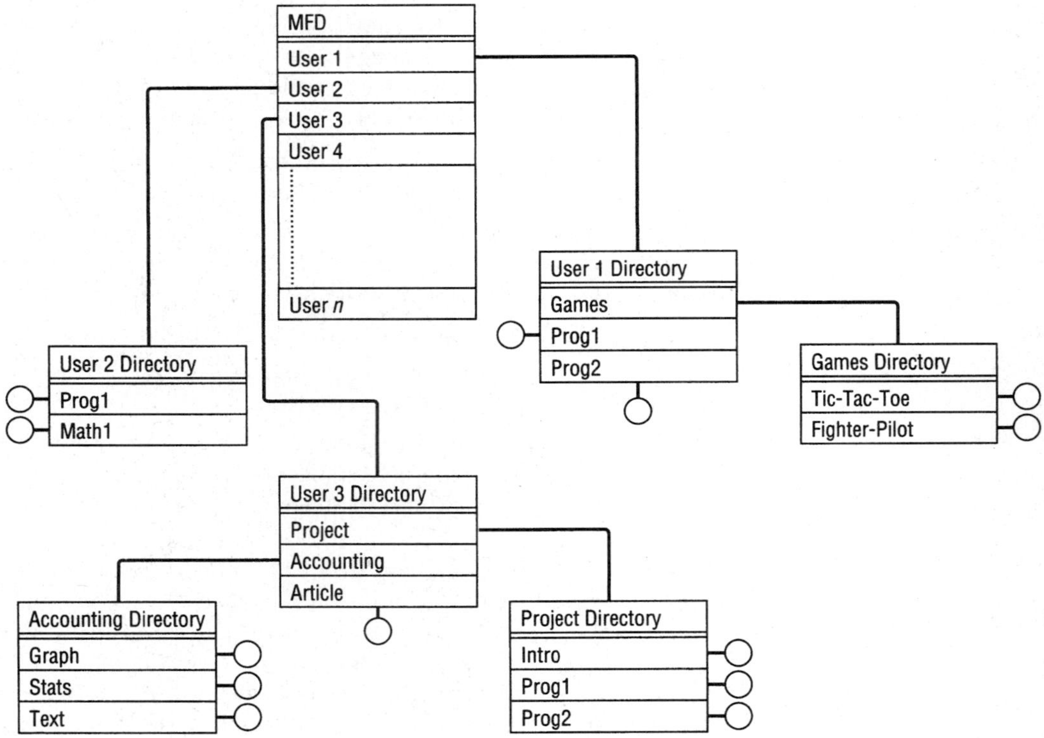

Tree structures allow the system to efficiently search individual directories because there are fewer entries in each directory. However, the path to the requested file may lead through several directories. For every file request the MFD is the point of entry. Actually, the MFD is transparent to the user — it's accessible only by the operating system. When the user wants to access a specific file, the file name is sent to the File Manager. The File Manager first searches the MFD for the user's directory and it then searches the user's directory and any subdirectories for the requested file and its location.

Regardless of the complexity of the directory structure, each file entry in every directory contains information describing the file; it's called the **file descriptor**. Information typically included in a file descriptor includes the following:

- File name — usually represented in ASCII code.
- File type — the organization and usage that are dependent on the system (e.g., files and directories).
- File size — although it could be computed from other information, the size is kept here for convenience.
- File location — identification of the first physical block (or all blocks) where the file is stored.
- Date and time of creation.
- Owner.
- Protection information — access restrictions based on who is allowed to access the file and what type of access is allowed.
- Record size — its fixed size or its maximum size, depending on the type of record.

FILE NAMING CONVENTIONS

The **complete file name** can be much longer than the user thinks it is. Depending on the level of sophistication of the File Manager, it can have from two to many components.

Two components are common to most File Managers: every file has a **relative file name** and often an **extension**. To avoid confusion, in the following discussion we'll refer to the **absolute file name**, the file's long name, as the "complete name" and the short name by which the user identifies the file as its "relative name."

The relative name is the name selected by the user when the file is created, such as `INVENTRY`, `TAXES89`, or `AUTOEXEC`. Generally, it can vary in length from 1 to 12 characters and can include any letters of the alphabet and digits. Every operating system has specific rules that affect the length of the relative name and the characters allowed.

Experienced users try to select descriptive relative names that readily identify the contents or purpose of the file and are easy for users of the system to remember and use correctly. For example, `PROG1` is a poor choice as a file name; it's easily confused with `PROG7` and `PROG11`. `INVENTRY` would be a better name if the file is used to run the inventory control program.

The extension is usually two or three characters long and is separated from the relative name by a period. Its purpose is to identify the type of file or its contents. For example, in a system using MS-DOS a typical relative name with extension would be `INVENTRY.FOR` where `FOR` indicates to the operating system that this file was written in FORTRAN. Similarly, TAXES.COB indicates a COBOL file. AUTOEXEC.BAT is a batch file that's automatically executed by some operating systems when they're booted up. INVENTRY.DAT indicates that this is a file that contains data to be used with INVENTRY.FOR.

Some extensions, such as BAS, BAT, COB, FOR, and EXE, are recognized by the operating system because they constitute its standard set. Some of these extensions serve as a signal to the system to use a specific compiler or program to run these files. Other extensions, such as TXT, DOC, OUT, MIC, and KEY, are created by the users for their own identification. Users are generally advised to consult their operating system manual before naming files so they can select valid and useful extensions to avoid unpleasant surprises later on.

The number of other components required for a file's complete name depend on the operating system. Here's how a file named INVENTRY.FOR would be identified by three different operating systems:

1. Using a personal computer with three disk drives and an MS-DOS operating system, the file's complete name is composed of its relative name and extension preceded by the drive label and directory:

   C:\PARTS\INVENTRY.FOR

   This indicates to the system that the file INVENTRY.FOR requires the FORTRAN compiler and can be found in the directory PARTS in the volume residing on drive C.

2. In a networked VAX environment using a VMS operating system, its complete name could be:

   VAX2::USR3:[IMFST.FLYNN]INVENTRY.FOR;7

   The left-most entry, VAX2, indicates which node in the computer network holds this particular user. The second entry, USR3, indicates the volume or storage device where the file will be retrieved and stored. This is followed by the directory, IMFST, and subdirectory, FLYNN, and then by the relative name and extension, INVENTRY.FOR. The final entry is this file's version number — 7 — which, in this case, indicates that the file had one original version and six revisions.

3. A UNIX system might identify the file as:

   /usr/imfst/flynn/inventry.for

   The first entry, /, represents a special master directory. Next is the name of the first subdirectory, usr/imfst, followed by a sub-subdirectory, /flynn, in this multiple directory system. The final entry is the file's relative name.

As you can see, the names tend to grow in length as the file managers grow in flexibility. But very often, most files can be accessed simply by their short relative names. Why don't users need to type in these extremely long names every time they access a file? Most operating systems provide a two-step solution. First, the File Manager selects a directory for the user when the interactive session begins, so all file operations requested by that user start from this "home" or "base" directory.

Second, from this home directory, the user selects a subdirectory, which is called a **current directory** or **working directory**. Thereafter, the files are presumed to be located in this current directory. Whenever a file is accessed, the user types in the relative name and the File Manager adds the proper prefix. As long as the users reference files in the working directory, they can access their files without entering the complete name from the highest level to the lowest.

The concept of a current directory is based on the underlying hierarchy present in a tree structure as shown in Figure 8.2 and allows programmers to retrieve a file by entering `INVENTRY.FOR` rather than

```
VAX2::USR3:[IMFEST.FLYNN]INVENTRY.FOR;7
```

FILE ORGANIZATION

RECORD FORMAT

All files are composed of records. When a user gives a command to modify the contents of a file it is actually a command to access records within the file. Within each file the records are all presumed to have the same format: they can be of fixed length or of variable length. And these records, regardless of their format, can be blocked or not blocked.

Fixed-length records are the most common because they're the easiest to access directly. That's why they're ideal for data files. The critical aspect of fixed-length records is the size of the record. If it's too small — smaller than the number of characters to be stored in the record — the "left-over" characters are truncated. But if the record size is too large, larger than the number of characters to be stored, storage space is wasted.

Variable-length records don't leave empty storage space and don't truncate any characters, thus eliminating the two disadvantages of fixed-length records. But while they can easily be read, one after the other, they're difficult to access directly because it's hard to calculate exactly where the record is located. That's why they're used most frequently in files that are likely to be accessed sequentially, such as text files and program files, or files that use an index to access their records. The record format, how it's blocked, and other related information is kept in the file descriptor.

The amount of space that's actually used to store the supplementary information varies from system to system and it conforms to the physical limitations of the storage medium, as we'll see later in this chapter.

PHYSICAL FILE ORGANIZATION

The physical organization of a file has to do with the way records are arranged and the characteristics of the medium used to store it.

On magnetic disks, files can be organized in one of three ways: sequential, direct, or indexed sequential. To select the best of these file organizations, the programmer or analyst usually considers these practical characteristics:

- Volatility of the data — the frequency with which additions and deletions are made;
- Activity of the file — the percentage of records processed during a given run;
- Size of the file;
- Response time — the amount of time the user is willing to wait before the requested operation is completed. This is especially crucial when doing searches and retrieving information in an interactive environment.

Sequential record organization is by far the easiest to implement because records are stored and retrieved serially, one after the other. To find a specific record, the file is searched from its beginning until the requested record is found.

To speed the process some optimization features may be built into the system. One is to select a key field from the record and then sort the records by that field before storing them. Later, when a user requests a specific record, the system searches only the key field of each record in the file. The search is ended when either an exact match is found or the key field for the requested record is smaller than the value of the record last compared, in which case the message "record not found" is sent to the user and the search is terminated.

Although this technique aids the search process, it complicates the maintenance algorithms because the original order must be preserved every time records are added or deleted. And to preserve the physical order, the file must be completely rewritten or kept sorted dynamically every time it's updated.

A **direct record organization** uses **direct access files**, which, of course, can be implemented only on direct access storage devices. These files give users the flexibility of accessing any record in any order without having to begin a search from the beginning of the file to do so. It's also known as "random organization," and its files are called "random access files."

Records are identified by their **relative addresses** — their addresses relative to the beginning of the file. These **logical addresses** are computed when the records are stored and then again when the records are retrieved.

The method used is quite straightforward. The user identifies a field (or combination of fields) in the record format and designates it as the **key field** because it uniquely identifies each record. The program used to store the data follows a set of instructions, called a **hashing algorithm**, that transforms each key into a number, the record's logical address. This is given to the information manager, which takes the necessary steps to translate the logical address into a physical address (cylinder, surface, and record numbers) preserving the file organization. The same procedure is used to retrieve a record.

Of course, a direct access file can be accessed sequentially by starting at the first relative address and incrementing it by one to get to the next record.

Direct access files can be updated more quickly than sequential files because records can be quickly rewritten to their original addresses after modifications have been made. And there's no need to preserve the order of the records, so adding or deleting them takes very little time.

Telephone mail order firms use hashing algorithms to directly access their customer information. Let's say you're placing an order and you're asked for your customer number (let's say it's 152132727). The program that retrieves information from the data file uses that key in a hashing algorithm to calculate the logical address where your record is stored, let's say it's 348. So when the order clerk types 152132727 the screen soon shows a list of all current customers whose customer numbers generated the same logical address. If you're in the database the operator knows right away. If not, you will be soon.

The problem with hashing algorithms is that several records with unique keys (such as customer numbers) may generate the same logical address — and then there's a collision. When that happens the program must generate another logical address before presenting it to the File Manager for storage. Records that collide are stored in an overflow area that was set aside when the file was created. Although the program does all the work of linking the records from the overflow area to their corresponding logical address, the File Manager must handle the physical allocation of space.

The maximum size of the file is established when it is created, and eventually either the file may become completely full or the number of records stored in the overflow area may become so large that the efficiency of retrieval is lost. In either case the file must be reorganized and rewritten, which requires intervention by the programmer.

Indexed sequential record organization combines the best of sequential and direct access. It is created and maintained through an Indexed Sequential Access Method (ISAM) software package, which removes the burden of overflow handling and preservation of record order from the shoulders of the programmer.

This type of organization doesn't create collisions because it doesn't use the result of the hashing algorithm to generate a record's address. Instead, it uses this information to generate an index file through which the records are retrieved. This organization divides an ordered sequential file into blocks of equal size. Their size is determined by the File Manager to take advantage of physical storage devices and to optimize retrieval strategies. Each entry in the index file contains the highest record key and the physical location of the data block where this record, and the records with smaller keys, are stored.

Therefore, to access any record in the file, the system begins by searching the index file and then goes to the physical location indicated at that entry. We can say then that the index file acts as a pointer to the data file. An indexed sequential file also has overflow areas but they are spread throughout the file, perhaps every few records, so expansion of existing records can take place and new records can be located in close physical sequence as well as in logical sequence. Another overflow area is located apart from the main data area but is used only when the other overflow areas are completely filled. We call it "the overflow of last resort."

This last-resort overflow area can store records added during the lifetime of the file. The records are kept in logical order by the software package without much effort on the part of the programmer. Of course, when too many records have been added here, the retrieval process slows down because the search for a record has to go from the index to the main data area and eventually to the overflow area.

When retrieval time becomes too slow, the file has to be reorganized. That's a job that, although it's not as tedious as reorganizing direct access files, is usually delegated to programmers or systems analysts.

For most dynamic files, indexed sequential is the organization of choice because it allows both direct access to a few requested records and sequential access to many. A variation of indexed sequential files is the **B-tree**.

PHYSICAL STORAGE ALLOCATION

The File Manager must work with files not just as whole units but also as logical units or records. Records within a file must have the same format but they can vary in length, as shown in Figure 8.3.

FIGURE 8.3 *Every record in a file must have the same format but can be of different sizes, as shown in these five examples of the most common record formats. The supplementary information in* (**b**), (**c**), (**d**), *and* (**e**) *is provided by the File Manager when the record is stored.*

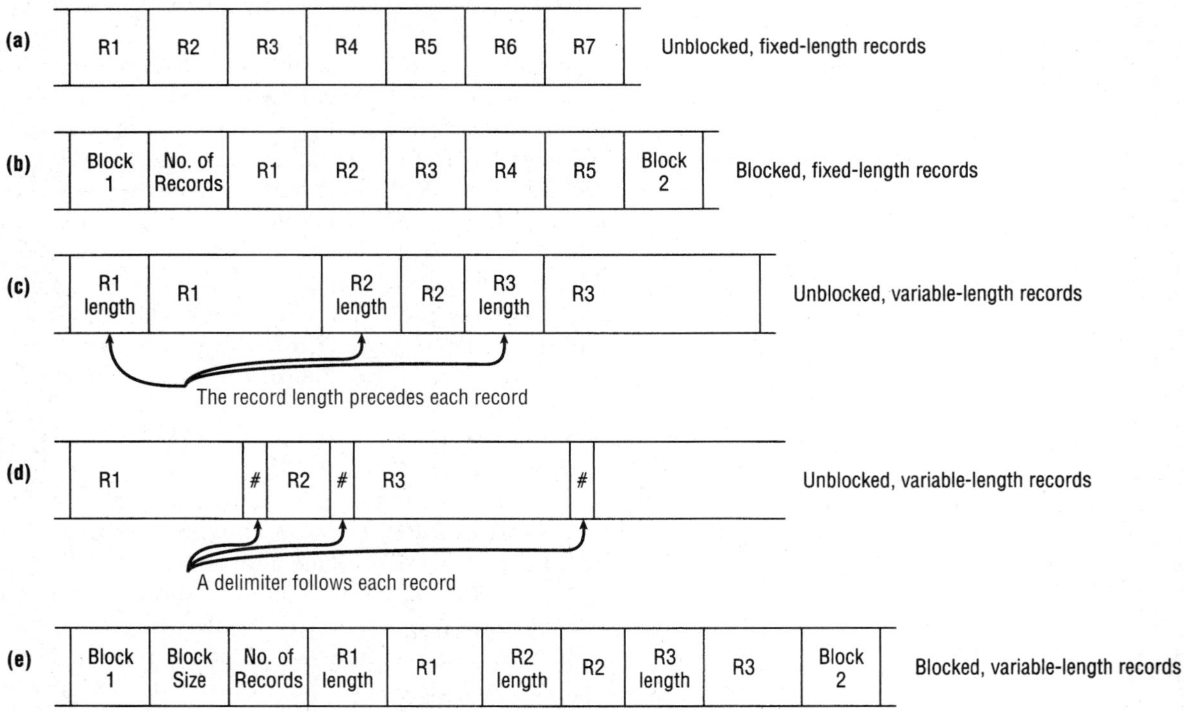

In turn, records are subdivided into fields. In most cases their structure is managed by application programs and not the operating system. An exception is made for those systems that are heavily oriented to database applications, such as PICK, where the File Manager handles field structure (Cook & Brandon, 1984).

So when we talk about file storage, we're actually referring to record storage. How are the records within a file stored? At this stage the File Manager and Device Manager have to cooperate to ensure successful storage and retrieval of records. In Chapter 7, on device management, we introduced the concept of logical versus physical records, and this theme recurs here from the point of view of the File Manager.

CONTIGUOUS STORAGE

When records use **contiguous storage** they're stored one after the other. This was the scheme used in early operating systems. It's very simple to implement and manage. Any record can be found and read once its starting address and size are known, so the directory is very streamlined. Its second advantage is its ease of direct access because every part of the file is stored in the same compact area.

The primary disadvantage is that files cannot be expanded unless there's empty space available immediately following it, as shown in Figure 8.4. Therefore, room for expansion must be provided when the file is created. If there's not enough room, the entire file must be recopied to a larger section of the disk every time records are added. The second disadvantage is fragmentation (slivers of unused storage space), which can be overcome by compacting and rearranging files. And, of course, the files can't be accessed while compaction is taking place.

FIGURE 8.4 *Using this example of contiguous file storage, File 1 can't be expanded without being rewritten to a larger storage area. File 2 can be expanded by only one record replacing the free space preceding File 3.*

Free Space	File 1 Record 1	File 1 Record 2	File 1 Record 3	File 1 Record 4	File 1 Record 5	File 1 Record 6	File 2 Record 1	File 2 Record 2	File 2 Record 3	File 2 Record 4	Free Space	File 3 Record 1	. . .

The File Manager keeps track of the empty storage areas by treating them as files — they're entered in the directory but are flagged to differentiate them from "real" files. Usually the directory is kept in order by sector number so adjacent empty areas can be combined into one large free space.

NONCONTIGUOUS STORAGE

Noncontiguous storage allocation allows files to use any storage space available on the disk. A file's records are stored in a contiguous manner if there's enough empty space. Any remaining records, and all other additions to the file, are stored in other sections of the disk. In some systems these are called the **extents** of the file and are linked together with pointers. The physical size of each extent is determined by the operating system and is usually 256 — or another power of two — bytes.

File extents are usually linked in one of two ways. Linking can take place at the storage level where each extent points to the next one in the sequence, as shown in Figure 8.5. The directory entry consists of the file name, the storage location of the first extent, the location of the last extent, and the total number of extents, not counting the first.

FIGURE 8.5 *Noncontiguous file storage with linking taking place at the storage level. File 1 starts in address 2 and continues in addresses 8, 20, and 18. The directory lists the file's starting address and ending address, and the number of extents it uses. Each block of storage includes its address and a pointer to the next block for the file, as well as the data itself.*

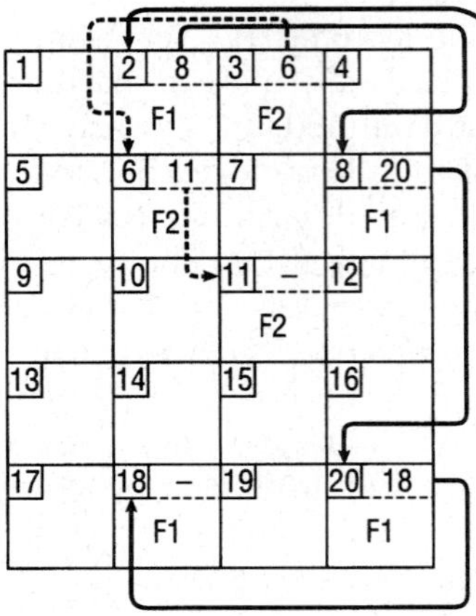

Directory

File No.	Start	End	No. extents
1	(2)	18	3
2	3	11	2

The alternative is for the linking to take place at the directory level, as shown in Figure 8.6. Each extent is listed with its physical address, its size, and a pointer to the next extent. A null pointer (–) indicates it's the last one.

Although both noncontiguous allocation schemes eliminate external storage fragmentation and the need for compaction, they don't support direct access because there's no easy way to determine the exact location of a specific record.

Files are usually declared to be either sequential or direct when they're created so the File Manager can select the most efficient method of storage allocation: contiguous for direct files and noncontiguous for sequential. Operating systems must have the capability to support both storage allocation schemes.

Files can then be converted from one type to another by creating a file of the desired type and copying the contents of the old file into the new using a program designed for that specific purpose.

INDEXED STORAGE

Indexed storage allocation allows direct record access by bringing together into an index block the pointers linking every extent of that file. Every file has its own index block, which consists of the addresses of each disk sector that make up the file. The index lists each entry in the same order in which the sectors are linked, as shown in Figure 8.7. For example, the third entry in the index block corresponds to the third sector making up the file (Calingaert, 1982).

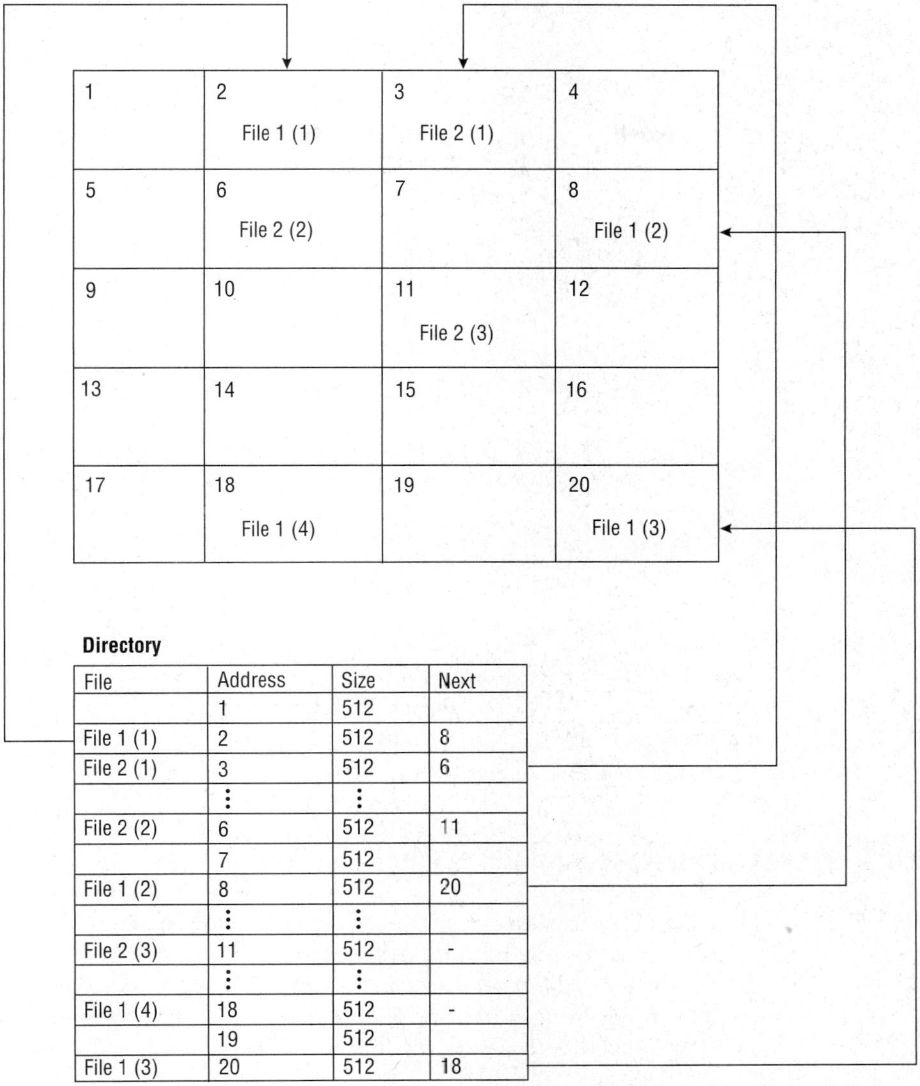

File	Address	Size	Next
	1	512	
File 1 (1)	2	512	8
File 2 (1)	3	512	6
	⋮	⋮	
File 2 (2)	6	512	11
	7	512	
File 1 (2)	8	512	20
	⋮	⋮	
File 2 (3)	11	512	-
	⋮	⋮	
File 1 (4)	18	512	-
	19	512	
File 1 (3)	20	512	18

FIGURE 8.6 *Noncontiguous storage allocation with linking taking place at the directory level for the files shown in Figure 8.5.*

When a file is created, the pointers in the index block are all set to null. Then, as each sector is filled, the pointer is set to the appropriate sector address — to be precise, the address is removed from the empty space list and copied into its position in the index block.

This scheme supports both sequential and direct access but it doesn't necessarily improve the use of storage space because each file must have an index block — usually the size of one disk sector. For larger files with more entries, several levels of indexes can be generated, in which case, to find a desired record, the File Manager accesses the first index (the highest level), which points to a second index (lower level), which points to an even lower level index and eventually to the data record.

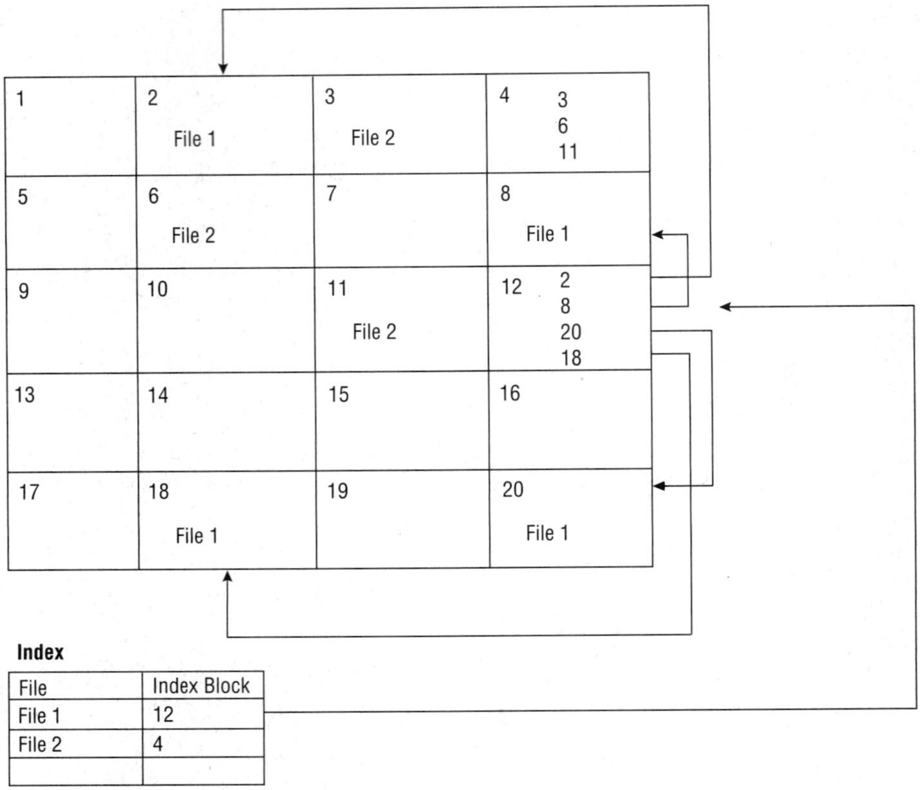

FIGURE 8.7 *Indexed storage allocation with a one-level index allowing direct access to each record for the files shown in Figures 8.5 and 8.6.*

DATA COMPRESSION

Data compression is a technique used to save space in files. Here are three methods for compressing data in databases.

Records with repeated characters can be abbreviated. For example, data in a fixed-length field might include a short name followed by many blank characters; it can be replaced with a variable-length field and a special code to indicate how many blanks were truncated.

Let's say the original string, ADAMS, looks like this when it's stored in a field that's 15 characters wide (*b* stands for a blank character):

ADAMS*bbbbbbbbbb*

When it's encoded it looks like this:

ADAMS*b*10

Numbers with many zeros can be shortened too with a code to indicate how many zeros must be added to recreate the original number. For instance, if the original entry is a number:

300000000

the encoded entry is this:

3#8

Repeated terms can also be compressed. One method is to use symbols to represent each of the most commonly used words in the database. For example, in a university's student database common words like "student," "course," "teacher," "classroom," "grade," and "department" could each be represented with a single character. Of course, the system must be able to distinguish between compressed and uncompressed data.

Front-end compression is a third type that is used in database management systems for index compression. For example, the student database where the students' names are kept in alphabetical order could be compressed as shown in Table 8.1.

TABLE 8.1 *With this compression scheme each piece of data builds on the previous piece of data. Each entry takes a given number of characters from the previous entry that they have in common and adds the characters that make it unique. So "Smithbren, Ali" uses the first six characters from "*Smith*berger, John" and adds "*ren, Ali.*" Therefore, the entry is* 6ren, Ali.

Original list	Compressed list
Smith, Betty	Smith, Betty
Smith, Gino	7Gino
Smith, Donald	7Donald
Smithberger, John	5berger, John
Smithbren, Ali	6ren, Ali
Smithco, Rachel	5co, Rachel
Smither, Kevin	5er, Kevin
Smithers, Renny	7s, Renny
Snyder, Katherine	1nyder, Katherine

There is a trade-off: storage space is gained but processing time is lost. Remember, for all data compression schemes the system must be able to distinguish between compressed and uncompressed data.

ACCESS METHODS

Access methods are dictated by a file's organization; the most flexibility is allowed with indexed sequential files and the least with sequential.

A file that has been organized in sequential fashion can support only sequential access to its records, and these records can be of either fixed or variable length, as shown in Figure 8.3. The File Manager uses the address of the last byte read to access the next sequential record. Therefore, the **current byte address (CBA)** must be updated every time a record is accessed, such as when the `READ` command is executed (Madnick & Donovan, 1974).

Figure 8.8 shows the difference between storage of fixed-length and of variable-length records.

FIGURE 8.8 *Fixed versus variable-length records.* (**a**) *Fixed length records have the same number of bytes so record length (RL) is a constant.* (**b**) *With variable length records RL_k is not a constant. Therefore, it is recorded on the tape immediately preceding each record.*

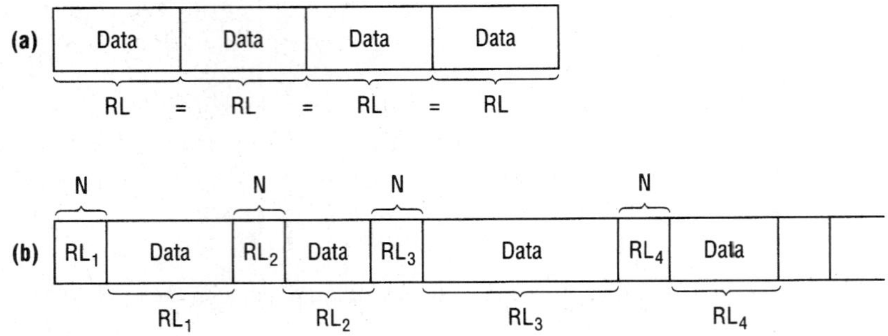

SEQUENTIAL ACCESS

For *sequential access of fixed-length records* the CBA is updated simply by incrementing it by the record length (RL), which is a constant:

$$CBA = CBA + RL$$

For *sequential access of variable-length records* the File Manager adds the length of the record (RL_k) plus the number of bytes used to hold the record length (N) to the CBA.

$$CBA = CBA + N + RL_k$$

DIRECT ACCESS

We've only looked at sequential access thus far. If a file is organized in direct fashion, it can be accessed easily in either direct or sequential order if the records are of fixed length. In the case of *direct access with fixed length records*, the CBA can be computed directly from the record length and the desired record number RN (information provided through the READ command) minus one:

```
CBA=(RN-1) * RL
```

For example, if we're looking for the beginning of the eleventh record and the fixed record length is 25 bytes, the CBA would be:

$$(11 - 1) * 25 = 250$$

However, if the file is organized for *direct access with variable-length records*, it's virtually impossible to access a record directly because the address of the desired record cannot be easily computed. Therefore, to access a record the File Manager must do a sequential search through the records. In fact, it becomes a half-sequential read through the file because the File Manager could save the address of the last record accessed and when the next request arrives it could search forward from the CBA — if the address of the desired record was between the CBA and the end of the file. Otherwise the search would start from the beginning of the file. It could be said that this semi-sequential search is only semi-adequate.

An alternative is for the File Manager to keep a table of record numbers and their CBAs. Then, to fill a request, this table is searched for the exact storage location of the desired record so the direct access reduces to a table lookup.

To avoid dealing with this problem, many systems force users to have their files organized for fixed-length records if the records are to be accessed directly.

Records in an *indexed sequential file* can be accessed either sequentially or directly, so either of the procedures to compute the CBA presented in this section would apply but with one extra step: the index file must be searched for the pointer to the block where the data is stored. Because the index file is smaller than the data file, it can be kept in main memory and a quick search can be performed to locate the block where the desired record is located. Then the block can be retrieved from secondary storage and the beginning byte address of the record can be calculated. In systems that support several levels of indexing to improve access to very large files, the index at each level must be searched before the computation of the CBA can be done. The entry point to this type of data file is usually through the index file.

As we've shown, a file's organization and the methods used to access its records are very closely intertwined, so when one talks about a specific type of organization one is almost certainly implying a specific type of access.

LEVELS IN A FILE MANAGEMENT SYSTEM

The efficient management of files cannot be separated from the efficient management of the devices that house them. This chapter and the previous one, on device management, have presented the wide range of functions that have to be organized for an I/O system to perform efficiently. In this section we'll outline one of the many hierarchies used to perform those functions.

The highest level module is called the "basic file system," and it passes information to the "logical file system," which, in turn, notifies the "physical file system," which works with the Device Manager. Figure 8.9 shows the hierarchy (Madnick & Donovan, 1974).

Each level of the file management system is implemented by using structured and modular programming techniques, which also set up a hierarchy — that is, the higher positioned modules pass information to the lower modules so that they, in turn, can perform the required service and continue the communication down the chain to the lowest module, which communicates with the physical device and interacts with the Device Manager. Only then is the record made available to the user's program.

Each of the modules can be further subdivided into more specific tasks, as we can see when we follow this I/O instruction through the file management system:

```
READ RECORD NUMBER 7 FROM FILE CLASSES INTO STUDENT
```

`CLASSES` is the name of a direct access file previously opened for input and `STUDENT` is a data record previously defined within the program and occupying specific memory locations.

Because the file has already been opened, the file directory has already been searched to verify the existence of `CLASSES` and pertinent information about the file has been brought into the operating system's active file table. This information includes its record size, the address of its first physical record, its protection, and access control information.

FIGURE 8.9
Typical modules of a file management system showing how information is passed from the File Manager at the top of the hierarchy to the Device Manager at the bottom.

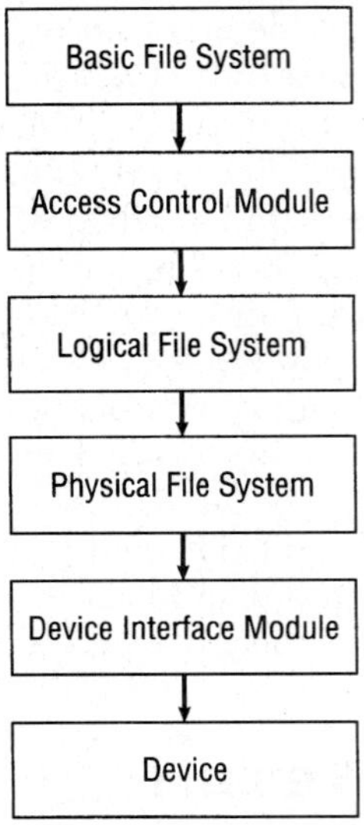

This information is used by the basic file system, which activates the **access control verification module** to verify that this user is permitted to perform this operation with this file. If access is allowed, information and control are passed along to the logical file system. If not, a message saying "access denied" is sent to the user.

Using the information passed down by the basic file system, the logical file system transforms the record number to its byte address using the familiar formula:

$$CBA = (RN-1) * RL$$

This result, together with the address of the first physical record and, in the case where records are blocked, the physical block size, is passed down to the physical file system, which computes the location where the desired record physically resides. If there's more than one record in that block, it computes the record's offset within that block using these formulas:

$$\text{block number} = \text{integer}\left[\frac{\text{byte address}}{\text{physical block size}}\right] + \begin{array}{l}\text{address of the first}\\ \text{physical record}\end{array}$$

$$\text{offset} = \text{remainder}\left[\frac{\text{byte address}}{\text{physical block size}}\right]$$

This information is passed on to the **device interface module**, which, in turn, transforms the block number to the actual cylinder/surface/record combination needed to retrieve the information from the secondary storage device. Once retrieved, here's where the device scheduling algorithms come into play as the information is placed in a buffer and control returns to the physical file system, which copies the information into the desired memory location. Finally, when the operation is complete, the "all clear" message is passed on to all other modules.

Although we used a READ command for our example, a WRITE command is handled in exactly the same way until the process reaches the device handler. At that point the portion of the device interface module that handles allocation of free space, the **allocation module**, is called into play because it is responsible for keeping track of unused areas in each storage device.

We need to note here that verification, the process of making sure that a request is valid, occurs at every level of the file management system. The first occurs at the directory level when the file system checks to see if the requested file exists. The second occurs when the access control verification module determines whether access is allowed. The third occurs when the logical file system checks to see if the requested byte address is within the file's limits. Finally, the device interface module checks to see whether the storage device exists.

Therefore, the correct operation of a simple user command requires the coordinated effort of every part of the file management system.

ACCESS CONTROL VERIFICATION MODULE

The first operating systems couldn't support file sharing among users. For instance, early systems needed ten copies of the FORTRAN compiler to serve ten FORTRAN users. Today's systems require only a single copy to serve everyone regardless of the number of active FORTRAN programs in the system. In fact, any file can be shared — from data files and user-owned program files to system files. The advantages of file sharing are numerous. In addition to saving space, it allows for synchronization of data updates, as when two applications are updating the same data file. It also improves the efficiency of the system's resources, because if files are shared in main memory then there's a reduction of I/O operations.

However, as often happens, progress brings problems. The disadvantage of file sharing is that the integrity of each file must be safeguarded; that calls for control over who is allowed to access the file and what type of access is permitted. There are five possible actions that can be performed on a file — the ability to READ only, WRITE only, EXECUTE only, DELETE only, or some combination of the four. Each file management system has its own method to control file access. The four most commonly used are the access control matrix, access control lists, capability lists, and lockword control.

ACCESS CONTROL MATRIX

The **access control matrix** is intuitively appealing and easy to implement, but it works well only for systems with a few files and a few users. In the matrix each column identifies a user and each row identifies a file. The intersection of the row and column contains the access rights for that user to that file, as Table 8.2 illustrates.

TABLE 8.2
The access control matrix showing access rights for each user for each file. User 1 is allowed unlimited access to File 1 but is allowed only to read and execute File 4 and is denied access to the three other files.

	User 1	User 2	User 3	User 4	User 5
File 1	RWED	R-E-	----	RWE-	--E-
File 2	----	R-E-	R-E-	--E-	----
File 3	----	RWED	----	--E-	----
File 4	R-E-	----	----	----	RWED
File 5	----	----	----	----	RWED

R = Read Access
W = Write Access
E = Execute Access
D = Delete Access
- = Access Not Allowed

(In the actual implementation, the letters RWED are represented by bits one and zero: a one indicates that access is allowed, and a zero indicates access is denied. Therefore, the code for User 4 for File 1 would read "1110" and not "RWE-.")

As you can see, it is a simple method, but as the numbers of files and users increase, the matrix becomes extremely large — sometimes too large to store in main memory. Another disadvantage is that a lot of space is wasted because many of the entries are all null, such as in Table 8.2, where User 3 isn't allowed into most of the files and File 5 is restricted to all but one user. A scheme that conserved space would have only one entry for User 3 or one for File 5, but that's incompatible with the matrix format.

ACCESS CONTROL LISTS

The **access control list** is a modification of the access control matrix and was used in the MULTICS operating system (Madnick & Donovan, 1974). Each file is entered in the list and contains the names of the users who are allowed to access it and the type of access each is permitted. To shorten the list, only those who may use the file are named; those denied any access are grouped under a global heading such as "WORLD," as shown in Table 8.3.

Some systems shorten the access control list even more by putting every user into a category: system, owner, group, and world. SYSTEM is designated for system personnel who have unlimited access to all files in the system. The OWNER has absolute control over all files created in the owner's account. An owner may create a GROUP file so that all users belonging to the appropriate group have access to it. WORLD is composed of all other users in the system, that is, those who don't fall into

TABLE 8.3 *An access control list showing which users are allowed to access each file. This method requires less storage space than does an access control matrix and explicitly names each user allowed access to each file. WORLD indicates that access is allowed to all users.*

File	Access
File 1	USER1 (RWED), USER2 (R-E-), USER4 (RWE-), USER5 (--E-), WORLD (----)
File 2	USER2(R-E-), USER3 (R-E-), USER4 (--E-), WORLD (----)
File 3	USER2(RWED), USER4 (--E-), WORLD (----)
File 4	USER1(R-E-), USER5(RWED), WORLD(----)
File 5	USER5(RWED), WORLD (----)

any of the other three categories. In this system the File Manager designates default types of access to all files at creation time and it is the owner's responsibility to change them as needed.

CAPABILITY LISTS

A **capability list** shows the access control information from a different perspective. It lists every user and the files to which each has access, as shown in Table 8.4.

TABLE 8.4 *A capability list that shows files for each user requires less storage space than an access control matrix and is easier to maintain than an access control list when users are added or deleted from the system.*

User	Access
User1	File1 (RWED), File4 (R-E-)
User2	File1 (R-E-), File2 (R-E-), File3 (RWED)
User3	File2 (R-E-)
User4	File1 (RWE-), File2 (--E-), File3 (--E-)
User5	File1 (--E-), File4 (RWED), File5 (RWED)

Of the three schemes described so far, the most commonly used is the access control list. However, capability lists, a more recent development, are gaining in popularity because they can control access to devices as well as to files.

Although both methods seem to be the same, there are some subtle differences best explained with an analogy. A capability list may be equated to a concert ticket, which allows the holder access to a seat in a specific part of the concert hall — orchestra, mezzanine, or rafters. On the other hand, an access control list can be equated to the reservation list in a restaurant; only those whose names appear on the list are allowed to be seated at a particular table (Bic & Shaw, 1988).

LOCKWORDS

The use of lockwords, or control words, to protect files is a very different method of access control. A **lockword** is similar to a password but protects a single file while a password protects access to a system. When the file is created, the owner can protect it by giving it a lockword, which is stored in the directory but isn't revealed when a listing of the directory is requested. Once it's protected, a user must provide the correct lockword to access the protected file.

The advantage of using lockwords is that they require the smallest amount of storage for file protection. But there are two disadvantages: lockwords can be guessed by hackers or passed on to unauthorized users. The second disadvantage is that a lockword generally doesn't control the type of access to the file: anyone who knows the lockword can read, write, execute, or delete the file — even if that wasn't the original intention of the owner.

CHAPTER EIGHT CONCLUSION

The File Manager controls every file in the system and processes the user's commands to interact (read, write, modify, create, delete, etc.) with any file on the system. It also manages the access control procedures to maintain the integrity and security of the files under its control.

To achieve its goals, the file management system must be able to accommodate a variety of file organizations, physical storage allocation schemes, record types, and access methods. And, as we've seen, this requires increasingly complex file management software.

In this chapter we discussed:

- Sequential, direct, and indexed sequential file organization;
- Contiguous, noncontiguous, and indexed file storage allocation;
- Fixed- versus variable-length records;
- Four methods of access control.

To get the most from a File Manager, it's important for users to realize the strengths and weaknesses of its segments — which access methods are allowed on which devices and with which record structures — and the advantages and disadvantages of each in overall efficiency.

Before exploring network operating systems in Chapter 10, in Chapter 9 we'll identify the hardware and software components and the common topologies of networked systems.

KEY TERMS

file
database
data file
directory
device independent
volume
master file directory (MFD)
subdirectory
file descriptor
complete file name
relative file name
extension
current directory
working directory
fixed-length record
variable-length record

sequential record organization
direct record organization
direct access files
relative address
logical address
key field
hashing algorithm
indexed sequential record organization
extents
data compression
current byte address (CBA)
access control matrix
access control list
capability list
lockword

EXERCISES

1. Explain what is meant by device independence.
2. Design a file lookup algorithm for each of the following cases:
   a. Files are listed in a unique directory.
   b. Files are listed in a two-level directory.
   c. Files are listed in a hierarchical directory.

   Provide for a path to be taken if the file is *not* found.
3. Three types of file organizations were presented in this chapter: sequential, direct, and indexed sequential. For each of the applications listed below, select the organization best suited to it and explain why you selected it.
   a. A data file containing employee payroll records.
   b. The circulation file in a library.
   c. A data file containing student transcript records.
   d. A bank's data file containing customers' checking account records.
   e. An inventory file in a local supermarket.
4. List the minimum information required in a directory to locate any one record in a file for each of the following cases:
   a. The file is stored in a simple contiguous form.
   b. The file is stored in a noncontiguous form with extents.
   c. The file is stored using the index method.
5. Some operating systems will automatically open and close files for users so that `OPEN` and `CLOSE` commands are unnecessary. List some problems generated by this procedure.
6. Many operating systems use the file command `RENAME` to allow users to give a new name to an existing file. Suppose this command wasn't available and files could be renamed only by using a combination of other file commands such as `LIST`, `TYPE`, `COPY`, `DELETE`, `SAVE`, and `CREATE`. Design a combination of commands that would perform the same function as `RENAME` and explain why you selected it.
7. Explain why it's difficult to support direct access to files with variable-length

records. Suggest a method for handling this type of file if direct access is required.

8. As was done in the section on access control in this chapter, list the steps required to satisfy the following requests:
   a. `READ RECORD NUMBER 10 FROM FILE INVENTORY INTO ITEM`
   b. `WRITE RECORD NUMBER 6 TO FILE ACCOUNT`

ADVANCED EXERCISES

9. If you were designing the file access control for a highly secure environment and were given a choice between the establishment of many access categories and just a few access categories, which would you select and why?
10. Compare and contrast dynamic memory allocation and the allocation of files in secondary storage.
11. When is compaction of secondary storage beneficial from the file manager's perspective? Give several examples. List some problems that could be presented as a result of compaction and explain how they might be avoided.
12. While sophisticated file managers implement file sharing by allowing several users to access a single copy of a file at the same time, others implement file sharing by providing a copy of the file to each user. List the advantages and disadvantages of each method.
13. Indexed sequential files are widely used in business applications because of their versatility. However, as records are added to the file and blocks are filled to capacity they have to be stored in an overflow area.
    a. How does this affect performance?
    b. What can be done to improve performance?

Chapter Nine

NETWORK ORGANIZATION CONCEPTS

FOUR MANAGERS

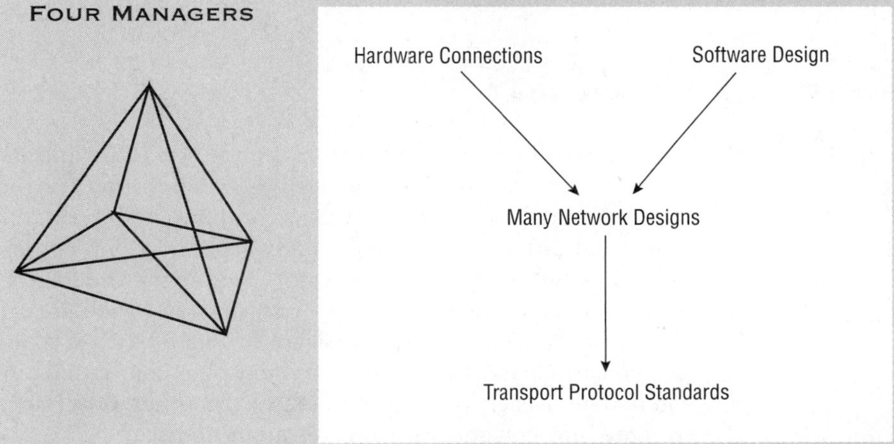

More and more stand-alone computers, typically uniprocessors, are linked through communication systems to form networks that can transmit and process all types of data and information among every user in the system. This chapter introduces the terminology and basic concepts of networks.

A common goal of networked systems is to provide a convenient way to share resources while controlling users' access to them. These resources include both hardware (such as CPU, memory, printers, tape, and disk drives) and software (such as programs and data files).

There are two basic kinds of operating system configurations for networks. In the first, the operating system for the network is built on top of existing local computer operating systems and is referred to as a **network operating system**. With this configuration users are conscious of the specific assortment of computers in the network and can access the resources by either logging on to an appropriate remote host or transferring data from the remote computer to their own.

With the second configuration, users do not need to be aware of every machine connected to the system; they can access remote resources as if they were local resources. This **distributed operating system** provides good control for distributed computing systems and allows their resources to be accessed in a unified way. A distributed operating system represents a total view across multiple computer systems for controlling and managing resources without local dependencies. Management is a cooperative process that encompasses every resource and involves every site.

A distributed operating system is comprised of the same four managers previously discussed but with a wider scope. At a minimum, it must provide the following components: process or object management, memory management, I/O management, device management, and network management. A distributed operating system offers several important advantages over traditional operating system environments including easy and reliable resource sharing, improved computation performance, adequate load balancing, good reliability, and dependable electronic communications among the network's users.

BASIC TERMINOLOGY

The merger between the fields of computer science and data communications that began in the late 1970s effectively eliminated the previously existing differences between data processing and data communication. In addition, it minimized fundamental differences among data, voice, and video communications, and blurred the lines between single processor computers and multiprocessor computers, as well as those between local area networks and wide area networks.

In general, a network is a collection of loosely coupled processors (as described in Chapter 6) interconnected by a communication network. In a distributed system each processor classifies the other processors and their resources as **remote** and considers its own resources **local**.

The size, type, and identification of processors varies. Processors are referred to as: **sites**, **hosts**, and **nodes** depending on the context in which they are mentioned. Usually, "site" indicates a specific location in a network containing one or more computer systems, "host" indicates a specific computer system found at a site whose services and resources can be used from remote locations, and "node" (or, more formally, "node name") refers to the name assigned to a computer system connected to a network to identify it to other computers in the network.

Typically, a host at one site, called the **server**, has resources that a host at another site, called the **client**, wants to use. Hosts can alternate between being clients or servers depending on their requirements.

NETWORK TOPOLOGIES

Sites in any networked system can be physically or logically connected to one another in a variety of topologies. The most common geometric arrangements are star, ring, bus, tree, and hybrid. In each topology there are tradeoffs between the need for fast communication among all sites, the tolerance of failure at a site or communication link, the cost of long communication lines, and the difficulty of connecting one site to a large number of other sites. Therefore, when deciding which configuration to use, system designers should keep in mind three criteria:

- Basic cost — the expense required to link the various sites in the system;
- Communications cost — the time required to send a message from one site to another;
- Reliability — the assurance that many sites can still communicate with each other even if a link or site in the system fails.

STAR

A **star topology**, sometimes called a "hub" or "centralized topology," is a traditional approach to interconnecting devices in which all transmitted data must pass through a central controller when going from a sender to a receiver, as shown in Figure 9.1. It permits easy routing because the central station knows the path to all other sites and, because there is a central control point, access to the network can be controlled easily and priority status can be given to selected sites. However, this centralization of control requires that the central site be extremely reliable and able to handle all network traffic, no matter how heavy.

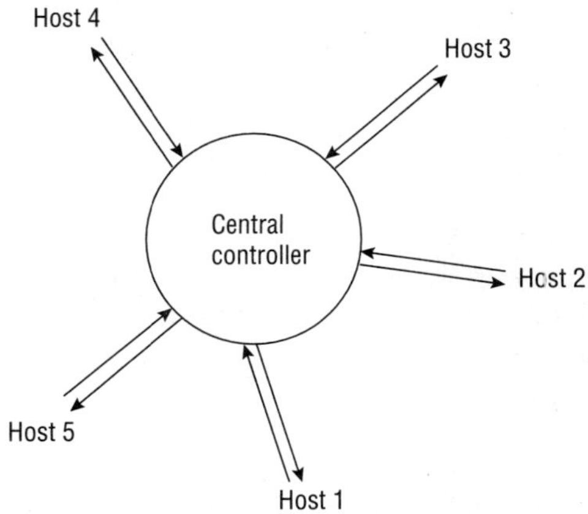

FIGURE 9.1 *Star topology. All sites are connected to one central controller, which assumes all responsibility for routing messages to the appropriate hosts.*

RING

In the **ring topology** all sites are connected in a closed loop, as shown in Figure 9.2, with the first site connected to the last. Data is transmitted in packets that also contain source and destination address fields. Each packet is passed from node to node in one direction only, and the destination station copies the data into a local buffer. Typically, the packet continues to circulate until it returns to the source station, where it is removed from the ring. There are some variations to this basic topology, such as the double loop network, shown in Figure 9.3, and a set of multirings bridged together, as shown in Figure 9.4. Both variations provide more flexibility, but at a cost.

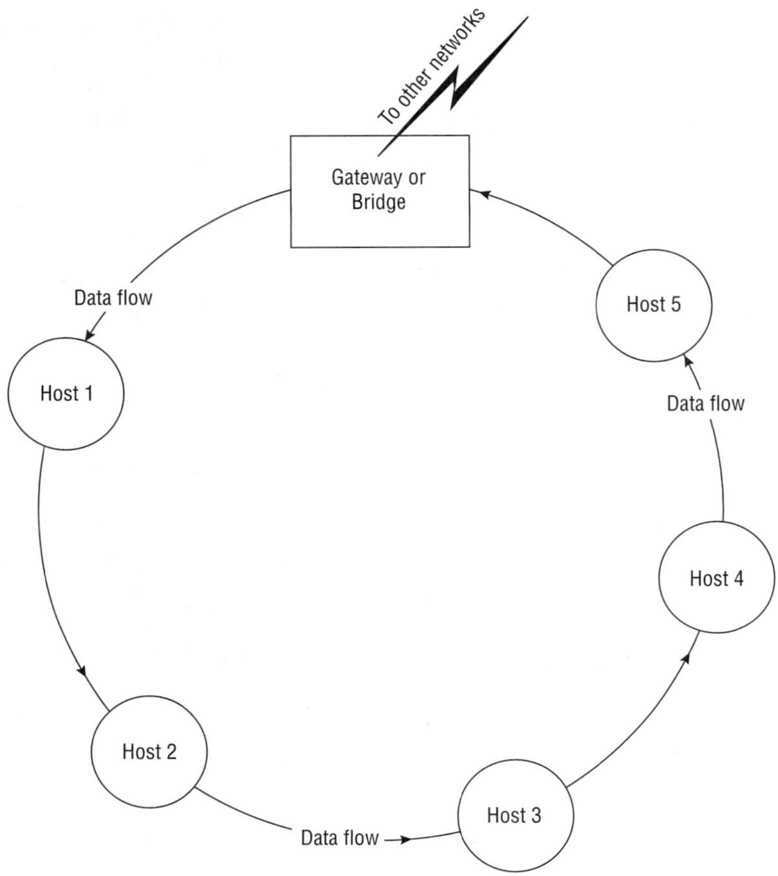

FIGURE 9.2
Ring topology. Each data packet is passed from one node to the next in one direction only.

Although ring topologies share the disadvantage that every node must be functional for the network to perform properly, rings can be designed that allow failed nodes to be bypassed.

BUS

In the **bus topology** all sites are connected to a single communication line running the length of the network, as shown in Figure 9.5. The topology physically connects the devices by means of cables that run between them, but the cables do not pass through a centralized controller mechanism; messages from any site circulate in both directions through the entire communication line and can be received by all other sites. Because all sites share a common communication line, only one of them can successfully send messages at any one time; therefore, a control mechanism is needed to prevent collisions. In this environment data may pass directly from one device to another, or it may be routed to an end point controller at the end of the line. This controller turns the messages around and sends them back down the cable in the opposite direction. With some bus networks each message must always go to the "end of the line" and then back down the communication

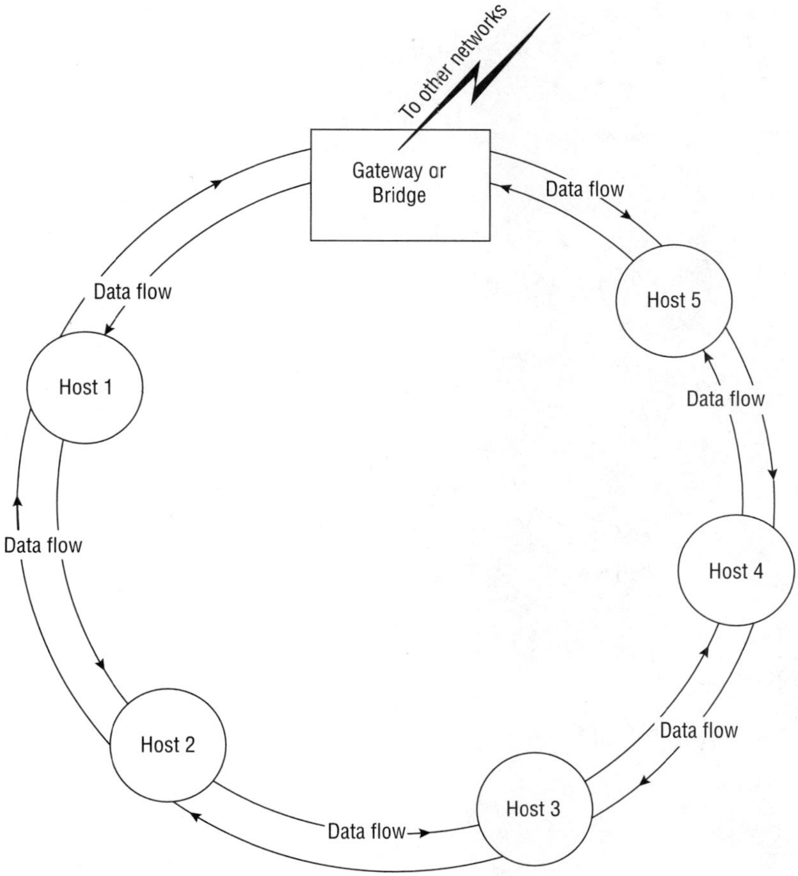

FIGURE 9.3
Double loop computer network using a ring topology. Data packets are passed in both directions.

line to whichever node it is addressed. However, other bus networks allow messages to be sent directly to the target node.

TREE

The **tree topology** is a collection of busses. The communication line is a branching cable with no closed loops, as shown in Figure 9.6. The tree layout begins at the "head end," where one or more cables start. Each cable may have branches that may, in turn, have additional branches, potentially resulting in quite complex arrangements. Using bridges as special fitters between busses of the same protocol and as translators to those with different protocols allows designers to create networks that can operate at speeds more responsive to the hosts in the network. In a tree configuration a message from any site circulates through the communication line, can be received by all other sites, and is absorbed at the end points. One advantage of bus and tree topologies is that even if a single node fails, message traffic can still flow through the network.

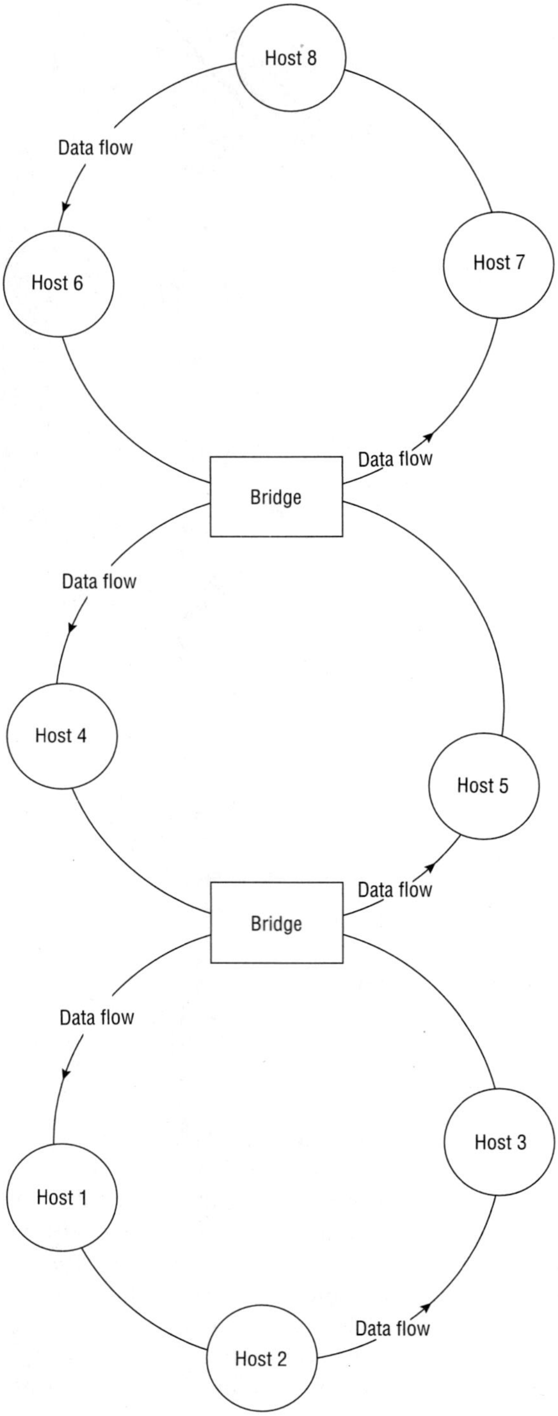

FIGURE 9.4 *Multirings bridged together. This variation of the ring topology allows several networks to be linked together.*

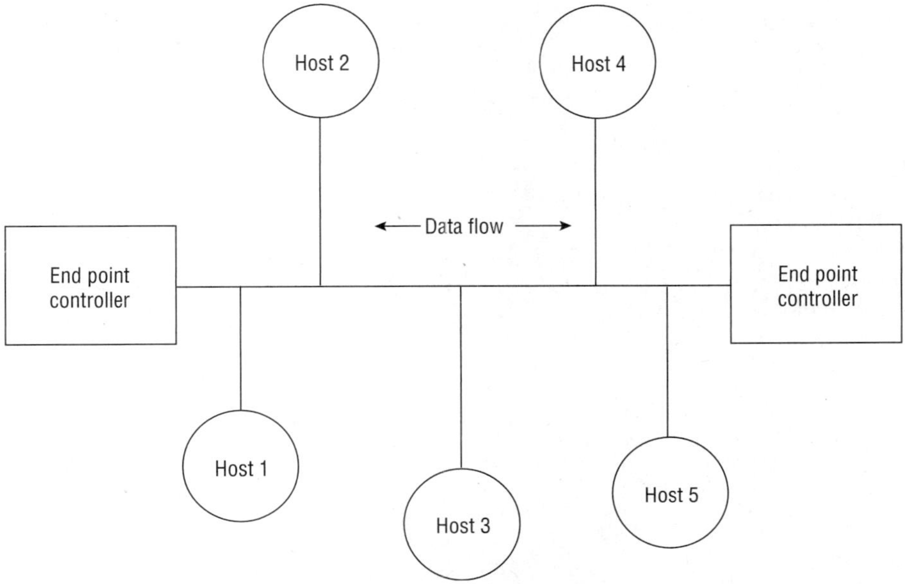

FIGURE 9.5
Bus topology. Data flows in both directions and is "turned around" when it reaches an end point controller.

HYBRID

A **hybrid topology** is some combination of any of the four topologies discussed here. For example, a hybrid can be made by replacing a single host in a star configuration with a ring, as shown in Figure 9.7. Or a star configuration could have a bus topology as one of the communication lines feeding its hub, as shown in Figure 9.8.

The objective of a hybrid configuration is to select among the strong points of each topology and combine them to meet that system's communications requirements most effectively.

NETWORK TYPES

It is often useful to group networks according to the physical distances they cover. Although the characteristics that define each group are becoming increasingly blurred as communications technology advances, networks are generally divided into local area networks, metropolitan area networks, and wide area networks.

LOCAL AREA NETWORK

A **local area network (LAN)** defines a configuration found within a single office building, warehouse, campus, or similarly enclosed computing environment. Such a network is generally owned, used, and operated by a single organization and allows computers to communicate directly through a common communication line. Typically, it is a cluster of personal computers or workstations located in the

FIGURE 9.6
Tree topology. Data flows up and down the branches of the trees and is absorbed by the controllers at the end points. Bridges help minimize differences between the various protocols used on the branches.

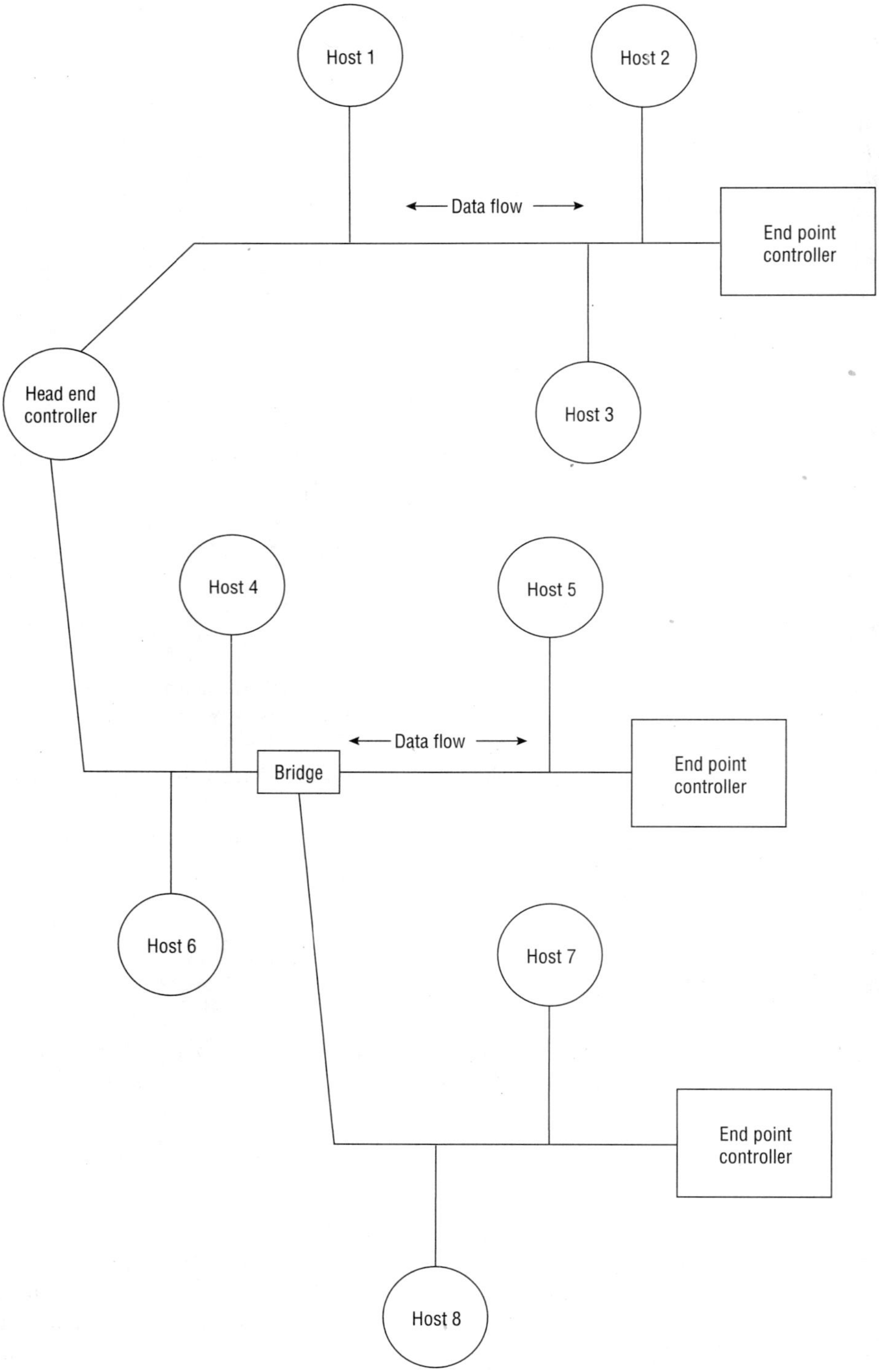

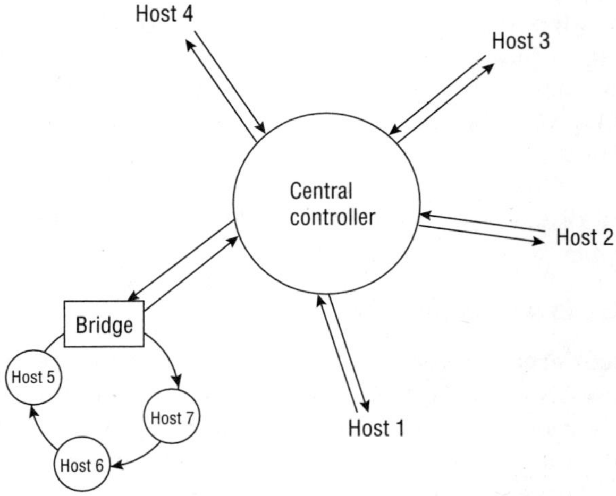

FIGURE 9.7
Example of a hybrid topology with a star and ring connected by a bridge.

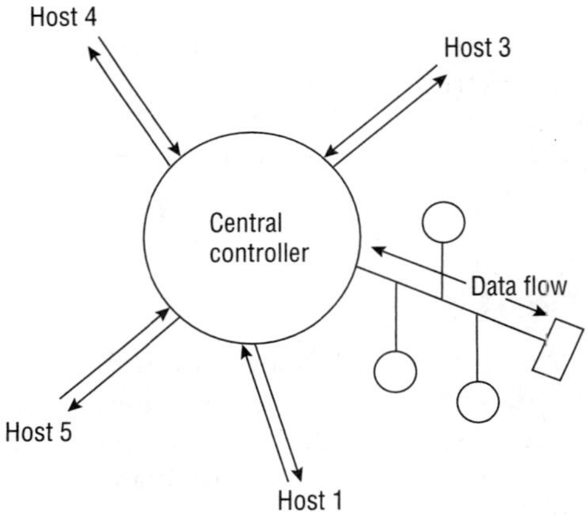

FIGURE 9.8
Example of a hybrid topology with a star and bus combination.

same general area. Although a LAN is physically confined to a well-defined local area, its communications are not limited to that area because the LAN can be a component of a larger communication network and can provide easy access to the outside through a bridge or a gateway.

A **bridge** is a device, and the software to operate it, that connects two or more geographically distant local area networks that use the same protocols. For example, a simple bridge could be used to connect two Ethernet local area networks.

A **gateway**, on the other hand, is a more complex device, and software, used to connect two or more local area networks or systems that use different protocols. A gateway will translate one network's protocol into another resolving hardware and software incompatibilities. For example, the systems network architecture (commonly called SNA) gateway can connect a microcomputer network to a mainframe host.

Today's LANs operate at speeds that vary from one megabyte per second to one gigabit per second. Because the sites are close to each other, bandwidths are available to support very high-speed transmission for fully animated, full-color graphics and video, digital voice transmission, and other high data-rate analog or digital signals. The previously described topologies — star, ring, bus, tree, and hybrid — are normally used to construct local area networks. The transmission medium used may vary from one topology to another; however, baseband coaxial cable and optical fiber are common to all. Factors to be considered when selecting a transmission medium are cost, data rate, reliability, number of devices that can be supported, distance between units, and technical limitations.

METROPOLITAN AREA NETWORK

A **metropolitan area network (MAN)** defines a configuration spanning an area larger than a LAN, ranging from several blocks of buildings to an entire city but not exceeding a circumference of 100 kilometers. A metropolitan area network may be owned and operated by a single organization and usually is used by many individuals and organizations. In some instances MANs are owned and operated as public utilities, providing the means for internetworking several LANs.

A MAN is a high-speed network typically configured as a logical ring. That means that depending on the protocol used, messages are either transmitted in one direction using only one ring, as illustrated in Figure 9.2, or in both directions using two counter-rotating rings, as illustrated in Figure 9.3, one always carrying messages in one direction and the other always carrying messages in the opposite direction.

WIDE AREA NETWORK

A **wide area network (WAN)** defines a configuration that interconnects communication facilities in different parts of a country or even different parts of the world, or that is operated as part of a public utility. WANs use the communications lines of "common carriers," which are government-regulated private companies such as telephone companies that already provide the general public with communication facilities. WANs use a broad range of communication media, including satellite and microwaves; in some cases the speed of transmission is limited by the capabilities of the communication line. WANs are generally slower than LANs.

The first WAN, **ARPAnet**, was developed in 1969 by the Advanced Research Projects Agency (ARPA); responsibility for its operation was transferred in 1975 to the Defense Communications Agency. Its successor, the **Internet**, is the most widely recognized WAN, but there exist other commercial WANs, such as Telenet.

SOFTWARE DESIGN ISSUES

So far we've examined the configurations of a network's hardware components. In this section we'll examine the four software issues that must be addressed by network designers:

- How do sites use addresses to locate other sites?
- How are messages routed and how are they sent?

- How do processes communicate with each other?
- How are conflicting demands for resources resolved?

ADDRESSING CONVENTIONS

Network sites need to determine how to uniquely identify their users so they can communicate with each other and access each other's resources. Names, addresses, and routes are required because sites are not directly connected to each other except over point-to-point links; therefore, addressing protocols are closely related to the network topology and geographic location of each site. In some cases (Pouzin & Zimmermann, 1978) a distinction is made between "local name," which refers to the name by which a unit is known within its own system, and "global name," the name by which a unit is known outside its own system. This distinction is useful because it allows each site the freedom to identify its units according to their own standards without imposing uniform naming rules, something that would be difficult to implement at the local level. On the other hand, a global name must follow standard name lengths, formats, and other global conventions.

Using an Internet address as a typical example, we can see that it follows a hierarchical organization, starting from left to right in the following sequence: from logical user to host machine, from host machine to net machine, from net machine to cluster, and from cluster to network. For example, in each Internet address — *mchoes@acm.org*, *ida@icarus.lis.pitt.edu*, or *igss12@aber.ac.uk* — the periods are used to separate each component. These electronic mail addresses, which are fairly easy to remember, must be translated (or "resolved," using a concept similar to that described in Chapter 3) to corresponding hardware addresses. This conversion is done by the networking section of the computer's operation system.

The examples given above follow the **Domain Name Service (DNS)** protocol currently in use, a general purpose distributed data query service whose principal function is the resolution of Internet addresses. If we dissect *ida@icarus.lis.pitt.edu* into its components, we have the following:

ida is the logical user,

icarus is the host for ida,

lis is the net machine for icarus,

pitt is the cluster for lis, and

edu is the network for the University of Pittsburgh.

We can see from the other two example addresses given that not all components need to be present in Internet addresses; nevertheless, the DNS is able to resolve them by examining them in reverse order.

ROUTING STRATEGIES

Routing allows data to get from one point on a network to another. It requires that each destination be uniquely identified. Once the data is at the proper network, then the router, a device that forwards data between networks, ensures that the correct node in the network receives it.

Routing protocols need to consider addressing, address resolution, message format, and error reporting. Most routing protocols are based on an addressing format that uses a network and a node number to identify each node. When a network is powered on, each **router** records in a table the addresses of the networks that are directly connected. Because routing protocols permit interaction between routers, sharing network destinations that each router may have acquired as it performs its services becomes easy. At specified intervals each router in the internetwork broadcasts a copy of its entire routing table. Eventually all of the routers know how to get to each of the different destination networks (Dickie, 1994).

Although the addresses allow routers to send data from one network to another, they cannot be used to get from one point in a network to another point in the *same* network. This must be done through address resolution, which allows a router to map the original address to a hardware address and store the mapping in a table to be used for future transmissions.

A variety of message formats are defined by routing protocols. These messages are used to allow the protocol to perform its functions, such as finding new nodes on a network, testing to determine whether they are working, reporting error conditions, exchanging routing information, establishing connections, and transmitting data.

Data transmission does not always run smoothly. For example, conditions may arise that cause errors such as inability to reach a destination because of a malfunctioning node or network. In cases such as this, routers and routing protocols would report the error condition although they would not attempt to correct the error; error correction is left to protocols at other levels of the network's architecture.

Two of the most widely used routing protocols in the Internet are routing information protocol and open shortest path first.

ROUTING INFORMATION PROTOCOL In **routing information protocol (RIP)**, selection of a path to transfer data from one network to another is based on the number of intermediate nodes, or hops, between the source and the destination. The path with the smallest number of hops is always chosen. This **distance vector algorithm** is easy to implement, but it may not be the best in today's networking environment because it does not take into consideration other important factors such as bandwidth, data priority, or type of network. That is, it can exclude faster or more reliable paths from being selected just because they have more hops. Another limitation of RIP relates to routing tables. The entire table is updated and reissued every 30 seconds, whether or not changes have occurred; this increases internetwork traffic and negatively affects the delivery of messages. In addition, the tables propagate from one router to another. Thus, in the case of an internetwork with 15 hops, it would take more than seven minutes for a change to be known at the other end of the internetwork. Because not all routers would have the same information about the internetwork, a failure at any one of the hops could create an unstable environment for all message traffic.

OPEN SHORTEST PATH FIRST In **open shortest path first (OSPF)**, selection of a transmission path is made only after the state of a network has been determined, so that if an intermediate hop is malfunctioning it is eliminated immediately from consideration until its services have been restored. Routing update messages are sent only when changes in the routing environment occur, thereby reducing the number of messages in the internetwork and reducing the size of the messages by not sending the entire routing table. However, memory usage is increased because OSPF keeps track of more information than RIP. In addition, the savings in bandwidth consumption are offset by the higher CPU usage needed for the calculation of the shortest path, which is based on Dijkstra's algorithm — simply stated as: find the shortest paths from a given source to all other destinations by proceeding in stages and developing the path in increasing path lengths (Stallings, 1994).

When a router uses Dijkstra's algorithm it computes all the different paths to get to each destination in the internetwork, creating what is known as a **topological database**. This data structure is maintained by OSPF and is updated whenever failures occur. Therefore, a router would simply check its topological database to determine whether a path was available, and would then use Dijkstra's algorithm to generate a "shortest path tree" to get around the failed link.

CONNECTION MODELS

A communication network is not concerned with the content of data being transmitted but with moving the data from one point to another. Because it would be prohibitive to connect each node in a network to all other nodes, the nodes are connected to a communication network designed to minimize transmission costs and to provide full connectivity among all attached devices. Data entering the network at one point is routed to its destination by being switched from node to node, whether by circuit switching or by packet switching.

CIRCUIT SWITCHING Circuit switching is a communication model in which a dedicated communication path is established between two hosts. The path is a connected sequence of links and the connection between the two points exists until one of them is disconnected. The connection path must be set up before data transmission begins; therefore, if the entire path becomes unavailable, messages cannot be transmitted because the circuit would not be complete. The telephone system is a good example of a circuit-switched network.

In terms of performance, there is a delay before signal transfer begins while the connection is set up. However, once the circuit is completed, the network is transparent to users and information is transmitted at a fixed rate of speed with insignificant delays at intermediate nodes.

PACKET SWITCHING Packet switching is basically a store-and-forward technique in which a message is divided into multiple equal-sized units called **packets**, which are then sent through the network to their destination, where they are reassembled into their original long format.

Packet switching is an effective technology for long-distance data transmission and provides more flexibility than circuit switching because it permits data transmission between devices that receive or transmit data at different rates. However, there is no guarantee that after a message has been divided into packets the packets will all travel along the same path to their destination, or that they will arrive in their physical sequential order. In addition, packets from one message may be interspersed with those from other messages as they travel toward their destinations. Therefore, a "header" containing pertinent information about the packet is attached to each packet before it's transmitted. The information contained in the packet header varies according to the routing method used by the network.

The idea is similar to sending a series of 30 reference books through a package delivery system. Six boxes contain five volumes each, and each box is labeled with its sequence number (e.g., box 2 of 6), as well as its ultimate destination. As space on passing delivery trucks becomes available, each box is forwarded to a central switching center, where it is stored until space becomes available to send it to the next switching center closer to its destination. Eventually, when all six boxes arrive they are put in their original order, the 30 volumes are unpacked, and the original sequence is restored.

Packet switching is fundamentally different from "message switching," also a store-and-forward technique, in which an entire message is accepted by a central switching node and forwarded to its destination when one of two circumstances occurs: all the circuits are free to send the entire message at once, or the receiving node requests its stored messages.

Packet switching provides greater line efficiency because a single node-to-node circuit can be shared by several packets and does not sit idle over long periods of time. Although delivery may be delayed as traffic increases, packets can still be accepted and transmitted.

That is also in contrast to circuit switching networks, which, when they become overloaded, refuse to accept new connections until the load decreases. Have you ever received a busy signal when trying to place a long distance telephone call during a major holiday? That problem is similar to a circuit switching network's overload response.

Packet switching allows users to allocate priorities to their messages so that a router with several packets queued for transmission can send the higher priority packets first. In addition, packet switching networks are more reliable than other types because most nodes are connected by more than one link, so that if one circuit should fail, a completely different path may be established between nodes.

There are two different methods of selecting the path: datagrams and virtual circuits. In the datagram approach, the destination and sequence number of the packet is added to the information uniquely identifying the message to which the packet belongs; each packet is then handled independently and a route is selected as each packet is accepted into the network. This is similar to the shipping label that's added to each package in the book shipment example. At their destination, all packets belonging to the same message are then reassembled by sequence number into one continuous message and finally are delivered to the addressee. Because the message cannot be delivered until all packets have been accounted for, it is up to the receiving node to request retransmission of lost or damaged packets. This routing method has two distinct advantages: it helps diminish congestion by sending incoming packets through less heavily used paths, and it provides more reliability, because alternate paths may be set up when one node fails.

In the "virtual circuit" approach, the destination and packet sequence number are not added to the information identifying the packet's message because a complete path from sender to receiver is established before transmission starts — all the packets belonging to that message use the same route. Although it's a similar concept, this is different from the dedicated path used in circuit switching because any node can have several virtual circuits to any other node. Its advantage over the datagram method is that its routing decision is made only once for all packets belonging to the same message — a feature that should speed up message transmission for long messages. On the other hand, it has a disadvantage in that if a node fails, all virtual circuits using that node become unavailable. In addition, when the circuit experiences heavy traffic, congestion is more difficult to resolve.

CONFLICT RESOLUTION

Because a network consists of devices sharing a common transmission capability, some method to control access is necessary to facilitate equal and fair access to this common resource. First we will describe some access control techniques: round robin, reservation, and contention. Then we will briefly examine the most common medium access control protocols used to implement access to resources: carrier sense multiple access; token passing; and distributed-queue, dual bus.

ACCESS CONTROL TECHNIQUES Round robin access control follows the same principles as round robin processor management, described in Chapter 4. In networks, round robin allows each node on the network to use the communication medium. If the node has data to send, it is given a certain amount of time to complete the transmission, at the end of which the opportunity is passed to the next node. If the node has no data to send, or if it completes transmission before the time is up, then the next node begins its turn. Round robin is an efficient technique when there are many nodes transmitting over long periods of time. However, when there are few nodes transmitting over long periods of time, the overhead incurred in passing turns from node to node can be substantial, making other techniques preferable depending on whether transmissions are short and intermittent, as in interactive terminal-host sessions, or lengthy and continuous, as in massive file transfer sessions.

The reservation technique is well suited for lengthy and continuous traffic. Access time on the medium is divided into slots and a node can reserve future time slots for its use. The technique is similar to that found in synchronous time-division multiplexing, used for multiplexing digitized voice streams, where the time slots are fixed in length and preassigned to each node. This technique could be good for a configuration with several terminals connected to a host computer through a single I/O port.

The contention technique is better for short and intermittent traffic. No attempt is made to determine whose turn it is to transmit so nodes compete for access to the medium. Therefore, it works well under light to moderate traffic, but performance tends to break down under heavy loads. This technique's major advantage is that it is easy to implement.

MEDIUM ACCESS CONTROL PROCEDURES Access protocols currently in use are based on the previously mentioned techniques and are discussed here with regard to their role in LAN environments.

Carrier sense multiple access (CSMA) is a contention-based protocol that is easy to implement. "Carrier sense" means that a node on the network will listen to, or test, the communication medium before transmitting any messages, thus preventing a collision with another node that is currently transmitting. "Multiple access" means that several nodes are connected to the same communication line as peers, on the same level and with equal privileges.

Although a node will not transmit until the line is quiet, two or more nodes could come to that conclusion at the same instant. If more than one transmission is sent simultaneously, creating a collision, the data from all transmissions will be damaged and the line will remain unusable while the damaged messages are dissipated. When the receiving nodes fail to acknowledge receipt of their transmissions, the sending nodes will know that the messages did not reach their destinations successfully and both will be retransmitted. The probability of this happening increases if the nodes are farther apart, making CSMA a less appealing access protocol for large or complex networks.

Therefore, the original algorithm was modified to include collision detection and was named carrier sense multiple access with collision detection (CSMA/CD). **Ethernet** is the most widely known CSMA/CD protocol. Collision detection does not eliminate collisions but it does reduce them. When a collision occurs, a jamming signal is sent immediately to both sending nodes, which then wait a random period before trying again. With this protocol the amount of wasted transmission capacity is reduced to the time it takes to detect the collision.

A different modification is CSMA with collision avoidance (CSMA/CA). Collision avoidance means that the access method prevents multiple nodes from colliding during transmission. However, opinion on its efficiency is divided. Some claim it is more efficient than collision detection, whereas others contend that it lowers a network's performance when there are a large number of nodes. CSMA/CA protocol is implemented in LocalTalk, Apple's cabling system, which uses a protocol called LocalTalk link access protocol. A terminal connected to an Apple CSMA/CA network would send out a three-byte packet to indicate that it wants to start transmitting. This packet tells all other terminals to wait until the first is finished transmitting before they initiate transmissions. If collisions do occur, they involve only the three-byte packets, not the actual data. This protocol does not guarantee the data will reach its destination, but it ensures that any data that is delivered will be error free.

In a token-passing network a special electronic message, called a "token," is generated when the network is turned on and is then passed along from node to node. Only the node with the token is allowed to transmit, and after it has done so, it must pass the token on to another node. These networks typically have either a bus or ring topology and are popular because access is fast and collisions are nonexistent.

In a **token-bus** network, the token is passed to each node in turn. Upon receipt of the token, a node attaches to it the data to be transmitted and sends the packet, containing both token and data, to its destination. The receiving node copies the data, adds the acknowledgment, and returns the packet to the sending node, which then passes the token on to the next node in logical sequence.

Initially node order is determined by a cooperative decentralized algorithm. Once the network is up and running, turns are determined by priority based on node activity. A node requiring the token frequently will have a higher priority than one that seldom needs it. A table of node addresses is kept in priority order by the network. When a transmission is complete, the token passes from the node that just finished to the one having the next lower entry in the table. When the lowest priority node has been serviced, the token returns to the top of the table and the process is repeated.

This process is similar to a train engine pulling into the station. If the station-master has a delivery to send, those cars are attached to the engine and the train is dispatched to its destination with no intermediate stops. When it arrives, the cars are detached and the engine is sent back to the point of origin with the message that the shipment was successfully received. After delivering that message to the shipment's originator, the engine proceeds to the next station to pick up a delivery.

Implementation of this protocol dictates higher overhead at each node than does CSMA/CD, and nodes may have long waits under certain conditions before receiving the token.

Token ring is the most widely used protocol for ring topology; it became better known than token bus when IBM made its Token-Ring Network commercially available. It is based on the use of a token that moves between the nodes in turn and in one direction only. When it's not carrying a message, the token is called a "free" token. If a node wants to send a message it must wait for the free token to come by. It then changes the token from "free" to "busy" and sends its message immediately following the busy token. Meanwhile, all other nodes must wait for the token to become free and come to them again before they are able to transmit a message.

The receiving node copies the message in the packet and sets the "copied" bit to indicate it was successfully received; the packet then continues on its way, making a complete round trip back to the sending node, which then releases the new free token on the network. At this point, the next node down the line with data to send will be able to pick up the free token and repeat the process.

The distributed-queue, dual bus (DQDB) protocol is intended for use with a dual-bus configuration, where each bus transports data in only one direction, and has been standardized by one of the Institute of Electrical and Electronics Engineers committees as part of its MAN standards. Transmission on each bus consists of a steady stream of fixed-size slots, as shown in Figure 9.9. Slots generated at one end of each bus are marked "free" and sent downstream, where they are marked "busy" and written to by nodes that are ready to transmit data. Nodes read and copy data from the slots, which then continue to travel toward the end of the bus, where they dissipate.

The distributed access protocol is based on a distributed reservation scheme and can be summarized as follows. If node C in Figure 9.9 wants to send data to node D, it would use Bus 1 because the slots are flowing toward D on that bus. However, if the nodes before C monopolize the slots, then C would not be able to transmit its data to D. To solve the problem, C can use Bus 2 to send a reservation

FIGURE 9.9 *Distributed-queue, dual bus protocol. Free slots are generated at one end of each bus and flow in only one direction. Using DQDB, if node C wants to send data to node D, it must wait for a free slot on Bus 1 because the slots are flowing toward node D on that bus.*

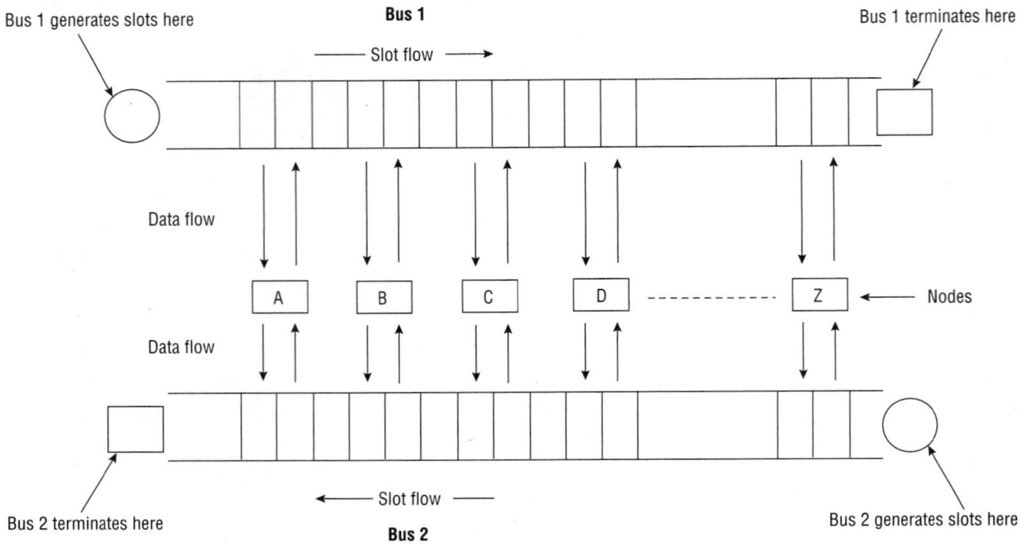

to its upstream neighbors. The protocol states that a node will allow free slots to go by until outstanding reservations from downstream nodes have been satisfied. Therefore, the protocol must provide a mechanism by which each station can keep track of the requests of its downstream peers.

This mechanism is handled by a pair of first-in, first-out queues and a pair of counters, one for each bus, at each of the nodes in the network. This is a very effective protocol providing negligible delays under light loads and predictable queuing under heavy loads. This combination makes the DQDB protocol suitable for MANs that manage large file transfers and will also satisfy the needs of interactive users.

TRANSPORT PROTOCOL STANDARDS

During the 1980s network usage began to grow at a fast pace, as did the need to integrate dissimilar network devices from different vendors, a task that became increasingly difficult as the number and complexity of network devices increased. Soon the user community pressured the industry to create a single universally adopted network architecture that would allow true multivendor interoperability. There are two competing standards, OSI and TCP/IP.

OSI REFERENCE MODEL

The International Organization for Standardization (ISO), which makes technical recommendations about data communication interfaces, took on the task of creating such a network architecture. Their efforts resulted in the open systems interconnection reference model, or **OSI reference model**, which serves as a framework for defining the services that a network should provide to its users. This model provides the basis for connecting "open" systems for distributed applications processing. The word "open" means that any two systems that conform to the reference model and the related standards can be connected, regardless of the vendor.

Once all services were identified, similar functions were collected together into seven logical clusters known as layers. One of the main reasons used to define the seven layers was to group easily localized functions so that each layer could be redesigned and its **protocols** changed in any way to take advantage of new advances in architecture, hardware, or software without changing the services expected from, and provided to, the adjacent layers. Boundaries between layers were selected at points that past experience had revealed to be effective. The resulting seven-layer OSI model is software that handles data transmission from one terminal or application program to another. Figure 9.10 shows how data passes through the seven layers and how they are organized: from the application layer, the one closest to the user, to the physical layer, the one closest to the cables, modems, and circuits. A brief description of each layer's function follows.

LAYER 1 — THE PHYSICAL LAYER Layer 1 is at the bottom of the model. This is where the mechanical, electrical, and functional specifications for connecting a device to a particular network are described. Layer 1 is primarily concerned with transmitting bits over communication lines, so voltages of electricity and timing factors are important. This is the only layer concerned with hardware, and all data must be passed down to it for actual data transfer between units to occur. Layers 2 through 7 all are concerned with software, and communication between units at these levels is only virtual. Examples of physical layer specifications are 10Base-T, RS449, and CCITT V.35.

LAYER 2 — THE DATA LINK LAYER Because software is needed to implement Layer 2, this software must be stored in some type of programmable device such as a front end processor, network node, or microcomputer. Bridging between two homogeneous networks occurs at this layer. On one side, the data link layer establishes and controls the physical path of communications before sending data to the physical layer below it. It takes the data, which has been divided into packets by the layers above it, and physically assembles the packet for transmission by completing its frame. Frames contain data combined with control and error detection characters so that Layer 1 can transmit a continuous stream of bits without concern for their format or meaning. On the other side it checks for transmission errors and resolves problems caused by damaged, lost, or duplicate message frames so that Layer 3 can work with error-free messages. Typical data link level protocols are High-Level Data Link Control (HDLC) and Synchronous Data Link Control (SDLC).

LAYER 3 — THE NETWORK LAYER Layer 3 provides services such as addressing and routing that move data through the network to its destination. Basically, the software at this level accepts blocks of data from Layer 4, the transport layer,

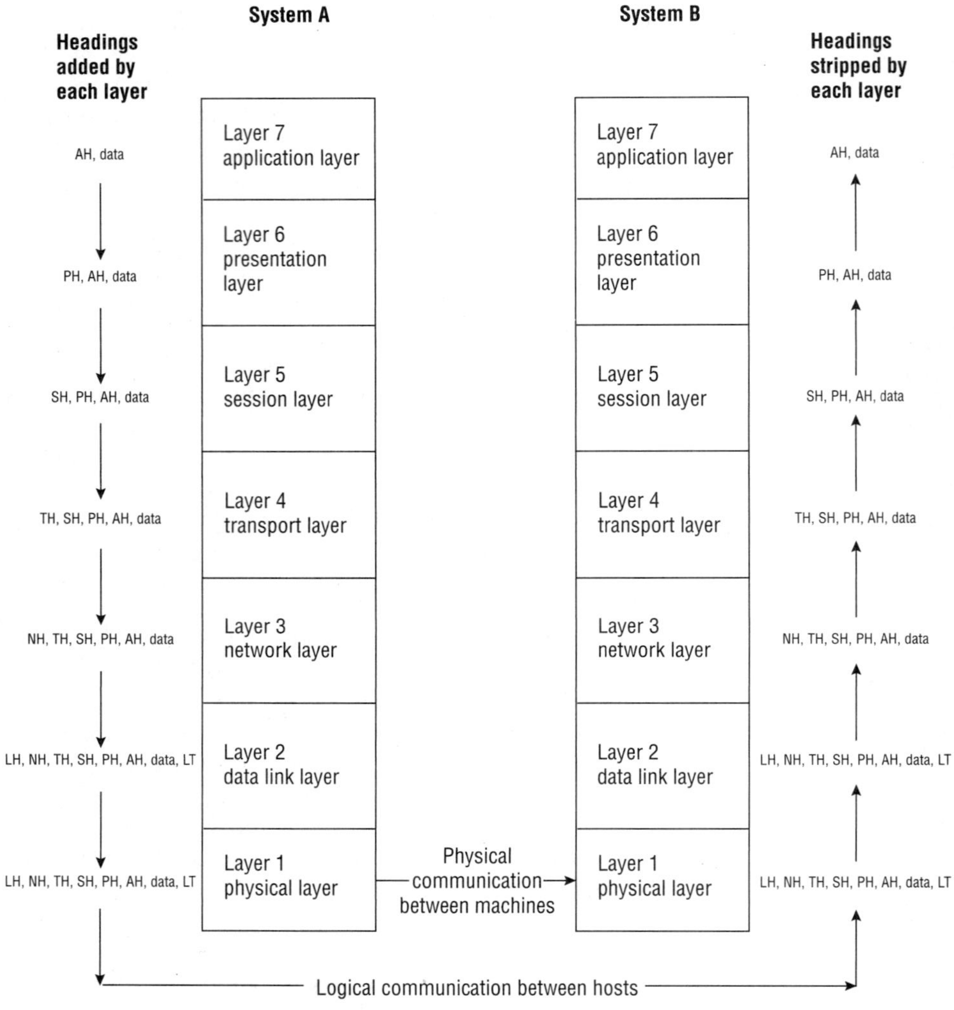

FIGURE 9.10
The OSI transport protocol standard. At every layer of the sending unit, System A, a new header is attached to the previous packet before it is passed on the next lower layer. Finally, at the data link layer, a link trailer (LT) is added, completing the frame, which is passed to the physical layer for transmission. Then the receiving unit removes each header or trailer until it delivers the data to the application program at Layer 7 on System B.

resizes them into shorter packets, and routes them to the proper destination. Addressing methods that allow a node and its network to be identified, as well as algorithms to handle address resolution, are specified in this layer. A database of routing tables keeps track of all possible routes a packet may take and determines how many different circuits exist between any two packet switching nodes. This database may be stored at this level to provide efficient packet routing and should be dynamically updated to include information about any failed circuit and the transmission volume present in the active circuits.

LAYER 4 — THE TRANSPORT LAYER Layer 4 is also known as the host-to-host or end-to-end layer because it maintains reliable data transmission between end users. A program at the source computer can send a virtual communication to a similar program at a destination machine by using message headers and control messages. However, the physical path still goes to Layer 1 and across to the destination computer. Software for this layer contains facilities that handle user addressing and ensures that all the packets of data have been received and that none have been lost. This software may be stored in front end processors, packet switching nodes, or host computers. In addition, this layer has a mechanism that regulates the flow of information so a fast host cannot overrun a slower terminal or an overloaded host. A well-known transport layer protocol is Transmission Control Protocol (TCP).

LAYER 5 — THE SESSION LAYER Layer 5 is responsible for providing a user-oriented connection service and transferring data over the communication lines. The transport layer is responsible for creating and maintaining a logical connection between end points. The session layer provides a user interface that adds value to the transport layer in the form of dialogue management and error recovery. Sometimes the session layer is known as the "data flow control" layer because it establishes the connection between two applications or processes, enforces the regulations for carrying on the session, controls the flow of data, and resets the connection if it fails. This layer may also perform some accounting functions to ensure that users receive their bills. The functions of the transport layer and session layer are very similar, and because the operating system of the host computer generally handles the session layer, it would be natural to combine both layers into one, as does TCP/IP.

LAYER 6 — THE PRESENTATION LAYER Layer 6 is responsible for data manipulation functions common to many applications, such as formatting, compression, and encryption. Data conversion, syntax conversion, and protocol conversion are common tasks performed in this layer. Gateways connecting networks with different protocols are presentation layer devices; one of their functions is to accommodate totally different interfaces as seen by a terminal in one node and expected by the application program at the host computer. For example, IBM's Customer Information Control System (CICS) teleprocessing monitor is a presentation layer service located in a host mainframe, although it provides additional functions beyond the presentation layer.

LAYER 7 — THE APPLICATION LAYER At layer 7, the application program's, terminals, and computers access the network. This layer provides the interface to users and is responsible for formatting user data before passing it to the lower layers for transmission to a remote host. It contains network management functions and tools to support distributed applications. File transfer and electronic mail are two of the most common application protocols and functions.

Once the OSI model is assembled, it allows nodes to communicate with each other. Each layer provides a completely different array of functions to the network, but all the layers work in unison to ensure that the network provides reliable transparent service to the users.

TRANSMISSION CONTROL PROTOCOL/INTERNET PROTOCOL (TCP/IP) MODEL

The transmission control protocol/Internet protocol (TCP/IP) model is probably the oldest transport protocol standard and the most widely used network layer protocol in use today. It was developed for the U.S. Department of Defense's ARPAnet and provides reasonably efficient and error-free transmission between different systems. Because it is a file-transfer protocol, large information files can be sent across sometimes unreliable networks with a high probability that the data will arrive error free. Some differences between the **TCP/IP model** and the OSI reference model are the significance that TCP/IP places in internetworking and in providing connectionless services and its management of certain functions such as accounting for use of resources.

The TCP/IP model organizes a communication system with three main components: processes, hosts, and networks. Processes execute on hosts, which can often support multiple simultaneous processes that are defined as primary units that need to communicate. These processes communicate across the networks to which hosts are connected. Based on this hierarchy, the model can be roughly partitioned into two major tasks: one that manages the transfer of information to the host in which the process resides and one that ensures it gets to the correct process within the host. Therefore, a network needs to be concerned only with routing data between hosts, as long as the hosts can then direct the data to the appropriate processes. With this in mind, the TCP/IP model can be arranged into four layers instead of OSI's seven, as shown in Figure 9.11. A brief description of their functions and how they relate to the OSI model follows.

NETWORK ACCESS LAYER The network access layer is equivalent to the physical, data link, and part of the network layers of the OSI model. Protocols at this layer provide access to a communication network. Some of the functions performed here are flow control, error control between hosts, security, and priority implementation.

INTERNET LAYER The Internet layer is equivalent to the portion of the network layer of the OSI model that is not already included in the previous layer, specifically the mechanism that performs routing functions. Therefore, this protocol is usually implemented within gateways and hosts. An example of a standard set by the DoD is the Internet Protocol (IP), which provides connectionless service for end systems to communicate across one or more networks.

HOST-HOST LAYER The host-host layer is equivalent to the transport and session layers of the OSI model. As its name indicates, this layer supports mechanisms to transfer data between two processes on different host computers. Services provided in the host-host layer also include error checking, flow control, and an ability to manipulate connection control signals. An example of a standard set by the DoD is the Transmission Control Protocol (TCP), which provides a reliable end-to-end data transfer service.

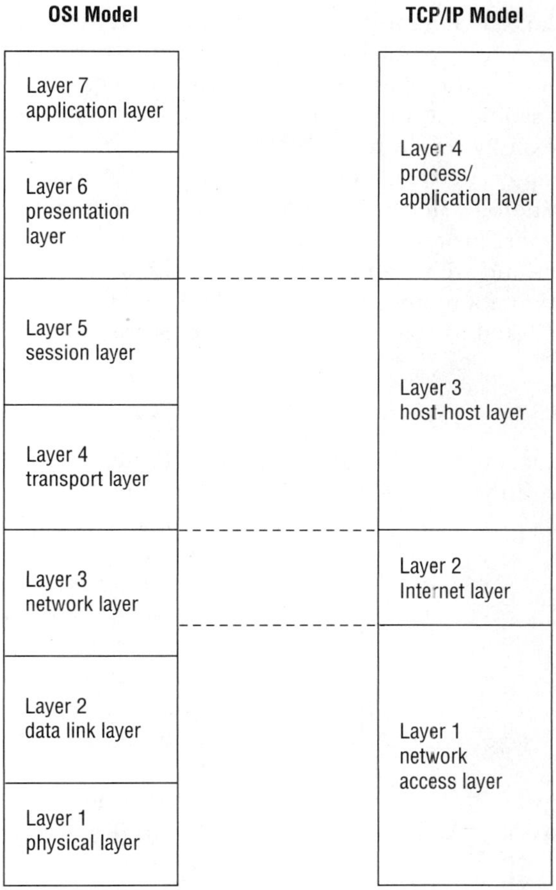

FIGURE 9.11 *Comparison of OSI and TCP/IP transport protocol standards and their functional layers.*

PROCESS/APPLICATION LAYER The process/application layer is equivalent to the presentation and application layers of the OSI model. It includes protocols for computer-to-computer resource sharing and terminal-to-computer remote access. Specific examples of standards set by the DoD for this layer are File Transfer Protocol (FTP), a simple application for transfer of ASCII, EBCDIC, and binary files; Simple Mail Transfer Protocol (SMTP), a simple electronic mail facility; and TELNET, a simple asynchronous terminal capability that provides remote log-on capabilities to users working at a terminal or a personal computer.

CHAPTER NINE CONCLUSION

Although operating systems for networks necessarily include the functions of the four managers discussed so far in this textbook — the Memory Manager, Processor Manager, Device Manager, and File Manager — they also include the need to coordinate all those functions among the network's many varied pieces of hardware and software, no matter where they are physically located.

There is no single gauge by which we can measure the success of a network's operating system, but at a minimum it must meet the reliability requirements of its owners. That is, when a node fails — and all networks experience node failure from time to time — the operating system must detect the failure, change routing instructions to avoid that node, and make sure every lost message is retransmitted until it is successfully received.

In this chapter we've introduced the basic network organization concepts: common terminology, network topologies, types of networks, software design issues, and transport protocol standards. Bear in mind, however, that this is a complicated subject and we've only just touched the surface in these few pages. For more information about any of the topics discussed here, refer to the texts cited in this chapter or listed as references at the end of the book.

KEY TERMS

network operation system (NOS)
distributed operating system (DOS)
remote
local
sites
hosts
nodes
star topology
ring topology
bus topology
tree topology
hybrid topology
local area network (LAN)
bridge
gateway
metropolitan area network (MAN)
wide area network (WAN)
ARPAnet
Internet
Domain Name Service (DNS)
router
routing information protocol (RIP)
distance vector algorithm
open shortest path first (OSPF)
topological database
packets
Ethernet
token-bus
token ring
OSI reference model
protocol
ISO
TCP/IP model

EXERCISES

1. Describe the primary functions of a network.
2. Compare the relative advantages and disadvantages of the five topologies discussed in this chapter.
3. Describe a hybrid topology and draw graphic illustrations of two examples.
4. Explain the major disadvantage of a star topology.
5. Describe the main differences between LANs, MANs, and WANs.
6. Discuss the difference between a bridge and a gateway and describe a topology that uses each.
7. Identify a network topology that would best suit each of the following environments and explain why.
   a. Dormitory floor

b. University campus

c. State or province

d. Nation

8. Explain the two ways in which packets can be routed and how they differ.
9. Although not explicitly discussed in the chapter, packet size would seem to have an impact on transmission time. Discuss whether or not this is true and explain why. Offer a comprehensive example comparing packet sizes and resulting transmission times.
10. Name three commercially available operating systems for networks and explain the topology each is designed to manage.

ADVANCED EXERCISES

11. Discuss what is wrong with the following logic: Packet switching requires control and address bits to be added to each packet, which causes considerable overhead in packet switching. In circuit switching a dedicated circuit is set up, and no extra bits are needed.

    a. Therefore, there is no overhead in circuit switching.

    b. Because there is no overhead in circuit switching, line utilization must be more efficient than in packet switching.
12. Describe the differences between CSMA/CD and CSMA/CA.
13. Explain the circumstances under which a token-ring network is more effective than an Ethernet network.
14. Contact the "network expert" at your school or place of work. Find out which topology, communication links, and configuration are used in that network. Is it a LAN, MAN, or WAN?
15. Even though the ISO model of networking specifies seven layers of functionality, most computer systems use fewer layers to implement a network. Why do they use fewer layers? What problems could be caused by the use of fewer layers?
16. Although security issues were not mentioned in this chapter, they must be considered by every network owner. Knowing that open networks allow all data to pass to every node, describe the possible security concerns of open network architectures. Include the implications of allowing log-on procedures, user IDs, and passwords to pass openly on the network.

Chapter Ten

MANAGEMENT OF NETWORK FUNCTIONS

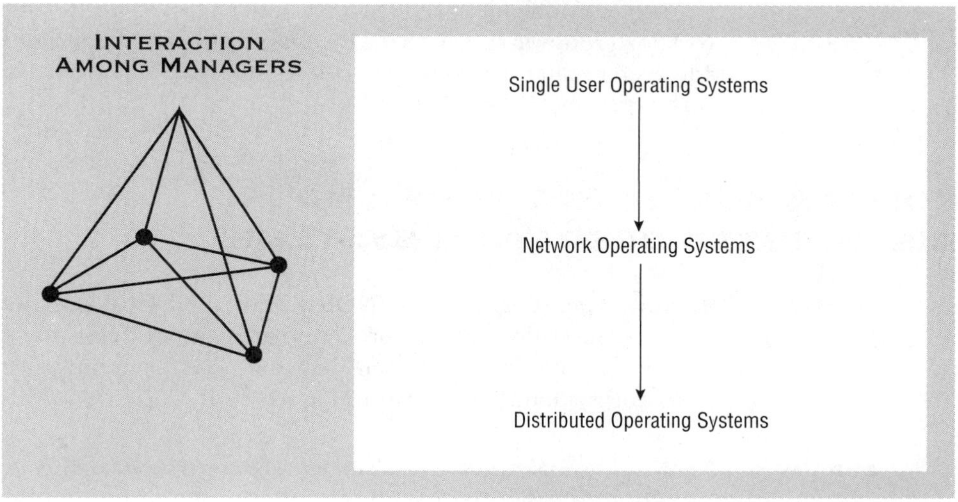

When organizations move toward completely decentralized systems, more and more computing devices are linked through complex networks of word processors, facsimile devices, copiers, teleconferencing equipment, microcomputers, mainframe host computers, and other equipment. But there are two problems with this expansion. First, a tremendous demand is placed on data communication networks by the staggering number of hardware interconnections. Second, there is constant pressure for these networks to operate with greater reliability and faster speed.

In this chapter we will: explore the differences between network operating systems and distributed operating systems; explain process-based and object-based operating system models and use them to define the roles of the Memory, Processor, Device, File, and Network managers present in distributed operating systems; and discuss the role of network operating systems.

HISTORY

Early networks focused on sharing expensive hardware resources such as large mainframes, laser printers, and sizable hard disks. The physical network, coupled with a network operating system, allowed organizations to increase the availability of these resources and spread the cost among many users. However, system owners soon realized that the real value of a network was not the hardware but the data and information stored in the files on the hard disks. Soon operating systems were enhanced with network capabilities to enable users throughout an organization to have easy access to centralized information resources. The first such development was the network operating system, followed by the more powerful distributed operating system.

Today applications collectively known as computer-supported cooperative work, or **groupware**, use a set of technologies called **distributed processing** to provide even greater access to centralized information and to assist users who need to work together to complete tasks.

COMPARISON OF NETWORK AND DISTRIBUTED OPERATING SYSTEMS

Network operating systems (NOSs) developed from the need to provide global resource allocation, global process management, and almost complete transparency of network access for users and their sites' operating systems, known as "local operating systems," as shown in Figure 10.1.

FIGURE 10.1 *In a NOS environment each node, shown here as triangles, is managed by its own local operating system, shown here as circles. Their respective network operating systems, shown here as squares, come into play only when one system needs to work with another.*

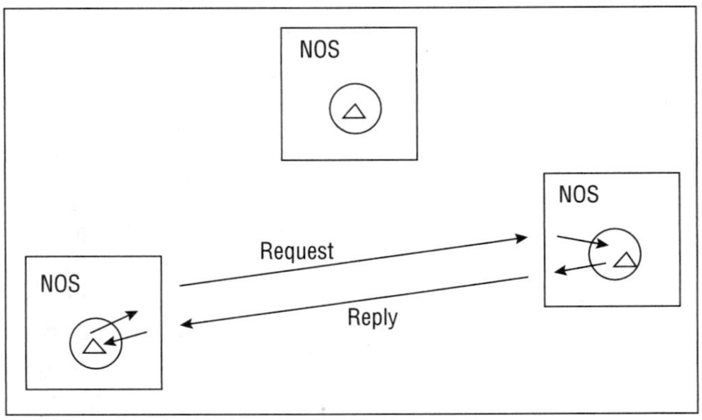

A network operating system provides local operating systems with the ability to accept a request for either processing or accessing data not available locally and determines where the resources are located. It then initiates the operation based on the request and returns the appropriate service to users and local environments. One of the goals of the NOS is to accomplish all this transparently. The local system views the action as having been performed locally because the network operating system handles all interfacing and coordination of the remote actions as well as communications between local operating systems by tracking the status and location of all entities in the system. As it receives service requests from local operating systems it completes them as if it were the actual wanted entity responding.

Because local operating systems are traditional operating systems designed to run a single computer, they can perform a task only if the process is part of their environment; otherwise, they will pass the request on to the network operating system to run it. To a local operating system, the NOS is the actual server performing the task, whereas in reality it is just the instrument for the actual task.

The NOS does not consider memory management, process management, device management, or file management from a global viewpoint. Rather, it sees them as autonomous local functions that must interact with each other but that do not direct each other. This limited view presents a problem because achieving true distributed computing or processing functions requires *global* control of all assets, not just those at the network communication level, a need that led to the development of a **distributed operating system (DOS)**. (Although they use the same acronym, this DOS must not be confused with MS-DOS, described in Chapter 12, or similar microcomputer operating systems.) Distributed operating systems provide an entire environment designed to optimize operations for the network as a whole, not just for local sites, as illustrated in Figure 10.2.

FIGURE 10.2 *A DOS views all nodes, shown here as triangles, as part of a globally managed operating system designed to optimize all system resources, with requests between nodes (shown here as triangles) handled entirely by the DOS. Therefore, every operation at every node is managed by the DOS.*

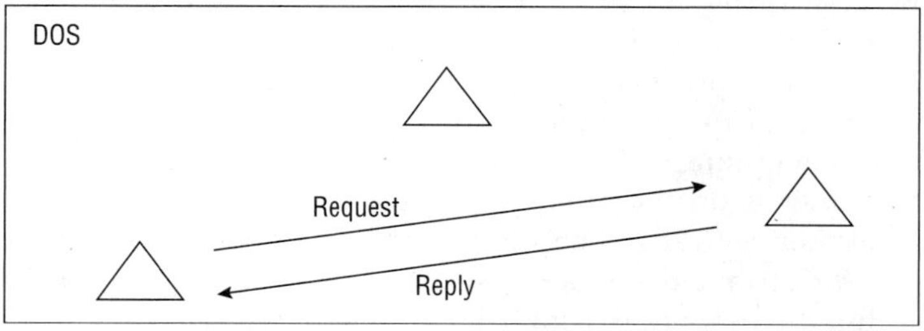

The major difference between a NOS and a DOS is in how each views and manages the local and global resources (see Table 10.1). Network operating systems build on capabilities provided by the local operating system and extend it to satisfy new needs. Access is performed using local mechanisms, with each system controlled and managed based on that system's policy. On the other hand, the DOS model views system resources as globally owned and manages them as such. Access uses global mechanisms rather than local mechanisms, with system control and management based on a single system policy.

TABLE 10.1 *Comparison of two types of operating systems used to manage networked resources.*

Network operating system (NOS)	Distributed operating system (DOS)
• Resources owned by local nodes	• Resources owned by global system
• Local resources managed by local operating system	• Local resources managed by a global DOS
• Access performed by local operating system	• Access performed by the DOS
• Requests passed from one local operating system to another via the NOS	• Requests passed directly from node to node via the DOS

For example, if an individual using a NOS wants to schedule a process to run at a remote site, the user must log onto the local network, may have to instruct the local system to migrate the process or data to the remote site, and then must send a request to the remote site to schedule the process on its system. Thereafter, the remote site will view the process as a newly created process within its "local" operating system's environment and will manage this process without outside intervention.

Based on its native set of resources and policies the local operating system makes all control decisions needed to process the given task. If synchronization with remote sites is required, the process would need to have embedded calls to the network service code. These calls are typically added on top of the local operating system and would provide the communications between the two processes on the different devices. This means that the job of synchronization is left up to the user and is only partially supported by the system.

On the other hand, a system managed by a DOS would handle the same example differently. If one site has a process that requires resources at another site, it presents this task to the operating system as a regular process. The DOS then examines the process control block to determine the specific requirements for this process. Using its process scheduler, the operating system determines how to best execute this process based on this site's current knowledge of the state of the total system. The process scheduler then takes this process, along with all other processes ready to run in the network, and recomputes the order of execution on the nodes to optimize global run time and prioritize the collection of global processes. Emphasis is on the global nature of operating system functionality, not just the local sites, with the goals of acting for the good of the total system.

A distributed operating system tries to manage the entire suite of resources within the network in a global fashion and is categorized by decentralization of the control of the network, so operating system functionality is not dependent on the knowledge or state of a single site or process. A distributed operating system is typically comprised of a replicated kernel operating system, normally low-level hardware-control software, called "firmware," with system-level software for resource management. These software components may be either unique or replicated within the system; their purpose is to allocate and manage the combination of global system resources so that system policies, not local policies, are maximized. Therefore, there is neither limiting local administrative control nor any requirement for users to know whether or not they are even on the network. The system must have a layer that hides the network and its intricacies from users so that users view the system as a logical single system and not as a collection of independent cooperating devices.

DOS DEVELOPMENT

Although the DOS was developed after the NOS, its global management of network devices is easy to understand and is therefore explained here first.

Because a DOS manages the entire group of resources within the network in a global fashion, it can be viewed as a logical single system rather than as a collection of independent cooperating systems. Control and allocation of resources is arrived at through negotiation and compromise among equally important peer sites in the distributed system. One advantage of this type of system is its ability to support file copying, electronic mail, and remote printing without requiring that the user install special server software on local machines; networking is an integral part of the operating system. Here is how operating system management is performed by a DOS.

MEMORY MANAGEMENT

The Memory Manager tracks available memory on each node by use of a kernel that performs a paging algorithm based on the goals of the local system. In addition, policies and mechanisms implemented at the local sites must be driven by the global system requirements. Therefore, memory allocation and deallocation will depend on the selected global scheduling and sharing schemes.

On a local level, the Memory Manager receives requests to allocate pages based on the policy in place on the machine and, from a global level, it receives requests from the Process Manager to provide memory to new or expanding client or server processes. The mechanism within the Memory Manager can be similar to that of a local operating system, but it must be extended to accept requests for memory from both local and global sources.

To control the stream of memory demands, the Memory Manager handles requests from the process manager to allocate and deallocate space based on the system's usage patterns. In a distributed environment, the combined memory for the entire system is made up of several subpools, one for each processor, and the Memory Manager has a subcomponent that exists on each processor. To allocate space, the Memory Manager examines the total free memory table. If the request can fit, allocation is performed and the table is adjusted to show the new allocation. To the outside world, the Memory Manager has two operations: allocate and deallocate space; however, it may also use local resources to do garbage collection in memory, perform compaction, decide which are the most and least active processes, and determine which processes to preempt to provide space for others.

The Memory Manager will allocate and deallocate virtual memory, read and write virtual memory, swap virtual pages to disk, get information about a range of virtual pages, lock virtual pages in memory, and protect specified pages. When an application tries to access a page not in memory, a page fault will occur and the Memory Manager will automatically bring that page into memory. If the application modifies the page, the virtual Memory Manager writes the changed page back to the file during its scheduled paging operations.

Extensive page protection mechanisms are implemented in either hardware or low-level memory management software existing in each site's kernel, which is summoned each time a process uses a memory address. As they're loaded into memory, several protection checks are performed on the pages loaded in memory:

- Read/write access allowed — allows users to have full access to the page's contents
- Read-only access allowed — allows users to read but not modify the page
- Execute-only access allowed — allows users to use the page. It means that a process cannot read or write to the page, but it can jump to an address within the page and start executing. This is appropriate for shared application software such as editors or compilers.
- Guard-page access allowed — used to facilitate automatic bounds-checking on stacks and other types of data structures
- No access allowed — prevents users from gaining access to the page. This is typically used by debugging software to prevent a process from reading from or writing to a particular page.

The last three controls are needed to ensure that processes do not write to pages that should be read only.

PROCESS MANAGEMENT

In a network, the Process Manager provides the policies and mechanisms to create, delete, abort, name, rename, find, schedule, block, run, and synchronize processes; to provide real-time priority execution, if required. In addition, it must manage the states of execution: ready, running, and waiting as described in Chapter 4. To do this, each CPU in the network is required to have its own run-time kernel that manages the lowest-level operation on the physical device, as indicated in Figure 10.3.

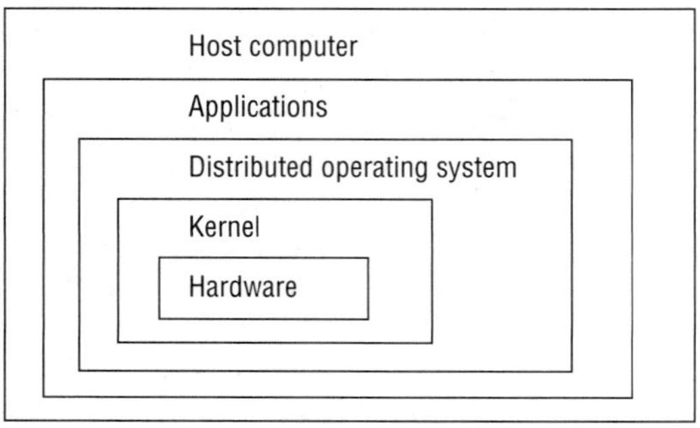

FIGURE 10.3 *Each computer or computational hardware device is operated by a kernel that controls its operation. The kernel is operated by the DOS, which is directed by the application software running on the host computer.*

The kernel actually controls and operates the CPU and manages the queues used for states of execution, although the mechanism directing how process control blocks (PCBs) are stored in the queues or how they are selected to run is driven by upper-level system policies. Therefore, the kernel is a fairly simple combination of hardware and software that aids in the effective run-time realization of the system's operational goals.

The kernel's states, in turn, are dependent on the external global system's process scheduler and dispatcher, which organize the queues within the local CPU and indicate which running policy to use in executing the processes on their queues. Typically, the scheduling function in the system contains three parts: a decision mode, a priority function, and an arbitration rule.

The decision mode determines which policies will be used when scheduling a resource. Options could include preemptive, nonpreemptive, round robin, and so forth.

The priority function component is used to describe the policy for assigning order to the execution cycle. The priority can be determined with a calculation based on occurrence of events; task recurrence; system loading levels; or program run time characteristics, such as most time remaining, least time remaining, and so on. The priority function is required to provide the proper order to the scheduling algorithm being used.

The arbitration rule is a policy to resolve conflicts between jobs of equal priority. This rule, such as LIFO or FIFO, would typically be structured as an order in which to execute jobs of the same priority.

Most advances on job scheduling for distributed systems have relied on one of three theories: queuing theory, estimation theory, or statistical decision theory. An example of estimation theory is a scheduler based on process priorities and durations. It uses the latter to compute and schedule the optimal interleaving of process chunks to maximize the system's throughput. Distributed scheduling is better achieved when migration of the scheduling function and policies considers all aspects of the system, including I/O, devices, processes, and communications.

Synchronization of processes in distributed operating systems is typically implemented through message passing or remote procedure calls. The creation of a process in a distributed system involves creation of a PCB with information similar to that discussed in Chapter 4, but with additional information to indicate the location of the process in the distributed system. The deletion or termination of a process requires finding the process control block and having the authority to access and delete it. Location of a process requires the use of a system directory or process that searches all kernel queue spaces, which requires system support for interprocess communications.

There are two ways of looking at the system: a **process-based DOS**, which is a large collection that includes all the system's processes and resources, and an **object-based DOS**, which clumps each type of hardware with its necessary operational software into discrete objects that are manipulated as a unit. Of the two, process-based DOS most closely resembles the theory described in Chapter 4.

PROCESS-BASED DOS A process-based DOS provides for process management through the use of client/server processes synchronized and linked together through messages and ports, also known as channels or pipes. The major emphasis is on processes and messages and how they are used to provide the basic features essential to process management such as process creation, scheduling, blocking, communication, and identification, to name a few. The issue of how to provide such features can be addressed in several ways. For example, the processes can be managed from a single copy of the operating system, from multiple cooperating peers, or from some combination of the two. Operating systems for distributed computers are typically configured as a kernel on each site. All other services, dependent on particular devices, are typically found on the sites where the devices are located. As users enter the system, they are provided with a unique process identifier and then assigned to a site for processing by the scheduling manager.

In a distributed system there is a high level of cooperation and sharing of actions and data maintained by the system sites in determining which process should be loaded and where it should be run; this is done through the exchange of messages between site operating systems. Once a process has been scheduled for service, it must be initiated at the assigned site, requiring the services of a dispatcher. The dispatcher's job is to take the directions from the operating system's scheduler, allocate the device to the process, and initiate its execution. This procedure may necessitate moving a process from memory in one site to memory at another site; reorganizing a site's memory allocation; reorganizing a site's ready, running, and waiting queues; and initiating the scheduled process. The system only recognizes processes and their demands for service and responds to them based on the established scheduling policy, which determines what must be done to manage the processes. As mentioned in earlier chapters, policies for scheduling must consider issues such as load balancing, communications minimization, memory loading minimization, first come first served, and least time remaining.

Synchronization is a key issue in network process management. For example, processes can coordinate their activities by passing messages. In addition, processes can pass synchronization parameters from port to port using **primitives** such as "send and receive" to implement the proper semantics for synchronization within the processes. For instance, when a process reaches a point at which it needs service from an external source, such as I/O, it will send a message searching for the service; during the time it is waiting, it is put in a wait state by the processor server.

Interrupts, which cause a processor to be assigned to another process, also are represented as messages that are sent to the proper process for service. For example, an interrupt may cause the active process to be blocked and moved into a wait state. The completion of the service for the interrupting requestor will cause the processor server to unblock and restore the process to a ready-to-process state.

OBJECT-BASED DOS An object-based DOS has a different way of looking at a computer system. Instead of being made up of resources and processes, the system is viewed as a collection of **objects**. The term *object* is meant to represent both hardware (such as CPUs, memory, printers, scanners, tape drives, and disks) and software (such as files, programs, semaphores, and data) or a combination of the two. Each object in the system has a unique name or identifier to differentiate it from all other objects in the system.

Objects are viewed as abstract entities, data types, that can go through a change of state, act according to set patterns, be manipulated, or exist in relation to other objects in a manner appropriate to the object's semantics in the system. This means that objects have a set of invariant properties that defines them and their behavior within the context of their defined parameters. For example, a tape drive has invariant properties that include the following: data can be written to a tape, data can be read from a tape, reading and writing cannot take place concurrently, and the data's beginning and ending points cannot be compromised. If we use these simple rules to construct a simulation of a tape drive, we have created an accurate representation of this object.

To determine the state of an object, one must perform an appropriate operation on it, such as reading or writing to a tape, because the object is identified by the set of operations one can send it. The combination of the operations with their internally defined data structures and computations represents an object's instantiation. Typically, systems using this concept have a large number of objects but a small number of operations on the objects, something on the order of one to ten.

Therefore, in an object-based DOS, process management becomes object management, with processes acting as discrete objects. Process management, in this case, deals with the policies and mechanisms for controlling the operations, creation, and destruction of objects in the system. Therefore, process management has two components: the kernel level and the process manager.

To provide the basic mechanisms for building the operating system, the collection of computers must have a kernel level that provides for object creation, destruction, capability management, operation, synchronization, communication, and scheduling.

An important job of the kernel is to provide the capacity to create and delete objects dynamically. When the object is created it is assigned all the resources needed for its operation and is given control until the task is completed. Once completed, it returns control to the kernel, which selects the next object to be executed.

Capability lists, discussed in Chapter 8, are an integral part of the kernel. Each site has both a capability manager that maintains the capability lists for objects that are found on it and a directory with location information on all capabilities in the system. This directory is used to guide local requests for capabilities to the site on which they are located.

To satisfy a request, the capability manager first determines whether a process has been previously granted rights and then, if the requester has access rights, grants it the right to access the requested object, such as a region in memory. Once granted, the requester directs the request for service to the named object. If the named object is at another site, the local capability manager will direct the requester, through a new address computation and message, to the proper capability manager.

Synchronization mechanisms and communication support are part of the kernel portion of a distributed operating system. Typically, synchronization has been implemented as some form of shared variable, such as the `wait` and `signal` codes discussed in Chapter 6.

Communication between distributed objects can be in the form of shared data objects, message objects, or control interactions. Most systems provide different communications primitives to their objects, which are either synchronous or asynchronous. That is, either the sender and receiver must be linked up and ready to send and receive, or there must be some shareable area such as a mailbox, queue, or stack to which the communicated information is sent. In some cases, the receiver periodically checks to see if anyone has sent anything. In other cases, the receiver waits, doing nothing else, until the communicated information arrives. There can also be a combination of these. For example, if instead of a receiver periodically checking the repository a mechanism could signal when a communication had arrived, then users could respond as they saw fit. The advantage is that the receiver need not periodically check the container, wasting time when nothing was there, it could check only when something was definitely waiting.

Finally, the kernel environment for distributed systems must have a scheduler with a consistent and robust mechanism for scheduling objects within the system according to its operations goals.

Assuming that the kernel level's operations exist, the Process Manager will include the following tasks: creation of objects, synchronization of operation on objects, scheduling of objects, dispatching of objects, deletion of objects, and communications among objects. To perform these tasks, the Process Manager uses the kernel environment, which provides the primitives it needs to capture the low-level hardware in the system. For example, to run a database called "object A," the Process Manager must do the following: (1) it must determine whether the object is in memory; (2) if not, it must find the object on secondary storage, allocate space in memory for it, and log it into all the proper locations; (3) it must provide the proper information for scheduling the object in the system; and (4) once the object has been scheduled, it will be pulled out by the kernel dispatcher to place it into the running state.

Thus far we have discussed the similarities between the object-based and process-based managers. The major difference between them is that objects contain all of their state information; that is, the information is not stored separately in another part of the system. For example, information does not need to be stored in a process control block or other data structure separate from the object.

DEVICE MANAGEMENT

In distributed systems, the actions performed at the physical device level are the same as those described in Chapter 7. Devices must be opened, closed, read from, and written to. In addition, status bits must be set or cleared and the parameters specific to each device must be initialized. These can be done on a global, cluster, or localized basis. From a distributed operating system perspective, users prefer to have devices they can request by name, and have the distributed operating system determine which device, from those available, contains a specific file and how to set it up. For example, if users need specific control of a device, then they should be able to call a device by name, such as disk 0 or tape 1. The control of the device would then be performed by the distributed operating system, which would obtain the device for the user when the *open* command is used.

Allocation is successfully completed only after examination of the device's status, when the distributed operating system returns to the requesting process a unique device ID, a name, that is used for further communication between process and device. Later, the device is released when the user issues a close command, at which point the DOS resets the device's state information and returns its device control block to the device's ready queue. Therefore, the DOS must keep a global accounting of devices and their availability, maintaining each device's status records and control blocks and distributing this information to all sites.

For example, when a user wants to print a file by executing a PRINT FILE ABC command, a DOS places a copy of the file in the distributed operating system spooler directory. The spooler selects the file from this directory and initiates an open request to the system's File Manager. Once it receives a message saying "OPEN OK," the spooler initiates another open request to the distributed operating system line printer Device Manager. Once the line printer is ready, the spooler sends the file to be printed from the system file repository to the printer's input buffer, which could be accomplished through a direct message transfer of the file or a packetized transfer, as described in Chapter 9. Once the printing is done, the copy of the file is deleted from the spooler, and the device is reset and closed. As shown in Figure 10.4, the DOS Device Manager is a collection of remote device drivers connected and associated with the devices, but controlled by status data from the DOS.

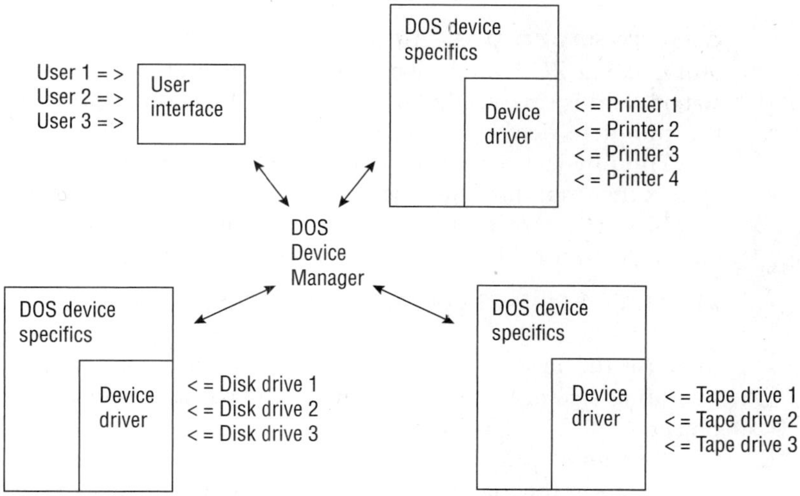

FIGURE 10.4
All systemwide devices are operated by their individual device managers but are controlled by the DOS Device Manager.

PROCESS-BASED DOS All resources in the process-based DOS are controlled by servers called "guardians" or "administrators." The job of these servers is to accept requests for service on their individual resource, process each request fairly with others, provide service to the requestor, and return to serve others, as shown in Figure 10.5.

However, not all systems have a simple collection of resources. Many have clusters of printers, and tape and disk drives. To control these, most process-based systems are configured around complex **server processes**, which manage multiple resources or divide the work among subordinate processes. The administrator process that controls the resources is configured as a device manager and includes the software needed to accept local and remote requests for service, decipher their meaning, and act on them. Typically a server process would be made up of one or more device drivers, a device manager, and a network server component.

FIGURE 10.5 *Requests move from the requestor to the process scheduler to the dispatcher to the server. Interrupt processing manages I/O or processing problems. The wait cycle is used to suspend and resume processing; it functions identically to the wait cycle described in Chapter 4.*

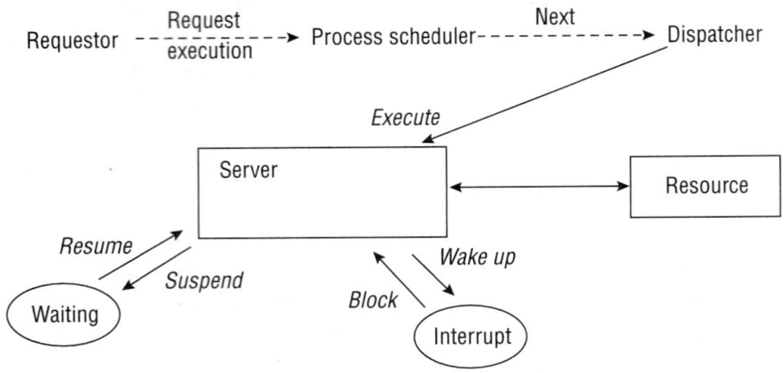

OBJECT-BASED DOS In object-based DOS, device management has a consistent make up. The physical device is viewed as an object, just like other items in the system, and is surrounded by a layer of software that provides to the outside world the complete view of the device object.

The physical device is manipulated by a set of "operations" — explicit commands that mobilize the device to perform its designated functions. For example, an object to control a tape unit would require operations to rewind, fast forward, and scan. To use a tape drive, users issue an operation on a tape object such as this:

```
WITH TAPE 1 DO FAST FORWARD(N) RECORDS
```

to cause the tape drive to advance *N* records. This assumes, of course, that the operating system has already granted the user access authorization to use the tape object.

The same sequence of events would apply to a disk drive. The user would send operations to the manager to create a new file, destroy an old file, open or close an existing file, read information from a file, or write to it. The user would not have to know the underlying mechanisms that implement the operations, just the operations themselves. The objects can be assembled to communicate and synchronize with each other to provide a distributed resource network, where each object is aware of its distributed peers, but only from a location point of view. If the local device manager cannot satisfy the need, the request is sent to another, a peer, device manager. The user does not need to know whether the resource it is using is centralized or distributed — only that it is providing adequate service.

For this system to be successful, the device manager object for each site must contain a directory of device objects on all sites. When a requesting object wants to use an output device to print something, for example, it presents this to its local device manager, which examines it to determine whether it can provide the proper service. If it can't meet the request locally — whether because of inadequate processing capacity or unavailability of the proper device — it sends the request to a peer device manager on a site that has the proper resources. The remote site will then process the request and perform the operation for the user.

FILE MANAGEMENT

The goal of distributed file management is to give users the illusion of a single logical file system implemented on an assortment of devices and computers spread over the network. Therefore, the main function of a distributed operating system File Manager is to provide transparent mechanisms to find, open, read, write, close, create, and delete files in the network.

To open a file, the File Manager first locates the file using a directory with information about stored files.

To read a file, the DOS sets up a channel to the file and attempts to read the data using simple file access schemes. A read operation will not be successful if the file is being written to concurrently.

To write to a file a process must have exclusive access to it, which can be accomplished by requesting that the file be locked, a technique frequently used in database systems.

To close a file, the File Manager sends a command to the remote server to release the lock on the particular file being accessed. This is typically accomplished by changing the information in the directory at the file's storage site.

To create a file requires the acquisition of a unique file identifier in the network and space on some storage device. Deletion causes the opposite. File management systems are a subset of database managers, which provide more capabilities to user processes than file systems and are being implemented as distributed database management systems as part of local area network systems.

Therefore, the tasks required by a DOS will include those typically found in a distributed database environment, which involve a host of controls and mechanisms necessary to provide consistent, synchronized, and reliable management of system and user information assets. These include: (1) concurrency control, (2) data redundancy and location transparency, (3) update synchronization, (4) distributed directory, (5) deadlock resolution or recovery, and (6) query processing.

Distributed database models give users a way to group sequences of actions into a logical execution unit. When this unit is executed on a database it must be controlled properly to maneuver the database from one consistent state to another. Maneuvering is accomplished through the concurrency control mechanisms, which provide the logical progression of actions on the system's databases and guard against simultaneous or erroneous operations on the elements of the database. Concurrence control techniques provide for the proper execution of a group of transactions to allow concurrent reads and writes, as long as they do not interfere with each other, thereby providing the "serial execution view" on a database.

Location transparency is related to response to users and distribution of data in the system. Location transparency is provided by mechanisms that map logical data items to physical locations. The mechanisms usually use information about data that is stored at all sites in the form of directories. Data redundancy is an issue related to data availability and reliability. It has positive effects on data access during the read cycle, by allowing the closest copy to be read. It also has beneficial aspects from a recovery viewpoint because if a site fails, the process can be restarted on another site that has the same information, and the failed site can be brought up to a consistent state by copying all updates done since the failure. The problem with redundant data is one of updating; when updates occur, they must be directed to all the sites and must be performed according to system-oriented reliability standards.

Based on the algorithm used and the method of recovery, the system can require that updates be performed at all sites before any reads occur to a master site or to a majority of sites. Some typically used update algorithms are: unanimous agreement, primary site copy, moving primary site, and majority site agreement.

A distributed directory manages transparency of data location and enhances recovery of data for users. It contains definitions dealing with the physical and logical structure for the stored data, as well as the policies and mechanisms for mapping between the two. In addition, it contains the systemwide names of all resources and the addressing mechanisms for locating and accessing them.

Deadlock detection and recovery, described in Chapter 5, are critical issues in distributed systems. The major goal is to detect and recover from the circular wait-for condition, which occurs when one device requests the use of one resource, whether file, disk, or tape, and also has exclusive use of another resource, while a second device requests use of any held resource and also holds the same resource under exclusive use.

Detection and correction, prevention, and avoidance are the known schemes used to deal with deadlocks. To recognize the condition, the system uses directed resource graphs and looks for cycles. To prevent cycles, the system tries to delay beginning execution of a transaction until it has all it needs to execute. To avoid cycles, the system tries to allow execution only when it finds a transaction that can be completed. To recover from deadlock, the system selects a victim, a transaction that when terminated will free enough resources so the others can finish.

Query processing examines the methods that minimize the functions needed to process requests for information. The techniques implemented deal with increasing the effectiveness of global query execution sequence, local site processing sequence, and device processing sequence, which relate directly to the global process scheduling problem. Therefore, to ensure consistency of the entire system scheduling scheme, the query processing strategy must be an integral part of the processing scheduling strategy.

COMMUNICATIONS MANAGEMENT

Communications management is a function unique to networked systems because stand-alone operating systems have no need for a communications manager. As part of a distributed operating system, the job of the communications manager is to provide the policies and mechanisms required to achieve intrasite and intersite communications among concurring processes. Typically, the communications manager must have the ability to provide identifiers to processes within the network and open or close logical paths from processes to other processes — in a one-to-one, one-to-few, one-to-many or one-to-all manner — while managing these paths in a dynamic fashion. The communications manager must be able to locate processes in the network, send messages throughout the network, and track media use. In addition, it must be able to reliably transfer data, code and decode messages, retransmit errors, perform parity checking, do cyclic redundancy checks, establish redundant links, and acknowledge messages and replies, if necessary.

To make all this happen, a process is registered or logged in the network when it is assigned a unique physical designator that can then be disseminated to the other sites. From that moment, it is logged with all sites in the network. For processes — or objects — to communicate with each other, the communications manager must be able to link the processes together. This is usually accomplished through a port — a logical door on one process that can be linked with the port on another process — establishing a logical path for communications between the two.

Ports are usually associated with physical buffers and I/O channels, and represent physical assets that must be used wisely by the communications manager. Ports can be assigned to one process or to many. However, due to the underlying network topology and location of processes, routing at some level is required. This could be as simple as a process-device pair address that associates a logical process with a physical site, or could incorporate many levels traversing multiple links in either a direct or a hop count form, as described in Chapter 9. Other functions that require management are routing, keeping statistics on network use (for use in message scheduling, fault localizations, and rerouting), and providing mechanisms to aid in process time synchronization. This is commonly known as a systemwide clock, which allows the distributed operating system components in the various sites to compensate for variations in time due to delays caused by distributed communications.

PROCESS-BASED DOS In a process-based DOS, interprocess communication is transparent to users of the network. The Network Manager has the functions of controlling the allocation of ports to processes, identifying the processes in the network, controlling the flow of messages, and guaranteeing the transmission and acceptance of the messages without errors. Normally, this component acts as the interfacing mechanism for the process in the system and provides the basics of message transfer, relieving the users of having to know where processes physically reside in the network. The Network Manager accepts each process's send and receive commands and interprets them. It transforms those commands into low-level actions that perform the actual transmission of the messages over the links.

OBJECT-BASED DOS A Network Manager object makes both intermode and intramode communications among cooperative objects easy. A process, the active code elements within objects, can begin an operation at a specific instance of an object by sending a request message. Knowing the location of the receiver is not necessary; only its name needs to be known for the Network Manager to provide for the proper routing of the message to the receiver. A process can also invoke an operation that is part of its local object environment.

Generally, some level of the following functions are implemented with Network Managers: send, receive, reply, and request.

- *Send* allows objects to send a message with operations to any object in the system.
- *Receive* warns objects of incoming communications from an object in the system.
- *Reply* allows objects to respond to requests for communications from another object, to respond to a send command they may not have been prepared for, or to indicate to someone that they are ready to accept a send command; that is, that a message can now be sent knowing that the receiver is awaiting it.
- *Request* provides a mechanism for objects to ask for particular services; for example, they could request that a message be sent.

The services supplied by this segment of the operating system are usually provided at the kernel level to better accommodate the many objects that will use them and to offer efficient service. Depending on the system, however, the communications manager may be a simple utility that handles only send and receive primitives, or it may be constructed using ports, or channels. A simple send-and-receive utility requires that users know the name of the objects they will communicate with, whereas the port or channel system requires users to know only the name of the port or channel with which the object is associated. For example, if a communications facility is supported by a port-object type mechanism, then objects are grouped as senders, receivers, ports, and messages, and they link together via capability lists.

NOS DEVELOPMENT

Many of the modern network operating systems (NOS) are true operating systems with all their common features, such as memory management, process scheduling, file management, and device management including disk and I/O operations. However, some earlier NOS did not provide general support for applications and focused on providing file and resource sharing for network clients. Network operating systems typically run on computers called **servers** and perform services for network workstations called **clients.**

Although programs can be run on NOSs, they differ from operating systems running on workstations in the types of services they are optimized to provide. For example, a single-user operating system such as MS-DOS (Chapter 12), or even a multiuser system such as UNIX (Chapter 14), focuses on a user's interaction with the system enabling applications to be run. Network operating systems, in contrast, focus on optimizing the ability to share applications and data stored on the server, as well as on the use of expensive shared resources such as printers and high-speed modems.

Some examples of modern network operating systems include Novell's NetWare, Microsoft's LAN Manager, IBM's LAN Server, and Banyan's VINES. In the following pages we will describe some of the features commonly found in a network operating system without focusing on any particular one. The choice of a specific NOS depends on several factors, including the applications to be run on the server, the service support required, and the user staff's level of training and their requirements for integration with other networking systems.

IMPORTANT FEATURES IN A NOS

Most network operating systems are implemented as either 16-bit or 32-bit software; software written to operate at 32 bits can take full advantage of modern processors. However, more important than the processor is the support a NOS provides for standard local area network technologies and client desktop operating systems.

As discussed in Chapter 9, several standards for LANs are available, such as Ethernet, token ring, LocalTalk, and Arcnet. As organizations take the first steps in building corporatewide information systems, many discover that a NOS, such as NetWare or LAN Manager, is a cost-effective way to provide this connection.

Networks are becoming increasingly heterogeneous; they support workstations that run MS-DOS, Windows, the Macintosh operating system, OS/2, and UNIX. For a NOS to serve as the networking glue in the organization, it must provide strong support for every computing system that makes up the corporate information network, sustaining as many current standards as necessary. Therefore, it must have an architecture that enables new technologies to be adapted easily.

For example, when a NOS provides services to a desktop operating system environment, it should preserve the user's model of interaction with the desktop system. Therefore, network resources should appear as simple extensions of the existing desktop computing environment. On an MS-DOS computer, a network drive should appear to be another hard disk with a different volume name, another drive letter. On the other hand, on a Macintosh computer it should appear as an icon for a volume on the desktop. And a UNIX system should view the drive as a mountable file system.

A NOS is designed to be used with a wide range of third-party hardware devices and software applications, including such devices as hard disk drives, tape backup systems, CD-ROM systems, and network interface cards. These products include software components providing multiuser network applications, such as electronic messaging, and networking expansions such as new protocol stacks.

In addition, a network operating system must be efficient and secure with core components designed to enable multiple network clients to quickly access data and resources without forgetting crucial security features necessary to safeguard applications and data.

MAJOR FUNCTIONS OF A NOS

A major function of a NOS is to allow users to access resources at a remote site. The Internet provides users with the **telnet** facility, which allows remote log in provided that they have an account at the site to which they are connected. For example, if students wanted to use the computer services provided at the University of Pittsburgh from their home computer, they would issue the command:

```
telnet vaxvm3.cis.pitt.edu
```

Security is usually a function of each local operating system that allows access to resources when users type in their current log-in names and passwords. For example, the telnet command above would establish a connection between the student's computer and the University of Pittsburgh VAXVM3 computer. Once the connection was established, the NOS would create a two-way communication line so that all commands entered by the student would be executed by the VMS operating system and all interactive output would be displayed on the student's monitor.

Typical operating system functions such as memory management, file management, and so forth are performed by the remote system, whereas the network operating system handles the functions described in Chapter 9. When accessing telnet, the user must know the appropriate commands for the remote system. For example, whenever users working on a UNIX system use telnet to reach a VMS system, they must use VMS commands exclusively while they're logged on to the VMS computer and return to using UNIX commands only after ending the telnet session.

Another important function of a NOS is to provide a procedure to transfer files from one computer to another. In this case, each system controls and manages its own file system and the files designated by a user are copied from one machine to another.

For example, the Internet provides the **File Transfer Protocol (ftp)** program. If programming students wanted to copy a data file from the university computer to their own desktop computers to complete an assignment, for instance, then each student would issue the following command:

```
ftp unixd.cis.pitt.edu
```

This would summon the ftp program, which would ask the student for a log-in name and password. Once this information was verified by the UNIX operating system, each student would be allowed to copy the file by using the command

`get` (filename.ext)

where "filename.ext" is the absolute file name and extension of the required data file. That means that a user must know exactly in which directory or subdirectory the file is stored because the file location is not transparent. To use ftp most effectively, users must learn special file access commands that are understood by the ftp program — a set entirely different, in some cases, from that of typical operating systems.

In addition, ftp allows users who do not have an account with the remote site to copy files through the **anonymous ftp** mode. In this case, the files to be copied must be placed in a special subdirectory with their protection lowered so that the general public can read them. When users want to copy files from this directory they use "anonymous" as the log-in name and their unique E-mail address as the password. Although the technique allows fast and easy widespread dissemination of information, the lower protection exposes the host to sophisticated break-in techniques and security vulnerabilities by unauthorized users, as described in Chapter 11. Therefore, the host operating system must have a strong security scheme to ensure that anonymous users do not take advantage of the easy access and compromise protected files or resources.

This "find and copy" technique is not considered true file sharing because all users wanting access to the data file must copy the file onto their own systems, thereby duplicating the code and wasting space. This practice also adds **version control** difficulties because when one user modifies the file in any way, those changes will not be reflected on other copies already stored in other directories unless each is replaced with the changed version.

CHAPTER TEN CONCLUSION

Network operating systems were developed to link freestanding independent systems. Although they were an adequate solution to early networking needs, they didn't take full advantage of the global resources available to all connected sites. Therefore, distributed operating systems were developed.

Every networked system, whether a NOS or a DOS, has requirements. Each must be secure from unauthorized access yet accessible to authorized users. Each must monitor its available system resources, including memory, processors, devices, and files as described in Chapters 2 through 8, as well as its communications links. In addition, because it is a networking operating system, it must perform the required tasks described in Chapter 9.

So far we've discussed each manager and each operating system function in isolation, but in reality, system performance depends on the combined effort of each piece. In the next chapter, the last in Part I, we'll look at the system as a whole and examine how each piece contributes to, or detracts from, overall system performance.

KEY TERMS

groupware
distributed processing
Network Operating Systems (NOS)
Distributed Operating Systems (DOS)
process-based DOS
object-based DOS
primitives
objects
server processes
servers
clients
telnet
file transfer protocol (ftp)
anonymous ftp
version control

EXERCISES

1. What are the advantages and disadvantages of process-based DOS?
2. What are the advantages and disadvantages of object-based DOS?
3. Name some of the advantages of distributed systems over centralized systems.
4. Name some of the disadvantages of distributed systems over centralized systems.
5. Give an example of a "communications" deadlock.

ADVANCED EXERCISES

6. If you were managing a hospital's network, what policies would you implement to protect your system. Keep in mind that as system manager, your job is to provide the correct level of accessibility to authorized users while denying access to unauthorized users.
7. Remembering the discussion of deadlocks in Chapter 5, if you were designing a networked system, how would you manage the threat of deadlocks in your network? Consider all of the following: prevention, detection, avoidance, and recovery.

Chapter Eleven

SYSTEM MANAGEMENT

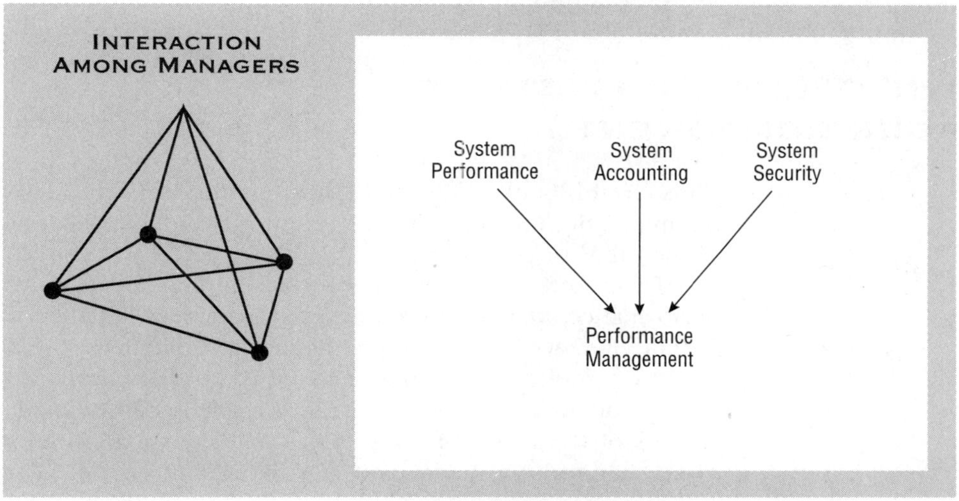

In Chapter 1 we introduced the four parts of the operating system: Memory Manager, Processor Manager, Device Manager, and File Manager. In Chapters 2 through 8 we studied how each component works — but we looked at them in isolation. In a real-life operating system, however, they don't work in isolation: each part depends on the other parts.

This chapter will show how they work together and how the system designer has to consider trade-offs to improve the system's overall efficiency. We'll begin by showing how the designer can improve the performance of one component, the cost of that improvement, and how it might affect the performance of the remainder of the system. Later, we'll describe some methods used to monitor and measure system performance, and we'll conclude with a discussion of accounting and security issues.

EVALUATING AN OPERATING SYSTEM

Every operating system is different. Most were designed originally to work with a certain piece of hardware or category of computer and were designed for specific groups of users to meet specific goals. However, most evolved over time to operate multiple systems and they now favor some users and some computing environments over others. For example, if the operating system was written for casual users to meet basic requirements, it might not satisfy more demanding users. Conversely, if it was written for programmers, then a business office's computer operator might find its commands obscure. If it serves the needs of a multiuser computer center, it might be inappropriate for a small research center. Or, if it's written to provide brief response time, it might provide poor throughput.

To evaluate an operating system, we need to understand its design goals, its history, how it communicates with its users, how its resources are managed, and what trade-offs were made to achieve its goals. In other words, we need to balance its strengths against its weaknesses.

THE OPERATING SYSTEM'S FOUR COMPONENTS

Thus far, this book has looked at the computer system's resources independently, but in practice the performance of any one resource depends on the performance of the other three.

If you were allowed to spend some money to upgrade a computer system's performance, what would you buy: more memory? a faster CPU? more disk drives? a whole new system? And if you bought a whole new system, what characteristics would you look for that would make it more efficient than the old one?

Of course, any improvement in the system can be made only after extensive analysis of the needs of the system's managers and its users. But whenever you make changes to a system, you may be trading one set of problems for another. The key is to consider the performance of the entire system and not just the individual components.

Memory management schemes were discussed in Chapters 2 and 3. If you increase memory or change to another memory allocation scheme you must consider the actual operating environment in which the system will reside. There's a trade-off between memory use and CPU overhead.

For example, if the system will be running student programs exclusively, and the average job runs for 100 milliseconds, your decision to adopt a relocatable partition scheme wouldn't speed up throughput if it takes 125 milliseconds to move one partition. Remember, as the memory management algorithms grow more complex, the CPU overhead increases and overall performance can suffer.

Processor management was covered in Chapters 4, 5, and 6. Let's say you decide to implement a multiprogramming system to increase your processor's utilization. If so, you'd have to remember that multiprogramming requires a great deal of synchronization between the Memory Manager, the Processor Manager, and the I/O devices. The trade-off: better use of the CPU versus increased overhead, slower response time, and decreased throughput.

There are several problems to watch for, among them the following:

1. A system could reach a saturation point if the CPU is fully utilized but is allowed to accept additional jobs — that would result in higher overhead and less time to run programs.

2. Under heavy loads, the CPU time required to manage I/O queues (which under normal circumstances doesn't require a great deal of time) could dramatically increase the time required to run the jobs.
3. With long queues forming at the channels, control units, and I/O devices, the CPU could be idle waiting for processes to finish their I/O.

Device management, covered in Chapter 7, includes several ways to improve I/O device utilization including buffering, blocking, and rescheduling I/O requests to optimize access times. But these are trade-offs: each of these options also increases CPU overhead and uses additional memory space.

Blocking reduces the number of physical I/O requests, and that's good. But it is the CPU's responsibility to block and later deblock the records, and that's overhead.

Buffering helps the CPU match the slower speed of I/O devices, and vice versa, but it requires memory space for the buffers, either dedicated space or a temporarily allocated section of main memory, and this in turn reduces the level of processing that can take place. For example, if each buffer requires 4K of memory and the system requires two sets of double buffers, we've dedicated 16K of memory to the buffers. At a university this might equal, or exceed, the size of several student programs. The trade-off is this: reduced multiprogramming versus better use of I/O devices.

Rescheduling requests is a technique that can help optimize I/O times; it's a "queue reordering technique." But it's an overhead function, so the speeds of the CPU and the I/O device must be weighed against the time it would take to execute the reordering algorithm (Madnick & Donovan, 1974). The following example illustrates this point. Table 11.1 lists three different CPUs with the speed for executing 1,000 instructions and four disk drives with their average access speeds.

TABLE 11.1 *A system with three CPUs and four disk drives of different speeds. Assuming the system requires 1,000 instructions to reorder I/O requests, the advantages of reordering vary depending on both the CPU and the disk.*

CPUs

Number	Time for 1000 Instructions
1	30.0 ms
2	1.2 ms
3	0.2 ms

Disk Drives

Number	Access Speed
A	35 ms
B	10 ms
C	5 ms
D	50 ms

Using the data in Table 11.1 and assuming that a typical reordering module consists of 1,000 instructions, which combinations of one CPU and one disk drive warrant a reordering module? To learn the answer we need to compare disk access speeds before and after reordering.

For example, let's assume that a system consisting of CPU 1 and Disk Drive A, as shown in Table 11.1, has to access Track 1, Track 9, Track 1, and then Track 9, and that the arm is already located at Track 1. Without reordering, Drive A requires approximately 35 ms for each access: 35 + 35 + 35 = 105 ms. After reordering (which requires 30 ms), the arm can perform both accesses on Track 1 before traveling, in 35 ms, to Track 9 for the other two accesses, resulting in a speed nearly twice as fast: 30 + 35 = 65 ms. In this case, reordering would improve overall speed.

However, when the same situation is faced by CPU 1 and the much faster Disk Drive C, we find the disk will again begin at Track 1 and make all four accesses in 15 ms (5 + 5 + 5) but, when it stops to reorder those accesses (which requires 30 ms), it takes 35 ms (30 + 5) to complete the task. Therefore, reordering requests is not always warranted.

Remember, when the system is configured, the reordering algorithm is either always on or always off. It can't be changed by the systems operator without reconfiguration, so the initial setting, on or off, must be determined by evaluating the system "on the average."

File management, discussed in Chapter 8, looked at how secondary storage allocation schemes help the user organize and access the files on the system. Almost every factor discussed in that chapter can affect overall system performance.

For example, file organization is an important consideration. If a file is stored noncontiguously and has several sections residing in widely separated cylinders of a disk pack, it could be a time-consuming task to sequentially access all of its records. Such a case would suggest that the files should be compacted so each section resides near the others, but recompaction takes CPU time and makes the files unavailable to users while it's being done.

Another file management issue that could affect retrieval time is the location of a volume's directory. For instance, some systems read the directory into main memory and hold it there until the user terminates the session. This poses a problem if the system crashes before any modifications have been recorded permanently in secondary storage. In such a case, the I/O time that was saved by not having to access secondary storage every time the user requested to see the directory has been negated by not having current information in the user's directory.

Similarly, the location of a volume's directory on the disk might make a significant difference in the time it takes to access it. For example, if directories are stored on the outermost track, then on average, the disk drive arm has to travel farther to access each file than if the directories were kept in the center tracks.

Overall, file management is closely related to the device on which the files are stored and designers must consider both issues at the same time when evaluating or modifying computer systems. Different schemes offer different flexibility, but the trade-off for increased file flexibility is increased CPU overhead.

MEASURING SYSTEM PERFORMANCE

Total system performance can be defined as "the efficiency with which a computer system meets its goals" — that is, how well it serves its users. But it isn't easy to measure system efficiency because it's affected by three major components: the user's programs, operating system programs, and hardware units. In addition, system performance can be very subjective and difficult to quantify — how, for instance, can anyone objectively gauge "ease of use"? While some portions of ease of use can be quantified — for example, time to log in — the overall concept is difficult to quantify.

Even when performance is quantifiable, such as the number of disk accesses per minute, it is not an absolute measure but a relative one based on the interactions of the three components and the workload being handled by the system.

MEASUREMENT TOOLS

Most designers and analysts rely on these measures of system performance: throughput, capacity, response time, turnaround time, resource utilization, availability, and reliability.

Throughput is a composite measure that indicates the productivity of the system as a whole; the term is often used by system managers. Throughput is usually measured under steady-state conditions and gives "the number of jobs processed per day" or "the number of on-line transactions handled per hour." Throughput can also be a measure of the volume of work handled by one unit of the computer system, an isolation that is useful when analysts are looking for bottlenecks in the system.

Bottlenecks tend to develop when resources reach their **capacity**, or maximum throughput level; the resource becomes saturated and the processes in the system aren't being passed along. Thrashing is a result of a saturated disk drive. Bottlenecks also occur when main memory has been overcommitted and the level of multiprogramming has reached a peak point. That means the working sets for the active jobs can't be kept in main memory, so the Memory Manager is continuously swapping pages between main memory and secondary storage. The CPU is processing the jobs at a snail's pace because it's very busy flipping pages.

Throughput and capacity can be monitored by either hardware or software. Bottlenecks can be detected by monitoring the queues forming at each resource: when a queue starts to grow rapidly, that's an indication that the arrival rate is greater than, or close to, the service rate and the resource is saturated. These are called "feedback loops," and we'll discuss them later in this chapter. Once the bottleneck is detected the appropriate action can be taken to resolve the problem.

To on-line interactive users **response time** is an important measure of system performance. Response time is the interval required to process a user's request: from when the user presses the key to send the message until the system indicates receipt of the message. For batch jobs this is known as **turnaround time**; that's the time from the submission of the job until its output is returned to the user. Whether on-line or batch, this measure depends on both the workload being handled by the system at the time of the request and on the type of job or request being submitted. Some requests, for instance, are handled faster than others because they require fewer resources.

To be an accurate measure of the predictability of the system, response time and turnaround time should include not just their average but also their variance.

Resource utilization is a measure of how much each unit is contributing to the overall operation. It is usually given as a percentage of time that a resource is actually in use. For example: Is the CPU busy 60 percent of the time? Is the line printer busy 90 percent of the time? How about each of the terminals? Or the seek mechanism on a disk? This data helps the analyst determine whether there is balance among the units of a system or whether a system is I/O-bound or CPU-bound.

Availability indicates the likelihood that a resource will be ready when a user needs it. For on-line users it may mean the probability that a port is free or a terminal is available when they attempt to log in. For those already on the system it may mean the probability that one or several specific resources, such as a plotter or a group of, say, seven tape drives, will be ready when their program makes its request. Availability in its simplest form means that a unit will be operational and not "out of service" when a user needs it.

Availability is influenced by two factors, **mean time between failures (MTBF)** and **mean time to repair (MTTR)**. MTBF is the average time that a unit is operational before it breaks down, and MTTR is the average time needed to fix a failed unit and put it back in service. They're calculated with simple arithmetic equations. For example, if you buy a terminal with an MTBF of 4000 hours (the number is given by the manufacturer) and you'll use it for 4 hours a day for 20 days a month, or 80 hours per month, then you would expect it to fail once every 50 months (4000/80) — not bad. The MTTR is the average time it would take to have a piece of hardware repaired and would depend on several factors: the seriousness of the damage, the location of the repair shop, how quickly you need it back, how much you are willing to pay, and so on. This is usually an approximate figure.

The formula used to compute the unit's availability (A) is:

$$A = \frac{\text{MTBF}}{\text{MTBF} + \text{MTTR}}$$

As indicated, availability is a ratio between the unit's MTBF and its total time (MTBF + MTTR). For our terminal, we could assume the MTTR is 2 hours; therefore:

$$A = \frac{4000}{4000 + 2} = 0.9995$$

So, on the average, this unit would be available 9,995 out of every 10,000 hours. In other words, you'd expect five failures out of 10,000 uses.

Reliability is similar to availability but it measures the probability that a unit will not fail *during a given time period* and it is a function of MTBF. The formula (Nickel, 1978) used to compute the unit's reliability is:

$$R(t) = e^{-(1/\text{MTBF})(t)}$$

where e is the mathematical constant approximately equal to 2.71828.

To illustrate how this equation works, let's say you absolutely need to use the terminal for the 10 minutes before your upcoming deadline. With time expressed in hours, the unit's reliability is given by:

$$\begin{aligned} R(t) &= e^{-(1/4000)(10/60)} \\ &= e^{-(1/24{,}000)} \\ &= 0.9999584 \end{aligned}$$

This is the probability that it will be available (won't fail) during the critical 10-minute time period — and 0.9999584 is a very high number. Therefore, if the terminal was ready at the beginning of the transaction, it will probably remain in working order for the entire period of time.

These measures of performance can't be taken in isolation from the workload being handled by the system unless you're simply fine-tuning a specific portion of the system. Overall system performance varies from time to time, so it's important to define the actual working environment before making generalizations.

FEEDBACK LOOPS

To prevent the processor from spending more time doing overhead than executing jobs, the operating system must continuously monitor the system and feed this information to the Job Scheduler. Then the Scheduler can either allow more jobs to enter the system or prevent new jobs from entering until some of the congestion has been relieved. This **feedback loop** has to be designed very carefully and can be either negative or positive (Deitel, 1984).

A **negative feedback loop** mechanism monitors the system and, when it becomes too congested, signals the appropriate manager to slow down the arrival rate of the processes.

People on vacation use them all the time. For example, if you're looking for a gas station and the first one you find already has too many cars waiting in line, you collect the data and you react negatively. Therefore your "processor" suggests that you drive on to another station (assuming, of course, that you haven't procrastinated too long and have enough gas to continue).

In a computer system a negative feedback loop monitoring I/O devices would inform the Device Manager that Printer 1 has too many jobs in its queue, causing the Device Manager to direct all newly arriving jobs to Printer 2, which isn't as busy. The negative feedback helps stabilize the system and keep queue lengths close to their estimated mean values.

A **positive feedback loop** mechanism works in the opposite way: it monitors the system, and when the system becomes underutilized, the positive feedback loop causes the arrival rate to increase. Positive feedback loops are used in paged virtual memory systems, but they must be used cautiously because they're more difficult to implement than negative loops.

Here's how they work. The positive feedback loop monitoring the CPU informs the Job Scheduler that the CPU is underutilized, so the Scheduler allows more jobs to enter the system to give more work to the CPU. However, as more jobs enter, the amount of main memory allocated to each job decreases. Soon, if too many new jobs are allowed to enter the job stream, the result can be an increase in page faults. And this, in turn, may cause CPU utilization to deteriorate. In fact, if the operating system is poorly designed, positive feedback loops can actually put the system in an unstable mode of operation. Therefore, the monitoring mechanisms for positive feedback loops must be designed with great care.

As this example shows, an algorithm for a positive feedback loop should monitor the effect of new arrivals in two places: the Processor Manager's control of the

CPU and the Device Manager's read and write operations. That's because both areas experience the most dynamic changes, which can lead to unstable conditions. Such an algorithm should check to see whether the arrival produces the anticipated result and whether system performance is actually improved. If the arrival causes performance to deteriorate then the monitoring algorithm could cause the operating system to adjust its allocation strategies until a stable mode of operation has been reached again.

MONITORING

Several techniques for measuring the performance of a working system have been developed as computer systems have evolved, and they can be implemented by either hardware or software components. Hardware monitors are more expensive but they have the advantage of having a minimum impact on the system because they're outside of it and attached electronically. They include hard-wired counters, clocks, and comparative elements (Lane & Mooney, 1988).

Software monitors are relatively inexpensive but because they become part of the system they can distort the results of the analysis. After all, the software must use the resources it's trying to monitor. In addition, software tools must be developed for each specific system, so it's difficult to move them from system to system.

In early systems, performance was measured simply by timing the processing of specific instructions. The system analysts might have calculated the number of times an ADD instruction could be done in one second. Or they might have measured the processing time of a typical set of instructions. (Typical in the sense that they would represent the instructions common to the system.) These measurements monitored only the CPU speed because in those days the CPU was the most important resource, so the remainder of the system was ignored.

Today, system measurements must include the other hardware units as well as the operating systems, compilers, and other system software. Measurements are made in a variety of ways. Some use "real" programs, usually production programs that are used extensively by the users of the system, and they are run with different configurations of CPUs, operating systems, and other components. The results are called **benchmarks** and are useful when comparing systems that have gone through extensive changes. Benchmarks are often used by vendors to demonstrate to prospective clients the specific advantages of a new CPU, operating system, compiler, or piece of hardware.

If it's not advisable or possible to experiment with the system itself, a simulation model is used to measure performance. This is typically the case when new hardware is being developed. A simulation model is a computerized abstraction of what is represented in reality. The amount of detail built into the model is dictated by time and money — the time needed to develop the model and the cost of running it.

Designers of simulation models must be careful to avoid the extremes of too much detail, which becomes too expensive to run, or of too little detail, which wouldn't produce enough useful information. If you'd like to write a program that's an example of a simulation model, see exercise 12 in Chapter 2.

ACCOUNTING

The accounting function of the operating system might seem a mundane subject, but it's not; it pays the bills and keeps the system financially operable. From a practical standpoint it might be one of the most important elements of the system.

Most computer system resources are paid for by the users. In the simplest case, that of a single user, it's easy to calculate the cost of the system. But in a multiuser environment, computer costs are usually distributed among users based on how much each one uses the system's resources. To do this distribution, the operating system must be able to set up user accounts, assign passwords, identify which resources are available to each user, and define quotas for available resources, such as disk space or maximum CPU time allowed per job. At a university, for example, students are sometimes given quotas that include maximum pages per job, maximum log-in time, and maximum number of jobs during a given period of time. To calculate the cost of the whole system, the accounting program must collect information on each active user.

Pricing policies vary from system to system. Typical measurements include some or all of the following:

Total amount of time spent between job submission and completion. In interactive environments this is the time from log-in to log-out, also known as **connect time**.

CPU time is the time spent by the processor executing the job.

Main memory usage is represented in units of time, bytes of storage, or bytes of storage multiplied by units of time — it all depends on the configuration of the operating system. For example, a job that requires 200K for 4 seconds followed by 120K for 2 seconds could be billed for 6 seconds of main memory usage, or 320K of memory usage, or a combination of K/second of memory usage computed as follows:

[(200 * 4) + (120 * 2)] = 1040K/second of memory usage

Secondary storage used during program execution, like main memory use, can be given in units of time or space, or both.

Secondary storage used during the billing period is usually given in terms of the number of disk tracks allocated.

Use of system software includes utility packages, compilers, and/or databases.

Number of I/O operations is usually grouped by device class: line printer, terminal, and disks.

Time spent waiting for I/O completion.

Number of input records read, usually grouped by type of input device.

Number of output records printed, usually grouped by type of output device.

Number of page faults are reported in paging systems.

Pricing policies are often used as a way to achieve specific operational goals.

For instance, by varying the price of system services, users can be convinced to distribute their workload to the system manager's advantage. Therefore, by offering reduced rates during off hours some users might be persuaded to run long jobs in batch mode inexpensively overnight instead of interactively during peak hours. Pricing incentives can also be used to encourage users to access more plentiful and cheap resources rather than those that are scarce and expensive. For example, by putting a high price on printer output, users might be encouraged to order a minimum of printouts.

Should the system give each user billing information at the end of each job or at the end of each on-line session? The answer depends on the environment.

Some systems only give information on resource use. Other systems also calculate the price of the most costly items, such as CPU utilization, disk storage use, and supplies (i.e., paper used on the line printer) at the end of every job. This gives the user an up-to-date report of expenses and, if appropriate, calculates how much is left in the user's account. Some universities use this technique to warn paying students of impending disaster.

The advantage of maintaining billing records on-line is that the status of each user can be checked before the user's job is allowed to enter the `READY` queue. If the user's financial status is questionable, the job will be rejected until the account is corrected.

The disadvantage is overhead, of course. When billing records are kept on-line and an accounting program is kept active, memory space is used and CPU processing is increased. One compromise is to defer the accounting program until off-hours, when the system is lightly loaded.

ETHICS

Unlike many disciplines, the computer industry is too young to have developed sufficient ethical concepts to guide an individual's use of the technology. For example, we take for granted that our medical doctor will keep our records private, but many of us don't have the same confidence in the computer-based companies that keep our credit records. Although ethics is a subject that's not often addressed in computer science classes, the implications are so vast they can't be ignored by users or systems administrators.

At issue are the seemingly conflicting needs of users: the individual's need for privacy, the organization's need to protect its proprietary information, and the public's right to know as illustrated in freedom of information laws.

For the system's owner, ethical lapses by authorized or unauthorized users can have severe consequences.

- Illegally copied software can result in lawsuits and fines of several times the retail price of each product for each transgression. Several industry associations publish toll-free numbers encouraging disgruntled employees to turn in their employers who use illegal software.
- Plagiarism, the unauthorized copying of copyrighted work, is illegal and punishable by law in the United States as well as in many other developed

nations. When the original work is on paper, most users know the proper course of action, but when the original is in electronic form, some people don't know what to do.

- Eavesdropping on E-mail, data, or voice communications is sometimes illegal and usually unwarranted, except under certain circumstances. If calls or messages must be monitored, the participants should always be made aware of that before the monitoring begins.
- "Cracking," sometimes called "hacking," gaining access to another's computer system to monitor or change data, is seldom ethical. Although it's seen as a sport by certain people, each break-in should cause the system's owner to question the validity of the system's data.
- Unethical use of technology, defined as unauthorized access to private or protected computer systems or electronic information, is a murky area of the law, but it's clearly the wrong thing to do. Legally, the justice system has great difficulty keeping up with each specific form of unauthorized access because the technology changes so quickly. Therefore, system owners can't rely on the law for guidance. Instead, they must aggressively teach their users about what is and is not ethical behavior.

How can we teach users to behave ethically? Only a continuing series of communications to computer users will effectively convey right and wrong behavior. Make sure your organization has a published policy clearly stating which actions will and will not be condoned. Consider teaching a regular seminar in the subject including real-life case histories. Discuss ethical questions such as: Is it okay to read someone else's E-mail? Is it right for someone else to read *your* E-mail? Is it ethical for a competitor to read your data? Is it okay if someone scans your bank account? Is it right for someone to change the results of your medical test? Is it acceptable for someone to copy your software program and put it on the Internet? Is it acceptable for someone to copy a Department of Defense document and put it on the Internet?

SYSTEM SECURITY

The system has conflicting needs: to share resources while protecting them. In the early days, security consisted of a lock and key: the system was physically guarded and only authorized users were allowed in the vicinity. With the advent of data communication, networking, the proliferation of personal computers, and modern telecommunications software, however, computer security has become much more difficult.

SYSTEM VULNERABILITIES

Systems that were once unaccessible have now become vulnerable to attack, and because system security is a relatively recent phenomenon, many systems have little protection built into them. The major problem is that system managers must balance two opposing needs: to keep the system accessible to its authorized users while protecting it from other people who have no right to access it.

Not all breaks in security are malicious; some are only the unauthorized use of resources. But some stem from a purposeful disruption of the system's operation, and others are purely accidental such as hardware malfunctions, undetected errors in the operating system, or natural disasters. Malicious or not, a break in security severely damages the system's credibility. Following are some types of security breaks that may occur.

Accidental incomplete modification of data occurs when nonsynchronized processes access data records and modify some but not enough of the record's fields. An example was given in Chapter 5 when we discussed the case of the deadlocked database.

Data values are incorrectly encoded when fields aren't large enough to hold the numeric value stored there. For example, when a field is too small to store a numerical value, FORTRAN will replace the number with a string of asterisks and COBOL will simply truncate the higher order digits. Neither error would be discovered at the time of storage — it would be discovered only when the value is retrieved. That's an inconvenient time to make such an unpleasant discovery.

Intentional unauthorized access is the most damaging break in security, and we'll devote the remainder of this chapter to some ways that can happen.

Browsing is when unauthorized users are allowed to search through storage, directories, or files for information they are not privileged to read. The storage refers to main memory or to unallocated space on disks or tapes. Sometimes the **browsing** occurs after the previous job has finished. When a section of main memory is allocated to a process, the data from a previous job often remains in memory — it isn't usually erased by the system — and so it's available to a browser. The same applies to data stored in secondary storage.

Wire tapping is nothing new. Just as telephone lines can be tapped, so can most data communication lines. **Wire tapping** can be "passive," where the unauthorized user is just listening to the transmission but isn't changing the contents. There are two reasons for passive tapping: to copy data while bypassing any authorization procedures and to collect specific information (such as passwords) that will permit the tapper to enter the system at a later date.

"Active" tapping is when the data being sent is modified. Two methods of active wire tapping are "between lines" transmission and "piggy back" entry. Between lines doesn't alter the messages sent by the legitimate user, but it inserts additional messages into the communication line while the legitimate user is pausing. Piggy back intercepts and modifies the original messages. This can be done by breaking the communication line and routing the message to another computer that acts as the host. For example, the tapper could intercept a log-off message, return the expected acknowledgment of the log-off to the user, and then continue the interactive session with all the privileges of the original user — and no one is any wiser.

Repeated trials is a method used to enter systems that rely on passwords. If an intruder knows the basic scheme for creating passwords such as length of password and symbols allowed to create it, then the system can be compromised with a program that systematically goes through all possible combinations until a valid combination is found. This isn't as long a process as one might think if the passwords are short or if the intruder learns enough about the intended victim-user. Because the intruder doesn't need to break a specific password, the guessing of any user's password allows entry to the system and access to its resources.

Trash collection is an evening pastime for those who enjoy perusing anything and everything thrown out by the computer department — the discarded computer tapes, disks, printer ribbons, and printouts of source code, programs, memory dumps, and notes. They all can yield important information that can be used to enter the system illegally.

Trap doors are unspecified and nondocumented entry points to the system. **Trap doors** can be caused by a flaw in the system design or they can be put there by a system programmer for future use. They may also be incorporated into the system by a destructive "virus" or by a "Trojan horse" program — one that is seemingly innocuous but that executes hidden instructions.

SYSTEM ASSAULTS: COMPUTER VIRUSES

Any assault on a system is a grave security risk. It raises questions about the integrity of the operating system, every file on the system, and the validity of any data. There are several kinds of assaults including viruses, worms, Trojan horses, and logic bombs.

A **virus** is any unauthorized program that is designed to: gain access to a computer system, lodge itself in a secretive way by incorporating itself into other legitimate programs, and replicate itself. Viruses need other programs to spread. A **worm** is like a virus — it replicates itself but is a self-contained program that is self-propagating. Worms thrive in network environments (Shoch & Hupp, 1982). A **Trojan Horse** is a virus that's disguised as a legitimate or harmless program that sometimes carries within itself the means to allow the program's creator to secretly access the user's system. A **logic bomb** is a destructive program with a time delay — it can spread throughout a network, often unnoticed, until a predetermined time when it "goes off" and does its damage. Regardless of the programmer's intent, any of these invasions destroys the integrity of the system.

These programs are very mobile on networked systems, such as the worm that infected more than 6,000 systems over a weekend in 1988. That program was installed by someone with access to a university computer and it spread literally overnight to hundreds of other universities. Many other destructive programs have been contracted from public "bulletin boards," where they can reproduce rather easily. Some have been included with illegal **"pirated" software**. For example, one virus was distributed in Pakistan to tourists as part of an illegally copied (and illegally bought) popular software package. The sellers said they did it to teach the buyers a lesson in ethics.

Viruses have even been found in legitimate applications software. One virus was inadvertently picked up at a trade show by a developer who unknowingly allowed it to infect the finished code of a completed commercial software package just before it was marketed. The package had to be quickly recalled.

There are measures that can be used to protect the system. The level of protection is usually in proportion to the importance of its data. Medical data should be highly protected. Undergraduate computer programs probably don't deserve the same level of security.

Software to combat viruses can be purchased for most systems. It can be preventive or diagnostic, or both. Preventive programs may calculate a "checksum" for each production program, putting the values in a master file. Later, before a program is executed, its checksum is compared with the master. Generally diagnostic software compares file sizes (checking for an added code when none is expected), looks for replicating instructions, and searches for unusual file activity. Some software may look for certain specific instructions and monitor the way the programs execute. But remember: soon after these packages are marketed, clever vandals start looking for ways to thwart them. Hence, only the most current software can be expected to uncover the latest viruses.

The most extreme protection for sensitive data is with **encryption** — putting it into a secret code. Total network encryption, also called communications encryption, is the most extreme form — that's when all communications with the system are encrypted. The system then decrypts them for processing. To communicate with another system, the data is encrypted, transmitted, decrypted, and processed. Partial encryption is less extreme and may be used between a network's entry and exit points or other vulnerable parts of its communication system. Storage encryption means that the information is stored in encrypted form and decrypted before it's read or used.

There are two disadvantages to encryption: it increases the system's overhead and the system becomes totally dependent on the encryption process itself — if you lose the key, you've lost the data forever. But if the system *must* be kept secure, then this procedure may be warranted.

MANAGING SYSTEMS

Most systems use a combination of several protection devices: passwords, backups, maintenance of written security policies, and carefully training users in proper data management.

Passwords are one of the easiest and most effective protection schemes to implement, but only if they're used correctly. A good password is unusual, memorable, and changed often. Ideally, the password should be a combination of characters and numbers, something that's easy for the user to remember but difficult for someone else to guess. The password should be committed to memory, never written down, and not included in a script file to log on to a network.

Historically, intruders have gained access to systems by using some innovative techniques to crack user passwords: trying words found in a file of dictionary terms; looking in and around the user's desk for a written reminder; trying the user identification as the password, searching log-on scripts; and even learning the names of a user's loved ones or the user's hobbies.

Good passwords are changed regularly and have at least six keystrokes including one or two numbers. There are several excellent techniques for generating a good password. You might try creating a misspelled word or bits of phrases that you'll easily remember. Another technique is to follow a certain pattern on the keyboard, generating new passwords easily by starting your sequence with a different letter each time. A third technique creates acronyms from memorable sentences, such as MDWB4YOIA which stands for: "MY Dog Will Be 4 Years Old In April." If your operating system differentiates between upper and lower case characters (as UNIX does), take advantage of that feature for maximum security creating passwords: MDwb4YOia.

Recent password technology includes development of the **smart card** — a credit card-sized calculator that displays a constantly changing multidigit number that's synchronized with an identical number generator in the system. To enter the correct password, the user must type in the number that appears at that moment on the smart card. Only if the numbers are identical is the user admitted to the system. For added protection, the smart card may require a secret number or code in addition to the displayed number.

Making **backups** and performing other archiving techniques should be standard operating procedure for any computing system. Most system managers use a layered backup schedule. That is, they back up the entire system once a week and back up every evening only the files that were changed that day. As an extra measure of safety, managers store copies of complete system backups for the previous three to six months in a safe off-site location.

Backups become particularly significant when a computer virus infects your system. If you discovered it early, you can empty the system and reload it with clean files from your backup disks or tapes. Of course, any changes made since the files were archived will have to be regenerated.

Perhaps most important to good system management is effective continuing user training and thorough written procedures. Most system failures are caused by honest mistakes made by well-intentioned users — not by malicious intruders. Written security procedures should recommend frequent password changes, reliable backup procedures, guidelines for loading new software, network safeguards, and rules for terminal access.

CHAPTER ELEVEN CONCLUSION

The operating system is more than the sum of its parts — it is the orchestrated cooperation of every piece of hardware and every piece of software. As we've shown, when one part of the system is favored, it's often at the expense of the others. So if a trade-off must be made, the system's managers must make sure they're using the appropriate measurement tools and techniques to verify the effectiveness of the system before and after modification, and then evaluate the degree of improvement.

We can't overemphasize the importance of keeping the system secure. After all, the system is only as good as the integrity of the data that's stored on it. A single breach of security — whether catastrophic or not, whether accidental or not — damages the users' perceptions of the system's integrity. And damaged perceptions are enough to threaten the future of the best-designed system, its managers, its designers, and its users. Prevention in the form of excellent security is the best medicine.

With this chapter we conclude Part I of this book. Thus far we've shown how operating systems are alike. In Part II we'll look at actual operating systems and show how they're different — and how each manages the components common to all operating systems. In other words, we'll see how close reality comes to the theory we've learned so far.

KEY TERMS

throughput
capacity
response time
turnaround time
resource utilization
availability
mean time between failures (MTBF)
mean time to repair (MTTR)
reliability
feedback loop
negative feedback loop
positive feedback loop
benchmarks
ethics
browsing
wire tapping
trap door
virus
worm
Trojan horse
logic bomb
"pirated" software
encryption
password
smart card
backups

EXERCISES

1. Describe how you would use a negative feedback loop to avoid eating too much food during each course of a very large meal.
2. Describe how a bank manager might use a positive feedback loop to direct waiting customers to five loan officers, being careful to (1) minimize waiting time for customers and (2) maximize the speed of loan processing. Include a description of how you would monitor the system and measure its success.
3. Using the information given in Table 11.1, calculate I/O access speed using CPU 1 and CPU 3 and each of the four disk drives as they evaluate the following track requests: 0, 31, 20, 15, 20, 31, 15. In each case, determine whether reordering the requests would be advantageous.
4. Give three examples of excellent passwords and explain why each would be a good choice to protect a system from unauthorized users.
5. Give three examples of inadequate passwords and explain why each would be a poor choice to protect a system from unauthorized users.
6. System managers can't protect their resources without recognizing all threats and even learning to "think like an hacker." Knowing that, and knowing that it's unethical to use a computer system without proper authorization, imagine that you are an unauthorized user who wants to break into your system. Describe how you might begin guessing the password of a legitimate user.
7. As a followup to the previous question, identify a friend who has chosen at least one computer password. On a piece of paper, list 20 possible passwords you might use if you were trying to access the friends' system. Then show the

list to your friend and ask if any of your guesses were correct. You might try combinations of names of family members and friends, favorite hobbies, automobiles, pets, birthdays, slang terms, favorite sayings, etc.

8. Describe how you would convince a university staff member to perform regular backups and manage archives appropriately.

ADVANCED EXERCISES

9. List 20 viruses and research three in detail, describing which files they infect, how they spread, and their intended effects.
10. Calculate the availability of a magnetic tape cartridge with an MTBF of 80 hours and an MTTR of 3 days (72 hours).
11. Calculate the reliability of a hard disk drive with an MTBF of 1050 hours during the last 40 hours of this month. Use Nickel's formula, shown on page 250, where $e = 2.71828$.
12. Calculate the availability of a hard disk drive with an MTBF of 1050 and an MTTR of 8 hours.
13. Assuming you had sufficient funds to upgrade only one component for a system with which you are familiar, explain which component you would choose to upgrade to improve overall system performance and why.

Part Two

OPERATING SYSTEMS IN PRACTICE

Thus far in this text we've explored how operating systems software works in theory — the roles of the Memory Manager, Processor Manager, Device Manager, and File Manager — and how they interact.

In Part II we'll see how they work in practice as we become acquainted with actual operating systems that run some of the most popular computer systems on the market today. For each system, our discourse will include the history of its development, its design goals, the unique properties of its four submanagers, and its user interface, the portion of the operating system that interacts with users. The user interface's commands and their formats vary from system to system, as you will see in the examples presented in this section. The user interface is probably the most changeable component of an operating system, which is why it was not presented until now.

The history of a system's development often illustrates its intrinsic strengths and weaknesses. For instance, a system that evolved from a rudimentary single-user system to a multifunctional multiuser system might perform simple tasks well but struggle when trying to meet the needs of a large computing environment. On the other hand, an elegant mainframe system that was later scaled down to accommodate a small computer might excel at complex tasks but prove overdesigned and cumbersome when executing tasks in the smaller environment.

The goals of the system's designers often indicate which users will find the system appealing, and in which environments. For example, a system written to make life easier for programmers will find a favorable audience in a "high-tech" computing environment, but it may not be as well received by a casual audience.

The tasks of the four submanagers are discussed briefly in light of the policies they follow and the trade-offs they make to keep the system running smoothly. Unfortunately, a complete discussion of these tasks isn't possible in the limited space we have here, so for more detailed information we suggest that you read the technical documentation for the version of your system.

At the end of each chapter we will review some of the user commands for each system. We've included only a few basic instructions — enough so the reader can compare, among the systems, the command structure, syntax, ease-of-use, and "appropriateness" to a given computing environment.

Obviously, our discussion in this section can't serve as an in-depth evaluation of an operating system. It's not designed to be. But it does present each system in a standard format to help the reader compare them; and it's important that the comparison be made because every operating system has strengths and weaknesses, as we'll see in the pages that follow.

Chapter Twelve

MS-DOS OPERATING SYSTEM

USER COMMAND INTERFACE

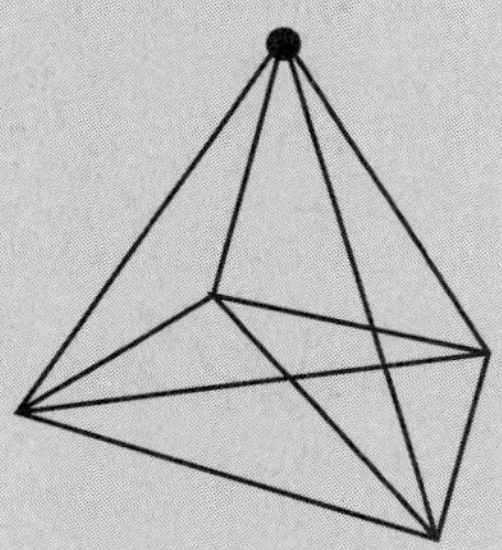

Design Goals

Memory Management

Processor Management

Device Management

File Management

User Interface

MS-DOS, also known as "PC-DOS" or simply "DOS," was developed to run single-user, stand-alone desktop computers. When the personal computer market exploded in the 1980s, MS-DOS was the standard operating system delivered with millions of these machines.

We will study this operating system first because it is one of the simplest to understand. In many ways, MS-DOS exemplifies early operating systems because it manages jobs sequentially from a single user. Its advantages are its fundamental operation and its straightforward user commands. With only a few hours of instruction a first-time user can learn to successfully manipulate a personal computer's files and devices.

It has two disadvantages. The first is its lack of flexibility and limited ability to meet the needs of programmers and experienced users. The second stems from its roots; it was written for a single family of microprocessors, the Intel family of chips: 8086, 8088, 80186, and 80286. When those microprocessors dominated the personal computer market, MS-DOS did too. But newer chips have made inroads. As a result, DOS must adapt or make way for other, more sophisticated, systems. Regardless of its future, DOS already has a historical significance as the primary operating system for a generation of microcomputers.

HISTORY

MS-DOS was the successor of the CP/M operating system. CP/M (for Control Program for Microcomputers) ran the first personal computers, 8-bit machines marketed by Apple Computer and Tandy Corporation. But when the 16-bit personal computers were developed in 1980, they required an operating system with more capability than CP/M, and many companies rushed to develop the operating system that would become the standard for the new generation of hardware.

IBM was the catalyst. When it searched for an operating system for its soon-to-be-released line of 16-bit personal computers, Digital Research offered the new CP/M-86 operating system and Softech offered their P-System. IBM looked carefully at both and began negotiations with Digital Research to buy the "new and improved CP/M" system. Meanwhile, Microsoft® discovered an innovative operating system, "86-DOS," designed by Tim Patterson of Seattle Computer Products, to run that company's line of 16-bit personal computers. Microsoft bought it, renamed it MS-DOS for Microsoft Disk Operating System, and made it available to IBM (Dettmann, 1988).

IBM chose MS-DOS in 1981, called it PC-DOS, and proclaimed it the standard for their line of personal computers. Eventually, with the weight of IBM's endorsement, MS-DOS became the standard operating system for most 16-bit personal computers sold.

This operating system has gone through many versions since its birth in Seattle. Some were needed to fix deficiencies; others were made to accommodate major hardware changes, such as increased disk-drive capabilities or different formats. Table 12.1 lists some of the major versions.

TABLE 12.1 *The evolution of MS-DOS (Tanenbaum, 1992).*

Version no.	Release date	Features
1.0	1981	CP/M compatible; supported only 1 directory
1.1	1982	Allowed double-sided 5 1/4" disks
2.0	1983	Eliminated some defects in version 1
3.0	1984	Increased memory requirement to 36K, supported PC/AT
3.1	1984	First release to support networking
3.2	1986	Supported token ring and 3 1/2" disks
3.3	1987	IBM PS/2 computer
4.0	1988	Supported hard disks larger than 32 megabytes
5.0	1991	Better use of extended memory
6.0	1993	Better use of conventional memory
6.22	1994	Provided users with capabilities previously available only as third party applications

Each version of MS-DOS is a standard version, so later versions of MS-DOS are compatible with earlier versions. Therefore, programs written to run on Version 2.0 can also be run on Version 3.3. It also means that among different manufacturers, the same commands elicit the same response from the operating system regardless of who manufactured the hardware running it.

DESIGN GOALS

MS-DOS was designed to accommodate a single novice user in a single-process environment (see Figure 12.1). Its standard I/O support includes a keyboard, monitor, printer, and secondary storage unit. Its user commands are based on English words or phrases and are indicative of the action to be performed. These commands are interpreted by the command processor, typically the only portion of the operating system with which most users interact.

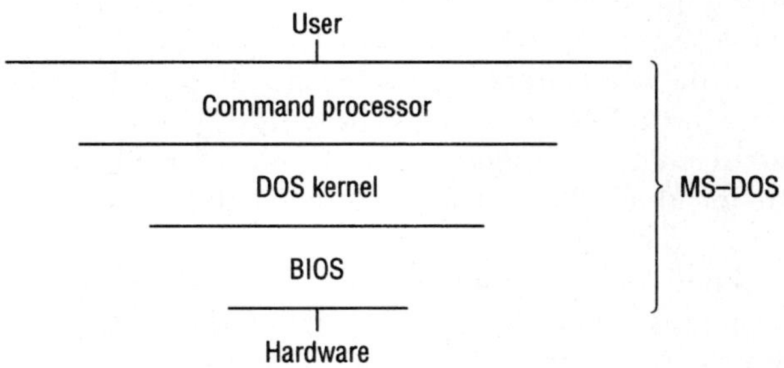

FIGURE 12.1 *The layered structure of MS-DOS: the command processor provides device independence; DOS kernel provides file management services; and BIOS provides device management services.*

The layering approach is fundamental to the design of the whole MS-DOS system, which is to "protect" the user from having to work with the bits and bytes of the bare machine that make up the bottom layer — the hardware that includes the electrical circuits, registers, and other basic components of the computer. Each layer is built on the one that precedes it, starting from the bottom up.

The bottommost layer of MS-DOS is BIOS (Basic Input/Output System). This layer of the operating system interfaces directly with the various I/O devices such as printers, keyboards, and monitors. BIOS contains the device drivers that control the flow of data to and from each device except the disk drives. It receives status information about the success or failure of each I/O operation and passes it on to the processor. BIOS takes care of the small differences among I/O units so the user can purchase a printer from any manufacturer without having to write a device driver for it — BIOS will make it perform as it should.

The middle layer, the DOS kernel, contains the routines needed to interface with the disk drives. It's read into memory at initialization time from the `MSDOS.SYS` file residing in the boot disk. The DOS kernel is a proprietary program supplied by Microsoft Corporation that implements MS-DOS. It's accessed by application programs and provides a collection of hardware-independent services, such as memory management, and file and record management. These are called "system functions." Like BIOS, it compensates for variations from manufacturer to manufacturer so all disk drives perform in the same way. In other words, the kernel makes disk file management transparent to the user so you don't have to remember in which tracks and sectors your files are stored — and which sectors of the disk are damaged and must be avoided. The kernel does that for you; it manages the storage and retrieval of files and dynamically allocates and deallocates secondary storage as it's needed.

The third layer, the command processor, is sometimes called the "shell." This is the part of the system that sends prompts to the user, accepts the commands that are typed in, executes the commands, and issues the appropriate responses. The command processor resides in a file called `COMMAND.COM`, which consists of two parts stored in two different sections of main memory. Some users mistakenly believe the `COMMAND.COM` file is the entire operating system because it's the only part that appears on the public directory. Actually, it's only one of several programs that make up MS-DOS; the rest are hidden.

It's the command processor's job to carry out the user's commands entered from the system prompt without having to wait for device-specific instructions. For example, when a user issues a `PRINT` command, the command processor directs the output to the line printer via BIOS; similarly, with a user command to `TYPE` a file the command processor directs the output to the monitor. In these cases the user doesn't need to compensate for the slow speed of the printer and the fast speed of the terminal; the user can interact with both devices and files in the same way.

The weakness of the command processor is that it isn't "interpretive." Programmers can't take shortcuts by abbreviating the commands. And new users must learn to enter each command completely and correctly. It's unforgiving to those who can't type, spell, or construct commands perfectly.

MS-DOS Version 4.0 introduced a menu-driven DOS shell to ease user's interaction with the system, but it was not widely accepted. When Version 5.0 was released, IBM and Microsoft also released a new operating system, OS/2, which was designed to replace MS-DOS. Although OS/2 offered several advantages over MS-DOS, such as using all of memory and supporting multiprogramming, it did not generate the interest that both companies expected.

The large collection of excellent quality application packages available for MS-DOS continue to make it a popular operating system. However, because technology is changing drastically, some authorities predict that MS-DOS has reached its final stages (Tanenbaum, 1992).

MEMORY MANAGEMENT

The Memory Manager has a relatively simple job because it's managing a single job for a single user. To run a second job, the user must close or pause the first file before opening the second. The Memory Manager uses a first-fit memory allocation scheme. First-fit was selected for early DOS versions because it's the most efficient strategy in a single-user environment. (Some systems accommodate "extended memory" capabilities and multitasking, features that are available with add-on hardware and software, but to keep our discussion succinct we won't include them here.)

Before we see how memory is allocated, let's see how it's structured. Main memory comes in two forms: Read Only Memory (ROM) and Random Access Memory (RAM).

ROM is usually very small in size and contains a program, a section of BIOS, with the sole task of starting up the system. The starting-up process is called **bootstrapping** because the system is effectively pulling itself up by its bootstraps. This program in ROM initializes the computer. It also retrieves the rest of the resident portion of the operating system from secondary storage and loads it into RAM.

RAM is the part of main memory where programs are loaded and executed. The RAM layout for a computer with one megabyte of memory is given in Figure 12.2.

FIGURE 12.2 *One megabyte of RAM main memory in MS-DOS. The interrupt vectors are located in low-addressable memory and the* COMMAND.COM *overlay is located in high-addressable memory.*

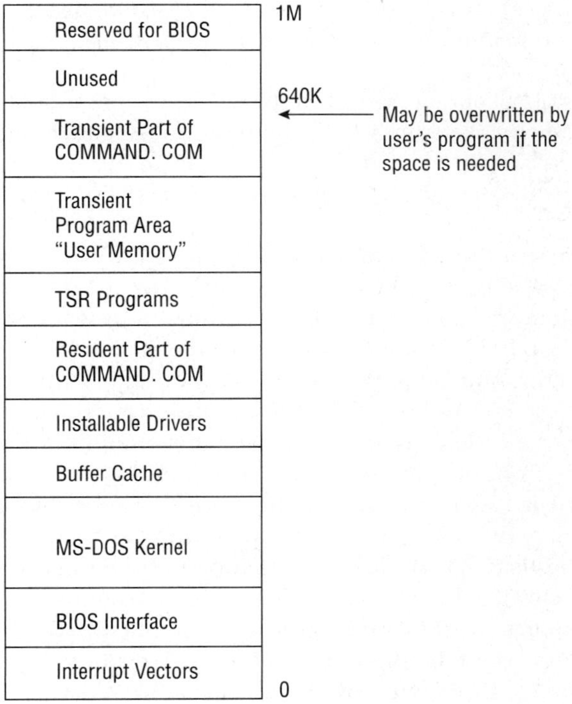

The lowest portion of RAM — known as low-addressable memory because this is where memory addressing starts: 0, 1, 2 . . . — is occupied by 256 interrupt vectors and their tables. An interrupt vector specifies where the interrupt handler program for a specific interrupt type is located. The use of interrupt handlers was discussed in Chapter 4. This is followed by BIOS tables and DOS tables, and the DOS kernel with additional installable drivers, if any, which are specified in the system's configuration file called `CONFIG.SYS`. This is followed by the resident part of the `COMMAND.COM` command interpreter — the section that is required to run application programs.

Any user application programs can now be loaded into the transient program area (TPA). If more space is required, the COMMAND.COM overlay area, located at the high-numbered memory location, can be taken over by the application program as well. The COMMAND.COM programs in this area are considered transient because they are used to execute commands, such as FORMAT, that can't be executed by the user when an application program is running, so they can be overlayed (or overwritten) by other programs; thus this space can be made available to large programs.

MAIN MEMORY ALLOCATION

The first versions of MS-DOS gave all available memory to the resident application program, but that proved insufficient because the simple contiguous memory allocation scheme didn't allow application programs to dynamically allocate and deallocate memory blocks. With Version 2.0, MS-DOS began supporting dynamic allocation, modification, and release of main memory blocks by application programs.

The amount of memory each application program actually "owns" depends on both the type of file from which the program is loaded and the size of the TPA (Duncan, 1986).

Programs with the COM extension are given all of the TPA, whether or not they need it.

Programs with the EXE extension are only given the amount of memory they need. These files have a header that indicates the minimum and maximum amount of memory needed for the program to run. Ideally, MS-DOS gives the program the maximum amount of memory requested. If that isn't possible, it tries to satisfy the minimum requirement. If the minimum is more than the amount of main memory space available then the program cannot be run.

Except for COM files, there can be any number of files in the TPA at one time. But this raises an interesting question: Why would a system have two programs in memory when it can run only one at a time? Answer: by having several files in memory at once, the user can quickly open one and work on it and close it before starting on the next. They can't both be open at the same time but by alternately opening and closing them the user can use two programs quickly and easily.

For example, a word processing program might allow a user to display two files on the screen at once by opening a window. Windows partition the screen into sections; in this example one would show the active file and the other the dormant file. If the user indicates that work should begin on the second (the dormant) file, then the first (the active) file is quickly closed and the second file is activated.

Here's a second example. Let's say your word processor's main program includes the code required to compose and print a document, but if you want to check your spelling, the "spell checker" program has to be loaded from the disk. When that's done, the "main" portion of the word processor is kept in memory and the second program is added without erasing the first one already there. Now you have two programs in memory but only one of them is executing at any given time. This is discussed in the section on Process Management later in this chapter.

If a program that is already running should need more memory, for additional

I/O buffers for example, the Memory Manager checks to see whether enough memory remains. If so, it will allocate it to the program while updating the memory block allocation table for that program. If not, then an error message is returned to the user and the program is stopped. Although initial memory allocation is handled automatically by programs written in BASIC, Pascal, or any other language supported by MS-DOS, the "shrinking" and "expanding" of memory allocation during execution time can be done only from programs written in either assembly language or C.

MEMORY BLOCK ALLOCATION

The Memory Manager allocates memory by using a first-fit algorithm and a linked list of memory blocks. But with Version 3.3 and beyond, a best-fit or last-fit strategy can be selected. When using last-fit, DOS allocates the highest addressable memory block big enough to satisfy the program's request (Dettmann, 1988).

The size of a block can vary from as small as 16 bytes (called a "paragraph") to as large as the maximum available memory. When a block is formed its first 5 bytes contain the following information:

byte 0	ASCII 90h if it's the last block, or ASCII 77h if not.
bytes 1–2	Includes the number zero to indicate a "busy" block and the pointer to the Program Segment Prefix (PSP) that is created by the `EXEC` function when the program is loaded.
bytes 3–4	Gives the number of paragraphs contained in the block.

Therefore, if a block contains four paragraphs and is the first of two blocks its code would be `7700000004h`.

The letter `h` indicates that the preceding value is in hexadecimal notation and is not recorded. The `77` (stored in byte zero) indicates this is not the last block. The `0000` (stored in bytes one and two) indicates this is a busy block and its pointer to the PSP is zero. The `0004` (stored in bytes three and four) indicates that this block contains four paragraphs.

Whenever a request for memory comes in, DOS looks through the free/busy block list (as shown in Figure 12.3) until it finds a free block that fits the request. If the list of blocks becomes disconnected, an error message is generated, and the system stops. To recover, the system must be rebooted (Dettmann, 1988).

FIGURE 12.3 *The linked list of memory blocks.*

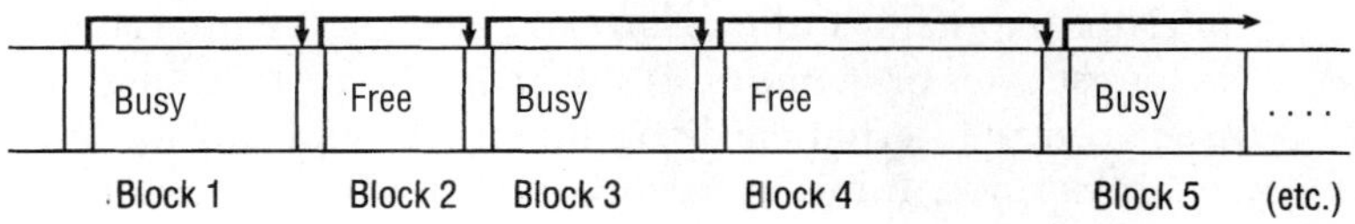

A well-designed application program will release the memory block it no longer needs. If two free memory blocks are contiguous, they are merged immediately into one block and linked to the list. A program that isn't well designed, however, will hoard its memory blocks until it stops running; only then can MS-DOS deallocate the memory blocks used by that program.

PROCESSOR MANAGEMENT

The Processor Manager has the relatively simple task of allocating the processor to the resident job when it's ready for execution.

PROCESS MANAGEMENT

MS-DOS wasn't written in **reentrant code**, discussed in the section on Virtual Memory in Chapter 3, because it was designed for a single-user, single-task environment. Reentrant code is the basis for **multitasking**, and MS-DOS doesn't support it; therefore, programs can't break out of the middle of a DOS internal routine and then restart the routine from somewhere else (Dettmann, 1988).

In our word processing/spell checker example the word processor's "parent" program called on the "child" spell checker program. The parent went to sleep, and remained asleep, while the child was running. There's no interleaving, so there's no need for sophisticated algorithms or policies to determine which job will run next or for how long. Each job runs in complete segments and is not interrupted mid-stream. In other words, there's no need to maintain a good job mix to balance system utilization.

However, although two jobs can't run together, some software programs give that illusion. Both Microsoft Windows and Borland's SideKick, for instance, appear to interrupt the parent program, change the screen displays, run unrelated programs, and then return to the parent — but this is not multitasking. (Multitasking is the microcomputer industry's synonym for multiprogramming.) These programs look and feel like multitasking operations because they retain their memory area and run executable programs, but they aren't both in the running state at the same time. In each case the parent program goes to sleep while the child runs along on its own. This synchronization is possible because the interrupt handlers built into MS-DOS give programmers the capability to save all information about the parent program that will allow its proper restart after the child program has finished.

INTERRUPT HANDLERS

Interrupt handlers are a crucial part of the system. One might say they are responsible for synchronizing the processes. A personal computer has 256 interrupts and interrupt handlers, and they are accessed via the interrupt vector table residing in the lowest bytes of memory, as shown in Figure 12.2. Interrupts can be divided into three groups: internal hardware interrupts, external hardware interrupts, and software interrupts. Internal hardware interrupts are generated by certain events occurring during a program's execution, such as division by zero. The assignment of such events to specific interrupt numbers is electronically wired into the processor and isn't modifiable by software instructions.

External hardware interrupts are caused by peripheral device controllers or by coprocessors such as the 8087/80287 (Duncan, 1986). The assignment of the external devices to specific interrupt levels is done by the manufacturer of the computer system or the manufacturer of the peripheral device. These assignments can't be modified by software because they are "hardwired" — implemented as physical electrical connections.

Software interrupts are generated by system and application programs. They access DOS and BIOS functions, which, in turn, access the system resources.

Some software interrupts are used to activate specialized application programs that take over control of the computer. Borland's SideKick is one such program. This type of interrupt handler is called Terminate and Stay Resident (TSR). Its function is to terminate a process without releasing its memory, thus providing memory-resident programming facilities. The TSR is usually used by subroutine libraries that are called once from the MS-DOS command level and then are available to provide services to other applications through a software interrupt. When a TSR starts running it sets up its memory tables and prepares for execution by connecting to a DOS interrupt; when all is ready the program determines how much memory it needs to keep. Later, when the program exits, a return code is passed back to the parent.

How are these interrupts synchronized? When the CPU senses an interrupt it does two things: (1) it puts on a stack the contents of the PSW (Program Status Word), the code segment register, and the instruction pointer register, and (2) it disables the interrupt system so that other interrupts will be put off until the current one has been resolved. The CPU uses the 8-bit number placed on the system bus by the interrupting device to get the address of the appropriate interrupt handler from the interrupt vector table and picks up execution at that address.

Finally, the interrupt handler reenables the interrupt system to allow higher-priority interrupts to occur, saves any register it needs to use, and processes the interrupt as quickly as possible.

Obviously, this is a delicate procedure. The synchronization of TSR activities with DOS functions already in progress must be carefully designed and implemented to avoid either modifying things that shouldn't be modified or crashing the system.

DEVICE MANAGEMENT

The ability to reorder requests to optimize seek and search time is not a feature of MS-DOS because it's designed for a single-user environment. All requests are handled on a first-come first-served basis. But, since Version 3.0, BIOS can support spooling so users can schedule several files to be printed one after the other. To do this, BIOS continuously transfers data from a specified memory buffer to the printer until the buffer is empty (Duncan, 1986).

MS-DOS was written for simple systems that use a keyboard, monitor, printer, mouse, one or two serial ports, and maybe a second printer. For storage, most personal computer systems use direct access storage devices, usually floppy disks or hard disks. Some systems also support a magnetic tape sequential access archiving system. The MS-DOS Device Manager can work with all of them.

These systems use only one of each type of I/O device for each port, so device channels are not a part of MS-DOS. And because each device has its own dedicated control unit, the devices do not require special management from the operating system. Therefore, **device drivers** are the only items needed by the Device Manager to make the system work. A device driver is a software module that controls an I/O device but handles its interrupts. Each device has its own device driver. BIOS is the portion of the Device Manager that handles the device driver software.

BIOS is stored in both ROM and RAM. In many MS-DOS systems the most primitive parts of the device drivers are located in ROM so they can be used by stand-alone applications, diagnostics, and the system's bootstrapping program. A second section is loaded from the disk into RAM and extends the capabilities of the basic functions stored in ROM so BIOS can handle all of the system's input and output requests.

Normally BIOS is provided by the system manufacturer adhering to Microsoft's specifications for MS-DOS and, because it's the link between the hardware and DOS, it uses standard operating system kernels regardless of the hardware. This means that programs with the standard DOS and BIOS interfaces for their system-dependent functions can be used on every DOS machine regardless of the manufacturer.

BIOS responds to interrupts generated by either hardware or software. For example, a hardware interrupt is generated when a user presses the "Print Screen" key — this causes BIOS to activate a routine that sends the ASCII contents of the screen to the printer.

Likewise, a software interrupt is generated when a program issues a command to read from a disk file. This causes the CPU to "tell" BIOS to activate a routine to read data from the disk and gives it: the number of sectors to transfer, track number, sector number, head number, and drive number. After the operation has been successfully completed it tells BIOS the number of sectors transferred and sends an "all clear" code. If an error should occur during the operation, an error code is returned so BIOS can display the appropriate error message on the screen.

Most device drivers are part of standard MS-DOS. Of course, you can always write your own device driver. All you need is knowledge of assembly language, information about the hardware, and some patience. This option might be necessary if you're using a system with an unusual combination of devices. For instance, in its early years of commercial availability, there was not a high demand for interfacing a computer with a videodisc player — so its device drivers were not incorporated into BIOS. Therefore, users who wanted to use a videodisc as an I/O device had to write (or buy) their own device drivers and load them when the system was booted up. These device drivers are called "installable" because they can be incorporated into the operating system as needed without having to "patch" or change the existing operating system. Installable device drivers are a salient feature of MS-DOS design.

FILE MANAGEMENT

MS-DOS supports sequential, direct, and indexed sequential file organization. Sequential files can have either variable- or fixed-length records. However, direct and indexed sequential files can only have fixed-length records.

FILE NAME CONVENTIONS

A file name contains no spaces and consists of the drive designation, the directory, any subdirectory, a primary name, and an optional extension. (DOS isn't case-sensitive so file names and commands can be entered in upper case, lower case, or a combination of both.)

The drive name (usually A, B, C, or D) is followed by a colon (:). Directories or subdirectories can be from one to eight characters long and are preceded by a back slash (\). The primary file name can be from one to eight characters long and the extension from one to three characters long. The primary name and extension are separated by a period. A file's extension can have a special meaning to DOS — the user should be aware of the standard extensions and their uses.

If no directories or subdirectors are included in the name, it's assumed that the file is in the current working directory. If no drive is designated, it's assumed the file is on the current drive. The root directory (see the next section, "Managing Files," for a discussion of this) is called by a single back slash \; the names of other directories are preceded by the \ symbol. The \ is a delimiter between names.

A file's relative name consists of its primary name and extension, if used. A file's absolute name consists of its drive designation and directory location (called its "path") followed by its relative name. When the user is working in a directory or subdirectory, it's called the "working directory" and any file in that directory can be accessed by its relative name. However, to access a file that's in another directory, the absolute name is required.

For example, if your working directory includes a file called JORDAN.DOC then you can identify that file by typing: JORDAN.DOC. However, if you changed to another working directory, then you would have to include the directory name when you called the file (shown in Figure 12.4, page 277):

```
\JOURNAL\CHAP9\JORDAN.DOC
```

And if you changed to another drive and wanted to call the file, you would have to include the drive designation as well:

```
C:\JOURNAL\CHAP9\JORDAN.DOC
```

The DOS commands require that the file names have no spaces within them. So to copy the file from the C drive to the B drive the command would look like this: COPY C:\MEMO\DEAN.DOC B:DEAN.DOC

A simpler way to access files is to select a working directory first and then access the files within that directory by their relative names. Later, when you're finished with one directory, you can issue the "change directory" command to move to another working directory.

Of course, there are many variations. For complete details, refer to a MS-DOS technical manual.

MANAGING FILES

The earliest versions of MS-DOS kept every file in a single directory. This was slow and cumbersome, especially as users added more and more files. To retrieve a single file, the File Manager searched from the beginning of the list until either the file was found or the end of the list was reached. If a user forgot how the file was named there was a good chance that it would never be seen again.

To solve this problem, Microsoft implemented a hierarchical directory structure in Version 2.0 — an inverted tree directory structure. (It's "inverted" because the root is at the top and the "leaves" are on the bottom.)

When a disk is formatted (using the `FORMAT` command) its tracks are divided into sectors of 512 bytes each. (This corresponds to a buffer size of 512 bytes.) Single-sided disks have one recording surface, double-sided disks have two recording surfaces, and hard disks have from two to four platters, each with two recording surfaces. The concept of *cylinders,* presented in Chapter 7, applies to these hard disks because the read/write heads move in unison.

The sectors (from two to eight) are grouped into "clusters" and that's how the File Manager allocates space to files. When a file needs additional space, DOS allocates more clusters to it. Besides dividing up the disk space, `FORMAT` creates three special areas on the disk: the boot record, the root directory, and the FAT, which stands for File Allocation Table (Dettmann, 1988).

The *boot record* is the first sector of every logical disk, whether it's an entire physical unit (such as a floppy disk or hard disk) or only a virtual disk (such as a "RAM disk"). Beginning with Version 2.0, the boot record contains the disk boot program and a table of the disk's characteristics.

The *root directory* is where the system begins its interaction with the user when it's booted up. The root directory contains a list of the system's primary subdirectories and files, including any system-generated configuration files and any user-generated booting instructions that may be included in an `AUTOEXEC.BAT` file. This is a batch file containing a series of commands defined by the user. Every time the CPU is powered up or is reset, the commands in this file are executed automatically by the system. A sample `AUTOEXEC.BAT` file is discussed later in this chapter.

The information kept in the root directory is: (1) the file name, (2) the file extension, (3) the file size in bytes, (4) the data and time of the file's last modification, (5) the starting cluster number for the file, and (6) the file attribute codes. The first four items are displayed in response to the `DIR` command, as shown in Table 12.2.

TABLE 12.2

Directory listing of a root directory, which includes three subdirectories and three files. Notice that the listing follows no particular order.

Volume in drive C is: MINE				
Director of C:\				
PROGRAMS		<DIR>	3-08-87	1:35p
MEMOS		<DIR>	3-08-87	1:36p
AUTOEXEC	BAT	45	8-22-88	10:12a
PHASES	DOC	210	2-12-86	5:15p
JOURNAL		<DIR>	12-18-88	11:27a
GEORGE	DOC	8644	10-15-85	3:00p
	6 File(s)		4077216 bytes free	

The number of entries in a root directory is fixed. For instance, only 512 entries are allowed for a 20M hard disk. The size of the root directory is limited because DOS needs to know where the disk's data area begins. Beginning with Version 2.0, users can avoid this limitation by creating subdirectories that have no size limit (Dettmann, 1988).

Each subdirectory can contain its own subdirectories and/or files, as shown in Figure 12.4.

FIGURE 12.4 *The directory system: the root directory listing has six entries, as shown in Table 12.2. The directory listing for* JOURNAL *has four entries: its three files and its subdirectory* CHAP9. *The directory listing for* CHAP9 *has three entries for its three files.*

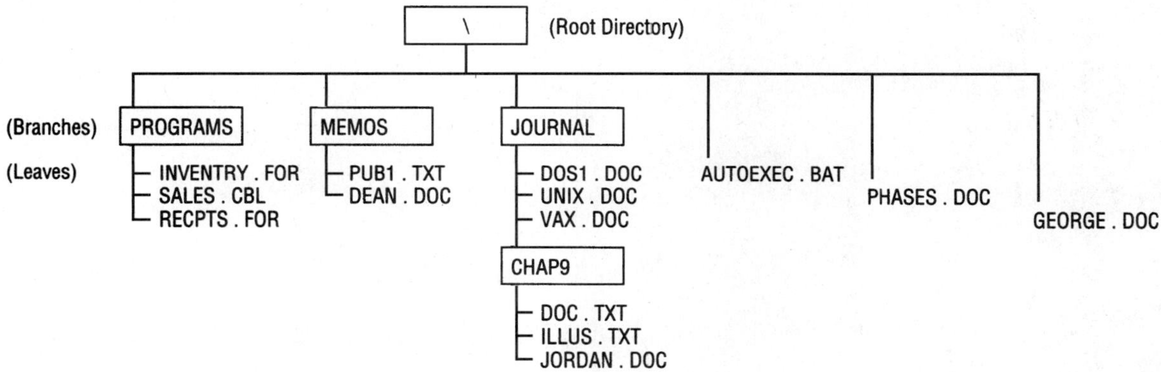

The directory listing shown in Table 12.2 was generated by the user's command: DIR. Note how the three subdirectories are distinguished from the three files. Note, also, that the system maintains the date and time when it was most recently modified. Some software security programs use this data to detect any viruses or other unauthorized or unusual modifications of the system's software.

MS-DOS supports "hidden files" — files that are executable but not displayed in response to DIR commands. Some of MS-DOS's system files are hidden files; they're used to run the operating system but they don't show up on the directory listings. COMMAND.COM is the only system file that isn't hidden and so it's always displayed on public directories.

The *File Allocation Table (FAT)* contains status information about the disk's sectors: which are allocated, which are free, and which can't be allocated because of formatting errors.

The directory notes the number of the first sector or cluster of the file — this number is recorded there when the file is created. All successive sectors or clusters allocated to that file are recorded in the FAT, and are linked together to form a chain, with each FAT entry giving the sector/cluster number of the next entry. The last entry for each chain contains the hexadecimal value FF to indicate the end of the chain. As you can see in Figure 12.5, a file's sectors don't have to be contiguous.

MS-DOS looks at data in a disk file as a continuous string of bytes. Therefore I/O operations request data by relative byte (relative to the beginning of the file) rather than by relative sector. The transformation from physical sector (or cluster)

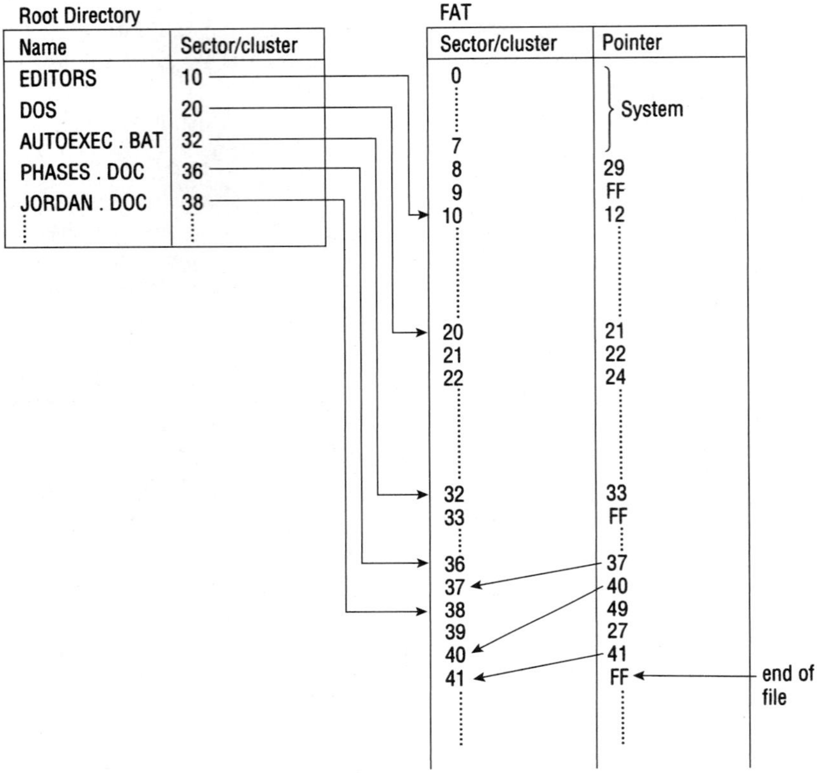

FIGURE 12.5 *For each file, the directory includes the first sector/cluster location in the File Allocation Table so it can be accessed quickly. The FAT links every sector for each file. Notice that the sectors for the file* `PHASES.DOC` *are not contiguous (the arrows are a visual aid to show their linking).*

to relative byte address is done by the File Manager so data on a disk appears to be accessed just like data in main memory.

As we mentioned a moment ago, MS-DOS supports noncontiguous file storage and will dynamically allocate disk space to a file, provided there's enough room on the disk. Unfortunately, as files are added and deleted from the disk, a file may become quite fragmented, making it increasingly cumbersome and time-consuming to retrieve.

Compaction became a feature of MS-DOS Version 6.0 with the inclusion of `DEFRAG.EXE`, a utility used to defragment a disk by picking up the fragments of a file and repositioning them as a single piece in a contiguous space. This program, created by Symantec Corporation, had previously been shipped with its Norton Utilities.

Another command can be used to determine the need for compaction. Given `CHKDSK (filename)` the system will respond with the number of noncontiguous blocks in which the file is stored. It's up to the user to compact the file, if necessary, so it's stored in as few noncontiguous blocks as possible to speed access time and reduce maintenance on the seek mechanism.

Restricting user access to the computer system and its resources isn't built into MS-DOS. Add-on security software is available but, for most users, data is kept secure by keeping the computer physically locked up or by removing the disks and keeping them in a safe place.

USER INTERFACE

MS-DOS is command-driven. Table 12.3 shows some of the most common commands. Users type in their commands at the system prompt. The default prompt is the drive indicator and the > character; therefore, C> is the standard prompt for a hard drive system and A> is the prompt for a computer with one disk drive. The default prompt can be changed with the PROMPT command.

TABLE 12.3 *Some common MS-DOS user commands. In general, commands can be entered in either upper- or lower-case characters, although in this text we will use all capital letters to make our notation consistent. Check the technical documentation for your system for proper spelling and syntax.*

Command	Stands for	Action to be performed
DIR	Directory	List what's in this directory.
CD or CHDIR	Change Directory	Change the working directory.
COPY	Copy	Copy the following file or files.
DEL or ERASE	Delete	Delete the following file or files.
RENAME	Rename	Rename a file.
TYPE	Type	Display the text file on the screen.
PRINT	Print	Print one or more files on printer.
DATE	Date	Display and/or change the system date.
TIME	Time	Display and/or change the system time.
MD or MKDIR	Make Directory	Create a new directory or subdirectory.
FIND	Find	Find a string. Search files for a string.
COPY	Copy	Copy a file. Append one to another.
FORMAT	Format Disk	Logically prepare a disk for file storage.
CHKDSK	Check Disk	Check disk for disk/file/directory status.
PROMPT	System Prompt	Change the system prompt symbol.
DEFRAG	Defragment Disk	Compact fragmented files.
(filename)		Run/Execute the file.

When the user presses the "Enter" key, the shell called COMMAND.COM interprets the command and calls on the next lower level routine to satisfy the request.

User commands include some or all of these elements in this order:

command source-file destination-file switches

The "command" is any legal MS-DOS command. The "source-file" and "destination-file" are included when applicable and, depending on the current drive and directory, might need to include the file's complete path name. The "switches" begin with a slash (i.e., /P /V /F) and are optional; they give specific details about how the command is to be carried out. Most commands require a space between each of their elements.

The commands are carried out by the COMMAND.COM file, which is part of MS-DOS. As we said before, when COMMAND.COM is loaded during the system's initialization, one section of it is stored in the low section of memory; this is the resident portion of the code. It contains the command interpreter and the routines needed to support an active program. In addition it contains the routines needed to process CTRL-C, CTRL-BREAK, and critical errors.

The transient code, the second section of COMMAND.COM, is stored in the highest addresses section of memory and can be overwritten by application programs if they need to use its memory space. Later, when the program terminates, the resident portion of COMMAND.COM checks to see if the transient code is still intact. If it isn't, it loads a new copy.

As a user types in a command, each character is stored in memory and displayed on the screen. When the "Enter" key is pressed the operating system transfers control to the command interpreter portion of COMMAND.COM, which either accesses the routine that will carry out the request or displays an error message. If the routine is residing in memory, then control is given to it directly. If the routine is residing on secondary storage, it's loaded into memory and then control is given to it.

Although we can't describe every command available in MS-DOS, some features are worth noting to show the flexibility of this operating system.

BATCH FILES

By creating customized "batch files," users can quickly execute combinations of DOS commands to configure their system, perform routine tasks, or make it easier for nontechnical users to run software.

For instance, if a user routinely checks the system date and time, loads a device driver for a mouse, moves to a certain subdirectory, and loads a program called MAIL.COM, then this program, called START.BAT, would perform each of those steps in turn.

```
DATE
TIME
DEVICE=MOUSE.SYS
CD\FLYNN\BOOK
MAIL
```

To run this program the user needs only to type START at the system prompt. To have this program run automatically every time the system is restarted, then the file should be renamed AUTOEXEC.BAT and loaded into the system's root directory. With batch files any tedious combinations of key strokes can be reduced to a few easily remembered customized commands.

REDIRECTION

MS-DOS can redirect output from one standard input or output device to another. For example, the DATE command sends output directly to the screen, but by using the redirection symbol (>) the output is redirected to another device or file instead.

The syntax is: command > destination.

For example, if you want to send a directory listing to the printer, you would type: DIR > PRN and the listing would appear on the printed page instead of the screen. Likewise, if you want the directory of the default drive to be redirected to a file on the diskette in the B drive, you'd type: DIR > B:DIRFILE and a new file called DIRFILE would be created on drive B and it would contain a listing of the directory.

You can redirect and append new output to an existing file by using the append symbol (>>). For example, if you've already created the file DIRFILE with the redirection command and you wanted to generate a listing of the directory and append it to the previously created DIRFILE, you would type: DIR >> B:DIRFILE.

Now DIRFILE contains two listings of the same directory.

Redirection works in the opposite manner as well. If you want to change the source to a specific device or file, use the < symbol. For example, let's say you have a program called INVENTRY.EXE under development that expects input from the keyboard, but for testing and debugging purposes you want it to accept input from a test data file, then you would type: INVENTRY < B:TEST.DAT.

FILTERS

Filter commands accept input from the default device, manipulate the data in some fashion, and send the results to the default output device. A commonly used filter is SORT, which accepts input from the keyboard, sorts that data, and displays it on the screen. This filter command becomes even more useful if it can read data from a file and sort it to another file. This can be done by using the redirectional parameters. For example, if you wanted to sort a data file called STD.DAT and store it in another file called SORTSTD.DAT then you'd type:

```
SORT < STD.DAT > SORTSTD.DAT.
```

The sorted file would be in ascending order (numerically or alphabetically) starting with the first character in each line of the file. If you wanted the file sorted in reverse order then you would type: SORT /R < STD.DAT > SORTSTD.DAT

You can sort the file by column. For example, let's say a file called EMPL has data that follows this format: the ID numbers start in Column 1, the phone numbers start in Column 6, and the last names start in Column 14. (A column is defined as characters delimited by one or more spaces.) To sort the file by last name the command would be: SORT /+14 < EMPL.DAT > SORTEMPL.DAT
and the file would be sorted in ascending order by the field starting at Column 14.

Another common filter is MORE, which causes output to be displayed on the screen in groups of 24 lines, one screen at a time, and waits until the user presses the "Enter" key before displaying the next 24 lines.

PIPES

A pipe can cause the standard output from one command to be used as standard input to another command; its symbol is a vertical bar (|). You can alphabetically sort your directory and display the sorted list on the screen by typing: DIR | SORT.

You can combine pipes and other filters, too. For example, to display on the screen the contents of the file INVENTRY.DAT one screen at a time, the command would be: TYPE INVENTRY.DAT | MORE.

You can achieve the same result using only redirection by typing:

```
MORE < INVENTRY.DAT
```

You can sort your directory and display it one screen at a time by using pipes with this command: `DIR | SORT | MORE`.

Or you can achieve the same result by using both pipes and filters with these two commands:

```
DIR | SORT > SORTFILE

MORE < SORTFILE
```

ADDITIONAL COMMANDS

FIND

FIND is a filter command that searches for a specific string in a given file or files and displays all lines that contain the string from those files. The string must be enclosed in double quotes and must be typed exactly as it is to be searched; upper- and lower-case letters are taken as entered.

For example:

`FIND "AMNT-PAID" PAYROLL.COB`
: will display all the lines in the file PAYROLL.COB that contain the string AMNT-PAID.

`FIND /C "AMNT-PAID" PAYROLL.COB`
: will count the number of lines in the file PAYROLL.COB that contain the string AMNT-PAID and display the number on the screen.

`FIND /N "AMNT-PAID" PAYROLL.COB`
: will display the relative line number, as well as the line in the file PAYROLL.COB that contains the string AMNT-PAID.

`FIND /V "AMNT-PAID" PAYROLL.COB`
: will display all of the lines in the file PAYROLL.COB that *do not* contain the string AMNT-PAID.

`DIR B: | FIND /V "SYS"`
: will display the names of all files on the diskette in drive B that *do not* contain the string SYS.

PRINT

The PRINT command allows the user to set up a series of files for printing while freeing up COMMAND.COM to accept other commands. In effect, it's a spooler. As the printer prints your files, you can type other commands and work on other applications. The PRINT command has many options but to use the following two they must be given the first time the PRINT command is used after booting the system:

`PRINT /B`

allows you to change the size of the internal buffer. Its default is 512 bytes but increasing its value speeds up the `PRINT` process.

`PRINT /Q`

specifies the number of files allowed in the print queue. The minimum value for Q is 4 and the maximum is 32.

`TREE`

The `TREE` command displays directories and subdirectories in a hierarchical and indented list. It also has options that allow the user to delete files while the tree is being generated. The display starts with the current or specified directory with the subdirectories indented under the directory that contains them. If we issue the command `TREE` for the system illustrated in Figure 12.4, the response would be

```
PROGRAMS
MEMOS
JOURNAL
  CHAP9
```

To display the names of the files in each directory, use the switch `/F`:

```
TREE /F
```

The `TREE` command can also be used to delete a file that's duplicated on several different directories. For example, to delete the file `PAYROLL.COB` anywhere on the disk the command would be:

```
TREE PAYROLL.COB /D /Q
```

The system displays the tree as usual but whenever it encounters a file called `PAYROLL.COB`, it pauses and asks if you want to delete it. If you type `Y` then it will delete the file and continue. If you type `N` it continues as before.

For illustrative purposes, we've included only a few MS-DOS commands. For a complete list of commands, their exact syntax, and more details about those we've discussed here, see a technical manual on the appropriate version of MS-DOS.

CHAPTER TWELVE CONCLUSION

MS-DOS has enjoyed years of popularity. It was written to serve users of several generations of personal computers, from the earliest IBM PCs to the more sophisticated stand-alone machines introduced in the late 1980s. As such, it was a huge success.

The strength of MS-DOS is that it was the first standard operating system to be adopted by most manufacturers of personal computing machines. As the standard it has also supported, and been supported by, legions of software design groups.

The weakness of MS-DOS is that it was designed for single-user/single-task systems and can't support multitasking and other sophisticated applications required of computers of every size — even including personal computers. MS-DOS started as a simple system and has tried to evolve into a more complex one.

Next we'll look at Windows NT, an operating system that combines a graphical user interface similar to its Windows predecessors with robust support for networks.

Chapter Thirteen

WINDOWS NT

WINDOWS NT

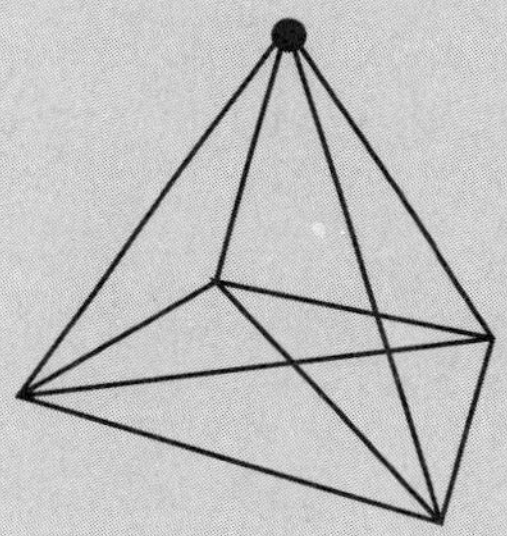

Windows NT is a complete network operating system that uses a graphical user interface (GUI) as its primary method of communication with the user. The first Windows GUI, Windows 1.0, was introduced in 1985 and ran on PC-compatible microcomputers "on top of" MS-DOS; it was followed by increasingly sophisticated versions of Windows that were designed to run powerful desktop computers. Because of its commercial success, Microsoft Corporation used Windows as a base from which it developed other specialty products and operating systems, including Windows NT.

This chapter concentrates on Windows NT, the network operating system. However, we have included, where possible, information comparing and contrasting it to Windows 95, a single-user operating system that supports a very similar graphical user interface. (Many acronyms are used throughout this chapter — they are defined in Appendix C.) For a comparison of interfaces, see Appendix D.

HISTORY

The first widely adopted Windows product, Windows 3.0, standardized a "windows" interface similar to the one made popular by Apple's Macintosh computer.

Windows became the "entry-level" product intended for single-user installations found in single-user or small-business environments.

Microsoft developed and released several Windows products to appeal to specific subaudiences (see Table 13.1). The first was Windows for Workgroups, which looks like Windows 3.0 to the user but contains extra programs and features for small local area networks. For example, a Windows for Workgroups system can easily share directories, disks, and printers among several interconnected machines. The system also allows for personal intercommunication through E-mail and "chat" programs. It is intended for small or mid-sized groups of PCs as typically seen in small businesses or departments of larger organizations.

TABLE 13.1 *The evolution of Microsoft Windows.*

Year	Product	Features
1985	Windows 1.0	First retail shipment of the first Windows product; required MS-DOS
1990	Windows 3.0	Improved performance and advanced ease-of-use; required MS-DOS
1992	Windows 3.1	Widely adopted, commercially successful GUI with more than 1,000 enhancements over 3.0; required MS-DOS
1992	Windows for Workgroups	GUI for small networks; required MS-DOS
1993	Windows NT	True client-server operating system with support for Intel, RISC, and multiprocessor systems
1995	Windows 95	True operating system designed to replace Windows 3.x, Windows for Workgroups, and MS-DOS for single-user desktop computers

Both Windows 3.x and Windows for Workgroups are built to run "on top" of the MS-DOS operating system. That is, MS-DOS is the true operating system but it takes its direction from the Windows program being run on it. However, this layering technique has been proven a disadvantage because although it helped Windows gain market share among MS-DOS users, MS-DOS has little built-in security, cannot perform multitasking, and has no interprocess communications capability. In addition, that system was written to connect closely to the microcomputer's hardware, making it difficult to move the operating system to other platforms. Windows New Technology (NT) was Microsoft's answer to these problems. It is a complete operating system, with no separate modules, and it does not rely on MS-DOS for support (Brain, 1994).

In the fall of 1988 Microsoft hired David Cutler to lead the development of the Windows NT operating system. An experienced architect of minicomputer systems, Cutler had spent 17 years at Digital Equipment Corporation developing several operating systems and compilers, including the VAX/VMS operating system. Together with Microsoft chairman Bill Gates and other Microsoft strategists, Cutler identified the primary market requirements for this new product: portability, multiprocessing capabilities, distributed computing support, compliance with government procurement requirements, and government security certification. The finished product was introduced in 1993.

A FEW WORDS ABOUT WINDOWS 95

Like Windows NT, Windows 95 cut its ties to MS-DOS but, unlike the other Windows operating systems, it is designed to run on the average user's computer system. In addition, entering a niche previously held by OS/2 and UNIX, it is a 32-bit preemptive multitasking operating system. To ease customers' migration from simpler operating systems to Windows 95, the earliest versions contained both 32-bit and 16-bit codes, thus creating an optimal transition from 16-bit MS-DOS/Windows 3.1 to an entirely 32-bit Windows 95 operating environment (Houlette et al., 1995).

DESIGN GOALS

For the system to fulfill its market requirements, certain complex features such as security had to be incorporated from the outset. Therefore, the designers of Windows NT very carefully assembled a set of software design goals that would facilitate decision making as the coding process evolved. For example, if two design options conflicted, the design goals would be used to help determine which was better.

The design of Windows NT was influenced by several operating system models, and thus used existing frameworks while introducing new features. It uses a client/server model to provide a variety of operating system environments such as Windows, MS-DOS, OS/2, and POSIX to its users. It uses an object model to manage operating system resources and to allocate them to users in a consistent manner. It uses symmetric multiprocessing (SMP) to achieve maximum performance from multiprocessor computers. To accommodate the various needs of users and to optimize resources, the Windows NT team had five design goals: extensibility, portability, reliability, compatibility, and performance.

EXTENSIBILITY

Knowing that operating systems must change over time to support new hardware devices, such as CD-ROM drives, or new software technologies, such as graphical user interfaces, the design team decided to produce an operating system that would be easily enhanced. This feature is called **extensibility**. To ensure the integrity of the code of Windows NT the designers separated the functions of the operating system into a privileged executive process and a set of nonprivileged processes called protected subsystems (Custer, 1993). The term "privileged" refers to a processor's mode of operation. Most processors have a privileged mode in which all machine instructions are allowed and system memory is accessible, and a nonprivileged mode in which certain instructions are not allowed and system memory is not accessible. In Windows NT terminology, the privileged processor mode is called "kernel" mode and the nonprivileged processor mode is called "user" mode.

Usually operating systems execute only in kernel mode and application programs execute only in user mode except when they call operating system services.

In Windows NT the protected subsystems execute in user mode as if they were applications, which allows protected subsystems to be modified or added without affecting the integrity of the executive process.

In addition to protected subsystems, Windows NT includes four features to ensure its extensibility:

- a modular structure so new components can be added to the executive process;
- "objects" — abstract data types manipulated by a special set of object services allowing system resources to be managed uniformly;
- drivers for new file systems, devices, and networks that can be added to the system at any time;
- a remote procedure call that allows an application to call remote services regardless of their location on the network.

PORTABILITY

Portability relates to the ability of a user to move an entire operating system to a machine that is based on a different processor or configuration with minimal recoding. To achieve this goal the operating system must follow certain guidelines. First, it must be written in a standardized, high-level language available in all machines. For instance, assembler language code is normally not portable. Second, the system must consider the hardware to which it will be ported. For example, an operating system built on a 32-bit addressable machine could not be ported to a 16-bit addressable machine. Third, code that interacts directly with the hardware should be minimized. Fourth, all hardware-dependent code should be isolated into modules that can be easily modified when the operating system is ported.

Windows NT was written for ease of porting to machines that use 32-bit linear addresses and provide virtual memory capabilities. It has the following features:

- Windows NT code is modular; that is, the code that must access processor-dependent data structures and registers is contained in small modules that can be replaced by similar modules for different processors.
- The majority of Windows NT is written in C, a programming language that is standardized and readily available. The graphic component and some portions of the networking user interface are written in C++. Assembly language code is used only for those parts of the system that must communicate directly with the hardware.
- Windows NT contains a hardware abstraction layer (HAL), a dynamic-link library that provides isolation from hardware dependencies furnished by different vendors. The HAL abstracts hardware, such as caches, with a layer of low-level software so that higher-level code need not change when moving from one platform to another.

RELIABILITY

Reliability refers to the robustness of a system — that is, its predictability in responding to error conditions, even those caused by hardware failures. It also refers to an operating system's ability to protect itself and its users from accidental or deliberate damage by user programs.

Structured exception handling is one way to capture error conditions and respond to them uniformly. Whenever such an event occurs, either the operating system or the processor issues an exception call, which automatically invokes the exception handling code that is appropriate to handle the condition, ensuring that no harm is done to either user programs or the system. In addition, the following features strengthen the system:

- A modular design that divides the executive into individual system components that interact with each other through specified programming interfaces. For example, the memory manager could be replaced by a new memory manager that would implement the same interfaces.
- A new file system called the NT File System (NTFS), which can recover from all types of errors including those that occur in critical disk sectors. To ensure recoverability it uses redundant storage and a transaction-based scheme for storing data.
- A U.S. government-certifiable security architecture that provides a variety of security mechanisms, such as user log on, resource quotas, and object protection.
- A virtual memory strategy that provides every program with a large set of memory addresses and prevents one user from reading or modifying memory occupied by another user unless the two are explicitly sharing memory.

COMPATIBILITY

Compatibility usually refers to an operating system's ability to execute programs written for other operating systems or for earlier versions of the same system. However, for Windows NT compatibility is a more complicated topic.

Through the use of protected subsystems, Windows NT provides execution environments for applications that are different from its primary programming interface — the Win32 Application Program Interface (API). When running on Intel processors, Windows NT's protected subsystems supply binary compatibility with existing Microsoft applications. Windows NT also provides source-level compatibility with POSIX applications that adhere to the POSIX operating system interfaces defined by IEEE. (POSIX is the Portable Operating System Interface for Computer Environments, an operating system API that is a set of calling conventions that define how a service is invoked through a software package developed by IEEE to increase the portability of application software).

In addition to compatibility with programming interfaces, Windows NT supports existing file systems, including the MS-DOS file allocation table (FAT), the

OS/2 high-performance file system (HPFS), the CD-ROM file system (CDFS), and the recoverable NT file system.

PERFORMANCE

To give users fast response times when dealing with CPU-bound applications, fast hardware is not enough — the operating system's **performance** must be fast and efficient too. Several features help Windows NT achieve good performance levels.

- System calls, page faults, and other crucial processes were tested and optimized to ensure the fastest possible processing speeds.
- A mechanism called the local procedure call (LPC) was incorporated into the operating system to guarantee that communication among the protected subsystems is fast and does not restrain performance.
- The speed of frequently used system services was maximized by carefully designing the environment subsystem.
- Critical elements of Windows NT's networking software were built into the privileged portion of the operating system to realize the best possible performance. However, these components can also be loaded and unloaded from the system dynamically.

MEMORY MANAGEMENT

Every operating system uses its own view of physical memory and makes its application programs access memory in specified ways, as exemplified in Figure 13.1. The challenge for Windows NT is to run application programs written for Windows, MS-DOS, POSIX, or OS/2 without crashing into each other in memory. Each of Windows NT's environment subsystems provides a view of memory that matches what its applications expect. The NT executive has its own memory structure, which the subsystems access by calling NT's inherent services.

In Windows NT, the operating system resides in high virtual memory and the user's code and data reside in low virtual memory, as shown in Figure 13.1. A user process cannot read or write to system memory directly. All user-accessible memory can be paged to disk, as can the segment of system memory labeled *paged pool.* However, the segment of system memory labeled *nonpaged pool* is never paged to disk because it is used to store critical NT objects, such as the code that does the paging, as well as major data structures.

USER-MODE FEATURES

The Virtual Memory (VM) Manager allows user-mode subsystems to share memory efficiently and provides a set of native services that a process can use to manage its virtual memory in the following ways:

- Allocate memory in two stages. First by "reserving" memory and then by "committing" memory, as needed. This two-step procedure allows a process to reserve a large section of virtual memory without being charged for it until it's actually needed.

- Read and/or write protection for virtual memory allowing processes to share memory when needed.
- Lock virtual pages in physical memory. This ensures that a critical page will not be removed from memory while a process is using it. For example, a database application that uses a tree structure to update its data may lock the root of the tree in memory, thus minimizing page faults while accessing the database.
- Retrieve information about virtual pages.
- Protect virtual pages. Each virtual page has a set of flags associated with it that determines the types of access allowed in user mode. In addition, Windows NT provides object-based memory protection. Therefore, each time a process opens a section object, a block of memory that can be shared by two or more processes, the security reference monitor checks whether the process is allowed to access the object.
- Rewrite virtual pages to disk. If an application modifies a page, the VM Manager writes the changes back to the file during its normal paging operations.

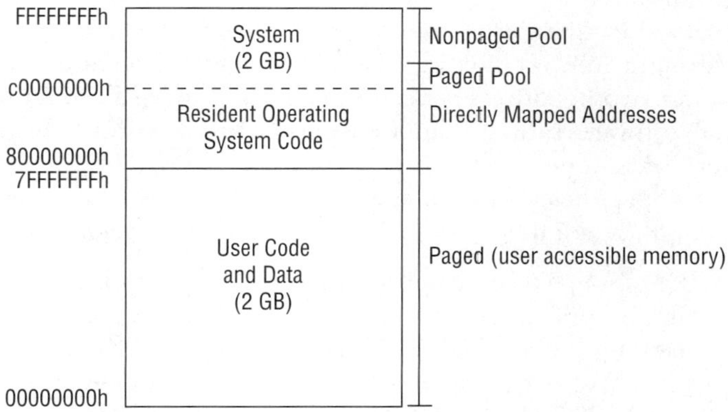

FIGURE 13.1 *Layout of Windows NT Memory. This is a virtual memory system based on 32-bit addresses in a linear address space. Each process's virtual address space is four gigabytes, with two gigabytes each allocated to program storage and system storage. When physical memory becomes full, the VM Manager pages some of the memory contents to disk, freeing physical memory for other processes.*

VIRTUAL MEMORY IMPLEMENTATION

The Virtual Memory Manager relies on address space management and paging techniques.

ADDRESS SPACE MANAGEMENT As shown in Figure 13.1, the upper half of the virtual address space is accessible only to kernel-mode processes. Code in the lower part of this section, kernel code and data, is never paged out of memory. In addition, the addresses in this range are translated by the hardware, providing exceedingly fast data access. Therefore, the lower part of the resident operating system code is used for sections of the kernel that require maximum performance, such as the code that dispatches units of execution, or "threads," for execution in a processor.

When users create a new process they can specify that the VM Manager initialize their virtual address space by duplicating the virtual address space of another process. Therefore, environment subsystems can present to their client processes views of memory that do not correspond to the virtual address space of a native NT process.

PAGING The pager is the part of the VM Manager that transfers pages between page frames in memory and disk storage. As such, it's a complex combination of both software policies and hardware mechanisms. Software policies determine *when* to bring a page into memory and *where* to put it. Hardware mechanisms include the exact manner in which the VM Manager translates virtual addresses into physical addresses.

Because the hardware features of each system directly affect the success of the VM Manager, implementation of virtual memory varies from processor to processor. Therefore, this portion of the operating system is not portable and must be modified for each new hardware platform. To ease transition, Windows NT keeps this code small and well isolated. The processor chip that handles address translation and exception handling looks at each address generated by a program and translates it into a physical address. If the page containing the address is not in memory, then the hardware generates a page fault and issues a call to the pager. The translation lookaside buffer (TLB) is a hardware array of associative memory (explained in Chapter 3) used by the processor to speed memory access. As pages are brought into memory by the VM Manager, it creates entries for them in the TLB. If a virtual address is not in the TLB, it may still be in memory. In that case, virtual software rather than hardware is used to find the address, resulting in slower access times.

Paging policies in a virtual memory system dictate *how* and *when* paging is done and are composed of fetch, placement, and replacement policies.

- The *fetch policy* determines when the pager copies a page from disk to memory. Several fetch policies were presented in Chapter 3. The VM Manager uses a demand paging algorithm with locality of reference, called "clustering," to load pages into memory. This strategy attempts to minimize the number of page faults that a process will encounter.
- The *placement policy* is the set of rules that determines where the virtual page will be loaded in memory. If memory is not full, the VM Manager selects the first page frame from a list of free page frames. This list is called the page frame database, and is an array of entries numbered from zero through $n - 1$, with n equaling the number of page frames of memory in the system. Each entry contains information about the corresponding page frame, which can be in one of six states at any given time: valid, zeroed, free, standby, modified, or bad. Valid and modified page frames are those currently in use. Those zeroed, free, or on standby represent available page frames; bad frames cannot be used.

  Of the available page frames, the page frame database links together those that are in the same state, thus creating five separate homogeneous lists. Whenever the number of pages in the zeroed, free, and standby lists reaches a preset minimum, the modified page writer process is activated to write the contents of the modified pages to disk and link them to the standby list. On the other hand, if the modified page list becomes too short, the VM Manager shrinks each process's working set to its minimum working set size and adds the newly freed pages to the modified or standby lists to be reused.

- The *replacement policy* determines which virtual page must be removed from memory to make room for a new page. Of the replacement policies considered in Chapter 3, the VM Manager uses a local FIFO replacement policy and keeps track of the pages currently in memory for each process — the process's working set. The FIFO algorithm is local to each process, so that when a page fault occurs, only page frames owned by a process can be freed. When it is created, each process is assigned a minimum working-set size, which is the number of pages the process is guaranteed to have in memory while it is executing. If memory is not very full, the VM Manager allows the process to have the pages it needs up to its working set maximum. If the process requires even more pages, the VM Manager removes one of the process's pages for each new page fault the process generates.

Certain parts of the VM Manager are dependent on the processor running the operating system and must be modified for each platform. These platform-specific features include page table entries, page size, page-based protection, and virtual address translation.

A FEW WORDS ABOUT WINDOWS 95

One goal of Windows 95 is to maintain compatibility with applications written for MS-DOS and Windows 3.x environments. However, this is a significant challenge because there are no set standards among applications on how to treat memory resources. Typically, programmers want memory to be available in infinite quantities.

Windows 95 memory architecture is defined as a demand-paged virtual memory system, based on a four-gigabyte flat linear address memory model using a 32-bit addressing scheme (Houlette et al., 1995). Although four gigabytes is the amount of memory that is physically addressable, actual memory limits are determined by hardware costs and platform limitations. A flat linear address memory model eliminates the need to view memory as made up of separate segments. It provides memory addressing starting at a physical location — zero for example — and continuing to the application limit, using an incremental memory addressing scheme. Hardware facilities that support this scheme were incorporated in the 80386 and later chips; therefore, Windows 95 cannot execute on the pre–Intel-386 class of microprocessors. Unlike Windows NT, Windows 95 does not support other non-Intel hardware platforms equipped with extremely different internal hardware.

Also unlike Windows NT, Windows 95 does not support POSIX or OS/2 applications, only Windows 3.x, Win32s, Win32, and DOS applications. One benefit of this is a reduction in kernel and operating system demands, freeing up application memory. One disadvantage is the effect on the file system. Although four megabytes, the minimum memory configuration for Windows 95, is sufficient to support several open applications, the operating system tends to degrade after three applications. One way to determine appropriate memory size for normal office applications is to divide the size of memory by one million and subtract one. So four megabytes would support three open applications, whereas eight megabytes would support seven open applications. As the cost increases to upgrade memory, say, from 16 to 32 megabytes, most users feel that a 12- to 16-megabyte configuration provides an adequate cost/performance tradeoff. Most standard applications are designed to stay within the four- to eight-megabyte range.

The VM Manager handles allocation and deallocation of physical memory. It is responsible for protecting individual process memory space, sharing memory among applications and the operating system, protecting the Windows 95 kernel, eliminating memory fragmentation, and swapping unused pages to hard disk using three major structures: the page directory, the page table, and the page frame.

- The page directory is a table containing addresses for the page table.
- The page table entries contain physical addresses and physical memory status flags. Each process has its own set of page table entries with status flags to indicate the following conditions: present, read/write, privilege, accessed, modified, available.
- The page frame is uniquely addressed by a page table entry and points to the physical memory address. The TLB is a 64-kilobyte hardware cache buffer built into the microprocessor (80386 and above) and performs the same function as the TLB in Windows NT.

To swap pages to disk, Windows 95 uses the least recently used (LRU) algorithm, as described in Chapter 3. The VM Manager uses the information in the page table to identify the type of usage and time stamp of each page and prioritizes the pages based on the amount of time since the last access. It also makes a distinction between modified and nonmodified pages when identifying pages to be swapped to disk — nonmodified pages will be swapped before modified pages.

PROCESSOR MANAGER

Mark Lucovsky, who designed and wrote NT's executive process manager, states that its essential goal is to "provide a set of native process services that environment subsystems can use to emulate their unique process structures" (Custer, 1993). This goal goes hand-in-hand with the objective of Windows NT to provide different operating system environments that run in user mode. The following properties point to the differences between native NT processes and those in other operating systems (Custer, 1993):

- NT processes are implemented as objects and are accessed using object services.
- An NT process can have multiple threads executing within its address space.
- Both process objects and thread objects have built-in synchronization capabilities.

- The NT process manager does not maintain parent/child or other relationships among the processes it creates.

In general, a process is the combination of an executable program, a private memory area, and system resources allocated by the operating system as the program executes. However, a process in Windows NT requires a fourth component before it can do any work: at least one "thread of execution." A thread is the entity within a process that the NT kernel schedules for execution; it could be roughly equated to a "task." Multiple threads, also called multithreading, allow a programmer to break up a single process into several executable segments and also to take advantage of the extra CPU power available in computers with multiple processors.

We introduced the idea of multiprocessing in Chapter 6, but the concept of multithreading is slightly different. To explain it, let's look at its evolution.

Microsoft Windows 3.1 is a cooperative multitasking operating environment. This means that several processes appear to be running at the same time, so as a word processor functions in one window a spreadsheet appears to run in another. The word "cooperative" indicates that each program controls the resources and their releases, which presents problems if one program monopolizes a resource for a long time, to the detriment of other programs. A major problem of cooperative systems is that if one program becomes deadlocked, it cannot release its resources, resulting in a deadlocked system.

UNIX is a preemptive multitasking operating system that allocates the CPU to running programs based on preset time slices. That system can have numerous programs running at the same time and still operate smoothly. Even if one process becomes deadlocked, it doesn't affect the execution of other processes because the operating system can still control the allocation and deallocation of system resources.

Windows NT is a preemptive multitasking, multithreaded operating system. It enhances the smoothness of operation and process independence of UNIX by allowing a process to break up into several "threads of execution." By default, a process contains one thread, which is composed of: a unique identifier, the contents of a volatile set of registers indicating the processor's state, two stacks used during the thread's execution, and a private storage area used by subsystems and dynamic-link libraries. These components are called the thread's "context"; the actual data forming this context varies from one processor to another. The NT kernel then schedules threads for execution on a processor. For example, when you use the mouse to "double click" on an icon in the Program Manager, NT creates a process, and that process has one thread that runs the icon's code. The process is like a container for the global variables, the environment strings, the heap owned by the application, and the thread. The thread is what actually executes the code (Brain, 1994). Figure 13.2 shows a diagram of a process with a single thread.

A process can have as many threads as there are CPUs available in the system. The overhead incurred by a thread is minimal. In some cases, it is actually advantageous to split an application into multiple threads because the entire program is then much easier to understand. The creation of threads is not as complicated as it

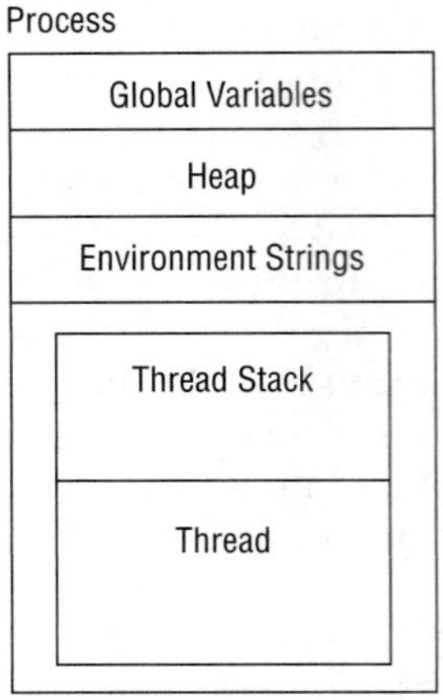

FIGURE 13.2 *Unitasking on Windows NT. Here's how a process with a single thread is scheduled for execution on the system's single processor.*

may seem. Although each thread has its own stack, all threads belonging to one process share its global variables, heap, and environment strings, as shown in Figure 13.3.

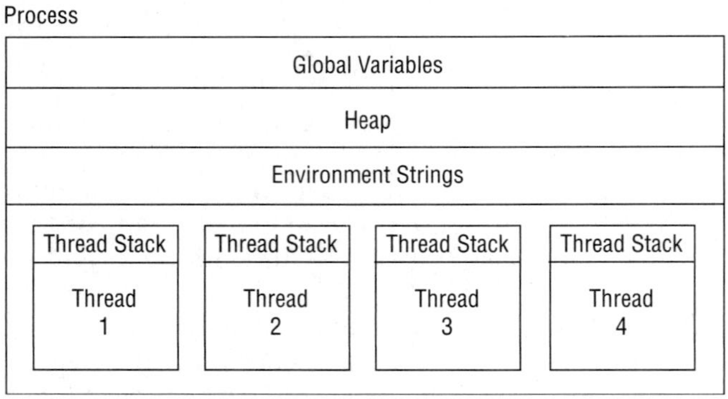

FIGURE 13.3 *Multitasking using multithreading. Here's how a process with four threads can be scheduled for execution on the system's four processors.*

Multiple threads can present problems because it is possible for several different threads to modify the same global variables independently of each other. To prevent this, Windows NT includes some very robust synchronization mechanisms to guarantee exclusive access to global variables as multithreaded processes are executed. For example, let's say the user is modifying a database application. When the user enters a series of records into the database, the cursor will change into a combination of hourglass and arrow pointer, indicating that a thread is writing the last record to the disk while another thread is accepting new data. Therefore, even as processing work is going on, the user can perform other tasks. The concept of overlapped I/O is now occurring on the user's end, as well as on the computer's end. Multithreading is even more advantageous when doing database searches because when the system has several threads of execution searching an array simultaneously, especially if each thread has its own CPU, faster data retrieval results. Programs written to take advantage of these enhancements must be designed very carefully to minimize contention, as when two CPUs attempt to access the same memory location, or when two threads compete for single shared resources, such as a hard disk.

Client/server applications tend to be CPU-intensive for the server because although queries on the database are received as requests from a client computer, the actual query is managed by the server's processor. Therefore, if ten users send their database queries at the same time, the system will have difficulty searching for the data and transmitting it from disk to memory. The multiprocessing environment of Windows NT would be able to satisfy those requests by providing additional CPU resources.

A FEW WORDS ABOUT WINDOWS 95

Windows 95 is a preemptive multitasking operating system using predetermined time slices (time quantums) to allocate the CPU to each process. The Windows 95 default time slice is 20 milliseconds. A process is defined as "an instance of an executing program." Therefore, each button in the task bar represents a process. Just as in Windows NT, in Windows 95 each process is divided further into subprocesses called threads, so that any process may contain more than one thread. Multithreading is achieved by having the threads share a single CPU, unlike in Windows NT, which allows for several processors within one system to operate at once.

Each active thread is assigned a priority that is used to determine when it will be scheduled to run. Threads are scheduled for execution by two schedulers: the primary scheduler, which evaluates priorities assigned to threads and schedules them for execution based on priority order, and the time slice scheduler, which regularly adjusts priorities for each thread to ensure that time slices are allocated fairly to all threads. When it comes time to switch the CPU from one thread to another, the processor manager examines the queues containing threads of equal priority. It looks at the highest priority queue and activates the next thread waiting there. The processor manager then goes through each waiting thread from queue to queue until all have been served, as described in Chapter 4.

To ensure smooth system performance, the schedulers can raise the priority of a thread when certain conditions have been met; for example, when a thread enters a critical region. This type of priority upgrade is called "dynamic priority boosting." In addition, threads can inherit priorities from other threads, which is called "priority inheritance." This technique is implemented when a low-priority thread is holding resources needed by high-priority threads. In this case, the low-priority thread temporarily inherits the priority of the high-priority thread to speed up its completion and release the needed resources to the high-priority thread. Then, after the low-priority thread has finished, its original priority is restored.

The problem of "contention," which is when separate threads are trying to access the same resources at the same time, is resolved through several synchronization techniques. One such technique demands that the thread notify the system that it needs to use a certain shared resource and then goes into a waiting state. When the operating system discovers that the resource is available, it allocates that resource to the waiting thread and restarts it. A similar technique puts a thread in a waiting state until a certain event has occurred, such as when input from the user is completed.

DEVICE MANAGEMENT

Darryl Havens, who designed and implemented operating system components for more than 12 years, designed the I/O Manager, which consolidates into one system physical I/O elements with logical file principles. When designing the I/O system for Windows NT, Havens borrowed some features from other systems he had worked on, such as DEC's VAX/VMS and VAX ELN operating systems. In addition, the I/O design was influenced by having to support Win32, OS/2, and POSIX (Custer, 1993).

The I/O system must accommodate the needs of existing devices — from a simple mouse to keyboards, printers, graphic display terminals, disk drives, CD-ROM drives, and networks. In addition, it must consider future storage and input technologies. The NT I/O system provides a uniform high-level interface for executive-level I/O operations and protects application programs from differences among physical devices. It shields the rest of the operating system from the details of device manipulation and thus minimizes and isolates hardware-dependent code.

The NT I/O system was designed to provide the following:

- Multiple installable file systems including the MS-DOS FAT system, the high-performance file system, the CD-ROM file system, and the NT file system
- Services to make device-driver development as easy as possible yet workable on multiprocessor systems
- Ability for system administrators to add drivers to the system or remove them from the system dynamically
- Fast I/O processing while allowing drivers to be written in high-level language
- Mapped file I/O capabilities for image activation, file caching, and application use

The I/O system is packet driven, which means that every I/O request is represented by an I/O request packet (IRP) as it moves from one I/O system component to another. An IRP is a data structure that controls how the I/O operation is processed at each step. The I/O manager creates an IRP that represents each I/O operation, passes the IRP to the appropriate driver, and disposes of the packet when the operation is complete. On the other hand, when a driver receives the IRP, it performs the specified operation and then either passes it back to the I/O manager or passes it through the I/O manager to another driver for further processing.

In addition to creating and disposing of IRPs, the I/O manager supplies code, common to different drivers, that they call to carry out their I/O processing. It also manages buffers for I/O requests, provides time-out support for drivers, and records which installable file systems are loaded into the operating system. It provides flexible I/O facilities that allow subsystems such as Win32 or POSIX to implement their respective I/O application programming interfaces. Finally, the I/O manager allows device drivers and file systems, which it perceives as "device" drivers, to be loaded dynamically based on the needs of the user, as shown in Figure 13.4.

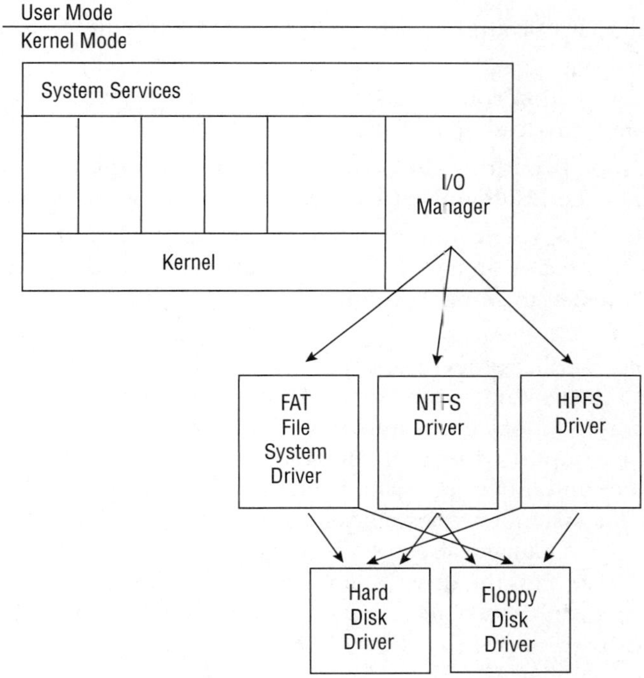

FIGURE 13.4 *An example showing how Windows NT supports the MS-DOS FAT and OS/2's HPFS drivers as well as its own NTFS driver. Drivers are modular and can be layered on top of each other, allowing different file systems to call the same disk driver to access files.*

To ensure that the operating system will work with a wide range of hardware peripherals, Windows NT provides a very rich device-independent model for I/O services. This model takes advantage of a concept, a "multilayered device driver," that is not found in more conventional operating systems, such as MS-DOS, with their monolithic device drivers. NT's drivers provide a large and complex set of services that are understood by an intermediate layer of the operating system. In a monolithic model, commands presented at this layer are relatively high-level functions, such as "open file" and "read from file." When these commands are issued, the device driver communicates directly with the hardware and provides the necessary hardware interface to perform file operations. The physical actions needed to fill these requests are hidden within the driver (Ruley et al., 1994). A monolithic model works well when there is only one type of file system.

Because Windows NT is designed to use a variety of file system formats, it would not be safe for a device driver to make assumptions about the underlying file organization. Therefore, NT combines multilayer device drivers with the I/O manager so application programs, and intermediate levels of the operating system, communicate with the I/O manager, which in turn communicates with the device drivers.

Each NT driver is made up of a standard set of routines including the following:

- Initialization routine, which creates system objects used by the I/O manager to recognize and access the driver.
- Dispatch routine, functions performed by the driver, such as read or write. This is used by the I/O manager to communicate with the driver when it generates an IRP after an I/O request.
- Start I/O routine, used by the driver to initiate data transfer to or from a device.
- Completion routine, used to notify a driver that a lower-level driver has finished processing an IRP.
- Unload routine, which releases any system resources used by the driver so that the I/O manager can remove them from memory.
- Error logging routine, used when unexpected hardware errors occur such as a bad sector on a disk; the information is passed to the I/O manager, which writes all this information to an error log file.

When a process needs to access a file, the I/O manager must determine from the file object's name which driver should be called to process the request, and it must be able to locate this information the next time a process uses the same file. This is accomplished by a driver object, which represents an individual driver in the system and a device object, which represents a physical, logical, or virtual device on the system and describes its characteristics.

The I/O manager creates a driver object when a driver is loaded into the system and then calls the driver's initialization routine, which records the driver entry points in the driver object and creates one device object for each device to be handled by this driver, as shown in Figure 13.5.

FIGURE 13.5 *The driver object is connected to device objects with the last device object pointing back to the driver object.*

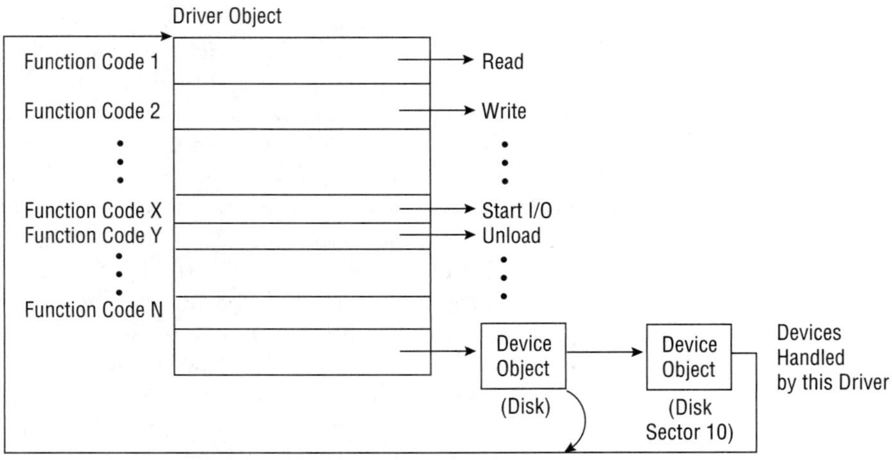

Example: Application instruction: READ "MYFILE.TXT"
Translate: READ = FUNCTION CODE 1
"MYFILE.TXT" = DISK SECTOR 10
Action: Access DRIVER OBJECT (1) = Activate READ routine = Access DISK SECTOR 10

Figure 13.5 illustrates how the last device object points back to its driver object, telling the I/O manager which driver routine to call when it receives an I/O request. It works in the following manner: When a process requests access to a file it uses a file name, which includes the device object where the file is stored. When the file is opened the I/O manager creates a file object and then returns a file handle to the process. Whenever the process uses the file handle the I/O manager can immediately find the device object, which points to the driver object representing the driver that services the device. Using the function code supplied in the original request the I/O manager indexes into the driver object and activates the appropriate routine because each function code corresponds to a driver routine entry point.

A driver object may have multiple device objects connected to it. The list of device objects represents the physical, logical, and virtual devices that are controlled by the driver. For example, each sector of a hard disk has a separate device object with sector-specific information. However, the same hard disk driver is used to access all sectors. When a driver is unloaded from the system, the I/O manager uses the queue of device objects to determine which devices will be affected by the removal of the driver.

Using objects to keep track of information about drivers frees the I/O manager from having to know details about individual drivers — it just follows a pointer to locate a driver. This provides portability and allows new drivers to be easily loaded. Another advantage to representing devices and drivers with different objects is that it is easier to assign drivers to control additional or different devices if the system configuration changes.

Figure 13.6 shows how the I/O manager interacts with a layered device driver to write data to a file on a hard disk (Custer, 1993). First, an application issues a command to write to a disk file at a specified byte offset within the file. Second, the I/O manager passes the file handle to the File System Driver. Third, the I/O manager translates the file-relative byte offset into a disk-relative byte offset and calls the next driver. Fourth, the function code and the disk-relative byte offset are passed to the disk driver. Fifth, the disk-relative byte offset is translated into the physical location and data is transferred. You may want to relate this process to the discussion about levels in a file management system in Chapter 8.

The NT I/O manager knows nothing about the file system. The process described in this example will work exactly the same if an NTFS driver is replaced by a FAT driver, a UNIX file system driver, a CD-ROM driver, a Macintosh file system driver, or any other driver.

Keep in mind that there is overhead involved with the I/O manager passing requests for information back and forth. So for simple devices, such as serial and parallel printer ports, NT provides a single-layer device driver approach in which the I/O manager can communicate with the device driver, which, in turn, will return information directly. But for more complicated devices, particularly for devices such as hard drives that depend on a file system, a multilayered approach is a better choice.

Another device driver feature that is unique to Windows NT is that almost all low-level I/O operations are asynchronous. That means that when an application issues an I/O request it does not have to wait for data to be transferred, but it can continue to perform other work while data transfer is taking place. Asynchronous I/O must be specified by the process when it opens a file handle. During asynchro-

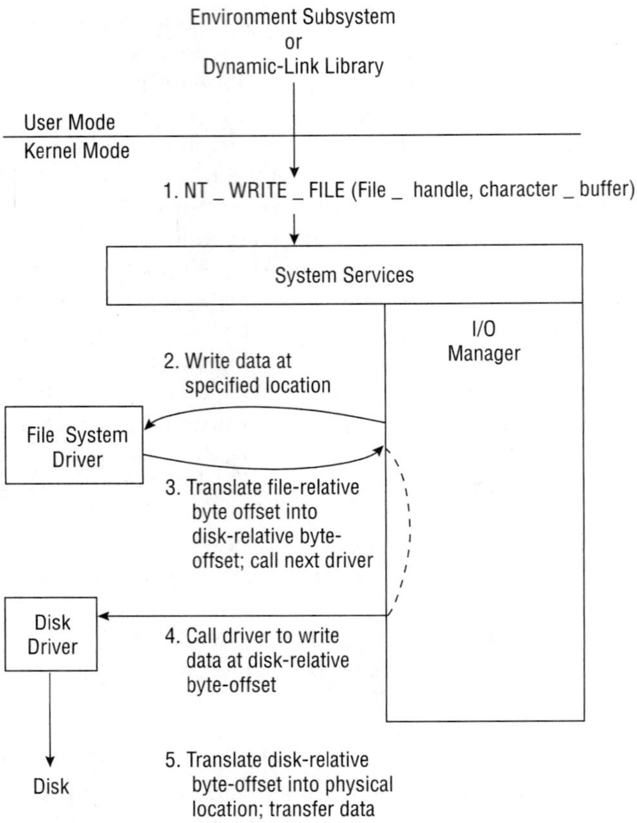

FIGURE 13.6 *Details of the layering of a file system driver and a disk driver first shown in Figure 13.4. These are the five steps that take place when the I/O manager needs to access a secondary storage device to satisfy the user command shown here as number 1. (Adapted from Custer, 1993.)*

nous operations, the process must be careful not to access any data from the I/O operation until the device driver has finished data transfer. Asynchronous I/O is useful for operations that take a long time to complete or for which completion time is variable.

For example, the time it takes to list the files in a directory varies according to the number of files. Because Windows NT is a preemptive multitasking system that may be running many tasks at the same time, it is vital that the operating system not waste time waiting for a request to be filled if it can be doing something else. The various layers in the operating system use the preemptive multitasking and multithreading characteristics of NT to enable themselves to get more work done in the same time. In NT's symmetric multiprocessing environment, it is theoretically possible for all the CPUs to attempt simultaneous device driver access, causing contention. To avoid this problem, device drivers, like other components of the NT executive, make use of synchronization objects, in particular semaphores and spin locks. A **spin lock** is a locking mechanism associated with a global data structure, such as the deferred procedure call (DPC) queue. Before entering a critical region, the kernel must get the spin lock associated with the protected DPC queue. If the spin lock is not available, the kernel keeps trying to get it until it succeeds. As the name of this protection mechanism implies, the process is held in limbo, spinning, until it gets the lock. Spin locks reside in global memory and are coded in assembly language for speed and to take advantage of whatever locking mechanisms are provided by the underlying processor architecture. On many processors spin locks are implemented with a hardware-supported test-and-set operation, as described in Chapter 6.

The last unique feature of NT device drivers considered here is the provision for power failure recovery. When most systems lose power while they are running, they crash, losing any I/O operations that were in progress. Windows NT is equipped with an uninterruptible power supply (UPS) that gives users ample warning of impending power failures and then shuts everything down in a systematic way. If the computer has a battery back-up for memory, NT provides a "**warm boot**" that allows the I/O manager to recover I/O operations that were in progress when the failure happened (Custer, 1993).

For example, if there is a power failure while the computer is writing a disk file, NT notifies all device drivers of the failure. The device drivers then set themselves to their stable states and continue with the I/O operations that were outstanding when the power failed. With this capability in place, a power outage does not significantly affect a Windows NT system, because operations continue from where they were and carry on transparently after power is fully restored.

A FEW WORDS ABOUT WINDOWS 95

The block input/output subsystem, which is part of the File Management Subsystem, handles access to the hard drive. The uppermost layer of the block I/O subsystem is called the input/output supervisor (IOS); it manages access of the higher-layer components in the file management subsystem within the hard disk. Below the IOS layer are the components that allow direct access to the disk hardware, the miniport driver, and the small computer system interface (SCSI) layer. The SCSI layer contains the functions that are common to all SCSI devices. The miniport driver contains the functions that are specific to an individual SCSI device. Therefore, the miniport driver is the only component that is hardware dependent.

Windows 95 introduced a new technology called "Plug and Play" that allows PC hardware and connected devices to work together with minimal direction from the computer operator. This feature is implemented in the hardware, in the operating system, and in the supporting software such as drivers and BIOS. These systems are able to configure hardware devices automatically and respond to dynamic configuration events; applications are able to adjust their configurations to reflect the addition or elimination of devices.

FILE MANAGEMENT

Typically, an operating system is associated with the particular file structure that it uses for mass storage devices, such as hard disks. Therefore, we speak of a UNIX file system (i-nodes) or an MS-DOS file system (FAT). Although there is a resident NT file system (NTFS), Windows NT is designed to be independent of the file system on which it operates.

Windows NT supports multiple file systems for hard disks including MS-DOS's FAT file system and OS/2's high performance file system (HPFS), as well as NTFS, which extends the capabilities of both the FAT and the HPFS file systems by adding the following features:

- File system recovery that allows for quick restoration of disk-based data after a system failure
- The ability to handle large storage media, on the order of approximately 17 billion gigabytes in size
- Security features, including execute-only files
- Unicode filenames, which allow documents to be transferred from one computer to another internationally without distorting their file names or path names
- Support for the POSIX operating system environment, including hard links, case-sensitive names, and information about when a file was last opened
- Features for future extensibility, such as transaction-based operations to support fault-tolerant applications, user-controlled version numbers for files, multiple data streams per file, flexible options for file naming and file attributes, and support for popular file servers (Custer, 1993).

In addition, Windows NT supports a CD-ROM file system, eliminating the need for the MSCDX patch to the file system required by all CD-ROM drives used with MS-DOS machines. The NTFS advanced server emulates the Macintosh file system and handles network services as though they were file systems (Ruley et al., 1994). Windows NT provides access to files on the LAN manager network through a file system called the Windows NT redirector, which accepts requests for remote files and directs them to a LAN manager server on another machine. Windows NT is capable of running all of these file systems simultaneously.

The primary concept in file handling in Windows NT, first introduced in UNIX, was the "virtual file," which refers to any source or destination for I/O that is treated as if it were a file. In Windows NT, programs perform I/O on virtual files, manipulating them by using file handles. Although not a new concept, in Windows NT a file handle actually refers to an executive file object that represents all sources and destinations of I/O. Processes call native NT file object services such as those to read from or write to a file. The I/O manager directs these virtual file requests to real files, file directories, physical devices, or any other destination supported by the system. File objects have hierarchical names, are protected by object-based security, support synchronization, and are handled by object services.

When opening a file, a process supplies the file's name and the type of access required. This request moves to an environment subsystem that in turn calls an NT system service. The object manager starts an object name lookup and turns control over to the I/O manager to find the file object. The I/O manager checks the security subsystem to determine whether or not access can be granted. The I/O manager also uses the file object to determine whether asynchronous I/O operations are requested.

The creation of file objects helps bridge the gap between the characteristics of physical devices and directory structures, file system structures, and data formats. File objects provide a memory-based representation of shareable physical resources. When a file is opened the I/O manager returns a handle to an NT file object. The NT object manager treats file objects like all other objects until the time comes to write to or read from a device, at which point the object manager calls the I/O manager for assistance to access the device. Figure 13.7 illustrates the contents of file objects and the services that operate on them; Table 13.2 describes the attributes of the file object (Custer, 1993).

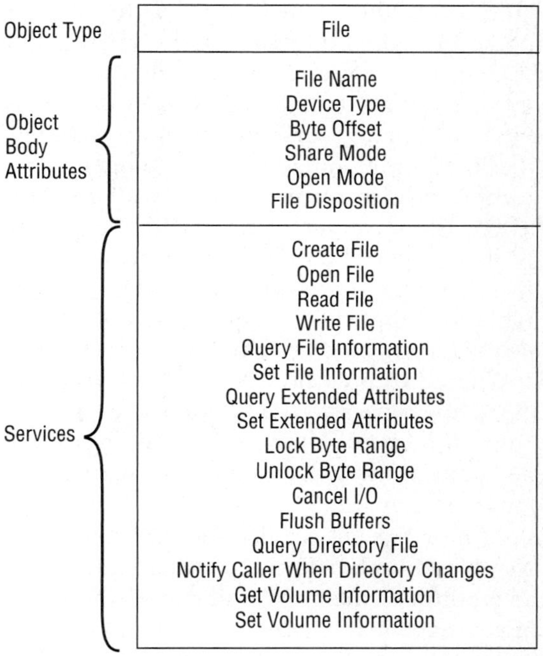

FIGURE 13.7 *Illustration of a file object, its attributes, and the services that operate on them.*

TABLE 13.2 *Description of the attributes of file objects shown in Figure 13.7.*

Attribute	Purpose
File name	Identifies the physical file to which the file object refers
Device type	Indicates the type of device on which the file resides
Byte offset	Identifies the current location in the file (valid only for synchronous I/O)
Share mode	Indicates whether other callers can open the file for read, write, or delete operations while this caller is using it
Open mode	Indicates whether I/O will be synchronous or asynchronous, cached or noncached, sequential or random, etc.
File disposition	Indicates whether to delete the file after closing it

A distinction should be made between a file object, a memory-based representation of a shareable resource that contains only data unique to an object handle, and the file itself, which contains the data to be shared. Each time a process opens a handle, a new file object is created with a new set of handle-specific attributes. For example, the attribute byte offset refers to the location in the file where the next read or write operation using that handle will occur. One may regard file object attributes as being specific to a single handle.

Although a file handle is unique to a process, the physical resource is not. Therefore, processes must synchronize their access to shareable files, directories, and devices. For example, if a process is writing to a file, it should specify exclusive write access to it or could lock portions of the file while writing to it, to prevent other processes from writing to that file at the same time.

Mapped file I/O is an important feature of the I/O system and is achieved through the cooperation of the I/O system and the VM Manager. At the operating system level, file mapping is typically used for file caching, loading, and running executable programs. The VM Manager allows user processes to have mapped file I/O capabilities through native services. Memory mapped files exploit virtual memory capabilities by allowing an application to open a file of arbitrary size and treat it as a single contiguous array of memory locations without buffering data or performing disk I/O. For example, a file of 100 megabytes can be opened and treated as an array in a system with only 20 megabytes of memory. At any one time only a portion of the file data is physically present in memory — the rest is paged out to the disk. When the application requests data that is not currently stored in memory, the VM Manager uses its paging mechanism to load the correct page from the disk file. When the application writes to its virtual memory space, the VM Manager writes the changes back to the file as part of the normal paging. Because the VM Manager optimizes its disk accesses, applications that are I/O bound can speed up their execution by using mapped I/O — writing to memory is faster than writing to a secondary storage device.

A component of the I/O system called the cache manager uses mapped I/O to manage its memory-based cache. The NT cache expands or shrinks dynamically depending on the amount of memory available. Using normal working-set strategies, the VM Manager expands the size of the cache when there is memory available to accommodate the application's needs, and reduces the cache when it needs free pages. The cache manager takes advantage of the VM Manager's paging system, avoiding duplication of effort.

NTFS supports long file names that can include spaces and special characters. Therefore, users can name a file "Spring 1996 Student Grades" instead of something cryptic like S96STD.GRD. Because the use of long file names could create compatibility problems, NTFS and Windows 95 automatically convert long file names to the standard eight-character file name and three-character extension required by DOS and Windows 16-bit applications.

A FEW WORDS ABOUT WINDOWS 95

This file management subsystem is made up of the following components:

- The installable file system (IFS) manager, which communicates with permanent storage devices and manages various types of file systems available on the system. Each file system is implemented as a 32-bit protected mode virtual device driver, resulting in a file system more solid than the MS-DOS file system. In addition, if a user decides to attach other storage devices to an existing system, such as a WORM drive, IFS can install and manage the new file systems needed to accommodate those devices.

- The virtual file allocation table (VFAT) is the new 32-bit FAT file system and manages all floppy and hard disks in the system. It runs in protected mode and maintains fast, direct access to a disk through the disk controller card.
- The new 32-bit CD-ROM file system, also called CDFS, replaces the MS-DOS CD-ROM extensions (MSCDEX). It multitasks more efficiently and provides much higher throughput than previous CD file systems.
- Any network file system for which a user has installed the redirector.

Using algorithms similar to those found in NT, both VFAT and CDFS work with VCACHE to provide caching of data in a dynamic memory pool, speeding up the process of reading information from disks.

To preserve compatibility with the MS-DOS file system, Windows 95 maintains both a DOS format (eight-character file name and three-character extension) and a long file name for each file. VFAT and CDFS build special directory entries containing long file names that can have up to 255 characters.

NETWORK MANAGEMENT

Windows NT networking software is not an add-on layer to an existing operating system. Rather, it is an integral part of the NT executive providing services such as user accounts, resource security, and mechanisms used to implement communication between computers, such as with "**named pipes**" and "**mailslots**." Named pipes provide a high-level interface for passing data between two processes regardless of their locations. Mailslots provide one-to-many and many-to-one communication mechanisms useful for broadcasting messages to any number of processes.

Microsoft Networks, informally known as "MS-NET," was released in 1984 and became the model for the NT Network Manager (Custer, 1993). Three MS-NET components — the redirector, the server message block (SMB) protocol, and the network server — were extensively refurbished and incorporated into Windows NT.

The NT redirector, coded in the C programming language, is implemented as a loadable file system driver and is not dependent on the system's hardware architecture. Its function is to direct an I/O request from a user or application to the remote server that has the appropriate file or resource needed to satisfy the request. NT networking can incorporate multiple redirectors, each of which directs I/O requests to remote file systems or devices. A typical remote I/O request might result in the following progression. 1) The user-mode software issues a remote I/O request by calling local NT I/O services. 2) After some initial processing, the I/O manager creates an I/O request packet (IRP) and passes the request to the Windows NT redirector, which forwards the IRP to the transport drivers. 3) Finally, the transport drivers process the request and place it on the network. The reverse sequence is observed when the request reaches its destination.

The SMB protocol is a high-level specification for formatting messages to be sent across the network and correlates to the application layer (layer 7), and the presentation layer (layer 6) of the OSI model described in Chapter 9. An API called NetBIOS interface is used to pass I/O requests structured in the SMB format to a remote computer. Both the SMB protocols and the NetBIOS API were adopted in several networking products before appearing in Windows NT.

The Windows NT server is written in C for complete compatibility with existing MS-NET and LAN manager SMB protocols, is implemented as a loadable file system driver, and has no dependency on the hardware architecture on which the operating system is running.

A basic peer-to-peer network server that handles SMB protocol is included in Windows NT's networking software. Windows NT can also load other network servers and run them alongside its built-in server. For high-end or large networked environments, a new product — tentatively called "LAN Manager for Windows NT" — will transform a peer-to-peer networked workstation into an advanced domain server (Custer, 1993). A domain server can share user accounts and security information with multiple associated systems grouped together in a network domain and with other trusted network domains.

Figure 13.8 (adapted from Custer, 1993) shows how the seven layers of the OSI reference model are implemented in Windows NT. As discussed in Chapter 9, each layer of the hierarchy assumes that it is communicating to the same layer on another machine and uses a common protocol. In reality, however, a message must pass down each layer on the client machine, be transmitted across the network, and then pass up each layer of the destination machine until the request is satisfied.

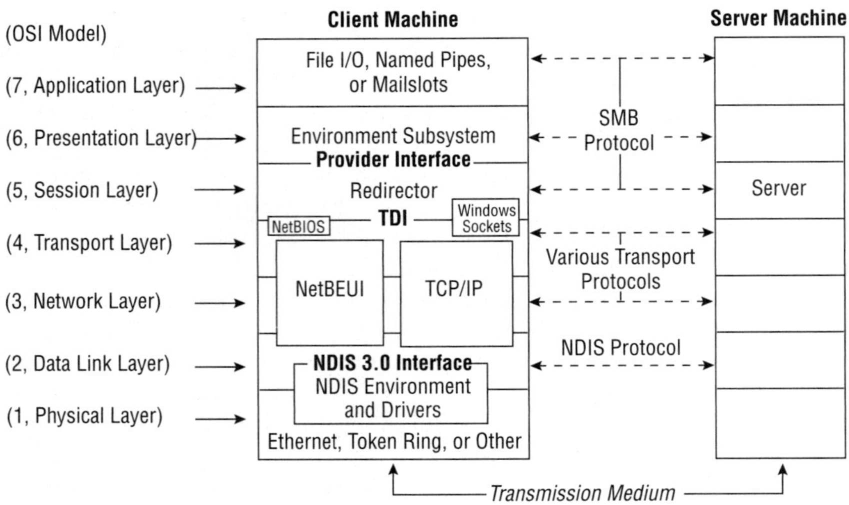

FIGURE 13.8 *Implementation of the seven layers of the OSI reference model in Windows NT. (Adapted from Custer, 1993.)*

The redirector calls transport driver interface (TDI) routines to transmit SMBs to the various transport drivers loaded into Windows NT. One of these routines, the NetBIOS API, provides compatibility with MS-DOS, 16-bit Windows, and OS/2 applications that send data across the network. A new 32-bit version is also present. Another is the new Windows Sockets API, which provides 16-bit and 32-bit **sockets**, a standard UNIX-style networking interface. Lower layers of code that support

UNIX applications and allow Windows NT to take part in the Internet are also included. This part of Windows NT corresponds to layer 5, the session layer.

In Windows NT, transport protocols are implemented as drivers and can be loaded into and out of the system. Two of the transports supplied by Microsoft are NetBEUI (NetBIOS Extended User Interface), a local area transport developed by IBM to operate below Microsoft's NetBIOS network interface, and TCP/IP (Transmission Control Protocol/Internet Protocol), commonly used in UNIX-based networks. Several other transports are under development, such as IPX/SPX (Internet Packet Exchange/Sequenced Packet Exchange), used by Novell Corporation's NetWare software; DECnet, a proprietary protocol used by Digital Equipment Corporation; AppleTalk, a protocol developed by Apple Computer, Inc.; and XNS (Xerox Network System), a transport developed by Xerox Corporation. This part of the networking system relates to the transport layer (layer 4) and the network layer (layer 3) of the OSI model.

Windows NT provides the network driver interface specification (NDIS), an interface, and an environment that supply the path between the network layer and the physical layer. This allows users to communicate with different network protocols using just one network card and one network driver. NDIS version 3.0 is written in C, is updated to use 32-bit addresses, and is multiprocessor enabled. Like the earlier versions, it is capable of handling multiple independent network connections and multiple simultaneously loaded transport protocols. This part of Windows NT corresponds to layer 2, the data link layer (Custer, 1993).

Using remote procedure calls (RPC), Windows NT allows users to create and execute distributed applications. RPC applications can handle library procedures that execute remotely as well as locally. This means that the RPC facility automatically transmits requests across the network, handles network protocols, deals with network errors, waits for results, and handles other details that, in the past, were the responsibility of the application programmer.

A FEW WORDS ABOUT WINDOWS 95

As Figure 13.9 shows, many of the features in Windows NT are also found in Windows 95.

Windows 95 networking was almost completely rewritten from Windows for Workgroups 3.11 and is quite similar to Windows NT. Most components maintain compatibility with 16-bit components but have been designed as 32-bit protected-mode Virtual Device drivers. The new design is also more modular and follows the layered approach of the OSI model.

Windows 95 provides support for a large number of concurrent network servers through the network provider interface (NPI), which is positioned between application developers and network providers so the user interface is consistent in its presentation of resources and servers. Therefore, printers and other peripherals are treated the same regardless of the underlying network configuration. In addition, an installable file system (IFS) supports multiple loadable drivers that provide access to specific types of file systems.

The Novell compatible protocol IPX/SPX is the default protocol for Windows 95; NetBEUI protocol and TCP/IP are also accommodated.

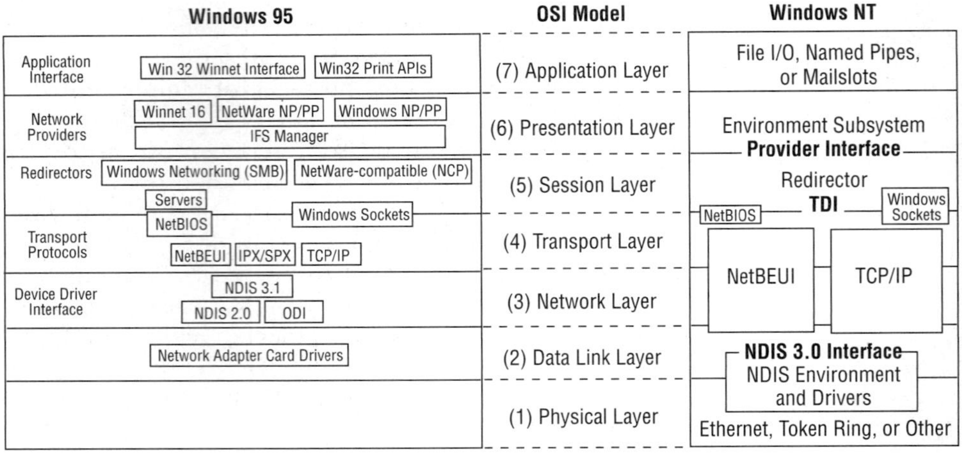

FIGURE 13.9 *Correlation of features common to Windows NT and Windows 95.*

SECURITY MANAGEMENT

Windows NT provides an object-based security model. That is, a security object can represent any resource in the system: a file, device, process, program, or user. This allows system administrators to give precise security access to specific objects in the system while allowing them to monitor and record how objects are used.

The U.S. Department of Defense has identified and categorized into seven levels of security certain features that make an operating system secure. Early versions of Windows NT targeted Class C2 level with a plan to evolve to Class B2 level — a more stringent level of security in which each user must be assigned a specific security level clearance and is thwarted from giving lower-level users access to protected resources.

To comply with the Class C2 level of security, Windows NT includes the following features:

- A secure log-on facility requiring users to identify themselves by entering a unique log-on identifier and a password before they are allowed access to the system
- Discretionary access control allowing the owner of a resource to determine who else can access the resource and what they can do to it
- Auditing ability to detect and record important security-related events or any attempt to create, access, or delete system resources
- Memory protection preventing anyone from reading information written by someone else after a data structure has been released back to the operating system

Windows NT strives to prevent access by unauthorized users while allowing entry to legitimate users by supporting a multilayered security system. Its Password Management is the first layer of security.

If a hard disk is formatted with the NTFS, users encounter a second layer of security that deals directly with file access security. At this level, the user can create a file and establish various combinations of individuals to have access to it because NT makes distinctions between owners and groups. The creator of a file is its **owner**. The owner can designate a set of users as belonging to a **group** and allow all the members of the group to have access to that file. Conversely, the owner could prevent some of the members from accessing that file.

In addition to determining who is allowed to access a file, users can decide what type of operations a person is allowed to perform on a file. For example, one may have "read only" access, while another may have "read and write" privileges. As a final measure, NT gives the user auditing capabilities that automatically keep track of who uses files and how.

NT SECURITY TERMINOLOGY

When someone logs in to an NT system, the system returns an **access token**. Thereafter, every time that the user creates a process, the process contains a copy of that person's access token. Access tokens are significant because they not only identify individuals and their rights, but also the group or groups to which they belong. The list of rights found in each individual's access token is assembled by the system and created by copying from each group that user's privileges.

Most objects in NT have a security descriptor. Each user creates a **security descriptor** and passes it along to the object when it is created. The owner of an NT object can always set its security information, even if it has been accidentally changed. A security descriptor contains the following information:

- An owner-identifier that identifies the current owner of the object
- A primary group-identifier
- A system access control list (SACL) that contains auditing information
- A discretionary access control list (DACL) that determines which users and groups can and cannot access the object

The DACL controls who can and cannot access the objects in an access control entry (ACE). Each ACE indicates one user or group and their privileges for that object. If a user has read access to a file, then the ACE is called an "access allowed ACE." Correspondingly, there can be an "access denied ACE," which prevents a specific individual or group from accessing designated objects.

The SACL also contains ACEs that are used to determine who will be audited and why. So an ACE in a SACL is called an "audit access ACE."

An access token identifies a process and its threads to the operating system, whereas a security descriptor lists which of these processes, or groups of processes, can access an object. When a thread opens a handle to an object, the object manager and the security system put this information together to determine whether the caller should be given the handle it is requesting. This check takes place only when a handle is opened, not every time the handle is used (Custer, 1993).

Because of the potential for sharing proprietary data in a client/server environment, ensuring security is extremely important. In Windows NT, server processes provide a secure access by taking on the identity of the client. That way, the client user can access only those files that are appropriate to that individual. This technique is called "**impersonation**" and is transparent to both programmers and end users. It does not interfere greatly with normal system operations, although it involves a certain amount of overhead.

A FEW WORDS ABOUT WINDOWS 95

Windows 95 is designed to blend into several networking environments with built-in functionality and **pass-through security**. The new security of Windows 95 allows users to share resources on the share-level and the user-level. The share-level is similar to that used in Windows for Workgroups, but the user-level is new. It is very important that the system administrator determine which level of security is required before setting any resource sharing parameters because only one level can be in effect at any one time — and changing between them erases the previous level's share and security information (Houlette et al., 1995).

Although Windows 95 security is stronger than that of Windows for Workgroups, the stand-alone Windows 95 system is still susceptible to illegal access because it uses the FAT file system, which has no inherent security of its own. Therefore, for example, files on the hard disk can be read after booting the computer system from a floppy disk. The only change to the FAT file system in Windows 95 is the file system's ability to handle long file names. Windows 95 relies on the security available on existing network servers, such as Novell or Windows NT, to provide security to networked computer users.

The designers of Windows 95 made the assumption that most PCs would be stand-alone and that sharing capabilities would not be needed. However, if PCs are networked, then network resources must be enabled with every PC set individually so that each user has a personal desktop configuration. Once this is done, a log on dialog box will appear asking the user for the name, password, and other information required by the server being used, and which will then be validated against the network user database. In some cases a Windows 95 workstation can be configured to require that a user's name and password be passed to a Netware server or a Windows NT server before continuing. This constitutes pass-through security and allows Windows 95 to take advantage of the existing networking hardware and software that are part of external network servers.

Share-level security is similar in Windows 95 and Windows for Workgroups. Windows 95 can be configured to perform share-level peer services. It can be implemented in a network consisting solely of workstations running Windows 95 only, whereas user-level security involves a network server. To use share-level security, the network access control setting must be activated. The icon for devices or folders that have been set for sharing will appear on the desktop with a hand icon added.

Windows 95 uses the log-on procedure to control several services, such as file sharing, printer sharing, and network and system management. User-level security is the ability to share a resource by specifying the names of users or groups that are authorized to use it and is the highest level of security that can be implemented. To enable user-level security, a Windows NT or Netware server must be present, and it must contain all user profiles so pass-through security can be implemented.

The new security features allow a Network Manager to effectively administer a network's users and resources.

USER INTERFACE

Users familiar with Windows 3.1 or Windows for Workgroups will find the NT desktop familiar, because all three products share the same look (Columbus & Simpson, 1995). The Windows NT desktop contains the icons for the tools and applications one can use to get work done. Getting around the desktop can be done using the mouse, the keyboard, or both. Most novice users prefer the mouse, while some experienced users rely on keyboard shortcuts to access both menus and commands quickly.

Windows NT provides a consistent series of dialog boxes and menus, regardless of the specific application, which makes it easy to learn. To start an application, users double-click on its icon. To quit an application they can select Exit from the file menu.

Although a detailed description of the tools present on the desktop is beyond the scope of this chapter, we will take a brief look at the Program Manager because it is the key application of the Windows NT desktop and it is the window that will always be present. Figure 13.10 shows a typical Program Manager window, which performs the following functions:

- Organizes files and programs into logical groups
- Sets up applications to be launched whenever a user logs in

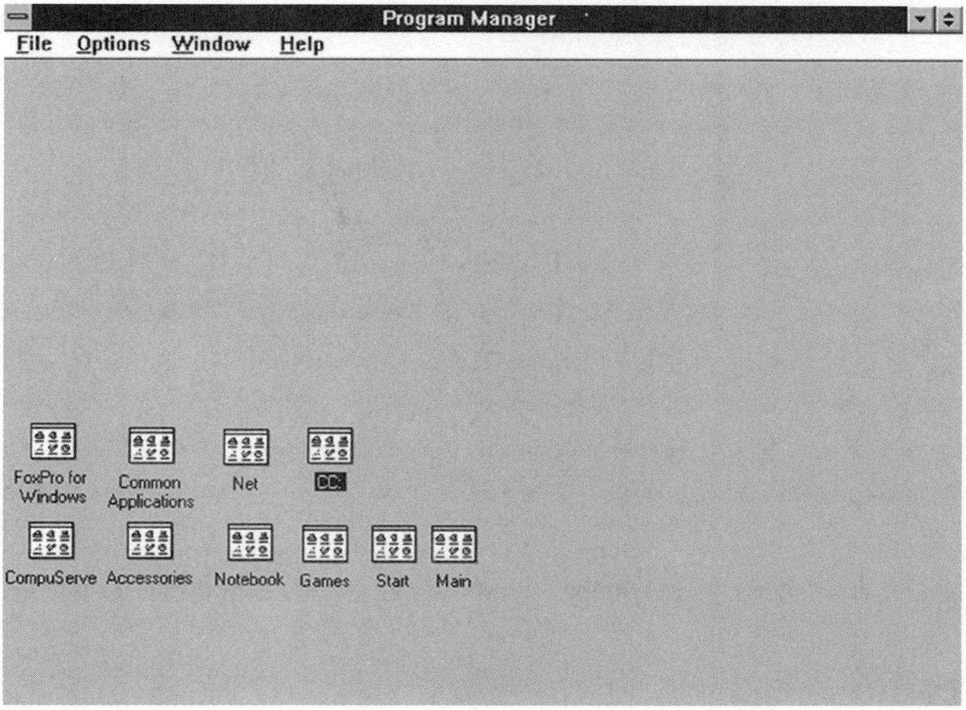

FIGURE 13.10 *The Windows NT Program Manager window with all its subwindows closed.*

- Launches applications either directly or through an associated data file
- Customizes the launch of applications to use specific switches and directories
- Logs out or temporarily exits Windows NT
- Totally shuts down or restarts Windows NT

A program group is similar to a file folder used to organize related documents, images, or applications that are represented as icons. When the user double-clicks on a program group, it becomes a window that contains icons for files and programs found on the hard disk, as shown in Figure 13.11. An application can be started by double-clicking on its icon.

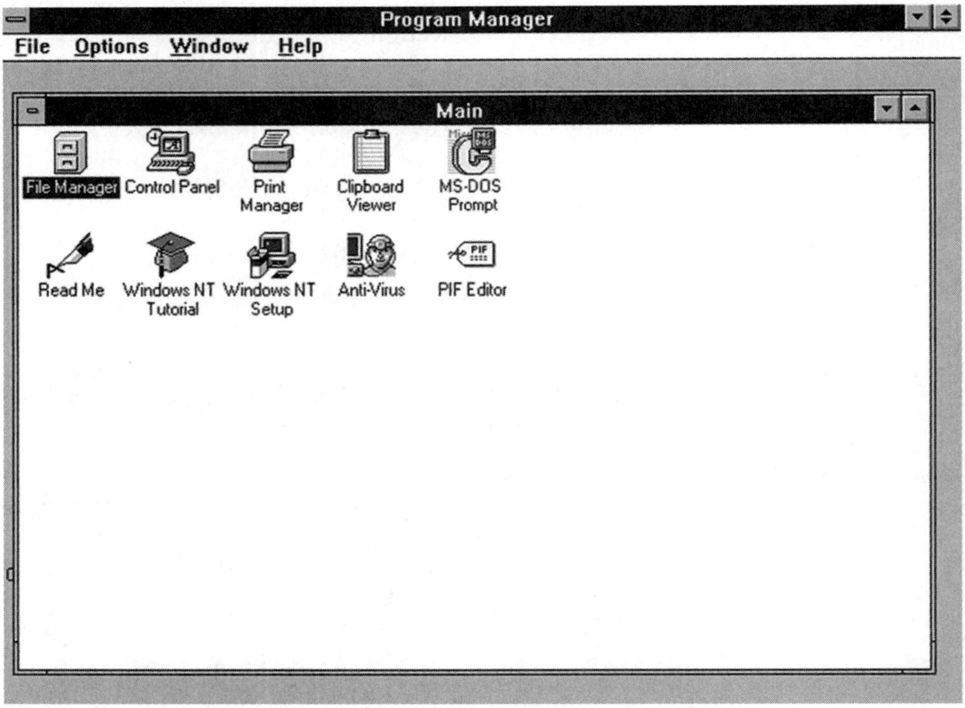

FIGURE 13.11 *The Windows NT Program Manager with the main window open showing its programs or data files as icons.*

The Program Manager also contains a series of pull-down menus along the top that are used to complete specific tasks.

- File: contains menu items for creating and manipulating program groups, as well as log-off and shutdown options
- Options: contains items that regulate how the Program Manager will behave when the user launches applications from it or changes its configuration
- Window: allows the user to automatically lay out the Program Manager window or quickly access any program group
- Help: accesses the Windows NT help system

For example, to add new program groups or items within existing groups the user would activate the file function of the program manager. Figure 13.12 shows the pull-down menu for the file option.

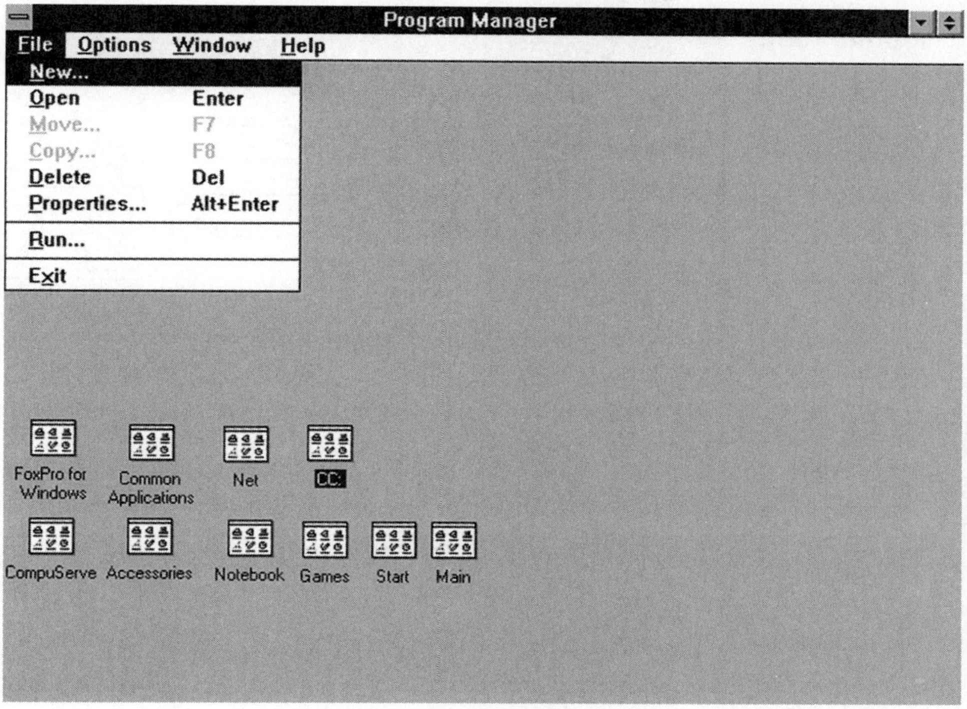

FIGURE 13.12 *The file pull-down menu showing six currently valid options in dark type and two currently invalid options in light type and the keyboard shortcuts for five of them.*

To create a new group you would select **New . . .** , which would then display the new program object dialog box on the screen (as shown on Figure 13.13), used to create both new program items and groups.

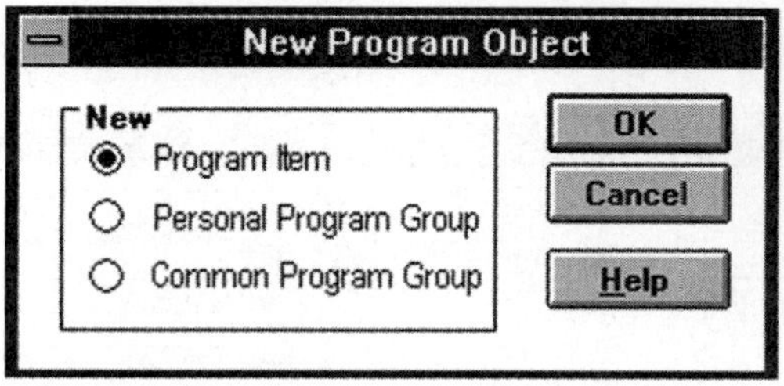

FIGURE 13.13 *The dialog box used by Windows NT to create a new group.*

At this point you have several choices, but because you are creating a personal program group, you would follow these steps:

1. Click once on the personal program group radio button; the program group properties dialog box, as shown in Figure 13.14, will be displayed on the screen.
2. Click once on the **Description:** entry and type the name of the program

group you want to create — for example, Chapter Seven. The **Group File:** entry in this dialog box is optional. Click once on **OK** to complete the process.

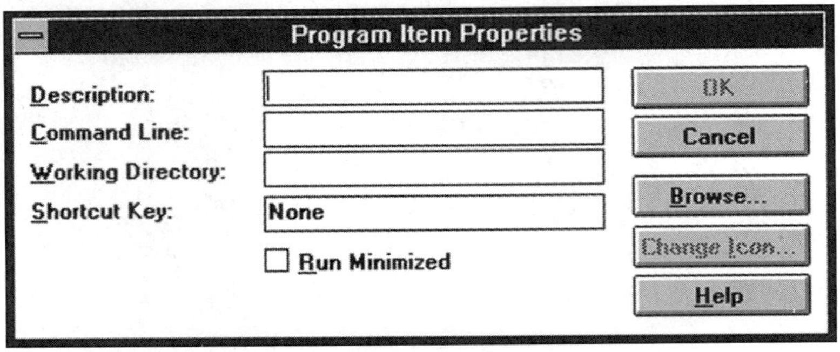

FIGURE 13.14 *The dialog box used by Windows NT to identify a new program's properties.*

Windows NT has two types of program groups: a personal group, which is available only to its creator, and a common group, which is seen in the program manager of anyone logged in to the system.

The process described above can be modified to create a new program item. To do so, use the dialog box shown in Figure 13.13 and follow these steps:

1. Click once on the **Program Item** button and click once on **OK**. The program item properties dialog box will appear on the screen, as shown in Figure 13.14.
2. Click once on the **Description:** entry and type the name of the program item you are creating. This can be any text, including spaces and punctuation.
3. If you know the exact location and name of the file you are going to use, type this information in the **Command Line** field; otherwise click once on **Browse . . .** and the browse dialog box will be displayed on the screen, as shown in Figure 13.15.

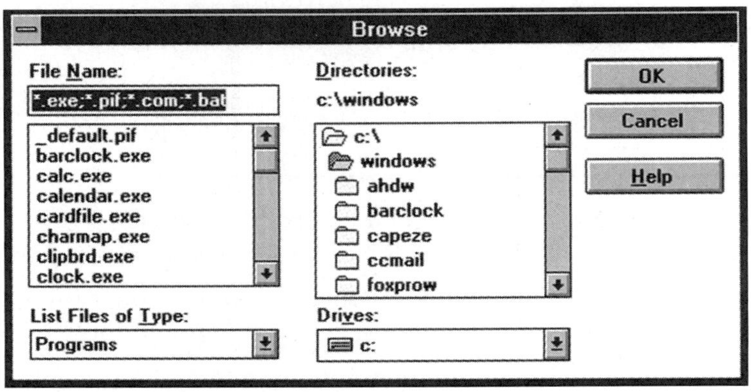

FIGURE 13.15 *The dialog box used to browse through the file system to identify the new program's location.*

4. Using the options in the browse dialog box, scroll through the executable files until you find the one you want to have represented as an icon on the desktop. Click once on **OK**.
5. The new program item will appear in the currently active program group.

Program items can also be data files. The easiest way to add a data file to a program group is just to drag it from the file manager window and the file will show up with the icon of its parent application. For example, a file with the extension ".doc" would show up with the icon identifying it as requiring the Microsoft Word application program. If the file is not associated with any applications it will have a blank icon.

You can also use the commands within the file menu to move, copy, and delete icons from the Program Manager's desktop, as shown in Figure 13.12. This is a bonus to users who learned their first applications on UNIX, DOS, or another command-driven operating system. Some people are so familiar with the commands that they can type commands faster than the system can execute them. Although it's not apparent, one can use a pseudocommand interface in Windows NT that resembles an MS-DOS shell. Therefore, anything that can be done from MS-DOS can be done in Windows NT. In addition, Windows NT provides many keyboard shortcuts to help users navigate, should the mouse become impaired. For a guide, look for keyboard shortcuts on the pull-down menus, such as the one shown in Figure 13.12, which identifies **ALT+Enter** as the keyboard shortcut to change a file's properties.

CHAPTER THIRTEEN CONCLUSION

Windows NT, the only network operating system profiled in this text, is a robust system incorporating GUI ease-of-use with the technical power to operate a network across several existing platforms. Because it was designed to evolve modularly and consistently over time, Windows NT's portability will facilitate its migration to new hardware platforms.

To make the operating system a fully international one, capable of accommodating the characters from many languages, an effort is underway to provide a single system binary. In addition, work is proceeding on fonts to support Asian languages as well as input editors that translate multiple keystrokes into individual characters such as accented vowels.

Windows NT's significant security controls have helped it gain inroads with organizations requiring consistent protection for their data and applications. Its authentication model supports new user interfaces from bank teller machines to fingerprint or retinal scanners. It also allows the implementation of different security architectures such as the Kerberos model, on top of the operating system, further extending Windows NT's reach into the market.

Next we'll look at UNIX, which began as a complex operating system for minicomputers and has since been adapted for use in mainframes, minicomputers, and personal computer systems.

Chapter Fourteen

UNIX OPERATING SYSTEM

USER COMMAND INTERFACE

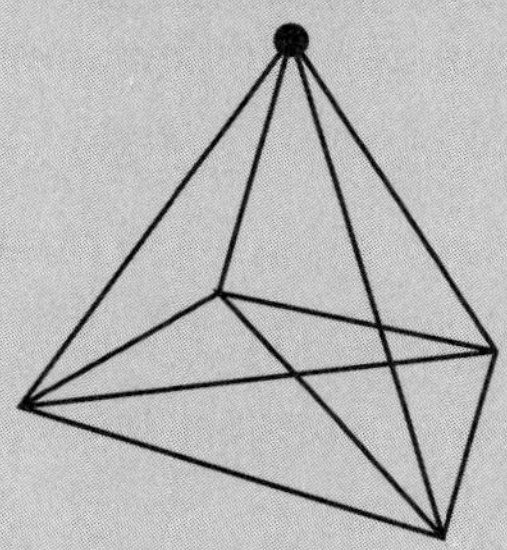

Design Goals

Memory Management

Processor Management

Device Management

File Management

User Interface

Unlike many operating systems, UNIX is not limited to specific computers using a particular microprocessor as a CPU. Instead, it runs on all sizes of computers using a wide range of microprocessors.

UNIX has three major advantages: (1) it is portable from large systems to medium-sized systems to single-user systems, (2) it has very powerful utilities, and (3) it is device independent.

Its portability is attributed to the fact that it's written in a high-level language, C, instead of assembly language as are most operating systems. Its utilities are brief, single-operation commands that can be combined to achieve almost any desired result — a feature that many programmers find endearing. And because it includes the device drivers as part of the operating system, and not as part of the devices, UNIX can be configured to run any device.

UNIX also has disadvantages: (1) its commands are so brief that novice users find it unfriendly, and (2) there's no single standardized version of the operating system. The problem of standardization was being addressed in the late 1980s by a standards committee proposing a standard set of specifications for AT&T's UNIX V (Bourne, 1987).

As of 1990, there existed about two dozen versions of UNIX, among them AT&T's UNIX System V, A/UX (UNIX System V for the Macintosh II), Ultrix (UNIX for DEC's VAX system), Microsoft's XENIX (a UNIX-based operating system for microcomputers using Intel processors), and the University of California at Berkeley's UNIX Versions 4.1 bsd, 4.2 bsd, and 4.3 bsd. Berkeley UNIX is an expanded version of AT&T's Version 7. It was designed originally to run on VAX computers and has become quite popular in many academic circles. Although it's a UNIX derivative, in some areas, such as file store structure and communications, it is very different from AT&T's System V. Some enhancements such as the "vi" editor and the "curses" screen handling package (loosely derived from "cursor motion optimization," it provides the highest level of screen control) have been incorporated into releases of System V (Haviland & Salama, 1987).

Throughout our discussion we'll describe AT&T's version of UNIX unless otherwise specified.

Note: UNIX is case-sensitive — it's strongly oriented toward lower-case characters. Therefore, throughout this chapter all file names and commands are typed in lower case.

HISTORY

The story of UNIX starts with a research project begun in 1965. It was a joint venture between Bell Laboratories (the research and development group of AT&T), General Electric, and MIT with a goal to develop the MULTICS operating system for the large and powerful GE-645 mainframe computer. MULTICS had a grand ambition: to serve the needs of a diverse group of users, but its ambition proved its undoing — it soon became too intricate, too complex, and too large to be of commercial value.

Bell Laboratories withdrew from the project in 1969, and AT&T management decided not to undertake the development of any more operating systems. But that didn't stop two young veterans of the MULTICS project, Ken Thompson and Dennis Ritchie. (Some people say they needed a new operating system to support their favorite game: Space Travel.) Regardless of their reasons for developing it, UNIX has become one of the most widely used operating systems in history (Seyer & Mills, 1986).

Thompson and Ritchie originally wrote the operating system in assembly language for a Digital Equipment Corporation PDP-7 computer and it was named "UNIX" by a colleague, Brian Kerningham, as a play on words from MULTICS (Seyer & Mills, 1986).

The first official version, presented in 1971 by Thompson and Ritchie, was designed to run on the DEC PDP-11 minicomputer and included all of the features found in current versions, with the exception of pipes and filters, which were added with Version 2. Before long, UNIX became known as a major operating system. Table 14.1 shows how UNIX evolved in the early days.

For Version 3, Ritchie took the innovative step of developing a new program-

TABLE 14.1 *The historical roots of UNIX, its features, and modifications (Seyer & Mills, 1986). Most modern versions of UNIX have evolved from these early systems. Note: the Berkeley UNIX is not included here; it was originally developed from Version 7, although some features from Berkeley versions have been integrated into System V.*

Year	Internal release	External release	Features	Language
1971	Version 1		Based on MULTICS; introduced shell concept	Assembly
1972	Version 2		Added pipes and filters	Assembly
1973	Version 3			Kernel and I/O written in C
1973	Version 4	UNIX V4		All in C
1974	Version 5		(Not publicly released)	All in C
1975	Version 6	UNIX V6	First version to become commercially available	All in C
1979	Version 7	UNIX V7	More powerful shell added: string variables, structured programming, trap handling	All in C
1980	Release 3.0	UNIX System III	Could be used in 16-bit microcomputers	All in C
1981	Release 4.0		First available for a mainframe	All in C
1982	Release 5.0		(Not publicly released)	All in C
1983		UNIX System V Release 1	Added more software tools (small general-purpose programs)	All in C
1984		UNIX System V Release 2	Added features from Berkeley version: shared memory, more commands, vi editor, termcap database, flex file names	All in C

ming language, C, and wrote a compiler for the C language so UNIX could be rewritten in this faster, high-level language. C was specifically designed to meet the needs of systems designers who weren't familiar with writing programs in assembly language code.

As UNIX grew in fame and popularity, AT&T found itself in a difficult situation. At the time it was forbidden by government antitrust regulations to sell software — but it could, for a nominal fee, make the operating system available first to universities and later to independent developers who, in turn, transformed it into a commercial product. Between 1973 and 1975 several "improved" versions were developed — the most popular version was developed at the University of California at Berkeley and it became known as "BSD." Its popularity in universities created a demand for it in business and industry — a demand AT&T was able to meet beginning in 1984 with the federal government's deregulation of its business.

AT&T entered the computer industry by offering a line of personal computers powered by UNIX System V — their version of UNIX with additional features from the Berkeley version. At that time, AT&T tried to promote their version of UNIX as the standard version, but by then UNIX had already been adopted and adapted by too many designers for too many machines.

By 1993 Berkeley had released 4.4BSD based on AT&T's UNIX, requiring customers to obtain licenses from AT&T to use it. Shortly thereafter, Novell acquired UNIX from AT&T and released 4.4BSD-Lite, which is "freely redistributable." In general, UNIX versions are identified as being more AT&T-like or more Berkeley-like, but because the operating system is easily modifiable, each version has peculiarities of its own.

The original "do one thing well" position of the early commands has been modified in current releases, and recent commands offer many options and controls. This factor has pros and cons — although commands become more difficult to use, they can be adapted to new situations with relative ease. In essence, the key features of the early systems, such as pipelines, have been preserved, while the potential of the commands has increased to meet new needs.

The new releases offer full support for local area networks, and comply with international operating system standards. In addition, system security has been greatly improved and meets many of the U.S. government security requirements.

To date there are several "standards," each supported by a coalition of vendors. Therefore, the multitude of UNIX versions, a problem that was to be solved with industry standards, has not been resolved.

DESIGN GOALS

Thompson and Ritchie envisioned UNIX as an operating system by programmers for programmers, and they had both short-term and long-term design goals for it.

The immediate goals were (1) to develop an operating system that would support software development and (2) to keep its algorithms as simple as possible (without becoming rudimentary).

To achieve their first goal, they included utilities in the operating system for which programmers typically need to write code. Each utility was designed for simplicity — to perform only one function but to perform it very well. And they were designed to be used in combination with each other so that programmers could select and combine any appropriate utilities that might be needed to carry out specific jobs.

This concept of small manageable sections of code fit right in with the second goal: to keep the operating system simple. To do this, Thompson and Ritchie selected the system's algorithms based on simplicity instead of speed or sophistication. As a result, UNIX can be understood by experienced programmers in a matter of weeks.

Their long-term goal was to make the operating system, and any application software developed for it, portable from machine to machine. The obvious advantage of portability is that it reduces conversion costs and doesn't cause application packages to become obsolete with every change in hardware. This goal was finally achieved with Version 4 because it was written entirely in C, a high-level language that is hardware independent, instead of in assembly language that is hardware dependent.

MEMORY MANAGEMENT

UNIX was originally designed for single users but, beginning with Version 4, it was made available for multiuser environments as well. It has since evolved into a powerful multiuser operating system.

For multiprogramming systems, most UNIX operating systems use either swapping or demand paging memory management techniques. The best choice depends on the kind of applications that will run on the system: if most jobs are small then swapping could be the best choice, but if the system will be running many large jobs then demand paging is best (Seyer & Mills, 1986).

Swapping requires that the entire program be in main memory before it can be executed, and this imposes a size restriction on programs. For example, if there is 2M of memory and the operating system takes up half of it (1M), then the size of the programs must be less than one megabyte. Swapping uses a round robin policy — when a job's time slice is up, or when it generates an I/O interrupt, the entire job is swapped out to secondary storage to make room for other jobs waiting in the READY queue. That's fine when there are relatively few processes in the system, but when traffic is heavy this swapping back and forth can slow down the system.

Paging requires more complicated hardware configurations; it increases the system overhead and under heavy loads might lead to thrashing. But it has the advantage of implementing the concept of virtual memory.

Figure 14.1 shows the typical internal memory layout for a single user-memory part UNIX image. An "image" is an abstract concept that can be defined as a computer execution environment composed of: a user-memory part (all of which is depicted in Figure 14.1), general register values, status of open files, and current directory. This image must remain in memory during execution of a process (Ritchie & Thompson, 1978).

FIGURE 14.1
This is how the user-memory part of an "image" is stored in main memory.

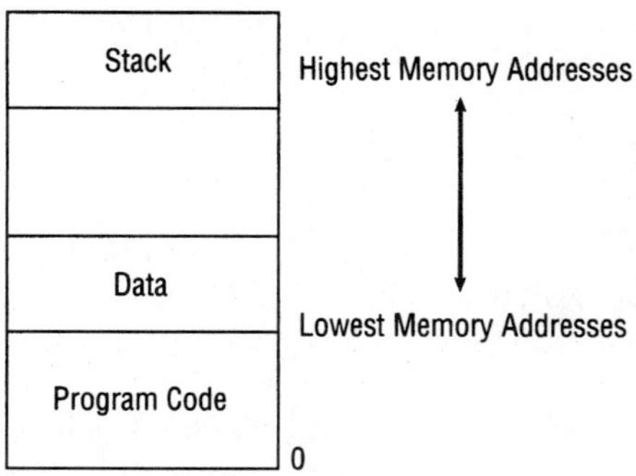

The segment labeled *program code* is the sharable portion of the program. Because this code will be physically shared by several processes it must be written in **reentrant code**. This type of code is protected so that its instructions are not modified in any way during its normal execution. In addition, all data references are made without use of absolute physical addresses.

The Memory Manager gives the program code special treatment. Because several processes will be sharing it, the space allocated to the program code can't be released until *all* of the processes using it have completed their execution. UNIX uses a "text table" to keep track of which processes are using which program code, and the memory isn't released until the program code is no longer needed. The text table is explained in more detail in the next section on Processor Management.

The *data* segment shown in Figure 14.1 starts after the program code and grows toward higher memory locations as needed by the program. The *stack* segment starts at the highest memory address and grows downward as subroutine calls and interrupts add information to it. A stack is a section of main memory where process information is saved when a process is interrupted. The data and stack are nonsharable sections of memory, so when the original program terminates the memory space is released.

Of course, while each process is in memory, the Memory Manager protects them from each other so they don't overlap.

The *UNIX kernel*, which permanently resides in memory, is the part of the operating system that implements the "system calls" to set up the memory boundaries so several processes can coexist in memory at the same time. The processes use these system calls to interact with the File Manager and to request I/O services.

The kernel is the set of programs that implements the most primitive of that system's functions, and it is the only part of the operating system to permanently reside in memory. The remaining sections of the operating system are handled in the same way as any large program. That is, pages of the operating system are brought into memory on demand, only when they're needed, and their memory space is released as other pages are called. UNIX uses the least-recently-used (LRU) page replacement algorithm.

Although we've directed this discussion to large multiuser computer systems, the same memory management concepts are used by UNIX systems for networked personal computers and single-user systems. For example, a single personal computer with a UNIX operating system, using a demand paging scheme, can support up to three users and 12 active windows in a true **multitasking** environment (Seyer & Mills, 1986).

PROCESSOR MANAGEMENT

The Processor Manager of the UNIX system kernel handles the allocation of the CPU, process scheduling, and the satisfaction of process requests. To perform these tasks, the kernel maintains several important tables to coordinate the execution of processes and the allocation of devices.

Using a predefined policy, the Process Scheduler selects a process from the `READY` queue and begins its execution for a given time slice. Remember, as we discussed in Chapter 4, the processes in a time-sharing environment can be in any of five states: `HOLD`, `READY`, `WAITING`, `RUNNING`, or `FINISHED`.

The process scheduling algorithm picks the process with the highest priority to be run first. Since one of the values used to compute the priority is accumulated CPU time, any processes that have used a lot of CPU time will get a lower priority than those that have not. The system updates the compute-to-total-time ratio for each job every second. This ratio divides the amount of CPU time that a process has used up by the total time the same process has spent in the system. A result equal to or greater than 1 would indicate that the process is CPU-bound. If several processes have the same computed priority, they are handled round-robin (low-priority processes are preempted by high-priority processes). Interactive processes typically have a low compute-to-total-time ratio, so interactive response is maintained without any special policies.

The overall effect of this negative feedback is that the system balances **I/O-bound** jobs with **CPU-bound** jobs to keep the processor busy and to minimize the overhead for waiting processes.

When the Processor Manager is deciding which process from the READY queue will be loaded into memory to be run first, it chooses the process with the longest time spent on the secondary storage.

When the Processor Manager is deciding which process, currently in memory and ready to be run, will be moved out temporarily to make room for a new arrival, it chooses the process that is either waiting for disk I/O or currently idle. If there are several processes to choose from, the one that has been in memory the longest is moved out first.

If a process is waiting for the completion of an I/O request and isn't ready to run when it is selected, UNIX will dynamically recalculate all process priorities to determine which inactive but ready process will begin execution when the processor becomes available. This is to avoid discrimination against I/O-bound jobs (Christian, 1983).

These policies seem to work well and don't impact on the running processes. However, if a disk is used for secondary file storage as well as a "swapping area," then heavy traffic can significantly slow disk I/O because job swapping may take precedence over file storage.

PROCESS TABLE VERSUS USER TABLE

UNIX uses several tables to keep the system running smoothly, as shown in Figure 14.2. Information on simple processes, those with nonsharable code, is stored in two sets of tables: the process table, which always resides in memory, and the user table, which resides in memory only while the process is active.

Each entry in the process table contains the following information: process identification number, user identification number, process memory address or secondary storage address, size of the process, and scheduling information. This table is set up when the process is created and is deleted when the process terminates.

For processes with sharable code, the process table maintains a subtable, called the text table, which contains the following information: memory address or secondary storage address of the text segment (sharable code) and a count to keep track of the number of processes using this code. Every time a process starts using this code, the count is increased by one; and every time a process stops using this code, the count is decreased by one. When the count is equal to zero the code is no longer needed and the table entry is released together with any memory locations that had been allocated to the code segment.

A User Table is allocated to each active process. It is kept in the transient area of memory and contains information that must be accessible when the process is running. This information includes the user and group identification numbers to determine file access privileges; pointers to the system's File Table for every file being used by the process; a pointer to the current directory; and a list of responses for various interrupts. This table, together with the process data segment and its code segment (which is present if the process has sharable code), can be swapped into or out of main memory as needed.

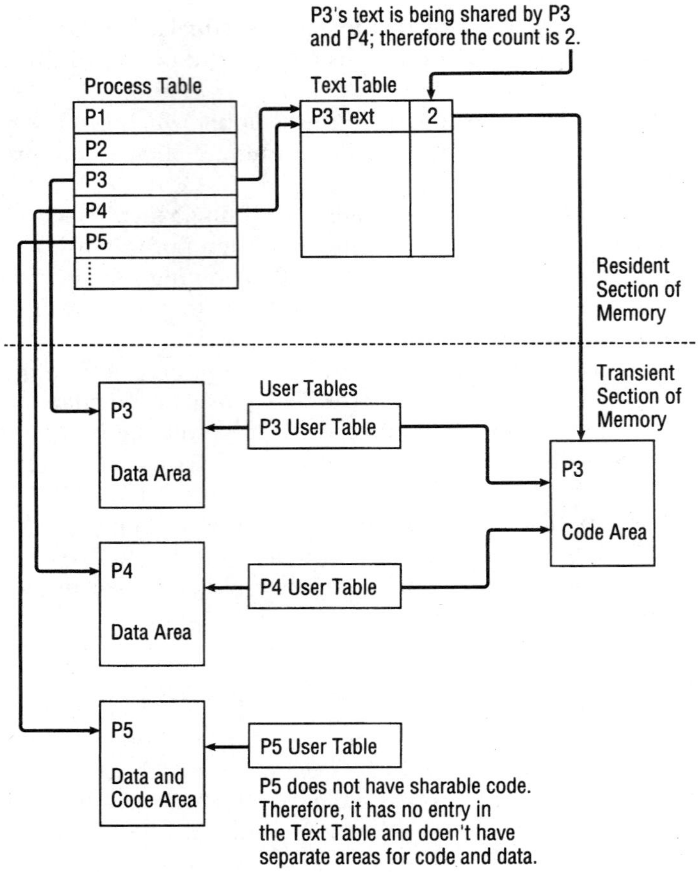

FIGURE 14.2 *The process control structure showing how the process table and text table interact for processes with sharable code, as well as for those without sharable code. Processes P3 and P4 show the same program code indicated in the text table by the number 2. Their data areas and user tables are kept separate while the code area is being shared. Process P5 is not sharing its code with another process; therefore it is not recorded in the text table, and its data and code area are kept together as a unit (Thompson, 1978).*

SYNCHRONIZATION

UNIX is a true multitasking operating system. It achieves process synchronization by requiring that processes wait for certain events. For example, if a process needs more memory, it is required to wait for an event associated with memory allocation. Later, when memory becomes available, the event is signaled, and the process can continue. Each event is represented by integers that, by convention, are equal to the address of the table associated with the event.

A **race** may occur if an event happens during the process's transition between deciding to wait for the event and entering the `WAIT` state. In this case the process is waiting for an event that has already occurred and may not recur. Although this isn't a problem in single-processor environments, it may pose a problem in multiprocessor environments.

`fork`, `wait`, AND `exec` COMMANDS

`fork`

An unusual feature of UNIX is that it gives the user the capability of executing one program from another program using the `fork` command. This command gives the second program all the attributes of the first program, such as any open files, and saves the first program in its original form.

The system command `fork` splits a program into two copies, which are both running from the statement after the `fork` command. When `fork` is executed a "process id" (called "pid," for short) is generated, which ensures that each process has its own unique ID number.

Figure 14.3 shows what happens after the fork. The original process (Process 1) is called the "parent" process and the resulting process (Process 2) is the "child" process. A child inherits the parent's open files and runs asynchronously with it unless the parent has been instructed to wait for the termination of the child process.

FIGURE 14.3 *When the* `fork` *command is received, the parent process shown in* (**a**) *begets the child process shown in* (**b**) *and Statement 2 is executed twice.*

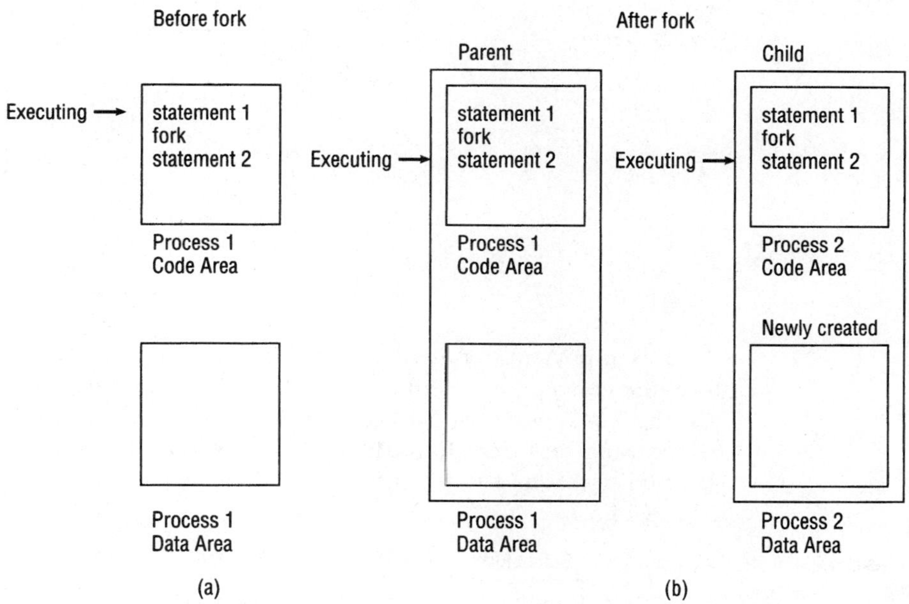

`wait`

A related command, `wait`, allows the programmer to synchronize process execution by suspending the parent until the child is finished, as shown in Figure 14.4.

In a program, the IF-THEN-ELSE structure is controlled by the value assigned to pid: a pid greater than zero indicates a parent process, a pid equal to zero indicates a child process, and a negative pid indicates an error in the `fork` call.

`exec`

The `exec` family of commands — `execl`, `execv`, `execls`, `execlp` and `execvp` — are used to start execution of a new program from another program. Unlike `fork`, which results in two programs being in memory, a successful `exec` call will overlay the second program over the first, leaving only the second program in memory. The second program can be considered a new process but, in fact, it takes on the pid of the first program.

FIGURE 14.4 *The* `wait` *command used in conjunction with the* `fork` *command will synchronize the parent and child processes.* (**a**) *shows the parent process,* (**b**) *shows the parent and child after the* `fork`, *and* (**c**) *shows the parent and child during the* `wait`.

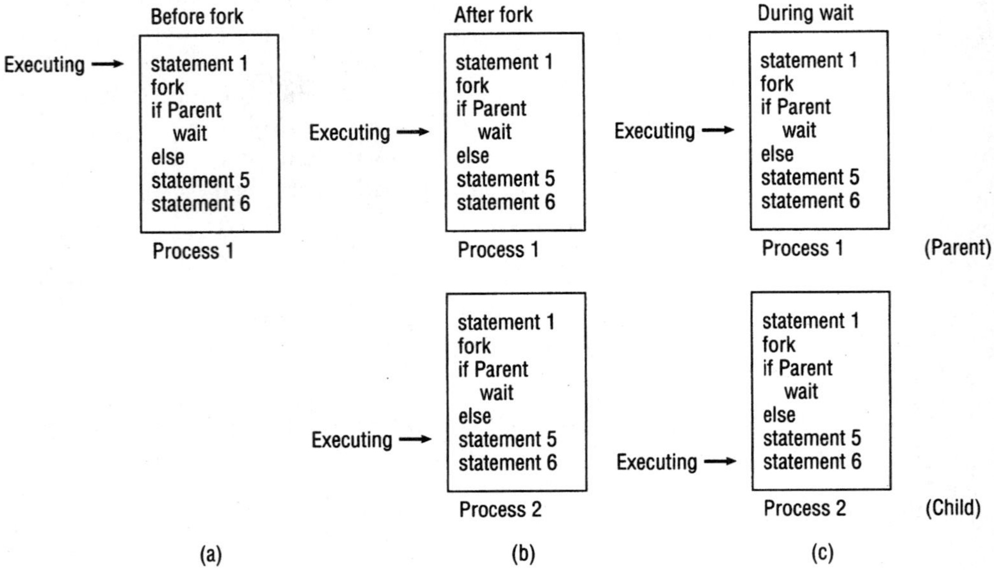

It is important to note that there's no return from a successful `exec` call; therefore, the concept of parent-child does not hold here. However, a programmer can use the `fork`, `wait`, and `exec` commands in this order to create a parent-child relationship and then have the child be overlaid by another program that, when finished, awakens the parent so that it can continue its execution, as shown in Figure 14.5.

FIGURE 14.5 *The* `exec` *command used after the* `fork` *and* `wait` *combination.* (**a**) *shows parent before* `fork`, (**b**) *shows parent and child after* `fork`, *and* (**c**) *shows how the child process (Process 2) is overlaid by the* `ls` *program after the* `exec` *command.*

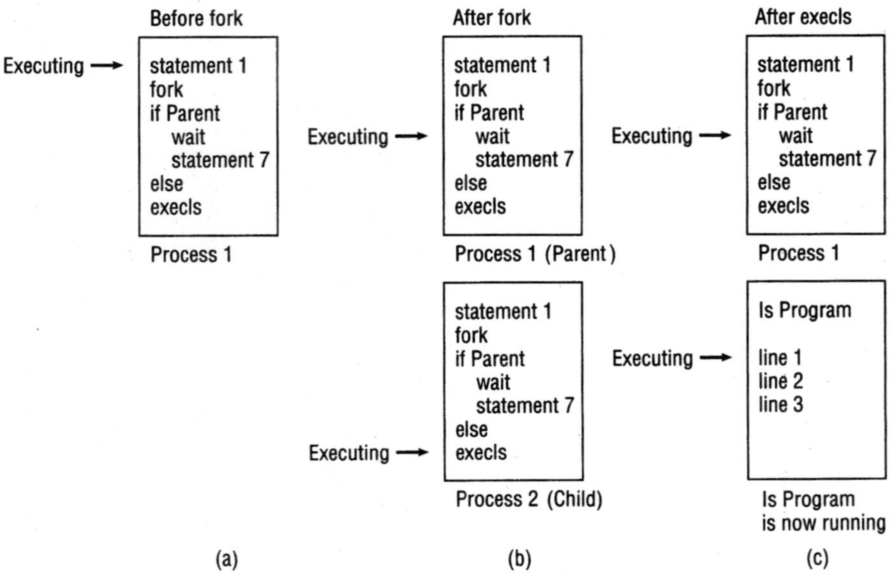

The `ls` command generates a listing of the current directory. When the `exec` call has been executed successfully, processing begins at the first line of the called program. Each `exec` call is followed by a test to ensure that it was completed successfully; if it was unsuccessful, the test would then indicate actions to be performed. Once the `ls` program is finished, control returns to the executable statement following `wait` in the parent process.

These commands illustrate the flexibility of UNIX that programmers find extremely useful. For example, a child process can be created to execute a procedure in the parent program, as was done in Figure 14.5, without having to load or find memory space for a separate program.

DEVICE MANAGEMENT

DEVICE DRIVERS

An innovative feature of UNIX is its treatment of devices — it is truly device independent. It achieves this independence by treating each I/O device as a special type of file. (Other operating systems control devices with a "hard coded" program built into each device.) Every device that's installed in a UNIX system is assigned a name that's similar to the name given to any other file. But while device files are given "descriptors," other files are not. These descriptors identify the devices, contain information about them, and are stored in the device directory.

The subroutines that work with the operating system to supervise the transmission of data between main memory and a peripheral unit are called the **device drivers**. They are written in C and are part of the UNIX kernel.

When a UNIX operating system is purchased, it comes with device drivers to operate the most common peripheral devices. However, if the computer system should include peripherals that are not on the standard list, their device drivers must be purchased or written by an experienced programmer and installed on the operating system.

The actual incorporation of a device driver into the kernel is done during the system configuration. Recent versions of UNIX have a program called `config` that will automatically create a `conf.c` file for any given hardware configuration. This `conf.c` file contains the parameters that control resources such as the number of internal buffers for the kernel and the size of the swap space. In addition, the `conf.c` file contains two tables: `bdevsw` (short for "block I/O devices") and `cdevsw` (short for "character I/O devices"), which provide the UNIX system kernel with the ability to adapt easily to different hardware configurations by installing different driver modules (Christian, 1983).

DEVICE CLASSIFICATIONS

UNIX divides the I/O system into two separate systems: the "block I/O" system (sometimes called the "structured I/O" system); and the "character I/O" system (sometimes called the "unstructured I/O" system).

Each physical device is identified by a minor device number, a major device number, and a class — either block or character — as shown in Figure 14.6.

FIGURE 14.6
The hierarchy of I/O devices in UNIX.

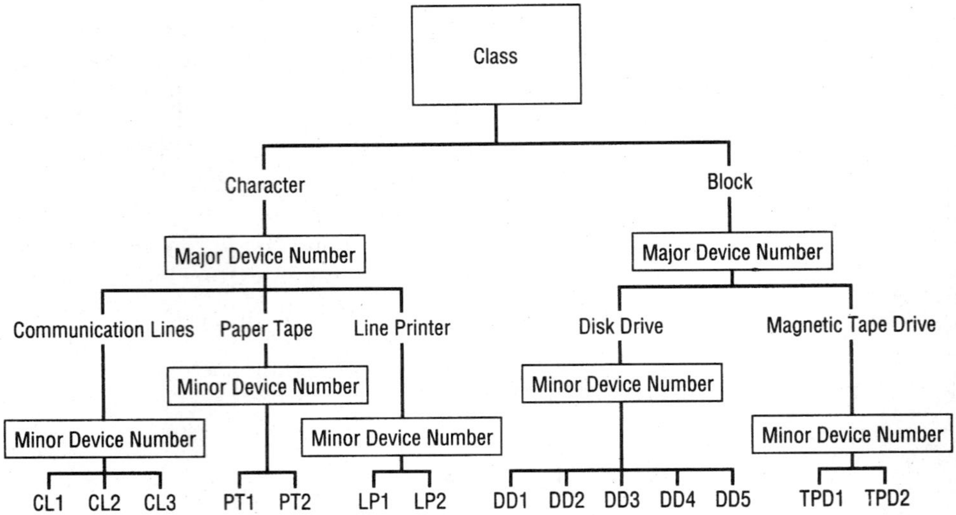

Each *class* has a Configuration Table that contains an array of entry points into the device drivers. This table is the only connection between the system code and the device drivers and it is an important feature of UNIX because it allows the systems programmers to create new device drivers quickly to accommodate differently configured systems (Thompson, 1978).

The *major device number* is used as an index to the array to access the appropriate code for a specific device driver.

The *minor device number* is passed to the device driver as an argument and is used to access one of several identical physical devices.

As its name implies, the block I/O system is used for devices that can be addressed as a sequence of 512-byte blocks. This allows the Device Manager to use buffering to reduce the I/O traffic. UNIX has from 10 to 70 buffers for I/O, and information related to these buffers is kept on a list.

Every time a `read` command is issued, the I/O buffer list is searched. If the requested data is already in a buffer then it is made available to the requesting process. If not, then it is physically moved from secondary storage to a buffer. If a buffer is available, the move is made. If all buffers are busy then one must be emptied out to make room for the new block. This is done by using an LRU policy, so the contents of frequently used buffers will be left intact, which, in turn, should reduce I/O traffic.

Devices in the character class are handled by device drivers that implement character lists. Here's how it operates: a subroutine puts a character on the list, or queue, and another subroutine retrieves the character from the list.

A terminal is a typical character device that has two input queues and one output queue. The two input queues are labeled the "raw queue" and the "canonical queue," and they are needed to synchronize the user's input speed with that of communication lines. It works like this. As the user types in each character, it's collected in the raw input queue. When the line is completed and the "Enter" key is pressed, the line is copied from the raw input queue to the canonical input queue, and the CPU interprets the line. Similarly, the section of the device driver that handles characters going to the output module of a terminal stores them in the "output queue" until it holds the maximum number of characters.

The I/O procedure is synchronized through hardware completion interrupts. Each time there's a completion interrupt, the device driver gets the next character from the queue and sends it to the hardware. This process continues until the queue is empty.

Some devices can actually belong to both classes: block and character. For instance, disk drives and tape drives can be accessed in block mode using buffers or the system can bypass the buffers when accessing the devices in character mode. Device drivers for disk drives use a seek strategy to minimize the arm movement, as explained in Chapter 7.

FILE MANAGEMENT

UNIX has three types of files: directories, ordinary files, and special files. Each file enjoys certain privileges.

Directories are files used by the system to maintain the hierarchical structure of the file system. Users are allowed to read information in directory files, but only the system is allowed to modify directory files.

Ordinary files are those in which users store information. Their protection is based on a user's requests and related to the read, write, execute, and delete functions that can be performed on a file.

Special files are the device drivers that provide the interface to I/O hardware. Special files appear as entries in directories. They're part of the file system, and most of them reside in the `/dev` directory. The name of each special file indicates the type of device with which it is associated. For example, `/dev/lp` is for the line printer. Most users don't need to know much about special files, but system programmers should know where they are and how to use them.

UNIX stores files as sequences of bytes and doesn't impose any structure on them. Therefore, text files (those written using an editor) are strings of characters with lines delimited by the line feed, or new line, character. On the other hand, binary files (those containing executable code generated by a compiler or assembler) are sequences of binary digits grouped into words as they will appear in memory during execution of the program. Therefore, the structure of files is controlled by the programs that use them, not by the system.

The UNIX file management system organizes the disk into blocks of 512 bytes each and divides the disk into four basic regions: (1) the first region (address 0) is reserved for booting; (2) the second region contains the size of the disk and the boundaries of the other regions; (3) the third region includes a list of file definitions, called the "i-list," which uses a combination of major and minor device numbers and i-numbers to uniquely identify a file; and (4) the remaining region holds the free blocks available for file storage. The free blocks are kept in a linked list where each block points to the next available empty block. Then, as files grow, noncontiguous blocks are linked to the already existing chain.

Whenever possible files are stored in contiguous empty blocks. And since all disk allocation is based on fixed-size blocks, allocation is very simple and there's no need to compact the files until the files become large and more dispersed — so that file retrieval becomes cumbersome. When that happens, the system operator might choose **compaction** to bring retrieval time back to normal.

Each entry in the i-list is called an "i-node" and contains 13 disk addresses. The first ten addresses point to the first ten blocks of a file. However, if a file is larger than ten blocks, the eleventh address points to a block that contains the addresses of the next 128 blocks of the file. For larger files, the twelfth address points to another set of 128 blocks, each one pointing to 128 blocks. For files larger than 8M there is a thirteenth address allowing for a maximum file size of over 100 megabytes (Thompson, 1978).

Each i-node contains information on a specific file, such as owner's identification, protection bits, physical address, file size, time of creation, last use and last update, number of links, and whether the file is a directory, an ordinary file, or a special file.

FILE NAMES

Most versions of UNIX allow file names to be a maximum of 14 characters long, including any suffixes and the period. (Some versions allow longer names.) Although UNIX doesn't impose any naming conventions on files, some system programs, such as compilers, expect files to have specific "suffixes" (they are the same as "extensions" described in Chapter 8). For example, `prog1.bas` would indicate the file to be a BASIC program because of its suffix `.bas` while the suffix in `backup.sh` would indicate the file to be a "shell" program.

UNIX supports a hierarchical tree file structure. The root directory is identified by a slash (/); the names of other directories are preceded by the (/) symbol, which is used as a delimiter. A file is accessed by starting at a given point in the hierarchy and descending through the branches of the tree (subdirectories) until reaching the leaf (file). This path can become very long and it's sometimes advantageous to change directories before accessing a file. This can be done quickly by typing two periods ("`..`") if the file needed is in the parent directory of the current directory (which is the directory one level up from the present directory in the hierarchy). Typing `../..` will move you up two branches toward the root in the tree structure.

In multiuser systems UNIX assigns the user to a appropriate directory when logging on to the system. Thereafter, any file operations that are requested by this user are started from this "home directory."

For instance, to access the file `checks` in the system illustrated in Figure 14.7, the user can simply type the following:

```
/programs/pay/checks
```

The first slash indicates that this is an absolute path name that starts at the

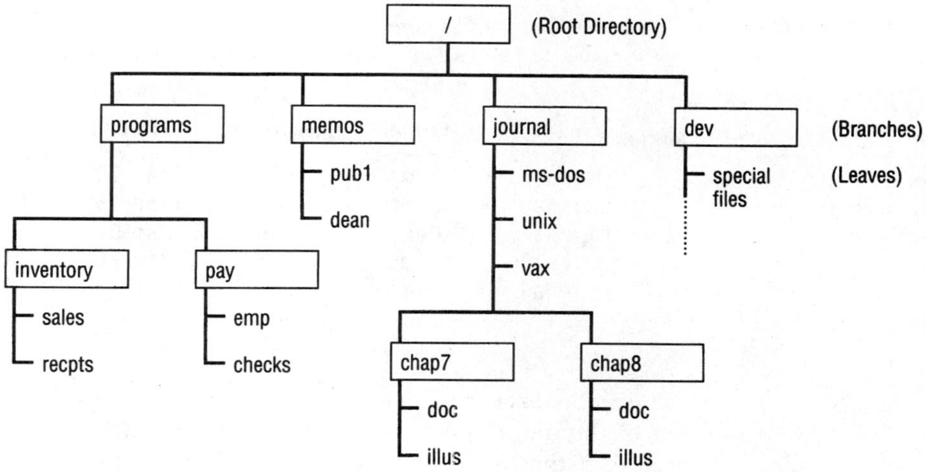

FIGURE 14.7 *The file hierarchy with (/) as the root, the directories as branches, and the files as leaves.*

root directory. A relative path name is one that doesn't start at the root directory. Two examples of relative path names from Figure 14.7 are:

```
pay/checks

journal/chap8/illus
```

A few rules apply to all path names:

1. If the path name starts with a slash, the path starts at the root directory.
2. A path name can be either one name or a list of names separated by slashes. The last name on the list is the name of the file requested.
3. Using two periods (`..`) in a path name will move you upward in the hierarchy (closer to the root). This is the only way to go up the hierarchy; all other path names go down the tree.
4. Spaces are not allowed within path names.

FILE DIRECTORIES

As shown in Table 14.2, a complete listing of files in a directory shows eight pieces of information for each file: the access control, the number of links, the name of the group and owner, the byte size of the file, the date and time of last modification, and, finally, the file name. Notice that the list is displayed in alphabetical order by file name.

The first column shows the type of file and the access privileges for each file. The first character in the first column describes the nature of the file or directory; `d` indicates a directory and `-` indicates an ordinary file. Other codes that can be used are:

`b` to indicate a block special file

`c` to indicate a character special file

`p` to indicate a named pipe file

TABLE 14.2 *This is the long listing of files stored in the directory* journal *from the system illustrated in Figure 14.7. The command* `ls -l` *(that's short for "listing-long") was used to get this listing.*

Access control	No. of links	Group	Owner	No. of bytes	Date	Time	File name
drwxrwxr-x	2	journal	comp	128	Jan 10	19:32	chap7
drwxrwxr-x	2	journal	comp	128	Jan 15	09:59	chap8
-rwxr-xr-x	1	journal	comp	11904	Jan 6	11:38	ms-dos
-rwxr--r--	1	journal	comp	12556	Jan 20	18:08	unix
-rwx------	1	journal	comp	10362	Jan 17	07:32	vax

The next three characters (`rwx`) show the access privileges granted to the owner of the file: `r` stands for read, `w` stands for write, and `x` stands for execute. Therefore if the list includes `rwx` the user can read, write, and/or execute that program.

Likewise, the following three characters describe the access privileges granted to other members of the user's group. (In UNIX, a "group" is defined as a set of users who have something in common: the same project, same class, same department, etc.) Therefore, `rwx` for characters 5–7 means other users can also read, write, and/or execute that file. However, a hyphen `-` indicates that access is denied for that operation. In Table 14.2 the `r--` means that the file `unix` can be read by other group members but cannot be altered or executed.

Finally, the last three characters in column one describe the access privileges granted to users at large, those system-wide. Thus, at-large users cannot modify the files listed in Table 14.2, nor can they modify or execute the file called `unix`. What's more, the `vax` file can't be read, modified, or executed by anyone other than the owner.

The second column in the directory listing indicates the number of links, also known as the number of aliases, that refer to the same physical file. Aliases are an important feature of UNIX; they support file sharing when several users work together on the same project. In this case it's convenient for the shared files to appear in different directories belonging to different users even though only one "central" file descriptor (containing information on the file) exists for that file. The file name may be different from directory to directory since these names aren't kept in the file descriptor, but the numbers of links kept there is updated so the system knows how many users are sharing this file. Eventually this number will indicate when the file is no longer needed and can be deleted.

The next three columns show, respectively, the name of the group, the name of the owner, and the file size in bytes. The sixth and seventh columns show the date and time of the last modification, and the last column lists the file name.

DATA STRUCTURES FOR ACCESSING FILES

The information presented in the directory isn't all kept in the same location. UNIX divides the file descriptors into parts, with the hierarchical directories containing only the name of the file and the "i-number," which is a pointer to another location, the "i-node," where the rest of the information is kept. Therefore, everything you see in Table 14.2, with the exception of the file name and the addition of the device's physical addresses for the file contents, is kept in the i-node. All i-nodes are stored in a reserved part of the device where the directory resides, usually in Block 1. This structure is illustrated in Figure 14.8, which uses the directory `memos` from Figure 14.7 as an example.

FIGURE 14.8 *Example of UNIX hierarchy for directories, i-nodes, and file blocks. Although the file blocks are represented here in physical serial order, they actually may be stored noncontiguously.*

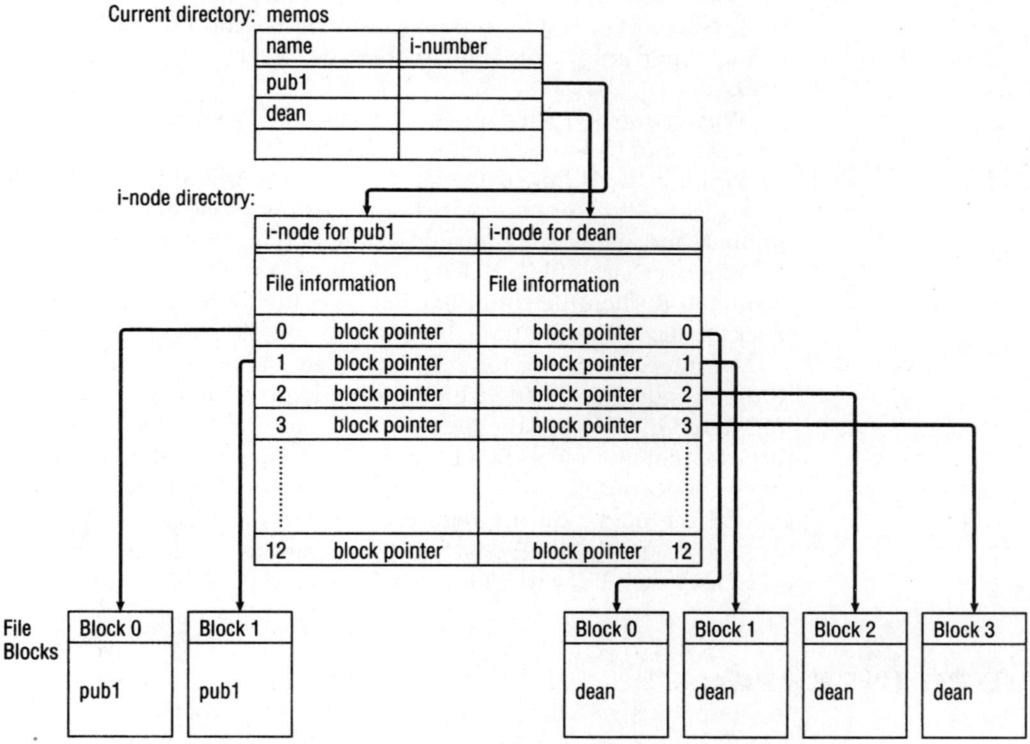

Each i-node has room for 13 pointers (0–12). The first ten block numbers stored in the i-node list relate to the first ten blocks of a file.

For the file called `pub1` in Figure 14.8, only the first two entries have pointers to data blocks and all the others are zeros because this is a small file that occupies only two blocks of storage. If a file is larger than ten blocks then the eleventh entry points to a block that contains a list of the next 128 blocks in the file. Because it's an extra step in the path to the data this block is called an "indirect block."

For files larger than 138 blocks, the twelfth entry points to a block that contains a list of 128 indirect blocks (each one containing pointers to 128 file blocks). Because this block introduces two extra steps in the path to the data it's called a "double indirect block." Finally, for extremely large files of more than 16,522 blocks, the thirteenth entry points to a "triple indirect block." This schema allows for 2,113,674 blocks to be allocated to a single file, for a total of 1,082,201,088 bytes (Christian, 1983).

Therefore, carrying this one step further, we can see that the bytes numbered below 5120 can be retrieved with a single disk access. Those in the range between 5120 and 70,656 require two disk accesses. Those in the range between 70,656 and 8,459,264 require three disk accesses, bytes beyond 8,459,264 require four disk accesses. This would give very slow access to large data files but, in reality, the system maintains a rather complicated buffering mechanism that considerably reduces the number of I/O operations required to access a file.

When a file is opened, its device, i-number, and read/write pointer are stored in the System File Table, residing in memory, and indexed by the i-node, so that during other read/write calls to the file the i-node information can be readily accessed.

When a file is created an i-node is allocated to it, and a directory entry with the file name and its i-node number is created.

When a file is linked (which happens when another user begins sharing the same file), a directory entry is created with the new name and the original i-node number, and the link-count field in the i-node is incremented by one.

When a shared file is deleted, the link-count field in the i-node is decremented by one. And when the count reaches zero, the directory entry is erased and all disk blocks allocated to the file, along with its i-node block, are deallocated.

An interesting note for system analysts is that linking files presents a problem to the accounting system, which must charge someone for the space occupied by the shared file. Should the file's owner, or those who used it, be charged? Charging the owner may not be fair because the owner may delete the file even though other users continue to share it. On the other hand, even though the user who created the file is still the registered owner, the space could be charged to those who are currently sharing it. Some installations divide the charges equally among every user with links to a file. Others avoid the issue by not charging any fees.

USER INTERFACE

UNIX is a command-driven system and its user commands (as shown in Table 14.3) are usually very short: either one character (usually the first letter of the command) or a group of characters (an acronym of the words that make up the command). In addition, the system prompt is very economical, often only one character, such as a dollar sign ($) or percent sign (%). Error messages are also quite brief; they assume the user doesn't need much assistance from the system.

The general syntax of commands is this:

command   optional arguments   optional file names

The "command" is any legal UNIX command and the "arguments" are required for some commands and optional for others. The "file name" can be a relative or absolute path name.

TABLE 14.3 *UNIX user commands can't be abbreviated or spelled out and must be in the correct case (commands must be in all lower-case letters). Check the technical documentation for your system for proper spelling and syntax.*

Command	Stands for	Action to be performed
(filename)	Run File	Run/Execute a file.
`ls`	List Directory	Show a listing of this directory.
`cd`	Change Directory	Change working directory.
`cp`	Copy	Copy a file into another file or directory.
`rm`	Remove	Remove/delete a file or directory.
`mv`	Move	Move or rename a file or directory.
`more`	Show More	Type the file's contents to the screen.
`lpr`	Print	Print out a file.
`date`	Date	Show date and time.
`date -u`	Universal Date/Time	Show date and time in universal format (Greenwich Mean Time).
`mkdir`	Make Directory	Make a new directory.
`grep`	"Global Regular Expression/ Print"	Find a specified string in a file.
`cat`	Catenate	Create a file or append to an existing file.
`format`	Format	Format a volume.
`diff`	Different	Compare two files.
`pwd`	Path Working Directory	Show the path name of this directory.

Commands are interpreted and executed by the "shell," one of the two most widely used programs in the UNIX system. The shell is technically known as the "command interpreter," because that is its function. But it isn't only an interactive command interpreter, it is also the key to the coordination and combination of UNIX system programs. In fact, it is a sophisticated programming language in itself.

The other frequently used program is the editor. The earliest versions of UNIX had only a line editor, which was called with the command `ed`. Current versions of UNIX feature a screen editor as well, which is called with the command `vi`, and was a feature introduced with the Berkeley version. Although the screen editor is easier to use than the line editor, it still requires some technical expertise to master it. To accommodate new users, some versions have added an "interpreter" with menus to help users build commands from lists of valid command options. These menu-based editors can be added to almost any UNIX system.

SCRIPT FILES

Command files, often called shell files or "script files," can be used to automate repetitious tasks. Each line of the file is a valid UNIX instruction and can be executed by the user simply by typing `sh` and the name of the script file. Another way to execute it is to define the file as an executable command and simply type the file name at the system prompt.

Here is an example of a simple script file that's designed to configure the system for a certain user:

```
set term=vt100
setenv DBPATH /u/nealm/lumber:.:/zdlf/product/central/db
setenv TERMCAP $INFODIR/etc/termcap
stty erase '^H'
set savehistory
set history=20
alias h history
alias 4gen infogen -f
setenv PATH /usr/info/bin:/etc
```

In this example, the terminal is identified as a model "VT 100," the working directory paths are set, the history is set to 20 lines and is given an alias of "h" (so the user can perform the "history" command simply by typing `h`). Similarly, "4gen" is established as an alias for the command "infogen -f." Finally, the path is defined as: `/usr/info/bin:/etc`.

If this script file is included in the user's configuration file, it will be automatically executed every time the user logs on to the system. The exact name of the user configuration file varies from system to system, but two common names are `.profile` and `.login`. See the documentation for your system for specifics.

Script files are used by the programmers, analysts, and the system manager to automate repetitive tasks and to simplify complex procedures.

REDIRECTION

If you're an interactive user, most of the commands used to produce output will automatically send it to your screen and the editor will accept input from the keyboard. There are times when you may want to send output to a file or to another device. In UNIX this is done by using the symbol > between the command and the destination to which the output should be directed. For example, the command: `ls > myfiles` will list the files in your current directory to the file named `myfiles` instead of listing them on the screen. Your screen will not display the listing.

The following command will copy the contents of `chapt1` and `chapt2` into a file named `sectiona`:

```
cat chapt1  chapt2  >  sectiona
```

The command `cat` is short for "catenate." If `sectiona` is a new file it is automatically created. If it already exists, the previous contents will be overwritten. (When `cat` is used with a single file and redirection is not indicated then it displays the contents of that file onto the screen.) Another way to achieve the same result is with the "wild card" symbol like this:

```
cat chapt* > sectiona
```

The asterisk symbol (*) indicates that the command pertains to all files that begin with "chapt" — in this case that means `chapt1` and `chapt2`.

The symbol >> will append the new file to an existing file. Therefore either of these commands

```
cat chapt1 chapt 2 >> sectiona
cat chapt* >> sectiona
```

will copy the contents of `chapt1` and `chapt2` onto the end of whatever already exists in the file called `sectiona`. If `sectiona` doesn't exist then the file will be created as an empty file and will then be filled with `chapt1` and `chapt2`, in that order.

The reverse redirection is to take input for a program from an existing file instead of from the keyboard. For example, if you have written a memo and need to mail to it several people, the command:

```
mail ann neal roger < memo
```

will send the contents of the file `memo` to the people listed between the command `mail` and the symbol <.

By combining the power of redirection with system commands, you can achieve results not possible otherwise. For instance: `who > temporary` will store in the file called `temporary` the names of all users logged on to the system. And the command `sort < temporary` will sort the list stored in `temporary` and display the sorted list on the screen as it's generated.

In each of these examples, it's important to note that the interpretation of < and > is done by the shell and not by the individual program (such as `mail`, `who`, or `sort`). This means that input and output redirection can be used with any program because the program isn't aware that anything unusual is happening. This is one instance of the power of UNIX — the ability to combine many operations into a single brief command.

PIPES

With Version 2, the addition of pipes and filters made it possible to redirect output or input to selected files or devices based on commands given to the command interpreter. UNIX does that by manipulating I/O devices as special files.

For the example just presented, we listed the number of users on-line into a file called `temporary` and we then sorted the file. There was no reason to create this file other than that we needed it to complete the two-step operation required to see the list in alphabetical order on the screen. However, a "pipe" can do the same thing in a single step.

A pipe is UNIX's way to connect the output from one program to the input of another without the need for temporary or intermediate files. A pipe is an open file connecting two programs: information written to it by one program may be read immediately by the other, with synchronization, scheduling, and buffering handled automatically by the system. In other words, the programs are executing concurrently, not one after the other. By using a pipe, indicated by the symbol, |, the last example can be rewritten as: `who | sort` and a sorted list of all users logged onto the system will be displayed on the screen.

A *pipeline* is when you have several programs simultaneously processing the same I/O stream. For example: `who | sort | lpr` takes the output from `who` (a list of all logged-on users), sorts it, and prints it on the line printer.

FILTERS

UNIX has many programs that read some input, manipulate it in some way, and generate output; they're called "filters." One example is `wc`, which counts the lines, words, and characters in a file. For example, the following command: `wc journal` would respond with: `10 140 700`, meaning that the file `journal` has 10 lines, 140 words, and 700 characters. (A "word" is defined as a string of characters delimited by blanks.) A shorter version of `wc` to count just the number of lines in the file is: `wc -l`.

Another filter command is `sort` (it's the same command we used to demonstrate pipes). If a file name is given with the command, the contents of the file are sorted and displayed on the screen. If no file name is given with the command, `sort` accepts input from the keyboard and directs the output to the screen. When it's used with redirection `sort` accepts input from a file and writes the output to another file. For example, this command: `sort < names > sortednames` will sort the contents of the file called `names` and send the output to the file `sortednames`. The data in `names` will be sorted in ASCII order, that is, using the ASCII collating sequence on each line so that lines with leading blanks will come first (in sorted order), lines with lower case characters will follow, and lines beginning with upper case characters will be last. To sort the list in alphabetical order the `sort` command would be: `sort -f < names > sortednames`.

To obtain a numerical sort in ascending order the command is:

```
sort -n < numbs > sortednums
```

To obtain a numerical sort in descending order the command is:

```
sort -nr < numbs > sortednums
```

In every example presented here, `sort` uses each entire line of the file to conduct the sort. However, if a user knows the structure of the data stored in the file then the sort can use other key fields.

For example, let's say a file called `empl` has data that follows the same column format: the ID numbers start in column 1, phone numbers start in column 10, and last names start in column 20. To sort the file by last name (the third "field") the command would be:

```
sort +2f < empl > sortedempl.
```

The file `empl` will be sorted alphabetically by the third field and the output will be sent to the file called `sortedempl`. (A field is delimited by at least one blank). The `+2` tells `sort` to skip the first two fields and the `f` says the list should be sorted in alphabetical order. The integrity of the file is preserved because the entire line is sorted — so each name keeps the correct phone and ID number.

ADDITIONAL COMMANDS

grep

One of the most-used UNIX commands is `grep`—it stands for "global regular expression and print" and it looks for specific patterns of characters. It's one of the most helpful (and oddly named) UNIX acronym-based commands. It's the equivalent of the MS-DOS command `FIND` and the VAX/VMS command `SEARCH`. When the desired pattern of characters is found, the line containing it is displayed on the screen.

Here's a simple example: if you need to retrieve the names and addresses of everyone with a Pittsburgh address from a large file called `maillist`, the command would look like this:

```
grep Pittsburgh maillist
```

As a result, you would see on your screen the lines from `maillist` for entries that included "Pittsburgh." And if you wanted the output sent to a file for future use, you could use the redirection command.

This command, `grep`, can also be used to list all the lines that *do not* contain a certain string of characters. Using the same example, the following command will display on the screen the names and addresses of all those who do not have a Pittsburgh address: `grep -v Pittsburgh maillist`.

Similarly, the following command will count all the people who live in Pittsburgh and will display that number on the screen. But it doesn't print out each line: `grep -c Pittsburgh maillist`.

As we said before, the power of UNIX is its ability to combine commands. Here's how the `grep` command can be combined with the `who` command. Suppose you want to see if your friend Sam is logged on. The command to display Sam's name, device, and the date and time he logged in would be: `who | grep sam`.

Combinations of commands, though effective, can appear confusing to the casual observer. For example, if you wanted a list of all the subdirectories (but not the files) found in the root directory, the command would be: `ls -l / | grep '^d'`.

This command is the combination of `ls` for list directory; `-l`, which is the long option of list and includes the information shown in Table 14.2; / to indicate the root directory; | to establish a pipe; the command `grep`; and `'^d'`, which says that `d` is the character we're looking for (because we only want the directories), the `^` indicates that the `d` is at the beginning of each line (and the quotes are required because we used the symbol `^`).

pg OR more

When files are very long, UNIX will send the output to the screen continuously and without pausing to allow the user to read the output one screen at a time—there is no "pause" function built into it. However, most UNIX versions have added a command to display output one screen at a time. It isn't part of the standard UNIX, perhaps because UNIX was first developed at a time when terminals used paper instead of screens.

The System V Release 2 has a `pg` command to display a file one screen at a time. The Berkeley versions offer a `more` command that does the same thing.

`nohup`
If a program's execution is expected to take a long time, you can start its execution and then log off the system without having to wait for it to finish. This is done with the command `nohup`, which is short for "no hangup." Let's say, for example, you want to copy a very large file but you can't wait at the terminal until the job is finished. The command would be:

```
nohup cp oldlargefile newlargefile &
```

The copy command (`cp`) will continue its execution copying `oldlargefile` to `newlargefile` in the background even though you've logged off the system. For this example, we've indicated that execution should continue in the background; the ampersand (`&`) is the symbol for running the program in "background" mode.

`nice`
If your program uses a large number of resources and you are not in a hurry for the results, you can be "nice" to other users by lowering its priority with the command `nice`. This will put the process in background mode and will free up your terminal for different work. For example, you want to copy `oldlargefile` to `newlargefile` and want to continue working on another project at the same time. The command

```
nice cp oldlargefile newlargefile &
```

would allow you to do that; however, you may not log off when using the `nice` command until the copy is finished because the program execution would be stopped.

The command `nohup` automatically activates `nice` by lowering the process's priority. It assumes that since you've logged off the system, you're not in a hurry for the output. The opposite is not true — when `nice` is issued it doesn't automatically activate `nohup`. Therefore, if you want to put a very long job on the background, work on some other jobs, and log out before the long job is finished, `nohup` is the command to use.

We've included only a few UNIX commands here. For a complete list of commands for a specific version of this operating system, their exact syntax, and more details about those we've discussed here, see a technical manual for the appropriate version.

CHAPTER FOURTEEN CONCLUSION

UNIX was written by programmers for programmers, and it's quite popular among those fluent in the ways of programming.

Many of its proponents cite its advantages: the user interface, device independence, and portability. They like its lack of verbosity and the powerful combinations of commands. UNIX is certainly an extremely portable operating system — there are versions of UNIX on the market today that can operate very large multiuser systems and single-user systems, and every size in between.

Those unfamiliar with UNIX often have the opposite opinion. They cite as disadvantages its system commands and the existence of many versions of UNIX with varying degrees of compatibility. According to them, the commands are too brief and the system lacks a friendly human/computer interface that would make it easier for those with less-than-expert programming skills to use.

The UNIX system does not follow the current trend of hiding the system from the user. Window and menu-oriented interfaces help to mask the commands, file system, and other functions from the user. In UNIX, the more aware users are of the system's internal functions, the better they can control them and improve their productivity. However, because UNIX has been adopted by a diverse community, facilitating tools called "user agents" have been furnished to shield novice users from many of the system's intricacies.

Chapter Fifteen

VAX/VMS OPERATING SYSTEM

USER COMMAND INTERFACE

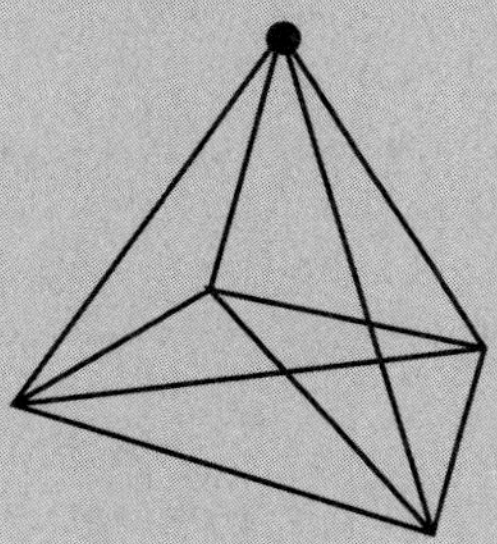

The VMS operating system we'll study in this section was written for the VAX-11 computer developed by the Digital Equipment Corporation.

VMS was developed to be completely compatible with the computers it operates. It runs on all VAX processors because they all share the same attributes — the same instruction set, addressing modes, data types, and memory management algorithms. This combination of a common architecture and a single operating system allows VAX/VMS programs to be ported from one VAX system to another without reprogramming, recompiling, or relinking.

Its disadvantage is tied to its dependence on the VAX hardware; it can't be ported to other computers outside the VAX family. We include it here because it is a major operating system and was designed to take every advantage of the hardware on which it runs.

HISTORY

The history of VMS is closely tied to the history of its hardware, the VAX family of computers.

When Digital Equipment Corporation (known as "Digital" or DEC) dominated the minicomputer market in the early 1970s, its PDP-11 (with 64K of addressable memory space) was ensconced in thousands of educational institutions and businesses that needed a multiuser computer but didn't need the power of a large mainframe.

However, by the early 1980s, as the 16-bit microprocessors began to invade the minicomputer market, DEC realized its need to upgrade the PDP-11 or lose its lead in the mid-sized computer market. It responded by committing its corporate resources to the creation of a family of computers for the next generation of computer users.

DEC's mandate to its design team was to create a new computer around the existing PDP-11 hardware. The result was the VAX-11, a state-of-the-art machine that could be built from an upgraded PDP-11.

They saw three advantages to this approach. First, they hoped to protect their existing customers' hardware investments and improve their software by expanding their machine's virtual address space to eliminate overlays and program segmentation. Second, they hoped to attract new customers by making their system easy to operate. Third, they hoped their new system would serve a wider range of applications than any other minicomputer — from end users to distributed processing environments to Original Equipment Manufacturers (OEM) who purchase computers and peripherals for use as components in other products that they sell to customers.

The result was a family of "super-minicomputers" named VAX, derived from Virtual Address Extension. The VAX group consists of 32-bit virtual memory computers; that means each computer has more than 4 *billion* bytes of available address space. The machine's architecture was built on the existing instruction set and addressing modes of the PDP-11. To support the needs of compiler writers and commercial and scientific applications programmers, additional data formats and instructions were created. In addition, the architecture was designed to support the needs of a virtual-memory operating system, VMS (Leonard, 1987).

The VMS operating system was written by the computer's designers to take the best advantage of the computer's virtual memory capabilities. As a result, the VAX hardware and VMS software work together in unison to provide users with an efficient environment. In fact, the VAX includes several CPU instructions created especially to support VMS commands that provide a large variety of system services, file management techniques, and queue management techniques.

As shown in Table 15.1, enhancements to the operating system were necessary to support the increase in memory size and the number of interactive users. The system performance varies with the size of the computer system. For example, the VAX 8600 delivers up to 4.2 times the performance of the VAX-11/780.

In addition to VMS, other operating systems can be used to run VAX computers including ULTRIX, a version of UNIX, and ELN, designed to support the de-

TABLE 15.1 *VMS has evolved, as have the VAX processors, which necessitated upgrades in the operating system.*

Model	Year	Physical memory	Features
PDP-11	1970	64K	2 interactive users
VAX-11/725	1978	3M	8 interactive users
VAX-11/750	1981	8M	64 interactive users
VAX-11/780	1984	12M	100 interactive users
VAX 8600	1985	68M	Several hundred interactive users
VAX 8800	1987	512M	Dual processor system
VAX 9000	1989	4096M	Can be configured with up to four processors; first VAX series to have vector processing instructions

velopment of dedicated, real-time applications. But VMS is the only one that takes full advantage of the VAX architecture (Leonard, 1987).

To support the growing numbers of interactive users, VAX clusters, a collection of VAXes with associated peripherals, were created. The VAX cluster design falls in between a loosely coupled system (one that is interconnected by a network) and a tightly coupled system (e.g., a parallel computer where multiple processors share main memory) (Shah, 1991).

The need for supporting high-speed computing, that resulted in the creation of the 64-bit Alpha AXP processors, and the need for open computing that supports the processing of applications on multiple platforms, made it necessary for the VMS operating system to undergo a significant set of changes. These changes can be likened to those that occurred during the PDP to VAX transition during the late 1970s. The existing VMS operating system was modified to support the new Alpha AXP architecture while maintaining compatibility with the existing VAX architecture. Open VMS VAX and Open VMS AXP support VAX and Alpha platforms respectively. Some of the major strengths of Open VMS are its user-friendliness, ample availability of reliable tools for software development and transportability of programs written in VMS for VAX platforms to Alpha AXP-based platforms (Bhargava, 1995).

DESIGN GOALS

The first major goal of the VAX architecture and VMS operating system was to be highly compatible with the PDP-11 computer to protect the capital investment of DEC's customers.

The second goal was to make the VAX/VMS system extendable. This would ensure longevity of the system because new data types and operations could be efficiently added to the existing set. Software engineers find this an attractive feature because it means that programs written for an earlier VAX model can also be run on newer models.

A third goal was to improve the interaction between the hardware and the operating system. Therefore, the architecture of the VAX and its operating system, VMS, were designed and developed concurrently. Every VAX processor offers

32-bit virtual addressing, a sophisticated memory management and protection mechanism, and hardware-assisted process scheduling and synchronization. All of these features are fully exploited by VMS.

A fourth goal was to enhance program performance, and this was accomplished in four ways: (1) the VAX/VMS has a powerful variable-length instruction set and various data types that allow compilers to quickly generate compact and efficient code, so users' programs can run faster and give a better performance; (2) VMS comes with a set of powerful tools to assist and streamline program development; (3) the VAX language processors allow programs written in one language to call procedures written in other languages; and (4) its information management software provides a sophisticated system for managing data and sharing files (*VAX hardware handbook,* 1982).

VMS is a multiuser operating system that's easy to learn and use. It's command-driven: all commands are English verbs that describe their function. Commands can be typed in upper or lower case (although for editorial clarity we'll use only upper case in this text), and may be abbreviated to their first three characters to simplify them.

The commands typed by the users are accepted and interpreted by the "command handler," one of the modules of the operating system, which acts as the interface between the users and the other modules of the operating system — the Memory Manager, Processor Manager, File Manager, and Device Manager.

MEMORY MANAGEMENT

The VAX computer has a very large virtual address space, on the order of 4 gigabytes. To satisfy the requirements of a multiuser, multiprogramming environment, the VMS Memory Manager divides the virtual address space into 512-byte sections called "pages." The size of a page is identical to the size of a sector on a disk (called a "block"), which is identical to a "page frame" in physical memory. As a matter of fact, in VMS the word "page" is often used to identify all three. A page is the basic unit of relocation and protection (*VAX architecture handbook,* 1981).

The major functions of the Memory Manager are to map virtual pages into physical pages in memory, to control the paging activities of the active processes, and to protect memory space. To do these, VMS relies on several submodules including the "pager," which handles the paging function by each process, and the "swapper," which moves entire jobs and processes into and out of memory.

Since the VAX's architecture is based on 32-bit longwords, its virtual address space consists of 2^{32} bytes — that's 4.3 billion bytes — which is divided into "system space" and "process space" with each consisting of 2^{31} bytes, as illustrated in Figure 15.1. In addition, the space for each process is subdivided into the "program region" and the "control region." As the names suggest, the program region contains procedures and data, and the control region contains process control structures and information maintained by the system.

The Memory Manager generates a Page Table for each active process. The entries in the table, one for each page, contain a "valid" bit, which indicates whether the page is actually in main memory — a value of one indicates a valid

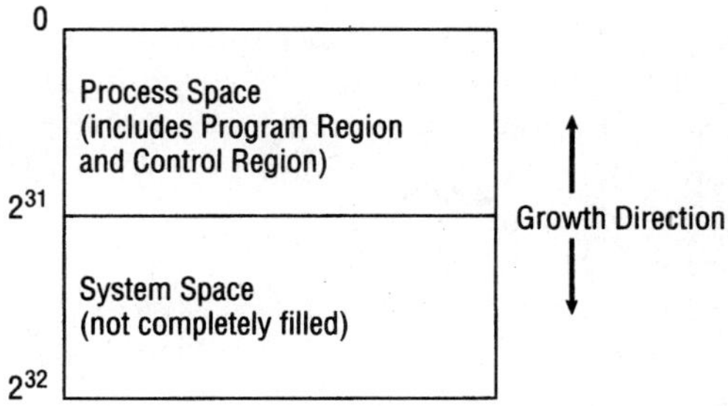

FIGURE 15.1 *Virtual address space is divided into process space and system space.*

page that's in memory and a zero indicates that it is not. If a page *is* in memory, its entry also contains the page frame number where the virtual page is mapped out. If a page is *not* in memory, the entry contains the information needed to locate the page in secondary storage.

The Memory Manager determines the minimum number of pages that have to be in a process's working set; the system manager determines the maximum number of pages. The size of the working set determines the amount of main memory allocated to a process and affects its paging and swapping performance. When the working set resides in memory, its pages can be accessed directly without incurring a page fault (*VAX architecture handbook*, 1981).

THE PAGER

Page faults are automatically handled by the "pager," a submodule of the Memory Manager, that reads into memory requested pages and, when necessary, removes pages from memory.

When an active process requests a page not in memory, the pager moves into action: (1) it looks in the Page Table entry and retrieves the disk address of the requested page; (2) it compares the number of pages in the working set to the maximum number of pages allowed and if the "less than" condition is true, it locates an empty page frame in memory and copies the page from secondary storage into it; (3) it updates the Page Table entry and returns control to the process so it can continue to execute.

If the "less than" condition is false, the pager has to choose a page to remove from the process's working set to make room for the new one. VMS doesn't use the least-recently-used (LRU) scheme — it doesn't have a reference bit in the Page Table entries; instead, it uses a first-in first-out (FIFO) scheme. However, the designers of VMS took steps to protect it against unexpected **FIFO anomalies** (as mentioned in Chapter 3) by having the Memory Manager maintain two more lists: a free page list and a modified page list, which are checked by the pager when page faults occur.

The system tries to keep a minimal number of free pages at all times. This free list is checked by the pager when it needs to locate an empty page frame during (2) above (*VAX software handbook,* 1982).

When a page is removed from a process's working set, the pager first checks the modified bit. If it's zero, meaning that the page has not been modified, then the page is immediately released and linked at the end of the free page list. In other words, the free page list acts as a fast backup store (a cache) of recently used pages. If the modified bit has a value of one, meaning that the page *has* been changed, then it must be written to secondary storage before it's released.

The writing doesn't take place immediately to conserve I/O time; instead, the page is linked to the end of the modified page list. When the list reaches a predefined maximum size all the modified pages are written to the disk at the same time, and the page frames are linked to the free page list. This "clustering" greatly reduces the number of I/O operations and minimizes the amount of time the disk is busy.

How does this addition of lists help prevent the FIFO anomaly? A page removed from a working set actually remains in memory for some time before it's either written to secondary storage or reused. Therefore, if a process requests a page that's in one of the lists, it's retrieved and incorporated into the working set without too much difficulty. To a certain degree, the size of these lists has a significant effect on system and process performance because it reduces fault time and paging I/O.

It should be noted that the largest number of page faults occurs when a new program starts up and begins loading its working set. VMS addresses the situation like this: when the first page of a new program is requested, the Memory Manager begins by reading several pages into memory at the same time, thus reducing the number of initial page faults. In addition, the Memory Manager dynamically adjusts the size of the working set of a program as it executes. The adjustment is based on the page fault rate of the process over a certain period of time. If the process has a large fault rate then its working set is increased. On the other hand, if it has a small fault rate then its working set size is decreased, giving more memory to other processes. When only a few processes are active each one can have an unlimited working set, but as activity increases the Memory Manager begins to reduce the size of the working sets to accommodate the new arrivals (*VAX software handbook,* 1982).

THE SWAPPER

In addition to paging, which affects each process individually, the Memory Manager also swaps entire jobs (that is, their entire working set is swapped) between memory and secondary storage. This is done by the "swapper," another module of the Memory Manager. The decision of which process should be swapped is based on three conditions: (1) its priority, (2) its status, and (3) the expiration of its time quantum.

The system strives for a balance between CPU-bound and I/O-bound programs. The name for all active processes residing in memory is the "balance set." If a process is waiting for I/O to terminate, it's swapped out to secondary storage by the swapper, making room for a process that's ready to execute. When swapping takes place, the entire working set of the job to be swapped out is written to secondary storage and the entire working set of the job to be swapped in is loaded into memory, thus minimizing the number of page faults as well as the time spent waiting for disk I/O operations.

The swapper is responsible, both for maintaining the free page list and the modified page list and for swapping processes from secondary storage to memory (called an "inswap") and vice versa (called an "outswap"). Because the swapper is activated by incoming, departing, and waiting jobs, it works closely with the Processor Manager and will be further explained in the next section (*VAX software handbook,* 1982).

PROCESSOR MANAGEMENT

In VMS, process scheduling is event-driven, preemptive, and priority controlled. The operating system defines 32 levels of priorities related to process scheduling. These priorities are numbered from 0 to 31, which is the highest priority. These priorities are divided into two groups: priorities 0 to 15 are allocated to interactive and background processes, and priorities 16 to 31 are allocated to real-time processes. Real-time processes are scheduled strictly by priority so a higher priority process always preempts one of lower priority. Interactive and background processes are scheduled using a modified preemptive algorithm to achieve a better balance of CPU-bound and I/O-bound jobs.

PROCESS SCHEDULER

Each process has a Process Control Block (PCB) that links it to the proper queue and defines the process's status within the system. Figure 15.2 shows the 32 priority queues with PCBs linked to four of them.

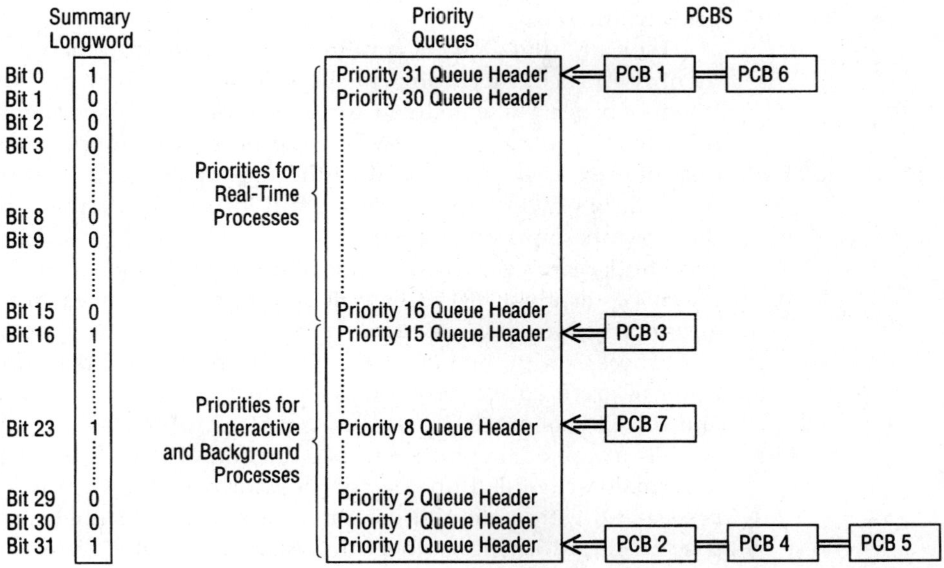

FIGURE 15.2 *The queue system. The summary longword indicates which queues are clear and which are not. Only one instruction is needed to locate the first nonempty queue, thus locating the highest-priority process. In this example, the queue for priority 31 is active, indicated by Bit 0, which is on; it has a value of 1. (Adapted from* VAX software handbook, *1982.)*

Processes are selected in order from high-priority to low-priority queues. Within each queue the selection is on a **FCFS** basis. For example, in Figure 15.2, the processes would be scheduled in this order: PCB1, PCB6, PCB3, PCB7, PCB2,

PCB4, and PCB5. A lower priority queue won't be serviced until all other queues above it have been satisfied. In a way, it's just like having a single queue; however, the subdivision makes it easier to search through the queues for PCBs because the Process Scheduler needs only to check the "summary longword" to see whether a queue is clear. If the bit is zero, the queue is empty and the scheduler bypasses it; if the bit is one, the scheduler knows that a PCB is in that queue (*VAX software handbook,* 1982).

As we mentioned in Chapter 4, processes go through several states while in the system. In VAX/VMS a process also changes states according to events that are caused by the process itself (such as a `READ` command prompting an I/O wait) or one caused by the operating system (such as the termination of a time quantum prompting the process to be "rescheduled"). Regardless of the event, the preempted process is placed at the end of the appropriate priority queue. This forces a rotation of processes within a priority and the available processor time is distributed more evenly among processes in the same priority.

A time quantum is used for interactive and background jobs to ensure a minimum amount of time during which processes can run and to rotate CPU-bound jobs. Real-time processes aren't limited by a time quantum, and their priority remains unchanged during their execution.

However, the Process Scheduler uses a modified preemptive priority algorithm to handle all other processes. This algorithm "floats" the process's priority based on its recent execution history. This means that the scheduler will dynamically change the current priority of a process as it executes, checking that the current priority isn't any lower than the one originally assigned when the process was created, nor any higher than 15 because that would put the process into the real-time priority queues.

Typically, when a `WAIT` condition is satisfied, the scheduler increases the priority of the process according to the priority increment of the satisfied condition. When a process is scheduled for execution, the scheduler decreases its current priority by one unit so that when the process is stopped (such as when its time quantum expires) it is placed at the end of the next lower priority queue. This policy favors I/O-bound processes and forces CPU-bound processes to remain in their own base priority queues.

The largest priority increments are given for terminal `READ` completion, followed by terminal `WRITE` completion, and the smallest priority increments are given for disk or magnetic tape I/O.

Processes with the same base priority are scheduled according to the following order of preferences: response to terminal input, terminal display, file I/O-bound, and file CPU-bound (*VAX software handbook,* 1982).

The swapper, mentioned in conjunction with Memory Management, is actually a normally scheduled process with a priority of 16, the lowest of all real-time processes, and with code and data areas that are contained in the operating system space. Figure 15.3 shows where the swapper falls in the process scheduling scheme.

Unless needed, the swapper is in hibernation and is awakened only when one of the following events occurs: a job terminates and exits from the system, the free page list becomes too big or too small, the modified page list becomes too big, a predefined unit of time passes, a new job enters the system, or a resident process

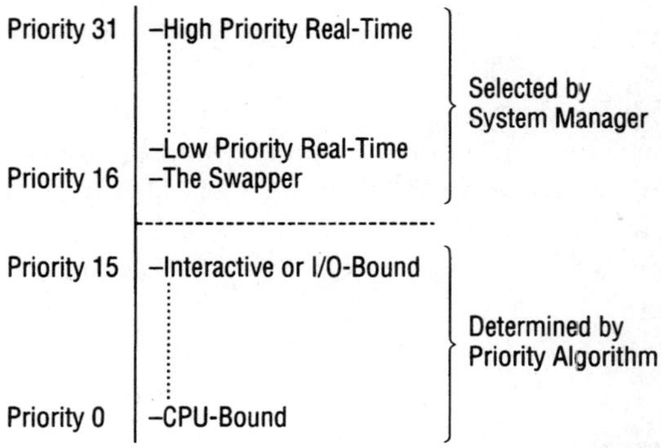

FIGURE 15.3 *The hierarchy of process priorities. Notice that since the swapper is part of the real-time priorities, it will not be preempted while executing. (Adapted from* VAX software handbook, *1982.)*

enters a WAIT state. Before any inswapping can take place, the swapper must determine whether there is enough memory for the new process's working set and, if there isn't, it must select a suitable outswap candidate. It does this by scanning the state queues containing resident processes in a predefined order. The candidate is chosen using a first-come first-served scheme with certain exceptions. For example, queues containing processes waiting for a free page, or processes in their initial time quantum, are automatically exempted as outswap candidates.

THE RESCHEDULER

A context switch is initiated whenever a process with higher priority becomes executable or when the time quantum of an active process expires. The routine that handles context switching is called the "rescheduler." Figure 15.4 shows the relationship between a process state, the rescheduler, and the swapper. It is similar to Figure 4.2 as processes move among the RUNNING state (1), the WAIT state (2), and the READY state (3).

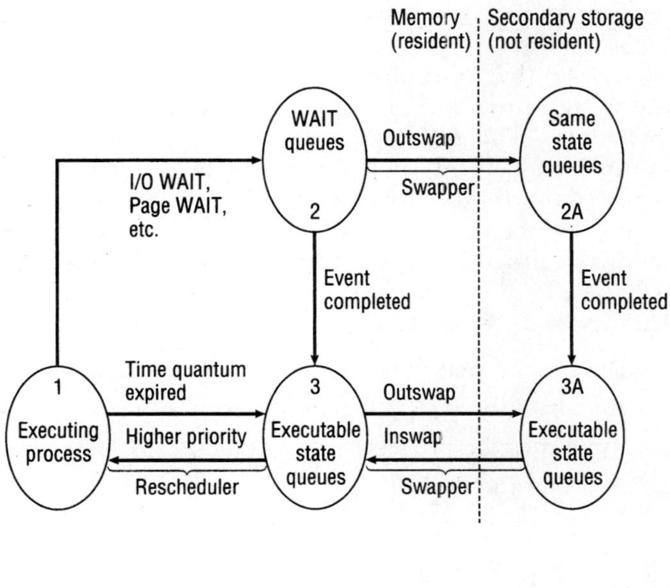

FIGURE 15.4 *This diagram shows how the swapper removes processes from both the* WAIT *(2) and* READY *(3) queues and stores them in secondary storage to open up main memory. The rescheduler activates processes in the* READY *(3) queue on a high-priority basis. (Adapted from* VAX software handbook, *1982.)*

For example, consider the path of Process X when its time quantum expires. It goes from RUNNING (1) to READY (3) and is placed in the next lower priority queue; the rescheduler performs a context switch and activates another process that's in the READY state (3). Then, if Process X becomes a candidate for an outswap, its PCB is linked to the proper queue (3A) by the swapper. Eventually Process X will be inswapped, find its way back into memory, and be assigned the processor once again. A process that issues an I/O command would follow an entirely different path.

DEVICE MANAGEMENT

VMS users don't interact directly with devices or their drivers when issuing input or output commands; instead, there are several levels between them and the physical devices. The highest level is called Record Management Services (RMS), which is accessed by processes when they issue I/O requests. RMS, in turn, interfaces with the Queue I/O Systems Service, which passes information along to the device drivers that actually manage the physical devices.

Our discussion of the VMS I/O Device Manager concentrates on its three logical components, the Queue I/O Systems Service, the device drivers, and the I/O Postprocessing Routine. RMS will be discussed in the File Management section that follows.

The Queue I/O Systems Service (QIO) queues the I/O requests to the device drivers. It's accessed through RMS by the majority of users, although QIO may be invoked directly by programmers who choose to perform their own record blocking, to control buffer allocation, or to optimize special record processing. The basic functions of QIO are to validate the argument provided by the process and to build an I/O Request Packet (IRP) that contains all the information needed by the device driver to perform the actual I/O function (READ or WRITE) on the specific device (tape, printer, disk, etc.).

The device driver (there is one for each type of device) is a set of routines and data structures that control the operation of the device. The device driver executes at a high processor-priority level, and it can't be interrupted by the Process Scheduler. The registers and program counter for each driver are kept within the Unit Control Block (UCB) for the device. The UCB serves the same function for the device driver that the PCB serves for the process. Thus, for every active device the unit's UCB contains information on the state of the executing driver process and on the status of the unit (*VAX software handbook*, 1982).

The device driver performs the following functions, among others:

1. Defines the peripheral device for the operating system;
2. Initializes the device at system startup time or after a power failure;
3. Translates the processes' I/O requests into device-specific commands;
4. Activates the device;

5. Responds to hardware interrupts generated by the device;
6. Returns data and status messages from the device to the process.

The operating system and device drivers share a common I/O database when processing an I/O operation. The database describes the specifications and functions of each device in terms familiar to VMS and consists of two main sections, the driver tables and the system data structures.

The first section includes three driver tables: the driver prologue table, which describes the driver and the device type; the driver dispatch table, which lists the entry point addresses of standard driver routines; and the function decision table, which lists all valid function codes and buffered codes for the device.

The second section is composed of system data structures that describe each bus adapter, device unit, and logical path to a device or group of devices. Device drivers may reference one or several of these control blocks: the Device Data Block, which contains information common to all devices of a given type connected to a single controller; the Unit Control Block, which describes the characteristics and state for a single device; the Channel Request Block, which defines the state of a controller and indicates which device unit is transferring data and which units are waiting; the Interrupt Dispatch Block, which is an extension of a controller and describes its current activity; and the Adapter Control Block, which defines the characteristics of a bus adapter.

Figure 15.5 is an example of the interaction between control blocks and tables. The sequence of steps is performed by the QIO service routine when satisfying an I/O request.

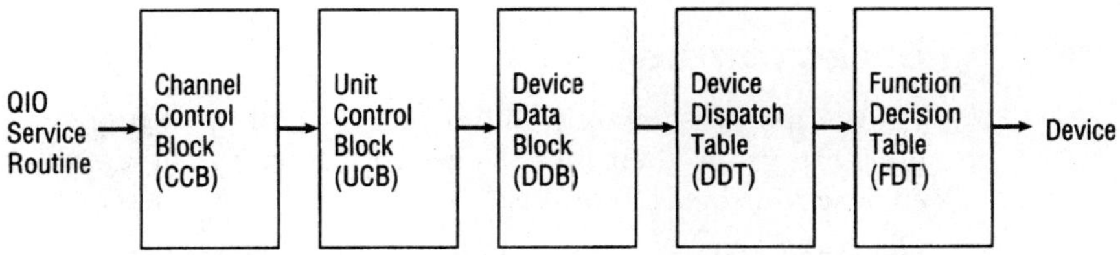

FIGURE 15.5 *Steps performed by QIO service routine when responding to an I/O request. Once an FDT routine validates that the user has access to the requested data area, the I/O request is completed. (Adapted from* VAX software handbook, *1982.)*

The I/O Postprocessing Routine is used for final processing of all device requests and returns the final status and data to the user process memory space (*VAX software handbook,* 1982).

QIO processing is extremely fast because the system both (1) minimizes the code needed to initiate and complete requests, thus optimizing use of the device, and (2) overlaps seeks with I/O requests, thus optimizing use of the disk controller. User processes can queue requests to a device driver at any time and, if the driver is free, the request will be satisfied; if the driver is busy, the I/O request will be placed on a waiting queue according to the priority of the requesting process. I/O requests are processed on a first-come first-served basis within priority. After an I/O request has been queued, the issuing process doesn't have to wait for the I/O operation to complete and can continue processing while the request is in progress.

FILE MANAGEMENT

VMS follows many standard naming conventions for its files and directories.

FILE NAMES

File names are selected by users and can be no more than nine alphanumeric characters — the only legal characters are the letters A through Z and digits 0 through 9. VMS isn't case-sensitive so file names can be given in upper or lower case. In the following pages we'll use all upper case.

The file's type is indicated by its extension, which can be up to three characters in length and is separated from the file name by a period. It's advisable that you check with a manual for your system before you assign your own extensions to a file because many three-character combinations have a specific meaning to the system.

In addition to a file name and extension, VMS provides a version number with every file, starting with number one and incrementing it every time the file is modified. Only the two most recent versions of the file are kept in the user's directory. For instance, if the directory listing for a data file named `INVENTORY` includes these two file names:

```
INVENTORY.DAT;2
INVENTORY.DAT;3
```

then it means that the directory contains the last two versions of the file, the most recent of which is version number 3.

DIRECTORIES

VMS supports a hierarchical tree structure of up to nine levels of subdirectories so users can group their files as needed. Directory names (shown in Figure 15.6) are enclosed in square brackets:

`[MCHOES]`, `[MCHOES.FIGURES]`, and `[MCHOES.FIGURES.TABLES]`

The complete name of a file contains all the information the system needs to locate and identify it. Because a disk can contain files belonging to several users, each disk is separated into directories, one for each user, that are created when the user is accepted into the system. In addition, a computer system usually has several disks, so each device is given a name when the system is configured. Therefore, the complete name for `INVENTORY.DAT;3` would include its disk name and directory:

```
DMA3:[MCHOES]INVENTORY.DAT;3
```

which tells the system that the file is stored on device DMA3 — disk model RK07, attached to controller A, unit 3 — on the directory called `MCHOES`. Note: VMS's punctuation requirements are stringent, so each colon, bracket, period, and semicolon must be entered correctly to separate the various components of the file specification.

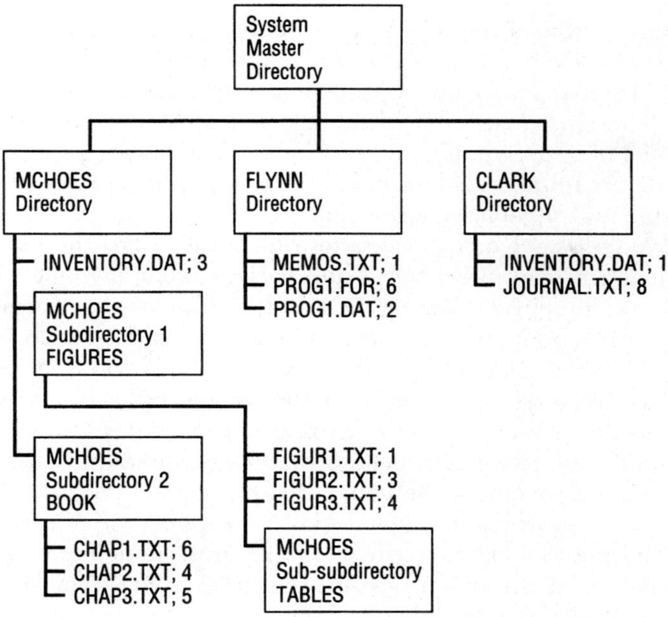

FIGURE 15.6 *The VMS directory and subdirectory structure.*

As you can see, this can be a cumbersome way to access files. To make life a bit easier, when users log on to the system they're automatically connected to the device in which their directories reside. This is the "home directory" and as long as the user accesses files in this directory the relative file name is sufficient; so `INVENTORY.DAT` is enough to access the most recent version of the data file called `INVENTORY`. The complete file name is needed only when accessing files on other users' directories.

To simplify the specification of directories a user can set a default working directory using the `SET DEFAULT` command followed by the directory name: `SET DEFAULT [MCHOES.FIGURES]`.

To access a subdirectory within that default directory a user uses the `DIRECTORY` command followed by the subdirectory name preceded by a period:

```
DIRECTORY [.TABLES]
```

The `DIRECTORY` command, or `DIR` for short, gives an alphabetical listing of all the files in the current directory. For example, in Figure 15.6, if user `FLYNN` asked for a directory listing, the screen would display:

```
          Directory DMA3:[FLYNN]
MEMOS.TXT;1   PROG1.DAT;2   PROG1.FOR;6
```

THE RMS MODULE

VMS uses a module called Record Management Services (RMS), which consists of procedures that can be invoked by a user program through the `OPEN`, `CLOSE`, `READ` `WRITE`, `GET`, and `PUT` statements. RMS provides a device-independent interface for general-purpose files and record processing on any secondary storage device. RMS software automatically blocks and deblocks records, thus enabling programs to process logical records without any extra attention by the programmer.

RMS provides extensive capabilities for data storage, retrieval, and modification. Therefore, users may easily select from sequential, relative, and indexed sequential file organization and from sequential, direct, or dynamic access modes. If the file organization isn't stated, the system assigns the default of sequential organization and sequential access mode.

VMS allows dynamic access to a file; that means the user can switch from sequential access to direct access and back again at any time while accessing the records in a program's data file that had been defined as having relative or indexed sequential organization. For example, a user could sequentially access a series of records within a data file by (1) accessing the first record directly, (2) accessing the following records sequentially until the last-desired record is read, and (3) switching back to direct access mode to bypass a group of records and access another one directly. The number of switches from one mode to the other is determined by the application program — the system doesn't impose any limit. The only restriction is that the file organization must be able to support the direct access mode.

The physical characteristics of a file must be defined when the file is created either through a user's program or an RMS utility. Typical characteristics are file name, protection code, file organization and size, record format and size, and key if the organization is indexed.

If the protection code (access code) isn't specified, the system sets it to the default of `READ WRITE EXECUTE DELETE (RWED)` for the system and owner. No other user has privileges on the file.

If the size of the file isn't given, RMS allocates the minimum amount of storage needed for the file, which can be increased dynamically during the life of the file.

If the record format and size aren't given, RMS will use its default characteristics. A user may select from fixed-length, variable-length, and "stream." Stream record format is used for sequential files only. In stream format, the records are of variable length and are separated by special character sequences called "terminators," which become part of the record they delimit.

Although files on magnetic tape can't be shared, all other RMS files allow sharing by any number of users who are reading, but not modifying, the file. Sequential files allow for single writers and multiple readers. Relative and indexed files allow for multiple readers and writers. Information on file sharing is applied to RMS by a user's program when it opens the file. To provide protection to sensitive data, RMS can lock records so that while a process is adding, deleting, or modifying a record other processes can't access it. The lock remains in effect until the program accesses another record, when RMS unlocks the first record and locks the second one automatically (*VAX software handbook,* 1982).

USER INTERFACE

VMS commands are entered by the user at the system prompt, which is a dollar sign (`$`).

The commands are English words or their abbreviations that describe the function they perform. Many users choose to type in the abbreviations of the commands, usually the first three letters, rather than the full word. Commands can be typed in either upper or lower case, but for editorial clarity, we'll use only upper case in this text.

TABLE 15.2 *VAX/VMS user commands can be in upper or lower case and many can be abbreviated. Check the technical documentation for your system for proper spelling and syntax.*

Command	Action to be performed
`RUN`	Run/Execute a file.
`DIRECTORY`	List directory files.
`SET DEFAULT`	Change the working directory.
`COPY`	Copy a file into another file or directory.
`DELETE`	Delete a file.
`RENAME`	Rename a file.
`CREATE`	Create a directory file.
`TYPE`	Display a file on the user's screen.
`PRINT`	Print out a file on a printer.
`SHOW TIME`	Show date and time.
`SEARCH`	Find a specified string in one or more files.
`APPEND`	Append to an existing file.
`MERGE`	Combine from two to ten similarly sorted files into a single file.
`HELP`	Provide on-screen help.

To make it easier for new users to learn the command language, an extensive `HELP` facility is available, which will be discussed in detail at the conclusion of this section.

The general format of a command is this:

[label:]command[/qualifiers] [parameter 1] . . . [parameter *n*]

The square brackets indicate optional entries, the ellipses (. . .) indicate more entries of the same type.

Labels are used to transfer the flow of control using the `GOTO` command. They are found most often in command procedures, not in interactive sessions.

Commands are reserved words that perform a specific task (see Table 15.2).

Commands may have *qualifiers,* which are key words that restrict or modify the function of a command; they're separated from the command by a slash (/). For example, in the command:

```
CREATE/DIRECTORY   [MCHOES.FIGURES]
```

`DIRECTORY` is the qualifier of the command `CREATE`. This command would create the subdirectory `FIGURES` within the directory `MCHOES`. The square brackets are required. No spaces are allowed between qualifiers, but the last qualifier is separated from the parameters by a space.

Most commands also have *parameters* that are file names or key words that the system recognizes. If the user omits the parameter on a command that requires one, the system will ask for it.

Although VMS is a standardized operating system, there may be variations from one system to the next. For complete instructions on command syntax, see the technical documentation for your system.

COMMAND PROCEDURE FILES

Command procedure files can be used to automate tedious or repetitious series of commands. These files contain VMS commands and, sometimes, data. Each line of instruction starts with a dollar sign, except for those lines containing data. The user can execute the file by typing the name of the file preceded by the "at" symbol (@). The default extension of a command procedure file is COM, although it may be overridden by a user-supplied extension.

For example, let's say the user often wants to check the system date and time, run the electronic mail program, see the system news, set up a default working directory, and review the list of files in that directory. A command procedure file like the following would do that. Comments are delimited by an exclamation point (!).

```
$SHOW TIME                             ! display date and time
$RUN [SYSTEM]MAIL                      ! run mail program
$TYPE [SYSTEM]DAILYNEWS.DAT            ! display any news from
                                       !computer center
$SET DEFAULT [MCHOES.BOOK.FIGURES]     ! set working director to
                                       !"FIGURES"
$DIR                                   ! list all files in "FIGURES"
```

If the program was named START.COM, then to run this program, the user simply types @START at the system prompt.

To make a customized command procedure file, like this one, run automatically every time the user logs on to the system, simply give the file the name LOGIN.COM and copy it to the user's home directory. Thereafter, every time the user logs on to the system, the LOGIN file will be executed. This technique can be used to perform certain commands automatically and/or set defaults before the user starts a working session.

Programmers take advantage of command procedure files to save themselves repetitious typing, and system managers use them to simplify complex maneuvers so they can be executed easily by any computer operator.

REDIRECTION

VAX/VMS defines its input and output resources using certain logical names to define them. For instance, the logical name of the system's input device is SYS$INPUT. Similarly, SYS$OUTPUT is the logical name for the output device. The default input device is the terminal keyboard, and the default output device is the terminal screen.

To redirect output, or input, the user simply reassigns the logical names to other devices or files using the ASSIGN command. For instance, a user can send the output from an interactive session to a file, instead of the screen, by using the ASSIGN command to redirect the output. (If you print out the file later, you'll have a printed record of your interactive session even if a printer isn't available when you're on-line.) The redirection command looks like this:

```
ASSIGN SESSION.OUT SYS$OUTPUT.
```

Now, all responses from the system will be redirected from your terminal screen to the output file SESSION.OUT and your screen will remain blank. For instance, to send a directory listing to your output file, enter the directory listing command DIR and the listing of files in the current directory is sent to the file called SESSION.OUT although the screen will remain blank.

To return the screen to normal, use the DEASSIGN command to restore the original default output device, as follows: DEASSIGN SYS$OUTPUT.

You can use ASSIGN commands in command procedures files too. Suppose you have an inventory program that runs at the end of every month and uses several weekly files for its input and generates a weekly output file for each input file. In this program you have used the names INFILE and OUTFILE to refer to the input and output files respectively, so the OPEN, READ, WRITE, and CLOSE statements refer to INFILE and OUTFILE. Before executing the program, you must equate those logical names, INFILE and OUTFILE, with the actual names of the files found in secondary storage. For example, WEEK1.DAT, WEEK2.DAT, WEEK3.DAT, and WEEK4.DAT can all be input files and WKOUT1.DAT, WKOUT2.DAT, WKOUT3.DAT, and WKOUT4.DAT can all be output files. The assignment takes place in a program that looks like this:

```
$ASSIGN WEEK1.DAT INFILE
$ASSIGN WKOUT1.DAT OUTFILE
$RUN INVENTRY
  .
  .
  .
$ASSIGN WEEK2.DAT INFILE
$ASSIGN WKOUT2.DAT OUTFILE
$RUN INVENTRY
  .
  .
  .
  (etc.)
```

When these commands are saved in a file with the COM extension, the user can execute them simply by typing the name of the file. If this program is named INVENTORY.COM then a user can run it by typing @INVENTORY.

FILTERS AND PIPES

Unlike the two other operating systems described thus far in this book, VAX/VMS did not accommodate filters or pipes as of 1995.

ADDITIONAL COMMANDS

APPEND

The APPEND command is used to attach the contents of one or more files to the end of an existing file. For example:

```
APPEND CHAPT1FIG.DAT CHAPT1TXT.DAT
```

will append the contents of CHAPT1FIG.DAT to the end of the file called CHAPT1TXT.DAT. (In this example both files are located in the same disk and current directory so the relative names of the files are sufficient.)

COPY

The COPY command creates a new file from one or more existing files. The simplest format of the command is:

```
COPY CHAPT1FIG.DAT CHAPT1FIG.BAK
```

where the contents of the first file are copied and named CHAPT1FIG.BAK. Both files reside in the same directory. If the user doesn't give the file names in the copy command, the system will prompt for them. For instance, if the name of the destination file was missing, the system would respond with: To: and wait for the user to type in the destination file name.

Multiple files can also be copied from one user to another. For example, COPY *.* DISK2:[MCHOES.BOOK] is the command to copy all the files from the current directory to the MCHOES.BOOK directory, which resides on the device DISK2. The *.* indicates that all files should be copied and because no names have been indicated for the new files they will have the same names as those from the default directory. For the command to work, the user issuing this command must have "write access" to the MCHOES.BOOK directory.

SORT

The SORT command can be used to reorder the records from an existing file and store the sorted records in a new file. For example, let's say a file called EMPL.DAT has the following format: the ID numbers start in column 1, phone numbers start in column 10, last names start in column 20, and first names start in column 40. This file can be sorted on any of these fields like this:

```
SORT/KEY = (POSITION:1,SIZE:9) EMPL.DAT IDSORT.DAT.
```

This command will sort the original file EMPL.DAT in alphanumeric order using the ID number as the key field; the POSITION indicates the starting point of the key field (1), and the SIZE indicates the number of characters to be used when sorting the records (9). IDSORT.DAT is the name of the sorted new file.

Likewise, the command

```
SORT/KEY=(POSITION:20,SIZE:18)/KEY=(POSITION:40,SIZE:15) EMPL.DAT NAMSORT.DAT
```

will sort the original file EMPL.DAT in alphanumeric order using the last name as the first key and the first name as the second key. The new file will be called

NAMSORT.DAT and will contain the employee records sorted by last name and then by first name within each last name.

MERGE

The MERGE command will combine from two to ten similarly sorted files into just one output file. All files to be merged must be sorted. For example, if we had two separate employee files already sorted by ID number and we wanted to merge them into a master file using the ID number as the key field, we would give the following command:

```
MERGE/KEY = (POSITION:1,SIZE:9) IDSORT1.DAT IDSORT2.DAT IDSORTMS.DAT
```

SEARCH

The SEARCH command looks for a specific string, or strings, in one or more files and lists all the lines containing the string or strings. For example, if a file named MAILLIST.DAT contains names and addresses of customers and you want to extract those who live in London, the command would be: SEARCH MAILLIST.DAT LONDON to display each line of the file containing the word LONDON. If you had two separate files containing customer names and addresses and you wanted to search both for LONDON, then you would enter: SEARCH MAIL1.DAT, MAIL2.DAT LONDON and all the lines containing LONDON from both files would be displayed on the screen.

The list of customers who live in London can also be generated and stored in a disk file for future reference with this command:

```
SEARCH/OUTPUT = LONDON.DAT  MAILLIST.DAT  LONDON
```

In this example the output of the search has been directed to the file LONDON.DAT and won't be displayed on the screen.

Sometimes, when you search for strings in a full text document you may want to see more than just the line where the string occurs. To see the surrounding text as well, use the WINDOW qualifier of the SEARCH command. For example:

```
SEARCH/OUTPUT = EXTRACT.DAT/WINDOW=3 CHAPT3.TXT "OPERATING SYSTEM"
```

will search for the words "OPERATING SYSTEM" in the file CHAPT3.TXT (the string must be enclosed in quotes if it contains a blank). The 3 means the size of the window is three lines. Therefore, one line preceding the string and one line following it will be copied to the EXTRACT.DAT file.

HELP

The VMS HELP command is extremely useful and geared to help advanced users as well as those just learning the system. It provides information and examples about specific DCL (Digital Command Language) commands, and because it's accessed interactively from the terminal, it's very convenient for users who don't have ready access to reference manuals. The help facility initially displays, in alphabetical order, the commands used most. To see the list of these commands on your screen, type HELP and the system will respond with -Topic?

This allows you several options:

1. Type in the name of the command or topic for which you need help.
2. Type `INSTRUCTIONS` for more detailed instructions on how to use the help facility.
3. Type `HINTS` if you aren't sure of the name of the command or topic for which you need help.
4. Type a question mark (?) to redisplay the most recently requested text.
5. Press the "Return" key to exit from `HELP`.

The specific DCL commands contained in the `HELP` file vary from installation to installation. For specific information refer to the technical documentation for that system.

CHAPTER FIFTEEN CONCLUSION

The main advantage of VMS is its compatibility across every computer in the VAX family. VAX system owners like VMS because they can invest in new VAX hardware, to keep up with advances in technology, knowing they won't need extensive alterations to the existing software.

System managers like VMS because it's an easy operating system to install. VMS comes prebuilt and it's self-installing and autoconfiguring, so no special configurations are necessary. In addition, many parameters, such as working set size, can be adjusted to suit specific needs.

System programmers like VMS because their software won't need to be significantly altered or rewritten when the hardware is upgraded from one model to the next, so program maintenance is kept low. New users like VMS because of its extensive help facility and simple, coherent commands.

Fast CPU speeds, new technology for a companion memory interface and Digital's effort to smooth the transition from VAX to AXP have made users interested in migrating their applications to the new architecture. This transition continues a trend of compatibility that had started with the PDP family of computers.

Chapter Sixteen

IBM/MVS OPERATING SYSTEM

USER COMMAND INTERFACE

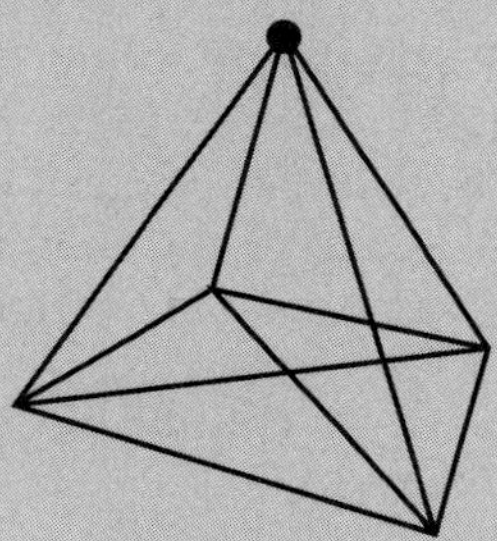

Design Goals

Memory Management

Processor Management

Device Management

File Management

User Interface

The MVS operating system was developed by IBM to operate the company's line of large mainframe computers. We include it in this book for two reasons: it is still widely used as an industry standard, and it has served as the basis for operating systems developed later by IBM.

MVS is famous for its heritage — it's the descendant of a long line of operating systems developed to run IBM's large computer mainframes. Its roots go back to the days of punched cards and batch input and, as we'll see in this chapter, those roots are evident from its line-by-line (previously card-by-card) command structure. It is unlike the other operating systems we have studied thus far because of its historical development. Its orientation is toward multiprogramming commercial computing environments, and it can make repetitive tasks fairly easy to run.

The disadvantage of MVS is its lack of succinct user command structure and simple key words. MVS is littered with terminology that new users find difficult, at first, to comprehend. But with practice, most new programmers quickly learn that they need to use a relatively few commands to perform most tasks.

Note: It would be inappropriate to describe the MVS operating system without using IBM's terminology for the system's hardware components and software. Unfortunately for those unfamiliar with the system, the standard terminology includes many acronyms and abbreviations, which can make any explanation cumbersome. Therefore, throughout this chapter, we have defined all of the acronyms and abbreviations when they are introduced, and thereafter we have referred to them as they are more commonly known. For your reference, Appendix B spells out all of the IBM vocabulary used in the chapter.

HISTORY

The MVS (multiple virtual storage) operating system was originally designed to support two classes of the company's mainframe computers — 360 and 370 computers. Table 16.1 is a simplified table showing only the operating systems (and mainframes) directly related to MVS.

IBM's 360 mainframe computers were large multiuser mainframe computers that became an industry standard. Their popularity spanned the years from 1964 to 1969. Contributing to their popularity in commercial data processing environments was their identical architecture — that is, they had the same instruction set, operating system, and I/O devices. Therefore, any programs that could run on one 360 computer could run on any other 360 computer. This was an important advantage when one computer was replaced with another — there was no need to modify the existing software (Prasad, 1989).

In addition, IBM provided several database management system software packages such as Customer Information Control Systems (CICS) and Information Management System (IMS), which are still widely used.

Because they were designed to be general-purpose machines, the 360 computers could operate equally well in both commercial and scientific environments. However, in time, the needs of the commercial world demanded more sophistication than was possible from the 360 family. It was time for a system that could handle time-sharing and multiple CPUs to speed up processing.

The 370 family was introduced in 1970 to solve those problems. In essence, the new architecture kept the 360 instruction set and the I/O concepts and made enhancements to storage techniques. The MVS operating system was introduced to take advantage of the concepts of virtual storage and multiple CPU operation. In addition, two new software packages were introduced: VTAM (Virtual Telecommunications Access Method) and VSAM (Virtual Storage Access Method) to manage telecommunications processing and files, respectively. And CICS and IMS were upgraded and rewritten for the new architecture.

The business community made further demands on the 370 machines, and in 1980 the new 370/XA was introduced (XA stands for Extended Architecture).

The 370/XA computers were architecturally different from the 370 in that they (1) supported true multiprocessing, (2) used a larger address, and (3) used more sophisticated I/O principles of operation, which resulted in better performance. The 308X and 3090 series were among the most powerful IBM main-

TABLE 16.1 *The historical evolution of IBM mainframes and operating systems having a direct impact on the development of MVS.*

Year	Computer	Operating system	Features
1964	IBM 360 Series	OS/PCP (Primary Control Program)	Batch, single-task systems
		DOS (Disk Operating System)	
1967		OS/MFT (Multiprogramming with a Fixed number of Tasks)	Descendant of PCP; introduced multiprogramming; used fixed-partition memory management
		DOS-2314	Descendant of DOS
1968		OS/MVT (Multiprogramming with a Variable number of Tasks)	Descendant of PCP; introduced spooling; used dynamic memory management
1969		OS/MFT-11	Descendant of MFT
		DOS/MP (DOS with Multi-Programming)	Descendant of DOS-2314
1970	IBM 370 Series	TSO (Time-Sharing Option for MVT Operating System)	Incorporated into MVT Operating System; introduced teleprocessing and time-sharing
1972		SVS (Single Virtual Storage System)	Incorporated into MVT operating system; introduced virtual storage concept
		OS/VS1 (Virtual Storage System 1)	Descendant of MFT-11; programs loaded into fixed partitions
		OS/VS2 (Virtual Storage System 2)	Descendant of MVT; dynamic allocation of memory at job's run time
1973		VM (Virtual Machine)	New operating system; introduced the "virtual machine" concept
		DOS/VS (DOS with Virtual Storage)	Descendant of DOS/MP
1974		MVS (Multiple Virtual Storage System)	Descendant of VS2
1981		MVS/XA (Multiple Virtual Storage System with Extended Architecture)	Expanded version of MVS
1983		MVS/ESA (Enterprise Systems Architecture)	Expanded storage could be accessed directly by application programs
1990	System/390	MVS/ESA	New I/O channel architecture, Enterprise System Connection (ESCON), made use of point-to-point fiber-optic links
1996		OS/390 (Open Server)	Provided integrated client/server functions, UNIX application environment support, and object programming support, among other features

frames. This family of computers ran under the MVS/XA operating system, which appeared to be generally accepted as the standard (Prasad, 1989).

As of 1990, the 370 architecture was supported by the 9370 computer series for small to medium systems, the 438X series for medium to large systems, and the 308X and 3090 series for very large systems. These last three series are designed to conform to the 370/XA architecture but can also operate as 370 modules.

The System/390 architecture was introduced in September 1990 to enhance System/370 XA, especially its network technology and cache controllers to continue the trend toward I/O decentralization. The MVS operating system expanded to MVS/ESA to support the new hardware (Houtekamer & Artis, 1993).

DESIGN GOALS

IBM had two design goals for MVS: to increase the productivity of the computer installation by dynamically allocating its resources and to increase the productivity of the human resources by automating the computer's operations and the management of data, resources, and workload.

MVS was designed to run the large computer systems of the 1970s with up to 64 megabytes of main memory, fast I/O devices with block multiplexer channels capable of transferring 3 megabytes of data per second. It was designed to support a large number of concurrent users working in either time-sharing or batch mode. And it was designed to satisfy the needs of the business community by providing innovative features without the cost of rewriting existing programs.

The computer's user interface wasn't designed with the casual user in mind. It was written for professionals — in fact, it's a complex language in itself. It's called the Job Control Language (JCL) and offers many options, but it requires time and effort on the part of the user to master it. JCL's statements can be divided into three basic functions:

1. `JOB` statements are used to separate and identify jobs.
2. `EXEC` statements are used to identify programs to be executed.
3. `DD` statements (data definition statements) are used to define in great detail the characteristics of each peripheral device requested by the job.

One tedious aspect of JCL is that every program must be preceded by these detailed commands — many of which are common from program to program. To relieve the user from typing the same commands over and over, MVS allows for typical sets of JCL statements to be stored in special library files. Later, the user can link these files to the program for processing. This feature helps smooth human/computer interaction.

MEMORY MANAGEMENT

Within the software structure of MVS, memory management falls under the functional area of supervisor management, which handles nine categories of activities:

Supervisor Control* (also included with Job and Data Management)
Task Management
Program Management
Virtual Storage Management*
Real Storage Management*
Auxiliary Storage Management*

Timer Supervisor

System Resource Management* (also included with Job and Data Management)

Recovery-Termination Management

The five modules marked with an asterisk (*) comprise the memory management section, which interacts with supervisor management through a system of tables, and are shown in Figure 16.1.

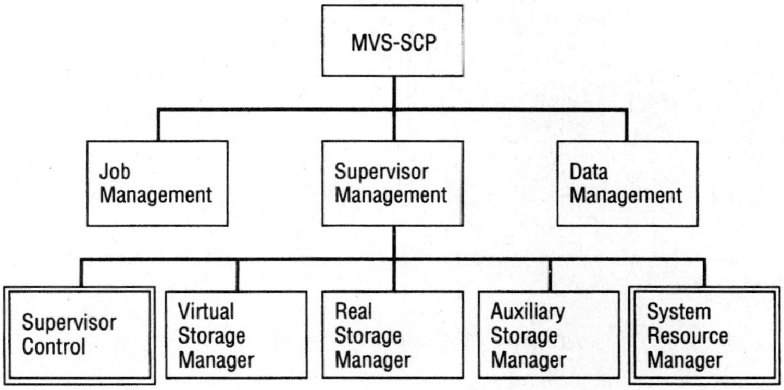

FIGURE 16.1 *Hierarchy of MVS with memory management functions highlighted and showing a subset of all the functions performed through MVS-SCP. Supervisor control and the system resource manager are included with job and data management as well. This diagram details the memory management functions.*

MVS allocates main memory using a segmented/page scheme. As illustrated in Figure 16.2, a virtual storage address space in MVS is divided into 256 segments of equal size, 64K each. Each segment is then subdivided into 16 pages of equal size, 4K each, where data or instructions are stored. Each user is assigned an address space that is 16M long (256 segments multiplied by 64K), so there are multiple virtual address spaces — hence the name of the operating system, Multiple Virtual Storage System, or MVS. Although in theory the number of virtual address spaces is unlimited, main storage and external page storage capacities restrict the maximum number of virtual storage address spaces. Figure 16.3 shows the format of MVS virtual addressing. As of 1990, MVS could support 1,635 virtual storage address spaces — therefore, that's the total number of batch jobs and on-line users that can access the system at one time.

When a program is said to have been "loaded into virtual storage," it means that the program occupies contiguous locations within the virtual storage address space. As it's being loaded, the program is subdivided into 4K pages, which are gathered into groups of 16 pages to make up segments. Main memory is divided into page frames of 4K each. Although the pages are contiguous within the confines of the virtual storage address space, they do not need to be contiguous in main storage.

VIRTUAL STORAGE MANAGEMENT

Once a job has started executing and has been "swapped in," its active pages are in page frames in main memory and its inactive pages are in External Page Storage

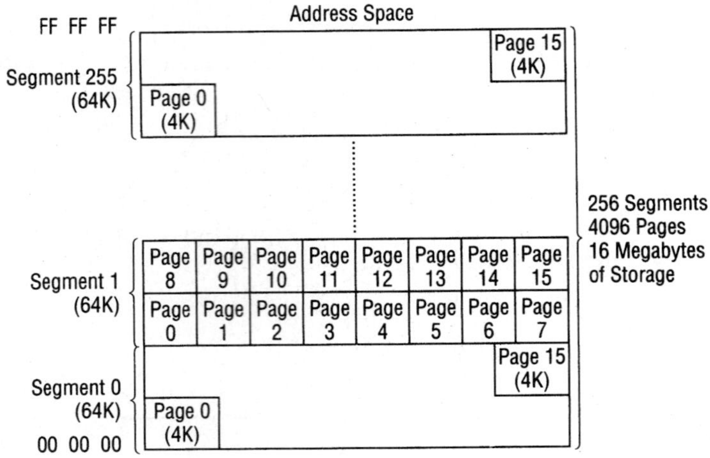

FIGURE 16.2 *A map of MVS virtual storage space.*

(EPS) page slots. If a job becomes inactive and is "swapped out," all of its pages reside in EPS page slots.

The Memory Manager needs to know three things to keep track of pages in an address space:

1. Is a segment or page allocated?
2. Where is a page located — in a main storage page frame or in an EPS page slot?
3. Is a particular page frame in main storage in use?

The information that will help answer these three questions resides in three software entities: Segment Tables, Page Tables, and External Page Tables. In addition, three hardware entities are used to support virtual storage: control registers, dynamic address translators, and a translation lookaside buffer.

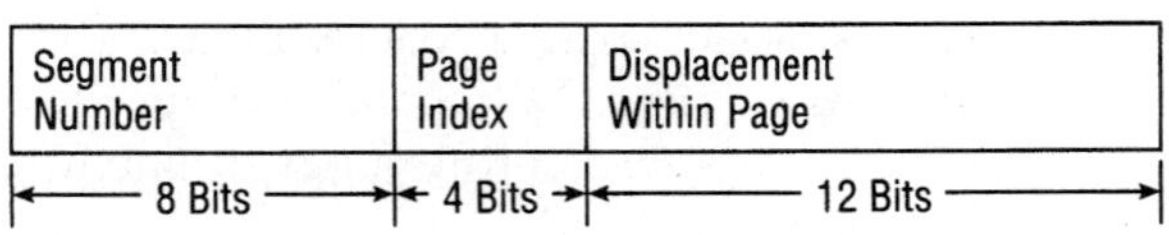

FIGURE 16.3 *MVS virtual address format. This configuration allows the Memory Manager to address any location within a 16M address space.*

The Segment Table has 256 entries, one per segment in an address space. Each entry is 4 bytes long and contains information about the length of the Page Table, the address of the Page Table, and whether or not the segment has been allocated. If it has been allocated, then a Page Table has been built for it and the page table address points to the Page Table for that segment in real storage. If the segment has not been allocated, no entry exists for either the page table length or the page table address for that segment.

There are 256 Page Tables for an address space, one per segment. However, only allocated segments will generate Page Tables, so, in general, the actual number of Page Tables is a fraction of the total. Each Page Table consists of 16 entries, one per page in a segment. Each entry is 2 bytes long and contains the page frame address, the "invalid bit," which indicates whether or not a page is in main memory, and the "get mained bit," which indicates whether or not a page has been allocated (Katzan & Tharayil, 1984).

The invalid bit can be zero (if the page is in main storage) or one (if the page is not in main storage). The get mained bit can be zero (if the page is not allocated) or one (if the page is allocated). Therefore, there are four possible combinations as shown in Table 16.2.

TABLE 16.2 *The four possible combinations of the invalid bit and the get mained bit indicate the status of the page.*

Invalid bit	Get mained bit	Means the page is . . .
0	0	In main storage and not allocated
0	1	In main storage and allocated
1	0	Not in main storage and not allocated
1	1	Not in main storage and allocated

The status of the page indicates where it can be found. For example, if both the invalid bit and the get mained bit are one, then the Memory Manager will have to search the External Page Table.

Every Page Table has a corresponding External Page Table consisting of 16 entries, one per page. External Page Tables are used to locate an allocated page that's not in main storage. Each entry is 12 bytes long and contains the address of the page slot in the EPS device where the page resides. The address is in cylinder/track/record format.

In the CPU, Control Register 1 is called the STOR register and is used to store the location and length of the Segment Table for an active address space. Figure 16.4 shows the relationship between the STOR register, the three tables, main storage, and external page storage.

As illustrated in Figure 16.4, MVS makes use of demand paging — only a program's active pages, its working set, are kept in main memory. All pages requested by a program and not in main memory cause a page fault and have to be fetched from secondary storage and moved into a page frame, if one is free. If a page frame is not free, then the control module of the program loader scans the Page Frame Table to locate the one that was least recently used. Before swapping the page out of memory, it checks to see whether its contents have been modified. If they haven't, then the control module can overlay the page frame with the new requested page. If the contents have been modified then the control module must first write the contents of the page frame to a page slot before the new requested page is brought into that page frame. This is called a "page-out."

To complete our discussion of memory allocation, we need to consider the two hardware components that facilitate demand paging: the one that performs Dynamic Address Translation (DAT) and the Translation Lookaside Buffer (TLB).

As we mentioned in Chapter 3, a virtual memory address needs to be translated into a main memory address. In MVS this is done by the DAT hardware mechanism using the Page and Segment Tables and information from the virtual address, which resides in the Program Status Word (PSW): segment number, page index, and displacement within the page.

It's a four-step process:

1. The translation begins by using the information in the STOR register to locate the Segment Table.
2. Once found, the segment number from the virtual address is used as an index to locate the address of the Page Table for that segment.
3. When that Page Table is located, the page index is used to find the appropriate page frame address.
4. This address, together with the displacement within the page, allows the CPU to access the appropriate instruction in the active program.

Figure 16.5 shows the process of dynamic address translation (DAT).

It should be noted that the procedure of dynamic address translation is further complicated by certain unexpected events. The first of these is that the segment's invalid bit could be set to one, indicating that the segment has not yet been allocated, thus generating an interrupt and halting dynamic address translation until this condition is cleared up. The second occurs at the Page Table entry where DAT checks the get mained bit to see if the page has been allocated. If it hasn't been, then an interrupt occurs and the dynamic address translation is halted until this condition is cleared up. If the page has been allocated, DAT checks the page's invalid bit to see whether the page is in main memory. If it is, the page frame address is extracted and concatenated with the displacement, and the instruction is presented to the CPU for processing. If it is not in main memory, an interrupt occurs, and DAT presents the external page storage slot address to the Control Module, which takes over. The Control Module then fetches the page from secondary storage, does any necessary page-outs, and updates the entry in the Page Table. Once this is done, DAT proceeds to concatenate the displacement and inform the CPU that all is ready.

Although this seems like a lengthy procedure, it's reasonably fast because it's done by the DAT hardware. To further speed up the process, MVS uses TLB — in other systems they're called "associative registers." The actual number of these registers varies depending on the CPU model. These buffers contain the address of the most recently used page frames and the segment and page numbers to which they relate. When DAT starts the process of dynamic address translation, a parallel search through the TLB begins, and the segment and page numbers from the virtual address are compared to those in the buffers. If a match is found, the DAT process is halted and the page frame number is used to generate the address in main memory. If a match is not found, the DAT process continues to completion and the address of the new page frame is stored in the TLB that was least recently used (Katzan & Tharayil, 1984).

ORGANIZATION OF STORAGE

MVS's virtual storage layout is presented in Figure 16.6. A virtual storage address is divided into three major areas: a systems area, a private area, and a common area.

The systems area is divided into two sections: one is where the nucleus load modules reside (it's mapped one-to-one with addresses in main memory and is

FIGURE 16.4 *MVS's virtual storage support structure (Katzan & Tharayil, 1984).*

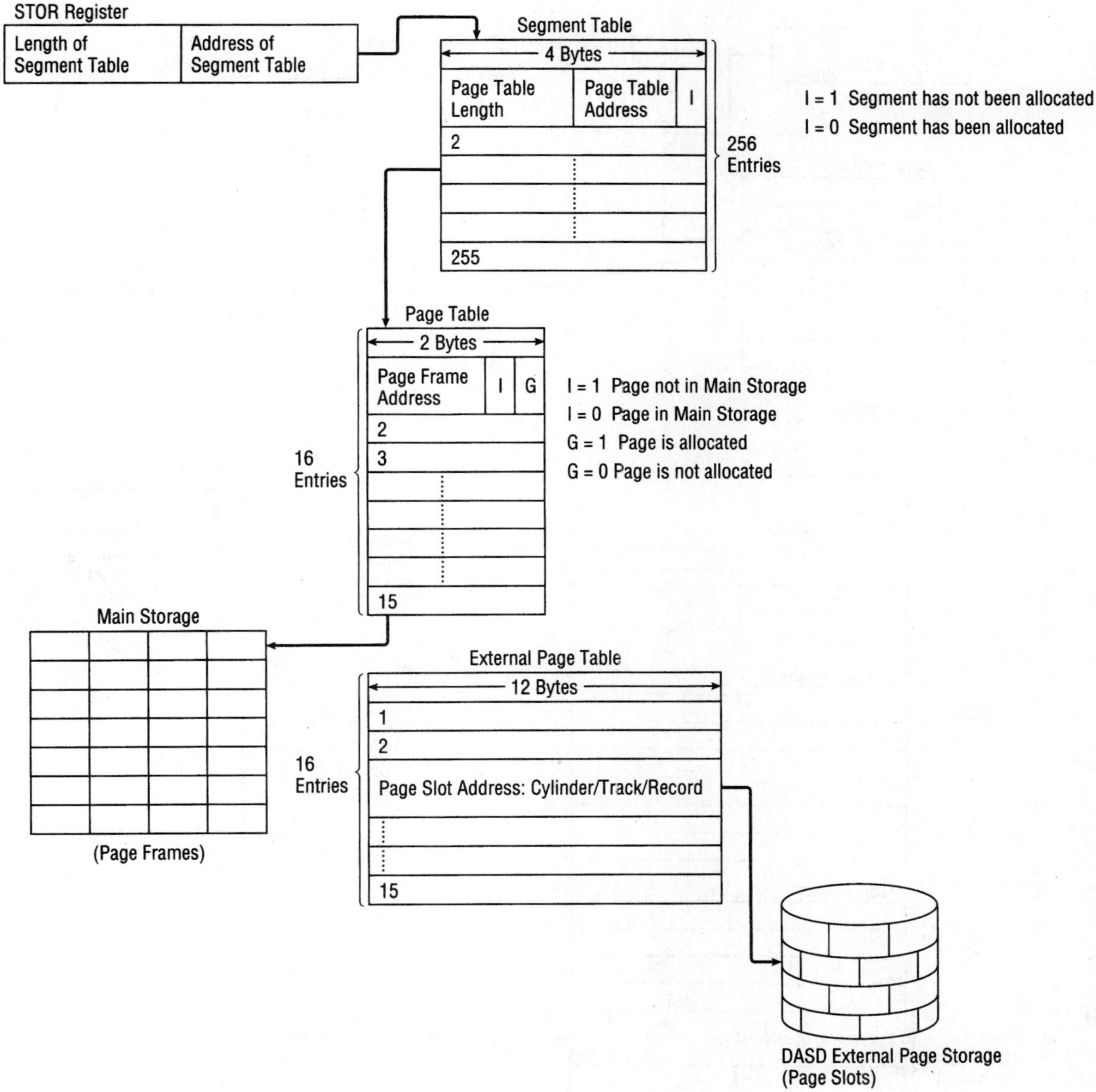

fixed in main memory); the other is called the "nucleus extension" and starts on a 64K boundary above the nucleus — it's also fixed in main memory.

The private area is the user's region, which contains information about the user and the user's programs. The amount of virtual storage given to the user depends on what the user specified in the execution statement for the job. The

FIGURE 16.5 *Dynamic address translation (Katzan & Tharayil, 1984).*

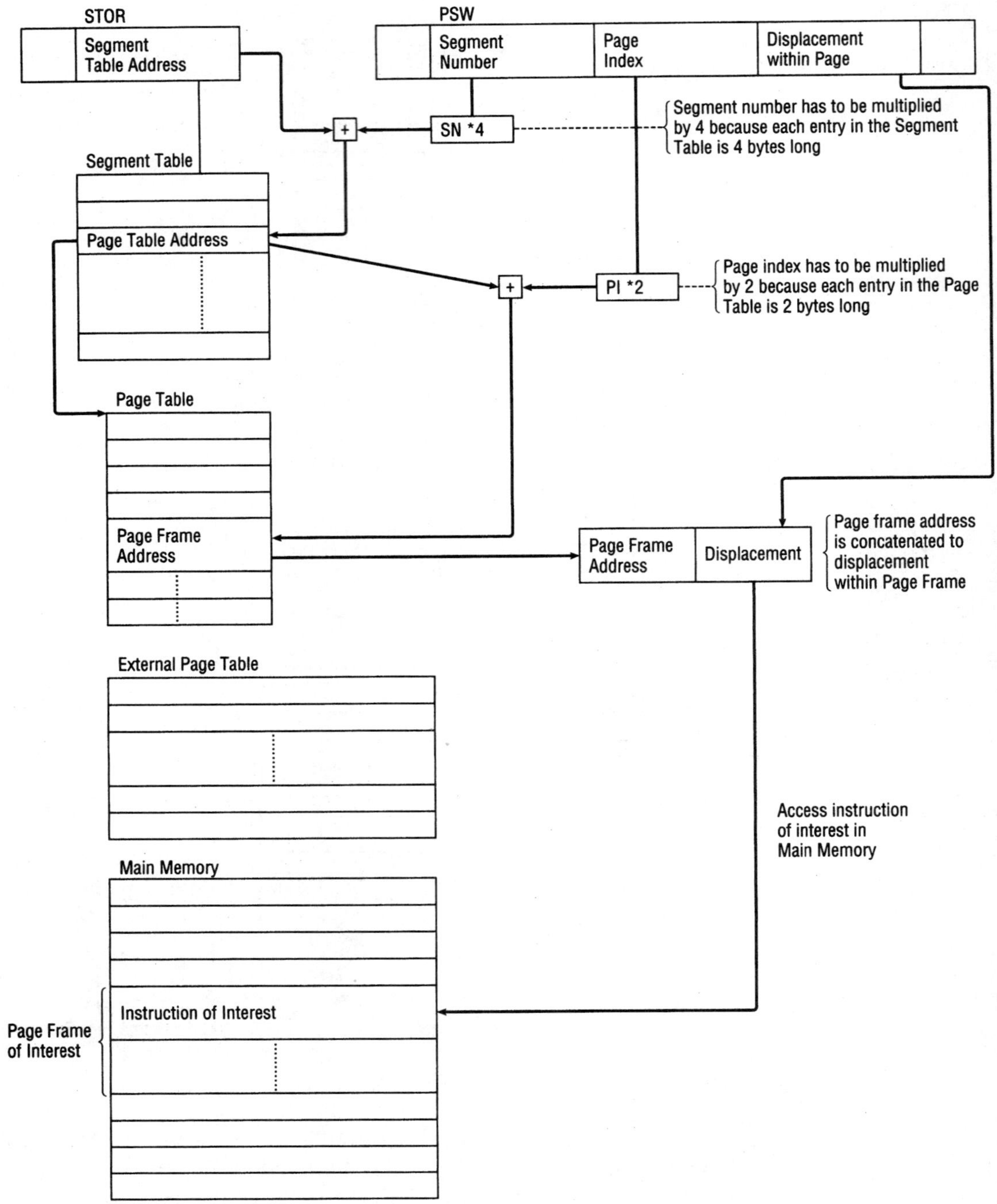

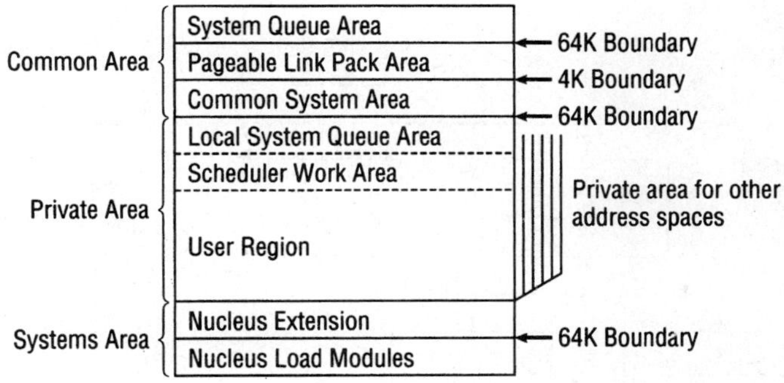

FIGURE 16.6 *Organization of virtual storage.*

user's region can be of the V=R type (it stands for "virtual equals real"), which means that there is a direct, one-to-one mapping with addresses in main memory so that the job is fixed in main memory and can't be paged out. Special time-dependent applications use this. The user's region can also be of the V=V type ("virtual equals virtual"), which means that the job is subject to page faults. Most application programs use the latter configuration.

The private area also contains the Local System Queue Area (LSQA), which contains control blocks and tables related to the address space, and the Scheduler Work Area (SWA).

As its name implies, the "common area" is common to all address spaces and is divided into three parts: (1) the System Queue Area (SQA), which contains tables and queues related to the whole system and is fixed in main memory; (2) the Pageable Link Pack Area (PLPA), which contains Supervisor Call (SVC) routines and access method routines; and (3) the Common System Area (CSA), which is used by the Job Entry Subsystem (JES) and the Telecommunication Access Method (TCAM) to communicate with private address spaces to perform their operations (Katzan & Tharayil, 1984).

PROCESSOR MANAGEMENT

The functional hierarchy of MVS is such that some of the processor management tasks performed by the Processor Manager, as described in Chapters 4 and 5, fall under the control of job management, while others fall under the control of supervisor management, as shown in Figure 16.7.

Job management provides an interface between application programs and the supervisor management routines. This is the section of the processor management that is known to the user who must learn the structure and syntax of the Job Command Language (JCL) in order to get work done on the computer system.

The functions of the Command Processing Module are to (1) read a command from the user's console or from a program and (2) schedule it for processing. The command is executed upon calling on the Master Scheduler, which is one of the key routines in the Job Processing Module and determines which job gets control of a processor after any interrupt.

The functions of the Job Processing Module are divided among several components. The first function of the JES is to read the job's JCL instructions, check

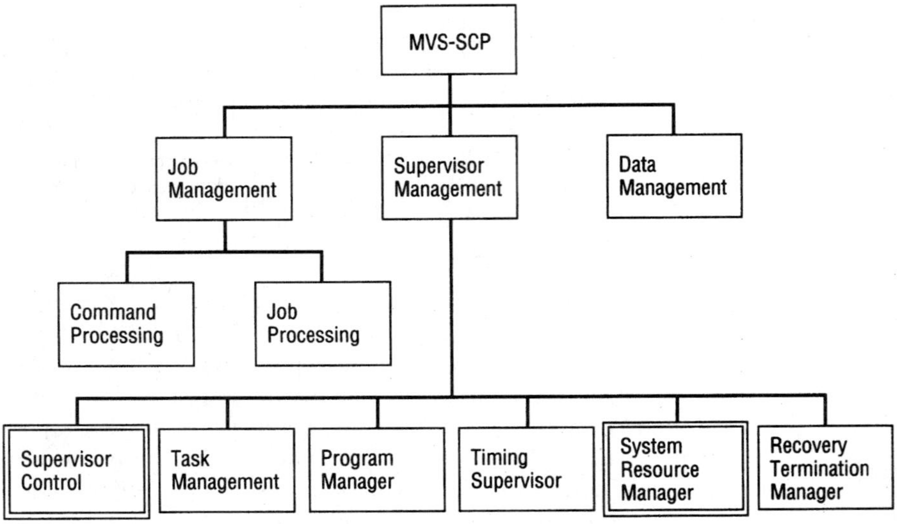

FIGURE 16.7 *Hierarchy of MVS with processor management functions highlighted. Supervisor control and the system resource manager are included with memory management and data management as well.*

them for accuracy, either cancel the job before it enters the system (if errors are found) or spool the job into an auxiliary DASD (if all is well), and give control to the "converter," which changes each JCL statement into machine language.

When the "initiator" requests a job for execution, JES performs its second function and selects a job according to its priority. The name of the job is then released to the initiator, which calls on the "interpreter" to set up control blocks for this new job. Jobs can't execute unless certain control blocks have been created because it's only through them that the system is aware of a job's presence.

Once the job has reached this point, data sets are allocated to it, and it's then ready to execute. The initiator calls on the Task Management Module, which supports the program as it runs.

Any output produced by a job as it's executing is passed on to JES, which performs its third function: it collects all output for a job and spools it into a DASD for printing at the end of the job. When the job is finished, the "terminator," together with JES, makes sure that all resources used by the terminating job are returned to the system.

Job management, task management, and application programs communicate through a series of control blocks. The Communications Vector Table (CVT) contains the addresses of the other control blocks and tables used by the system's supervisors and constitutes the major control block in the system. In addition, each virtual memory region has its own Task Control Block (TCB), and the contents of a given region are described by a series of request blocks generated from the Task Control Block. The presence of an active task is indicated by a Program Request Block (PRB), whereas the fact that a supervisor call interrupt is being processed is indicated by the presence of a Supervisor Request Block (SVRB). Figure 16.8 shows how these control blocks are linked together.

Request control blocks indicate active modules, if the request block queue is empty, the region isn't active and the job has terminated (Davis, 1987).

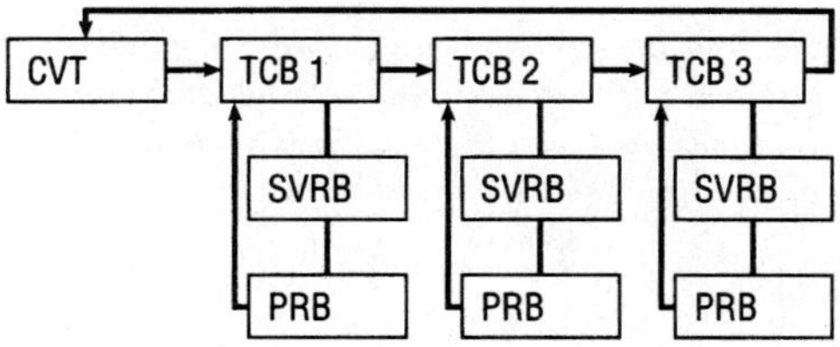

FIGURE 16.8 *The Task Control Blocks (one per region) are linked by pointers. Additional details about a region are given in a request block queue linked to the TCB.*

TASK MANAGEMENT

Once a job has been loaded, task management takes over and handles any interrupts generated during its run. It also determines which task will have access to the CPU, referred to as "dispatching"; this task is performed by a module called the dispatcher. It dispatches a task according to the status of that task: `READY`, `RUNNING`, or `WAITING`. A `WAITING` task is one that can't be dispatched because it's waiting for the completion of an event (I/O, page swap, etc.). A `READY` task is one that can be dispatched as soon as its turn comes up, while a `RUNNING` task is one that is currently executing. Once in the `READY` queue, tasks are dispatched according to their priority, which is determined by job control and control program parameters. The dispatcher keeps track of tasks that are sent to each CPU, prevents the same process from being sent to two CPUs, and maintains the accounting information for all active tasks.

PROGRAM MANAGEMENT

The Program Manager searches for load modules, schedules them, synchronizes exit routines to the supervisor, and fetches modules into storage. Load modules are located by looking through control blocks on different queues. The Program Manager keeps track of modules that have been loaded into virtual storage together with their names, starting addresses, entry points, and other information. If a load module isn't in virtual storage, the Program Manager calls on the "program fetch" routine to perform the load function.

Program Manager functions are activated through `LINK` and `LOAD` macros and are as follows:

1. Program fetch;
2. Link (load a module and pass control to it);
3. Exit from a linked program;
4. Load a module into virtual storage;
5. Delete a module from virtual storage;
6. Load and transfer control through a module.

DEVICE MANAGEMENT

Device management falls under the control of the Data Management module, as shown in Figure 16.9.

FIGURE 16.9 *Hierarchy of MVS with device and file management functions highlighted. Supervisor control and the system resource manager are included with job and processor management as well. Modules indicated with a check mark apply to device management only.*

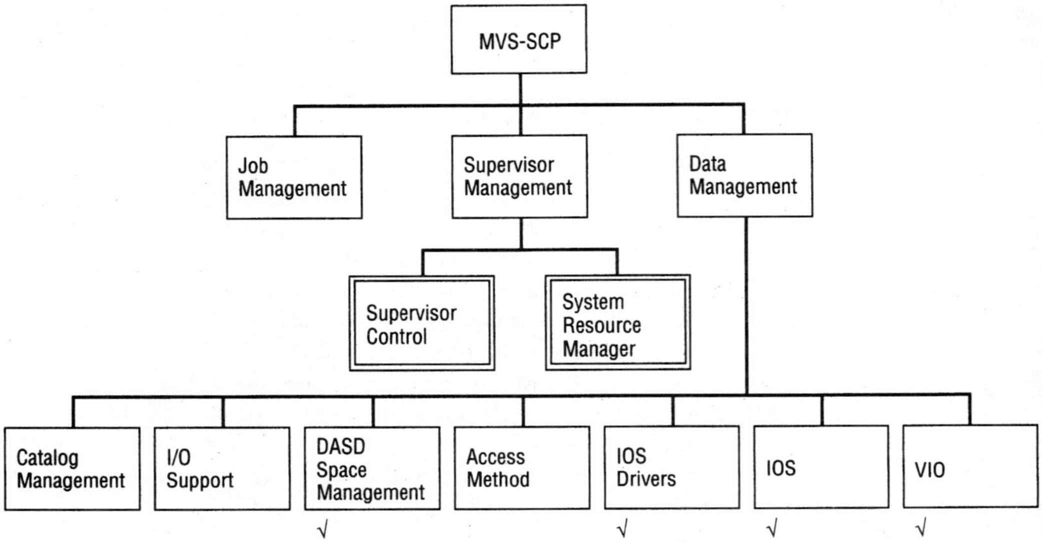

As shown in Figure 16.9, data management activities can be separated into seven categories. The activities directly related to device management are performed by the following four submodules: DASD space management, I/O Supervisor (IOS), IOS drivers, and Virtual I/O (VIO).

DASD SPACE MANAGEMENT

The functions of space management are handled by several routines that control the allocation and deallocation of space in direct access storage devices.

For example, the `ALLOCATE` routine provides the amount of space requested by a job and creates the file label, the Data Storage Control Block (DSCB), that will be stored in the Volume Table of Contents (VTOC), the name given to the main directory of every DASD volume. The `EXTEND` routine increases the size of an already existing file by allocating it more space (not necessarily contiguous). The `SCRATCH` routine releases the space occupied by a deleted file and removes its file label from the VTOC. Each DSCB contains file characteristics and the physical tracks at which the file is stored.

I/O SUPERVISOR

To appreciate the functions of the I/O Supervisor let's look at the I/O hardware structure of MVS, as shown in Figure 16.10.

The 370/XA architecture introduced the concept of the channel subsystem.

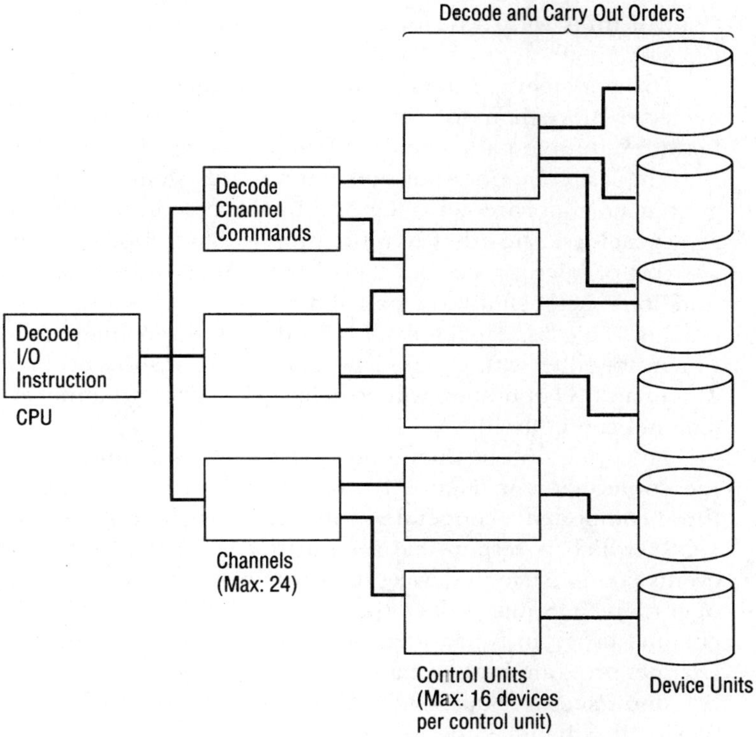

FIGURE 16.10 *A sample I/O hardware configuration indicating the function allocated to each unit in MVS.*

Upgrades in hardware components have made it possible to optimize the handling of I/O operations by distributing their execution among the microprocessors contained in the channels, control units, and devices that constitute the channel subsystem.

In this configuration, the role of the channel became one of path selector and executor of Channel Command Words (CCW). The functions performed by the channel are error detection and correction, command retry, and multiple requesting. This last function allows a block multiplexer channel to perform concurrent I/O operations on disk drives attached to the same control unit. For example, if a SEEK command is being executed and there is a rotational delay caused by the position of the record with respect to the position of the read/write head, then the disk drive performing the SEEK can be temporarily disconnected from the channel and the control unit can initialize an I/O operation on a different disk drive.

Current control units use multiple microprocessors and support internal caches that allow them to perform sophisticated data management functions such as error detection and correction, command retry, multiple track operation, channel switching, and string switching. These last two functions greatly improve access to secondary storage devices by providing multiple paths from channels to devices and vice versa.

Having multiple paths reduces the probability that an I/O operation will be delayed because a channel leading to the requested device is busy, since another channel (also connected to that device) may be available to execute the request.

Control units with two, four, and eight channel switches are presently available (Prasad, 1989).

String switching refers to the case in which a string of disk drives can be connected to more than one control unit, which increases the availability of the system because multiple paths are established between device and channel.

The last component of the channel subsystem, the disk drive, also has undergone major improvements. One is the increase in density, allowing for larger storage capacities. The other is in the support of multiprocessing, a direct result of the low cost of microprocessors. This evolution provides disk drives with sophisticated functions such as multiple paths, rotational position sensing, and dynamic reconnection. This last capability allows a device to reconnect to any available channel, which, together with channel switching, reduces the probability that the completion of an I/O operation will be delayed because a channel is busy. Instead another channel can be used.

An input/output operation is regarded as a unit of work distributed among the components in Figure 16.10. When a program issues an I/O command all those components cooperate in its execution, beginning with the I/O Supervisor (IOS), which is responsible for starting I/O operations and for monitoring the events taking place in devices, control units, and channels. Before starting an I/O operation, IOS makes sure that a data path to the device is available and that a channel program is provided by the IOS drivers. It then stores the address of the channel program in the Channel Address Word (CAW), a special location in memory, and issues a "Start I/O" (SIO) instruction. When the I/O operation is completed, IOS handles the termination process and restores the availability of I/O resources: channels, control units, and devices.

I/O SUPERVISOR (IOS) DRIVER

These are the programs and access methods that interface directly with IOS. Most of the access methods use Execute Channel Programs (EXCP) to interface with IOS. The driver fixes control blocks in real storage and converts the virtual storage address of the Channel Command Words (CCW) into a real storage address. It then signals IOS to issue a "Start I/O" (SIO) command. At this point IOS gets control and, if a path is available, it starts the I/O operation. If the request can't be started immediately, IOS puts the request on a queue for future execution.

VIRTUAL I/O

Virtual I/O (VIO) is a module in MVS used to handle temporary files by using only virtual storage or paging space. The application program isn't aware that it's not using a real DASD file because VIO simulates a virtual track for the DASD device and writes to auxiliary storage only when the virtual track is full.

One of the advantages of VIO is the elimination of device allocation and data management overhead — that's because VTOC search and update have been eliminated. Another advantage is more efficient use of DASD space if the virtual track size is less than 4,096 bytes (Katzan & Tharayil, 1984).

FILE MANAGEMENT

File management falls under the control of the data management module, as shown in Figure 16.9. File management activities are performed by catalog management, I/O support, and access method submodules.

CATALOG MANAGEMENT

Catalog management routines are used by other components of the system and by the application programs to locate and update information in a catalog. In MVS the master catalog is a VSAM (Virtual Storage Access Method) file that contains an entry for each cataloged file. The following example will help illustrate this.

Each file used by a program must be described in a special DD (Data Definition) statement, which is part of the JCL statements preceding any job. The DD statement tells the system which I/O device to use, the volume serial number of any specific volume needed, the data set name, whether old data is being read or new data generated, and what to do with the data when the job ends. This is a typical DD statement:

```
//DATAIN DD DSN=TESTDAT,DISP=(OLD,KEEP),
//    UNIT=2314, VOL=SER=PACK10
```

In this example,

DATAIN is the name of the DD statement;

DD means this is a Data Definition statement;

DSN stands for "Data Set Name" ("data sets" is the name used for files in this environment);

TESTDAT is the name of the file requested;

DISP stands for "Disposition" for this file;

OLD,KEEP indicates that the file TESTDAT is an "old" file and should be "kept" after being used;

, the comma at the end means this instruction is continued on the next line;

// the space after the two slashes means this is continued from the previous line;

UNIT=2314 says that the file resides on a Model 2314 disk pack;

VOL=SER=PACK10 means PACK10 is the serial number of the volume or disk pack.

If the user had cataloged the file TESTDAT during a previous execution by activating the catalog management routine with the DISP=(NEW,CATL) parameter, then the file's name and location and the type of I/O devices needed are already stored in the catalog. Therefore the DD statement is shorter and doesn't include the second line shown above. The DD statement for a cataloged file would be:

```
//DATAIN DD DSN=TESTDAT,DISP=(OLD,KEEP)
```

In this example, the user is accessing the file using its name, TESTDAT, without specifying the type of I/O unit or the volume and serial number. They are not needed because that information is recorded in the system's catalog, which is searched by catalog management, and establishes the connection between a file name and its physical location. Users communicate with catalog management through the DISP parameter of the Data Definition JCL (Davis, 1987).

I/O SUPPORT

The OPEN and CLOSE commands in users' programs activate the routines classified under I/O support. All files must be opened before they can be used and closed after processing is completed. When a file is opened, the OPEN routine creates all the internal tables needed to keep track of the I/O operations, positions the file to the starting point, and gets the file ready for processing by passing control to the routines that execute access methods.

When a file is closed, the CLOSE routine releases all buffers and tables associated with it, deallocates any tape drives used, releases temporary DASD, writes end of file marks, and updates file labels. And in the case of direct access storage, it updates information in the Volume Table of Contents (VTOC).

To accommodate multivolume files, MVS provides an End of Volume (EOV) command, which becomes part of the DD statement. This command makes it possible for application programs to process multivolume files without knowing when the end of one volume has been reached and the next volume's processing has started. The following example will illustrate this point.

```
// DATAIN DD DSN=TESTDAT,DISP=(OLD,KEEP),
//    UNIT=TAPE,VOL=SER=(004001,004002),CHKPT=EOV
```

This instruction says that the file TESTDAT resides on two tapes, 4001 and 4002. The CHKPT=EOV says that a checkpoint will be taken at the end of tape 4001, at which point the routine EOV will write the trailer file labels, rewind the tape, and request the operator to mount the next tape. This example is for an input file. If it had been an output file, the EOV would have requested the operator to mount a new tape for the additional output.

If the file had been a DASD output file, EOV would get more space on a new volume and would update the VTOC entry for that file.

ACCESS METHODS

Access method routines are used to move data between main memory and an I/O device. MVS provides two ways of reading and writing: basic and queued.

When in the *basic access method,* a READ or WRITE command from the user's program starts the transfer of data between main memory and the I/O device. I/O operations are overlapped with CPU functions so the program may continue to execute while the I/O operation is being completed. It's the user's responsibility to provide the buffers and to synchronize the I/O. That means that the user must ensure that a buffer is completely written before moving more data into it. This type of access method gives the user almost complete control over I/O, but it requires detailed effort on the part of the individual.

In the *queued access method* the system does all the buffering and synchronization. The program GETs or PUTs (those are the READ and WRITE operations, respectively) a record, and the system does all the I/O, buffering, blocking, and deblocking. This type of access is the easiest to use and is provided in all the language compilers supported by MVS (Katzan & Tharayil, 1984).

In addition to being grouped into basic or queued, there are five access methods that reflect the types of file organizations.

SEQUENTIAL ACCESS There are two sequential access method routines.

BSAM — Basic Sequential Access Method is used for files with records that are sequentially organized and are stored or retrieved in physical blocks.

QSAM — Queued Sequential Access Method is the queued version of BSAM with the addition of being able to perform logical, buffered record operations.

INDEXED SEQUENTIAL ACCESS There is one indexed sequential access method routine.

ISAM — Indexed Sequential Access Method is used for files with records that are logically ordered according to a key and where indices are maintained to facilitate record retrieval by using the key field.

Access to ISAM files can be through either QISAM (Queued Indexed Sequential Access Method), which provides sequential access to the records, or BISAM (Basic Indexed Sequential Access Method), which provides direct access to the records.

DIRECT ACCESS There is one direct access method routine.

BDAM — Basic Direct Access Method is used for files with records that are organized in a way to meet the user's needs and where the user must provide an address to access a record on the direct access device.

PARTITIONED ACCESS MVS has one partitioned access method routine.

BPAM — Basic Partitioned Access Method is used most often for subroutines and program libraries since one subroutine or program can be selected or replaced without disturbing the others. The partitioned file consists of a directory of all the files included in the set. Each entry contains the file's name and a pointer to its location within the set. Each file in the set is called a "member" and can be concatenated, thus allowing for the whole set of files to be processed sequentially. Figure 16.11 shows the partitioned organization.

The four access methods discussed thus far were present in earlier systems, MFT and MVT (see Table 16.1), and are supported by MVS for compatibility reasons.

VIRTUAL STORAGE ACCESS With VSAM — Virtual Storage Access Method — MVS provides an access method specifically designed to take advantage of virtual storage.

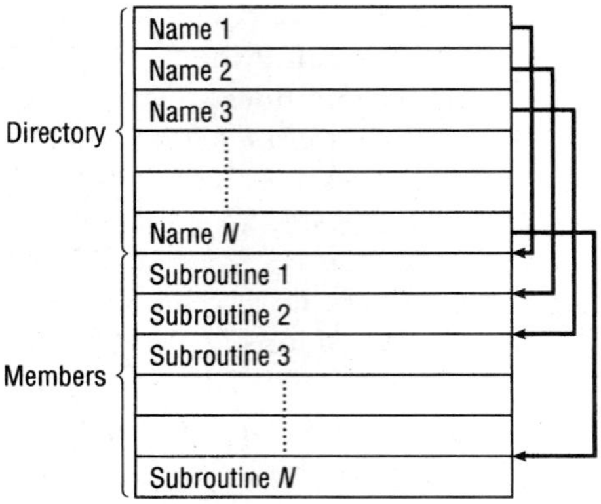

FIGURE 16.11 *Partitioned organization. Once a member has been located through the directory it's read sequentially.*

VSAM can process three different types of files: key-sequenced, entry-sequenced, and relative record.

In key-sequenced files, each record has a "key" that is used to load records in sequence. When new records are added, the sequence is preserved.

For entry-sequenced files, records are loaded sequentially and new records are appended at the end of the file. Under this mode VSAM stores the record and returns its relative byte address to the user's program, which, in turn, may create its own index to allow it to directly access each record.

Relative record files have their records loaded according to a relative record number, which can be assigned by VSAM or by the user's program. If VSAM assigns the relative record number, then new records are appended to the end of the file. On the other hand, if the user's program assigns the relative record numbers, new records are loaded in relative record sequence.

In the case of relative record files, the records occupy fixed-length storage locations that are numbered from one to the maximum number of records in the file. Record storage and retrieval is done through storage location number, which allows for either sequential or direct record access. Direct record access in this type of file is a much faster way to retrieve records than direct access in key-sequenced files.

VSAM provides for the creation of alternate indices to support multiple entries to files that use either the key-sequence or entry-sequence record organization. This eliminates the need to keep several copies of the same file to accommodate different application programs.

In general, the advantage of these access method routines is that they remove device-dependent coding, channel programming, and buffer management from application programs and thereby greatly enhance data management.

SPACE ALLOCATION

A Volume Table of Contents (VTOC) is maintained by data management on each DASD volume. This is a directory of existing files and free space. The VTOC usually occupies two cylinders and is located either at the beginning or in the middle of the disk pack. Placing the VTOC in the first cylinders maximizes the largest contiguous amount of space that can be allocated. Placing it in the middle minimizes seek time because, on the average, the arm has half as far to travel between

VTOC and a requested file. The position of the VTOC is determined when the volume is initialized, which must be done before it's ready to be used. When a volume is initialized: (1) the volume label is created, (2) space for the VTOC is allocated, and (3) each track is initialized.

Storage on DASD volumes is allocated by tracks; the minimum amount allocated is one track. When space is requested the VTOC is searched for free space entries, the space is allocated, and the VTOC is updated. If contiguous space isn't available, data management tries to satisfy the request with up to five noncontiguous blocks of storage, called extents.

Space for any file is done in JCL through the `SPACE` statement. Depending on whether you need a cylinder, track, or block of space, the format is this (Brown, 1977):

```
//SPACE=(CYL, (primary, secondary, [index or directory]))
//SPACE=(TRK, (primary, secondary, [index or directory]))
//SPACE=(BLOCKSIZE, (primary, secondary, [index or directory]))
```

The first parameter (`CYL`, `TRK`, or `BLOCKSIZE`) offers a choice of requesting cylinders, tracks, or blocks of space. If `CYL` or `TRK` are not specified, `BLOCKSIZE` is assumed. In fact, it's usually the most convenient way of requesting space since a block corresponds to the way in which a program will handle storage of the data. `BLOCKSIZE` is a device-independent way to request space so that the same amount of space is allocated regardless of the device type.

The second and third parameters (primary, secondary) found in each of the statements indicate the amount of space to be allocated to the "primary storage area" and "secondary storage area." The primary storage area is where the file will be stored when first created. When this space is completely filled up, the file can continue to grow into the secondary storage area.

When computing the amount of space required, the user must consider the device type, track capacity, tracks per cylinder, cylinders per volume, block size, key length, and device overhead. Device overhead refers to address markers and interblock gaps and varies with each device. This isn't as bad as it sounds because all installations have tables with the information needed and the formulas used to carry out the computation.

The third parameter found in each of the statements (index or directory) provides a choice of requesting either an index (for ISAM files), or a directory (for partitioned files). Space for the directory is allocated in units of 256-byte blocks, which can hold up to five member names. To estimate the number of directory blocks, divide the total number of members by 5 and round up the quotient to the next integer. Space for the index is computed by the user using the appropriate formula and is based on the number of records to be stored, the number of tracks per cylinder, and the number of index entries per track.

For instance, the following `SPACE` statement shows how to request space for a partitioned file with 32 members:

```
//SPACE=(1000, (10,20,7))
```

Since neither of the reserved words `TRK` or `CYL` are present, this is a request for blocks of space: 10 blocks of 1000 bytes each for primary storage area, 20 blocks of 1000 bytes each for every extent (used for secondary storage areas), and 7 directory blocks.

USER INTERFACE

Unlike the other operating systems we've discussed so far, MVS is used primarily for very large mainframes running numerous batch jobs concurrently. Although time-sharing is supported by the Time-Sharing Option (TSO) the user/computer interface still reflects its early development to process batch programs.

The user's command language statements perform six primary functions: introduce a job to the operating system, identify its owner, request peripheral device support, identify files that will be used during the execution of the job, request secondary storage space, and execute the job.

The system operator has access to additional commands to intervene as a program runs, if problems should occur.

The system's database administrator, who is considered a "super user," has access to the full set of commands. In a hierarchical structure, the database administrator can use the complete set of commands, the operator has access to a subset, and the users have access to the smallest subset (Brown, 1977).

JCL is a complex language — it allows skilled experts to perform almost any task. JCL is also repetitive: the average programmer needs to use only a small subset of the command language statements to perform basic activities. It has few default values and makes few or no assumptions for the user. Therefore, it must be told explicitly what to do with every job. It consists of individual parameters, each of which has an effect that may take pages to describe.

Some familiarity with a high-level language such as Pascal, COBOL, or FORTRAN is helpful, but not necessary, to understand JCL.

JCL statements can be grouped as follows:

1. `JOB` statements are primarily used to separate and identify jobs. Two of their secondary functions are to pass information to the system accounting and to pass priority information to the operating system. This is the first command in the list.
2. `EXEC` statements are used to identify programs to be executed. They follow the `JOB` statement.
3. `DD` statements are used to define in detail the characteristics of each peripheral device used by the job. They request the allocation of I/O devices (Davis, 1987).

The general format of a JCL statement is this:

```
//NAME  OPERATION  OPERAND  COMMENTS
```

The two slashes (//) always fall in the first two columns of the statement.

The NAME field identifies the statement so that other statements or systems control blocks can refer to it. The NAME can range from one to eight alphanumeric characters. The first character of the name must immediately follow the two slashes (must be in column 3) and must be an alpha character.

The OPERATION field specifies the type of statement: JOB, EXEC, or DD.

The OPERAND field contains parameters separated by commas and provides detailed information about the job, job step, or file. This field has no fixed length or column requirements.

The COMMENTS field is optional, but it can only be coded if there is an OPERAND field.

All fields must be separated by a space, and the information coded can't extend beyond column 71 (Brown, 1977).

If a statement must be continued on the next line, then the first line must end with a comma and the second line must begin with two slashes (//) followed by a blank space. Comment lines can be interspersed between command statements by starting the line with //* followed by a blank space.

EXAMPLE 1

```
//INVENT JOB 3943,MCHOES,CLASS=A,TIME=3
//*     Written by IMF, 2-6-90
```

The name of the job is INVENT.

This is a new job.

The cost of running this job will be charged to account 3943.

The name of the programmer is McHoes.

The CLASS parameter is used to improve the efficiency of a batch system by allowing the operating system to group jobs with similar resource needs.

The TIME parameter is included to specify the number of minutes or seconds a job is to run. In this example, 3 minutes have been requested.

The entire second line is a comment line and is not executable.

All parameters in the operand field must be separated by commas without any spaces in between.

This statement uses two kinds of parameters. CLASS and TIME are "keyword parameters," meaning that they are identified by their reserved words — they can be positioned in any order in the JOB statement. On the other hand, the accounting parameters (account number, programmer name, etc.) are "positional parameters"; that means they are identified by their position and must be coded in the order prescribed by the JCL manual. This example includes only a few of the many parameters that can be used with the JOB statement.

EXAMPLE 2

```
//STEP6 EXEC PROG=SORTNAME
```

The first entry indicates the "stepname." This is an optional field that is included only if subsequent JCL statements refer to this job step or if the programmer wishes to restart the job from that step.

EXEC indicates that the program or procedure named next is to be executed.

PROG=SORTNAME names the program to be executed. This entry can be substituted with PROC=FORTRAN if a cataloged procedure is to be used. In this case the operating system searches the procedure library for the procedure that's named and replaces this EXEC statement with a set of precoded JCL statements.

EXAMPLE 3

```
//PRINTER DD UNIT=008
```

This statement requests a printer identified as device number 8 on channel 0. Every peripheral device attached to an IBM system is identified by a three-digit hexadecimal number — the number for this specific printer is 008.

EXAMPLE 4

```
//OUTPUT DD UNIT=3330,DCB=(DSORG=PS,LRECL=80,
// BLKSIZE=1600,RECFM=FB)
```

In the example, UNIT=3330 identifies any disk device model number 3330 available.

DCB stands for Data Control Block, and the parameters following it will be included in the program Data Control Block when the file is opened.

DSORG stands for Data Set Organization and indicates the organization of the file (or data set). In this example, the file organization is PS, which stands for Physical Sequential.

LRECL stands for Logical Record Length and specifies the length of the logical record in bytes. It is used when defining either fixed- or variable-length records, and it's omitted for records of undefined length. In this case each logical record is 80 bytes long.

BLKSIZE stands for Block Size and specifies the size of the block in bytes. The block size must be a multiple of the logical record length and can range from 1 to 32,760 bytes for direct access storage devices (Brown, 1977).

RECFM stands for Record Format and is composed of one or more characters, each indicating a specific characteristic of the record described. In this example, F indicates fixed-length records and B indicates that the records are blocked.

Three other parameters used in the DD statements are (1) the disposition (DISP) parameter, which tells the system what to do with a disk file — for example, KEEP or DELETE or CATLG — and tells the system the status of the file — for example, NEW if the file is to be created or OLD if the file already exists; (2) the VOLUME or VOL parameter, which specifies a particular disk pack by its serial number; (3) the SPACE parameter, which requires programmers to estimate their secondary storage space requirements by indicating the number of tracks, the number of cylinders, or the number of bytes needed.

Magnetic tape DD statements are very similar to those used for direct access storage devices. Although it was once the most common secondary storage medium, magnetic tape is now used primarily for backup and to transmit files between computer centers.

Under the Time-Sharing Option (TSO) users can allocate and deallocate files during execution by providing the number of files to be dynamically allocated using the DYNAMNBR parameter in the EXEC statement. They can also ask the system to notify them when their batch jobs terminate by using the NOTIFY parameter in the JOB statement.

CHAPTER SIXTEEN CONCLUSION

For the large mainframes it was designed to operate, the MVS has been improved over the years to give better performance. It has also kept up with the changing demands of users with the incorporation of time-sharing and telecommunication facilities.

Part of its success can be attributed to the portability of software from version to version throughout its evolution. MVS has been designed to allow software from older systems to run on the new machines.

A weakness of MVS is its Job Control Language, which is difficult and very time-consuming to master.

Appendix A

COMMAND TRANSLATION TABLE FOR MS-DOS, UNIX, AND VAX/VMS

Although each operating system has a unique collection of user commands, many are comparable across systems and perform approximately the same functions. Here is a general comparison of MS-DOS, UNIX, and VAX/VMS commands. (IBM's Job Control Language doesn't have comparable commands and Windows NT is menu driven.) Be aware, however, that most commands require additional information, such as parameters, arguments, switches, and so on. And many UNIX commands are version- and vendor-specific. For complete command construction, see a technical manual for your system.

Command	MS-DOS	UNIX	VAX/VMS
1. Execute a file	(file name)	(file name)	RUN (file name)
2. List files in this directory	DIR	ls	DIRECTORY
3. Change directory	CD *or* CHDIR	cd	SET DEFAULT
4. Copy a file	COPY	cp	COPY
5. Delete a file	DEL *or* ERASE	rm	DELETE
6. Rename a file	RENAME	mv	RENAME
7. List the contents of a file to the screen	TYPE	more *or* cat	TYPE
8. Print files on a printer	PRINT	lpr	PRINT
9. Show system date	DATE	date	SHOW TIME
10. Show system time	TIME	date	SHOW TIME
11. Make a new directory	MD *or* MKDIR	mkdir	CREATE
12. Search files for a string	FIND	grep	SEARCH
13. Append one file to another	COPY	cat	APPEND
14. Format a volume	FORMAT	format *or* mkfs	—
15. Check the disk	CHKDSK	du	—
16. Compare two files	COMP	diff	—
17. Change the system prompt symbol	PROMPT	*	—
18. Provide help	—	help	HELP

*The user can change the UNIX system prompt by placing the appropriate command in the user's profile or login file. The exact command varies from system to system. See your documentation for details.

NOTES:

1. MS-DOS commands can be in upper or lower case but cannot be abbreviated.
2. UNIX commands must be in lower case. Although file names can be in upper or lower case, all lower-case names are the norm.
3. VAX/VMS commands can be in upper or lower case. Many commands can be abbreviated — see a technical manual for details.
4. A dash — indicates that there is no comparable command available.

Appendix B

GUIDE TO IBM/MVS VOCABULARY

To work with an IBM operating system, one must learn the acronyms used in Chapter 16 to describe hardware and software. Here are the full names for the terms used in this book in alphabetical order. For more detail refer to the technical documentation for your system.

BDAM	Basic Direct Access Method
BISAM	Basic Indexed Sequential Access Method
BLKSIZE	Block Size
BPAM	Basic Partitioned Access Method
BSAM	Basic Sequential Access Method
CAW	Channel Address Word
CCW	Channel Command Word
CICS	Customer Information Control Systems
CSA	Common System Area
CVT	Communications Vector Table
DAT	Dynamic Address Translation
DCB	Data Control Block
DD	Data Definition
DISP	Disposition Parameter
DSCB	Data Storage Control Block
DSORG	Data Set Organization
EOV	End of Volume
EPS	External Page Storage
EXCP	Execute Channel Programs
IMS	Information Management System
IOS	I/O Supervisor
ISAM	Indexed Sequential Access Method
JCL	Job Control Language
JES	Job Entry Subsystem
LRECL	Logical Record Length
LSQA	Local System Queue Area
MVS	Multiple Virtual Storage System
MVS/XA	Multiple Virtual Storage System with Extended Architecture
PLPA	Pageable Link Pack Area
PRB	Program Request Block
PSW	Program Status Word

RECFM	Record Format
QISAM	Queued Indexed Sequential Access Method
QSAM	Queued Sequential Access Method
SIO	Start I/O
SVC	Supervisor Call
SVRB	Supervisor Request Block
SQA	System Queue Area
SWA	Scheduler Work Area
TCAM	Telecommunication Access Method
TCB	Task Control Block
TLB	Translation Lookaside Buffer
TSO	Time-Sharing Option
VIO	Virtual I/O
VSAM	Virtual Storage Access Method
VTAM	Virtual Telecommunications Access Method
VTOC	Volume Table of Contents
XA	Extended Architecture

Appendix C

GUIDE TO MICROSOFT VOCABULARY

Here are the acronyms and full names used in Chapters 12 and 13, on Microsoft's operating systems MS-DOS and Windows NT, in alphabetical order. For more detail refer to the technical documentation for your system.

ACE	Access Control Entry
ACL	Access Control List
API	Application Program Interface
BIOS	Basic Input/Output System
CDFS	CD-ROM File System
CP/M	Control Program for Microcomputers
DACL	Discretionary Access Control List
DLL	Dynamic Link Library
DOS	Disk Operating System
DPC	Deferred Procedure Call
FAT	File Allocation Table
GUI	Graphical User Interface
HAL	Hardware Abstraction Layer
IFS	Installable File System
IOS	Input/Output Supervisor
IRP	I/O Request Packet
LPC	Local Procedure Call
NetBEUI	Net BIOS Extended User Interface
NDIS	Network Driver Interface Specification
NPI	Network Provider Interface
NT	New Technology
NTFS	New Technology File System
PSP	Program Segment Prefix
RAM	Random Access Memory
ROM	Read Only Memory
RPC	Remote Procedure Call
SACL	System Access Control List
SCSI	Small Computer System Interface
SMB	Server Message Block
SMP	Symmetric Multiprocessing
TCP/IP	Transmission Control Protocol/Internet Protocol

TDI	Transport Driver Interface
TLB	Translation Lookaside Buffer
TPA	Transient Program Area
UPS	Uninterruptible Power Supply
VFAT	Virtual File Allocation Table

Appendix D

GUIDE TO GRAPHICAL USER INTERFACES

Many popular graphical user interfaces (GUIs) share several similarities in both appearance and operation. Here are samples of windows from three popular operating systems: Windows NT, Macintosh System 7, and Windows 95.

A Windows NT desktop with one open window. To close a window double click on the square in the upperleft corner. To minimize a window click on the upside-down triangle in the upper right. To maximize a window click on the triangle in the upper right. To run an application, double click on its icon or click once and press the Enter key.

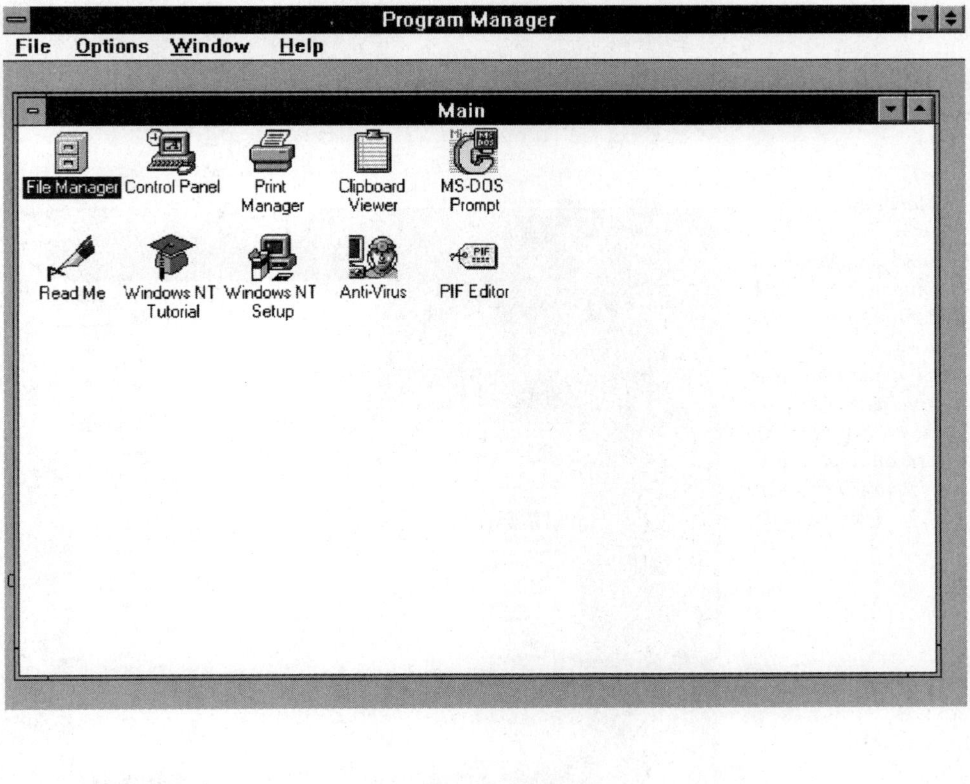

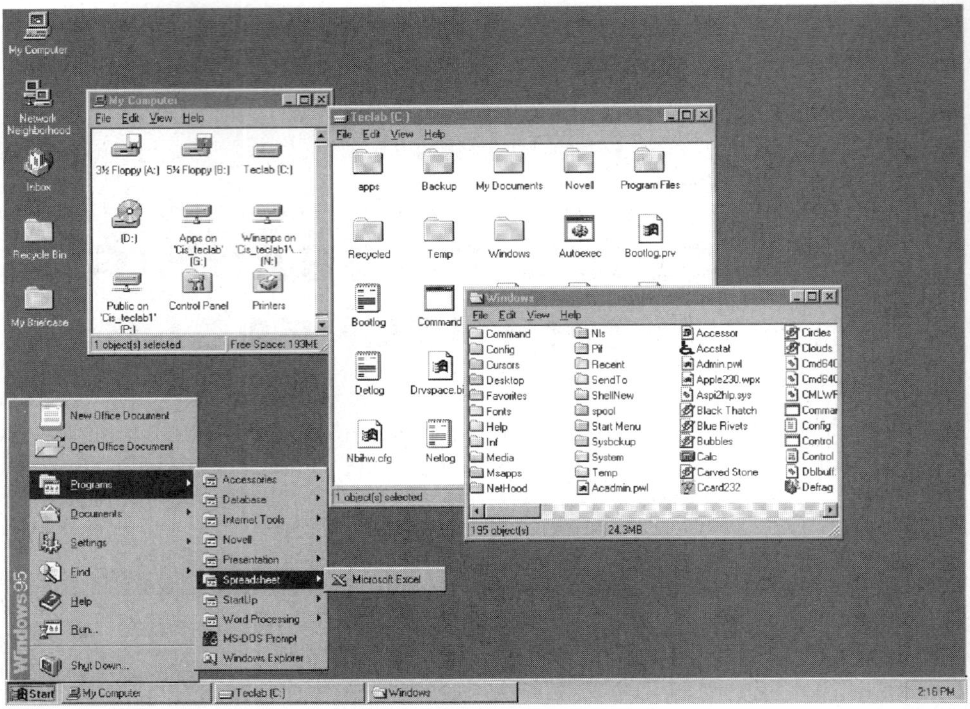

A Windows 95 desktop with several windows. To close the window double click on the 'x' in the upper right corner. To minimize the window click on the minus sign in the upper right. To maximize a window click on the square (located between the 'x' and the minus sign) in the upper right. To run an application, double click on its icon or click once and press the Enter key.

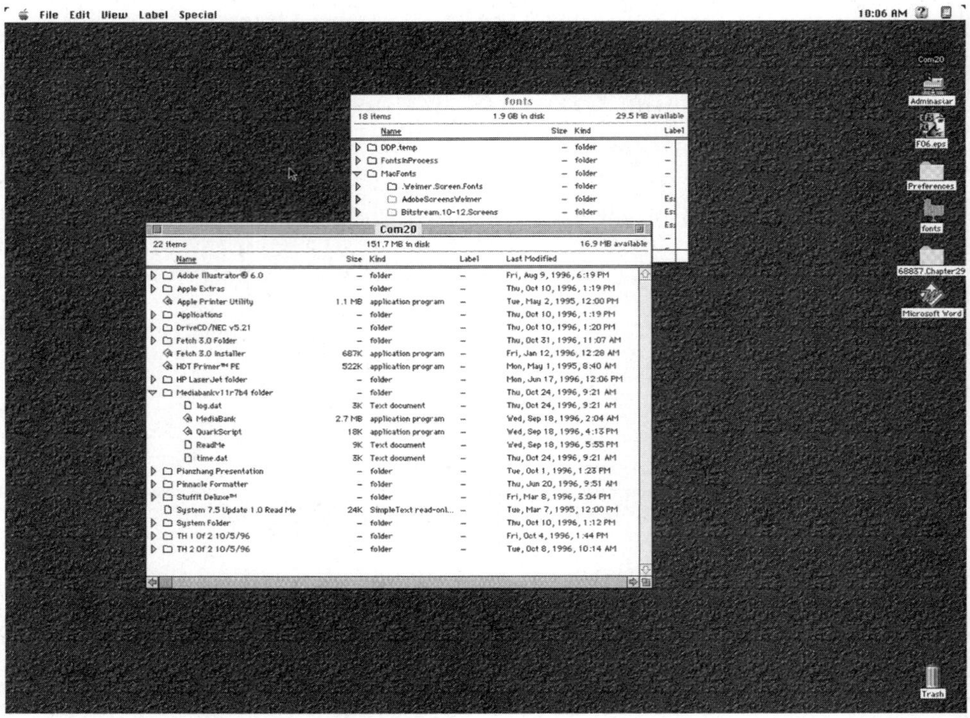

Macintosh System 7 desktop with two open windows. To close a window click on the square in the upper left corner. To resize a window click on the intersecting squares in the upper right. To run an application, double click on its icon or name.

Glossary

absolute file name: a file's name, as given by the user, preceded by the directory (or directories) where the file is found and, when necessary, the specific device label.

access control list: an access control method that lists each file, the names of the users who are allowed to access it, and the type of access each is permitted.

access control matrix: an access control method that uses a matrix with every file (listed in rows) and every user (listed in columns) and the type of access each user is permitted on each file, recorded in the cell at the intersection of that row and column.

access control verification module: the section of the File Manager that verifies which users are permitted to perform which operations with each file.

access time: the total time required to access data in secondary storage. For a direct access storage device with movable read/write heads, it's the sum of seek time (arm movement), search time (rotational delay), and transfer time (data transfer).

access token: an object in Windows NT that uniquely identifies a user who has logged on. An access token is appended to all the user's processes and contains the user's security ID, the names of the groups to which the user belongs, any privileges the user owns, the default owner of any objects the user's processes create, and the default access control list to be applied to any objects the user's processes create.

active multiprogramming: a term used to indicate that the operating system has more control over interrupts designed to fairly distribute CPU utilization over several resident programs. It contrasts with *passive multiprogramming.*

activity: the term used by UNIVAC to describe a process.

Ada: a high-level concurrent programming language developed by the Department of Defense and made available to the public in 1980.

address: a number that designates a particular memory location.

address resolution: the process of changing the address of an instruction or data item to the address in main memory at which it is to be loaded or relocated.

Advanced Research Projects Agency network (ARPAnet): a pioneering long-distance network funded by ARPA (now DARPA). It served as the basis for early networking research, as well as a central backbone during the development of the Internet. The ARPAnet consisted of individual packet switching computers interconnected by leased lines.

aging: a policy used to ensure that jobs that have been in the system for a long time in the lower level queues will eventually complete their execution.

algorithm: a set of step-by-step instructions used to solve a particular problem. It can be stated in any form, such as mathematical formulas, diagrams, or natural or programming languages.

allocation module: the section of the File Manager responsible for keeping track of unused areas in each storage device.

allocation scheme: the process of assigning specific resources to a job so it can execute.

anonymous ftp: a use of ftp that allows a user to retrieve documents, files, programs, and other data from anywhere in the Internet without having to establish a user ID and password. By using the special user ID of "anonymous" the network user is allowed to bypass local security checks and have access to publicly accessible files on the remote system.

ARPAnet: see *Advanced Research Projects Agency network.*

assembler: a computer program that translates programs from assembly language to machine language.

assembly language: a programming language that allows users to write programs using mnemonic instructions that can be translated by an assembler. It is considered a low-level programming language and is very computer dependent.

associative memory: the name given to several registers, allocated to each active process, whose contents associate several of the process segments and page numbers with their main memory addresses.

availability: a resource measurement tool that indicates the likelihood that the resource will be ready when a user needs it. It's influenced by mean time between failures and mean time to repair.

avoidance: the strategy of deadlock avoidance. It is a dynamic strategy attempting to ensure that resources are never allocated in such a way as to place a system in an unsafe state.

backup: the process of making long-term archival file storage copies of files on the system.

batch system: a type of system developed for the earliest computers that used punched cards or tape for input. Each job was entered by assembling the cards together into a "deck" and several jobs were grouped, or "batched," together before being sent through the card reader.

Belady's anomaly: points to the fact that for some paging algorithms the page fault rate may increase as the number of allocated page frames increases. Also called *FIFO anomaly.*

benchmarks: a measurement tool used to objectively measure and evaluate a system's performance by running a set of jobs representative of the work normally done by a computer system.

best-fit memory allocation: a main memory allocation scheme that considers all free blocks and selects for allocation the one that will result in the least amount of wasted space. It contrasts with the *first-fit memory allocation.*

blocking: a storage-saving and I/O-saving technique that groups individual records into a block that's stored and retrieved as a unit. The size of the block is often set to take advantage of the transfer rate.

bootstrapping: the process of starting an inactive computer by using a small initialization program to load other programs.

bounds register: a register used to store the highest location in memory legally accessible by each program. It contrasts with *relocation register.*

bridge: a data-link layer device used to interconnect multiple networks. A bridge is used to create an extended network so that all individual networks appear to be part of one larger network.

browsing: a system security violation in which unauthorized users are allowed to search through secondary storage directories or files for information they should not have the privilege to read.

B-tree: a special case of a binary tree structure used to locate and retrieve records stored in disk files. The qualifications imposed on a B-tree structure reduce the amount of time it takes to search through the B-tree, making it an ideal file organization for large files.

buffers: the temporary storage areas residing in main memory, channels, and control units. They're used to store data read from an input device before it's needed by the processor and to store data that will be written to an output device.

bus: (1) the physical channel that links the hardware components and allows for transfer of data and electrical signals; or (2) a shared communication link onto which multiple nodes may connect.

bus topology: a network architecture in which elements are connected together along a single link.

busy waiting: a method by which processes, waiting for an event to occur, continuously test to see if the condition has changed and remain in unproductive, resource-consuming wait loops.

cache memory: a small, fast memory used to hold selected data and to provide faster access than would otherwise be possible.

capability list: an access control method that lists every user, the files to which each has access, and the type of access allowed to those files.

capacity: the maximum throughput level of any one of the system's components.

Carrier Sense Multiple Access with Collision Avoidance (CSMA/CA): a method used to avoid transmission collision on shared media such as networks. It usually prevents collisions by requiring token acquisition.

Carrier Sense Multiple Access with Collision Detection (CSMA/CD): a method used to detect transmission collision on shared media such as networks. It is used to detect transmission collision and require that the affected stations stop transmitting immediately and try again after delaying a random amount of time.

CD-ROM: compact disk read only memory; a direct access storage medium that can store large quantities of data including pictures and audio.

Central Processing Unit (CPU): the component with the circuitry, the "chips," to control the interpretation and execution of instructions. In essence, it controls the operation of the entire computer system. All storage references, data manipulations, and I/O operations are initiated or performed by the CPU.

channel: see *I/O channel.*

channel program: see *I/O channel program.*

Channel Status Word (CSW): a data structure that contains information indicating the condition of the channel, including three bits for the three components of the I/O subsystem — one each for the channel, control unit, and device.

circuit switching: a communication model in which a dedicated communication path is established between two hosts, and on which all messages travel. The telephone system is an example of a circuit switched network.

circular wait: one of four conditions for deadlock through which each process involved is waiting for a resource being held by another; each process is blocked and can't continue, resulting in deadlock.

client: a user node that requests and makes use of various network services. A workstation requesting the contents of a file from a file server is a client of the file server.

C-LOOK: a scheduling strategy for direct access storage devices that's an optimization of C-SCAN.

`COBEGIN`: used with `COEND` to indicate to a multiprocessing compiler the beginning of a section where instructions can be processed concurrently.

`COEND`: used with `COBEGIN` to indicate to a multiprocessing compiler the end of a section where instructions can be processed concurrently.

collision: when a hashing algorithm generates the same logical address for two records with unique keys.

compaction: the process of collecting fragments of available memory space into contiguous blocks by moving programs and data in a computer's memory or disk. Also called *garbage collection.*

compatibility: the ability of an operating system to execute programs written for other operating systems or for earlier versions of the same system.

compiler: a computer program that translates programs from a high-level programming language (such as FORTRAN, COBOL, Pascal, C, or Ada) into machine language.

complete file name: see *absolute file name.*

compression: see *data compression.*

concurrent processing: execution of a set of processes in such a way that they appear to be happening at the same time. It's typically achieved by interleaved execution.

concurrent programming: a programming technique that allows for the simultaneous execution of sets of instructions.

connect time: in time-sharing, the amount of time that a user is connected to a computer system. It is usually measured by the time elapsed between log on and log off.

contention: a situation that arises on shared resources in which multiple data sources compete for access to the resource.

context switching: the acts of saving a job's processing information in its PCB so the job can be swapped out of memory and of loading the processing information from the PCB of another job into the appropriate registers so the CPU can process it. Context switching occurs in all preemptive policies.

contiguous storage: a type of file storage in which all the information is stored in adjacent locations in a storage medium.

control cards: cards that define the exact nature of each program and its requirements. They contain information that direct the operating system to perform specific functions, such as initiating the execution of a particular job. See *job control language.*

control unit: see *I/O control unit.*

control word: a password given to a file by its creator.

C programming language: a general purpose programming language developed by D. M. Ritchie. It combines high-level statements with low-level machine controls to generate software that is both easy to use and highly efficient. It is the primary language of UNIX.

CPU: an abbreviation for *Central Processing Unit.*

CPU-bound: a job that will perform a great deal of nonstop processing before issuing an interrupt. A CPU-bound job can tie up the CPU for long periods of time while all other jobs must wait. It contrasts with *I/O-bound.*

cracker: an individual who attempts to access computer systems without authorization. These individuals are often malicious, as opposed to "hackers," and have several means at their disposal for breaking into a system.

critical region: the parts of a program that must complete execution before other processes can have access to the resources being used. It's called a critical region because its execution must be handled as a unit.

C-SCAN: a scheduling strategy for direct access storage devices that's used to optimize seek time. It's an abbreviation for circular SCAN.

CSMA/CA: see *Carrier Sense Multiple Access with Collision Avoidance*

CSMA/CD: see *Carrier Sense Multiple Access with Collision Detection*

current byte address (CBA): the address of the last byte read. It is used by the File Manager to access records in secondary storage and must be updated every time a record is accessed, such as when the `READ` command is executed.

current directory: the directory or subdirectory in which the user is working.

cylinder: for a disk or disk pack, it's when two or more read/write heads are positioned at the same track, at the same relative position, on their respective surfaces.

DASD: an abbreviation for *direct access storage device.*

database: a group of related files that are interconnected at various levels to give users flexibility of access to the data stored.

data compression: a procedure used to reduce the amount of space required to store data by reducing encoding or abbreviating repetitive terms or characters.

data file: a file that contains only data.

deadlock: a problem occurring when the resources needed by some jobs to finish execution are held by other jobs, which, in turn, are waiting for other resources to become available. The deadlock is complete if the remainder of the system comes to a standstill as a result of the hold the processes have on the resource allocation scheme. Also called *deadly embrace.*

deadly embrace: a colorful synonym for *deadlock.*

deallocation: the process of freeing an allocated resource, whether memory space, a device, a file, or a CPU.

dedicated device: a device that can be assigned to only one job at a time; it serves that job for the entire time it's active.

demand paging: a memory allocation scheme that loads into memory a program's page at the time it's needed for processing.

detection: the process of examining the state of an operating system to determine whether a deadlock exists.

device: a computer's peripheral unit such as printer, plotter, tape drive, disk drive, or terminal.

device driver: a device-specific program module that handles the interrupts and controls a particular type of device.

device independent: programs that are devoid of the detailed instructions required to interact with any I/O device present in the computer system. This is made possible because the operating system provides an I/O interface that supports uniform I/O regardless of the type of device being used.

device interface module: transforms the block number supplied by the physical file system into the actual cylinder/surface/record combination needed to retrieve the information from a specific secondary storage device.

Device Manager: the section of the operating system responsible for controlling the use of devices. It monitors every device, channel, and control unit and chooses the most efficient way to allocate all of the system's devices.

Dijkstra's algorithm: a graph theory algorithm that has been used in various link state routing protocols. This allows a router to step through an internetwork and find the best path to each destination.

direct access file: see *direct record organization.*

direct access storage device (DASD): any secondary storage device that can directly read or write to a specific place. Also called a *random access storage device.* It contrasts with a *sequential access storage device.*

directed graph: a graphic model representing various states of resource allocations. It consists of processes and resources connected by directed lines (lines with directional arrows).

direct memory access (DMA): an I/O technique that allows a control unit to access main memory directly and transfer data without the intervention of the CPU.

directory: a storage area in a secondary storage volume (disk, disk pack, etc.) containing information about files stored in that volume. The information is used to access those files.

direct record organization: files stored in a direct access storage device and organized to give users the flexibility of accessing any record at random regardless of its position in the file.

disk pack: a removable stack of disks mounted on a common central spindle with spaces between each pair of platters so read/write heads can move between them.

displacement: in a paged or segmented memory allocation environment, it's the difference between a page's relative address and the actual machine language address. It's used to locate an instruction or data value within its page frame. Also called *offset.*

distributed operating system (DOS): an operating system that provides control for a distributed computing system (two or more computers interconnected for a specific purpose), allowing its resources to be accessed in a unified way.

distributed processing: a method of data processing in which files are stored at many different locations and in which processing takes place at different sites.

DNS: see *domain name service.*

Domain Name Service (DNS): is a general purpose distributed, replicated, data query service. Its principal function is the resolution of Internet addresses based on fully qualified domain names such as .com (commercial) or .edu (educational).

DOS: see *distributed operating system.* Also used to identify the MS-DOS operating system.

double buffering: a technique used to speed I/O in which two buffers are present in main memory, channels, and control units.

dynamic partitions: a memory allocation scheme in which jobs are given as much memory as they request when they are loaded for processing, thus creating their own partitions in main memory. It contrasts with *static partitions,* or *fixed partitions.*

elevator algorithm: see *LOOK.*

embedded computer systems: a dedicated computer system that often resides in large physical systems such as jet aircraft or ships. It must be small and fast and work with real-time constraints, fail-safe execution, and nonstandard I/O devices. In some cases it must be able to manage concurrent activities, which requires parallel processing.

encryption: translation of a message or data item from its original form to an encoded form thus hiding its meaning and making it unintelligible without the key to decode it. It's used to improve system security and data protection.

Ethernet: a 10MB standard for LANs, initially developed by Xerox and later refined by Digital Equipment Corporation, Intel, and Xerox. All hosts are connected to a coaxial cable where they contend for network access using CSMA/CD.

explicit parallelism: a type of concurrent programming that requires that the programmer explicitly state which instructions can be executed in parallel. It contrasts with *implicit parallelism.*

extensibility: one of an operating system's design goals that allows it to be easily enhanced as market requirements change.

extension: in some operating systems, it's the part of the file name that indicates which compiler or software package is needed to run the files. UNIX calls it a *suffix.*

extents: any remaining records, and all other additions to the file, that are stored in other sections of the disk. The extents of the file are linked together with pointers.

external fragmentation: a situation in which the dynamic allocation of memory creates unusable fragments of free memory between blocks of busy, or allocated, memory. It contrasts with *internal fragmentation.*

external interrupts: interrupts that occur outside the normal flow of a program's execution. They are used in preemptive scheduling policies to ensure a fair use of the CPU in multiprogramming environments.

FCFS: an abbreviation for *first come first served.*

feedback loop: a mechanism to monitor the system's resource utilization so adjustments can be made.

field: a group of related bytes that can be identified by the user with a name, type, and size. A record is made up of fields.

FIFO: an abbreviation for *first in first out.*

FIFO anomaly: an unusual circumstance through which adding more page frames causes an increase in page interrupts when using a FIFO page replacement policy. Also called *Belady's anomaly.*

file: a group of related records that contains information to be used by specific application programs to generate reports.

file descriptor: information kept in the directory to describe a file or file extent. It contains the file's name, location, and attributes.

File Manager: the section of the operating system responsible for controlling the use of files. It tracks every file in the system including data files, assemblers, compilers, and application programs. By using predetermined access policies, it enforces access restrictions on each file.

file server: a dedicated network node that provides mass data storage for other nodes on the network.

File Transfer Protocol (FTP): a protocol that allows a user on one host to access and transfer files to or from another host over a TCP/IP network.

FINISHED: a job status that means that execution of the job has been completed.

firmware: software instructions or data that are stored in a fixed or "firm" way, usually implemented on *Read Only Memory* (ROM). Firmware is built into the computer to make its operation simpler for the user to understand.

first come first served (FCFS): (1) the simplest scheduling algorithm for direct access storage devices that satisfies track requests in the order in which they are received; (2) a nonpreemptive process scheduling policy (or algorithm) that handles jobs according to their arrival time; the first job in the READY queue will be processed first by the CPU.

first-fit memory allocation: a main memory allocation scheme that searches from the beginning of the free block list and selects for allocation the first block of memory large enough to fulfill the request. It contrasts with *best-fit memory allocation.*

first generation (1940–1955): the era of the first computers characterized by their use of vacuum tubes and their very large physical size.

first-in first-out (FIFO) policy: a page replacement policy that removes from main memory the pages that were brought in first. It's based on the assumption that these pages are the least likely to be used again in the near future.

fixed-length record: a record that always contains the same number of characters. It contrasts with *variable-length record.*

fixed partitions: a memory allocation scheme in which main memory was sectioned off in early multiprogramming systems. At system initialization memory was divided into fixed partitions of various sizes to accommodate programming needs of users. Also called *static partitions.* It contrasts with *dynamic partitions.*

floppy disk: a removable flexible disk that provides low-cost, direct access secondary storage for personal computer systems.

fragmentation: a condition in main memory where wasted memory space exists within partitions, called *internal fragmentation,* or between partitions, called *external fragmentation.*

ftp: the name of the program a user invokes to execute the File Transfer Protocol.

FTP: see *File Transfer Protocol.*

garbage collection: see *compaction.*

gateway: a communications device or program that passes data between networks having similar functions but different protocols.

group: a property of operating systems that enables system administrators to create sets of users that share the same privileges. A group can share files or programs without allowing all system users access to those resources.

groupware: software applications that support cooperative work over a network. Groupware systems must support communications between users and information processing. For example, a system providing a shared editor must support not only the collective amendment of documents, but also discussions between the participants about what is to be amended and why.

graphical user interface (GUI): a user interface that allows the user to activate operating system commands by clicking on a desktop icon using a pointing device such as a mouse or touch screen. GUI evolved from command-driven user interfaces.

GUI: see *graphical user interface.*

hacker: a person who delights in having an intimate understanding of the internal workings of a system — computers and computer networks in particular. The term is often misused in a pejorative context, where "cracker" would be the correct term.

hard disk: a direct access secondary storage device for personal computer systems. It's generally a high-density, nonremovable device.

hardware: the physical machine and its components, including main memory, I/O devices, I/O channels, direct access storage devices, and the central processing unit.

hashing algorithm: the set of instructions used to perform a key-to-address transformation in which a record's key field determines its location. See also *logical address.*

high-level scheduler: another term for the *Job Scheduler.*

`HOLD`: one of the process states. It is assigned to processes waiting to be let into the `READY` queue.

hop: a node network through which a packet passes on the path between the packet's source and destination nodes.

host: the Internet term for a network node that is capable of communicating at the application layer.

hybrid system: a computer system that supports both batch and interactive processes. It appears to be interactive because individual users can access the system via terminals and get fast responses, but it accepts and runs batch programs in the background when the interactive load is light.

hybrid topology: a network architecture that combines other types of network topologies, such as tree and star, to accommodate particular operating characteristics or traffic volumes.

impersonation: in Windows NT, the ability of a thread in one process to take on the security identity of a thread in another process and perform operations on that thread's behalf. Used by environment subsystems and network services when accessing remote resources for client applications.

implicit parallelism: a type of concurrent programming in which the compiler automatically detects which instructions can be performed in parallel. It contrasts with *explicit parallelism.*

indefinite postponement: means that a job's execution is delayed indefinitely because it's repeatedly preempted so other jobs can be processed.

index block: a data structure used with indexed storage allocation. It contains the addresses of each disk sector used by that file.

indexed sequential record organization: a way of organizing data in a direct access storage device. An index is created to show where the data records are stored. Any data record can be retrieved by consulting the index first.

indexed storage: the way in which the File Manager physically allocates space to an indexed sequentially organized file.

interactive system: a system that allows each user to interact directly with the operating system via commands entered from a keyboard. Also called *time-sharing system.*

interblock gap (IBG): an unused space between blocks of records on a magnetic tape.

internal fragmentation: a situation in which a fixed partition is only partially used by the program. The remaining space within the partition is unavailable to any other job and is therefore wasted. It contrasts with *external fragmentation.*

internal interrupts: also called "synchronous" interrupts, they occur as a direct result of the arithmetic operation or job instruction currently being processed. They contrast with *external interrupts.*

internal memory: see *main memory.*

International Organization for Standardization (ISO): a voluntary, non-treaty organization founded in 1946 that is responsible for creating international standards in many areas, including computers and communications. Its members are the national standards organizations of the 89 member countries, including ANSI for the United States.

Internet: the largest collection of networks interconnected with routers. It is a three level hierarchy composed of backbone networks (e.g., NSFNET), mid-level networks (e.g., NEARnet) and local networks. The Internet is a multi-protocol internetwork.

Internet Protocol (IP): the network-layer protocol used to route data from one network to another. It was developed by the United States Department of Defense.

interrecord gap (IRG): an unused space between records on a magnetic tape. It facilitates the tape's start/stop operations.

interrupt: a hardware signal that suspends execution of a program and activates the execution of a special program known as the interrupt handler. It breaks the normal flow of the program being executed.

interrupt handler: the program that controls what action should be taken by the operating system when a sequence of events is interrupted.

inverted file: a file generated from full document databases. Each record in an inverted file contains a key subject and the document numbers where that subject is found. A book's index is an inverted file.

I/O: an abbreviation for input/output.

I/O-bound: a job that requires a large number of input/output operations, resulting in much free time for the CPU. It contrasts with *CPU-bound*.

I/O channel: a specialized programmable unit placed between the CPU and the control units. Its job is to synchronize the fast speed of the CPU with the slow speed of the I/O device and vice versa, making it possible to overlap I/O operations with CPU operations. I/O channels provide a path for the transmission of data between control units and main memory, and they control that transmission.

I/O channel program: the program that controls the channels. Each channel program specifies the action to be performed by the devices and controls the transmission of data between main memory and the control units.

I/O control unit: the hardware unit containing the electronic components common to one type of I/O device, such as a disk drive. It is used to control the operation of several I/O devices of the same type.

I/O device: any peripheral unit that allows communication with the CPU by users or programs, including terminals, line printers, plotters, card readers, tape drives, and direct access storage devices.

I/O device handler: the module that processes the I/O interrupts, handles error conditions, and provides detailed scheduling algorithms that are extremely device dependent. Each type of I/O device has its own device handler algorithm.

I/O scheduler: one of the modules of the I/O subsystem that allocates the devices, control units, and channels.

I/O subsystem: a collection of modules within the operating system that controls all I/O requests.

I/O traffic controller: one of the modules of the I/O subsystem that monitors the status of every device, control unit, and channel.

IP: see *Internet Protocol.*

ISO: see *International Organization for Standardization.*

job: a unit of work submitted by a user to an operating system.

job control language (JCL): a command language used in several computer systems to direct the operating system in the performance of its functions by identifying the users and their jobs and specifying the resources required to execute a job. The JCL helps the operating system better coordinate and manage the system's resources.

Job Scheduler: the high-level scheduler of the Processor Manager that selects jobs from a queue of incoming jobs based on each job's characteristics. The

Job Scheduler's goal is to sequence the jobs in the READY queue so that the system's resources will be used efficiently.

job status: the condition of a job as it moves through the system from the beginning to the end of its execution: HOLD, READY, RUNNING, WAITING, or FINISHED.

job step: units of work executed sequentially by the operating system to satisfy the user's total request. A common example of three job steps is the compilation, linking, and execution of a user's program.

Job Table (JT): a table in main memory that contains two entries for each active job — the size of the job and the memory location where its page map table is stored. It's used for paged memory allocation schemes.

K: 1,024 bytes or 2^{10} bytes.

key field: (1) a unique field or combination of fields in a record that uniquely identifies that record; or (2) the field that determines the position of a record in a sorted sequence.

LAN: see *local area network.*

leased line: a dedicated telephone circuit for which a subscriber pays a monthly fee, regardless of actual use.

least-frequently-used (LFU): a page-removal algorithm that removes from memory the least frequently used page.

least-recently-used (LRU) policy: a page-replacement policy that removes from main memory the pages that show the least amount of recent activity. It's based on the assumption that these pages are the least likely to be used again in the immediate future.

LFU: an abbreviation for *least-frequently-used.*

link: a generic term for any data communications medium to which a network node is attached.

local area network (LAN): a data network intended to serve an area covering only a few square kilometers or less. Because the network is known to cover only a small area, the networking signaling protocols can be optimized to permit rates up to 100 MB.

local station: the network node to which a user is attached.

locality: behavior observed in many executing programs in which memory locations recently referenced, and those near them, are likely to be referenced in the near future.

locking: a technique used to guarantee the integrity of the data in a database through which the user locks out all other users while working with the database.

lockword: a sequence of letters and/or numbers provided by users to prevent unauthorized tampering with their files. The lockword serves as a secret "password" in that the system will deny access to the protected file unless the user supplies the correct lockword when accessing the file.

logic bomb: a virus with a time delay. It spreads throughout a network, often unnoticed, until a predetermined time, when it "goes off" and does its damage.

logical address: the result of a key-to-address transformation. See also *hashing algorithm.*

LOOK: a scheduling strategy for direct access storage devices that's used to optimize seek time. Sometimes known as the elevator algorithm.

loosely coupled configuration: a multiprocessing configuration in which each processor has a copy of the operating system and controls its own resources.

low-level scheduler: another term for *Process Scheduler.*

LRU: an abbreviation for *least-recently-used.*

magnetic tape: linear secondary storage medium that was first developed for early computer systems. It allows only for sequential retrieval and storage of records.

mailslots: a high-level network software interface for passing data among processes in a one-to-many and many-to-one communication mechanism. Mailslots are useful for broadcasting messages to any number of processes.

main memory: the memory unit that works directly with the CPU and in which the data and instructions must reside in order to be processed. Also called *primary storage* or *internal memory.*

mainframe: the historical name given to a large computer system. It was characterized by its large size, high cost, and high performance.

logical address: the result of a key-to-address transformation. See also *hashing algorithm.*

MAN: see *metropolitan area network.*

master file directory (MFD): a file stored immediately after the volume descriptor. It lists the names and characteristics of every file contained in that volume.

master/slave configuration: an asymmetric multiprocessing configuration consisting of a single processor system connected to "slave" processors each of which is managed by the primary "master" processor, which provides the scheduling functions and jobs.

mean time between failures (MTBF): a resource measurement tool; the average time that a unit is operational before it breaks down.

mean time to repair (MTTR): a resource measurement tool; the average time needed to fix a failed unit and put it back in service.

Memory Manager: the section of the operating system responsible for controlling the use of memory. It checks the validity of each request for memory space and, if it's a legal request, allocates the amount needed to execute the job.

Memory Map Table (MMT): a table in main memory that contains as many entries as there are page frames and lists the location and free/busy status for each one.

metropolitan area network (MAN): a data network intended to serve an area approximating that of a large city.

microcomputer: a complete, small computer system, consisting of hardware and software, developed for single users in the late 1970s.

middle-level scheduler: a scheduler used by the Processor Manager to manage processes that have been interrupted because they have exceeded their allocated CPU time slice. It's used in some highly interactive environments.

minicomputer: a small to medium-sized computer system developed to meet the needs of smaller institutions. It was originally developed for sites with only a few dozen users.

modem: an electronic device that connects a terminal or computer to a communication line. The word comes from MOdulation/DEModulation, which is what the modem does: it converts a binary bit pattern generated by a terminal or computer into electrical signals that can be transmitted over communication lines, and then reconverts them into binary bit patterns when they reach their destination.

module: a logical section of a program. A program may be divided into a number of logically self-contained modules that may be written and tested by a number of programmers.

monoprogramming system: a single-user computer system.

most-recently-used (MRU): a page-removal algorithm that removes from memory the most recently used page.

MTBF: an abbreviation for *mean time between failures.*

MTTR: an abbreviation for *mean time to repair.*

multiple level queues: a process scheduling scheme (used with other scheduling algorithms) that groups jobs according to a common characteristic. The processor is then allocated to serve the jobs in these queues in a predetermined manner.

multiprocessing: when two or more CPUs share the same main memory, most I/O devices, and the same control program routines. They service the same job stream and execute distinct processing programs concurrently.

multiprogramming: a technique that allows several programs to reside simultaneously in main memory and interleaves their execution by overlapping I/O requests with CPU requests.

multitasking: a synonym for multiprogramming.

mutex: (from MUTual EXclusion) a condition that specifies that only one process may use a shared resource at a time to ensure correct operation and results. It's typically shortened to "mutex" in algorithms describing synchronization between processes.

mutual exclusion: one of four conditions for deadlock in which only one process is allowed to have access to a resource.

named pipes: a high-level software interface to NetBIOS, which represents the hardware in network applications as abstract objects. Named pipes are represented as file objects in Windows NT and operate under the same security mechanisms as other NT executive objects.

natural wait: common term used to identify an I/O request from a program in a multiprogramming environment that would cause a process to wait "naturally" before resuming execution.

negative feedback loop: a mechanism to monitor the system's resources and, when it becomes too congested, to signal the appropriate manager to slow down the arrival rate of the processes.

NetBIOS interface: a programming interface that allows I/O requests to be sent to and received from a remote computer. It hides networking hardware from applications.

network: a system of interconnected computer systems and peripheral devices that exchange information with one another.

network operating system (NOS): the software that manages network resources for a node on a network and may provide security and access control. These resources may include electronic mail, file servers, and print servers.

no preemption: one of four conditions for deadlock in which a process is allowed to hold on to resources while it is waiting for other resources to finish execution.

node: a network-layer addressable device attached to a computer data network.

noncontiguous storage: a type of file storage in which the information is stored in nonadjacent locations in a storage medium. Data records can be accessed directly by computing their relative addresses.

nonpreemptive scheduling policy: a job scheduling strategy that functions without external interrupts so that once a job captures the processor and begins execution, it remains in the RUNNING state uninterrupted until it issues an I/O request or it's finished.

NOS: see *network operating system.*

N-step SCAN: a variation of the SCAN scheduling strategy for direct access storage devices that's used to optimize seek times.

null entry: an empty entry in a list. It assumes different meanings based on the list's application.

object: any one of the many entities that constitute a computer system, such as CPUs, terminals, disk drives, files, or databases. Each object is called by a unique name and has a set of operations that can be carried out on it.

object-based DOS: a view of distributed operating systems where each hardware unit is bundled with its required operational software, forming a discrete object to be handled as an entity.

offset: in a paged or segmented memory allocation environment, it's the difference between a page's address and the actual machine language address. It's used to locate an instruction or data value within its page frame. Also called *displacement.*

open shortest path first (OSPF): a protocol designed for use in Internet Protocol networks, it is concerned with tracking the operational state of every network interface. Any changes to the state of an interface will trigger a routing update message.

open systems interconnection (OSI) reference model: a seven-layer structure designed to describe computer network architectures and the ways in which data passes through them. This model was developed by the ISO in 1978 to clearly define the interfaces and protocols for multi-vendor networks, and to provide users of those networks with conceptual guidelines in the construction of such networks.

operating system: the software that manages all the resources of a computer system.

optical disc: a secondary storage device on which information is stored in the form of tiny holes called "pits" laid out in a spiral track (instead of a concentric track as for a magnetic disk). The data is read by focusing a laser beam onto the track.

optical disc drive: a drive that uses a laser beam to read information recorded on compact optical discs.

OSI reference model: see *open systems interconnection reference model.*

OSPF: see *open shortest path first.*

overlay: a technique used to increase the apparent size of main memory. This is accomplished by keeping in main memory only the programs or data that are currently active; the rest are kept in secondary storage. Overlay occurs when segments of a program are transferred from secondary storage to main memory for execution, so that two or more segments occupy the same storage locations at different times.

owner: one of the three types of users allowed to access a file. The owner is the one who created the file originally. The other two types are "group" and "everyone else," also known as "world" in some systems.

P: an operation performed on a semaphore, which may cause the calling process to wait. It stands for the Dutch word *proberen,* meaning "to test," and it's part of the P and V operations to test and increment.

packet: a unit of data sent across a network. Packet is a generic term used to describe units of data at all layers of the protocol stack, but it is most correctly used to describe application data units.

packet switching: a communication model in which messages are individually routed between hosts, with no previously established communication path.

page: a fixed-size section of a user's job that corresponds to page frames in main memory.

paged memory allocation: a memory allocation scheme based on the concept of dividing a user's job into sections of equal size to allow for noncontiguous program storage during execution. This was implemented to further increase the level of multiprogramming. It contrasts with *segmented memory allocation.*

page fault: a type of hardware interrupt caused by a reference to a page not residing in memory. The effect is to move a page out of main memory and into secondary storage so another page can be moved into memory.

page frame: individual sections of main memory of uniform size into which a single page may be loaded.

page interrupt handler: part of the Memory Manager that determines if there are empty page frames in memory so that the requested page can be immediately copied from secondary storage, or determines which page must be swapped out if all page frames are busy.

Page Map Table (PMT): a table in main memory with the vital information for each page including the page number and its corresponding page frame memory address.

page replacement policy: an algorithm used by virtual memory systems to decide which page or segment to remove from main memory when a page frame is needed and memory is full. Two examples are FIFO and LRU.

page swap: the process of moving a page out of main memory and into secondary storage so another page can be moved into memory in its place.

parallel processing: the process of operating two or more CPUs in parallel: that is, more than one CPU executing instructions simultaneously.

parity bit: an extra bit added to a character, word, or other data unit and used for error checking. It is set to either 0 or 1 so that the sum of the one bits in the data unit is always even, for even parity, or odd for odd parity, according to the logic of the system.

partition: a section of main memory of arbitrary size. Partitions can be static or dynamic.

passive multiprogramming: a term used to indicate that the operating system doesn't control the amount of time the CPU is allocated to each job, but waits for each job to end an execution sequence before issuing an interrupt releasing the CPU and making it available to other jobs. It contrasts with *active multiprogramming*.

pass-through security: used to perform remote-validation activities in Windows 95. Log on information is passed to the appropriate networking protocol for processing that enables Windows 95 to use existing network hardware and software with all the security that is built into these external network servers.

password: a user-defined access control method. Typically a word or character string that a user must specify in order to be allowed to log on to a computer system.

path: the sequence of routers and links through which a packet passes on its way from source to destination node.

PCB: an abbreviation for *Process Control Block*.

peer (hardware): a node on a network that is on an equal level with other nodes on that network. For example, all nodes on a local area network are peers.

peer (software): a process that is communicating to another process residing at the same layer in the protocol stack on another node. For example, if the processes are application processes they are said to be application-layer peers.

performance: the ability of an operating system to give users good response times under heavy loads and CPU-bound applications such as graphic and financial analysis packages, both of which require rapid processing.

pirated software: illegally obtained software.

pointer: an address or other indicator of location.

polling: a software mechanism used to test the flag, which indicates when a device, control unit, or path is available.

portability: the ability to move an entire operating system to a machine based on a different processor or configuration with as little recoding as possible.

positive feedback loop: a mechanism used to monitor the system. When the system becomes underutilized, the feedback causes the arrival rate to increase.

POSIX: Portable Operating System Interface for Computer Environments is an operating system application program interface developed by IEEE to increase the portability of application software.

preemptive scheduling policy: any process scheduling strategy that, based on predetermined policies, interrupts the processing of a job and transfers the CPU to another job. It is widely used in time-sharing environments.

prevention: a design strategy for an operating system where resources are managed in such a way that some of the necessary conditions for deadlock do not hold.

primary storage: see *main memory*.

primitives: well-defined, predictable, low-level operating system mechanisms that allow higher-level operating system components to perform their functions without considering direct hardware manipulation.

priority scheduling: a nonpreemptive process scheduling policy (or algorithm) that allows for the execution of high-priority jobs before low-priority jobs.

process: an instance of execution of a program that is identifiable and controllable by the operating system.

Process Control Block (PCB): a data structure that contains information about the current status and characteristics of a process. Every process has a PCB.

process identification: a user-supplied unique identifier of the process and a pointer connecting it to its descriptor, which is stored in the PCB.

process-based DOS: a view of distributed operating systems that encompasses all the system's processes and resources. Process management is provided through the use of client/server processes.

processor: (1) another term for the CPU (Central Processing Unit); or (2) any component in a computing system capable of performing a sequence of activities. It controls the interpretation and execution of instructions.

Processor Manager: a composite of two submanagers, the Job Scheduler and the Process Scheduler. It decides how to allocate the CPU, monitors whether it's executing a process or waiting, and controls job entry to ensure balanced use of resources.

Process Scheduler: the low-level scheduler of the Processor Manager that sets up the order in which processes in the `READY` queue will be served by the CPU.

process scheduling algorithm: an algorithm used by the Job Scheduler to allocate the CPU and move jobs through the system. Examples are FCFS, SJN, priority, and round robin scheduling policies.

process scheduling policy: any policy used by the Processor Manager to select the order in which incoming jobs will be executed.

process state: information stored in the job's PCB that indicates the current condition of the process being executed.

process status: information stored in the job's PCB that indicates the current position of the job and the resources responsible for that status.

Process Status Word (PSW): information stored in a special CPU register including the current instruction counter and register contents. It is saved in the job's PCB when it isn't running but is on `HOLD`, `READY`, or `WAITING`.

process synchronization: (1) the need for algorithms to resolve conflicts between processors in a multiprocessing environment; or (2) the need to ensure that events occur in the proper order even if they are carried out by several processes.

producers and consumers: a classic problem in which a process produces data that will be consumed, or used, by another process. It exhibits the need for process cooperation.

program: a sequence of instructions that provides a solution to a problem and directs the computer's actions. In an operating systems environment it can be equated with a job.

program file: a file that contains instructions.

protocol: a set of rules to control the flow of messages through a network.

PSW: an abbreviation for *process status word.*

queue: a linked list of PCBs that indicates the order in which jobs or processes will be serviced.

race: a synchronization problem between two processes vying for the same resource. In some cases it may result in data corruption because the order in which the processes will finish executing cannot be controlled.

random access storage device: see *direct access storage device.*

read only memory (ROM): a type of primary storage in which programs and data are stored once by the manufacturer and later retrieved as many times as necessary. ROM does not allow storage of new programs or data.

readers and writers: a problem that arises when two types of processes need to access a shared resource such as a file or a database. Their access must be controlled to preserve data integrity.

read/write head: a small electromagnet used to read or write data on a magnetic storage medium, such as disk or tape.

READY: a job status that means the job is ready to run but is waiting for the CPU.

real-time system: an extremely fast computing system that's used in time-critical environments that require immediate decisions, such as navigation systems, rapid transit systems, and industrial control systems.

record: a group of related fields treated as a unit. A file is a group of related records.

recovery: the steps that must be taken, when deadlock is detected, by breaking the circle of waiting processes.

reentrant code: code that can be used by two or more processes at the same time; each shares the same copy of the executable code but has separate data areas.

register: a hardware storage unit used in the CPU for temporary storage of a single data item.

relative address: in a direct organization environment, it indicates the position of a record relative to the beginning of the file.

relative file name: a file's simple name and extension as given by the user. It contrasts with *absolute file name.*

reliability: (1) a standard that measures the probability that a unit will not fail during a given time period. It's a function of MTBF; (2) the ability of an operating system to respond predictably to error conditions, even those caused by hardware failures; or (3) the ability of an operating system to actively protect itself and its users from accidental or deliberate damage by user programs.

relocatable dynamic partitions: a memory allocation scheme in which the system relocates programs in memory to gather together all of the empty blocks and compact them to make one block of memory that's large enough to accommodate some or all of the jobs waiting for memory.

relocation: (1) the process of moving a program from one area of memory to another; or (2) the process of adjusting address references in a program, by either software or hardware means, to allow the program to execute correctly when loaded in different sections of memory.

relocation register: a register that contains the value that must be added to each address referenced in the program so that it will be able to access the correct memory addresses after relocation. If the program hasn't been relocated, the value stored in the program's relocation register is zero. It contrasts with *bounds register.*

remote log in: the ability to operate on a remote computer using a protocol over a computer network as though locally attached.

remote station: the node at the distant end of a network connection.

repeated trials: repeated guessing of a user's password by an unauthorized user. It's a method used to illegally enter systems that rely on passwords.

resource holding: one of four conditions for deadlock in which each process refuses to relinquish the resources it holds until its execution is completed even though it isn't using them because it's waiting for other resources. It's the opposite of *resource sharing.*

resource sharing: the use of a resource by two or more processes either at the same time or at different times.

resource utilization: a measure of how much each unit is contributing to the overall operation of the system. It's usually given as a percentage of time that a resource is actually in use.

response time: a measure of an interactive system's efficiency that tracks the speed with which the system will respond to a user's command.

ring topology: a network topology in which each node is connected to two adjacent nodes. Ring networks have the advantage of not needing routing because all packets are simply passed to a node's upstream neighbor.

RIP: see *routing information protocol.*

root directory: (1) for a disk, it's the directory accessed by default when booting up the computer; or (2) for a hierarchical directory structure, it's the first directory accessed by a user.

rotational delay: a synonym for *search time.*

rotational ordering: an algorithm used to reorder record requests within tracks to optimize search time.

round robin: a preemptive process scheduling policy (or algorithm) that allocates to each job one unit of processing time per turn to ensure that the CPU is equally shared among all active processes and isn't monopolized by any one job. It's used extensively in interactive systems.

router: a device that forwards traffic between networks. The routing decision is based on network-layer information and routing tables, often constructed by routing protocols.

routing: the process of selecting the correct interface and next hop for a packet being forwarded.

routing information protocol (RIP): a routing protocol used by IP. It is based on a distance-vector algorithm.

`RUNNING`: a job status that means that the job is executing.

safe state: the situation in which the system has enough available resources to guarantee the completion of at least one job running on the system.

SCAN: a scheduling strategy for direct access storage devices that's used to optimize seek time. The most common variations are N-step SCAN and C-SCAN.

scheduling algorithm: see *process scheduling algorithm.*

search strategies: algorithms used to optimize search time in DASD. See also *rotational ordering.*

search time: the time it takes to rotate the drum or disk from the moment an I/O command is issued until the requested record is moved under the read/write head. Also called *rotational delay.*

second generation (1955–1965): the second era of technological development of computers when the transistor replaced the vacuum tube. Computers were smaller and faster and had larger storage capacity than first-generation computers and were developed to meet the needs of the business market.

sector: a division in a disk's track. Sometimes called a "block." For floppy disks, the tracks are divided into sectors during the formatting process.

security descriptor: a Windows NT data structure appended to an object that protects the object from unauthorized access. It contains an access control list and controls auditing.

seek strategy: a predetermined policy used by the I/O device handler to optimize seek times.

seek time: the time required to position the read/write head on the proper track from the time the I/O request is issued.

segment: a variable-size section of a user's job that contains a logical grouping of code. It contrasts with *page.*

Segment Map Table (SMT): a table in main memory with the vital information for each segment including the segment number and its corresponding memory address.

segmented memory allocation: a memory allocation scheme based on the concept of dividing a user's job into logical groupings of code to allow for noncontiguous program storage during execution. It contrasts with *paged memory allocation.*

semaphore: a type of shared data item that may contain either binary or nonnegative integer values and is used to provide mutual exclusion.

sequential access medium: any medium that stores records only in a sequential manner, one after the other, such as magnetic tape. It contrasts with *direct access storage device.*

sequential record organization: the organization of records in a specific sequence. Records in a sequential file must be processed one after another.

server: a node that provides to clients various network services such as file retrieval, printing, or database access services.

server process: a logical unit composed of one or more device drivers, a device manager, and a network server module needed to control clusters or similar devices, such as printers or disk drives, in a process-based distributed operating system environment.

shared device: a device that can be assigned to several active processes at the same time.

shortest job first (SJF): see *shortest job next.*

shortest job next (SJN): a nonpreemptive process scheduling policy (or algorithm) that selects the waiting job with the shortest CPU cycle time. Also called *shortest job first.*

shortest remaining time (SRT): a preemptive process scheduling policy (or algorithm) similar to the SJN algorithm that allocates the processor to the job closest to completion.

shortest seek time first (SSTF): a scheduling strategy for direct access storage devices that's used to optimize seek time. The track requests are ordered so the one closest to the currently active track is satisfied first and the ones farthest away are made to wait.

site: a specific location on a network containing one or more computer systems.

SJF: an abbreviation for shortest job first. See *shortest job next.*

SJN: an abbreviation for *shortest job next.*

socket: a feature added to UNIX to support network services. Sockets are abstract communication interfaces that allow applications to communicate while hiding the actual communications from the applications.

smart card: a small credit-card-sized device that uses cryptographic technology to control access to computers and computer networks. Each smart card has its own personal identifier, which is known only to the user, as well as its own stored and encrypted password.

software: a collection of programs used to perform certain tasks. They fall into three main categories: operating system programs, compilers and assemblers, and application programs.

spin lock: a Windows NT synchronization mechanism used by the kernel and parts of the executive that guarantees mutually exclusive access to a global system data structure across multiple processors.

spooling: a technique developed to speed I/O by collecting in a disk file either input received from slow input devices or output going to slow output devices such as printers. Spooling minimizes the waiting done by the processes performing the I/O.

SRT: an abbreviation for *shortest remaining time.*

SSTF: an abbreviation for *shortest seek time first.*

stack: a sequential list kept in main memory. The items in the stack are retrieved from the top using a last-in first-out (LIFO) algorithm.

stack algorithm: an algorithm for which it can be shown that the set of pages in memory for n page frames is always a subset of the set of pages that would be in memory with $n + 1$ page frames. Therefore, increasing the number of page frames will not bring about Belady's anomaly.

star topology: a network topology in which multiple network nodes are connected through a single, central node. The central node is a device that manages the network. This topology has the disadvantage of depending on a central node, the failure of which would bring down the network.

starvation: the result of conservative allocation of resources in which a single job is prevented from execution because it's kept waiting for resources that never become available. It's an extreme case of *indefinite postponement.*

static partitions: another term for *fixed partitions.*

station: any device that can receive and transmit messages on a network.

store-and-forward: a network operational mode in which messages are received in their entirety before being transmitted to their destination, or to their next hop in the path to their destination.

subdirectory: a directory created by the user within the boundaries of an existing directory. The ability to dynamically create and delete any number of subdirectories is a popular feature of recent file systems.

subroutine: also called a "subprogram," a segment of a program that can perform a specific function. Subroutines can reduce programming time when a specific function is required at more than one point in a program.

subsystem: see *I/O subsystem.*

suffix: see *extension.*

symmetric configuration: a multiprocessing configuration in which processor scheduling is decentralized and each processor is of the same type. A single copy of the operating system and a global table listing each process and its status is stored in a common area of memory so every processor has access to it. Each processor uses the same scheduling algorithm to select which process it will run next.

synchronous interrupts: another term for *internal interrupts.*

task: (1) the basic unit of Ada programming language that defines a sequence of instructions that may be executed in parallel with other similar units; or (2) the term used by IBM to describe a process.

TCP/IP reference model: a common acronym for the suite of transport-layer and application-layer protocols that operate over the Internet Protocol.

test-and-set: an indivisible machine instruction known simply as "TS," which is executed in a single machine cycle and was first introduced by IBM for its multiprocessing System 360/370 computers to determine whether the processor was available.

third generation: the era of computer development beginning in the mid-1960s that introduced integrated circuits and miniaturization of components to replace transistors, reduce costs, work faster, and increase reliability.

thrashing: a phenomenon in a virtual memory system where an excessive amount of page swapping back and forth between main memory and secondary storage results in higher overhead and little useful work.

throughput: a composite measure of a system's efficiency that counts the number of jobs served in a given unit of time.

time quantum: a period of time assigned to a process for execution. When it expires the resource is preempted, and the process is assigned another time quantum for use in the future.

time-sharing system: a system that allows each user to interact directly with the operating system via commands entered from a keyboard. Also called *interactive system.*

time slice: another term for *time quantum.*

token: a unique bit pattern that all stations on the LAN recognize as a "permission to transmit" indicator.

token bus: a type of local area network with nodes connected to a common cable using a CSMA/CA protocol.

token ring: a type of local area network with stations wired into a ring network. Each station constantly passes a token on to the next. Only the station with the token may send a message.

track: a path along which data is recorded on a magnetic medium such as tape or disk.

transfer rate: the rate with which data is transferred from sequential access media. For magnetic tape, it is the equal to the product of the tape's density and its transport speed.

transfer time: the time required for data to be transferred between secondary storage and main memory.

transport speed: the speed that magnetic tape must reach before data is either written to or read from it. A typical transport speed is 200 inches per second.

trap door: an unspecified and nondocumented entry point to the system. It represents a significant security risk.

Trojan horse: a computer program that is disguised as harmless and that carries within itself a means to allow the creator of the trojan horse to access the system on which it resides.

turnaround time: a measure of a system's efficiency that tracks the time required to execute a job and return output to the user.

unsafe state: a situation in which the system has too few available resources to guarantee the completion of at least one job running on the system. It can lead to deadlock.

user: anyone who requires the services of a computer system.

V: an operation performed on a semaphore that may cause a waiting process to continue. It stands for the Dutch word *verhogen,* meaning "to increment," and it's part of the P and V operations to test and increment.

variable-length record: a record that isn't of uniform length, doesn't leave empty storage space, and doesn't truncate any characters, thus eliminating the two disadvantages of fixed-length records. It contrasts with a *fixed-length record.*

verification: the process of making sure that an access request is valid.

victim: an expendable job that is selected for removal from a deadlocked system to provide more resources to the waiting jobs and resolve the deadlock.

virtual device: a dedicated device that has been transformed into a shared device through the use of spooling techniques.

virtual memory: a technique that allows programs to be executed even though they are not stored entirely in memory. It gives the user the illusion that a large amount of main memory is available when, in fact, it is not.

virus: a program that replicates itself on a computer system by incorporating itself into other programs, including those in secondary storage, that are shared among other computer systems.

volume: any secondary storage unit, such as disks, disk packs, hard disks, or tapes. When a volume contains several files it's called a "multifile volume." When a file is extremely large and contained in several volumes it's called a "multivolume file."

`WAIT` **and** `SIGNAL`**:** a modification of the test-and-set synchronization mechanism that's designed to remove busy waiting.

`WAITING`**:** a job status that means that the job can't continue until a specific resource is allocated or an I/O operation has finished.

waiting time: the amount of time a process spends waiting for resources, primarily I/O devices. It affects throughput and utilization.

warm boot: a feature of Windows NT that allows the I/O system to recover I/O operations that were in progress when a power failure occurred.

wide area network (WAN): a network usually constructed with long distance, point-to-point lines, covering a large geographic area.

wire tapping: a system security violation in which unauthorized users monitor or modify a user's transmission.

working directory: the directory or subdirectory in which the user is currently working.

working set: a collection of pages to be kept in main memory for each active process in a virtual memory environment.

worm: a computer program that replicates itself and is self-propagating in main memory. Worms, as opposed to viruses, are meant to spawn in network environments.

Bibliography

Anderson, R. E. (1991). *ACM code of ethics and professional conduct: Communications of the ACM. 35* (5), 94–99.

Barnes, J. G. P. (1980). An overview of Ada. *Software Practice and Experience, 10,* 851–887.

Belady, L. A., Nelson, R. A., & Shelder, G. S. (1969, June). An anomaly in space-time characteristics of certain programs running in a paging environment. *CACM, 12*(6), 349–353.

Ben-Ari, M. (1982). *Principles of concurrent programming.* Englewood Cliffs, NJ: Prentice-Hall.

Bhargava, R. (1995). *Open VMS: architecture, use, and migration.* New York: McGraw-Hill.

Bic, L., & Shaw, A. C. (1988). *The logical design of operating systems* (2nd ed.). Englewood Cliffs, NJ: Prentice-Hall.

Bourne, S. R. (1987). *The UNIX system V environment.* Reading, MA: Addison-Wesley.

Brain, M. (1994). *Win32 system services. The heart of Windows NT.* Englewood Cliffs, NJ: Prentice Hall.

Brinch Hansen, P. (1973). *Operating system principles.* Englewood Cliffs, NJ: Prentice-Hall.

Brown, G. D. (1977). *System/370 job control language.* New York: Wiley.

Calingaert, P. (1982). *Operating system elements: A user perspective.* Englewood Cliffs, NJ: Prentice-Hall.

Christian, K. (1983). *The UNIX operating system.* New York: Wiley.

Columbus, L., & Simpson, N. (1995). *Windows NT for the technical professional.* Santa Fe: OnWord Press.

Cook, R., & Brandon, J. (1984, October). The Pick operating system: Part I: Information management. *BYTE, 9*(11), 177–198.

Courtois, P. J., Heymans, F., & Parnas, D. L. (1971, October). Concurrent control with readers and writers. *CACM, 14*(10), 667–668.

Custer, H. (1993). *Inside Windows NT.* Redmond, WA: Microsoft Press.

Davis, W. S. (1987). *Operating systems — a systematic view* (3rd ed.). Reading, MA: Addison-Wesley.

Deitel, H. M. (1984). *An introduction to operating systems* (rev. ed.). Reading, MA: Addison-Wesley.

Dettmann, T. R. (1988). *DOS programmer's reference.* Indianapolis, IN: Que Corporation.

Dickie, M. (1994). *Routing in today's internetworks. The routing protocols of IP, DECnet, NetWare, and AppleTalk.* New York: Van Nostrand Reinhold.

Dijkstra, E. W. (1965). *Cooperating sequential processes.* Technical Report EWD-123, Technological University, Eindhoven, The Netherlands. Reprinted in Genuys (1968), 43–112.

Dijkstra, E. W. (1968, May). The structure of the T.H.E. multiprogramming system. *CACM, 11*(5), 341–346.

Duncan, R. (1986). *Advanced MS-DOS.* Redmond, WA: Microsoft Press.

Finkel, R. (1986). *An operating systems vade mecum.* Englewood Cliffs, NJ: Prentice-Hall.

FitzGerald, J. (1993). *Business data communications. Basic concepts, security, and design* (4th ed.). New York: Wiley.

Forinash, D. E. (1987). *An investigation of Ada run-times supportive of real-time multiprocessor systems.* Unpublished master's thesis, Department of Statistics & Computer Science, West Virginia University, Morgantown.

Fortier, P. J. (1986). *Design of distributed operating systems.* New York: McGraw-Hill.

Habermann, A. N. (1976). *Introduction to operating system design.* Chicago: Science Research Associates.

Havender, J. W. (1968). Avoiding deadlocks in multitasking systems. *IBMSJ, 7*(2), 74–84.

Haviland, K., & Salama, B. (1987). *UNIX system programming.* Reading, MA: Addison-Wesley.

Hoare, C. A. R. (1974, October). Monitors: An operating system structuring concept. *CACM, 17*(10), 549–557. Erratum in (1975, February), *CACM, 18*(2), 95.

Holt, R. C. (1972, September). Some deadlock properties of computer systems. *ACM Computing Surveys, 4*(3), 179–196.

Houlette, F., et al. (1995). *Insider's guide to Windows 95 programming.* Indianapolis: Que Corporation.

Hugo, I. (1993). *Practical open systems. A guide for managers* (2nd ed.). Oxford, England: NCC Blackwell Ltd.

Katzan, H., Jr., & Tharayil, D. (1984). *Invitation of MVS: Logic and debugging.* New York: Petrocelli Books.

Lane, M. G., & Mooney, J. D. (1988). *A practical approach to operating systems.* Boston: Boyd & Fraser.

Leonard, T. E. (Ed.). (1987). *VAX architecture reference manual.* Bedford, MA: Digital Equipment Corporation.

MacLennan, B. J. (1987). *Principles of programming languages: design, evaluation, and implementation* (2nd ed.). New York: Holt, Rinehart & Winston.

Madnick, S. E., & Donovan, J. J. (1974). *Operating systems.* New York: McGraw-Hill.

Nemeth, E., Snyder, G., Seebass, S., & Hein, T. R. (1995). *UNIX system administration handbook* (2nd ed.). Upper Saddle River, NJ: Prentice-Hall.

Nickel, W. E. (1978, November). Determining network effectiveness. *Mini-Micro Systems, 11.*

Patil, S. S. (1971, February). *Limitations and capabilities of Dijkstra's semaphore primitive for coordination among processes.* M.I.T. Proj. MAC Computational Structures Group Memo 57.

Peterson, J. L., & Silberschatz, A. (1987). *Operating system concepts* (2nd ed.). Reading, MA: Addison-Wesley.

Pinkert, J. R., & Wear, L. L. (1989). *Operating systems concepts, policies, and mechanisms.* Englewood Cliffs, NJ: Prentice-Hall.

Pouzin, L., & Zimmermann, H. (1978, November). A tutorial on protocols. *Proceedings of the IEEE. 66*(11), 1346–1370.

Prasad, N. S. (1989). *IBM mainframes: Architecture and design.* New York: McGraw-Hill.

Ritchie, D. M., & Thompson, K. (1978, July–August). The UNIX time-sharing system. *The Bell Systems Technical Journal, 57*(6), 1905–1929.

Ruley, J. D., et al. (1994). *Networking Windows NT.* New York: Wiley.

Seyer, M. D., & Mills, W. J. (1986). *DOS:UNIX systems becoming a super user.* Englewood Cliffs, NJ: Prentice-Hall.

Shah, J. (1991). *VAXclusters: architecture, programming, and management.* New York: McGraw-Hill.

Shah, J. (1991). *VAX/VMX concepts and facilities.* New York: McGraw-Hill.

Shelly, G. B., & Cashman, T J. (1984). *Computer fundamentals for an information age.* Brea, CA: Anaheim Publishing Company.

Silberschatz, A. & Galvin, P. B. (1994). *Operating systems concepts* (4th ed.). Reading, MA: Addison-Wesley.

Shoch, J. F., & Hupp, J. A. (1982, March). The "worm" programs — early experience with a distributed computation. *Communications of the ACM, 25*(3), 172–180.

Smith, B. (1989, May). The UNIX connection. *BYTE, 14*(5), 245–253.

Spencer, D. D. (1983). *The illustrated computer dictionary* (rev. ed.). Columbus, OH: Charles E. Merrill.

Stallings, W. (1994). *Data and computer communications* (4th ed.). New York: Macmillan.

Tanenbaum, A. S. (1987). *Operating systems: Design and implementation.* Englewood Cliffs, NJ: Prentice-Hall.

Tanenbaum, A. S. (1992). *Modern operating systems.* Englewood Cliffs, NJ: Prentice-Hall.

Teorey, T. J., & Pinkerton, T. B. (1972, March). A comparative analysis of disk scheduling policies. *CACM, 15*(3), 177–184.

Thompson, K. (1978, July–August). UNIX implementation. *The Bell Systems Technical Journal, 57*(6), 1905–1929.

U.S. Department of Defense. (1982, April). *Ada Programming Language.* (MIL-STD-1815), Washington, D.C.

VAX architecture handbook. (1981). Bedford, MA: Digital Equipment Corporation.

VAX hardware handbook. (1982). Bedford, MA: Digital Equipment Corporation.

VAX software handbook. (1982). Bedford, MA: Digital Equipment Corporation.

Yourdon, E. (1972). *Design of on-line computer systems.* Englewood Cliffs, NJ: Prentice-Hall.

Additional Readings

Allen, A. O. (1978). *Probability, statistics, and queueing theory with computer science applications.* New York: Academic Press.

Anderson, D. A. (1981, June). Operating systems. *Computer, 14*(6), 69–82.

Atwood, J. W. (1976, October). Concurrency in operating systems. *Computer, 9*(10), 18–26.

Auerbach guide to operating systems. (1974). Philadelphia, PA: Auerbach Publishers.

Bach, M. J. (1986). *The design of the UNIX system.* Englewood Cliffs, NJ: Prentice-Hall.

Barron, D. W. (1984). *Computer operating systems for micros, minis, and mainframes* (2nd ed.). New York: Chapman & Hall.

Bashe, C. J., Johnson, L. R., Palmer, J. H., & Pugh, Emerson W. (1986). *IBM's early computers.* Cambridge: Massachusetts Institute of Technology.

Bassler, R. A., & Joslin, E. O. (1975). *An introduction to computer systems* (3rd ed.). Arlington, VA: College Readings.

Bayer, R., Graham, R. M., & Seegmüller G. (1979). *Operating systems: An advanced course.* New York: Springer-Verlag.

Beck, L. (1982, October). A dynamic storage allocation technique based on memory residence time. *CACM, 25*(10), 714–724.

Belady, L., et al. (1981, September). The IBM history of memory management technology. *IBMJRD, 25*(5), 491–503.

Bell, C. G., et al. (1978, January). The evolution of the *DEC system 10. CACM, 21*(1), 44–63.

Benford, T. (1995, September). Forecast for a Hex speed heyday: From 4X to 6X and beyond. *CD-ROM Professional, 8*(9), 109–110.

Bersoff, E. H., et al. (1980). *Software configuration management.* Englewood Cliffs, NJ: Prentice-Hall.

Biedny, D. (1994, March). CD recording systems. *NewMedia,* Multimedia Tool Guide, 115–120.

Birch, J. P. (1973). Functional structure of IBM virtual storage operating systems. Part III: Architecture and design of DOS/VS. *IBMSJ, 12*(4), 401–411.

Bobrow, D. G., et al. (1972, March). TENEX, a paged time sharing system for the PDP-10. *CACM, 15*(3), 135–143.

Bolsky, M. I. (1985). *The UNIX system user's handbook.* Englewood Cliffs, NJ: Prentice-Hall.

Borgerson, B. R., et al. (1978, January). The evolution of the Sperry Univac 1100 series: A history, analysis, and projection. *CACM,* 21(1), 25–43.

Bourne, S. R. (1982). *The UNIX system.* Reading, MA: Addison-Wesley.

Brinch H. P. (1970, April). The nucleus of a multiprogramming system. *CACM, 13*(4), 238–241.

Brown, R. L., et al. (1984, October). Advanced operating systems. *Computer, 17*(10), 173–190.

Bunt, R. B. (1976, October). Scheduling techniques for operating systems. *Computer, 9*(10), 10–17.

Burke, F. (1987). *UNIX system administration.* San Diego: Harcourt Brace Jovanovich.

Buzen, J. P., & Gagliardi, U. O. (1973). The evolution of virtual machine architecture. *Proceedings of the National Computer Conference,* 42, 291–300.

Canon, M. D., et al. (1980, February). A virtual machine emulator for performance evaluation. *CACM, 23*(2), 71–80.

Card, C., et al. (1983, February). The world of standards. *BYTE, 8*(2), 130–142.

Cederquist, G. N. (1970, Spring). CPS — An operating system for DEC minicomputers. *DECUS,* 153–163.

Cheriton, D. R., et al. (1979, February). THOTH: A portable real-time operating system. *CACM, 22*(2), 105–155.

Cheriton, D. R. (1982). *The Thoth system: multiprocess structuring and portability.* Amsterdam: North Holland.

Claybrook, B. G. (1983). *File management techniques.* New York: Wiley.

Coffman, E. G., et al. (1971, June). System deadlocks. *ACM Computing Surveys, 2*(3), 67–78.

Coffman, E. G., & Denning, P. J. (1973). *Operating systems theory.* Englewood Cliffs, NJ: Prentice-Hall.

Comer, D. (1984). *Operating system design: The XINU approach.* Englewood Cliffs, NJ: Prentice-Hall.

Cook, R., & Brandon, J. (1984, November). The Pick operating system: Part 2. System control. *BYTE, 9*(12), 132, 474.

Cutler, D. N., et al. (1976). The nucleus of a real-time operating system. *Proceedings of ACM Annual Conference,* 241–246.

Dahlgren, Kent. (1989, April). Demand paged virtual memory. *Dr. Dobb's Journal, 14*(4), 32–34.

Daney, C., & Foth, T. (1984). A tale of two operating systems. *BYTE, 9*(9), 42–56.

Datapro management of applications software. (1985). Delran, NJ: Datapro Research Corporation.

Datapro reports on microcomputers. (1985). Delran, NJ: Datapro Research Corporation.

Datapro reports on minicomputers. (1973). Delran, NJ: Datapro Research Corporation.

Denning, P. J., & Brown, R. L. (1984, September). Operating systems. *Scientific American, 251*(3), 94–106.

Ferrari, D. (1987). *Computer system performance evaluation.* Englewood Cliffs, NJ: Prentice-Hall.

Fiedler, D. (1983, August). The UNIX tutorial: Part 1. An introduction to features and facilities. *BYTE, 8*(8), 186–210.

Fiedler, D. (1983, October). The UNIX tutorial: Part 3. UNIX in the microcomputer marketplace. *BYTE, 8*(10), 132–156.

Fiedler, D. (1989, May). Future imperfect. *BYTE, 14*(5), 227–237.

Fogel, M. H. (1974, January). The VMOS paging algorithm: A practical implementation of the working set model. *Operating Systems Review, Newsletter of the ACM Special Interest Group on Operating Systems, 8*(1), 8–17.

Gaines, R. S. (1972, March). An operating system based on the concept of a supervisory computer. *CACM, 15*(3), 150–156.

Genuys, F. (Ed.). (1968). *Programming languages.* London: Academic Press.

Gerding, D. (1995, January). Ultimedia: Creating your multimedia dream machine. *CD-ROM Today, 3*(1), 43–53.

Glatzer, H. (1994, September). Jukeboxes: Bulking up on CD-ROM. *NewMedia, 4*(9), 51–53.

Goldberg, R. P. (1974, June). A survey of virtual machine research. *Computer, 7*(6), 34–45.

Grant, B. (1989). Choosing the right operating system. *Microage Quarterly, 4*(2), 34–37.

Habermann, A. N. (1969, July). Prevention of system deadlocks. *CACM, 12*(7), 373–385.

Hellerman, H., & Conroy, T. E. (1975). *Computer system performance.* New York: McGraw-Hill.

Hoare, C. A. R. (1985). *Communicating sequential processes.* Englewood Cliffs, NJ: Prentice-Hall.

Hoare, C. A. R., & Perrot, R. J. (Eds.). (1972). *Operating systems techniques.* New York: Academic Press.

Horowitz, E. (1983). *Programming languages: A grand tour.* Rockville, MD: Computer Science Press.

Janson, P. A. (1985). *Operating systems: Structure & mechanisms.* New York: Academic Press.

Jerram, P. (1994, June). CD-ROM Titles. *NewMedia, 4*(6), 40–46.

Joseph, M., et al. (1984). *A multiprocessor operating system.* Englewood Cliffs, NJ: Prentice-Hall.

Kaisler, S. H. (1983). *The design of operating systems for small computer systems.* New York: Wiley.

Kane, G. (1986). *Guide to popular operating systems.* Glenview, IL: Scott, Foresman.

Katzan, H., Jr. (1973). *Operating systems: A pragmatic approach.* New York: Van Nostrand Reinhold.

Katzan, H., Jr. (1986). *Operating systems, a pragmatic approach* (2nd ed.). New York: Van Nostrand Reinhold.

Kenah, L. J., & Bate, S. F. (1984). *VAX/VMS internals and data structures.* Maynard, MA: Digital Press.

Kernighan, B. W., & Pike, R. (1984). *The UNIX programming environment.* Englewood Cliffs, NJ: Prentice-Hall.

Kernighan, B. W., & Ritchie, D. (1978). *The C programming language.* Englewood Cliffs, NJ: Prentice-Hall.

Kokkonen, K. (1989, April). More memory for DOS Exec. *Dr. Dobb's Journal, 14*(4), 14–23.

Lamport, L. A. (1974, August). A new solution of Dijkstra's concurrent programming problem. *CACM, 17*(8), 453–455.

Lamport, L. A. (1981, November). Password authentication with insecure communication. *CACM, 24*(11), 770–772.

Lampson, B. W., & Sturgis, H. E. (1976, May). Reflections on an operating system design. *CACM, 19*(5), 251–265.

Leemon, S. (1982, November). An alternative to Atari DOS. *Creative Computing, 8*(11), 148–151.

Leeson, M. (1978). *Computer operations procedures and management.* Chicago: Science Research Associates.

Levy, H. M., & Eckhouse, Richard H., Jr. (1980). *Computer programming and architecture: The VAX-11.* Bedford, MA: Digital Equipment Corporation.

Levy, N. M., & Lipman, P. H. (1982, March). Virtual memory management in the VAX/VMS operating system. *Computer, 15*(3), 35–41.

Little, J. (1978, July). A module approach to microcomputer operating systems. *Computer Design, 23*(8), 217–224.

London, K. R. (1973). *Techniques for direct access.* Philadelphia, PA: Auerbach Publishers.

Loomis, M. E. (1983). *Data management and file processing.* Englewood Cliffs, NJ: Prentice-Hall.

Mak, N. (1989, April). Swap. *Dr. Dobb's Journal, 14*(4), 44–49.

Maekawa, M., et al. (1987). *Operating systems: Advanced concepts.* Menlo Park, CA: Benjamin/Cummings.

Mandell, S. L. (1983). *Computers and data processing today with BASIC.* St. Paul, MN: West Publishing.

Margulis, N. (1989, April). Advanced 80386 memory management. *Dr. Dobb's Journal, 14*(4), 24–31.

Martin, J. (1973). *Design of Man — Computer dialogues.* Englewood Cliffs, NJ: Prentice-Hall.

McKeag, R. M., et al. (1976). *Studies in operating systems.* New York: Academic Press.

Milenkovic, M. (1987). *Operating systems concepts and design.* New York: McGraw-Hill.

Miller, R. (1978, July). UNIX — A portable operating system? *Operating Systems Review, Newsletter of the ACM Special Interest Group on Operating Systems, 12*(3), 32–37.

Moir, D. (1989, June). Maintaining system security. *Dr. Dobb's Journal, 14*(6), 75–76.

Morris, R., & Thompson, K. (1979, November). Password security: A case history. *CACM, 22*(11), 594–597.

Olson, R. (1985, July). Parallel processing in a message based operating system. *Software, 2*(4), 39–49.

Organick, E. I. (1972). *The Multics system: An examination of its structure.* Cambridge, MA: MIT Press.

Pajari, G. E. (1989, May). Interrupts aren't always best. *BYTE, 14*(5), 261–265.

Peterson, G. L. (1981, June). Myths about the mutual exclusion problem. *Information Processing Letters, 12*(3), 115–116.

Peterson, S. A memory allocation compaction system. *Dr. Dobb's Journal, 14*(4), 50–57.

Patterson, T. (1983, June). An inside look at MS-DOS. *BYTE, 8*(6), 230–252.

Plattner, B., & Nievergelt, J. (1981). Monitoring program execution: A survey. *Computer, 14*(11), 76–92.

Pressman, R. (1987). *Software engineering: A practitioner's approach* (2nd ed.). New York: McGraw-Hill.

Prieve, B. G., & Fabry, R. S. (1976, May). VMIN — An optimal variable-space page replacement algorithm. *CACM, 19*(5), 295–297.

Raynal, M. (1986). *Algorithms for mutual exclusion.* Cambridge, MA: MIT Press.

Redell, D. D., et al. (1980, February). Pilot: An operating system for a personal computer. *CACM, 23*(2), 81–92.

Ricart, G., & Agrawala, A. K. (1981, January). An optimal algorithm for mutual exclusion in computer networks. *CACM, 24*(1), 9–17.

Ritchie, D. M., & Thompson, K. (1974, May). The UNIX timesharing system. *CACM, 17*(5), 365–375.

Roberts, B. (1983, October). The UNIX operating system. *BYTE, 8*(10), 130–132.

Ruff, L. B., & Weitzer, M. K. (1986). *Understanding and using MS-DOS/PC DOS.* St. Paul, MN: West Publishing.

Savage, J. E., Magidson, S. & Stein, A. M. (1986). *The mystical machine: Issues and ideas in computing.* Reading, MA: Addison-Wesley.

Sayers, A. P. (Ed.). (1971). *Operating system survey.* Princeton, NJ: The Comtre Corporation Auerbach.

Schindler, G. E., & Fry, J. B. (Eds.). (1978, July–August). UNIX time-sharing system. *The Bell System Technical Journal, 57*(6).

Schneider, W. (1989). Computer viruses: What they are, how they work, how they might get you, and how to control them in academic institutions. *Behavior Research Methods, Instruments & Computers, 21*(2), 334–340.

Shaw, A. (1974). *The logical design of operating systems.* Englewood Cliffs, NJ: Prentice-Hall.

Sherrod, P., & Brenner, S. (1984, August). Minicomputer system offers timesharing and realtime tasks. *Computer Design, 23*(9), 223–228.

Shiell, J. (1986). Virtual memory, virtual machines. *BYTE, 11*(11), 110–112.

Shneiderman, B. (1987). *Designing the user interface: Strategies for effective human-computer interaction.* Reading, MA: Addison-Wesley.

Sisk, J. E., & Van Arsdale, S. (1985). *Exploring the PICK operating system.* Hasbrouck Heights, NJ: Hayden Book.

Sommerville, I. (1986). *Software engineering* (2nd ed.). Reading, MA: Addison-Wesley.

Steel, T. B., Jr. (1964, May). Operating systems. *Datamation, 10*(5), 26–28.

Svoboda, L. (1976). *Computer performance measurement and evaluation methods: Analysis and applications.* New York: Elsevier.

Theaker, C. J., & Brookes, G. R. (1983). *A practical course on operating systems.* New York: Springer-Verlag.

Thomas, R. & Yates, J. (1982). *A user guide to the UNIX system.* Berkeley, CA: Osborne/McGraw-Hill.

Toong, H. D., & Gupta, A. (1982, December). Personal computers. *Scientific American, 247*(6), 86–107.

Turner, R. W. (1986). *Operating systems: Design and implementations.* New York: Macmillan.

Udell, J. (1993, February). Start the presses. *BYTE, 18*(2), 116–134.

Unger, J. (1989, May). One man's experience. *BYTE, 14*(5), 237–245.

Van Tassel, D. (1972). *Computer security management.* Englewood Cliffs, NJ: Prentice-Hall.

Vasilescu, E. N. (1987). *Ada programming with applications.* Newton, MA: Allyn & Bacon.

Wallis, P. J. L. (1982). *Portable programming.* New York: Wiley.

Waring, B. (1994, March). CD-ROM drives. *NewMedia,* Multimedia Tool Guide, 109–113.

Weinberg, G. M., & Geller, D. P. (1985). *Computer information systems: An introduction to data processing.* Boston: Little, Brown.

Weizer, N. (1981, January). A history of operating systems. *Datamation,* 118–126.

White, E., & Grehan, R. (1987, June). Microsoft's new DOS. *BYTE, 12*(6), 116–126.

Wolverton, V. (1985). *Running MS-DOS.* Bellevue, WA: Microsoft Press.

Wong, W. G. (1986, March/April). Program interfacing to MS-DOS: Part VI. Device drivers — Why and how. *Micro/Systems Journal, 2*(2), 50–53.

Wood, P. (1989, May). Safe and Secure? *BYTE, 14*(5), 253–260.

Yourdon, E. N. (Ed.). (1979). *Classics in software engineering.* New York: Yourdon Press.

Index